PAUL McCARTNEY

Also by Philip Norman

Biography and journalism

Shout! The True Story of the Beatles
The Stones
The Road Goes On For Ever
Tilt the Hourglass and Begin Again
Your Walrus Hurt the One You Love
Awful Moments
Pieces of Hate
Elton
The Life and Good Times of the Rolling Stones
Days in the Life: John Lennon Remembered
The Age of Parody
Buddy: the Biography
John Lennon: the Life
Mick Jagger

Autobiography

Babycham Night: A Boyhood at the End of the Pier

Plays and musicals

Words of Love
The Man That Got Away
This is Elvis: Viva Las Vegas
Laughter in the Rain: the Neil Sedaka Story

PAUL McCARTNEY

THE BIOGRAPHY

PHILIP NORMAN

WEIDENFELD & NICOLSON

A W&N PAPERBACK
First published in Great Britain in 2016
by Weidenfeld & Nicolson
This paperback edition published in 2017
by Weidenfeld & Nicolson,
an imprint of Orion Books Ltd,
Carmelite House
50 Victoria Embankment
London EC4Y 0DZ

An Hachette UK company

1 3 5 7 9 10 8 6 4 2

© Philip Norman 2016

A CIP catalogue record for this book
is available from the British Library.

ISBN   978 1 7802 2640 8

Typeset by Input Data Services Ltd, Somerset

Printed and bound by CPI Group (UK) Ltd, Croydon, CRO 4YY

MIX
Paper from
responsible sources
FSC® C104740

www.orionbooks.co.uk

CONTENTS

PROLOGUE

All Our Yesterdays

On 4 December 1965, the Beatles appeared at Newcastle-on-Tyne's City Hall during what would be their last-ever British tour. I was a 22-year-old reporter in the Newcastle office of the *Northern Echo*, a daily paper circulating throughout the north-east. Orders from my newsdesk were 'Go along and try to get a word with them.'

I set out on the assignment with zero hope. The Beatles had already been the biggest story in pop music – and, increasingly, beyond it – for more than two years. From my lowly, limited vantage-point, what new insight could I hope to add? As for getting 'a word' with them, this tour came in the wake of their *Rubber Soul* album, their second smash-hit film *Help!*, their historic performance to 55,000 people at New York's Shea Stadium and their investiture as MBEs by the Queen. I'd be competing not only with Tyneside's own heavyweight media but also the national newspapers and broadcasters who had offices there. Even if I did manage to get close to them, why would they waste a second on some nobody from the *Northern Echo*?

Like almost every young male in the Western Hemisphere, my daily fantasy was to swap lives with a Beatle. And there was no question as to which one. Paul, a year my senior, was the most obviously good-looking; John for all his magnetism could never be called that while George had good bone-structure but unsightly teeth and Ringo was ... Ringo. If the adolescent female frenzies that engulfed them had any rational focus, it was the left-handed bass guitarist whose delicate face and doe-like eyes were saved from girliness by the five o'clock shadow dusting his jawline.

Paul wore his Beatle gear with greatest elegance: the high polo necks and long-collared, button-down shirts, the corduroy once confined to farm labourers, the black leather jackets still uncomfortably reminiscent of Nazi storm troopers, the elastic-sided boots last seen on Edwardian men-about-town. He also seemed the one most enjoying the band's (presumably) mounting riches; I remember with what inexpressible envy I read this gossip snippet in the *New Musical Express*: 'On order for Beatle Paul McCartney – Aston Martin DB5.'

He'd become known as their PR man, before we quite understood what PR men were, with his charm, good humour, impeccable manners and air of what could only be called refinement. There was always something aspirational about him, as in his dating of a classy young actress, Jane Asher; at the same time, none of the others seemed happier amid the mindless, balcony-buckling, seat-wetting mayhem of their live shows. A friend who saw them at Portsmouth Guildhall told me how, in the crazed opening moments, someone threw a teddy bear onto the stage. Paul picked it up, sat it on the neck of his bass guitar and kept it there throughout their performance.

So now here I was on a slushy December night in Newcastle, waiting outside the City Hall's rear entrance with a knot of reporters including my friend David Watts from the *Northern Echo's* evening stablemate, the *Northern Despatch*. Forty-five minutes before showtime, a black Austin Princess limousine, which had driven from Glasgow through heavy snow, drew up and from it emerged the four most famous haircuts on earth. The only one to acknowledge us was John, who shouted a sarcastic greeting. Despite the cold, he wore no topcoat, only jeans and a white T-shirt, the first I ever saw with something printed across the front. I couldn't make out what it said, but I got the impression that was sarcastic also.

In those innocent days, the only security was a single elderly stage-door keeper. Dave and I between us easily talked our way past him and a few minutes later found ourselves in the corridor outside the Beatles' – totally unguarded – dressing-room. Some other media people had also got this far, but no one dared knock on the closed door, let alone barge in. As we loitered there indecisively, a rising crescendo of shrieks and stamping feet from the adjacent concert hall warned that potential interview time was running out.

Then suddenly Paul came along the passage wearing a black polo neck, just like on the *With the Beatles* album cover, and unwrapping a stick of Juicy Fruit gum. As he opened the door, Dave said 'I know that face' and, as he paused with a grin, I managed to ask, 'Can we come in and talk to you?'

'Sure,' he replied in the Liverpudlian voice that was so conspicuously higher and softer than the others. So, scarcely believing our luck, we followed him.

It wasn't a dressing-room, in fact, but a spacious lounge with green leather sofas and armchairs and a wall of French windows looking on to nothing. The Beatles had just finished a meal of steak and chips and trifle and the plates were being cleared by a squad of brisk Geordie waitresses in black dresses and white aprons. There were no other females present, nor any visible trace of alcohol or drugs. The only entertainment provided was a TV set showing an episode of *The Avengers*, its only audience George's pale, unsmiling face.

I started talking to Ringo, who was sitting in one of the green leather chairs, then John perched on an arm and joined in. Both now also wore their stage uniform of black polo necks and were astonishingly friendly and easy: I felt I had every bit as much right to be there as the *Melody Maker* big shot who'd come up specially from London. (John's patience seems especially remarkable now that I know what pressures he was under at the time.) George never looked up from *The Avengers* and Paul moved around restlessly, chewing Juicy Fruit and looking for one of the Moody Blues who were also appearing that night. 'Anyone seen the Moodies?' he kept asking. I recall staring at his jeans and wondering if they were the everyday kind they seemed, or custom-made with specially reinforced seams and rivets to prevent them being torn to shreds by frantic hands.

On a nearby sofa lay the Hofner 'violin' bass whose long-necked Stradivarius silhouette had become his particular trademark. I'd once played guitar myself, in a no-hope band on the Isle of Wight, and to show my kinship with the Beatles I asked him if the bass was heavy to wear onstage. 'No, it's light,' he said. 'Here . . . try it.' With that, he picked it up and tossed it over to me. I'm a hopeless catcher, but I somehow managed to grab its fretboard and shoulder-strap together. For a few moments I found myself fingering the same frets Paul McCartney did, and thumbing the same steel-wound strings. I asked whether violin-shaped basses were more expensive than regular ones. 'Only 52 guineas [£54.60],' he said. 'I'm a skin-flint, you see.'

The three were just as nice when I found a blank page in my notebook and requested an autograph for my young sister. 'You're her favourite,' I blurted, as Paul added his surprisingly grown-up signature. 'I'll be all right then, won't I,' he murmured, 'if I'm her favourite.' It was the gentlest possible put-down.

Like all their interviewers, I felt I got on better with them than anyone ever had before. 'Is it OK if I stick around for a bit?' I asked Paul, then looked at John. 'Sure,' they both nodded. Just then, a hollow-cheeked man in a yellow shirt with leg o' mutton sleeves entered the room and noticed me. This was their roadie, Neil Aspinall, one of whose main functions on the road was saying to journalists what the lovely, cuddly Fab Four couldn't possibly say themselves. More than likely he'd received one of their secret signals that a visitor was becoming tiresome.

'You,' he said with a jerk of his thumb. '*Out!*'

'But . . . they just told me I could stay,' I protested.

'Well, *I'm* telling you you've got to go,' he snapped, then glanced down at a newspaper, forgetting my existence.

As I made my ignominious exit, I consoled myself that at least

I had a Beatles angle none of my rivals did: how Paul McCartney threw me his violin bass and told me he was a skinflint.

For the rest of the Sixties, and the century, our paths were never to cross again. At the London *Sunday Times*, where I went on to work, all Beatles coverage was jealously guarded by older colleagues. So I wrote not a line about the flowering of Lennon and McCartney's songwriting after they stopped touring in 1966, which brought their album masterpiece, *Sgt. Pepper's Lonely Hearts Club Band*, and superlative 'Paul' songs like 'Penny Lane', 'Eleanor Rigby' and 'She's Leaving Home'. It was for others – so many others – to chronicle the two eventful years after Brian Epstein's death, with Paul seemingly running the band, that saw their journey to a Himalayan ashram, their *Yellow Submarine* cartoon film, their White Album, their *Magical Mystery Tour* and their launch of a business called Apple, which had nothing whatever to do with computers.

All that time, I remained just another of the countless young males for whom Paul McCartney's life seemed like paradise, and whose girlfriends mortifyingly melted at any sight of him (especially the 'Fool on the Hill' film sequence with those melting brown eyes in extreme close-up). There were already fears that the Beatles mightn't last for ever; an awareness that their life together maybe hadn't brought the supreme happiness we all presumed and that strange discontents and doubts were starting to gnaw at them. But one, at least, seemed to stand for continuity. George might have found Indian religion and lost his sense of humour; John might have dumped his pleasant wife for a Japanese performance artist and be off with her on all kinds of weird tangents. But Paul stuck with lovely Jane Asher, still maintained a flawless Beatle cut, wore the latest Carnaby suits, attended West End first nights, signed autographs and kept smiling.

Then, as the Sixties ran out, even his sense of public duty seemed to weaken. He parted from Asher, who had seemed so perfect for him in every way, and took up with an unknown American photographer named Linda Eastman. On their sudden wedding day in

1969, millions of heartbroken young women weren't the only ones to feel let down. Dry-eyed young men like me, who'd lived his life vicariously since 1963, also wondered what on earth he could be thinking of.

That same year, I was finally commissioned to write a Beatles story in a national publication, though not yet a British one. America's *Show* magazine asked me to investigate their Apple organisation, the fortunes it was devouring and the resultant blizzard of rumour about their imminent break-up. I approached their press officer, Derek Taylor, expecting the fact I'd published nothing about them, save long ago in the *Northern Echo*, to count against me. However, Taylor liked some *Sunday Times* pieces I'd written on other subjects, notably the strong man Charles Atlas, and agreed to give me accreditation. For several weeks that summer, I was allowed to hang around Apple's London headquarters, 3 Savile Row, the Georgian townhouse which seemed the ultimate expression of Paul's good taste.

By that point, his taste was all that remained of him there. John and Yoko were in almost every day, running their peace campaign from the front ground-floor office; George and Ringo both dropped by frequently. But there was no sign of Paul. Disgusted by John's appointment of Allen Klein as the Beatles' manager, he'd left London with Linda, to go to ground on his Scottish farm and record his first solo album. Though I didn't realise it at the time, I had a ringside seat at the Beatles' break-up.

A few months into the bleak, hung-over morning-after we were learning to call 'the Seventies', I received a phone call from Tony Brainsby, a freelance publicist known for his bumptiousness and shock of bright red hair. Brainsby now represented the solo Paul McCartney who was putting together a new band, to be named Wings, and asked if I would care to interview him about it for the *Sunday Times*? I answered no without a qualm. Then, and for years to come, the Beatles were considered immeasurably greater than any individual member. The only story of interest was when they'd get back together.

For the *Sunday Times Magazine* I went on to interview many major names in rock, country and blues – Mick Jagger, Bob Dylan, Eric Clapton, the Beach Boys, David Bowie, Bob Marley, Elton John, James Brown, Stevie Wonder, Johnny Cash, Rod Stewart, B.B. King, the Everly Brothers, Diana Ross, Little Richard, Fats Domino, Fleetwood Mac, Aretha Franklin, Bill Haley – but was never offered another talk with Paul, and never sought one. I shared the media's feeling of offence that he should have started another band – adding insult to injury by putting Linda in it in place of John – and resolution to give it no encouragement. As the (daily) *Times's* first-ever rock critic, I had ample opportunities to talk to him at press launches for the early Wings albums, yet somehow never did. In 1973, I had to concede his triumph with *Band on the Run*, even if some of the rhymes ('And the county judge/ held a grudge . . .') seemed a comedown for the creator of 'Penny Lane'.

Otherwise I echoed the view that Paul McCartney had turned into a self-satisfied lightweight and mourned the loss of his Beatle magic, and his increasing attacks of sentimentality and whimsy. Soon after the release of 'Mull of Kintyre', I wrote a satirical poem about him in the *Sunday Times Magazine* whose last verse now looks horrifically tasteless:

> Oh, deified scouse with unmusical spouse
> For the cliches and cloy you unload
> To an anodyne tune may they bury you soon
> In the middlemost midst of the road.

Has anyone ever more thoroughly burned his bridges?

In 1979, an industrial dispute closed down the *Sunday Times* for a year, which I decided to spend writing a biography of the Beatles. Colleagues and friends urged me not to waste my time; by then, the words written and spoken about them must have run into the billions; everything there was to know must already be known.

I approached the ex-Beatles for interviews, but got the same response from all four via their respective PRs: they were more interested in their solo careers than raking up the past. In fact – as we hadn't yet learned to say – they were still in denial of what had happened to them in the Sixties, an experience finally monstrous more than miraculous. The turn-down from Paul via Tony Brainsby may also have been influenced by that recent verse in the *Sunday Times*. My conversations with Brainsby grew increasingly tense until one day he shouted 'Philip . . . fuck off!' and banged down the phone.

I delivered my book, *Shout!*, to the publishers in late November 1980, just two weeks before John was murdered in New York. After five years out of the music business, he'd just released a new album, *Double Fantasy*, and was doing extensive promotional interviews. I'd kept *Shout!* open-ended in case he'd agree to talk to me for a postscript.

I did get inside his apartment at the Dakota Building – but not in the way I'd hoped. When the book came out in America the following spring, I went to New York to appear on the *Good Morning America* television show. During the interview, I said that in my view John hadn't been one quarter but three-quarters of the Beatles. Yoko saw the broadcast and phoned me at the ABC studio to tell me that what I'd said was 'very nice'. 'Maybe you'd like to come over and see where we were living,' she added.

That afternoon, I found myself at the Dakota, being shown round the huge white seventh-floor apartment where John had raised their son, Sean, while Yoko tended to their finances. Later in her ground-floor office, seated in a chair modelled on an Egyptian pharaoh's throne, she talked at length about his phobias and insecurities and the bitterness he'd felt towards his old bandmates, especially his other half in pop's greatest songwriting partnership. As often happens with the recently bereaved, some of the partner she'd lost seemed to have gone into her; listening to Yoko, I often felt I was hearing John. And any mention of Paul brought a wintry bleakness to her face. 'John always used to say,' she told me at one point, 'that no one ever hurt him the way Paul hurt him.'

The words suggested a far deeper emotional attachment between the two than the world had ever suspected – they were like those of a spurned lover – and I naturally included them in my account of my visit for the *Sunday Times*. After it appeared, I returned to my London flat one evening to be told by my then girlfriend, 'Paul phoned you.' She said he wanted to know what Yoko had meant and that he'd seemed upset rather than angry. As with John, I was being offered access much too late and in a way I'd never imagined. However, at that time I fondly believed I'd written my last word on the Beatles and their era. So I didn't attempt to get his formal response to Yoko's quote, and afterwards heard no more about it.

The main criticisms of *Shout!*, by the lyricist Sir Tim Rice among others, were its over-glorification of Lennon and bias against McCartney. I replied that I wasn't 'anti-Paul', but had merely tried to show the real human being behind the charming, smiley façade. Actually, if I'm honest, all those years I'd spent wishing to be him had left me feeling in some obscure way that I needed to get my own back. The pronouncement that John had represented three-quarters of the Beatles, for instance, was (as Tim Rice pointed out) 'mad'. Paul himself hated the book, so I heard, and always referred to it as *Shite*.

And in the end – to quote his sum-up on the *Abbey Road* album – all his critics were confounded. Wings became a chart success and live concert attraction as big as the Beatles had ever been. Shrewd self-management and investment in other musical catalogues (while anomalously not owning copyright in his own best-known songs) earned him a fortune vastly bigger than any of his fellow Beatles, or anyone else in the business, an estimated £1 billion. Ancient rumours of his tight-fistedness (hadn't he told me 'I'm a skinflint' in 1965?) were put to rest by his frequent involvement in charity concerts and, most spectacularly, his creation of a performing arts academy, to bring on young singers, musicians and songwriters, on the site of his old school in Liverpool.

His marriage to Linda, viewed as such a disastrous misstep at the time, became by far the happiest and most durable in pop. Despite the immensity of his fame and wealth, the couple managed to lead a relatively normal domestic life and prevent their children from becoming the usual pampered, neglected, screwed-up rock-biz brats. If the public never quite warmed to Linda, thanks mainly to her militant vegetarianism and animal-rights activism, she was acknowledged to have been the right one for him, just as Yoko had been for John.

He seemed to have achieved everything possible, not only in pop music but in the wider creative world: his classical oratorio performed in Liverpool Cathedral and accepted into the repertoire of symphonies all over the world; his painting exhibited at the Royal Academy; his collected poems published in hardback, prompting suggestions that he'd be an overwhelmingly popular choice as Poet Laureate. In 1997, his lengthy record of drug-busts (including a nine-day prison term in Japan) was brushed aside to allow him to receive a knighthood for services to music. He had indeed, as *Rolling Stone* magazine said, 'done less to fuck up his good luck than any other rock star who ever existed'.

Then, in his late fifties, his life suddenly veered off its perfectly-polished rails. In 1998, Linda died after a long struggle against breast cancer. Four years later, he married the charity campaigner and former model Heather Mills, to the evident consternation of his children; six years after that, the couple divorced amid a tabloid tumult uglier than even the pop world had seen before. For the first time ever, it felt good *not* to be Paul McCartney.

Since Yoko had invited me to the Dakota Building in the aftermath of John's death, she'd given me several further exclusive interviews. In 2003, we met in Paris and she agreed to co-operate with me in what would be the first large-scale, serious Lennon biography. Even without my troubled history with McCartney, I assumed there'd have been no hope of any input from him. Despite their public displays of solidarity, his relations with Yoko stayed deep in the Ice Age over issues like the order of the Lennon–McCartney songwriting credit and John's share of royalties from

Paul's 'Yesterday'. If she was with me, that surely must mean he'd be agin me.

Nonetheless, I thought it only courteous to send him a message via his then PR, Geoff Baker, saying I was doing a biography of John and that it would not be in any way 'anti-McCartney'. Two weeks later, my office phone rang and a familiar Scouse-Lite voice said "Ullo . . . it's Paul here.' Would that I'd had the balls to answer 'Paul who?'

My astonished silence elicited a faint chuckle. 'Yeah . . . I bet you never thought you'd hear from me, did you?'

He was phoning out of curiosity, he told me, 'to see what this fellow who seems to hate me so much is like'. We ended up talking for about 15 minutes. But it wasn't the conversation of a writer and the world's biggest pop star. I had no hope that he'd help me with the Lennon biography, so employed none of the guile with which journalists try to extract quotes from celebrities. I talked to him bloke-to-bloke, without deference but with growing respect. Rock megastars never have to do anything unpleasant or uncomfortable for themselves if they don't want to, yet, despite all the aides at his disposal, he'd bothered to pick up the phone.

When I told him I wasn't expecting him to give me an interview for the Lennon book, he did not demur: 'Otherwise it'd look as if I was rewarding you for writing bad stuff about me.' But, I said, there were certain specific factual questions that only he could answer: would he at least do that by e-mail?

'Okay,' he said.

As I'd learned in 1965, backstage at Newcastle City Hall, a Beatle's 'yes' didn't always mean yes. But in this case it did. I would e-mail my questions to his PA, Holly Dearden, and dictated replies would immediately come back, varying from half a dozen words to a couple of hundred.

Some resolved crucial issues about the Beatles' early history. In their Hamburg days, for example, he was said to have been the only witness when a drunken, pill-crazed John allegedly kicked their then bass-player Stu Sutcliffe in the head, maybe triggering

Sutcliffe's later fatal brain haemorrhage. No, he could not recollect any such incident. Other less sensational points were no less revealing. Was it true, I asked, that when they started writing songs together, left-handed Paul could play John's right-handed guitar and vice versa? If so, it was a perfect metaphor for the creative symbiosis between two otherwise totally different characters that enabled one to finish a song the other had started.

Yes, he replied, it was true.

In June 2012, I watched the now 70-year-old Sir Paul headline over pop music's other knights, Sir Elton John, Sir Cliff Richard and Sir Tom Jones, in the Queen's Diamond Jubilee concert at Buckingham Palace; wearing a dark blue military tunic like a sobered-up Sergeant Pepper and still playing his 'skinflint's' Hofner violin bass. John's 'Imagine' might be the world's favourite secular hymn but his 'Hey Jude' was by now an alternative national anthem. Two months later, again in the Queen's presence, he and 'Hey Jude' provided the finale of the London Olympics' £27 million opening ceremony. Apart from the sparkly little woman in the Royal box, there was no national treasure Britain was keener to show off to the world.

Yet being honoured and loved on this scale brings with it what one might call the Curse of Yesterday. The Beatles broke up longer ago than John Lennon's whole lifetime, their career representing barely a fifth of McCartney's total one. All his solo success since then has not changed a general view that his talent peaked in his early twenties, with John looking over his shoulder; that there can never again be a Paul McCartney song to match 'Yesterday', 'Penny Lane' or even 'When I'm Sixty-Four'.

Lesser figures from the do-it-yourself songwriting boom Lennon and McCartney instigated are happy to bask in the glow of their old hits, but not McCartney. Although his back catalogue is pop music's equivalent of the works of Shakespeare, he still feels as great a need to prove himself as the rawest beginner. In common with so many of rock's enduring monoliths – Mick Jagger, Elton John – adulation seems to go through him like Chinese food, leaving him always ravenous for more. That day he telephoned me, he mentioned he was currently 'back at Abbey Road, making records'. As I write, in late 2015, the world tour on which he has been more or less continuously for the past 15 years still shows no sign of coming to an end.

The dozens of books that have been written about him almost all focus on his role in the Beatles' story – what their publicist, Derek Taylor, rightly called 'the 20th century's greatest romance' – and treat the four decades which followed as merely an afterthought. His own official biography, *Many Years from Now*, written by Barry Miles, followed the same pattern, devoting only some 20 pages out of more than 600 to his post-Beatle years and ending in 1997, the year before Linda's death.

So there has been no comprehensive quality biography of pop music's greatest living emblem as well as greatest nonconformist. And for all the millions of words written about him, in and out of the Beatles, the page remains strangely blank. This seemingly most open and approachable of all mega-celebrities is actually one of the most elusive. From his apparent 'normality' and 'ordinariness' he has constructed ramparts of privacy rivalled only by Bob Dylan. Now and again, behind the eternal Mr Nice Guy, we glimpse someone who, for all his blessings and honours, can still feel frustration, even insecurity, and who on the inside niggles and festers just like the rest of us. But for the most part, that smile and cheery thumbs-up have camouflaged everything.

At the end of 2012, I e-mailed McCartney, care of his publicist, Stuart Bell, saying I'd like to write his biography as a companion volume to *John Lennon: The Life*. If he didn't want to talk to me directly – and it was hardly likely he could face ploughing through the whole Beatles story yet again – then perhaps he'd give me tacit approval, so I could interview people close to him who'd never be accessible otherwise. I admitted I might be his very last choice as a biographer, but said I hoped the Lennon book had made some amends for my less than fair treatment of him in *Shout!* Bell agreed to pass on my request, warning that a response might take some

time as McCartney was on tour in America. Oh, yes, I thought . . .
the old runaround . . .

A couple of weeks later, a response came back, e-mailed by a PA
at his dictation:

Dear Philip

Thanks for your note. I'm happy to give tacit approval and
maybe Stuart Bell will be able to help.

All the best
Paul

It was the biggest surprise of my career.

PART ONE

Stairway to Paradise

I

'Hey, mister, gimme a quid and I'll show you Paul McCartney's house'

The pale blue minibus that starts out from Liverpool's Albert Dock promises 'the only tour to go inside the childhood homes of Lennon and McCartney'. On its side are two cartoon faces, outlined in the vaguest black and white yet still as instantly recognisable all over the world as Mickey Mouse. By now, perhaps even more so.

For many years, Liverpool was strangely reluctant to capitalise on its most famous sons. But no longer. At Albert Dock, the Beatles Story museum recreates the whole saga so realistically, one could almost think one had shared in it. Mathew Street, renamed 'the Cavern Quarter', is a teeming boulevard of souvenir shops and themed bars, with a near-as-dammit replica of the Cavern a few metres from the site of the original. In North John Street, the luxurious Hard Day's Night Hotel has both a John Lennon and a Paul McCartney Suite, each costing around £800 per night and always reserved for months ahead.

In addition, there is a huge choice of Magical Mystery Tours around the city centre's main Beatle landmarks – the Pier Head, St George's Hall, Lime Street station, the Empire Theatre – then out to the suburbs, where the most sacred shrines are located.

This one by blue minibus is a cut above the rest, being operated by the National Trust, a body normally dedicated to preserving and restoring Britain's ancient stately homes. The two homes for which we're bound are neither ancient or stately, yet between them attract as many paying visitors, proportionate to their size, as any Tudor palace or eighteenth-century Palladian mansion in the Trust's care.

Here, for once, the two names' fixed order of precedence didn't apply. Paul's childhood abode, 20 Forthlin Road, Allerton, was the first to be acquired by the Trust and, in 1996, opened to public view as the place where Lennon and McCartney's songwriting partnership began. For some years afterwards, it was felt that 251 Menlove Avenue, Woolton, where John was brought up, did not qualify as a national monument because no specific Beatles track could be proved to have been composed there (even though Paul and he used to rehearse endlessly in its glassed-in front porch). Finally, in 2002, John's widow, Yoko Ono, bought the house and presented it to the Trust, together with an allowance for its restoration and upkeep.

This Sunday morning's blue minibus contingent are the mix of nationalities and ages one would expect. A group of four from French-Canadian Montreal is led by broadcasting executive Pierre Roy, a 'Paul' person to his manicured fingertips: 'I'm a Gemini like him, I'm left-handed, too, and my first girlfriend's name was Linda.'

A pair of young women in their mid-twenties hail respectively from Dublin and Teesside (the latter rather shamefacedly admitting she actually prefers George). Bernard and Margaret Sciambarella, a married couple in their forties, have merely crossed the Mersey from the Cheshire Wirral, bringing their 21-year-old student daughter. Despite both being hardcore Beatles fans they've taken this tour only once before. 'It's always the same if something's right on your doorstep, isn't it?' Margaret says.

We head off along Liverpool's revitalised waterfront, passing on one side the old dock basin, now ringed by espresso bars and boutiques; on the other, Victorian commercial buildings now transformed into desirable river-view apartments. At the corner of James Street is the former headquarters of the White Star shipping line where, one day in 1912, a company official stood on the balcony, reading the *Titanic*'s casualty-list through a megaphone to the stunned crowds beneath.

Broadcasting technology a century ago turns out to have been rather more reliable than today's. 'Guys, I'm sorry . . .' is our driver's opening announcement. 'The bus only just came back from a service and the CD player isn't connected up yet. That means that unfortunately there won't be any music to go with the places you'll be seeing on the tour.'

So out of Beatle City in silence we go: through gangster-haunted Toxteth, past the magnificent iron gateway to Sefton Park, along Smithdown Road, where Paul's mother did her nurse's training. A turning left leads to Queen's Drive and the former family home of Brian Epstein which, disgracefully, no one has ever thought worth preserving for the nation.

'Right, guys,' our driver says, 'we're just coming up to a place you'll all recognise. I'm sorry there's no tape of Penny Lane to go with it.'

Who cares? The song rings out of collective memory louder and clearer than the purest stereo. Penny Lane is in our ears and in our eyes, even if its 'blue suburban skies' this morning tend more towards dish-mop grey.

It is arguably Paul's masterpiece, twinned with a John masterpiece, 'Strawberry Fields Forever', on the greatest-value pop single ever released. And Penny Lane the place competes with the site of the old Strawberry Field Salvation Army home as Liverpool's most-visited Beatle shrine. Over the decades, its street-sign has been stolen so many times that the local authority took to simply painting the name on buildings. Latterly, a supposedly thief-proof sign has proved little more successful than the old type.

It has always seemed the sweetest of song-titles, evoking an innocent 1950s world when Britain used big copper penny coins that often dated back to Queen Victoria's reign, confectioners sold penny chocolate bars or 'chews' and women did not pee but 'spent a penny', the cost of using a public toilet. In reality, the name commemorates James Penny, an eighteenth-century Liverpool slave-trader. Nor is the song really about Penny Lane, but Smith-down Place, where the lane (which, anyway, has more associations with John than Paul) widens into a shopping 'parade' and a terminus for several bus-routes.

Every topographical feature listed in the lyric is still here, for each of us instantly triggering a mental soundtrack of nostalgic piano, old-fashioned brass or the tripping notes of a piccolo trumpet solo. There's still a barber, 'showing photographs of every head he's had the pleasure to know', even if hairstyles have moved on from 'Tony Curtises' and 'ducks' arses' and the shop's name is no longer Bioletti, as during Paul's childhood, but Tony Slavin. There's a branch of Lloyds TSB, where the banker might well not own 'a mac' (raincoat, that is, not laptop) and nowadays is perhaps even more likely to be laughed at behind his back.

Here is the traffic island behind whose shelter 'a pretty nurse' could well be 'selling poppies from a tray' (and every one of us knows whom *she* represented). To the left, along Mather Avenue, there's still a fire-station where even now some dragoon-helmeted officer might be watching the time in an hourglass as he polishes his 'clean machine . . . in his pocket . . . a portrait of the Queen'.

Paul's and John's childhood homes lie less than a mile apart but in separate suburbs whose social differences remain very noticeable. Allerton, on this side at least, consists predominantly of working-class council estates whereas Woolton is a well-heeled enclave of industrialists, professionals and academics from Liverpool University. When John first met Paul in 1957, that distinction was multiplied a thousandfold.

On the blue minibus, after our McCartney prologue, we have reverted to the traditional pecking-order. First stop is 'Mendips', the semi-detached villa with faux Tudor flourishes where John, that supposed 'working-class hero', spent an irreproachably middle-class and rather pampered boyhood in the care of his forceful Aunt Mimi.

Not for almost two hours do we leave Woolton's leafy boulevards, drive down Mather Avenue and pull up outside 20 Forthlin Road. Another, identical, minibus is waiting to collect an earlier tour group who are just emerging through the minuscule front garden. The intoxicated buzz of their conversation includes French, Spanish and Russian, or perhaps Polish. 'Well, she was just seventeen . . .' sings a Dutch-accented male voice. 'You know what I mean . . .' an international chorus responds.

To modern British ears, the term 'council house' tends to signify society's lower rungs, but in the years just after the Second World War, these local authority-built and -subsidised dwellings represented a miraculous upward leap from overcrowded and insanitary back-to-back slums.

Twenty Forthlin Road is a classic example of the terraced variety: two-storeyed plain-fronted (which in the Fifties meant ultramodern) with a large downstairs window, two small upper ones and a glass-paned front door under a wedge-shaped porch. Although a national monument, it does not rate one of the blue plaques handed out by the National Trust's complementary body, English Heritage, to mark the homes of great figures in history. Blue plaques are conferred only where the great figure is dead or a centenarian.

Like 'Mendips', the house has a resident custodian who also acts as tour-guide. Most are devoted fans for whom living in John's or Paul's old home, restored to its 1950s character, is beyond Heaven. For some years, indeed, Forthlin Road had a custodian with an uncanny facial resemblance to Paul though his name, confusingly, was John.

Today, our guide is a motherly-looking woman with pale, curly hair who introduces herself as Sally, then tactfully relieves us of our bags and cameras, promising they'll be kept safe 'in the very same place where the McCartneys used to put their hats and coats'.

When the National Trust acquired the house, Paul's only stipulation was that it shouldn't be just a shrine to the Beatles but a memorial to a family. 'And at the beginning,' Sally reminds us, 'this was a very sad place for him.' In the little hallway above the front door hangs a simple wooden plaque:

In loving memory of
Mum and Dad
Mary and Jim

To the left is the sitting-room where Paul first began writing songs with John (though he'd tried writing them by himself even before that). It is a tiny space, almost every square inch filled by a chunky 'three-piece suite' of sofa and two matching armchairs, a fringed standard lamp and a wood-encased, tiny-screen TV set. On a side table stands the weighty black dial-telephone (Garston 6922) that, for some time, was the only one in the whole street. The yellow willow pattern wallpaper was chosen by the National Trust as typical of such a room in the early Fifties; then, as it was being decorated, some of the McCartneys' original silver-blue chinoiserie paper came to light. A section of this is mounted on card under plastic, which a privileged member of each tour group gets to hold up for the others to see.

Against the inside wall is an upright piano, the kind that once stood in so many British front parlours. 'It was in this room that 16-year-old Paul sat at the piano and wrote "When I'm Sixty-Four",' Sally says. 'And, as you probably know [*probably?*], the piano came from the North End Road Music Stores, or NEMS, which was owned by Brian Epstein's family. No, this isn't the same piano,' she adds before anyone can ask. 'Paul has got that.'

Above the TV set hangs his brother Michael's photograph of him and John in their facing armchairs, poring over their right- and left-handed guitar fretboards, it's said, during the composition of 'I Saw Her Standing There' (hence that singing Dutchman outside). 'The two of them had a rule that if they couldn't remember a new song the next day, then it wasn't worth keeping,' Sally continues. 'If it was, Paul would write it down in his school exercise book. And he's still got that school exercise book.'

Folding wooden doors lead to a tiny dining-room and, beyond, a kitchen stocked with 1950s products like Rinso detergent, Robin starch and Lux soap. After the McCartneys moved out in 1964, a family named Smith occupied the house for 30 years and installed modern kitchen fitments including a stainless steel sink unit. When the National Trust took over, the original wooden draining-boards were discovered in the roof-cavity. Then the porcelain sink that went with them turned up in the back garden, being used as a plant-holder.

The garden is a modest grass rectangle, its view still the police training-college in Mather Avenue. 'Of course, there were police horses kept there when Paul was a boy,' Sally says. 'So lots of nice manure for his dad's roses.' The wooden shed used to hold a scullery – where clothes were scrubbed by hand, then fed through the rollers of an iron-framed 'mangle' – and an outside toilet. Now it holds a visitors' 'rest room' ('This is a long tour after all,' Sally says) and a guide's cubbyhole, where she's parked her lunch of a focaccia and sun-dried tomato sandwich.

She shows us the drainpipe which, late at night, Paul would shin up to climb through the inside toilet window and let John in at the front door without waking his father. This must be the only National Trust property where the drainpipe is pointed out as being of historical interest.

We go upstairs to the large back bedroom Paul ceded to his younger brother, Michael, though both kept their clothes there. Slung over the bed-head is a set of black Bakelite radio-headphones like those which first piped in the heavenly contagion of rock 'n' roll. Paul's old room, overlooking the street, isn't much wider than its narrow single bed. On the coverlet lie a scatter of significant artefacts including a paperback of Dylan Thomas's *Under Milk Wood* (i.e. good English student) and a replica of his very first guitar, the reddish sunburst f-hole Zenith. 'Paul still has the original one,' Sally hardly needs to tell us.

Here each group is allowed a few minutes for what in church would be called 'silent reflection'. And it usually is silent or, anyway, wordless. 'Some people laugh, some people cry,' Sally says. 'Mostly they're just very, very moved.'

In all the years 20 Forthlin Road has been open to the public,

Paul has never seen its restored interior, though he's paid several incognito visits to look at it from outside. Once, when he brought his son James, he was accosted by a small boy from a neighbouring house. Not realising who it was, the boy tried a hustle with all the Liverpudlian cheek of the Beatles in their prime:

'Hey, mister, gimme a quid and I'll show you Paul McCartney's house.'

2

'Apple sandwiches with sugar'

Although surnames with the prefix Mac or Mc, meaning 'child of', usually denote Scots, Paul's origins on both his father's and mother's side are Irish. Throughout history there has been a close relationship between the two races, forged mainly by common resentment of the English. They overlap in numerous ways, from their shared Gaelic language to their fondness for whisky and the passion and sentimentality of their native music, which both make with the aid of bagpipes. Scottish-descended families can be found all over Ireland and vice versa.

One of the most controversial songs Paul ever wrote was 'Give Ireland Back to the Irish' – yet in truth his forebears were deprived of their homeland willingly enough.

His paternal great-grandfather, James McCartney, was part of the mass emigration of the late nineteenth century when Ireland's horrific poverty drove thousands abroad in hopes of finding a better life. James was one of many who crossed the Irish Sea to Liverpool, whose teeming port and factories upheld its claim to be 'the second city of the British Empire'. He arrived in the early 1880s, settling in the humble Everton district and working as a house-painter. James's son, Joseph, grew up to become a leaf-cutter at Cope's tobacco factory and, in 1896, to marry a local fishmonger's daughter, Florence Clegg. She bore nine children of whom two, Ann and Joseph junior, died in infancy (their names being re-assigned to another boy and girl who came later). Joseph and

Florrie's second surviving son and fifth child, born in 1902, was Paul's father, James, ever afterwards known as Jim.

Home for Jim and his six siblings, Jack, Joe junior, Edith, Ann, Millie and Jane – nicknamed 'Gin' – was a tiny terrace house in Solva Street, in the poorest part of Everton. Later in life, he would recall how the McCartney children possessed two pairs of shoes between them, one for the boys, one for the girls. As their school forbade its pupils to go unshod, they took turns to attend in the precious footwear, then came home at night and repeated the day's lessons aloud to the others.

Despite the family's extreme poverty, and the many dubious influences of the neighbourhood, Jim grew up to be honest, modest and punctiliously courteous, earning the nickname 'Gentleman Jim' even from his own brothers and sisters. When he left school aged 14, his headmaster's report '[couldn't] find a word to say against him'. His one childhood misadventure was falling off a wall at the age of ten and damaging his right eardrum, which left him permanently deaf on that side.

Since the eighteenth century, Liverpool's prosperity had been largely founded on cotton, brought by ship from the Americas and Asia and sold on to textile mills and clothes manufacturers all over northern Britain. Jim joined one of the city's oldest-established cotton brokers, A. Hannay & Son, as a 'sample boy', taking samples of newly-arrived cargoes around to prospective buyers. To supplement his six shilling (30p) per week wage, he sold programmes at Everton's Theatre Royal and occasionally operated the limelight, the piercing beam reserved for top artistes at extra special moments.

For the son he was to have one day the world would pour out almost its whole stock of limelight. But a little fell on Jim, too. His father, Joseph, had been a keen amateur musician, playing the E-flat tuba in the Cope's factory's own brass band and organising concerts and sing-songs for neighbours. Despite Jim's partial deafness, he proved to have a natural musical ear which allowed him to teach himself both the trumpet and the piano. Just after the

Great War, in which he'd been too young to serve, he formed a semi-professional dance band that included his older brother, Jack, on trombone.

To begin with, they wore Zorro-style black masks and called themselves the Masked Music Makers, but the heat of performing made the dye in the masks trickle down their faces, so they hurriedly relaunched as the Jim Mac Jazz Band. They would perform at local dances and occasionally for silent movie shows, improvising tunes to fit the action on the screen. Jim's father and brother Jack had good singing voices but he attempted no vocals, preferring to stick to his 'horn'. A family photograph shows the Jim Mac Jazz Band sometime in the 1920s, wearing tuxedos and wing collars, with a group of their female followers around a bass drum very like the future Sgt. Pepper's. The bandleader's fragile face and wide-open eyes are a further portent of astonishing things to come.

By the outbreak of the Second World War in 1939, Jim was 37 and, despite the matchmaking efforts of his mother and five sisters, seemed happy to remain what used to be called, without any ulterior meaning, a 'confirmed bachelor'. At Hannay's, he had risen to the rank of cotton salesman, dividing his time between Liverpool's Cotton Exchange in Old Street and the docks where consignments were unloaded, with interludes of visiting clients at mills in Manchester, 35 miles to the east. One of his jobs was checking the length of the cotton staple, or fibre, a longer staple being more suitable for spinning. Despite his hearing impairment, he became able to do this aurally. 'He could fluff a bit of cotton against his good ear and instantly be able to grade it,' his adopted daughter, Ruth McCartney, remembers.

As Britain's principal port for Atlantic food convoys and a major armaments-manufacturing centre, Liverpool was a prime target for Hitler's Luftwaffe, enduring a Blitz almost as ferocious as that visited on London. Jim was over the age for military service and further exempted by his partial deafness. When Hannay's shut down for the duration, he operated a lathe in a munitions factory and did night shifts as a volunteer fireman.

One day, while visiting his widowed mother in Norris Green, he met a hospital nurse of similarly Irish origins named Mary Patricia Mohin, who was boarding with his sister Gin. Though the worst of Liverpool's Blitz had passed by now, raids still continued intermittently. While Jim and Mary were getting acquainted, the sirens began to wail, forcing them to continue their conversation in the Anderson shelter in the garden. As they huddled together inside the Anderson's flimsy corrugated-iron walls, 'Gentleman Jim' finally fell.

Mary's father Owen, a coal deliveryman, had come over from County Monaghan at the turn of the century, changing his name from Mohan to Mohin to make it sound less Irish. In what was to prove an unhappy precedent, Mary's mother died when she was ten, leaving her and two brothers, Wilfred and Bill (two sisters having not survived). Her father remarried and started a second family, but her stepmother cared little for Mary, finally freezing her out of home altogether.

After this, it was perhaps no surprise she should have felt a vocation to care for others. At the age of 14, she became a nursing trainee at Smithdown Road Hospital. She went on to a three-year course at Walton General Hospital in Rice Lane, qualifying as a state registered nurse and becoming a ward sister aged only 24.

When Mary met Jim McCartney, she was 31, an age when most women in those days resigned themselves to what used to be called spinsterhood. But to Jim, on the cusp of 40, she was a catch with her very Irish good looks – the kind suggesting forebears from Spain or Italy – and shy, gentle manner. Nonetheless, it was Mary who took the initiative in their courtship. 'My dad said he had really fancied my mum and he took her out for a long time,' Paul would remember. 'Then he suddenly twigged that she'd been getting him to take her around to dances . . . She was going to joints and she wasn't that kind of girl. It turned out to be where my father was playing. She was following him round as a fan. [Later] it made me think "God, *that's* where I get it all from!"'

The romance might have ended as soon as it began, for Mary had been brought up as a Catholic while the McCartneys were Protestant. Among Liverpool's Irish population, the sectarian divide was as fiery as back in the Old Country; Catholics and 'Orangemen' each held triumphalist parades and marches that usually ended in violence, and intermarriage was deplored by both communities. However, Mary had no close family on hand to make difficulties and Jim anyway declared himself agnostic: they were married at St Swithin's Roman Catholic chapel in April 1941.

Their first child, a boy, was born on 18 June the following year at Walton General Hospital. Mary had once been sister in charge of the maternity unit there, so was given the luxury of a bed in a private ward. When the baby arrived, he was in a state of white asphyxia, caused by oxygen-deficiency in the brain, and appeared not to be breathing. The obstetrician was ready to pronounce him dead but the midwife, who knew Mary well and was also a Catholic, prayed fervently to God and after a few moments he revived.

Jim was on fire-watching duty and didn't reach the hospital until some hours later, by which time the baby was definitely breathing and no longer deathly white. 'He had one eye open and he squawked all the time,' his father was to recall with true Liverpudlian candour. 'They held him up and he looked like a horrible piece of red meat.'

Learning of the miracle that had occurred, Jim raised no objection when Mary wanted him baptised into the Catholic church. He was given his father's and great-grandfather's first name of James and the saintly middle name Paul, by which he would always be better known.

His first home was a set of furnished rooms at 10 Sunbury Road, Anfield, close to the cemetery where hundreds of Liverpool's air-raid victims had been buried. Soon afterwards, Jim left the munitions factory and became an inspector with the Corporation's Cleansing Department, checking that refuse-collectors did not skimp their rounds. In a city where 20,000 homes had been destroyed by bombs, accommodation was a continual problem. The McCartneys had four further temporary addresses on both sides of the River Mersey, never staying longer than a few months. The pressure increased in January 1944, when Mary returned to Walton General to have a second son, Peter Michael, always to be called Mike.

After the war, A. Hannay & Son reopened and Jim returned to his old job of cotton salesman. But five years of global conflict had left the cotton market severely depressed and he was lucky to bring home £6 per week. To augment his pay packet, Mary used her nursing experience to become a health visitor with the local authority, treating people for minor ailments in their own homes.

In 1947, when Paul wasn't quite five, she became a domiciliary (i.e. resident) midwife on the new housing estate at Speke, some eight miles south-east of Liverpool's city centre. The chief attraction of the job was that a rent-free council house went with it. When the McCartneys moved into their new home at 72 Western Avenue, the estate was still only half-constructed, a wilderness of muddy roads and roofless brick shells. His imagination already vivid, Paul felt they were 'like a pioneer family in a covered wagon'.

One of his earliest memories was being cold – the icy winter winds off the Mersey, the burn of chapped lips, ears and knees exposed by the short trousers to which all small boys in those days were condemned.

Nineteen forty-seven was the hardest of Britain's post-war austerity years, when a battle-exhausted, bankrupted nation seemed to have no warmth, no food, no fun, no colour but the bleary black and white of cinema newsreels. Liverpool felt like the austerity capital of the UK with its acres of shattered buildings and gaping craters. In common with most urban children, Paul and Mike's main outdoor playgrounds were bomb sites, known in Scouse slang – which refuses to take anything too seriously – as 'bombies'.

Inside 72 Western Avenue it was never cold, for Mary McCartney gave her two sons the loving, secure home she herself never had. Paul was to remember 'lots of hugs and kisses' from his mother, combined with a nurse's brisk practicality that always knew just what to do if he or his brother fell and hurt themselves or developed a temperature. More comforting even than a hug was the brisk professional way she applied bandages or sticking-plaster, and shook the thermometer vigorously before popping it under his tongue.

Mary was tireless in caring for her maternity patients, a job which became ever more demanding as the new estate began to fill up. Paul always retained a vision of her going out to deliver a baby late one snowy winter's night, pedalling off on her bicycle, with a basket in front for her birthing requisites and a little lamp glimmering above. Her aura to him seemed almost saintly, for grateful patients were always leaving gifts of flowers or hard-to-obtain sweets on the doorstep of number 72 like offerings at a shrine.

It was a curiosity of Britain's class system in the 1940s and 1950s that nurses of whatever background became honorary members of the middle class and considered the acquisition of a genteel accent to be part of their training. Thus, despite being so integral to the Speke community, Mary was also somewhat apart from it, and Paul and Mike came to feel the same. Their mother's particular concern was that they shouldn't talk the same glottal Liverpudlian as other children on the estate, and should always be more polite and punctilious than was the general Merseyside way. After a couple of years in Western Avenue, the family were moved to another council house, 12 Ardwick Road, just a few streets away. It was no larger than their previous home, and still had only an outside toilet, but Mary considered the neighbourhood a better one.

Despite having come so late to parenthood, Jim turned out to be a dutiful and loving father. His manner was rather serious, befitting one who went off each day in a business suit to 'the City', but, according to Mike McCartney, 'he had a subtle underground bubbling sort of fun which could explode at any minute'. The boys discovered early on, for instance, that it was no good competing to 'pull tongues' with Dad, as he had much the fattest tongue and could poke it out much farther.

Jim had had to give up the trumpet-playing when he lost his teeth, but the piano remained a passion with him. In pride of place in the living-room stood a sturdy upright model, bought on the instalment-plan from NEMS' music store in Walton. Paul's earliest inklings of melody were his father's exuberant cross-handed versions of old standards like George Gershwin's 1922 hit 'Stairway to Paradise'.

Though the boys never knew either of their McCartney grandparents, they were well provided with aunts and uncles through Jim's two brothers, Jack and Joe, and four sisters, Edie, Annie, Millie and Ginny. Tall, romantically handsome Uncle Jack, onetime trombonist in the Jim Mac Jazz Band, now a rent-collector for Liverpool Corporation, had been gassed in the Great War and ever afterwards was unable to speak above a whisper. Aunt Millie had married one of Jim's Cotton Exchange colleagues, Albert Kendal, so Paul really did have the 'Uncle Albert' he would later put into a song. The family reprobate was Aunt Edie's husband, Will Stapleton, a ship's steward who – like most of that profession – pilfered extravagantly from the vessels on which he served and eventually served three years in jail for stealing £500 from a cargo of banknotes on route to West Africa. Not for half a century was another family member to experience life behind bars.

The most vivacious of the aunts was Ginny or Gin, Paul's favourite from the beginning – and also destined to be named in one of his songs. She was the matriarch of the family, the one to whom all the others turned for advice. 'Mam was a very wise woman,' her son, Ian Harris, remembers, 'and she always knew how to get what she wanted. Once she even persuaded Liverpool Corporation to change a bus-route, so that the bus would run down our street.'

The children of the family, Harris recalls, were 'like nomads, because we were always staying at one another's houses. I spent a lot of time at Paul's and Mike's. Their mum, Aunt Mary, was very strict – but a lovely, kind woman.' There were frequent get-togethers in the Liverpool style, with lashings of drink and singing, dancing and laughing into the small hours. Uncle Jack would tell jokes in his intriguing whisper while Jim thumped away at the piano. When New Year's Eve was celebrated at Uncle Joe's house in Aintree, midnight would be signalled by the wheezy wail of a Scottish piper outside the front door. Gin's voice would always be loudest in the answering chorus of 'Let 'imin!'

Mary's Catholicism would normally have meant her sons being brought up and educated 'in the faith'. But here, as in all things, she deferred to her nominally agnostic but fundamentally Protestant husband. After their Catholic baptisms, and a few classes at Catholic Sunday school when they were very small, Paul and Mike had no further involvement with their mother's church. Instead, they were sent to Stockton Road Infants School, a short walk from their home, where the religious instruction was exclusively Anglican. Infants from other settler families were being enrolled at such a rate at Stockton Road that it soon became Britain's most overcrowded junior school, with 1500 pupils. Paul and Mike were among a contingent transferred to Joseph Williams Primary School in Gateacre, a half-hour bus ride away.

Paul had turned out to be left-handed, a fact that could easily have blighted his early education. Left-handed children used to be regarded as deliberately perverse, if not slightly sinister (the Latin word for left is 'sinistra'), and would often be forced to use their right hand, even held up to ridicule with terms like 'cack-handed' and 'leftie'. But at Joseph Williams, he was allowed to go on working with his left hand. As a result, his writing became meticulously neat – as his mother's was – and he showed a marked talent for drawing and painting.

From the start, he found his lessons easy and was popular with his teachers, thanks both to his impish good looks and the politeness and decorum Mary had instilled. The only criticism made of him then was one that would recur throughout his life – being too much reliant on his facility and charm and so never quite achieving the results he was capable of. One of his school reports described him as 'a very intelligent boy who, with a little more care and application, could easily be first'.

Among his classmates at Joseph Williams Primary was a tall, flaxen-haired girl named Bernice Stenson whose mother knew Mary McCartney and sometimes helped her with her midwifery duties. On one occasion, they had to deliver a baby whose mother was deaf. Mary showed her usual calm and patience, delegating Mrs Stenson to handle the paperwork while she 'got on down below'.

Bernice remembers how, by the age of six or seven, Paul was already known for his 'strong, clear' singing voice, and would always be given the lead role in school shows and pantomimes and the Christmas carol service. He had inherited his father's passion for music, instinctively singing the harmony line with songs he heard on the radio. When he turned 11, Jim hoped he might get into the choir at Liverpool Cathedral, the great sandstone edifice towering over the city that had somehow escaped Hitler's bombs. He was one of 90 boys who auditioned for the cathedral's director of music, Ronald Woan, by performing the Christmas carol 'Once in Royal David's City'. When his turn came, something made him deliberately fluff a high note he was perfectly capable of reaching and he was turned down; it would be almost another 40 years before the cathedral opened its doors to him.

Meanwhile, he had to settle for the choir of St Barnabas' Church, known as 'Barney's', in Mossley Hill, near Penny Lane. The services implanted a deep love of Anglican hymns with their sonorous organ chords and often high poetic words. Years later, when he began writing songs that echoed all round the world, people would often say the more serious ones 'sounded like hymns'. But at the time, Barney's main attraction was that choristers received payment for singing at weddings and funerals. 'If you did a wedding, it was 10 shillings [50p],' he would recall. 'I waited weeks – months – but I never got a wedding.'

Jim McCartney was understandably keen for him to learn the piano – learn it 'properly' rather than picking it up by ear, as Jim himself had done. No music lessons being available at Joseph Williams Primary, Paul began having private piano tuition from an elderly woman teacher. He soon gave up, complaining that it just added to his homework and that his teacher's house 'smelt of old people'.

In the end, what little formal musical tuition he ever had came mainly from his father and the upright piano in their living-room. While playing 'Stairway to Paradise' or some other old favourite, Jim would shout out the names of the chords, show him their shapes on the ebony and ivory keys and commentate on their sequences. His dad also loved brass band music and would take Paul to recitals in Liverpool's spacious parks, so passing on another deeply traditional taste that stuck.

But Jim always insisted he wasn't a 'real' musician, having had no professional training. Occasionally, he'd depart from his beloved Gershwin and Irving Berlin standards to play something he'd written himself back in his Jim Mac Jazz Band days, a pensive little tune named 'Eloise'. He refused to say he'd 'written' it, however: for him – as for the world in general – songwriters were a mystical freemasonry, found only in London or New York. All he'd done, he insisted with the modesty of another age, was 'make it up'.

The McCartneys were far from affluent. Jim's £6 per week from Hannay & Co. was unaugmented by commission or any other perks. Mary's pay as a midwife was six shillings (30p) more – a source of some embarrassment to them both – but still little enough for the long hours she worked.

However, in north-west England, just after the Second World War, a family of four could live quite comfortably on their combined earnings. Meat was not expensive, and formed the basis of

Mary's catering: lamb, pork, steaks, liver and Sunday roast beef with Yorkshire pudding, which she also served in the northern manner as a dessert, spread with Tate & Lyle's Golden Syrup. Paul ate every sort of meat with relish except tongue, which looked altogether too much like his own. Fruit came mainly from tins, peaches, pears and mandarin segments, drowned in custard or condensed milk, his special favourite. For years, the only orange juice he knew was a concentrate which the government had issued to children during the war in small, official-looking bottles, and was still widely available. 'You were supposed to dilute it,' he would remember. 'But we liked swigging it straight from the bottle.'

The brothers were always immaculately dressed, and lacked for nothing their schoolmates had. Every summer, Mary and Jim took them away on holiday, either to nearby North Wales or one of Butlin's seaside holiday camps. This being before Britain discovered leisure clothes, the boys wore their school shirts and short trousers to play on the beach while Jim sat in a deck-chair in his business suit.

Both of them joined Liverpool's 19th City Scout troop, which meant another uniform on top of their school one, and regular trips away to camp. Paul proved adept in Scout activities like tying knots and lighting fires, and took pleasure in the accumulation of badges proclaiming his multifaceted competence.

A snapshot taken on a Welsh hillside shows a prototypical 1950s family – Jim wearing a tweed jacket and open-necked shirt, looking rather like a pipe-puffing Fred Astaire; Mary in the rather formal frock for which she's exchanged her usual starched apron. Nine-year-old Paul sits up straight with arms akimbo, at ease with the camera even then. Mike has laughed as the shutter clicked, so is slightly out of focus.

Though their mother ran their lives, Jim was the head of the household whose every word was law. He insisted they should be polite in old-fashioned ways that even then were dying out, such as raising their school caps to 'ladies', even perfect strangers queuing at a bus-stop. 'We'd say "Aw, Dad, why do we have to do this? None

of the other boys do,'" Paul would remember. 'But we still did it.'
Total honesty over even the smallest things was another of Jim's
unbendable rules. 'I once found a £1 note in the street and he made
me hand it in at the police station.'

In even the best British homes of this era, children were subjected to corporal punishment without any interference from
outsiders. The blameless Jim had received his share of 'good hid-
ings' in his boyhood, and in turn did not scruple to wallop his sons
hard on the bottom or bare legs when they seriously misbehaved
– though Mary never did. Generally it would be Mike, the more
uninhibited and impulsive of the two, who felt the flat of their
father's hand whereas Paul usually managed to talk his way out
of trouble.

That ability helped him navigate his way through the rough
and tumble of primary school largely unscathed. Mike was always
getting into fights, but something about Paul made even the worst
bullies hesitate to pick on him. It didn't work every time. Near his
home, a narrow path called Dungeon Lane ran down to a stretch
of the Mersey known as the Cast Iron Shore, because it was littered with metal fragments from a nearby ship-breakers. Here one
day when he was on his own, two bigger boys waylaid him and
robbed him of his cherished wristwatch. Both boys lived near the
McCartneys; there was a police prosecution and Paul had to identify them in open court. Even if he was no bruiser, he didn't lack
courage.

Mary McCartney continued to devote herself to her midwifery
so selflessly that Jim worried her own health might suffer. Eventually, to his relief, she took a different job with the local health
authority, accompanying school doctors on their rounds in the
Walton and Allerton area. That meant a normal nine-to-five
day rather than turning out on her bike at all hours and in all
weathers.

At the clinic where she was now based, Mary made friends with
Bella Johnson, a youthful widow whose teenage daughter, Olive,
was a secretary at the Law Society in central Liverpool, working

just around the corner from Jim at the Cotton Exchange. She was a sophisticated young woman who owned her own car and spoke with – to Mary – an impressively 'posh' accent. She became Paul and Mike's unofficial big sister, joining in their games, taking them for trips in her car and rowing on the lake at Wilmslow.

Bella would often join them for high tea at 12 Ardwick Road, when Mary served a special treat: sandwiches filled with sugar-sprinkled sliced apple. Both boys clearly adored their mother, though it always seemed to Olive that Michael had greater need of her. 'I remember Mike sitting at Mary's feet. He was the one you always felt you wanted to love and protect. With Paul, you loved him but you knew you'd never have to protect him.'

In 1952, Paul faced the hurdle of the Eleven Plus examination which decided the educational future of all British children in the state system, sending bright 11-year-olds to grammar schools and consigning the others to 'secondary modern' ones or technical colleges where they learned trades like carpentry or plumbing.

For his final terms at Joseph Williams Primary, he had an inspirational teacher named F.G. Woolard, who got all but one of a 40-strong class through the Eleven Plus. Paul was one of only four out of 90 candidates from Joseph Williams to be awarded places at Liverpool Institute High School for Boys – actually a grammar school, the most prestigious in the city, though known with typical Scouse familiarity as 'the Inny'. Later, Mike would scrape in there, too.

June 1953 brought the coronation of 26-year-old Queen Elizabeth II, the moment when austerity finally ended for Britain. Like thousands of other people, Jim and Mary bought their first television set to watch the (rain-soaked) Coronation procession through London and the crowning in Westminster Abbey on a minute black and white screen. Bella and Olive Johnson were among the crowd of friends and relatives invited to 'look in' (as TV-watching used to be known) in a cinema-like atmosphere with rows of chairs, every light extinguished and the curtains drawn.

Getting a place at the Inny had not been Paul's only recent

triumph. He was also one of 60 Liverpool children to win a prize in a Coronation essay competition and receive it in a ceremony at the city's Picton Hall. He would remember how hearing his name called to go up onto the stage made him shake with fear – not a reaction he'd often have in similar situations thereafter.

The page-long essay 'by Paul McCartney, age 10 years, 10 months', already shows a talent for telling a story in a short space and is a model of neatness, its spelling and punctuation almost perfect:

On the Coronation Day of William the Conquerer, senseless Saxon folk gathered round Westminster Abbey to cheer their Norman king as he walked down the aisle. The Normans thinking this was an insult turned upon the Saxons killing nearly all of them. But on the Coronation of our lovely young queen, Queen Elizabeth II, no rioting nor killing will take place because present day royalty rule with affection rather than force. The crowds outside Buckingham Palace will be greater than they have been for any other Coronation, so will the processional route to the Abbey. Preparations are going on all over the world, even in Australia people are preparing to take that long voyage to England. In London, children, for a Coronation treat, are being given a free seat by the roadside. But the London children are not the only lucky children, for youngsters in other parts of Britain are receiving mugs with a portrait of the Queen engraved on the china. Souvenirs are being made ready for any tourists who come to see this marvellous spectacle, one of these being the Coronation Loving Cup which is designed to show both Queen Elizabeth the Second on the front and Queen Elizabeth the First on the back. Another is a goblet which is being made in Edinburgh and has a bubble enclosed in its stem, and the fancy letters, ER, is engraved in the glass. One alteration is that the diamonds, rubies, emeralds and sapphires in the crown are being dismantled, polished and replaced by expert jewellers. But after

all this bother, many people will agree with me that it was well
worth it.

That 'portrait of the Queen' would reappear in another much-
praised composition, 14 years later. And the whole thing might be
paraphrased as 'Her Majesty's a pretty nice girl'.

3

'I learned to put a shell around me'

Liverpool Institute High School for Boys was housed in a neoclassical building in the heart of the city's once affluent, still elegant Georgian quarter. It had been founded in 1837 as an adult education 'institute', which later split into a boys' school and Liverpool College of Art. The two shared the same L-shaped block while functioning independently with separate entrances – the Inny's mini-Parthenon colonnade in Mount Street, the art college around the corner in Hope Street.

As a grammar school in the best Victorian tradition, it educated its pupils free of charge yet with the same refinements as public (which in Britain denotes private) schools like Eton and Harrow. There was a uniform of black blazers, green-and-black striped ties and caps; there were teachers known as 'masters' in black scholastic gowns, licensed to administer ritual public chastisement with a cane. An ethos of public service was expressed in a Latin motto which for two of its pupils was to prove eerily prophetic: 'Non Nobis Solum Sed Toti Mundo Natior' – 'not for ourselves alone but for the whole world were we born'.

Over the decades, the school had produced an impressive crop of politicians, industrial tycoons and academics, most notably the Nobel prize-winning physicist Professor Charles Glover Barkla. Another old boy was Arthur Askey, one of many nationally famous professional comedians to come out of Liverpool. At one stage in his school career, Paul would sit at the same wooden, slope-topped classroom desk Askey had used 40 years earlier.

New boys at the Inny spent a year in its Lower School, then were sorted into streams according to their academic aptitudes. The A-stream's syllabus revolved around classics, Latin and/or Greek, and the B-stream's around modern languages. Though Paul was clearly bright enough for either, he went into the B-stream. One of his earliest school friends was a fellow B-streamer named Ian James, from Elswick Street in the humble quarter of south Liverpool known as the Dingle. Classroom desks being arranged in alphabetical order, the two sat near each other and attended the same lessons except that Ian took French while Paul took German. They both learned Spanish from a teacher named Miss Inkley whose thick make-up, in her class's perfervid imagination, concealed scars acquired as a wartime secret agent. She taught them a silly little Spanish song about three bunny rabbits in a tree, 'Tres conejos en un árbol', that would stay imprinted on Paul's memory for ever.

Ian James remembers him as a highly personable, popular figure with an appeal by no means limited to their fellow juniors. 'He was a brilliant mimic,' says James. 'We were just starting to get the *Goon Show* on the radio, and Paul could do all the voices from it, like Eccles and Bluebottle. In the mornings, you'd see him in the playground with a little crowd around him, acting out the show he'd heard the night before. He was an entertainer even then.'

Schoolboy nicknames derive either from mockery and contempt or respect and affection. Paul's nickname of Maca – with one 'c' rather than its familiar two – definitely belonged to the second category even though, after a year, he had to share it with his brother Michael.

Yet, despite the promise he'd shown in primary school, he did not shine particularly brightly at the Inny. None of his lessons was a problem to him, and he could easily have come top, or nearly, in every subject. The problem was one belied by his innocent face and always polite, conciliatory manner: he hated being told what to do. Even in his two strongest subjects, his performance fell below expectations. Ian James, who shared his English class, saw little sign of the care and enthusiasm he'd expended on his Coronation essay. 'Our English master, Mr Jones, had the same initials as the Queen's on the Coronation mugs, E.R. [Elizabeth Regina], so we used to call him Lizzie. You were each given a certain number of good-conduct marks that were taken away for bad behaviour. Paul and I used to chatter so much in Lizzie's class that we'd both lose nearly all our good-conduct marks.'

Nor did the Inny much develop the talent for drawing and painting he'd had since kindergarten or his keen interest in all the visual arts. His Coronation essay prize had included a book token, which he'd used to buy a grown-up volume about Picasso, Salvador Dalí and Victor Pasmore. He'd also since won a prize for a drawing of St Aidan's Church in Speke, an oasis of beauty among the raw council estates.

At school, he felt a powerful attraction to the art cupboard with its blocks of cartridge paper and bundles of virgin pencils and paintbrushes. But the lessons themselves were lost on him. He turned his talent, instead, to drawing caricatures of his teachers and classmates and the characters he observed each day from the top deck of his bus to school.

The Inny's distinguished alumni included several who had made their mark in music, like the conductor and composer Albert Coates, the baritone Sir Charles Santley and the folk singer and composer Stan Kelly-Bootle. The school's prospectus in the mid-Fifties recorded that its music room 'has a piano where boys can play by arrangement with the teacher. It also has a gramophone player on which boys can play records after 1.30 p.m.' The music master from 1955, Noel 'Neddy' Evans, is remembered by other former pupils, such as newsreader Peter Sissons, as 'a fantastic teacher'.

But none of this was to figure in Paul's musical development. He decided early on that Mr Evans wasn't worthy of his attention and 'Neddy' seemingly made little effort to change his mind.

*

British children at that time were subjected to nothing like the deluge of erotica that nowadays saturates even the youngest. Most boys of Paul's generation did not reach puberty until the start of their teens and many didn't learn about sex until even later. As a rule, enlightenment came from their fathers – as uncomfortable as their own fathers had been in the same situation – wrapped up in evasive metaphors about 'the seed of life' and 'the birds and bees'.

Reserved, rather straitlaced Jim McCartney was particularly ill-equipped for this most important talk with his elder son. As Paul would remember, Jim's idea of sex-education was advising him to watch dogs 'at it' in the street. For amplification, he'd secretly consult *Black's Medical Dictionary*, which his mother used in her midwifery, leafing through gruesome chapters on boils and haemorrhoids to a section with illustrations of the female anatomy. Even to a 13-year-old crackling with testosterone, they could not be called erotic, though the term mons Veneris, once he'd discovered it meant 'mound of Venus', set his imagination racing.

Ever since kindergarten, he'd been aware of his attractiveness to girls and the infallible effect of turning his brown eyes full on them. A slight blip occurred in his early teens when, for no discernible reason, he suddenly ballooned in size. The chubbiness soon disappeared, never to return, but the self-consciousness it brought lingered long afterwards. Years later, when writing about the most important encounter of his life, he would describe himself on that day at St Peter's church fete as 'a fat schoolboy'.

By now, he was attracting girls by the flock. Bernice Stenson, his former classmate at Joseph Williams Primary, had a crush on him, so did most of her friends. 'He had this angelic-type face and we'd see it peering out from the top deck of the 86 bus as it passed us [when] he was on his way to Liverpool Institute and we were waiting for our bus to Aigburth Vale High School,' Bernice recalls. 'We'd all jump up and down and wave and shout at him.'

In 1955, Mary McCartney's good name with the local authority took her family another step up the housing ladder. They left Speke for 20 Forthlin Road, Allerton – part of a council estate, like their two previous homes, but in an area that was predominantly middle class, in places even 'posh'. This meant an enormous amount to Mary in her constant battle to raise the sights of her two sons; as Paul would remember, 'She hoped some of the poshness would rub off on us.' Much as he loved, even revered, his mother, he'd reached the age when all young people criticise their parents without mercy. He would tease Mary about her genteel speech mannerisms, for example the way she always pronounced 'ask' as 'ah-sk'. 'That's "ask", Mum,' he once corrected her, using Scouse pronunciation, as in 'Askey'. All his life, he was to reproach himself for so thoughtlessly hurting her feelings.

Twenty Forthlin Road was the McCartneys' first home with an inside toilet. Though small, it was built to a high standard, with three bedrooms and a dining- as well as a sitting-room. Its rear windows overlooked Mather Avenue's police training school, whose extensive grounds lent a rather countrified atmosphere. The weekly rent was 26 shillings, or less than £1.50. A telephone was installed so that Mary could always be contacted by the health authority in an emergency. It was the only private phone in the street, so a constant stream of neighbours would always be dropping by to make calls, each leaving three old pennies in payment.

The police training school over the back garden wall did not take long to make its presence felt. On their first night in the house, Paul and Mike slept in twin beds in the large back bedroom. Next morning, they were awoken by dogs barking and what sounded like a gunshot. 'We looked out, and there was a policeman running away from a big Alsatian like a wolf,' Mike McCartney remembers. 'He was turning and firing a gun at it, and we could see he had a big thick glove on. Bang, bang! went the gun, but it was firing blanks. They were training dogs to grab the arm of someone trying to escape and getting them used to the noise of guns. We thought it was a pretty exciting way to say "Hello".'

The family saw 20 Forthlin Road as the start of a bright new era and refurbished it extensively, though there wasn't much money to spare. For a sitting-room carpet, they could afford only runners

– narrow offcuts in different patterns – while the wallpaper was a selection of 'roll-ends' in various designs including silver-grey willow pattern. Mary couldn't decide which paper she preferred, so the samples were hung together in a patchwork to help her make up her mind. Sadly, she never would.

After Michael's birth, she had suffered from mastitis, an inflammation of the breast-tissue caused by breastfeeding. Recently, she had begun to feel similar pain, which at first she'd thought no more than heartburn and tried to treat with the indigestion remedy Bisodol. When that had no effect, she decided the menopause (in those days more delicately known as 'the Change') must be to blame. In the summer of 1956, 14-year-old Paul and 12-year-old Michael, as usual, went away to Boy Scout camp together. The weather was unusually cold and wet, and Mary told her clinic colleague Bella Johnson she was concerned they might be suffering under canvas. She was so worried that Bella's daughter, Olive, offered to drive her to the camp to make sure they were all right.

They were quite all right, but Mary wasn't: on the return journey to Liverpool she was in such pain that she had to lie down on the car's back seat. When she got home, she went straight to bed. Trained nurse that she was, she already suspected the worst. 'Oh, Olive,' she whispered to her friend, 'I don't want to leave the boys *just* yet.'

The pain seemed to subside but, in a few days, came back worse than ever. Paul and Michael had by now returned from camp, with no idea anything was wrong, for Mary seemed her usual brisk, capable self – and, as everyone knew, nurses never got sick. The only giveaway was her sudden yearning for the Catholic faith she'd all but abandoned since her marriage. Michael was mystified one day to find her sitting on her bed weeping, holding a crucifix and a picture of a relative who'd recently become a priest.

Finally Jim persuaded her to use her contacts in the health service to get a quick appointment with a specialist. He diagnosed breast cancer and arranged for her immediate admission to Liverpool's Northern Hospital. From her own medical training, Mary knew he'd as good as pronounced a death sentence. Before leaving her precious new home – whose array of sitting-room wallpaper samples still awaited her decision – she cleaned it from top to bottom and washed and ironed all Jim's and the boys' clothes.

She was rushed straight into the operating theatre for a mastectomy, which wasn't carried out: the cancer had spread too far. There was no hope. Paul and Michael hadn't been told what was wrong with her, and now weren't told she was dying. When Jim took them to see her in hospital, she did her best to be cheerful and reassuring, but Paul, the ever observant, saw blood on her bedsheet and guessed the truth.

Mary received the last rites from a Catholic priest and asked for a rosary to be put around her wrist. Before she slipped into a coma, her last thoughts were of her sons and how she would have loved to see them grow up. She died on 31 October 1956, aged 47.

Suddenly Paul's and Michael's world no longer had its warm centre of hugs, nice meals, gentle fingers on their foreheads when they felt ill, thermometers comfortingly shaken and popped under their tongues. Everything the word 'mum' calls to mind – and that teenage boys still need as much as newborn infants – was gone, except for that last pile of lovingly laundered shirts and towels back at Forthlin Road.

For Jim McCartney, the blow was devastating. Mary had not only been the love of his life but its organiser. Outside of his beloved garden, he had always left domestic matters to her. Now he faced the task of caring for Paul and Michael and steering them through adolescence and its numerous problems – all without the second wage packet Mary had always provided. When the awful news was broken, Paul couldn't help blurting out, 'What are we going to do without her money?'

At first, Jim seemed unable to come to terms with his loss, sobbing that he wanted 'to be with Mary', almost as if he meant to end his own life, too. Men in that era, especially northern men, were not supposed to show emotion, and his sons had never known him other than totally composed behind his pipe.

'That was the worst thing for me,' Paul would remember. 'Seeing my dad cry.' But, grief-stricken though he was, the brown eyes shed no public tears. 'I was determined not to let it affect me. I carried on. I learned to put a shell around me.'

4

Puttin' On the Style

Rock 'n' roll did many things for British boys when it burst on the unsuspecting 1950s. For Paul, it turned a shell into a suit of shiny armour.

Jim McCartney's collapse was short-lived. After Mary's funeral – the Catholic one she'd requested on her deathbed – Jim dried his eyes and buckled down to his new responsibilities. Since their mother's death, Paul and Michael had been staying with their Auntie Gin and Uncle Harry in Huyton. When they returned to Forthlin Road, their dad seemed back to his old disciplined, under-stated self.

On his small salary, there was no question of employing a housekeeper. So, at the age of 55, he had to teach himself to cook and do all the other household jobs that men of his generation, especially in the north of England, regarded as 'women's work'. His sons pitched in to help like the Boy Scouts they were, Paul now the proud holder of a 'bivouac badge' for building a fire and cooking over it. Their plentiful uncles and aunts rallied round with frequent morale-boosting visits and invitations to meals, Every Tuesday, Gin and Millie would clean the house from top to bottom and have a hot dinner waiting when Paul and Mike came in from school.

The home Jim created was rough and ready, but never gloomy. 'The house was full of laughter,' Mike McCartney says. 'There was always music playing – Dad with his records or on the piano, or the relatives around for a sing-song. Dad could have his moments [of grieving for Mary] but Auntie Gin would be there, or someone else, and it'd soon be all right again.'

In the otherwise male atmosphere, Jim perpetuated Mary's many hospital-inspired rules for hygiene and health – for example, only white tablecloths and towels because coloured ones got dirty without showing it. He also carried on her concern over her sons' diet, urging them to eat healthily, with plenty of roughage, and inquiring every day whether their bowels were working satisfactorily. Unlike most bachelor establishments, too, the house always smelt of lavender, which Jim grew in the back garden, then rubbed between his fingers to unlock its scent.

Bereaved families often find a pet dog helps to ease the pain, but Paul and Mike had no need of that: the sound of barking from the nearby police training school went on almost around the clock. The wide grassy tract behind their house provided a constant spectacle of dogs being trained or stately police horses at exercise. There were regular public displays of horse-riding and obedience-trials, always culminating with the routine the boys had seen on their first morning – the pistol-firing fugitive pursued by an Alsatian, grabbed by his outsize glove and sent sprawling onto the grass. Paul and Mike would put chairs on the flat roof of their concrete garden shed and see the whole show for nothing. Paul particularly loved the vast chestnut police horses whose duties, in those riot-free days in Liverpool, were purely ceremonial. Watching them go through their dignified paces, he little dreamed of the thoroughbreds he himself would one day own and ride.

Jim McCartney might be a humble cotton salesman who'd left school aged 14, but he had a capacious mind and memory and a thirst for knowledge he'd always striven to pass on to his sons. He prided himself on his vocabulary and religiously filled in the crossword puzzles in his morning *Daily Express* and evening *Liverpool Echo*. When an unfamiliar word cropped up, he'd send the boys to check its spelling in the multivolume *Newnes Family Encyclopaedia*, which for him represented the fount of all knowledge. Paul, as a result, was the one in his class at the Inny who knew how to spell 'phlegm'. His cousin, Bert Danher, caught the crossword bug from Jim sufficiently to become a puzzle-compiler in later life.

Jim was a treasury of proverbs and sayings, which in Liverpool can verge on the surreal: 'There's no hair on a seagull's chest . . .'; 'It's imposausigable. . .'; 'Put it there if it weighs a ton' (shake hands); 'You're about as useful as a one-legged man in an arse-kicking contest'. If ever Paul or Mike wanted to postpone a boring task, their father's response was always 'D.I.N.', for 'Do it now'; if they were quarrelling, he'd tell them to 'let it be', or forget it. Another oft-repeated maxim summed up Jim's whole civilised approach to life: 'The two most important "-ations" in life are "toler-" and "moder-".'

'Dad was always encouraging us to make something of ourselves,' Mike McCartney says. 'That was his mantra – giving us the confidence to go out there and be something in that big old world.'

But even for a singular boy like Paul, the world of his boyhood seemed to hold little promise or excitement. Mid-Fifties Britain may have had a stability later generations would envy, but its downside was stifling dullness and predictability. The British had had quite enough excitement with the Second World War, and now wished only for everlasting peace to enjoy all the commodities that had lately come off the ration, like eggs, butter and sugar.

Youth had none of the power it would later enjoy – in fact, was barely recognised at all. Around the age of 16, boys turned into men and girls into women, dressing and talking like their parents, adopting the same values, seeking the same amusements, soon marrying and 'settling down' in their turn. Only university and college students, a tiny minority, were permitted any drawn-out transition from adolescence to maturity, albeit still in the same tweed jackets and frumpy frocks as their elders.

The war had made popular music a vital part of everyday life, but as yet it had no specific appeal to the young. The BBC's Light Programme gave employment to dozens of dance orchestras and bands, all of whom performed live on-air, in programmes still with a wartime flavour: *Calling All Forces, Workers' Playtime, Music While*

You Work. Record-sales were already big business: the *New Musical Express* had started a 'Top 12' chart in 1952 and extended it to a Top 20 in 1954. Every new song was also issued as sheet music so that it could be reproduced, Victorian-style, on parlour pianos at home.

The biggest hits were by American artistes like Guy Mitchell, Frankie Laine and Doris Day, though Sinatra-esque British crooners like Dennis Lotis and Dickie Valentine inspired large female followings. The songs – written by those mysterious 'professionals' for whom Jim McCartney had such respect – tended to be faux-Italian or -Irish ballads, themes from the newest Disney film or novelty numbers like 'How Much Is That Doggie in the Window?'

A few successful vocalists came from Liverpool, notably Frankie Vaughan, Michael Holliday and Lita Roza. But, like the comedians for which the city was more famous – Robb Wilton, Tommy Handley, Arthur Askey – they were advised to lose their Scouse accents and never mention their birthplace in their acts. Showbusiness superstition held that anything glamorous or desirable had to come, or seem to come, from London. The last place it could conceivably come from was a sooty seaport on a muddy river, far away in the north-west.

Paul's thirteenth birthday present from his father was a trumpet. The instrument with which Jim led his little dance band before the war still had greatest prestige on the bandstand, thanks to America's Harry James and Britain's Eddie Calvert, aka 'the Man with the Golden Trumpet'. Calvert's instrumental version of 'Cherry Pink and Apple Blossom White', from the film *Underwater*, had been number one in Britain's new Top 20 for four weeks in 1955.

However, Jim had no idea of launching Paul on a musical career, even one as modest as his own had been. Rather, the trumpet would be a social asset in a city where much of the best entertainment took place in private homes. 'If you can play something, son,' he advised, 'you'll always get invited to parties.'

Rock 'n' roll first crept up on Britain in the dark. During mid-1955, showings of an American film called *Blackboard Jungle* caused disturbances among young members of its audience that left a trail of wrecked cinemas across the country. This reaction was not to the film, which concerned delinquent high school students in New York, but to a song played over the opening credits, 'Rock Around the Clock' by Bill Haley and his Comets.

In hindsight, the record seems innocent enough, a conventional, intelligible tenor voice simply chanting the hours in the day when one can rock – i.e. dance. To adult British ears at the time, its slap-bass beat and braying saxophone were a din almost as destructively hideous as the recent war's bombs. Indeed its consequences were to be almost as traumatic, and much longer lasting.

The war had not made Britain any less rigidly class-bound, and rock 'n' roll music initially affected only the working class. Its first enthusiasts, the instigators of those cinema riots, were Teddy boys: young men who defied the drab national dress code by sporting Edwardian-style velvet-collared jackets and narrow 'drainpipe' trousers, with accessories often including switchblade knives, razors, brass knuckles and bicycle chains. 'Teds' responding to rock 'n' roll awoke fears of a juvenile delinquency problem on the same scale as America's, not to mention an older, darker fear of proletarian uprising.

But, as was soon apparent, the musical malignancy had spread much wider. 'Rock Around the Clock' went to number one in the new Top 20, and was followed by a string of further Bill Haley hits, all using 'rock' in the title and all unleashing further mayhem. When Haley visited Britain in 1956, arriving by ocean liner, he was greeted by crowds that even the young Queen would hardly attract. That was his big mistake. In total contrast with his music, he proved to be a chubby, benign-looking man with a kiss-curl plastered on his forehead and not the faintest whiff of danger or subversion. When, soon afterwards, his record-sales went into decline, Britain's parents breathed a sigh of relief, thinking the crisis had passed.

But by now America had a new rock 'n' roller of a very different stamp. Like Bill Haley, the bizarrely-named Elvis Presley wore a guitar but, unlike any vocalist – that is, any *white* vocalist – he used his body, especially his hips and buckling knees, to underline the amorous fervour of what he sang. He was, in other words, raw sex on crêpe soles. While Haley's deleterious effect had largely been on males, Presley's was overwhelmingly on females, rousing previously decorous, tight-corseted Fifties young womanhood to hysterical screams, reciprocal bodily writhings and an apparent common compulsion to tear the singer's clothes from his back.

Presley's 'Heartbreak Hotel', recorded in January 1956, was the first rock 'n' roll song truly reflecting the adolescent psyche in all its self-dramatisation and self-pity. Presley did not (and never would) follow Bill Haley's example of meeting his British public, but film footage showed him to be the ultimate Teddy boy, with black backswept hair, brooding eyes, a top lip permanently curled as if in disdain for the entire adult world that hated, feared, mocked and execrated him. Over the next two years, he would enjoy a run of UK hits no other act would match until the following decade.

Paul was an instant convert to Elvis, hereafter known by Christian name alone. 'I first saw his picture in a magazine – I think it was an ad for "Heartbreak Hotel" and I thought, "Wow! He's so good looking . . . he's perfect. The Messiah has arrived."' When thoughts of his mother began gnawing at him, 'Hound Dog', 'Blue Suede Shoes', 'Teddy Bear', or especially 'All Shook Up' (with its glorious – and prophetic – mumble of 'Mm-hm-hm hm yay-yay-*yeah*') were infallible balm.

He also loved Little Richard, the first black rock 'n' roller, who combined a demented shriek with outrageous camp that went completely over most British heads. Though Paul's voice was the lightest alto, he found he could do spot-on imitations of both the Presley mumble and the Richard scream. The crowd now gathered round him in the Inny playground not to hear a radio but a rock show.

Today, pop music is an unavoidable element of daily life, playing on perpetual loops in shops, offices, bars, restaurants and public spaces, buzzing in the earpieces of bus- and train-travellers, thumping out of cars, ringing around construction sites, whispering inside lifts and tinkling down telephone lines. But in rock 'n' roll's early days in Britain, it received public airing only in the disreputable haunts of Teddy boys – espresso bars, bikers' cafes, pinball arcades and fairgrounds.

In America, it had received instant circulation via the country's hundreds of commercial radio stations. But British radio was the monopoly of the traditionally stuffy, puritanical BBC which – with all those conventional bands and orchestras to protect – excluded it completely. Its sole mouthpiece was Radio Luxembourg, beamed from far away in mainland Europe, which operated a nightly English language service playing all the new American releases, somewhat blurred by intrusive French or Belgian voices and static.

Like most families in that pre-transistor era, the McCartneys had only one radio, a bulky, valve-operated apparatus housed in a wooden cabinet and known as a 'wireless'. Unfortunately, this was sited immovably in the sitting-room, where Jim McCartney liked to play his kind of music on the gramophone during Luxembourg's evening transmission hours. An inveterate handyman, Jim kept a drawer full of electronic oddments he thought 'might come in useful someday'. One evening, he came up to Paul's and Mike's rooms – they'd stopped sharing by then – and presented each of them with a set of black Bakelite headphones.

'There were wires disappearing through the floorboards to the radio below, so that we'd be able to listen to Radio Luxembourg in our bedrooms,' Mike McCartney remembers. 'So Dad would have his Mantovani downstairs while upstairs we'd have Elvis, Little Richard, Fats Domino and Chuck Berry . . . and our kid [Paul] would be singing along or trying to write down the lyrics. I sometimes think that if it hadn't been for those Bakelite headphones, there wouldn't have been any Beatles.'

Though the music no longer destroyed cinemas, the press kept up an unremitting tirade against it, supported by opportunistic politicians, teachers, clergy and 'real' musicians of Jim's generation. Its lyrics, mostly nonsensical enough to have been written by Lewis Carroll, were condemned as 'obscene' and its rhythm as 'jungle-like' – a racist allusion to its origins in black rhythm and blues. Rock 'n' roll singers were ridiculed as inarticulate morons, controlled by unscrupulous managers (all too true in most cases), whose fraudulence was summed up by their inability to play the guitars they flourished and spun about them. Every commentator agreed: it couldn't be long before young people saw through the con-trick that was being perpetrated on them and the whole noisy nuisance blew over.

But there was no going back. Thanks to Elvis, and the Teds, British boys en masse had discovered something previously unknown in their stodgy, sleepy country, except to a tiny metropolitan elite. They had discovered style. So Paul joined the queue at Bioletti's barber shop, beside the Penny Lane roundabout, waiting for his former boyish tousle to be shaped into a toppling Elvis quiff and combed back at the sides into the two interwoven rear flaps known as a 'duck's arse', or DA. Unfortunately, like many another 14-year-old would-be Elvis, he spent his weekdays in a school uniform whose cap was designed to be worn squarely on the head, to the ruination of any coiffure let alone this springy, aerated one.

The Institute had a strict dress code, personally enforced by its headmaster, J. R. Edwards, popularly known as 'the Baz' (short for 'bastard'). Nowhere was he more of a baz than over caps, which had to be worn at all times on pain of severe punishment. The only way Paul could do so without harming the precious cockade was to clamp his cap onto the back of his head like a Jewish yarmulka.

Grammar school boys, too, now craved the Teds' drainpipe trousers that British parents hated almost as much as they did rock 'n' roll music. Even the easy-going Jim could not abide 'drainies' and insisted Paul's dark grey school trousers should retain their billowy 24-inch cuffs (although in Jim's own pre-Great War boyhood, every Englishman from the prime minister downwards had been slim-shanked).

Other boys were having furious arguments with their fathers on the subject – but not Paul. Few men's outfitters yet sold tapered trousers ready to wear; the usual thing was for an alterations tailor to 'take in' a conventional baggy pair. Paul had his school ones taken in a little at a time, first to 20 inches, then 18, then 16, so that Jim wouldn't notice the erosion.

He found other ways of taking in his dad as well, without ever actually lying. 'Near my house there was a tailor who'd do the job while you waited,' Ian James remembers. 'Paul used to leave for school wearing ordinary-width trousers, then have them altered at lunch-time. If Jim said anything about them when he got home, he'd say, "They're the same pair you saw me go out in this morning."'

Most days on his bus journey to school, Paul sat next to a fellow Institute pupil, a pale, solemn-looking boy named George Harrison who lived in Upton Green, Speke, not far from the McCartneys' former home in Ardwick Road, and whose father, Harry, worked as a bus-driver for Liverpool Corporation. Often, when the number 86 stopped on Mather Avenue to pick up Paul, Mr Harrison would be behind the wheel, so he'd get a free ride.

George was a year his junior and in the class below his at the Inny, so during the day there was a wide social gap between them. But on the journey to and from school they could be friends. Paul was much impressed by an episode illustrative of their very different families. After some misdemeanour, George had received the Inny's commonest corporal punishment, one or more strokes on the palm of the hand with a wooden ruler. 'The teacher missed his hand and caught him on the wrist, and made a big red weal. The next day, his dad came to the school and punched the teacher on the nose. If I'd complained to my dad that I'd been beaten, he'd have said, "You probably deserved it."'

After 'Heartbreak Hotel' came out, much of Paul and George's conversation revolved around Elvis – his astounding voice, his amazing clothes, the guitar that seemed his indispensable accomplice in whipping up female frenzy. George revealed that his bus-driving dad had learned to play the guitar while serving in the Merchant Navy and that he himself now possessed one. Paul in return made the rather less sensational announcement that he was learning the trumpet.

Out of school hours, his main friend continued to be Ian James. They were both good-looking, and both equally obsessed by their hair and clothes. Among the new records currently on Radio Luxembourg was 'A White Sport Coat', by the American country singer Marty Robbins (anglicised into 'A White *Sports* Coat' by Britain's King Brothers). Paul had searched high and low for such a garment and finally found one in silver-flecked oatmeal, cut in daring Teddy boy 'drape' style with a flap on its breast pocket. Ian had a similar Elvis quiff and DA and a similar jacket in pale blue.

He also had access to a guitar just at this moment when the eyes of British boys were becoming riveted to the instrument. His grandfather had been bandmaster to the local Salvation Army in the Dingle and he'd grown up with a Spanish guitar around the house – then considered nothing but a background rhythm-maker. When the skiffle craze arrived, and Paul finally got a guitar of his own, Ian looked like his natural musical partner.

Skiffle derived from American folk music during the Great Depression when poor whites who couldn't afford conventional instruments would improvise them from kitchen washboards, jugs, and kazoos. In its British reincarnation, it became a mash-up of blues, country, folk, jazz and spirituals – all genres about which most young Britons had little or no previous knowledge.

Its biggest, in fact only, star was Lonnie Donegan – like Paul, of mixed Irish and Scots origins – who had previously played banjo with Chris Barber's jazz band. In 1956, Donegan and a rhythm section from the Barber band recorded a skiffle version of 'Rock Island Line' by the blues giant (and convicted killer) Huddie 'Lead Belly' Ledbetter. Its subject matter, railroad-tolls on Rock Island, Illinois, could hardly have been more mundane, but that word 'rock', in any context, now set schoolboy hormones aflame. 'Rock Island Line' went to number eight in Britain and also became a hit across the Atlantic, an unprecedented example of British musicians selling Americana back to the Americans.

Skiffle offered the romance of America – chiefly represented by freight trains, penitentiaries and chain-gangs – but without the taint of sex and Teddy boy violence attached to rock 'n' roll. The BBC relented so far as to put on a radio programme called *Saturday Skiffle Club* and an early-evening TV show especially for teenagers titled like a train, the *Six-Five Special*, with skiffle theme music. Whereas rock 'n' roll was an unknowable alchemy created by incomprehensible beings, skiffle could be played by anyone with a cheap acoustic guitar and mastery of the three simple chords of 12-bar blues. Its other essential instruments were literally home-made: 'basses' improvised from resonant empty boxes, broom-handles and bits of string, and serrated kitchen washboards, scrubbed with fingers capped by steel thimbles to create a scratchy, frenetic percussion.

The effect was galvanising on bashful British boys with no previous musical leanings who, hitherto, would rather have committed hara-kiri than get up in public and sing. All over the country, juvenile skiffle groups sprang – or, rather, strummed – into life under exotically homespun names, like the Vipers, the Nomads, the Hobos, the Streamliners and the Sapphires. The guitar rocketed even further in popularity, so much so that at one point a national shortage was declared.

In November 1956, when Lonnie Donegan appeared at Liverpool's Empire Theatre, Paul was in the audience. Before the show, he hung around the Empire stage-door, hoping for a glimpse of Donegan arriving for rehearsal. Some local factory hands had sneaked out of work with the same idea; Donegan paused to talk to them and on learning they'd gone AWOL he wrote a note to their foreman, asking that they shouldn't be penalised because of him. Paul had expected metaphorical stars to be as cold and distant as the real thing, and Donegan's friendliness and graciousness to those fans made a profound impression on him.

By now, the 'King of Skiffle' had dropped all 1930s-hobo visuals from his act, performing the ragged-arsed repertoire of Lead Belly and Woody Guthrie in black tie, with a tuxedoed trio that included a virtuoso electric guitarist, Denny Wright. That touch of sophistication was Paul's Damascene moment; from then on, he burned to play a guitar and sing – an impossibility with a trumpet. So after the Donegan show, he asked his dad if he could swap his birthday present for a guitar. To Jim McCartney, as to all musicians of his generation, rock 'n' roll and skiffle were undifferentiated cacophony. But, remembering how his own dad, the brass band E-flat tuba man, had once ridiculed his love of jazz and swing, he resolved to be tolerant. So Paul returned the trumpet to Rushworth and Draper's music store and in its place selected a Zenith acoustic guitar with f-holes and a red sunburst finish, price £15.

For instruction he turned to Ian James, who now owned a superior Rex model with a cutaway body, for reaching the tinkliest treble notes at the bottom of the fretboard. Ian showed him the first basic one-finger chords, G and G7, and how to tune the Zenith – which, with his natural musical ear, presented no problem. To begin with he played as Ian did, with his guitar-neck pointing leftwards, but found it extremely awkward and laborious. Then he happened to see a picture of the American country star Slim Whitman, a 'leftie' like himself, and realised he should be holding his guitar the other way around, fingering the fretboard with his right hand and strumming with his left. That, of course, put the bottom string where the top one ought to be, so he had to remove all six and put them into reverse order. The white scratch plate – over which the strummer's hand slides after each stroke – proved too firmly screwed in place to be switched over, so it had to be left upside-down.

All this was less than a month after Mary's death. And for Paul, in his buttoned-up grief, the Zenith came as salvation with six strings. He played it at every possible moment, even when sitting on the toilet, both the inside and outside ones. 'It became an obsession . . . took over his whole life,' remembers Mike McCartney. 'It came along at just the right moment and became his escape.'

He also began to sing as he played, not mimicking Elvis or Little Richard now, but in his real voice. This was high and pure, like no one currently in the charts or anywhere in popular music except perhaps the jazz singer Mel Tormé, though he found he could give it a sandpapery rock 'n' roll edge.

And he'd already written – or, as his dad would say, made up – a song. Called 'I Lost My Little Girl', it seemed to be in the usual idiom of teenage heartbreak, but actually was a way of channelling his grief over his mother's death. It revolved around chords Ian James had taught him, G, G7 and C, and Ian was one of the first people he played it to, in his bedroom at Forthlin Road. 'I was really impressed,' James remembers. 'I'd always thought all songwriters were old blokes on Tin Pan Alley. That was something no one else I knew would have thought of doing.'

Despite his obsession with his guitar, he kept up his interest in the piano, now suddenly the least cool of instruments. He had often asked his father to teach him, but Jim, modest and self-deprecating as ever, insisted he could only learn 'properly' by finding a teacher and going through all the groundwork he had shirked as a small boy. Remembering the camphor-scented old lady teachers he'd so disliked then, Paul made sure he had lessons from a man this time, and started on a back-to-basics course, determined to be able to read music at the end of it. But he felt no more interested now than he had at the age of eight – and, meantime, songs kept coming into his mind for which he could always find the piano-chords by instinct. 'Something was making me make it up,' he would recall, 'whether I knew how to do it or not.'

Rock 'n' roll films, too, were now coming from America and finding their way to Merseyside cinemas. They were a genre known as 'exploitation movies', hastily put out to catch the craze before its universally-predicted demise. Most were cheap black and white affairs, with feeble plots and cliché characters, serving only as a showcase for the music acts involved. But *The Girl Can't Help It*, filmed in colour and CinemaScope and on general release all over Britain in the summer of 1957, was like no exploitation movie before.

Intended primarily as a vehicle for the monumentally-endowed Jayne Mansfield, it was a satire on rock 'n' roll, with in-performance appearances by Little Richard, Fats Domino, the Platters and Freddie Bell and the Bell Boys. It had all the sexiness for which the music was condemned, but wrapped in witty double entendre, verbal and visual, that went completely over the censors' heads. In its most famous scene, Little Richard shrieked the title song in voice-over as Mansfield sashayed down a street, making men's spectacles shatter in their frames and milk spurt orgasmically from bottles.

The film's performance sequences included two instant rock 'n' roll classics. One was 'Be-Bop-A-Lula' by Gene Vincent and His Blue Caps, the first rock band whose sidemen were as young and hip, in their blue 'cheesecutter' caps, as the lead singer. The other was 'Twenty Flight Rock' by Eddie Cochran, an Elvis lookalike with a white sports coat, a red guitar – and a novel line in humour and self-mockery. His girlfriend lived on the top floor, the elevator was broken, so he had to walk up 20 flights and his feet were killing him.

Paul and Ian James were among the first in line to see *The Girl Can't Help It*. Afterwards, Ian bought the single of 'Twenty Flight Rock' from Currys in Elliott Street, playing it over and over again until he'd worked out its guitar chords and Paul had managed to decipher and write down all its words. 'After a couple of run-throughs, he got it,' James remembers. 'He *was* Eddie Cochran.'

At the beginning of July 1957, Lonnie Donegan was in the charts yet again with a double-sided hit, 'Gamblin' Man' and 'Puttin' On the Style'. Skiffle groups had started up all over Liverpool, but none so far had attempted to recruit Paul, and he seemed in no hurry to join one.

Two boys he knew at the Inny, Ivan Vaughan and Len Garry, were sharing the role of tea chest bassist in a group called the Quarrymen. 'Ivy', a formidably bright 'A' streamer, was his special friend: they shared the same sense of humour and the same birthday, 18 June. And it so happened that Ivan's home in Vale Road, Woolton, backed on to that of the Quarrymen's leader, John Lennon, with whom he was equally good friends.

On 6 July, the Quarrymen were to play at a garden fete organised by Woolton's parish church, St Peter's. Ivan suggested Paul should come along and he'd introduce him to John with a view to his possibly joining the line-up. Paul agreed, but asked Ian James to meet him there, thinking there might be places for both of them in the group – and also for a bit of protection.

5

'Chalkandcheese!'

He already knew John Lennon by sight; with homes only a quarter of a mile apart, they could hardly miss each other. But until now, the age gap between them had ruled out any socialising. Paul was only just 15 while John was three months shy of 17. Although still at school – just – he looked like a Teddy boy and displayed all the touchy aggression that went with it. 'This Ted would get on the bus,' Paul was later to remember. 'I wouldn't stare at him too hard in case he hit me.'

St Peter's church fete seemed the least likely rendezvous with such a hard case. It was an event organised mainly for children, with its fancy dress procession, turn-outs by local Scouts, Girl Guides and Brownies and ceremonial crowning of a juvenile 'Rose Queen'. Its chief musical attraction was the 25-piece military band of the Cheshire Yeomanry, but a skiffle group had been added to the programme to attract the parish's teenaged element. The Quarrymen got the gig because, unlikely as it might seem, their leader had once attended the church's Sunday school and sung in its choir.

Though the summer of 1957 was a gloriously hot, sunny one in Britain, Saturday, 6 July, turned out cloudy and humid. Paul arrived for the rendezvous by bike, wearing his silver-flecked oatmeal jacket and the narrowest black drainies he'd yet smuggled past his father. He later admitted he was thinking less about meeting John Lennon than his chances of picking up a girl afterwards.

Despite its closeness to the city, Woolton had some of the atmosphere of a country village. The neo-Gothic sandstone church stood
on a hill, its 90-foot bell-tower crowned with four pinnacles said to
be the highest point in Liverpool. The weathered headstones in its
churchyard included one commemorating various members of a
local family, among them:

ELEANOR RIGBY . . .

THE BELOVED WIFE OF THOMAS WOODS

. . . DIED 10TH OCTOBER, 1939, AGED 44 YEARS

Behind the church was a sloping field, littered with all the innocent
paraphernalia of an English garden fete: stalls selling home-made
cakes, jams and knitted tea-cosies, and amusements like quoits, skit-
tles and 'shilling-in-the-bucket'. Near the bottom was a makeshift
stage on which the Quarrymen performed two sets, bookending
a display by the City of Liverpool Police dogs – the same that the
McCartney brothers could hear in the training college over their
back garden fence.

Now at last Paul could inspect the tough guy of the 86 bus at leisure without fear of reprisals. He wore a plaid shirt and jeans, and
played an undersized, steel-strung Spanish guitar, nowhere near
as impressive as Paul's own cello-style Zenith. Under the toppling
Elvis quiff, his wide-set eyes stared challengingly at his juvenile
audience, as if he'd gladly have picked a fight with any one of them.
Unlike most skiffle vocalists, he didn't try to sound American, but
sang in a Liverpool accent whose thin yet resonant tone burned
like acid through the ambient sounds of children's voices, clinking
teacups and birdsong.

The Quarrymen were better-equipped than many skiffle groups,
having, in addition to the requisite washboard and tea chest bass,
a second guitarist, a banjo-player and a drummer with a full,
though undersized, kit. They did all the skiffle standards, including a version of 'Puttin' On the Style' even more uproarious than
Lonnie Donegan's original. But their front man seemed always to

be prodding them towards rock 'n' roll. Among his repertoire was 'Come Go With Me', a recent hit by an American doo-wop group the Del-Vikings, in which he twisted the doo-wop lyric into skiffle-ese: 'Come, come, come, come and go with me . . . down to the Penitentiar-ee'.

After their second set, the group retired to the Church Hall, where they were also to play at a dance that evening. A few minutes later, Ivy Vaughan brought Paul in to meet John.

For someone without Paul's instinctive showmanship, the encounter might well have led nowhere. He had only Ivy for backup – Ian James hadn't yet arrived – while John was surrounded by fellow musicians who were almost all close cronies: washboard-player Pete Shotton, bassist Len Garry, guitarist Eric Griffiths, banjoist Rod Davis, drummer Colin Hanton and the group's manager, Nigel Walley.

There were introductions, as stiffly formal as only teenagers know how. 'John was always reserved, he never made the first move,' Colin Hanton remembers. 'People had to come to him.'

Paul broke the ice by picking up one of the group's two guitars – whether John's or Eric Griffiths's no one now remembers – and launching into Eddie Cochran's 'Twenty Flight Rock' in a perfect facsimile of Cochran's voice with its Elvis quiver and softened r's: 'We-e-e-e-ll, I gotta gal with a wecord machine . . . When it comes to wockin' she's the queen . . .' To sing and play the slap-bass rhythm simultaneously was impressive enough, never mind for a left-hander on a right-handed instrument.

'He gave a great performance – showing off, really, but not in a big-headed way,' Colin Hanton says. 'And you could see John thinking "Yes, you'll do."'

The Quarrymen's leader, in fact, had a rather shaming handicap. 'John found it really hard to play the guitar at first,' Hanton continues. 'His guitar was tuned for banjo chords [i.e. using only four strings] and he found it really hard to figure out guitar chords. In fact, I believe he was thinking of ditching the guitar, so when Paul turned up and played "Twenty Flight Rock" with all those six-string chords . . . well, that was it. John wanted to learn everything he could from him.'

Paul had something else to show in that perfectly judged 'not big-headed' way of his. Standing at the Church Hall's old upright piano, an instrument hitherto never resonating to anything stronger than 'All Things Bright and Beautiful', he began pounding out the rolling bass boogie of Jerry Lee Lewis's 'Whole Lot of Shakin' Goin' On'.

The last of John's reserve melted and he joined Paul at the keyboard, revealing himself a fellow piano enthusiast in a guitar-mad world. These close quarters also revealed that, in defiance of the fete's strict teetotalism, he'd managed to get hold of some beer. 'I remember John leaning over,' Paul says, 'contributing a deft right hand to the upper octaves and surprising me with his beery breath.'

Soon afterwards, Ian James turned up and everyone went to a nearby coffee bar. 'I seem to recall the Quarrymen being told their appearance at the dance that night had been cancelled,' James says. 'So I decided to go home.'

The dance appearance wasn't cancelled, and Paul hung out with the Quarrymen until early evening, getting a first flavour of what hanging out with John could mean. First they went to a pub where no one but the drummer, Colin Hanton, was old enough to be served alcohol and Paul had to lie that he was aged 18 along with the others. Then they received word that some tough Teds from Garston were coming over to Woolton, thirsting for skiffle-players' blood. Having set out that day to attend a church fete, Paul felt he'd ended up 'in Mafia land'.

After making such an impression, he might have been expected to go onstage with the Quarrymen at St Peter's Church Hall that very night. But John was in two minds about recruiting someone whose superior musicianship would inevitably overshadow him, maybe even pose a threat to his leadership. 'I'd been kingpin up to then,' he would later recall. 'The decision was whether to keep me strong or make the group stronger.'

Walking home later, he asked washboard-player Pete Shotton,

his closest crony, whether Paul should be let in, and Shotton emphatically voted yes. They agreed that the next one of them to see Paul would extend a formal invitation.

This didn't happen until a couple of weeks later, when Shotton came out of his family's house in Vale Road to see Paul cycling by. 'He stopped and we passed the time of day, chatted for a while, then I suddenly remembered what John and I had decided,' Shotton recalls. 'I said, "Oh, by the way Paul, do you want to join the band?" He thought for a moment, very casually, then said "Okay", jumped on his bike and rode off.'

In reality John Lennon was not the hard case he seemed, still less the 'working-class hero' he would one day style himself. His father Alfred, a ship's steward, had disappeared when John was seven and his mother, Julia, unable to cope, had given him over to her childless older sister, Mary, known as Mimi. He had grown up in Mimi's spotless Woolton home, provided with every comfort but ruled by his aunt's strict discipline and rigid social snobbery. Almost everything he did, or would ever do, was a kick against that repressive middle-class milieu.

He early proved himself a gifted boy, with the same talent for art and writing as Paul. The difference in John's case was his extreme short-sightedness, for which he was prescribed powerful spectacles he hated and refused to wear. The challenging stare he turned on the world was actually his constant effort to bring it into focus. His myopia largely accounted for the surreal quality of his pictures and prose and his compulsion to turn every other word into a pun.

He had attended Dovedale Primary School, near Penny Lane, then gone on to Quarry Bank High School, a grammar school of the same aspirational stamp as Liverpool Institute. There, abetted by Pete Shotton, he had been a notorious rebel and subversive, doing no work and running out reams of highly creative stories and cartoons lampooning his teachers.

Though his mother had given him away to her sister, she

remained a powerful presence in his life, living not far from Aunt Mimi's with a man friend by whom she had two further children. In contrast with her brisk older sister, Julia Lennon was glamorous and high-spirited, an accomplished amateur entertainer who could sing and play the banjo and ukulele. When John became smitten by Elvis and rock 'n' roll, Julia bought him a guitar and taught him his first chords, albeit only the four-string banjo kind. It was enough for him to form the Quarrymen, initially from among his classmates at Quarry Bank High School, taking the name from the school song in which the students hymned themselves as 'Quarry men, strong before our birth'.

By the time John met Paul, his guitar and rock 'n' roll were all he cared about. He had just crowned his school career by failing his GCE O-Level exams in every subject, and was about to embark on a form of higher education at that time easily available to such academic non-achievers. That September, he was to begin a course at Liverpool College of Art.

As things turned out, almost three months passed before Paul took his place among the Quarrymen. He had other commitments for the rest of his school holidays, including Boy Scout camp with Mike in the Peak District of Derbyshire and a week at Butlin's holiday camp in Filey, Yorkshire: the boys' first time back at Butlin's since their mother's death.

As a result, he missed the Quarrymen's August debut at a Liverpool cellar club called the Cavern, at that time an enclave of traditional jazz. Skiffle was seen as a branch of jazz, and so tolerated at the Cavern, but rock 'n' roll was banned. When John started up Elvis's 'Don't Be Cruel', he was passed a note from the manager, Alan Sytner, ordering him to 'cut out the bloody rock'.

At Butlin's in Filey, one of the entertainments team, known as Redcoats, was Paul and Michael's cousin by marriage, an ebullient, mustachioed man named Mike Robbins. During their stay, one of Robbins's duties was emceeing the camp's leg of a national talent contest, sponsored by the *People* newspaper and offering 'cash prizes of over £5000'. Paul, who had his guitar with him as always, entered himself and Michael as 'The McCartney Brothers', modelled on America's close-harmony Everly Brothers, Phil and Don.

The effect was rather spoiled by the younger McCartney Brother, who'd broken his arm at Boy Scout camp just before coming on holiday, and still wore it in a bulky sling. The pair did the Everlys' hit 'Bye Bye Love', then Paul soloed on Little Richard's 'Long Tall Sally'. They were under the contest's age-limit, and even their Redcoat relative couldn't save them from being disqualified. As a consolation, they came offstage to discover they'd acquired a fan, a girl named Angela from Hull. It wasn't Paul she turned out to fancy, however, but his wounded sibling.

Thus his first paid appearance with the Quarrymen didn't come until 18 October, when they played at the New Clubmoor Hall, Norris Green. Alas, nothing could have been less like his impressive display at the Woolton fete. John had granted him a solo instrumental spot, Arthur Smith's 'Guitar Boogie', a seeming doddle for someone who could simultaneously play and sing 'Twenty Flight Rock'. But midway through, he suffered an attack of sticky fingers and messed it up completely.

The Quarrymen at this point were getting two or three gigs a week if they were lucky, in one or other of the numerous urban villages that make up greater Liverpool. They travelled by double-decker bus, their guitars and washboard on their knees and Colin Hanton's drum-kit packed into the luggage-recess under the stairs.

The venue would be some municipal or church hall where, more than likely, Paul's father had fronted the Jim Mac Jazz Band 30 years earlier. The promoter was invariably a middle-aged man, with slicked-back hair and too-strong aftershave, who hated all young people's music and was simply cashing in on the brief time it *surely* now had left. The Quarrymen seldom received more than a couple of pounds between them, grudgingly counted out in half-crowns, shillings, pennies and even halfpennies. Some promoters gave them schoolmasterly written reports on their performance; all were vigilant for any excuse to cut their fee or withhold it altogether.

Their audience would be teenage girls in mumsy-looking full-skirted dresses and cardigans, with waved or 'home-permed' hair, jiving with boys still mostly wearing nothing more adventurous than blazers and grey flannels. Dancers and musicians alike kept a weather eye on the door in case the dreaded Garston Teds should suddenly arrive like drunken cowboys riding in to shoot up Dodge City. There were also occasional engagements at golf clubs, factory socials, private parties (no fee but free beer and food) and, once, at an abattoir.

After the show, a selection of their female followers would be usually waiting, game for a snog, a grope or, on very lucky nights, a 'knee-trembler' up against a wall. There were never enough for John, whose sexual appetite seemed insatiable and who boasted of having once masturbated nine times in a single day (so failing to win a bet with Pete Shotton that he could reach double figures).

John led the Quarrymen not only onstage but also in regular masturbation sessions, usually at Nigel Walley's house, in which Paul was now included. They would settle themselves in armchairs, put out the lights and each would wank independently, encouraging himself and his neighbours by calling out the names of sex-goddesses like Gina Lollobrigida or Brigitte Bardot. Often at the crucial moment, John would spoil the mood by shouting 'Winston Churchill!'

'When Paul joined the band, things changed . . . but it wasn't an overnight change,' Colin Hanton remembers. 'Paul was shrewd. He realised from the start that John liked to think of himself as the dominant force, but he needed Paul to teach him proper guitar chords, which was the way in to playing more rock 'n' roll material. He recognised John was the power in the group and that the best way to take him on was to do it subtly.'

Nothing could be done about those group-members who, possessing only the rudimentary musical talent of skifflers, were an obstacle to any meaningful further development into rock 'n' roll. Pete Shotton and his washboard were the most glaring example but, as John's partner-in-crime since toddlerhood, Pete's position was unassailable.

Nigel Walley was another Lennon childhood friend; originally the group's bass-player, now their manager, sending handwritten letters to potential bookers and giving out business cards ('The Quarrymen – Open for Engagements') yet still receiving a musician's share of their earnings. Paul suggested that Nigel's cut might be reduced to something more like a manager's 10 per cent but when John seemed unreceptive to the idea, he said nothing more about it. 'In those days, Paul was keen not to overstep the mark with John,' Colin Hanton says. 'I mean, he was the new boy and he had to be careful.'

In many ways, Paul and John were not the total opposites they appeared. Both had the same passion for rock 'n' roll and ambition to play it to the same standard as their American heroes. Both were artistic, bookish, fond of language and addicted to cartooning; both had the same sense of humour, nourished by the aural anarchy of Spike Milligan and Peter Sellers on BBC radio's *Goon Show*, although John's was ruthlessly cruel while Paul's was subtler and kindlier.

Paul's most immediate effect on the Quarrymen was in their presentation. 'You could see he had this show business side to him,' Colin Hanton says, 'while John just lived for the music.' The group had always worn what they liked onstage, but now John accepted Paul's suggestion of a uniform: black trousers, white Western-style shirts and black bootlace ties.

On 23 November, they had a return booking at the New Clubmoor Hall, where Paul had previously mucked up 'Guitar Boogie'. He was determined to cut a better figure this time. 'He had this sort of oatmeal jacket – he'd worn it to the Woolton fete – and he let it be known to John that when we did the gig, he was going to wear the jacket,' Hanton remembers. 'So the gig got nearer and then one day John turned up and he had got a cream jacket that was lighter than Paul's. It was John's way of saying "Hey, I'm cooler than you."'

That night, a photograph was taken of the Quarrymen onstage that would be endlessly reproduced in years to come. John is singing lead, with Paul apparently harmonising. They are the only two in the line-up wearing jackets. The others strum and plunk away in shirtsleeves, unaware that an officer class has been born.

With Paul's arrival, rehearsals became more frequent – and more serious. Mostly they took place at his house which, in itself, gave him a certain air of authority. With Jim McCartney banished to the kitchen, the tiny sitting-room at 20 Forthlin Road took on the appearance of a serious band room. Not wanting Mike to be left out, his father had got him a banjo first, then a full-size drum-kit in pale blue, which he set about mastering with his usual exuberance. Considerate as always, Paul would always go outside to check that the noise wasn't audible beyond a couple of houses' radius. However, the break in Mike's arm had left it permanently weakened, and he was never a threat to the Quarrymen's existing drummer, Colin Hanton.

The welcome was more uncertain when John called a rehearsal at his Aunt Mimi's house in Menlove Avenue, Woolton. Mimi had always been bitterly hostile to his music, refusing even to have a piano in the house because it would remind her of vulgar pubs. She could not see – nor, in fairness, could anyone her age – how skiffle might ever lead to a worthwhile career. 'The guitar's all very well, John,' she famously advised him, 'but you'll never make a living from it.'

These visits showed Paul the full panoply of middle-class gentility in which John had been raised. Mimi's 1930s semi-detached villa had a name, 'Mendips', rather than just a number; the interior resembled a miniature stately home with its grandly-named 'morning room', faux Tudor beams, stained glass windows and ceremonial displays of Spode and Royal Worcester china-ware. Some of the rooms even had bells with which, in pre-war times, the householder would ring for a maid.

The very name 'Mimi' to Paul suggested a Noel Coward world of fur stoles and long cigarette-holders (though her real name was

Mary, like his late mother's, and she too had once been a nurse). Mimi, for her part, regarded everyone John brought home as a potential bad influence, to be set alongside her special bête noire, Pete Shotton. Paul fell into this category simply because he'd once lived in the social no-go area of Speke. 'When I caught sight of him, when John brought him home for the first time, I thought "Oh-ho, look what the cat's dragged in,"' Mimi later recalled. 'He seemed so much younger than John – and John was always picking up waifs and strays. I thought "Here we go again, John Lennon . . . another Shotton."'

Even Paul's immaculate manners could not thaw her. 'Oh, yes, he was well-mannered – *too* well-mannered. He was what we call in Liverpool "talking posh" and I thought he was taking the mickey out of me. I thought "He's a snake-charmer all right," John's little friend, Mr Charming. I wasn't falling for it. After he'd gone, I said to John, "What are you doing with him? He's younger than you . . . and he's from *Speke*!"'

After that, when Paul appeared, she would always tell John sarcastically that his 'little friend' was here. 'I used to tease John by saying "chalk and cheese", meaning how different they were,' she remembered, 'and John would start hurling himself around the room like a wild dervish shouting "Chalkandcheese! Chalkandcheese!" with this stupid grin on his face.'

By far the Quarrymen's jolliest rehearsals were at the home of John's mother, Julia, on the Springwood estate, a couple of miles from Menlove Avenue, where she lived with her man friend, head waiter John Dykins, and their two small daughters. There John's group could always count on a welcome from the vivacious, auburn-haired woman who was just about his only grown-up ally.

Julia and John had lived apart for so many years that she'd become more like his older sister than his mother. Her comfortable, chaotic house in Blomfield Road was his bolt-hole whenever the wax-polished perfection of 'Mendips' and Aunt Mimi's anti-rock 'n' roll diatribes became too much for him. That Mimi called it witheringly 'the House of Sin' only added to its allure.

At Julia's, they tried rehearsing in different rooms, but found their puny acoustic instruments rang out loudest in the tiled bathroom – still more so if they stood together inside the actual tub. Julia made no objection to this hijacking of facilities which her small daughters, Julia junior and Jacqueline, made doubly essential. Even if she happened to be bathing the little girls together, she'd hustle them out of the tub and empty it so that the Quarrymen could climb in. When Paul joined, he was made as welcome as the others, and thought Julia 'gorgeous'. Often, after he'd left, she would shake her head sadly. 'Poor boy,' she'd say. 'Losing his mother like that . . .' He soon wouldn't be the only one.

The main change to the Quarrymen that Paul got past John, early in 1958, was George Harrison.

Over the past year, he had become not just friendly but friends with the Institute boy in the class below his who shared his daily bus journey to school and his obsession with guitars and rock 'n' roll. George was only 14, and looked even younger in his Inny uniform, but he passed all Paul's exacting tests of personality: he was thoughtful, observant, dryly humorous and a quiet rebel against authority in any form. Outside school hours, he dressed at the height of fashion: Italian-style high-buttoning suits, cuffless trousers and pointed shoes known as winkle-pickers because they looked sharp enough to pick the meat from that tiny, convoluted shellfish.

Paul and George were close enough to have been on a camping holiday together to the faraway south of England, carrying only a small backpack each, hitching rides and living on tinned spaghetti and creamed rice. One truck that picked them up had no passenger seat so George had to perch on the gearbox cover while Paul sat on the battery. They hadn't gone far when Paul let out a cry of agony. The battery had connected with the metal zips on his jeans' back-pockets, searing two zipper-shaped scorch marks into his buttocks.

They got as far south as Paignton in Devon, where they slept rough on the beach, then hitched back up to North Wales, hoping to make contact with Paul's cousin, Mike Robbins, who now worked at the Butlin's holiday camp in Pwllheli. They couldn't get into the camp, so moved on to Chepstow, by now so impoverished that they had to ask the local police to lend them a cell for the night. Denied even this, they ended up sleeping on a wooden bench at the town's football ground.

Paul had long marked down George as a potential Quarryman. He now owned a magnificent Hofner President guitar – worth several weeks' of his bus-driver father's salary – on which he was doggedly decoding the solos and riffs on American records that most British boy guitarists still found impenetrable. The Quarrymen's numbers were by now drastically reduced. Ivan Vaughan, despite his ebullient slogan 'Jive with Ive the Ace on the bass', had left to concentrate on his academic studies, as had banjo-player Rod Davis. Peter Shotton, the least musical of them all, had taken the hint when John broke his washboard over his head, and was now a cadet at the police academy in Mather Avenue whose training-field backed on to the McCartney home. But the third guitarist's place, behind John and Paul, was still filled by John's old school friend, Eric Griffiths.

Paul made John aware of George with the same subtlety that he acclimatised his father to new pairs of tapered trousers. George would turn up at Quarrymen gigs, seeming more faithful follower than potential recruit. Between times, Paul enthused to John about his school friend's prowess at 'single-string stuff', pointing out that to be taken seriously as a rock 'n' roll band they needed a proper lead guitarist, like Cliff Gallup in Gene Vincent's Blue Caps, rather than just their present collective skiffle strum. The problem was that George was two and a half years John's junior and, even when togged up in his sharpest box jacket and winkle-pickers, still looked absurdly young. To John, he became 'that bloody kid, hanging around all the time' – a view which would take many years to change.

In the end, musicianship won the day. George knew how to play a new American instrumental hit, Bill Justis's 'Raunchy' (a word which nobody in Britain then realised meant 'sexy'). John was so impressed that he made him play it again and again like a serious-faced wind-up toy. So Eric Griffiths was unceremoniously dumped, and 'the bloody kid' – or, more importantly, his Hofner President guitar – was in.

John, too, had been trying to write songs, but with the same conviction as Paul and his father: that it was an art which could only be properly practised by 'professionals'. Then both at once had their minds changed by an American rock 'n' roll act named after insects. These were the Crickets, a four-man group who scored a string of British hits from late 1957 into 1958. Their 21-year-old leader, Buddy Holly, not only sang in a unique stuttery, hiccuppy voice but also played heavily electrified lead guitar and wrote or co-wrote most of their material.

Holly came as a godsend to the Quarrymen, as to every other skiffle group struggling with the transition to rock 'n' roll. For all its thrilling novelty, his sound was built around basic guitar chords and simple sequences that they already knew. He recorded both with the Crickets and as a solo artist, which made him unusually prolific; within a few months, he'd given his British pupils a whole repertoire.

Biographical information about American music stars was scarce, and for some time almost nothing was known about Holly, not even his colour. Surprisingly, he turned out to be white, a gangling Texan who played a solid-body Fender Stratocaster more like a space ship than a guitar and wore thick black horn-rimmed glasses. With that, the schoolboy stigma of wearing glasses – which made John Lennon prefer to blunder around in a half-blind state – was wiped away. John immediately acquired some Holly-style horn-rims and, in Paul's words, 'saw the world'. But he wouldn't wear even those onstage or in public.

Both of them loved Holly's music: the guitar that could conjure such drama from its simple chords, the stuttery voice that was so easy to copy, the experiments with echo, multitracking and instrumentation never heard in rock 'n' roll before. But what fascinated them most was the idea of Holly as a songwriter. Here was no jaded middle-aged hack, rhyming 'moon' and 'June' in a Tin Pan Alley garret, but someone young and cool, turning out songs for his own band to play, each one more innovative and exciting than the last.

Summer 1958 brought Buddy Holly's barnstorming 'Rave On' – and a further sign of the Quarrymen's increased professionalism since Paul's arrival. Until then, they'd had no means of preserving their music so that they could listen to themselves at leisure and pick up mistakes. Other groups owned tape recorders and sent out tapes to prospective bookers. But the bulky reel-to-reel recorders of 1958 were hugely expensive. On their £2 gigs, the Quarrymen couldn't dream of such a luxury.

Then John heard about a Liverpool electrical retailer named Percy Phillips who operated a private recording studio not far from the city centre. Anyone could book time there and then get their recording made into a disc – a far more impressive calling-card than a tape.

The Quarrymen had recently lost another member when tea chest bassist Len Garry contracted a near-fatal case of meningitis and had to spend many weeks in hospital. That gave Paul a further opportunity to modernise the line-up by bringing in his Institute classmate John Duff Lowe, a former chorister at Liverpool Cathedral, who could play Jerry Lee Lewis-style arpeggios on the piano. So for their recording debut with Percy Phillips – John, Paul and George, plus pianist Lowe and drummer Colin Hanton – the Quarrymen were a rock band at last.

Phillips's studio was the sitting-room of his Victorian terrace house in Kensington, a Liverpool district named after the Royal London borough. As an A-side, the Quarrymen chose 'That'll Be the Day', the Crickets' first and greatest hit, with John singing Buddy Holly's lead vocal, Paul and George on harmonies and

George replicating – more or less – Holly's jangly solo guitar. The B-side was one of Paul's solo-written songs, 'In Spite of All the Danger', inspired by Elvis Presley's 'Tryin' to Get to You', which he'd heard at Boy Scout camp. Actually, it was a remarkably authentic-sounding Country and Western ballad featuring the already perfect vinaigrette harmony of Lennon and McCartney, with a rather shaky counter-harmony by George.

For eleven shillings and sixpence (about 67p) the Quarrymen received one ten-inch aluminium and acetate disc. Their name did not appear on its yellow 'Kensington' label: only the song-titles and composing credits, handwritten by Paul. 'In Spite of All the Danger' was credited to 'McCartney–Harrison' in recognition of the guitar fills George had contributed.

They couldn't afford to have copies made, so had to share that one disc on a rota-system, each keeping it for a week to play to family and friends, then surrendering it to the next in line. However, when it reached pianist John Duff Lowe, he failed to pass it on, nobody else claimed their turn, and Lowe drifted out of the band soon afterwards still with it in his possession. When it re-surfaced 23 years later, it would be rated the world's most valuable record.

Among the surviving participants there's some dispute about the exact date of the recording, but a plaque on Percy Phillips's old house, 38 Kensington, states it to have been 14 July 1958. If that is true, it had the most ghastly of sequels. The very next day, John's mother, Julia, was killed by a speeding car as she crossed the road a few yards from Aunt Mimi's front gate.

A cinema film about the young John, *Nowhere Boy*, released in 2009, showed him reacting to Julia's death like a typical, uncontrolled twenty-first-century adolescent, first punching Paul in the mouth, then clinging to him and sobbing hysterically on his shoulder. In reality, British boys in the 1950s, whatever their background, were still ruled by the Victorian code of the stiff upper lip. As devastated as John was, he kept his grief as secret as Paul had after Mary McCartney's death two years earlier.

But their empathy now had an extra, sad dimension. In future, after they'd become the world's darlings, they would sometimes drop their guard, discuss their common loss and allow the tears to harmonise in their eyes.

6

'Paul seemed to make John come alive when they were together'

John's arrival at Liverpool College of Art in the autumn of 1957 should have removed him from the sphere of the two Liverpool Institute schoolboys who now formed the nucleus of the Quarry-men. But actually it brought them closer. Their respective seats of learning shared the complex of neoclassical Victorian buildings that had started life as a 'mechanics institute', the art college in Hope Street backing onto the Inny in Mount Street. Each day as Paul and George sat in class, John was just on the other side of the wall.

Things still might have turned out differently if he had immersed himself in his new life as an art student. However, during his first terms at college, he remained as much a misfit as at school, sticking doggedly to his proletarian Teddy boy look, staying aloof from his fellow students – all but the prettier female ones – and refusing to think about anything except rock 'n' roll.

Though the art college and the Institute had long since been blocked off from each other, there was a connecting door between them, accessed through a small yard. Paul and George were thus able to meet up with John in the college for illicit guitar-practice during their lunch hour. Among crowds of art students, a uniformed Institute pupil would instantly have been spotted and sent back to his own territory. But the resourceful Paul had a blazer-badge

attached to his breast pocket only with pins, allowing it to be removed and replaced at will. If he also took off his green, gold and
black school tie, he could pass for a legitimate college denizen in a
plain black jacket and white shirt.

John's fellow student Helen Anderson remembers him ushering
Paul in, with George, their tag-along junior, usually following a
little later. The three would go into the cafeteria for a cheap lunch
of chips, then take their guitars into an empty life-drawing room,
which tended to be more spacious than others. Helen, being extraordinarily beautiful, was among the very few they allowed to
watch while they rehearsed. 'Paul would have a school notebook
and he'd be scribbling down words,' she says. 'Those sessions could
be intense because John was used to getting his way by being aggressive – but Paul would stand his ground. Paul seemed to make
John come alive when they were together.'

The pair's songwriting sessions, by contrast, generally took place
in private. They tried it first in John's tiny room at 'Mendips', seated
side-by-side on his narrow single bed, but there was so little space
that their guitars' machine-heads (the part with the tuning-pegs)
would keep colliding. Usually, too, Aunt Mimi would be in the
sitting-room directly underneath, chafing at the 'caterwauling' she
could hear through the ceiling. Before long, she banished them
to the only part of the house out of earshot – its glassed-in front
porch. The porch was bleak and draughty, with nowhere to sit, but
it lent their puny acoustic guitars a satisfying echo.

Mimi remained resolutely unimpressed by anything her nephew
composed with his 'little friend'. 'John would say, "We've got this
song, Mimi, do you want to hear it?"' she recalled. 'And I would
say, "Certainly not . . . front porch, John Lennon, front porch."'
What she overheard that clearly wasn't 'caterwauling' became another way of discomfiting John. '[He] got very upset with me when
I mentioned one night that I thought Paul was the better guitar
player. That set him off, banging away on his own guitar. There
was quite a bit of rivalry going on there.'

The only place where they could really concentrate was Paul's music-friendly home, especially during the afternoons when his father was at work. For John, cutting classes at the art college meant nothing, but it was the first time Paul had ever played truant – in Liverpudlian, 'sagged off' – from school. Now the partnership fully coalesced as they sat by the fireplace in their small facing armchairs, one guitar pointing leftward, the other rightward. 'Instead of looking into my own mind for a song, I could watch John playing,' Paul would remember, 'as if he was holding a mirror up to what I was doing.' Their voices created the same effect, John's acrid lead melding with Paul's high, supple harmony like vinegar with virgin olive oil.

For stimulation, they brewed endless cups of tea in the tiny kitchen and smoked cheap Woodbine cigarettes or Typhoo tea-leaves noxiously in a pipe belonging to Paul's dad. When musical inspiration temporarily failed, they wrote Goonish monologues and playlets on a portable typewriter – John was a surprisingly fast and accurate typist – or made elaborate hoax telephone calls to anyone they happened to dislike at the moment.

Jim McCartney soon discovered what was going on, but made no attempt to stop it, even though he would have been held responsible for Paul's truancy by the educational authorities if it had come to light. Jim, in fact, was just as worried by the friendship as Aunt Mimi, but was always hospitable to John, merely warning Paul privately (and, it would prove, all too accurately), 'He'll get you into trouble, son.'

Often the sessions went on into the evening, when Jim and Paul's brother were home. Mike McCartney had become a keen amateur photographer and snapped the songwriters continually, sometimes catching John in the Buddy Holly glasses he still hid from the world.

Just before Christmas, after a session with Paul that had lasted until almost midnight, he took off his glasses as always and walked home down Mather Avenue in his customary state of near-blindness. Next day, he remarked to Paul about the 'funny people' who lived in a house he passed en route and who, despite the late hour and the cold, had been 'out in their front garden, playing cards'. Paul took a look, and realised that what John had mistaken for a late-night outdoor card-school were models of Joseph, Mary and the infant Jesus in an illuminated Nativity creche.

Even now there were still some songs that Paul preferred to work on alone and keep to himself as they seemed too close to his father's traditional tastes to let John hear. 'I wasn't necessarily looking to be a rocker,' he would recall. 'When I wrote "When I'm Sixty-Four", I thought I was writing a song for Sinatra.'

Sagging off from school inevitably had consequences. In the summer of 1958, 16-year-old Paul took his GCE O-Level exams but passed in just one subject, French. That meant spending the best part of another year in the fifth form before he could re-sit the exam. By next time round, he'd pulled himself together sufficiently to pass English language, English literature, art and maths, but still failed history, geography, religious knowledge and German.

He then went into the Inny's sixth form for a two-year course ending in Advanced Level exams which normally led to university or other higher education. But Paul oddly seemed not to be considered university material; instead it was suggested he might train to become a teacher, as George's older sister Louise had done. What he might teach was suggested by his two A-Level subjects, art and English.

In the latter, he was taught by the Institute's head of English, Alan 'Dusty' Durband, an inspirational educator who, among other things, co-founded Liverpool's Everyman Theatre and authored numerous textbooks and study-guides. The impression Paul made was initially none too favourable. 'He'd slink into class,' Durband later remembered, 'as if he couldn't care less.'

His attitude changed when the class read Chaucer's *The Canterbury Tales* and Durband overcame their misgivings about the fourteenth-century English by pointing out the numerous bawdy references to arses and farts. 'Paul was inspired. You could see he found something with Chaucer, and then the other writers we looked at. He was passionate about words and using them and learning from how others had used them. I think he had that desire all along to write something that people would remember.'

Even to so enlightened a teacher, John Lennon and the Quarrymen represented nothing but a waste of valuable study-time for Paul, and 1959 would do little to alter that view.

Bad luck set in early. On the afternoon of 1 January, they were returning by bus from their old stamping ground, Wilson Hall, after playing at a New Year's Day party for the Speke Bus Depot Social Club. The date had been arranged through George's dad, who sat on the club committee, and its recompense included so much free beer that even Paul ended up almost incapable of performing. During the hung-over, recriminatory homeward journey, something was said that upset their drummer Colin Hanton, who disembarked with his kit one stop too early and never turned out for another gig.

Anyway, rock 'n' roll seemed to have run out of steam, vindicating all those who'd dismissed it as merely a passing fad and its stars as squalid fraudsters. Elvis had publicly repented by joining the US Army and having his gorgeous quiff and sideburns ritually planed off. Little Richard, the nonpareil shrieker and piano-pounder, had abandoned a world tour to train for the ministry. Jerry Lee Lewis's career had nosedived after a British tour, when he was found to be bigamously married to his 13-year-old cousin. Then on 3 February Buddy Holly died in a plane crash along with J.P. 'the Big Bopper' Richardson and 16-year-old Latino rocker Ritchie Valens. This last was a particular tragedy for the Quarrymen, who still relied heavily on Holly's instantly usable three-chord songs and riffs.

In America, the furores around the various performers, and a payola scandal involving several top disc-jockeys – among them Alan 'Moondog' Freed, the man who'd given rock 'n' roll its name – seemed to have tainted the music beyond redemption. The shrieking, flaunting, scowling rockers were replaced by blandly-pretty boy crooners, mostly called Bobby, whose every ingratiating breath proclaimed them utterly hygienic and harmless.

Viscerally exciting music survived only in blues, R&B and rockabilly records that British buyers as a rule could find only in expensive 'imports' at specialist London stores. But Liverpool had a back-door free supply thanks to its still-flourishing transatlantic liner trade. Ship's crews on the New York run – a self-consciously superior and stylish breed known as 'Cunard Yanks' – would bring home hot-off-the-press Stateside releases and pass them on to relatives or friends who played music. There was hot competition to be the first to learn the latest Chuck Berry, Carl Perkins, Bo Diddley or Coasters track and then perform it live.

Ranged against the still-skiffly Quarrymen were dozens of highly-accomplished rock bands with Yank-worshipping names – Kingsize Taylor and the Dominoes, Karl Terry and the Cruisers, Derry and the Seniors, Cass and the Cassanovas, Rory Storm and the Hurricanes. They tended to be slightly older working men with well-paid jobs on the docks or in factories who could afford to equip themselves with matching suits and impressive arsenals of guitars, saxes and amps from Hessy's music shop. And the first requirement for entry to this fraternity was a drummer. In Rory Storm's Hurricanes, he was Ritchie Starkey, a sad-eyed boy from the Dingle who used the stage name Ringo Starr.

The Quarrymen's Colin Hanton was not the greatest player, but his undersized kit had pardoned everything. And finding a replacement for him now seemed an impossibility. Even the most beaten-up second-hand drums couldn't be had for less than about £25. Anybody possessing such a prize would be looking to join some grown-up band with saxes and matching suits, not an art student and two schoolboys.

Too proud to jump off the bus after Colin and beg him to return, John, Paul and George carried on as a trio with just their three guitars, but quickly found their previous small trickle of gigs drying up. Every promoter they approached for work asked the same question: 'Where's your drummer?' Their reply that 'the rhythm is in the guitars' carried little conviction when the thunderous likes of Ringo Starr could be had for the same price.

Consequently, their only public appearance in around eight months – other than strumming together in empty lecture-rooms at Liverpool College of Art – was at a McCartney family party at the house of Paul's Auntie Gin. Among the guests was a friend of his cousin Ian named Dennis Littler, whose more successful group the three Quarrymen tried to join en bloc – but were turned down for being too young and inexperienced.

In an effort to shake off the skiffle image, they took to calling themselves Japage 3, an amalgam of their three Christian names, but no one seemed able to pronounce it correctly – 'Jaypage' – and the war was still close enough for the 'Jap' part to be undesir-able. By summer, George had become sufficiently disillusioned to moonlight with another group, the Les Stewart Quartet, who *did* have a drummer and played at a coffee bar named the Lowlands in the suburb of West Derby.

Towards the end of August, in nearby Hayman's Green, a woman named Mona Best decided to turn the cellar of her large Victorian house into a club-cum-coffee bar for her teenage sons, Rory and Peter, and their friends. The Les Stewart Quartet were booked for the opening night on 29 August, but at the last minute Stewart pulled out, so George rounded up John and Paul to take over the gig. Mrs Best was unfazed by their lack of a drummer and hired them, still as the Quarrymen, augmented by a defector from the Stewart Quartet, guitarist Ken Brown.

The four were also roped in to help her and her sons put the finishing touches to the new club's décor. John covered the walls of the dance area with Aztec-looking shapes while Paul – whose artistic tendencies his companions barely yet realised – painted rainbow stripes above the recess where they were to play. Mona Best's favourite film was *Algiers* with its famous chat-up line 'Come with me to ze Casbah', so that was the intriguing, sex-scented name she gave her cellar.

West Derby did not offer many amusements to teenagers and although the Casbah was intended to be private, a huge crowd turned up on its opening night to see John, Paul, George and Ken

Brown play in the cramped alcove under Paul's striped ceiling. Despite having no drummer, they went down so well that Mrs Best offered them a regular Saturday-night spot for £3 between them. When a story on the club appeared in the local paper, customers started trekking from neighbouring suburbs – even from the city centre – and other bands lined up to play there. Before long, Mrs Best had to hire a doorman to control the crowds and keep out the rougher element.

Paul by this time had had several casual girlfriends from the crowd who mooned over him at a distance. One was a slightly older, impressively-developed girl named Layla whom he would join when she was out babysitting – a useful means of access to some undisturbed hours on a sofa. Another, Julie Arthur, a niece of the comedian Ted Ray, brought him his first brush with celebrity. But it was at the Casbah that he met his first love.

She was Dorothy 'Dot' Rhone, an elfin 16-year-old from Childwall who'd recently left Liverpool Institute High School for Girls (an establishment strictly segregated from the boys' school) to work in a city chemist's shop. Dot was initially more attracted by John Lennon's 'rugged' looks but on finding that John was already going steady with fellow art student Cynthia Powell she agreed to date Paul instead.

This was an age of unchallenged male dominance, nowhere stronger than in Britain's industrial north. Liverpool girls, as a rule, were the most likely to stand up and speak out for themselves. But Dot came from a home tyrannised by her heavy-drinking father, a timekeeper on Liverpool docks, and so was excessively timid and unaware of her own bewitching prettiness.

As Paul's 'steady' – like the equally mild, malleable Cynthia with John – she was subject to an almost Victorian code of submissiveness and obedience. Paul wasn't anything like as controlling and possessive as John, who'd physically attack anyone he suspected of fancying Cyn. Nonetheless, at the Casbah Dot was forbidden to dance with other boys, even the most platonic of old friends. Like Cynthia, too, she had to change her appearance to resemble John and Paul's common fantasy, Brigitte Bardot, dyeing her hair blonde and wearing tight skirts and fishnet stockings.

On the far stronger credit side, Paul was loving and attentive, frequently sweeping her up and holding her in his arms like a doll. And after her own troubled, often violent home, she basked in the uncomplicated happiness of his, especially when the McCartney aunts, uncles and cousins would gather at 20 Forthlin Road for a party or a sing-song. 'I'd never known anything like it,' she recalls. 'It was wonderful.'

During the Quarrymen's two-month Casbah residency, they developed a close relationship with Mona Best and became friendly with her son, Pete, an 18-year-old whose brooding good looks rather resembled the Hollywood star Jeff Chandler. In their continuing drummerless state, it was a matter of great interest that Mrs Best had recently bought Pete a pale blue drum-kit on which he was already showing some ability.

Then on the evening of 10 October, fourth guitarist Ken Brown arrived at the club feeling unwell, so the motherly Mrs Best excused him from performing and put him on door-duty instead. At the evening's end, she insisted on giving him his full 15 shilling (75p) share of the band's £3 fee.

According to Brown, the thought of paying someone for not playing outraged Paul. 'He was always tight with his money – John never had any, Paul never spent any – and he kicked up a right stink . . . he stormed off, shouting, "Right, that's it! We'll never play here again!"'

Behind this haughty exit, in which John and George joined without protest, may well have been a belief that they'd soon have no further need of piddling £3 gigs. A few days later, they took part in a talent contest staged by Carroll Levis, an oleaginous Canadian whose eponymous 'Discoveries' were said to be guaranteed national stardom. Before going onstage at the Liverpool Empire, they impulsively changed their name to Johnny and the Moondogs, partly in homage to America's Johnny and the Hurricanes, partly to the recently-martyred Alan 'Moondog' Freed.

John had already tried to become a Carroll Levis Discovery with the pre-Paul Quarrymen, but they'd been beaten by a group featuring a midget who stood on his tea chest bass to play it. Despite the absence of a drummer, Johnny and the Moondogs fared much better, getting through the contest's preliminary round at the Empire and going forward to the semi-finals at Manchester's Hippodrome theatre on 15 November.

There they were sunk by their own poverty: the show ran late and they had to leave to catch their last train back to Liverpool instead of playing in the finale, on which the results depended. Then on the bus to the station, Paul discovered he hadn't enough money left to buy his train ticket.

The three were on the smokers' upper deck and a male passenger who was just getting off heard his lamentations and wordlessly pressed a two-shilling (10p) coin into his hand. Paul pursued this unknown benefactor to the top of the stairs and shouted down after him 'I love you!'

The group's future became even more uncertain that winter when John suddenly discovered there was more to art college than just a free rehearsal space. His tutors could claim little credit for this awakening, however; it was almost entirely due to a fellow student, Stuart Sutcliffe, with whom he'd been put into the Painting School to spend his second year.

Nineteen-year-old Sutcliffe was the college's most brilliant member, an abstract painter and sculptor with a talent so unique and fully-formed that most of the staff did not even try to teach him anything. Four years earlier, the young Hollywood star James Dean had been killed while driving his sports car at high speed, so becoming a pre-rock 'n' roll youth icon, an Elvis without music. Tiny and delicate, 'Stu' had some of Dean's brooding, poetic air – and was, alas, fated to be comparably short-lived.

Aside from his visual gifts, he was an omnivorous reader, with seemingly bottomless stores of literary and cultural knowledge. From the moment they were introduced, by fellow student Bill

Harry, he got through to the cynical, chippy Teddy boy as no conventional teacher ever had.

It was from Stu that John learned about the French Impressionists, the rock 'n' roll outcasts of their day, and about the American 'beat' writers who had infused the spirit of rock into poetry and prose before the music existed. The band that had been his *raison d'être* was relegated to 'a back seat' (Paul's disgruntled phrase) as he hung out with Stu, Bill Harry and a consciously arty circle, discussing Van Gogh, Picasso, Kerouac, Ferlinghetti and Corso with an earnest enthusiasm of which he'd never before seemed capable.

Most impressively, Stu motivated John to produce some actual art as opposed to grotesque cartoons, and was full of praise for the results. It was another snub for Paul, also a talented cartoonist, who had known about people like Matisse and Picasso since the age of about ten. If he and Stu hadn't been vying for John's attention, they might well have been best friends; as it was, an uneasy reserve always existed between them.

Though utterly self-assured in his work, Stu was full of personal insecurities about his appearance and small stature. And even with so impressive a friend, John could never resist homing in on insecurity and frailty. 'He generally toyed with people,' recalls Bill Harry. 'If you stood up to him, he respected that and wouldn't try it on again. If he detected any weakness, he took advantage. Stu was very mild and gentle, and John would put him down verbally in a way he never did other people in our circle, especially not Paul.'

As the 1950s ebbed away – to be replaced by who knew what? – there were other strains on the Lennon–McCartney partnership. John had moved out of Aunt Mimi's and was sharing a room with Stu in a huge, chaotic mixed-gender student flat near Liverpool Cathedral (though he always crept back to 'Mendips' whenever he needed food, money or his washing done). That temporarily put an end to songwriting sessions at 20 Forthlin Road with the two facing armchairs, the exercise book full of 'Lennon and McCartney Originals' and the pipefuls of Typhoo tea-leaves.

For John, leaving the orbit of his domineering aunt seemed to bring on the reaction to his mother's death that he'd been forced to suppress at the time. He had never been able to handle alcohol and now turned into an habitual and often violent drunk, given to acts of mindless vandalism like smashing up telephone-kiosks or urinating down the college lift-shaft. And college had introduced him to a new narcotic besides cigarettes and beer. Vick nasal inhalers, sold at any chemist's shop, had wicks impregnated with benzedrine which one could chew for a totally legal, medicinal-smelling 'high'. His reeking nostrils allowed him to stay up partying or manically talking all night and made his outbreaks of cruelty or self-destructiveness or violence even more unpredictable and extreme.

The John–Paul–George trio, meanwhile, was in limbo, still without a drummer or even a permanent stage name. Johnny and the Moondogs had been dropped as too redolent of that disappointing night in Manchester; if anything, they were known as 'the college band' since art college dances were their most regular gigs. John asked the students' union to provide a PA system for them to use and committee members Stu and Bill Harry pushed through a vote of funds to buy one, on condition it wouldn't be removed from the college (which it soon was, never to return).

After a time, the two Institute boys came to be regarded as honorary students, free to come and go in the college as they pleased. They also joined John, Stu and Bill in its 'Panto Days', when everyone took to the streets in fancy dress, collecting for charity (John simply pocketing the contents of his collection tin).

'I remember chatting to Paul one Panto Day,' Harry says. 'He was wearing a skirt around his trousers and a spotted headscarf.' He would always enjoy donning disguises, even after it became an essential security measure.

Resigned to being drummerless, they decided the next best sound-thickener would be one of the new electric bass guitars, whose throaty growl was increasingly to be heard on American pop records and even a few British ones. The problem was that bass guitars, if one could find them, cost even more than new drum kits; among even the highest-earning local rock combos they were still a rarity.

The solution was provided by Stu Sutcliffe's talent as an artist. In November 1959, one of Stu's paintings was chosen for the prestigious two-yearly John Moores Exhibition, sponsored by Liverpool's noted business magnate and philanthropist. The canvas was not only exhibited at the Walker Art Gallery but also purchased by the discerning Mr Moores for £65. It so happened that Hessy's music store currently had in stock a Hofner President bass, a splendiferous cello model, for the very same price. Although Stu had never played a guitar in his life, John persuaded him to buy the President and join the college band.

Bringing in a totally incompetent player was not appealing to Paul, especially one who already occupied so much of John's attention. But as George would remember, 'It was better to have a bass guitarist who couldn't play than not to have a bass guitarist at all.'

John and Paul's rapport always rekindled in vacation-times, when college and school loosened their respective holds. During the next Easter holidays, the pair decided to visit Paul's cousin Bett who, with her husband Mike Robbins, ran a pub, The Fox and Hounds, in Caversham, Berkshire, way down south. Bett, too, was a great music-lover, and had first introduced Paul to Rodgers and Hart's 'My Funny Valentine', whose couplet 'Don't change a hair for me/ Not if you care for me' would always be his idea of lyric-writing perfection.

They hitch-hiked the 200 miles to Berkshire, taking along their guitars, and spent a week at The Fox and Hounds, sharing a small single bed as innocently as children. Last thing each night, Mike Robbins would come into their room and tell them stories about his years with a radio vocal group called the Jones Boys before switching off the light.

In return for helping out around the pub, they were allowed to perform there as an acoustic duo. 'Playing on Sat . . . billed as the Nerk Twins,' Paul wrote on a postcard to his brother Michael, adding with almost equal excitement, 'May be serving behind bar.'

They designed their own publicity posters and drew on Robbins's experience as a holiday camp entertainments officer in deciding the playlist. His advice was not to plunge straight into Gene Vincent's 'Be-Bop-A-Lula', as they'd planned, but to start with something melodic, like Les Paul and Mary Ford's 'The World Is Waiting for the Sunrise', then work up to a rock 'n' roll climax.

The performance took place in The Fox and Hounds' taproom, or lowest-status bar, with Paul and John seated on a pair of bar-stools. Their self-deprecating name – 'nerk' in Liverpudlian means fool – had left unclear just what kind of entertainment was on offer, and just three people came in to watch them. A second show, at lunch-time on the Sunday, was only marginally better-attended.

But after they'd returned north, one of Mike Robbins's regulars asked him: 'Whatever happened to those Nerk Twins? They were bloody useless but at least they brought a bit of life into the pub.'

7

'Just who do you want to be, Paul?
Tommy Steele?'

Paul's instincts as a PR man were already beginning to show. Some time in April 1960, he drafted a letter to a local journalist named Low who'd requested details about the band with a view to giving them some publicity. Whether the fair copy was sent, or produced the desired article, isn't known. But the page and a half, in Paul's neat hand, reveals that they're still without a drummer or a name, and still pushing the 'rhythm is in the guitars' line:

Dear Mr Low

I am sorry about the time I have taken to write to you, but I hope I have not left it too late. Here are some details about the group.

It consists of four boys – Paul McCartney (guitar), John Lennon (guitar), Stuart Sutcliffe (bass) and George Harrison (another guitar) and is called the . . . This line-up may at first seem dull but it must be appreciated that as the boys have above-average ~~playing~~ instrumental ability they achieve surprisingly varied effects. Their basic beat is the off-beat, but this has recently tended to be accompanied by a faint on-beat; thus the overall sound is ~~rather~~ reminiscent of the 4 in the bar beat of Traditional jazz. This could possibly be put down to the influence on the group of Mr McCartney, who led one of the top local jazz bands (Jim Mac's Jazz Band) in the 1920's.

Modern music is, however, the group's delight and, as if to prove the point, John and Paul have written over 50 tunes, ballads and faster numbers, in the last three years.

John – described as their leader, despite coming second in the initial personnel list – is said to be an 'accomplished guitarist and banjo-player and an 'experienced cartoonist'. Of his 18-year-old self, Paul says he's reading English at Liverpool University and that, as well as the guitar, his specialities are piano and drums.

That fib about Liverpool University reveals his sensitivity about being the group's last remaining schoolboy. Although a year his junior, George Harrison had by now left Liverpool Institute to become an apprentice electrician at Blacklers, a city centre depart-ment store. Like John and Stu, George could stay out as late and get as drunk as he liked, whereas Paul always had to be thinking about the next morning's class and revising for his GCE A-Levels in July.

During the long hours when city centre pubs were closed, the still-nameless quartet hung out at a small coffee bar named the Jacaranda in Slater Street, where toast and jam cost only five old pennies, or 2p, per portion. At night, the basement became a club where prestigious bands like Cass and the Cassanovas and Derry and the Seniors would meet to unwind after their evenings' gigs.

The Jacaranda belonged to 30-year-old Allan Williams, a chunky Welsh Scouser with curly hair, a piratical black beard and a Chinese wife named Beryl, who ran its kitchen. Williams at the time knew little about Liverpool's music scene, and at first didn't realise that the four 'layabouts' who monopolised seats in his coffee bar for hour after hour without ordering anything *were* a band.

What first caught Williams's eye was Stu Sutcliffe's talent as an artist. At the time, the Welshman was planning to stage a Liver-pool Arts Ball, modelled on London's Chelsea Arts Ball at the Royal Albert Hall, when Chelsea's bohemian community gave Britain a rare glimpse of public drunkenness and nudity. For Williams's far drunker and more abandoned version at St George's Hall, he hired Stu to design and John, Paul and George to build and decorate the carnival floats that were ritually destroyed at the ball's end. He also set them to work painting a mural in the Jacaranda's ladies' toilet.

Allan Williams's emergence as a possible benefactor sharpened their need for a stage name that would stick. After more fruitless collective brainstorming, a decision was made privately by John and Stu and presented to Paul as a fait accompli one evening as they walked along Gambier Terrace towards the cathedral. In homage to Buddy Holly's Crickets, they had decided on the Beetles, but spelt with an 'a' as in beat music and beatnik. In a pun within a pun, it would be spelt 'Beatals' to suggest beating all competition.

Neither Paul nor the unassertive George offered any objection, But among the bands who congregated at the Jacaranda, the name received a unanimous thumbs-down. Brian Casser, charismatic front man of Cass and the Cassanovas, said they were mad to depart from the usual formula of so-and-so and the such-and-suches. They should use their leader's first name to create a Treasure Island effect and become Long John and the Silver Beatles.

John refused to identify himself in any way with the peg-legged villain of R.L. Stevenson's seafaring classic. However, a flash of bullion seemed to modify the entomological element that everyone so disliked, so they settled on the Silver Beatles.

They still lacked a drummer – but that was no longer their only handicap. Stu Sutcliffe was supposed to have filled the void with his expensive Hofner President bass, but Stu turned out to have no aptitude whatsoever for the instrument and, despite lessons from John, still had trouble in laying down even the most basic rhythm. His lack of skill so embarrassed him that he'd stand with his back to the audience to hide his inept fingering. Often the others would secretly unplug his amp, leaving him mute. Paul was becoming increasingly annoyed by having to carry such a passenger, convinced it would keep the band in its gig-less limbo for ever. But John would not hear a word against his artistic and cultural mentor and seemed unbothered by even the worst of Stu's fluffs.

Paul, in any case, had a weightier matter on his mind. Early in 1960, his steady girlfriend, the elfinly pretty Dot Rhone, had told him she was expecting a baby. She was 16, he was 17.

In those days, pregnancy outside marriage still carried the same stigma it had in Victorian times, nowhere more so than in Britain's respectable working-class north. And generally for the young man responsible, the only option was a hasty marriage to save the unborn child from being labelled, as it surely would be, 'a little bastard'.

Paul behaved well, never trying to claim the baby wasn't his – which anyway, with a girl like Dot, would have been an impossibility – nor proposing any of the degrading, often dangerous means by which unwanted pregnancies used to be terminated. The ordeal, especially for super-shy and unconfident Dot, was facing their respective families. As they were both little more than children themselves, there had to be a meeting between Dot's mother, Jessie, and Jim McCartney at Forthlin Road about what should be done. Mrs Rhone favoured giving up the baby for adoption, saying her daughter was 'too young to push a pram'. But Jim, lovely man that he was, threw his arms around Dot and told her he'd be proud to see her pushing his grandchild in one.

It was settled that Paul and Dot would have a quiet wedding at a register office, before the baby's birth that autumn, then live at Forthlin Road with Jim and Mike. Dot loved the prospect of joining the warm, party-loving McCartney clan, so different from her own violent father and troubled home. But the implications for Paul were clear: with a wife and baby to support, he'd have to leave school, forget all about further education and find a 'proper' job which could have nothing whatsoever to do with music.

It wasn't to be, however: three months into her pregnancy, Dot suffered a miscarriage. Paul was loving and attentive, rushing to her bedside with flowers and trying to conceal his relief. The stairway to Paradise still stretched ahead.

★

America's pioneer rock 'n' rollers whose careers had collapsed in their homeland continued to command a fanatical British following, and in March 1960 two of the most cherished, Gene ('Be-Bop-A-Lula') Vincent and Eddie ('Twenty Flight Rock') Cochran, toured the north together, stopping off for six consecutive nights at the Liverpool Empire.

The tour's promoter was Larry Parnes, at that time Britain's only notable pop music impresario. Parnes had discovered Tommy Steele, Britain's first rock 'n' roll star, but – since such a career couldn't possibly last – had swiftly turned Steele into an all-round entertainer and film actor. He now managed a string of pop vocalists in the new, blander style with stage-names designed to tickle the adolescent female psyche in every possible mood: Billy Fury, Marty Wilde, Dickie Pride, Duffy Power, Johnny Gentle, Vince Eager. His habit of boarding them at his Kensington flat led them to be dubbed 'the Larry Parnes stable'.

John and Paul were naturally at the Empire to see their two greatest musical heroes after Elvis and Buddy in the flesh. Paul would never forget the moment when the curtains opened to reveal Eddie Cochran with his back to the audience, running a comb through his hair. In fact, he was so drunk that the microphone-stand had to be threaded between him and his guitar to keep him upright.

The same evening marked Allan Williams's transition from coffee-bar owner to pop music entrepreneur. Untroubled by his total lack of experience, he struck a co-promotion deal with Larry Parnes to bring Cochran and Gene Vincent back to Liverpool on 3 May for a show at the city's boxing stadium. His role was the recruitment of top local bands like Rory Storm and the Hurricanes and Cass and the Cassanovas to support the American stars. But, despite their 'in' with Williams, the just-hatched Silver Beatles had no hope of being included without a drummer.

On 17 April, Cochran was fatally injured when his chauffeur-driven car hit a lamp-post en route from Bristol to London. Even so, it was decided the Liverpool boxing stadium concert should still go ahead with Gene Vincent – who'd suffered a broken collarbone in the crash – as sole headliner. To bulk out the programme, Allan Williams hastily booked further hometown attractions like the former Gerry Marsden Skiffle Group, now called Gerry and the Pacemakers. Even with the net thus widened, John, Paul, George and Stu resigned themselves in advance to being left out and watched the show miserably from the (standing) audience.

The event showed Larry Parnes that Liverpool possessed a wealth of good amateur musicians whom he could use to back his solo singers at attractively lower rates than London professionals. Less than a week later, he came back to Allan Williams with a request that galvanised every guitarist and dazzled every drummer on Merseyside: he needed a group to go on tour with the biggest name in his stable, Billy Fury. Williams was to organise a general audition at which Parnes and his star between them would choose the lucky sidemen.

Fury was Britain's leading male pop star after Cliff Richard: a 20-year-old combining the smoulder of Elvis with the pathos of Oliver Twist. He was actually a Liverpudlian, born Ronald Wycherley, who'd worked as a Mersey tugboat-hand before Larry Parnes discovered him at a concert in Birkenhead and rebaptised him. Obedient to long-time show business convention, however, he spoke in a vaguely American accent and his publicity omitted all reference to his birthplace. Most interestingly to John and Paul, he was the first British pop idol to bypass the professional songsmiths of Tin Pan Alley. Others had penned the odd original track but on Fury's debut album, *The Sound of Fury*, currently in the shops, every one was his own composition.

This time, the Silver Beatles wouldn't miss out; for, thanks to Brian Casser, they had a drummer at long last. He was Thomas Moore, a forklift truck-driver at the bottle-making factory in Garston. At 29, he seemed middle-aged to the two students, the apprentice and the schoolboy; nonetheless, they gobbled him up like bulimic piranhas.

The auditions took place on 10 May, in an old social club in Seel Street which Allan Williams planned to convert into an upscale nightspot. The cream of Liverpool's bands went through their paces as Parnes and Fury sat at a table taking notes like adjudicators at a music festival. To provide a photographic record, Williams had hired his Slater Street neighbour, Cheniston Roland, whose subjects were normally celebrities staying at the Adelphi Hotel, such as Marlene Dietrich and jazzman Dizzy Gillespie.

For this breathtaking opportunity, the Silver Beatles made a special sartorial effort: matching black shirts, black jeans with white-piped rear pockets and two-tone Italian shoes which Larry Parnes, in the twilight, mistook for 'tennis shoes'. They were painfully in awe of the star whose backing band they aspired to be, calling him 'Mr Fury' and reacting like scandalised maiden aunts when the photographer Cheniston Roland addressed him as 'Ronnie'; in earlier years, he'd been Roland's newspaper delivery boy.

Their new drummer, Tommy Moore, didn't arrive with them, having gone to fetch his kit from a club on the other side of town. When their turn came, Moore still hadn't appeared, so they were forced to borrow the Cassanovas' drummer Johnny Hutchinson, a noted tough guy who made no bones about disliking John and thinking the Silver Beatles 'not worth a carrot'.

Cheniston Roland's famous shot of them in mid-performance shows John and Paul frantically bouncing around in their little two-tone shoes as if trying to compensate for their bandmates' woodenness – serious-faced George; Stu Sutcliffe with his heavy bass, as usual turning away in embarrassment to hide his ineptitude; 'Johnny Hutch' on drums, in ordinary street-clothes and clearly bored to death.

Among the onlookers was the Cassanovas' new bass-player, John Gustafson. 'They had tinny little amps that hardly made a squeak,' Gustafson recalls. 'John and Paul didn't do any of their own songs that day, just straight rock 'n' roll, Carl Perkins, Chuck Berry, Larry Williams. But what sticks in my mind was Paul's voice. This pretty boy, who all the girls loved, would open his mouth and the most amazing Little Richard-type scream came out.'

They didn't get the coveted Billy Fury job, but Larry Parnes saw something in those leaping lads in 'tennis shoes'. Eight days later, through Allan Williams, Parnes offered them a week-long Scottish tour as backing group to another singer from his stable, Johnny Gentle. They'd have to decide quickly since the tour was scheduled to begin in 48 hours.

For the two art students, the electrical apprentice and the forklift truck-driver, there was no problem about seizing the opportunity. But for Paul, it came at the start of the Inny's summer term, with his A-Level exams just a few weeks ahead. Few fathers would have been likely to sanction such a jaunt, least of all one with a respect for education like Jim McCartney's.

Nonetheless, when the Silver Beatles caught a train for Scotland two days later, Paul went with them. He'd managed to convince Jim that he had an unexpected week off from school and the tour would be 'good for his brain'.

In the spirit of Larry Parnes protégés, three of them took stage-names of their own invention. Paul became Paul Ramon, thinking it had an exotic 1920s silent movie sound; George became Carl Harrison in tribute to Carl Perkins; and Stu Sutcliffe became Stuart de Stael after the abstract painter Nicolas de Stael. John and new drummer Tommy Moore didn't bother, although during the tour – according to Paul – John did once or twice hark back to the Treasure Island theme Brian Casser had proposed for the band and let himself be known as 'Long John'.

They travelled to Alloa, Clackmannanshire, in the Scottish Central Lowlands, where they met their temporary front man, Johnny Gentle, for the first time. There was then just half an hour to rehearse before they went onstage together at the Town Hall in nearby March Hill.

Twenty-three-year-old Gentle was yet another 'secret' Liver-pudlian, born John Askew and a carpenter and merchant seaman before moving to London, where Larry Parnes had found and re-branded him. Although only a minor member of Parnes's stable, he was hugely impressive to the Silver Beatles for having appeared with Eddie Cochran at the Bristol Hippodrome just hours before Cochran's death on the road back to London.

Gentle was less thrilled to find that of his promised five sidemen, only three were fully functioning musicians. Stu Sutcliffe still palpably struggled on bass guitar and while Tommy Moore was a serviceable enough drummer, his kit was so insecurely put together that a too-enthusiastic bang on the bass drum could detach it from its mounting and send it rolling away across the stage.

In the opening show, their performance was so bad that Parnes's Scottish co-promoter, a sometime poultry farmer named Duncan McKinnon, popularly known as 'Drunken Duncan', wanted to put them on the first train back to Liverpool. But Johnny Gentle insisted that he could work with them, hoping they might improve along the way.

The tour, which had sounded so glamorous, turned out to be a week of purgatory, travelling in a van up Scotland's bleak north-east coast and into the Highlands, performing in half-empty ballrooms and municipal halls and staying in cheerless small hotels or bed-and-breakfasts. Nor were their paltry audiences even aware of watching the Silver Beatles, still less of their fancy individual stage-names; at each venue, the posters simply advertised 'Johnny Gentle and his Group'. For their collective fee of £18, they had to work punishingly hard, opening the show with an hour on their own, backing Gentle for 20 minutes of Elvis and Ricky Nelson songs, then doing about another hour on their own, usually beset by disappointed cries for more 'Johnny!' The stamina John, Paul and George were forced to develop would serve them well in the months – and years – ahead.

Living at democratically close quarters with his group, Johnny Gentle soon became aware of the tensions within it. The disappointments and discomforts of the journey gave a special edge to John's acid tongue and malevolent humour, usually at the expense of his two most vulnerable bandmates. He teased Tommy Moore continually about his age, calling him 'dad' or 'grandad' and playing elaborate practical jokes on him. And Stu's distance from art college magnified his poor musicianship in John's eyes and disqualified him from respect, even consideration. In the back of the tour van, there weren't enough seats for everyone, so John always made Stu perch precariously on one of the metal wheel-arches.

The tour revealed Paul's ability – one he would keep all his life – to get the most out of even the poorest situation. However remote the venue and minuscule the audience, he always played the role of 'Paul Ramon' to the hilt, greeting the Highland girls with an unfailing smile and ever-ready joke Scottish accent, signing his first-ever autographs with euphoric loops of his schoolteachery signature and immediately sending a postcard to his dad about it.

He also took every opportunity to pump the good-natured Gentle about what a pop idol's life was like. 'He was inquisitive about everything . . . how I'd got my start . . . how you made records . . . where I thought he and the others in the band should go from here.

'I told him, "The best thing you can do is get down to London as soon as possible." In retrospect, of course, that was the very worst advice I could have given. But Paul said, oh no, they were determined to make it in Liverpool first.

'He was never in any doubt that the band would make it someday. He had this total focus and dedication, but he was realistic as well. He'd looked at the careers of the big rock 'n' roll names and knew how short they always were. "When we get to the top," he told me, "we'll have a couple of good years if we're lucky."'

At one point on the journey, he might easily have gone the way of Eddie Cochran. En route from Inverness to Fraserburgh, the van-driver, Gerry Scott, was incapacitated by a severe hangover so Johnny Gentle took over at the wheel. At a confusing road-fork, he took the wrong turn and hit an approaching car head-on. No one was wearing seat-belts but, miraculously, the only casualty was Tommy Moore, who had two teeth loosened by a flying-guitar case and had to be taken to the local hospital suffering from concussion.

It wasn't enough to excuse Tommy from his so-necessary duties at that night's show. While he was still being treated in the casualty department, John barged in, almost frog-marched him to the venue and pushed him onstage, still groggy from painkillers and with a bandage around his head.

Things went rapidly downhill from there. The group had by now spent all of their small subsistence allowance from Larry Parnes but had seen no sign of a promised second instalment that was to have come via Allan Williams. For the last couple of days, they became semi-vagrants, skipping out of hotels and cafés without paying (something which didn't bother John but mortified Paul) and sleeping in the van. George later recalled that they were 'like orphans . . . shoes full of holes, clothes a mess'. When Parnes finally did send some money, it wasn't enough to pay all their train-fares home, so Stu's mother had to be asked to make up the difference.

For Paul, it was the unhappiest introduction to a land that would one day give him boundless happiness.

The Scottish tour had promised to lift the Silver Beatles out of obscurity but it left them even worse off than before. Johnny Gentle had seen some sparks of talent in their playing and sent an enthusiastic report to Larry Parnes in London. However, Parnes had decided they were trouble and offered them no further work. Worst of all, the battered Tommy Moore resigned as their drummer to return to his better-paid job driving a forklift truck at Garston Bottle Works. They did their best to win him back, shouting apologies up at the windows of his flat until his girlfriend appeared and told them to fuck off, then pursuing his forklift around the bottle works yard, but on that question Tommy was immovable.

All hope now rested with Allan Williams who, thanks to his connection with Parnes, had become a figure of consequence in Liverpool entertainment circles. Through the summer of 1960, Williams set about trying to get them gigs, handicapped as they were by rhythm still only 'in the guitars' and a name that nobody liked or understood. The business cards he had printed called them the Beatles, though they were variously advertised as the Silver Beatles, the Silver Beetles and the Silver Beats.

Few of the venues Williams came up with seemed like any place for a Liverpool Institute boy like Paul. These were mainly ballrooms and municipal halls in Liverpool's toughest areas, where unreconstructed Teddy boys wanted to hear nothing but original hardcore rock 'n' roll, and faithfully kept alive its original spirit of violence and destruction.

What would be innocently billed as a 'dance', a 'hop' or a 'jive-session' almost always turned into a set-piece confrontation between Teds from the district and invaders from a neighbouring suburb. Often, a number from the band would unwittingly cause the 'bother'; their version of the Olympics' 'Hully-Gully', for example, always started beer-bottles, even whole beer-*crates*, flying.

One night at the misleadingly posh-sounding Grosvenor Ballroom in Wallasey, a huge Ted leapt onto the stage and grabbed Paul's puny little Elpico amplifier to use as a missile. His polite protest was answered by a snarl of 'One move and you're dead.'

Williams at the time had a business partner, a member of Liverpool's substantial West Indian community whose vast consumption of the cheapest brand of cigarette had earned him the nickname 'Lord Woodbine'. In Upper Parliament Street the pair operated a strip club, still illegal in Liverpool and so innocuously named the New Cabaret Artists Club. One evening when the strippers' regular accompanists failed to show, Williams put the Silver Beatles/Beetles/Beats on instead.

Paul would always remember the rather forbidding stripper named Janice who briefed them on her musical requirements. '[She] brought sheet music for us to play all her arrangements. She gave us a bit of Beethoven and the Spanish Fire Dance. We said, "We can't read music, sorry, but . . . we can play the Harry Lime Cha Cha, which we've arranged ourselves . . . and you can have Moonglow and September Song . . . and instead of the Sabre Dance, we'll give you Ramrod."

'Well, we played behind her . . . the audience looked at her, everybody looked at her just sort of normal. At the end of her act, she would turn round and . . . well, we were all just young lads, we'd never seen anything like it and we all blushed. Four blushing, red-faced lads.'

The best exposure Williams provided was in the basement club of his coffee bar, the Jacaranda, where, led by Stu Sutcliffe, they'd already painted surrealistic murals and redecorated the ladies' toilet. They appeared on Mondays, when the club's usual Jamaican steel band had the evening off, but without any advertisements or even billing outside. The tiny stage did not have stand-microphones, so Paul and John's girlfriends, Dot and Cynthia, would sit in front of them, each holding up a broom-pole with a hand-mic tied to its end. Bill Harry and his own girlfriend, Virginia, often witnessed this display of selflessness. 'Then later as we left, we'd see Paul necking with Dot in one doorway and John with Cynthia in another.'

At the Inny, Paul had sat his A-Level exams in two subjects, failing art but passing English literature. Though it was enough to get him to teacher-training college, a mood of unaccustomed sloth had come over him and he was considering marking time for an extra year in the sixth form. The idea had been prompted by one of John's college acquaintances, still studying art at the advanced age of 24.

'I thought if he could keep going without getting a job, then so could I.'

This plan was overturned by a sudden opportunity which would see Liverpool's worst band leap out of the Jacaranda's basement to West Germany, then back again, almost magically transformed into its very best.

The opportunity came from Hamburg, a port very like Liverpool in its raffish, cosmopolitan nature but with the addition of a sex district named St Pauli that was legendary throughout Europe. There, a club owner named Bruno Koschmider had recently asked

Allan Williams to supply a band for one of his establishments, the Kaiserkeller. Williams had sent over Derry and the Seniors, who at that time were Merseyside's top dance-hall attraction. Such was the German appetite for British rock 'n' roll that now Herr Koschmider wanted a second outfit, for a six-week engagement beginning on 17 August.

Williams's first thought was not of his recent mural-painters and toilet-decorators. He offered the gig to Rory Storm and the Hurricanes, who had to turn it down because of a prior commitment at a Butlin's holiday camp. Next on his list were Gerry and the Pacemakers, but their leader, Gerry Marsden, refused to quit his steady job with British Railways. So, scraping the bottom of the barrel, Williams turned to John, Paul, George and Stu.

Accepting the offer meant turning professional – an easy enough transition for three out of the four. John had no idea what he might do after graduating (or failing to) from art college and rejoiced in confounding his Aunt Mimi's prophecy by earning a living from his guitar. Stu would not have to turn his back on art, for the college assured its most promising student he could return and complete his diploma anytime he wished. For George, anything was preferable to an electrical apprenticeship at Blacklers.

Paul, on the other hand, seemed to have everything to lose. Becoming a full-time musician – with no prospects after the first six weeks – seemed no kind of substitute for teacher training. He would disappoint his father and, even worse, betray the memory of the mother who'd always so much wanted him to rise socially. On the other hand, he'd be getting £15 per week, a hefty wage for anyone in 1960; more than his dad earned, and most of his teachers too.

Jim McCartney was predictably horrified by the thought of Paul giving up school and, even more, of his taking employment in the country which had bombed Liverpool to ruins only 20 years earlier. And having only just turned 18, he couldn't go without written parental consent. However, his brother Michael pleaded eloquently on his behalf and Allan Williams visited 20 Forthlin

Road with assurances that 'the lads' would be well looked after. So Jim put aside his misgivings and signed the necessary paper.

There remained one major obstacle for the band who, for the sake of simplicity in a non-English-speaking environment, now called themselves simply the Beatles. Somehow or other, they would have to find themselves a drummer. They thought they'd struck lucky with a mysterious youth named Norman Chapman, whom they chanced to hear practising alone – and brilliantly – in an office building near the Jacaranda. Chapman sat in with them a couple of times, but then had to go into the army in Britain's final batch of National Service conscripts.

With their departure date looming, Paul was ready to take on the drummer's role, using odds and ends of kit left behind by previous incumbents. However, that would still leave them one body short: Herr Koschmider wanted a band exactly like the one Williams had previously sent him, and Derry and the Seniors were a quintet.

Then late one night, John, Paul and George happened to drop by the Casbah coffee club in Hayman's Green, their first visit since playing there as the Quarrymen the previous year and walking out in a Paul-led huff. They found Mona Best's basement venue still buzzy, now with a resident band named the Blackjacks, featuring her handsome, taciturn son Pete, on his pearly blue drum-kit. Afterwards, Paul contacted Pete Best – who, coincidentally, was also bound for teacher-training college – told him about the Hamburg gig and invited him to audition for the Beatles. This duly took place, at the same run-down club where they themselves had auditioned for Larry Parnes, but was the merest formality: Pete was in as suddenly as, two years later, he would be out. Blackjacked twice over.

At the Inny, the news that Paul was blowing out sixth form to become a rock musician caused a sensation among pupils and staff alike. Head of English 'Dusty' Durband was deeply disappointed by this apparently reckless sacrifice of the most worthwhile of careers. 'Just who do you want to be, Paul?' Durban inquired, quoting the least impressive pop name he could think of: 'Tommy Steele?'

Strictly speaking, it was Jim McCartney's job to give written notice to the headmaster, Mr Edwards, but Paul himself did so. He was, as always, polite and respectful to 'the Baz', but couldn't resist mentioning the affluence awaiting him in Hamburg: 'I am sure you will understand why I will not be coming back in September . . . and the pay is £15 per week.'

On the last day of term, his farewell was to climb onto his wooden desk – the one at which the famous funny man Arthur Askey used to sit – and perform 'Good Golly Miss Molly' in his lustiest Little Richard shriek.

8

'Everything's mad here. People never sleep'

Dear Dad and Mike

Well, it's not going too badly, but one disadvantage is that we never get up in time to buy things like writing paper etc!! (as you can see) We play pretty long hours but if we ever feel like going out we can do so because the majority of places stay open till about 7 or 8 in the morning.

I bought a cheap watch at a weekly market they have here, it's quite good, & keeps good time (cost about 22/- [£1.10])

Because we get up so late in the day, we don't have time to write, that's why I'm writing now at 10.30 [am] before I go to sleep.

To Mike.

Tony Sheridan, who was on Oh Boy! & the Empire is in Hamburg & we're quite good friends. He played with us the other night for a guest spot. Our club's big but the atmosphere at the place where Sheridan used to play (The Top Ten) is fabulous, & ours is pretty useless.

I'm getting pretty homesick, & even more so now because recently we've heard that we may be kept on & may be in Germany for ages! We really can't refuse if they give us the chance because the money is much better than at home. Everything's mad here. People never sleep. The food is . . .

just like English food gone wrong. Potatoes with salad, cold tomatoes, lettuce & that grand luxury dish – potatoes frittes or something ie. chips. Sausages are extremely long and are made with fish & meat. Ugh! Ah well, we can buy corn flakes, beefsteak, liver, mashed potatoes etc, at the local cafe now so we're eating well. We can get a glass of milk for about 13 pfennigs [1p] so that's cheap enough. Anyway, I'd rather be home.

Don't be frightened to write. I won't be annoyed if you do.

Love & Auf Wiedersehen
Paul

This innocent account of shopping for watches in open-air markets, buying cornflakes and drinking milk of course represents only a fraction of what Paul has been doing since his arrival in Hamburg. With typical considerateness, he doesn't want to worry or offend his father – still less risk being summarily ordered home. Here's just a little of what he left out:

He's in Hamburg's St Pauli district, home of the Reeperbahn, Europe's most notorious red-light area, surrounded by strip clubs, prostitutes, porno bookshops, blue movie shows, pimps, transvestites and gangsters . . . His new employer, Bruno Koschmider, is a circus clown turned strip-club owner who enjoys beating up customers with a cosh or a wooden chair-leg while thuggish waiters hold the victim helpless . . . The Beatles aren't appearing at Koschmider's large, busy Kaiserkeller club as they'd expected, but at a run-down strip joint nearby where they're being used virtually as slave labour, playing for four-and-a-half hours with only three 30-minute breaks each week-night, and for six hours at weekends. . . . The living accommodation provided for the five of them consists of two stone-walled, windowless, airless storerooms at the rear of a porno cinema called the Bambi Kino, with no washing facilities but the cinema's gents' toilet: all in all a scene of squalor and degradation that would have made his fastidious mother weep.

When the Beatles arrived in Hamburg, fellow Liverpudlians Derry and the Seniors had already been playing at the Kaiserkeller for some months. With their black singer, Derry Wilkie, they were a polished, highly professional outfit to whom John, Paul and George had always seemed like little boys, skiffling on the margin. Indeed, their sax-player Howie Casey was incredulous that Allan Williams should be sending over such a 'bum group' to play alongside them.

Not all Casey's bandmates were so disparaging – for instance, newcomer guitarist Brian Griffiths who, at 16, was even younger than George. Back in Liverpool, 'Griff' had been outside the Jacaranda one day when he heard a noise coming up through a pavement-grating. 'It was the Beatles, rehearsing in the basement,' he says. 'I'll always remember, Paul was singing "Roll Over Beethoven" in an amazing, pure voice that seemed to hit every note effortlessly – and yet it rocked! It rocked! It rocked!'

The Beatles' disappointing venue was called the Indra and located in a street off the main Reeperbahn named the Grosse Freiheit (meaning 'great freedom'). It had long been failing as a strip club and Bruno Koschmider wanted to change its image, though at first its regulars may well have misinterpreted that change: to German ears, 'Beatles' was easily confused with 'peedles', meaning little boys' willies.

The band took the stage in matching lavender-coloured jackets, tailored by the McCartneys' next-door neighbour, and the same black shirts they'd worn on the Johnny Gentle tour. Paul had a new guitar, a Rosetti Solid 7 with a red sunburst body and double cutaway which, unfortunately, looked a lot better than it sounded. Like the Zenith, it was a right-handed model, which he had to play upside-down with the strings in inverted order.

On this night of 17 August 1960, the five were still exhausted by their road trip from England in Allan Williams's ramshackle van as well as stunned by their first immersion in the Reeperbahn and deflated by the sordid little club, whose scatter of customers were mostly expecting its usual attraction, a stripper named Conchita.

Their opening numbers were so somnambulistic that Bruno Koschmider began clapping his hands and shouting '*Mach Schau!* [Make it a show]', an exhortation which in these parts usually caused tassels on bare breasts to whirl faster or heralded the climactic shedding of a G-string. John responded with an over-the-top parody of Gene Vincent, fresh from the Eddie Cochran death-crash, hunchbacked and dragging one calipered leg like a caterwauling Quasimodo. Blissfully unaware that they were being mocked, the Germans loved it.

A half-dead club wasn't instantly brought to life the way Elvis had done it in his best feature film, *King Creole*. The Beatles had to build an audience: first making enough noise to attract people in off the Grosse Freiheit, then pulling out all the stops to hold their attention, sometimes playing a whole set to a single occupied table. 'They had to be good,' says Hamburg musician Frank Dostall, 'or else the customers just left and went into the strip-joint or porno bookstore next door.'

Derry and the Seniors dropped by to watch during a break from their own equally punishing work schedule at the Kaiserkeller, further along the street. Saxophonist Howie Casey was amazed at the change in that 'bum group' he'd last seen at the Larry Parnes audition. 'Then, they'd seemed almost embarrassed about how bad they were. But they'd turned into a good stomping band.'

'Paul was really the one keeping them together,' Brian Griffiths says. 'John in those days wasn't such a good singer, George was very shy, Stu was still a learner on the bass and Pete Best had only just come into the band. Paul had the voice – and the musical technique. He knew all about minor and diminished seventh chords, whereas John was still hanging round guitarists in other bands, saying, "Go on, show us a lick."'

The Tony Sheridan mentioned in Paul's letter had been the first British musician on the Reeperbahn, with his backing band, the Jets. Born Anthony Esmond Sheridan McGinnity, he was a brilliant guitarist with an educated accent and a streak of self-destructive devilment that was to find a ready response in John. 'When the

Beatles walked into the club where I was playing, I recognised them as blood-brothers,' Sheridan remembered, 'although at first I wondered about Paul with that girlie face and those thin eyebrows. Was he gay or something?'

Sheridan gave the Liverpool boys a guided tour of the Reeperbahn's still unique depravities: the strip clubs where *everything* came off, the interracial sex-shows, the female mud-wrestling displays, the transvestite bars, the tributary street named the Herbertstrasse whose lighted shop windows displayed price-ticketed whores of every age and size.

They also discovered how the Reeperbahn's denizens, both British and German, managed to keep themselves going all through its neon-crazy night. They took a slimming tablet called Preludin whose amphetamine content stepped up the body's metabolic rate, creating both manic energy and a raging thirst. Apart from chewing Vick nasal inhalers, it was the first drug the Beatles had ever tried. John devoured it unthinkingly, taking five or six 'Prellys' in an evening, washed down with so many steins of beer that he'd sometimes foam at the mouth like a rabid dog.

But Paul exercised caution and restraint. Prellys induced such goggle-eyed wakefulness that the only way of getting any rest was to take a sleeping-pill. He hated that groggy morning-after feeling – for which the quickest cure was to pop another Prelly. So as not to be thought 'a cissy', he'd take just one of the tiny white pills then pretend to be as wired as John.

This ability to put a shell around himself, developed after his mother's death, also helped him endure the band's horrible sleeping quarters behind the Bambi Kino, where rats scuttled over the bare concrete floor and the smallest rain-shower came dribbling through the ceiling onto the dingy little cots below. He imagined himself a struggling artist, a young Picasso or Matisse, surviving in a Parisian attic. And one day, he thought, all of this would make 'a chapter for the memoirs'.

Even his self-control and fastidiousness, however, couldn't withstand what he later called Hamburg's 'sex shock'. He and the others had come from a country whose young women still encased themselves in impenetrable brassieres and corsets, believed premarital sex to be sinful and were haunted by a fear of getting pregnant. Now they were in a community of prostitutes, strippers and barmaids with no such inhibitions – or restrictive undergarments – who found these baby-Teddy boy musicians hugely attractive and, in forthright German style, made no bones about it. Here, sex was no longer an occasional stroke of luck but a 24-hour buffet.

Paul was later to admit he found his first sexual experience with one of these professionals thoroughly unnerving. '[She was] a shortish, dark-haired girl . . . I think she was a strip-teaser. I remember feeling very intimidated in bed with her . . . spent the whole night not doing an awful lot but trying to work up to it.'

Sometimes the girls had flats or rooms of their own, but often they'd have to be brought back to the Bambi Kino which offered no privacy whatever. When 17-year-old George lost his virginity, Paul, John and Pete were all in bed a few feet away: they kept quiet during the transaction, but cheered and clapped at its end. If Paul came in and saw 'a little bottom bobbling up and down', meaning John was athwart a lady friend, he'd mumble 'Sorry' and duck out again as if he'd blundered into a wrong classroom at the Inny. John wasn't always so considerate. 'When [he] found Paul in bed with a chick,' George later recalled, 'he went and got a pair of scissors and cut all her clothes in pieces, then wrecked the wardrobe.'

Even with such distractions, Paul's primary concern was always the band. 'I remember, John and I had been drinking for most of the night in this place called Carmen's Bar,' Brian Griffiths says. 'About nine o'clock the next morning, we were walking back to the Indra and as we get closer, we hear a noise . . . it's Paul, alone in the empty club, practising Elvis's big ballad of 1960, "It's Now or Never". John goes, "Oh, what the frig's he doing that sort of crap for?" To John, the only Elvis tracks worth anything were things like "That's All Right, Mama" and "Mystery Train". But Paul knew they couldn't get through the night only on rock 'n' roll and they had to appeal to the German audience. So he'd also do "Wooden Heart", from Elvis's GI Blues, complete with the verse in German.'

Both the Liverpool bands had entered West Germany without the necessary work permits. If challenged, the Beatles were to pose as students on vacation (which two of them really were) and Derry and the Seniors as plumbers who'd brought along musical instruments to entertain themselves between jobs.

Early in October, the Seniors' cover was blown and the West German immigration authorities ordered them out of the country. But, having spent every Deutschmark they'd earned, they were unable to get back to Britain. Deprived of their accommodation at the Kaiserkeller, they became homeless for several days before throwing themselves on the mercy of the British consul. Brian Griffiths spent one night on a park bench, then Paul offered him the use of his bed at the Bambi Kino during the hours when the Beatles were onstage. John made the same offer to the band's singer, Derry Wilkie, as did Pete Best to their drummer, Jeff Wallington.

'I'm in Paul's bed until about 6 a.m., then suddenly here he is, wanting it back,' Griff remembers. 'The only place I could find to sleep was in the cinema-stalls, freezing cold, with rats running around everywhere.'

To take over the Kaiserkeller residency, Allan Williams sent Rory Storm and the Hurricanes, who'd by now finished their Butlin's engagement. Rory – real name Alan Caldwell – was a tall blond Adonis afflicted by a severe stammer that fortunately disappeared while he was singing. Both athletic and eccentric, he would enliven his stage act by shinning up the nearest wall like a human fly or if the venue were a swimming-pool, doing a triple somersault from the top board mid-song in a pair of gold lamé briefs.

The Beatles knew Rory well, having shared a bill with him many times at the Casbah. Less well did they know the Hurricanes' drummer, Ritchie Starkey, whose penchant for wearing three or four chunky rings on each hand – together with the band's previous Wild West persona as the Ravin' Texans – had inspired his stage name of Ringo Starr.

Though Ringo was only a few months John's senior, he seemed much older and more worldly than any of them with his Ford Zephyr car and taste for American Lark cigarettes. George had always thought 'he looked like a tough guy ... with that grey streak in his hair and half a grey eyebrow and that big nose', and even John later admitted to having been a little in awe of him.

Paul would be hugely flattered when Ringo came to watch them perform, which he usually did late at night when they were on to very slow numbers like Duane Eddy's 'Three-30-Blues'. But never did it cross any of their minds that one day he would join them. A letter from George to a friend in Liverpool around this time voices the apparent consensus that 'Pete Best is drumming good'.

Rory Storm's golden hair and Ringo's doleful face seemed to bring the Beatles luck. Bruno Koschmider had been receiving increasingly angry complaints from an elderly war-widow who lived above the Indra Club and was disturbed by their music each night until the small hours. Wanting no trouble with the authorities, Koschmider closed down the Indra and put them on at the Kaiserkeller as support to the Hurricanes. As Paul had predicted in his letter home, their contract was extended to 31 December.

At the Kaiserkeller, their schedule was even more punishing than before: five-and-a-half hours per night with three half-hour breaks. The large basement club could contain up to 500 people, yet had no ventilation whatever. The heat was consequently horrendous, not to mention the body-odours and cigarette-smoke. The clientele were mostly sailors from a dock-area as extensive as Liverpool's (but rather more prosperous), and the frequent outbreaks of violence made Wallasey's Grosvenor Ballroom seem sedate by comparison. To contain it, Koschmider employed a team of waiters mainly recruited from local boxing and bodybuilding gyms and renowned for the ruthless speed with which they handled any disturbance. Specially fractious customers were not just thrown into the street but taken to the boss's office, where Koschmider himself would go to work on them with his rubber cosh or the antique chair-leg he kept secreted down his trousers. Unlike in Liverpool, however, musicians were granted automatic immunity from attack. Like those figures in Western films who continue calmly sipping their beer while saloon brawls rage around them, Paul would press doggedly on with 'It's Now or Never' as the fists flew and flick-knives flashed.

Also unlike Liverpool, the band were bought drinks by appreciative spectators while they played; so many drinks that by the end of their set the stage-front would be crowded with bottles and glasses. Usually it would be beer, though now and again someone in a prime side booth – traditionally reserved for the Reeperbahn's top gangsters, racketeers and porn-merchants – would send them a tray of schnapps, insisting that each shot be downed in one, with a ritual cry of 'Prost!'

This feeling of invulnerability prompted John to '*Mach Schau*' in ways that might have been expected to get him lynched in a city which had suffered wartime bombing even worse than Liverpool's. He'd goose-step around the stage shouting 'Fuckin' Nazis!' and 'Sieg Heil!' with a black comb pressed to his upper lip like a Hitler moustache. But the Germans either didn't get it or found it hilarious.

Baiting Bruno was a popular sport with all the musicians – and, again, seemed to bring no consequences. The Kaiserkeller's half-rotten wooden stage had already been stomped to pieces once by Derry and the Seniors; now the Beatles and Rory Storm's band had a competition to see who'd be first to do it again. Rory took the prize by leaping on top of his piano during a performance of 'Blue Suede Shoes'. Under their combined weight, the stage's anaemic timbers gave way and the piano sank from view like a foundering ship with Rory on its poop deck.

Paul took part in the onstage clowning while never going as far as John, or anywhere near it. 'Generally, if one started acting the fool, the other did, too,' Brian Griffiths says. 'But with Paul, it never interfered with the song – or the quality of his voice.'

He was later to admit doing 'a couple of loony things' in Hamburg. One of the looniest occurred on a night when he, John, George and Pete Best were all temporarily broke and John suggested solving their problem by robbing a drunken sailor. A suitable victim was found in the Kaiserkeller, then befriended and inveigled outside by promises of an even better place around the corner. But at that point, Paul and George lost their nerve and melted away, leaving the dirty deed to John and Pete Best. Unfortunately, the sailor was not as helplessly drunk as he'd first seemed, and proved to be armed with a tear-gas pistol, so they, too, fled.

'What Hamburg taught the Beatles was that they didn't have to copy anyone else any more,' Tony Sheridan said. 'They could be themselves – and the qualities they found in themselves surprised even them. Plus, they could rehearse for their future night after night, at the public's expense. Watching them, I used to think that Paul could probably make it without John, but John was never going to make it without Paul.'

The most significant episode in this first trip to Hamburg found Paul again relegated to a back seat. At the Kaiserkeller, in addition to the traditional Reeperbahn roughnecks, the Beatles began to attract middle-class boys and girls known as 'exis' (short for existentialists) who read Camus and Sartre, dressed in unisex black leather and wore their hair combed forward in what was then known as the French style.

The centre of the group was Astrid Kirchherr, a strikingly beautiful and stylish young photographer with close-cropped blonde hair. When Astrid first set eyes on the Beatles she fell headlong in love; not with Paul, the most obviously adorable one, but tiny Stuart Sutcliffe.

As an excuse for getting to know Stu better, she photographed all five Beatles on a foggy autumn morning, in Hamburg's closed and shuttered Dom fairground. Strangely, in what would not only become a timeless image of the baby Beatles but a blueprint for rock bands ever afterwards, Paul was given little prominence in comparison with Stu, John and even George. One shot shows him leaning against some heavy piece of fairground machinery on which the other three are perched; bereft of his usual ease with the camera, he stares off to one side, holding John's Club 40 guitar rather than his own inferior Solid 7. In the best-known close-up of him from the shoot, he looks strangely blank, perhaps aware that the photographer's attention is really on Stu, far in the misty background.

The addition of Astrid and male exis like graphic designer Klaus Voormann and photographer Jürgen Vollmer to the Beatles' social circle in effect recreated the art-studenty atmosphere from which Paul had felt excluded back in Liverpool. 'They were more interested in Stuart and John,' he would recall. 'I was a little bit too baby-faced and didn't attract them so much.'

Paul and Stu had always gotten along reasonably well, but now there began to be friction between them. 'Funnily enough, Paul has turned out the real black sheep of the whole trip,' Stu wrote to his art college friend Rod Murray just after first meeting Astrid. 'Everyone hates him and I only feel sorry for him.'

The problem for Paul was no longer Stu's ineptitude on bass guitar and John's stubborn blindness to it. By now he had become a reasonably competent player and was doing solos, even taking the odd vocal (like Elvis's 'Love Me Tender') and receiving applause. For a time, Koschmider had taken him out of the Beatles to play in an offshoot of Derry and the Seniors alongside the seasoned sax-player Howie Casey, who found no fault whatsoever with his musicianship.

The truth was that Stu had become bored with playing bass and was longing to return to painting, his true, unquestioned talent. At Astrid's insistence, he left the band's quarters at the Bambi Kino to move into the comfortable house she shared with her mother, where an attic room was turned into a studio for him. 'That was what made Paul upset with Stuart,' Astrid recalls. 'He wasn't serious enough about the band and he wouldn't practise.'

To sharpen Paul's sense of grievance, John no longer subjected

Stu to ruthless mockery and baiting, but nowadays treated him with – for John – extraordinary gentleness and tolerance. 'John,' Astrid remembers, 'was Stuart's guardian angel.'

In November 1960, Stu asked Astrid to marry him and was accepted. He wrote to a friend in Liverpool that when the Beatles left Hamburg, either to return home or play elsewhere in mainland Europe, he would stay behind and Paul would take over on bass.

By now, they had become weary of Bruno Koschmider and had set their sights on a rival music club, the Top Ten, on the main Reeperbahn, whose atmosphere, Paul had written to his brother, Mike, was 'fabulous'. After secretly auditioning for the Top Ten's go-ahead young owner, Peter Eckhorn, they were offered a residency, beginning immediately, at higher pay and with infinitely more civilised accommodation on the top floor of the club building.

Before that could come to fruition, three of the five Beatles were ignominiously kicked out of the country, seemingly queering their Hamburg pitch for good. On 21 November, the St Pauli police belatedly discovered George Harrison was under 18 and therefore banned from frequenting the Reeperbahn after 10 p.m. Since he'd defied this curfew every night for the past three months, he was immediately deported, leaving under his own steam, by train.

The others gave notice to Koschmider at 1.30 one morning after they came offstage at the Kaiserkeller. Koschmider agreed to let them go, on condition that they played nowhere else in West Germany until the end of their contract, 31 December. When they refused, he luckily didn't call his waiters or produce his antique chair-leg, but merely ordered them out of his office.

After the customary late-night meal, Paul and Pete Best returned to the Bambi Kino to collect their possessions for the transfer to the Top Ten, where John was already installed. Having packed their bags, even the two most well-behaved Beatles couldn't resist a small demonstration against the slum conditions they'd had to endure for all these weeks.

Paul has since said that he and Pete set light to a condom, though at the time he said it was 'a piece of cord nailed to the wall' of the passage. According to Pete, it was 'a bit of old sacking' which didn't even catch light, merely smouldered a bit at the edges. After a few seconds, they tired of the joke, extinguished the minute conflagration and climbed into their ratty beds one last time.

Next day, a squad of police arrived at the Top Ten club, arrested Paul and Pete and hauled them off to the Reeperbahn's main police station, where they learned Bruno Koschmider had charged them with attempted arson. Though Koschmider subsequently withdrew the charge, the police soon discovered they'd been working in West Germany for three months without the necessary permits. They, too, were sentenced to deportation, held in custody overnight and put on a flight back to Britain, leaving behind most of their clothes and Pete's drums.

It would be the only time Pete Best ever saw the inside of a prison cell. Sadly, the same can't be said of Paul.

9

'Sing "Searchin'", Paul!'

His condition when he arrived back at 20 Forthlin Road gave his father and younger brother a severe shock. Three months of flat-out exertion, irregular meals and scanty sleep had left him 'like an emaciated skeleton', Mike McCartney tautologically recalled. 'When he sat down, the ankles showing above the winkle-pickers were as thin and white as Dad's pipe-cleaners.'

He spent the next week at home, recuperating on a combination of Jim's cooking and cod-liver oil capsules. John, too, was by now back in Liverpool, having left West Germany of his own volition six days after Paul's enforced exit, but the pair were too depressed by what had happened even to get in contact. Meanwhile, George, the original deportee, didn't know the others had returned: he assumed they'd opened at the Top Ten club with some other lead guitarist in his place. Stu Sutcliffe alone remained in Hamburg, hiding out with Astrid and her mother.

After that heady dip into St Pauli's 'great freedom', the Beatles' prospects at home seemed little brighter than before. Nor could they look to Allan Williams for salvation this time. Back in the autumn, Williams had hatched another grand entrepreneurial scheme, a Liverpool version of the Reeperbahn's Top Ten club at which he'd promised them the job of house band. But they came home to find that Williams's new club had burned down – apparently 'torched' by some ill-wisher, possibly also in the club business – only six days after opening.

As a result, their engagements diary through Christmas and into the 1961 New Year looked thin. Most local dance promoters they'd previously worked for didn't recognise them under the name of the Beatles and weren't willing to take a chance on anyone sounding so peculiar. In addition, British pop group fashion had changed radically during their three-month absence. Every aspiring band now played dramatic-sounding instrumentals, wore matching shiny suits and performed synchronised dance-routines and high kicks like Cliff Richard's Shadows.

Even to a parent as easy-going and supportive as Jim McCartney, the Beatles seemed to have no future and with unusual sternness Jim ordered Paul to find proper employment or get out of the house. Compliant as ever, he took a temporary job on a parcel delivery-truck at £7 per week, then got himself hired by the maritime cable-winding firm of Massey & Coggins. He started at the bottom, sweeping the factory yard, but was soon marked down as potential management material.

John later claimed credit for aborting this career as a dockland white-collar worker. 'I was always saying, "Face up to your dad, tell him to fuck off, he can't hit you."' It was the advice of someone who'd grown up without a dad, which Paul was the least likely boy in the world to follow. But a blunt ultimatum from John did make him defy Jim for the first time ever. 'I told [Paul] on the phone, "Either come or you're out,"' John recalled. 'So he had to make a decision between me and his dad, and in the end he chose me.'

One, at least, of the band's old haunts remained open to them. Pete Best's mother, Mona, was still running the Casbah coffee club in Hayman's Green, where Paul, John and George had originally played as the Quarrymen, and John's and Paul's art still adorned the wall and ceiling. Mrs Best needed little persuasion to book her son's band (as she thought of it) and to plaster the neighbourhood with posters advertising 'the Beatles – direct from Hamburg'.

As Stu Sutcliffe still hadn't returned home, Paul might have been expected to continue playing bass, but instead the gap was filled by a friend of Pete Best's named Chas Newby, coincidentally also a left-handed player. The Bests, Pete and Mona, now effectively managed the band: the Casbah was their base camp as well as an ever-open venue and its doorman, Frank Garner, drove them to and from the outside gigs that were slowly building up again.

Lodging with the Best family was a young trainee accountant named Neil Aspinall who'd attended Liverpool Institute High School with Paul and George and was a close friend of Pete and his brother, Rory. Neil owned an old red and white van and to keep Frank Garner on door-duty at the Casbah he took over the job of driving the Beatles for a couple of pounds a night, somehow fitting it in with studying for his accountancy exams.

On the snowy night of 27 December 1960, Neil drove them to what seemed a routine booking at Litherland Town Hall; a 30-minute spot among well-regarded local bands like the Del Renas and the Deltones. Their billing was the same as Mona Best had given them: 'Direct from Hamburg – the Beatles.' Since they were virtually unknown by that name in their home city, most of the audience thought they must be German.

Among the audience that night was William Faron Ruffley, whose band, Faron's Flamingos, had a huge local following and were arch-practitioners of the slick, well-tailored Shadows style. Faron, aka 'the Panda-footed Prince of Prance', was resplendent in his trademark white suit and surrounded by his usual coterie of adoring girls.

As the stage-curtains parted to reveal the supposedly German group, there was a moment of palpable surprise and – just for an instant – disappointment. For here was not the expected line of ersatz Shadows, dancing the neat, synchronised two-step which, up to that moment, had been the height of performing cool. Here were defiantly asymmetric figures dressed all in black, like their Hamburg exi friends, but with none of the neatness or sleekness black usually creates. 'They were a right mess,' Faron remembers. 'Paul had a red guitar with three strings on it and it wasn't even plugged in . . . John hit his amp with a hammer to get it going.'

Since the earliest rock 'n' roll era – and the Swing era before that

– dance-hall practice had never changed: the band played while its audience danced. But as Paul started 'Long Tall Sally' in his best Little Richard scream –

> Gonna tell Aunt Mary 'bout Uncle John
> He said he had the misery but he had a lotta fun . . .

– the entire crowd rushed to the stage-front and just stood there, gazing and gaping upwards in the first recorded outbreak of Beatlemania. Turning round, Faron saw that even his personal harem had forsaken him.

Liverpool's Cavern club long ago surpassed Nashville's Grand Ole Opry as the most famous popular music venue of all time. Nor did the home of country music ever exert such a hold on the collective imagination as this far homelier home of the pre-Brian Epstein Beatles. Even for those who haven't seen its modern facsimile, the Cavern is as visible and tangible as anything in real life: they can almost believe they've descended its 18 stone steps . . . felt its heat and smelt its mingling odours . . . sat on one of its undersized wooden chairs with Paul, John and George on its tiny stage, close enough to reach out and touch.

By now, it's hardly necessary to add that the Cavern was located in Mathew Street, a cobbled lane through central Liverpool's warehouse district; that it was a former wine-storage cellar consisting of three connected brick tunnels with arches rather like those of Victorian sewers; and that its facilities or, rather, lack of them made the Reeperbahn's music clubs seem the height of luxury by comparison. Less well-known is the McCartney family connection with the Cavern just prior to its Beatle heyday. Paul's cousin, Ian Harris – son of his Auntie Gin – was a joiner who'd helped refurbish the club, installing a new floor and upgrading the toilets. By 1961, however, few of its clientele would have believed any refurbishment had taken place in their lifetime.

Paul had just missed appearing at the Cavern, back when he'd

joined the Quarrymen and the club was still ferociously dedicated
to traditional jazz. Since then, the anti-rock zealotry of its owner,
Ray McFall, had weakened, thanks partly to the decline in jazz
audiences and partly to the success of Mona Best's Casbah, whose
membership now stood at over 3000. During the Beatles' absence
in Germany, rock bands had been let into the Cavern, albeit as
gradually and reluctantly as tradespeople into Ascot's Royal Enclosure. In their post-Hamburg hiatus, it was Mrs Best – still working
tirelessly on behalf of 'Pete's group', as she saw it – who persuaded
Ray McFall to try them out.

McFall had had the bright idea of lunch-time live music sessions
to attract the young female office employees who commuted into
central Liverpool each day. The Beatles' debut was at such a session
on 9 February 1961, with Stu Sutcliffe (who'd returned home in
January) back playing bass.

A touch of the Ascot Royal Enclosure still lingered. Ray McFall
was scandalised by the Beatles' lack of matching suits, collars and
ties, and threatened not to allow them onstage. He relented when
the Cavern deejay, Bob Wooler, pointed out their great advantage
over other musicians, who had regular jobs during the day. Being
all unemployed, they were permanently available to play at lunch-
time. Wooler dubbed them 'a rock 'n' dole group'.

At the Cavern, they were required to perform for only an hour
at a time – a mere finger-snap after their marathon sets at the Indra
and Kaiserkeller. 'Mach Schau'-ing to the limit for 60 minutes still
left a huge overdrive of energy, manifested in clowning, repartee
with the audience or among themselves, and mimicking other
pop performers. Paul's speciality was taking off the Shadows'
trouble-prone bass-player, Jet Harris, who in a recent Cavern appearance had managed to fall off the stage.

'Everyone smoked in those days, and the Beatles all used to be
dragging on ciggies during their set,' remembers Cavern habitué
Frieda Kelly, who was then 19. 'George would put one behind his
ear for later, or wedge it in the head of his guitar. Paul smoked as
much as the others, but we knew he used to buy his cigarettes at

George Henry Lee, the department store, where they had a kiosk. That used to seem so much more sophisticated than going to an ordinary tobacconist's.'

To begin with, the Beatles weren't stars of the Cavern, just one in a rota of bands covering much the same American rock 'n' roll and R&B material, including Rory Storm and the Hurricanes, the Big Three (formerly Cass and the Cassanovas) and Gerry and the Pacemakers, who'd replaced them at the Hamburg Top Ten club. They stood out from the competition by the eclecticism of their material, playing the little-known B-sides of familiar A-sides, or songs associated with female performers – like the Shirelles' 'Boys' – or standards and show tunes never attempted by a rock band before.

Paul was always at the forefront of this experimentation, both its hard and soft side. On the one hand, he begged Bob Wooler to lend him – and him alone – Chan Romero's raucous 'Hippy Hippy Shake', the pièce-de-résistance of Wooler's import singles collection, so that he could replicate its joyous mindlessness. On the other, he carefully studied and copied two records by jazz diva Peggy Lee, borrowed from his cousin Bett: 'Fever' and 'Till There Was You', the latter a misty-eyed ballad from a hit Broadway show, *The Music Man*. But as yet few Lennon-McCartney compositions were included in their act, lest the Liverpool crowd objected to their wasting time that could have been filled by Chuck Berry or Carl Perkins.

For its former members, and millions of modern proxy ones, the Cavern needs no prose poem to recreate its purgatorial Paradise: the health and safety nightmare of an unventilated cellar packed full of chain-smokers and rife with dodgy electrical plugs, yet with no sprinkler system or even emergency exit; the men's toilet where one stood on a plank over a permanent foetid lake; the women's toilet where audacious rats sometimes rode atop swinging doors; the constant shower of flakes from the white-distempered ceiling, known as 'Cavern dandruff'; the energy and euphoria which – so unlike Hamburg – were fuelled by nothing stronger than coffee and Coca-Cola; the body-heat that rose up the 18 steps and sent clouds of steam billowing into Mathew Street; the mingled scents of sweat, mould, cheese-rind, rotting vegetables, mouse-droppings and disinfectant that impregnated clothes beyond the help of any dry cleaner.

'You could be on a bus, with two girls right at the other end,' Frieda Kelly remembers, 'and you'd know straight away they'd been to the Cavern.'

Frieda herself preferred the Beatles' lunch-time sessions, on Mondays, Wednesdays and Fridays, when the place was less crowded, the atmosphere more relaxed and the audience overwhelmingly female. The band played two sets: from 12 to 1 p.m. and 1.15 to 2.15. 'I used to time my lunch hour so I could see the second set. One of them might turn up late – usually George – so the first set wouldn't be a full hour. And by the second one, they'd really have warmed up.'

The central tunnel containing the stage was so narrow that, even on their kiddy-size wooden chairs, the girls could sit only seven abreast, like a bouffanted, mascara-ed kindergarten. Everyone had their allotted place, or 'spec', so there was little pushing or quarrelling. Those at the front always looked their very best for their idols, dressing up to the nines and arriving with just-washed hair in thickets of rollers which they didn't remove until the last seconds before their idols came on.

Frieda Kelly's spec was standing next to the left-hand wall, facing the door to the tiny backstage room where the bands changed and tuned up and Bob Wooler made his famously punning PA announcements ('Hi, all you Cavern-dwellers! Welcome to the *best* of cellars!') and played records from his own private collection during intermissions. 'It meant standing up for an hour, but that never bothered me. It always seemed to go by in about five minutes.'

Frieda, whose life was to be closely intertwined with the Beatles', remembers this as the time when Paul and John seemed closest. 'While they were playing, it was as if they could read each other's minds. One of them only had to play a note or say a word, or just nod, and the other knew what he wanted him to do. John, of course, was as blind as a bat, but never went onstage wearing glasses. When someone handed him a written request, he couldn't ever see it, so he'd hand it to Paul to read out.'

Many of the girls were so near that they made requests verbally, without shouting or even raising their voices. Paul still remembers a pair named Chris and Val who always asked for the same Coasters' song in thick Scouse. 'Sing "Searchin'", Paul,' they'd plead softly in unison, pronouncing it 'sea-urchin'.

The first Jim McCartney knew of the Cavern was finding Paul's shirts so drenched with sweat that they had to be wrung out over the kitchen sink. Jim's workplace at the Cotton Exchange was only a few minutes' walk from Mathew Street and at the first opportunity he dropped by the club during his own lunch hour. But the crowd in front of the stage was so large that he couldn't attract his son's attention.

John's Aunt Mimi saw the Beatles at the Cavern just once, then vowed never to set foot in it again. But Jim, who worked only a few streets away, often popped in at lunch-time. If he was cooking supper at 20 Forthlin Road that night, he'd drop off some chops or a pound of sausages for Paul to take home after the show and put into the fridge.

The Reeperbahn's door had not slammed on the Beatles irrevocably. Their engagement at the Top Ten club was still open, if some way could be found of lifting the one-year ban imposed on Paul and Pete Best as a result of the Bambi 'arson' episode. Paul therefore drafted a contrite letter to the West German foreign office on his and Pete's behalf. It was, as usual, literate and persuasive, but told rather a large white lie (that neither of them drank alcohol) to support his plea that a vengeful Bruno Koschmider had wildly exaggerated a stupid but harmless prank:

> We both swear that we had no intention whatsoever of burning the cinema or maliciously damaging its property. The whole

incident had no motive to prompt it, in fact there was no reason
at all behind the burning. It was just a stupid trick which
we feel we ought to have been punished for in a less drastic
manner.

Representations were also made in Hamburg by the Top Ten's
owner, Peter Eckhorn, and through the West German Consulate
in Liverpool by Allan Williams. As a result, the ban on Paul and
Pete was lifted on condition they promised to be of good behaviour
in future and Eckhorn paid back the costs of flying them home. So
on 1 April 1961, the Beatles began a 13-week stint at the Top Ten,
also doubling as backing band to its resident singer, Tony Sheridan.

This would have been the perfect moment for Paul to take
over from Stu Sutcliffe on bass guitar without rancour or embarrassment. Stu by now had had more than enough of playing an
instrument he would never fully master, and intended to waste no
more time away from his true métier. His plan was to return to
Liverpool College of Art, where he'd been so bright a star before
John lured him into rock 'n' roll. He would complete his interrupted
studies, then take the teacher-training course on which, thanks to
his brilliant record as a student, he'd been as good as promised a
place.

At the last moment, the college rejected him for the course.
Though no official explanation was ever given, it seemed he was
being blamed for the loss of the student union's PA system, which
the then Quarrymen had walked off with back in 1959. So he and
his weighty Hofner President bass stayed in the Beatles' line-up,
leaving Paul still in the rather awkward, skiffle-ish role of third
guitarist. It didn't last long. The red Rosetti Solid 7 that had done
duty both as a guitar and bass was by now almost falling apart
but not worth the expense of repairing. Accordingly – in a ritual
that would become part of later bands' stage-acts – John, George
and Pete joined Paul in smashing it to pieces. From then on, he
switched to the grand piano on the club's stage, using its bass keys
to provide the runs that Stu couldn't.

While diving zestfully back into St Pauli's sexual smorgasbord, John and Paul both had steady girlfriends back home. John's was his art college classmate, Cynthia Powell; Paul's was still the elfin Dot Rhone, who'd miscarried his child a year earlier while he was still at school. After that grown-up emotional trauma, they had returned to teenage dating, with Dot always at his beck and call, her hair and clothes always as he liked them. Since he'd brought her home a gold ring, she'd considered them engaged while never putting any pressure on him to set a wedding-date.

Dot and Cynthia had become friends and together led a life rather like service wives', writing long letters several times a week to their boys overseas, with snapshots to show they were keeping up their required Brigitte Bardot look; both remaining absolutely faithful without wondering too much whether the boys overseas were doing the same.

With the more civilised conditions of the Top Ten engagement, Cynthia and Dot could be invited to Hamburg for a short visit. Cynthia stayed with Astrid – who was welcoming and hospitable to both girls – but actually spent almost every night sharing John's bunk bed in the musicians' dorm in the attic of the club building. For the fastidious Paul, however, more elaborate arrangements were necessary.

He had become a special pet of Rosa, the elderly toilet attendant who'd also defected from Bruno Koschmider's employment to work for Eckhorn. Known to the Liverpudlians as 'Mutti' – mummy – Rosa kept an outsize glass jar of Preludin and Purple Hearts under her counter to sustain them through their long nights onstage. For Paul, her favourite, she'd also steal extra rations, sardines or bananas, as she walked through the market to work. Now, to save him from the squalor John never minded, she arranged for him and Dot to stay on a houseboat on the River Elbe, which Sheridan and some of the other musicians also used.

Though the two girls were shielded from St Pauli's more extreme entertainments, they were soon initiated into Preludin and other 'sweeties' from Mutti's glass jar. The result did not altogether please boyfriends accustomed to their meek silence. 'Usually, we hardly dared open our mouths,' Dot remembers. 'Now the two of us couldn't stop talking.'

Many young men in that era remodelled their girlfriends' appearance, as Paul and John had Dot's and Cynthia's. But with Astrid and Stu Sutcliffe, the opposite was the case. The boyishly beautiful blonde turned the delicate little Scot into her mirror-image. Her first step was to put Stu into the black leather she and her exi circle habitually wore despite its lingering associations with fascism and Hitler's SS. An accomplished seamstress, she made him a suit of blouson and trousers that, with his tiny stature and fine-boned face, turned him into more of a Hell's Cupid than Angel.

It was in fact an ideal outfit for boy rock 'n' rollers on the round-the-clock Reeperbahn, which could be worn both on- and offstage, absorb beer-splashes, sweat and other stains without a trace, even be slept in if necessary. John, Paul, George and Pete immediately had copies run up by a St Pauli tailor, setting them off with fancily-tooled cowboy boots and pink flat caps. John later recalled that they looked like 'four Gene Vincents' (though, in fact, Vincent hadn't worn leathers until British TV producer Jack Good suggested it).

They baulked, however, at Astrid's next creation for Stu, a high-buttoning jacket with a round collar, inspired by Pierre Cardin's recent Paris collection. To John and Paul, this still looked altogether too much like the upper half of a woman's two-piece 'costume'. 'Borrowed mum's jacket have we, Stu?' they would sneer whenever he appeared in it.

The last thing any of them had thought of copying was the forward-combed hair, known as the 'French' style, worn by most of their male exi friends. As handy with scissors as with a needle, Astrid had created her own version for her previous boyfriend, Klaus Voormann, mainly to hide Klaus's rather protuberant ears. Now she persuaded Stu to part with the Teddy boy cockade he'd had since his early teens and let her give him 'a Klaus'. For John and Paul, this was more extreme than a wardrobe full of 'mum's

Paul, aged 5, with brother Michael (right).

Paul (front) and Michael on holiday in north Wales.

Paul and Michael with their wonderful dad, Jim, in the back garden at 20 Forthlin Road.

Poster for Kaiserkeller club when rival Liverpool band Rory Storm and the Hurricanes headlined over the Beatles.

Paul at the piano in Hamburg. Note the bottles lining the stage-front. Stu Sutcliffe is on right.

George, Pete Best, Paul and John (*l to r*) after the transition to black leather. Paul has just bought his Hofner violin bass.

After Brian Epstein's takeover: out go rock 'n' roll black leathers, in come tailor-made suits of grey 'brushed tweed'.

'What are they writing about us?' Maybe that the Dave Clark Five have knocked them off number one.

Hard-core fans at the Cavern club. Despite their transports of ecstasy, they stay on their kindergarten-size chairs.

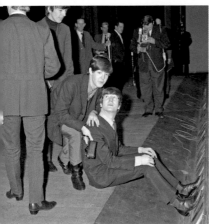

Paul says a cautioning word in John's ear, in the days when he still listened.

The camera loves him, even perched on the kitchen sink at 'Forthlin'.

Under the protective eye of Brian Epstein (far left), Ed Sullivan feigns interest in Paul's violin bass before the TV appearance that put America in the Beatles' pocket.

Surf broads: with fans during a rare rest-day in Miami.

Paul with Jane Asher, when he lodged in her parents' house in a 'Peter Pan world'.

With Wilfrid Brambell, his 'grandfather' in *A Hard Day's Night*; a chance to indulge his love of false beards.

The Beatles between floors at NEMS, the Epstein family's electrical store in Liverpool. 'You've already got a good business, Mr Epstein,' one record company boss advised Brian. 'Why not stick to that?'

jackets'. Only George, whose quietness had always belied his sty-
listic daring, came to Astrid and requested the same cut. But after
a couple of days with it, he lost his nerve and bared his forehead
again.

It was during the girlfriends' visit that the tension between Paul
and Stu finally boiled over. Stu's disillusionment with studying art
and his supposed renewed commitment to the Beatles had begun to
waver as soon as he returned to Hamburg and linked up again with
Astrid and the exis. He'd begun secretly attending drawing-classes
at the city's art college, whose tutors happened to include the renowned Scottish-Italian painter and sculptor Eduardo Paolozzi. So
impressed was Paolozzi by Stu's talent that he became his mentor,
even arranging for him to receive a grant from the West German
government.

This made Stu even more unreliable in attending rehearsals,
which had always been Paul's main gripe against him. At the same
time, Pete Best was dating a stripper and would disappear for hours,
similarly cutting band-practice and reappearing just in time for the
night's performance. One night, Stu and Pete were both playing
so erratically – while still drawing squeals from their respective
female followings – that Paul's patience finally snapped. Rounding
on each of them in turn, he hissed, 'You may look like James Dean
and *you* may look like Jeff Chandler, but you're both crap!'

An even more out-of-character incident occurred on an evening
when the two girlfriends were not watching the show in rapt admiration as usual, but having a hen-session at Astrid's. Between
songs, Paul made a remark about Astrid; what exactly he said no
one now remembers, but it caused the usually gentle, stoical Stu to
square up furiously to him.

According to Paul, it was no more than a scuffle: 'We gripped
each other fiercely until we were prised apart.' But Tony Sheridan, who was onstage with them, always described it as a serious
scrap, in which Stu came off decidedly worst. 'I've seen Paul fight,'
Sheridan recalled. 'Like this [miming cat-scratch] . . . with his
claws.' Stu, at any rate, took the fracas very seriously, telephoning

Astrid and telling her to order Paul's girlfriend out of her house.

About a third of the way through the Top Ten engagement, Stu resolved the problem by quitting the Beatles for good and Paul took over on bass – something which, he later said, he'd never really wanted. 'There's a theory that I ruthlessly worked Stu out of the group in order to get the prize chair of bass. Forget it . . . Nobody wants to play bass, or nobody did in those days. Bass was the thing that fat boys . . . were asked to stand at the back and play. So I didn't want to do it, but Stuart left and I got lumbered with it.'

Between the former onstage grapplers, friendly relations were sufficiently restored for Stu to lend Paul his bass until Paul could buy one of his own. Hofner guitars being manufactured in West Germany, he could pick up a 'violin' model (officially the 550/1) brand-new for the equivalent of about £30. As luck would have it, the Reeperbahn's main guitar dealers stocked one of the only two left-handed versions Hofner had ever produced. It arrived just in time for the Beatles' first professional recording-session.

Earlier that summer, Tony Sheridan, their Top Ten club colleague and occasional lead singer, had been signed up by the German Polydor label. His producer was to be Bert Kaempfert, an internationally famous bandleader and composer whose instrumental 'Wonderland by Night' had been an American number one in 1960. As at the Top Ten, Sheridan's backing band was to be the Beatles – renamed 'the Beat Brothers' because of that unfortunate assonance with 'peedles' or little boy's willies.

The recording session took place in the assembly hall of a Hamburg infants' school on 22 June 1961. In an unhappy augury for Pete Best, Bert Kaempfert didn't care for Pete's heavy 'Mach Schau' beat and (according to Tony Sheridan) stopped him using his bass drum pedal and limited him to brushes instead of sticks.

As Kaempfert was aiming solely at the unadventurous West German pop audience, the choice of material was not inspiring. The 'Beat Brothers' backed Sheridan on four tracks including two rocked-up old chestnuts, 'My Bonnie' and 'When the Saints', then were allowed to tape two numbers of their own. One was an instrumental, 'Cry for a Shadow', a parody of Cliff Richard's shiny-suited sidemen with George on lead guitar; the other was the jazz standard 'Ain't She Sweet', sung by John. Apart from the boom of his brand-new bass, Paul was unnoticeable.

This time when the Beatles returned from Hamburg, no one in Liverpool mistook them for Germans. During their absence, thanks largely to the revivified Cavern, there had been a huge increase in the number of local bands and the clubs, halls and 'jive hives' where they could perform. So much was going on that in July John's art school friend Bill Harry had started a fortnightly newspaper named *Mersey Beat* to cover it.

Mersey Beat naturally gave star treatment to the only Mersey beat-makers with anything resembling a recording deal. On page one of its second issue was a report about their session with Tony Sheridan for Bert Kaempfert, illustrated by one of Astrid's photographs of them at Hamburg fairground back in the autumn of 1960. Paul's surname was misspelt as 'McArtrey'.

To lighten the news of which bands were playing where and who'd quit one to join another, Bill Harry turned to John for the zany drawings and writing with which he'd always amused his cronies. The most famous of numerous columns and skits he contributed is 'A Short Essay on the dubious origins of the Beatles', purporting to explain the name that no one any longer thought a bad idea. It had come, John wrote, in a vision: 'a man appeared on a flaming pie and said unto them "From this day forward you are Beatles."' Fluent writer and clever cartoonist though Paul was, he found no similar niche in the paper – but half a century later, that 'flaming pie' line would come in useful.

Yet, for all their hometown celebrity, the Beatles seemed to have run into a brick wall – one 18 steps underground, steaming with condensation and odorous with rat-shit. They had parted acrimoniously from Allan Williams after refusing to pay his commission for the second Hamburg trip (arguing, not unreasonably, that they'd negotiated it themselves). Now, their only management was Mona

Best, assisted by her son, their drummer. And Mrs Best, for all her virtues, was not the one to launch them into the wider world beyond Liverpool and St Pauli. Never before or since, in fact, was a band such a plum ripe for picking.

This sense of having gone as far as they ever could seems to have made even Paul forget his usual punctilious professionalism. On 9 October, John turned 21 and received the munificent gift of £100 from his Aunt Elizabeth in Edinburgh. To spend it, he asked Paul to accompany him on a hitch-hiking trip down through France to Spain. Paul agreed, even though it meant reneging on several important Beatles gigs. He added a tip, learned on previous such journeys with George: that wearing some distinctive garment or headgear was the surest way of getting lifts. Accordingly the two just took off together, wearing matching bowler hats – the Nerk Twins reincarnated. George and Pete Best were so disgusted at being left in the lurch that both started looking around for other bands to join while Stu Sutcliffe in Hamburg told Astrid and several other people that the Beatles had broken up.

Having crossed the Channel by the Dover–Calais ferry, Paul and John found their bowler hats to be totally ineffective in hitching rides, so decided to take the train to Paris. For the British, this had always been the world capital of sex, and so it seemed to them, even after their Hamburg experiences. Neither spoke much French – surprisingly for the future composer of 'Michelle' – and their misadventures with the language were worthy of the Ealing film comedy *Innocents in Paris*. At one point, they chummed up with some prostitutes and were wildly excited to be offered '*une chambre pour la nuit*'. But, to Paul's regret, '*une chambre*' proved to be all that was on offer.

They dropped the idea of moving on to Spain when one of their Hamburg exi friends, Jürgen Vollmer, proved to be in Paris, studying photography. Jürgen gave them a guided tour of the city, showing them L'Opéra, where they danced around singing mock arias, and taking them to flea markets where they beheld their very first pair of bell-bottomed jeans.

One night, they went to a concert by France's only rock 'n' roll star, Johnny Hallyday, paying an astronomical seven shillings and sixpence (35p) each for seats at L'Olympia theatre, little dreaming they themselves would soon top the bill there.

Every cool young Frenchman seemed to have the combed-forward hairstyle which Astrid Kirchherr had given Stu Sutcliffe in Hamburg and which John and Paul had previously derided. Jürgen had one, too, and was as handy as Astrid with barber's scissors, so one day in his room at the Hotel de Beaune they asked him to shear off their Teddy boy quiffs. It was only a tentative version of what would become the Beatle cut but it transformed their faces, making John's more challenging and mocking, Paul's even rounder and more baby-innocent.

Actually the Beatle cut can be found adorning numerous historical figures from Julius Caesar to Napoleon. Much later in life, Paul would claim that, for him, its true begetter had been an icon of the art world, the painter, designer and film director Jean Cocteau.

Cocteau's 1959 film *The Testament of Orpheus* was a fantasy about that mythic minstrel of ancient Thrace, full of beautiful young men with Beatle cuts millennia before their time. Indeed, Orpheus was a musician who sang and played his stringed instrument with such maddening sweetness that young women fought literally to tear him limb from limb. Sound familiar?

10

'Oo, Vi, give me legs a comb'

Brian Epstein's discovery of the Beatles is always portrayed as the luckiest accident in entertainment history. One day in November 1961, so the story goes, a teenage boy walked into the record department which 27-year-old Brian ran in the basement of NEMS, his family's central Liverpool electrical store, and asked for a single called 'My Bonnie' by the Beatles.

Brian had never heard of the group or the record, but offered to order it for his young customer. In the process, he found that these Beatles were not foreigners, as he'd assumed from their weird name, but Liverpudlians who had made the track in Germany as backing musicians to Tony Sheridan. His curiosity aroused, Brian decided to go and see them at a Cavern club lunch-time session, only at that point realising that the Cavern was just a couple of hundred yards from his shop. So the young businessman in his bespoke suit ventured gingerly down the 18 steps – and stumbled on pure magic.

In reality, Brian was well aware of the Beatles long before he visited the Cavern. His record department thronged with their fans and also sold *Mersey Beat*, the local music paper whose pages they dominated (and to which he himself contributed a record column). He'd taken *Mersey Beat*'s editor, Bill Harry, out to lunch twice to pick Harry's brains about them and sent his personal assistant, Alistair Taylor, to the Cavern ahead of him to check them out. Taylor's advice was grab them before anyone else could.

Nor was it relevant that Brian had no qualifications for managing a pop group beyond an interest in theatre and a flair for design and presentation; nor that the still largely blue-collar world of pop was at the furthest possible extreme from his own genteel middle-class one. In Britain's nascent music business, almost every manager was a social cut above his artisan artistes, with little or no understanding of youth culture. Those first impresarios were making up the rules as they went along: Brian's, uniquely, would be all about quality, value for money and good taste.

Uniquely, too, he was not motivated primarily by money; the Epstein chain of NEMS shops generated all he could ever want. His needs were more complex and rooted in a private life as troubled as it was privileged. The elder son of highly respectable Jewish parents, he was gay in an era when sexual acts between males were a crime punishable by imprisonment as well as an offence against his religion. To compound his feelings of guilt and self-loathing, he was drawn to casual sex in its riskiest forms – soliciting in public toilets or kerb-crawling the Liverpool docks, where entrapment by the police and 'queer-bashing' gangs were continual hazards. His daily life as a dapper, sophisticated man-about-town had a dark underside of shame, fear and violence.

His epiphany at the Cavern therefore had little to do with the Beatles' music. In their all-over black leather, they were four delectable bits of juvenile 'rough trade'; a quadruple fantasy he could enjoy without his usual shame or fear of grievous bodily harm. He was to love them in a platonic, almost paternal way, calling them 'the Boys' until well after they became men, and dedicating himself to their welfare and protection.

But he was *in* love with just one. Not with Paul, the most obviously attractive, but with John, whose tough-guy exterior hid a middle-class upbringing not unlike Brian's own, and who'd needed an all-protecting father figure since the age of six. So, yet again, a back seat for Paul – one which this time he took with some relief.

*

On the Beatles' side, there was never any doubt that being managed by such a prominent local businessman, for whatever reasons, would be a major step forward. But, as lords of the Mathew Street underworld, they had developed a super-sized attitude from which even their most career-conscious and punctilious member was not immune. When an exploratory meeting with Brian was arranged at the NEMS store after hours, Paul failed to turn up. George telephoned 20 Forthlin Road to ask what had happened to him and learned he was taking a leisurely bath. Brian blushed with irritation – an unfortunate trait he had – and spluttered, 'He's going to be very late.'

'But very clean,' the deadpan George pointed out.

At further meetings which didn't clash with Paul's bath-time, Brian set out what he'd do for the Beatles if they put themselves in his hands: firstly, secure them a contract with a major British record label rather than an obscure West German one, then make them nationally famous. It was all pure bluff – and in the end, of course, incalculable understatement.

Paul was the one who questioned Brian most closely, asking if the plan involved changing the music they played or the way they played it. Reassured that they'd be left just as they were (a false promise, it would turn out), he deferred to John for the final verdict, delivered with typical Lennon directness: 'Right, Brian. Manage us.'

Although there were already two people with managerial claims on the Beatles, neither stood in Brian's way or tried to take any share of them. Allan Williams willingly gave them up without a penny but – still fuming over his unpaid Hamburg commission – advised Brian not to touch them 'with a bargepole'. Mona Best, Williams's successor, acknowledged that Brian could do more for them than she ever could, and was content with the benefit which would accrue to her son.

As Paul, like George and Pete, was under 21, Brian couldn't put him under contract without his father's consent. Jim McCartney offered no objection, believing in the popular stereotype of Jewish people as 'good with money'. It helped, too, that the McCartneys' upright piano, on which Jim showed Paul his first chords, and on which he wrote his very first songs, had come from the Epstein family's original NEMS shop in Walton.

Living on the fringe of Liverpool's underworld as they did, the Beatles knew all about Brian's secret gay life and quickly guessed his fixation on John. (Strangely, none of their families ever seemed aware of any of it.) Although John hadn't a gay bone in his body, he took malicious pleasure in playing up to Brian, pretending to lead him on, then rebuffing him as cruelly as only John knew how. John wasn't the only Beatle to arouse Brian's ardour: Pete Best has since claimed to have been propositioned by him on a car journey to Blackpool while John and Cynthia were sitting in the back. But never once would he show the tiniest flicker of attraction to Paul.

'I think Brian felt a bit guilty because he ought to have fancied Paul, but didn't,' a former NEMS employee recalls. 'That always seemed to make him a bit uneasy around Paul and try extra hard if he ever had to do anything for him.'

Soon after Brian's takeover, *Mersey Beat* announced a readers' poll for the most popular of Liverpool's 350-odd bands. Like many others, the Beatles sent in dozens of voting slips nominating themselves and putting their greatest rival, Rory Storm and the Hurricanes, last on the candidates list. Rory's band in fact received more votes but Bill Harry let the Beatles win by a landslide. Their picture occupied the upper half of *Mersey Beat*'s front page, in their Hamburg black leather suits (of which numerous Cavern habitués, girls as well as boys, now wore copies). Once again, Paul's surname was spelt 'McArtrey'.

In this heady atmosphere, a management contract was drawn up between John Winston Lennon, James Paul McCartney, George Harrison and Randolph Peter Best, binding them to NEMS Enterprises, a company newly created by Brian, for five years at a commission of 10 to 15 per cent. Though all four 'boys' signed the document, he himself forgot to do so, making the whole exercise pointless. Not until the following October would a proper contract be sealed, giving him 25 per cent. At Paul's instigation, the boys tried to beat him down to 20 per cent, but he argued the extra five was for the expenses he'd incur – on his crusade to make them 'bigger than Elvis'.

Their entourage, such as it was, also became absorbed into NEMS Enterprises. Apart from their driver/roadie, Neil Aspinall, this consisted of just one other, a droll teenager named Tony Bramwell, who'd known George since childhood – and had been one of the many babies delivered by Paul's mother. Bramwell followed them around to all their gigs, so ubiquitous that John nicknamed him 'Measles', and would carry their guitars for them. 'I'd been doing it for nothing for months,' he recalls. 'Now Brian offered to pay me to do it.'

Brian's first step was to make the Beatles run as efficiently as his record department at the family store. The smallest and lowest-paying of their gigs were now treated like Royal Command performances; before each one, they and Neil Aspinall would receive a detailed briefing, typed on Brian's headed notepaper, giving the address of the venue, the promoter's name, the rendezvous times with Neil and the duration of the performance. Every week, the NEMS wages clerk would make up regulation pay packets for them, each containing £20, which were hand-delivered by Tony Bramwell.

Brian also personally took over their promotion, designing lavish display ads for the *Liverpool Echo* and other local papers, and posters heralding the coming of 'Mersey Beat Poll Winners! Polydor Recording Artists! Prior to European Tour!' [i.e. Hamburg again]. 'Just billing them as Polydor recording artists instantly raised the level of their gigs,' Bramwell says. 'Now they weren't playing church halls any more, but Top Rank ballrooms.'

While keeping his promise not to interfere with their music, Brian (going back on that promise to Paul) revolutionised the band's stage-presentation or, rather, lack of it, decreeing there was to be no more onstage smoking, eating, clowning or backchat with the audience. Drinking, of course, couldn't be prevented, but between sets they must no longer adjourn to the nearest bar, where trouble – usually involving John – was always liable to start. Instead, Neil would bring them drinks and sandwiches backstage. So from here on the black-leather Cavern scruffs had a Green Room.

Brian's final target was those Hamburg-bought outfits which, ironically, had been one of the band's main excitements for him in the first place. It happened that Cliff Richard's Shadows, now a successful act in their own right, were appearing at the Liverpool Empire. Brian took John, Paul, George and Pete to the show, then told them that if they wanted to make it, they must wear the same kind of dapper matching suits.

Paul has always been portrayed as Brian's ally in smartening up the Beatles and so robbing their stage performance of an excitement and authenticity that only their Cavern audience fully experienced – the first step in the 'selling out' that John would condemn so bitterly in retrospect.

Paul certainly was all for going into suits, indeed had already made some sketches of a possible Beatles stage uniform. But John at that point was just as hungry to succeed by whatever means it took; he later admitted he would have worn 'a balloon if someone [was] going to pay me'. Besides, as Tony Bramwell points out, the suits Brian provided weren't 'tatty, flash stuff like other bands wore onstage', but tailor-made, in 'grey brushed tweed', costing £40 apiece, the equivalent of £1000 today. Nor did he object when Brian – supported by Paul – said they should end every show with a deep bow in unison like actors taking a curtain-call.

Brian was not working totally blind. Early on, he enlisted the help of Joe Flannery, a fellow member of Liverpool's clandestine gay community with whom, some years earlier, he'd had an atypically happy, stable relationship. Flannery already managed a band, Lee Curtis and the All Stars, fronted by his younger brother. 'I met up with Brian only about a week after he'd started managing the Beatles,' he remembers. 'It was at the Iron Door club [the Cavern's main rival, in Temple Street]. My brother's group needed to borrow a bass amp, so I asked Paul for a loan of his. But he just nodded at John and said, "Ask the boss."'

After late gigs, the Beatles would often crash out at Flannery's comfortable flat in Gardner Road. 'When they'd sleep in my sitting-room, I noticed there was a pecking-order. John always had the couch while Paul made do with two armchairs pushed together.

'I used to have a part-Norwegian housekeeper named Anne, who'd stay late to make them sandwiches, helped by her very attractive 17-year-old daughter, Girda. Paul took a fancy to Girda and would always be in the kitchen chatting to her. One night, her mother pointed the breadknife at him and said. "You shouldn't be out here. Get back in the sitting-room where you belong!"'

Flannery negotiated bookings with the tougher promoters who would have been put off by Brian's genteel accent. He also joined in Brian's little subterfuges to impress the Beatles – like telling him in front of them that Elvis Presley's manager, Colonel Tom Parker, was calling long distance from America.

But Brian was very far from being all bluff. Thanks to NEMS's reputation as one of the north's largest record retailers, he was able to get the Beatles an audition with the mighty Decca label almost immediately. A Decca producer named Mike Smith came up to Liverpool, saw them at the Cavern and was sufficiently impressed to offer them a studio audition on 1 January 1962.

On 31 December, they set off for London separately, Brian by train, the Beatles in Neil Aspinall's van. Unfortunately, Neil lost his way and a journey that should have lasted only about four hours took more than ten. Having finally reached central London, they got caught up in its traditionally rowdy New Year's Eve celebrations around the Trafalgar Square fountains. At one point, a man approached them, offering something called 'pot' which he suggested they should 'smoke' together in the back of Neil's van. The Liverpool lads turned and fled.

As a result, they were all viciously hung-over when they met up with Brian the next morning at Decca's studios in Broadhurst Gardens, St John's Wood – Paul's first glimpse of the leafy north London enclave he would one day call home. They were kept waiting a long time in reception, to Brian's blushing annoyance, then were informed that their amps weren't good enough to record, so they'd have to use the studio's own. They had just one hour to demo 15 songs, chosen (by Brian) from their huge repertoire of R&B and pop cover versions and standards, plus three Lennon–McCartney originals.

The Beatles' Decca audition has gone down in history as a disastrously below-par performance that gave no real idea of who or what they were. In fact, despite the hangovers and haste, it was a showcase of enormous versatility and charm, ranging from Barrett Strong's 'Money', delivered with all John's bitter brio, to Paul's heartfelt 'Till There Was You' and George's surprisingly sweet version of Bobby Vee's 'Take Good Care Of My Baby'; from the semi-comic 'Sheik Of Araby' and 'Three Cool Cats' to a quickstep version of Harry Warren's 'September In The Rain', sung by Paul as if there wasn't a rock 'n' roll bone in his body. The Lennon-McCartney songs were John's 'Hello Little Girl' and Paul's 'Like Dreamers Do' and 'Love of the Loved'.

In the end, versatility proved to be their undoing; the Decca people could see no way of marketing such an unfocused bunch of musical eccentrics in the simplistic British pop scene of 1962. That they hailed from so distant and inaccessible a part of the country also helped tip the balance against them. So the Beatles were turned down and a north London butcher named Brian Poole and his band, the Tremeloes, were signed instead.

The Liverpool bands who competed with each other so ferociously onstage were privately the best of friends who liked nothing better than to meet up and drink together after a long night at the Cavern or the Iron Door. Their favourite rendezvous – offering entertainment as good as any city nightspot – was the home of the Hurricanes' flamboyant front man, Rory Storm.

Rory carried his 'Mr Showmanship' tag into everyday life, having changed his name by deed poll from Alan Caldwell and even renamed his family's house in Broadgreen Road 'Stormsville'. His mother, Vi, was his most ardent fan and welcomed his musician friends to Stormsville at any hour of the night, providing non-stop food and hot drinks, plus a mixture of straight talking and zany humour that could put even John Lennon into the shade.

Often present at these sitting-room soirées would be Rory's younger sister Iris, a bubbly 17-year-old who'd had a childhood romance with George Harrison. Iris had kept up the family tradition of unconventionality by running away, joining a circus and becoming a trapeze artiste: she now worked as a dancer in pantomimes and summer variety shows, specialising in the French cancan.

'Paul and John used to love my parents,' she recalls. 'My dad was the most totally *good* man I've ever known. Each week, he used to open his pay packet, take only what he needed to feed and clothe us, then give the rest to charity. He'd usually have gone to bed when the Beatles arrived; they called him "the Crusher" because he had these nightmares that made him shout out and roll around the bed. And they called my mum "Violent Vi", I suppose because they could never best her in an argument.'

Iris had known Paul for years as a friend of Rory's but one night at a Beatles gig she noticed him looking at her in a different way. 'It was at the Operation Big Beat show at New Brighton Tower, when they were on with [black American singer] Davy Jones. The Twist had just come in and I demonstrated it with the Beatles backing me.

'People have always thought Paul wrote "I Saw Her Standing There" about me because I was "just seventeen" when he asked me out. But in the two years we were together, he always used to say he couldn't write a song about me, because the only thing that rhymed with "Iris" was "virus".'

It turned into another 'going steady' arrangement, fitted in between Beatles gigs and Iris's commitments as a dancer. 'We'd go to the cinema every Tuesday: Paul would pay one week, I'd pay the next. Or we'd go to the Empire if a big name was on – always sitting in the cheap seats. Paul liked what I thought were quite square entertainers, like Joe "Mr Piano" Henderson. He knew all of Joe's numbers and sang along with them, which I found a bit embarrassing.'

Even with the feisty Iris, he remained something of a couture control-freak. 'Because of being in show business, I was used to glamming myself up. But Paul only liked me to dress very plainly . . . dark skirts and jumpers, my hair in a bun. Later on, I laughed when I read that he'd turned into such a vegetarian. When we were going out, his favourite meal used to be lamb chops, chips and peas.'

Iris had always been a regular at the Cavern, cheering on both her brother's band and the Beatles. But that changed when Brian Epstein came along. Brian feared the Beatles' female fans would desert them if they were known to have wives or even girlfriends. 'He asked Rory to ask me not to go down the Cavern any more,' Iris recalls, 'in case anyone found out we were dating.'

Paul by now had a car of his own, bought with the aid of a loan from his father. The model he chose was typically aspirational: one of the new Ford Classics in a colour named Goodwood Green, after Britain's poshest motor racing circuit, and advertised as 'suitable for the golf-club car park'.

'Wherever we went, he always had to be the centre of attention,' Iris says. 'John used to love to imitate Quasimodo or what he called "Spassies" [spastics] and Paul had picked it up from him. One night we'd gone to this coffee bar in Birkenhead called The Cubic Club because everything was cube-shaped – the tables, the seats. Paul's showing-off got on my nerves so much that I picked up the sugar-bowl – the sugar was the one thing there *not* in cubes – and emptied it over his head.

'We were always having rows and breaking up. And whenever we did, George would be round the next day, asking me to go out with him again.'

Much of their time together was spent in the sitting-room at 'Stormsville', listening to the wild cries of Iris's dad having his spectacular nightmares in bed upstairs. 'My dad used to sleep-walk as well. One night he came downstairs in his pyjamas fast asleep and ran out into the street, saying he was looking for his car. Paul went after him and talked him back indoors and up to bed again.

'After the Beatles had been out on a gig, Paul used to like my mum to comb his legs. He's quite hairy, and having his legs combed seemed to relax him. He'd say "Oo, Vi, give me legs a comb" and roll up his trouser-leg, and Mum would get a comb and do it.

'She loved him but she wasn't afraid to speak her mind about the way he used his good looks and charm to get away with things – like always smoking other people's cigarettes instead of buying his own. I remember her saying to him once, "You've got no heart, Paul."'

Through her dancing, Iris moved in higher show business circles than young men who strummed guitars in Liverpool cel-lars. While going out with Paul, she also saw a lot of Frank Ifield, an Australian singer/yodeller whose 'I Remember You' topped the UK singles charts for seven weeks in early 1962. The friend-ship was purely platonic, though Ifield clearly wished it could be more.

'When Frank came to Liverpool to appear at the Empire, Paul told me he'd got tickets – and for a change, we weren't in the cheap seats but the front row. When Frank came onstage, he could see the two of us sitting there, cuddled up together and holding hands. He didn't give any sign of having seen us, but I knew the next song he sang was aimed directly at Paul. It was Jim Reeves's "He'll Have to Go".

'I was in two worlds at the same time. After the show, I'd be having drinks at the Lord Nelson [pub] with Frank and the Shadows and the other stars on the bill. Then I'd go outside and find Paul waiting for me, and we'd get fish and chips on the way home.

'When the week was over, I saw Frank off on the train from Lime Street station. Then I turned round and saw Paul coming along the platform, doing his Quasimodo act.'

11

'Just think – Little Richard's got on my shirt! I can't believe it!'

He was often to be found at Lime Street station during that early spring of 1962, if not always in the same jokey mood. With John, George and Pete, he'd meet Brian Epstein off the train from London; they'd go to a nearby coffee bar named the Punch and Judy and Brian would give them the usual depressing news. Armed with the Decca audition tape – which, since he'd paid for it, could now be termed a demo – Brian visited one London record company after another, pitching an act which, he said, was potentially 'bigger than Elvis'. The record company men smiled at that, smiled even more patronisingly at the idea of such a thing coming out of Liverpool. 'You've *got* a good business, Mr Epstein,' said one, meaning his family's NEMS electrical stores. 'Why not stick to it?'

At the same time, smoothing out his boys' rough edges was proving a laborious process. In April, they were booked for a two-week return visit to Hamburg – the first of three that year – to appear at the Reeperbahn's brand-new Star-Club. 'Don't be raping on the Reeperbahn,' Iris Caldwell's irrepressible mum admonished Paul when he called at 'Stormsville' to say adieu.

Under the band's new management, there were no more punishing trans-European journeys by road or rail. John, Paul and Pete flew out from Manchester on 11 April, leaving George, who had flu, to follow later with Brian. At Hamburg airport, the first-comers were met by Astrid and Klaus Voormann, who told them Stu Sutcliffe had died from a brain haemorrhage the previous day. His mother, Millie, was also en route from Liverpool to identify the body.

Stu's death was a devastating blow to John (who always regarded the premature demise of those he loved as a personal betrayal). Paul, for his part, suffered pangs of extreme guilt, remembering the friction there had often been between Stu and himself in their battle for John's attention. But in truth he had nothing to reproach himself for; the pity was that he and Stu, with their common passion for art, never became the friends they should have been.

Stu's fatal haemorrhage was attributed to 'trauma to the brain', generally believed to date back to a year earlier, when he still played bass with the Beatles and they would often be targeted by the disgruntled boyfriends of their female fans. After a gig at Lathom Hall, Stu had been alone backstage when he was set on by a gang of toughs, knocked to the ground and kicked in the head. John came to his rescue, fighting off the attackers with such reckless ferocity that he broke the little finger of his right hand.

Forty years after the event, however, Stu's younger sister, Pauline, published a different theory, allegedly based on what he'd told her and his mother shortly before his death. This was that during the Beatles' second stint in Hamburg, Paul, John and Stu had been out walking and John had attacked Stu without provocation or warning, knocking him down, then kicking him in the head with savagery enough to cause trauma to the brain and then some. John had immediately fled the scene, leaving Paul to pick up Stu – by now bleeding from the face and one ear – and help him back to the Beatles' dorm above the Top Ten club. As a result, John had always believed himself responsible for Stu's death and been haunted by guilt and remorse until his own dying day.

Yet no plausible explanation was forthcoming of why John, however unhinged by drink or pills, should have brutalised someone he loved, admired – and protected – as much as he did Stu. And had Paul truly been the sole eyewitness to such an incident, it would presumably have stayed seared on his memory for ever. 'It's possible Stu and John had a fight in a drunken moment,' he says now. 'But I don't remember anything that stands out.'

The Star-Club's manager, Horst Fascher, was one of St Pauli's most renowned tough guys, a former featherweight boxing champion who'd done time for accidentally killing a sailor in a street brawl. Fascher loved rock 'n' roll and adored the Beatles; consequently, they'd always been immune to any harm from the Reeperbahn's criminal community, both the gangsters and protection racketeers at its top and the muggers and pickpockets at its bottom.

Apart from a team of extra-brutal waiter/bouncers known as 'Hoddel's gang', Fascher's main innovation at the Star-Club was bringing over American rock 'n' roll legends whose careers had shrunk to almost nothing in their homeland. The first of those with whom the Beatles overlapped was their greatest hero after Elvis – Gene Vincent.

At close quarters, however, their hero turned into a bit of a nuisance: a borderline psychopath who always carried a loaded gun ('Not much point in carryin' it if it ain't loaded,' as he explained) and liked to show off the unarmed combat techniques he'd learned in the US Marines. He was particularly keen to use Paul to demonstrate how he could put someone 'out' simply by touching a couple of pressure-points. 'C'mon . . . it'll only last for a coupla' minutes,' wheedled the same sacred voice that had sung 'Be-Bop-A-Lula'. But Paul would have none of it, and got less and less polite about saying so.

At the Star-Club, the Beatles also shared the bill – and, often, the stage – with Roy Young, a high-octane singer/pianist, dubbed 'England's Little Richard', whom they'd once watched on the BBC's first all-rock 'n' roll television show, *Drumbeat*. 'I'd arrived to play at the Top Ten club a few months earlier, just as they were leaving after the trouble with Bruno Koschmider,' Young recalls.

'When I got out of my car outside the Top Ten, they ran over and lifted me bodily into the air.'

Paul loved Young's piano-playing and suggested Brian should offer him a permanent place in the Beatles. But he had already signed a three-year contract with the Star-Club's owner, Manfred Weissleder.

Young also worked for Weissleder, in a managerial capacity, booking American acts like Jerry Lee Lewis and Ray Charles, for which he was rewarded with a luxurious apartment and a swish Ford Taunus convertible. 'The Beatles were always asking me to take them for a drive to the seaside. When I did, they all started jumping around in the sea in their clothes and calling to me to do the same. I knew that if I didn't, I'd be thrown in. Then I turned around and saw John driving my brand-new Taunus down the beach towards the water . . . On the way back to Hamburg, I made them all sit forwards like little kids, so they wouldn't make the upholstery too wet.'

In the aftermath of Stu Sutcliffe's death, and without Brian around to restrain him, John's behaviour, both on and offstage, was more manic than even St Pauli had seen before. 'He'd take so many pills that he literally wouldn't be able to shut his eyes to go to sleep,' Roy Young says. 'Paul, on the other hand, would always want to be up early, to write songs or rehearse. And he used to worry that they weren't saving any of the money they earned – that they'd end up with nothing to show for all the struggle they'd had to get this far, and have to take ordinary everyday jobs that they hated.

'One night when the Beatles were due onstage, John wasn't anywhere to be seen. Eventually, Horst Fascher found him in a toilet near the stage, having sex with a girl inside one of the cubicles. Horst got a bucket of water and emptied it over the top of the door onto the two of them. In retaliation John wrenched off the toilet-seat, hung it around his neck and went onstage wearing it. Horst started screaming that the Beatles were fired and they'd better pack their bags and be on the next plane home.

'When I looked into their dressing-room, I found Paul in a corner

– in tears. He said he'd borrowed some money from his father to buy a car and if they were fired from the Star-Club, he wouldn't be able to pay it back.'

But the Reeperbahn forgave them yet again. And a few days later came the momentous (if not wholly truthful) telegram from Brian:

CONGRATULATIONS BOYS. EMI REQUEST
RECORDING SESSION. PLEASE REHEARSE
NEW MATERIAL

The Beatles weren't only the greatest pop band in history; they were also arguably the luckiest. Their first massive stroke of good fortune was acquiring Brian Epstein as their manager; their second came when Brian stumbled on Parlophone Records and George Martin.

In 1962, there wasn't another label boss in London with Martin's special combination of qualities. He was a trained classical musician who had studied piano and oboe at the prestigious Guildhall School and was a talented composer, arranger and conductor. Yet he also had a love of comedy in its more outrageous forms and felt something of a mission to capture it on record. Parlophone at that time was best-known for albums by the Goons – whose radio show had entranced John and Paul long before there was an Elvis – and live recordings of West End comedy hits like Flanders and Swann's *At the Drop of a Hat* and the groundbreaking satirical revue *Beyond the Fringe*.

Parlophone was the least significant in the constellation of labels belonging to the giant EMI organisation and Brian had already pitched the Beatles to the others without success. It was during what he'd decided would be his final foray to London on their behalf that everything changed. A chance tip-off led him to Martin, a tall, elegant man of 36 with a cultured accent and the aura (so he later recalled) of 'a stern but fair-minded schoolmaster'.

At Brian's assertion that the Beatles could be 'bigger than Elvis',

Martin's eyes glazed over – for he knew nothing could *ever* be bigger than that. But he heard something in their demo that no one else had, and agreed to give them a hearing at EMI's Abbey Road studios on 6 June after their return from Hamburg. That was the real meaning of 'EMI request recording session'.

For anyone who doesn't already know, Abbey Road studios are on a leafy boulevard through north London's wealthiest quarter, St John's Wood. Their frontage is an unassuming white townhouse with a spacious drive and steep front steps, behind which a maze of technical departments and offices occupies perhaps three times the area. In 1962, the place looked much as today except that its low white street-wall had yet to be covered with adoring graffiti and the nearby zebra pedestrian crossing was considered no different from any other.

The Beatles' reception there could not have been more unlike their Decca one six months earlier. Although George Martin spoke like a BBC announcer, he came from quite humble north London roots and, while crisp and authoritative, was genial and welcoming. He impressed the band by not treating them like hicks while they instantly won him over with their Scouser charm and cheek.

In Abbey Road's orchestra-sized Studio Two, they demoed three Lennon–McCartney compositions, 'Love Me Do', 'P.S. I Love You' and 'Ask Me Why', plus various cover versions including Paul's semi-comic version of 'Besame Mucho', a Mexican bolero dating from 1940 that was part of his musical legacy from his father.

Ironically, George Martin at this point was not seeking anything particularly original. The comedy albums in which Parlophone specialised – and which Martin usually produced personally – were hugely effortful to put together, yet only rarely achieved major sales or listing in the record charts. Meanwhile, over at EMI's prestigious Columbia label, Cliff Richard's producer, Norrie Paramor, turned out a golden stream of pop hits to a virtually identical formula. Martin's initial hope was that the Beatles might be his very own Cliff and the Shadows.

So the unsuspecting John, Paul and George were each tested singing solo, to see which of them might be moulded into a Cliff-style front man. 'I thought of making Paul the leader,' Martin recalled. 'Just because he was the prettiest.' Then – going against all pop fashion, and possibly his own interests, too – he decided to leave the pattern of their voices as was.

He also made a decision one cannot imagine from any other British record producer at the time. If and when the Beatles recorded on Parlophone, it must be Lennon–McCartney material they performed. Indeed, Paul and John were a bit surprised by Martin's preference for 'Ask Me Why' and 'Love Me Do' over 'Besame Mucho' or 'The Sheik of Araby'. Paul remembers how he and John still regarded their own songs as 'a bit wet' compared to those of Chuck Berry, Ray Charles and the other giants they covered.

There was a further caveat, for Brian's ears only. Martin had decided Pete Best wasn't a good enough drummer to record; if he did sign them to Parlophone, he'd want to use a session-player of his own. It was not a demand that Pete be dropped from the line-up only that he shouldn't play on the records. But it brought to the boil John, Paul and George's long-simmering ambition to sack Pete and replace him with Ringo Starr.

The main reason is said to have been Paul's insecurity about Pete's good looks and the numbers of female fans he attracted. It's certainly true that at more than one Liverpool gig his drums were placed at the front of the band rather than the back, and that screams of 'Pete!' could sometimes drown out those of 'Paul!' Such, anyway, would be Pete's solace in later life, when he possessed one of the world's most tragic pairs of eyes. Asked why he'd been dropped on the very eve of Beatlemania, he'd simply answer, 'Jealousy.'

But the truth was that Pete had never really fitted into the band: he was too quiet and self-contained and lacking in John's and Paul's verbal and intellectual sparkle. He had seemed even more of an outsider since the other three had started combing their hair forward over their eyes while his remained in a neat, no-nonsense cockade. In fact, he now says he would have been perfectly willing to copy the others but was never asked to because Astrid thought his hair too curly.

Ringo, by contrast, fitted the line-up like a comfortable old carpet slipper even before he joined it: he was friendly, easy-going and apparently devoid of self-importance or temperament – qualities that would prove more valuable than he knew. Although raised in Liverpool's tough Dingle area and robbed of education by childhood illness, he had a droll, dry wit and love of wordplay that chimed perfectly with John's and Paul's. They'd become friends in Hamburg when Ringo was there as one of Rory Storm's Hurricanes and, later, playing in Tony Sheridan's band; John, Paul and George had once even cut a demo record with Ringo drumming and the Hurricanes' Lu Walters on vocals (billed as 'the Beatles mit Wally').

But firing Pete and hiring Ringo had ramifications far beyond the inevitable outcry from Pete's Liverpool fans. After his stint in Hamburg with Tony Sheridan, Ringo had rejoined Rory Storm and the Hurricanes and was about to depart with them for a summer season at Butlin's holiday camp in Skegness, Lincolnshire. Poaching Rory's drummer, and perhaps jeopardising the Skegness gig, would be a tricky matter, the more so with Paul still dating Rory's sister, Iris.

Almost as big a problem was that Pete's best friend was Neil Aspinall, the Beatles' invaluable driver/roadie. What if Neil were to quit out of loyalty to Pete and the Best family, in whose home he lodged? In a further twist, worthy of Gilbert and Sullivan, Neil had been having a Mrs Robinson-style affair with Pete's mother, Mona, whose Casbah club had given the Beatles their first real break and who'd been their de facto manager before Brian Epstein came along. To cap the Gilbertian plot, Mrs Best was on the point of giving birth to Neil's child.

In fact, Pete's firing and Ringo's poaching were mainly orchestrated by George. Although Paul had long been unhappy with Pete's drumming – shown up in all its heavy-handedness on the first 'Love Me Do' demo – he was too civilised not to feel twinges of conscience, especially since Pete had no idea of what was in the wind. One evening, when the Beatles had met up at the Bests' house, he was talking excitedly about a new car he intended to buy. Paul looked uncomfortable and mumbled, 'You'd be better saving your money.'

It has since emerged that even before Martin first put the Beatles through their paces, their contract with Parlophone was a fait accompli. EMI's publishing arm, Ardmore and Beechwood, were already aware of Lennon and McCartney as songwriters but couldn't have them unless they were also signed as performers. Their recording contract was to last for seven years and pay a royalty of one old penny per double-sided record, 1.25 per cent of the retail price, rising by yearly increments of a farthing, or a quarter of a penny. Later, it would be held up as one of the stingiest contracts ever, but at that time, when even major artistes considered making records an honour rather than an earner, it was standard.

In the end, John, Paul and George couldn't face telling Pete he was out, but deputed Brian to do it. The task was doubly awkward for Brian, who'd relied on Pete as a kind of sub-manager to the band as well as once proposing they should sleep together. During their painful conversation in Brian's office, the telephone rang: it was Paul, asking whether the deed had been done yet. For Pete, that would always be final proof of Paul's culpability.

Thereafter, everything was sorted out with the ease of a less mercenary age. Rory Storm released Ringo from the Hurricanes with no ill will towards the Beatles, least of all his sister Iris's boyfriend. The Bests made no attempt to extract financial compensation from Brian, contenting themselves with his promise to put Pete into another band (the All Stars, fronted by the brother of his friend Joe Flannery). At Pete's unselfish urging, Neil Aspinall elected to remain the Beatles' roadie, while the baby boy Neil had fathered with Mona Best was christened Roag and brought up as a member of the Best family.

For some time after Pete's firing, the Beatles guiltily stayed away from the Bests' house. Then one evening, Paul – viewed by the whole family as the arch-villain of the affair – knocked on the front door and asked if he could park his car in their driveway. Mrs Best, as she later recalled, managed to hold her peace but Pete's girlfriend, Kathy, 'gave him a damned good talking-to'.

It was a different story with Pete's fans when *Mersey Beat* broke the news on 23 August. There were riots outside the Cavern and, unprecedentedly, heckling of the Beatles inside; as George Harrison made his way to the stage, someone 'nutted' him and gave him a black eye. Brian was the target of so many threats and recriminations that he hired a bodyguard.

The only film footage of the Beatles at the Cavern dates from this turbulent week, shot in grainy black and white by Manchester's Granada Television. Ringo, with his new Beatle cut, sits at his drums, clearly disconcerted by the audible shrieks of 'We want Pete!' To try to drown the protests, Paul and John do a good old R&B standard – the unwittingly appropriate 'Some Other Guy'.

Concurrent with the Pete Best problem was one which seemed to threaten the Beatles' career just as it was about to take flight. John had found himself in the same fix Paul had been in two years earlier, without the same providential get-out. He'd made his girlfriend, Cynthia, pregnant and saw no alternative but to marry her.

Back then, it was considered risky enough for a pop artiste to have a steady girlfriend, as Iris Caldwell was Paul's. Being married was thought to destroy any appeal for young women, whose fantasies depended on their idols being – at least theoretically – available and within reach. Such had been the fate of Marty Wilde, once kingpin of the Larry Parnes stable; Brian Epstein was determined it shouldn't happen to his lead Beatle at this pivotal moment in the band's career.

After John and Cynthia's lower-than-low-key civil marriage, therefore, the new Mrs Lennon spent her first months of pregnancy secreted in a flat in Falkner Street belonging to Brian (where in fact he'd once hoped for a first romantic tryst with John). To keep an eye on Cynthia, her friend Dot Rhone – Paul's former fiancée and so nearly the mother of his first child – agreed to move into the flat below, even though it would inevitably mean frequent painful encounters with Paul. He would later describe his first wife, Linda, as the kindest person he ever knew, but Dot certainly ran her close.

Everything had thus been beautifully tidied up by early September, when the new-look Beatles returned to Abbey Road studios to record their first single. There was some initial awkwardness when they filed into Studio Two to find a strange drum-kit already set up there. George Martin had previously been introduced to Ringo Starr but, unfortunately, did not find Ringo's drumming any more acceptable than Pete Best's and so had booked a session player, Andy White, to sit in with John, Paul and George. Ringo was relegated to bashing a tambourine and glumly thinking they'd 'done a Pete Best' on him.

As the A-side – the one considered more likely to chart – Martin had chosen 'Love Me Do', an early song of Paul's, originally titled 'Love Love Me Do', with atypically rudimentary lyrics and chords, although the title had a faintly literary ring. The B-side was to be 'P.S. I Love You', a joint John–Paul memory of writing billets-doux from Hamburg. 'Yes, "P.S. I Love You" was probably a better song,' Martin admits now. 'But it wasn't a hit.'

Through 'Love Me Do' ran a harmonica riff jointly inspired by Bruce Channel's 'Hey Baby' and 'I Remember You', the recent UK number one by Frank Ifield, Paul's main rival for Iris Caldwell's attention. (Quick off the mark as always, Paul had already added 'I Remember You' to the Beatles' stage act.) Their live version of 'Love Me Do' featured John playing the riff and singing the 'Whoa-oh love me do' chorus. But on record he didn't have time to do both, so Paul (though equally capable of playing harmonica) handled the 'Whoa-oh's'.

'Love Me Do' was scheduled for release on 5 October. At EMI, the fact that it came from Parlophone, and was by such a bizarrely-titled act, led most of the top brass to think it must be a comedy record. On the pop side, no one regarded it as a potential hit and everyone thought the name 'Beatles' almost self-destructively terrible. Still, the company promotion machine went through the motions: ahead of release-day, 250 advance copies were circulated among music journalists, radio deejays and television producers, crediting the writers as John Lennon and Paul McArtney.

For the Beatles, their families and hometown fans, it was astounding enough to have a single out and, still more so, to hear it on the radio, even if most of the deejays did add a sarky little dig at their name. So, for the first time, Paul could hear himself through his headphones in bed at 20 Forthlin Road, amid the same nocturnal barking of police dogs that had accompanied his first discovery of Elvis and Little Richard.

But now his favourite of all those rock 'n' roll ravers was no longer just a voice from far away. On 12 October, at New Brighton Tower Ballroom, Brian celebrated the release of 'Love Me Do' with a marathon concert headlined by Little Richard, who was currently touring Britain, with the Beatles as second on the bill. Merseyside could not mistake the euphoric message: now there was only one person who outranked and out-rocked their boys.

Richard was somewhat different from the anarchic figure of the mid-Fifties, having exchanged his baggy Dayglo suits and liquorice-whip hair for tailored sharkskin and a Nina Simone crop. Paul and John were initially so awed that they dared not even speak to him, let alone ask if they could all be photographed together. Instead, they begged help from Paul's brother, Mike, who'd proudly brought along his brand-new camera. '[Mike] found a hole in the scenery and shot pictures of Richard onstage while we stood in the wings, taking it in turns to try to get in the shot with him,' Paul would remember. 'It didn't work. Mike said Richard moved too fast for him to catch. I think one shot of Ringo and Richard's shoulder came out.'

Before long, they had forgotten their shyness and were all over the star like pin-collared puppies, plying him with questions. 'They asked me, "Richard, how does California look?"' Richard writes in his autobiography, *The Quasar of Rock*. "'Are the buildings in New York real tall? Have you ever met Elvis Presley? Is he nice-looking?"

'I developed a specially close relationship with Paul McCartney, but me and John couldn't make it . . . He would do his no-manners [fart] and jump over and fan it all over the room, and I didn't like it. He was different from Paul and George – they were sweet. Paul would come in and sit down and just look at me. Like he wouldn't move his eyes. And he'd say, "Oh, Richard! You're my idol. Just let me touch you." He wanted to learn my little holler [i.e. banshee scream] so we sat at the piano going "Ooooh! Ooooh!" until he got it. I once threw my shirt in the audience and Paul went and got one of his best shirts and he said, "Take it, Richard." I said "I can't take that" but he insisted, "Please take it, I'll feel bad if you don't take it. Just think – Little Richard's got on my shirt! I can't believe it!"'

The Little Richard/Beatles night was such a success that Brian staged a second one a week later, this time at the Liverpool Empire. Being on a Sunday, the show was subject to Britain's arcane sabbath entertainment laws which forbade performers to appear 'in costume'. To circumvent this, the Beatles simply took off their jackets, revealing shirts in a – for Liverpool – daring shade of pink. 'When the curtain went back, the stage was in complete darkness,' Frieda Kelly remembers. 'Then a spotlight lit up Paul's face as he sang "Besame Mucho". I remember thinking, "Wow, the Beatles at the *Empire*! Now they've *really* made it."'

All the Beatles' Cavern following bought 'Love Me Do' – even those, like Frieda, who didn't own a record-player. Brian reputedly ordered 10,000 copies for his two Liverpool stores, far more than he could ever sell, having been told that was the quantity needed to get it into the Top 10. Though EMI made no special promotional effort, the single aroused a smattering of interest in the trade press and on radio, slowly climbing the Top 40, breaking into the Top 20 in early November but then stalling at 17. That month, the Beatles were committed to a further two-week stint at the Hamburg

Star-Club, which meant going away just when the music media might have stepped up coverage of them. So Britain was only dimly aware of a new band who broke every mould with their peculiar hair and clothes, and whose bassist played an instrument more like a violin, its neck pointing in the wrong direction.

At least EMI now realised they weren't a comedy act and had potential enough to justify a second single. And George Martin believed he had the very song to do it: a perky ballad called 'How Do You Do It?' by the young songwriter Mitch Murray. Martin had sent an acetate of the song to Liverpool for the Beatles to learn before their September recording sessions; it had been taped along with 'Love Me Do', indeed for a time earmarked as their debut single. The good humour of the occasion had been slightly marred when John and Paul protested that 'How Do You Do It?' wasn't them and they wanted to do another of their own compositions. 'When you can write material as good as this, I'll record it,' Martin told them icily. 'But right now we're going to record *this*.'

Back in September, they'd submitted another possibility, 'Please Please Me', originally conceived by John as an angst-ridden ballad in the style of Roy Orbison and developed by the two of them sharing a piano keyboard. Paul had previously run it past Iris Caldwell, who remembers being far from enthusiastic. 'It went "Last night I said these words to my girl . . . you know you never even try, girl . . ." He asked me what I thought and I said, "I think it's bloody awful, Paul."' When Iris next saw Paul's rival, Frank Ifield, she tried the words on him. 'Do I have to worry?' Ifield asked – i.e. that the song might challenge him in the charts. Iris thought not.

Originally John and Paul had put forward 'Please Please Me' as a possible B-side to 'Love Me Do'. However, George Martin felt it wasn't right yet and suggested they should work on it some more in a new form which he suggested; speeding up the tempo, using a harmonica riff again and lengthening it by repeating the first verse at the end.

When the Beatles returned to Abbey Road on 26 November, with 'How Do You Do It?' still threatening to be their second single, John and Paul persuaded Martin to listen to a new version of 'Please Please Me' in which all his suggestions had been followed. The producer agreed to let them tape what was no longer in any way the lachrymose ballad it had started out as. After the eighteenth take, Martin switched on the intercom from a control room that was never again to be so much under his control.

'Gentlemen,' he told them, 'you have just made your first number one.'

PART TWO

The Barnum & Bailey Beatle

12

'Did you know he sleeps with his eyes open?'

Since 1963, so many globally-adored pop bands have come and gone – almost every one claimed at the time to be 'bigger than the Beatles' or 'new Beatles' – it's easy to forget in how many ways the actual Beatles were, and always will be, inimitable.

Their uniqueness, of course, stemmed from their own talent – or, rather, the prodigious joint one of Lennon and McCartney – but it had just as much to do with the Britain of the early 1960s in which they first found fame. An innocent place, it seems in retrospect, still in the iron grip of tradition and class, where almost nothing was known of celebrity culture, mass marketing or hype and no one yet fully realised the commercial power of young people, least of all young people themselves. Like some plump, willing Hamburg barmaid in their former life, it was all theirs for the taking.

Previous British pop stars like Cliff Richard and Billy Fury had had to struggle for years to reach a family audience, but with John, Paul, George and Ringo it took only months. In late 1962, they were just a 'beat group' with one minor hit single behind them. Early in 1963, along with 'Please Please Me' came a brief burst of notoriety over their clothes and hair, culminating with an incident when they were ejected from a Young Conservatives dance in Carlisle for the crime of wearing black leather jackets. By the end of the year, they had appeared at the London Palladium and in the Royal Variety Show, and no Fleet Street paper that cared about its circulation dared print an uncharitable word about them.

Their appearance, for that time, was more revolutionary than any other pop act band's had ever been or would be: not just their hair, but the round-collared jackets, the broad grins in place of traditional rock star moodiness, the asymmetric violin bass. Their innovative presentation, not as lead vocalist and sidemen but four (almost) equals, gave them a wholly unforeseen extra power. On top of their collective charm, each had a distinct character appealing to different sections of their audience: there was the 'clever' one, the 'cute' one, the 'quiet' one and what film producer Walter Shenson called 'the adorable runt of the litter'.

Together they were more articulate, charming and intelligent – above all funnier – than any pop artistes before, but this alone doesn't explain the British media's fixation on them during that rainy summer of 1963. It was a season of unremitting hard news, including the Profumo scandal, the biggest train robbery in history, the thwarting of Britain's attempt to join the European Economic Community, the resignation of Prime Minister Harold Macmillan and the resulting turmoil within the Tory government. Fleet Street initially turned to 'Beatlemania' (a term coined by the *Daily Mirror*) for a bit of light relief, thereby discovering to its surprise that pop-obsessed teenagers read newspapers, too. From then on, there was no surer way to shift copies.

Today, the '-mania' tag is attached to any pop star, or other sort of star, who draws an ardent crowd: 'Justin Bieber-mania', 'Leonardo DiCaprio-mania', 'One Direction-mania', 'Prince Harry-mania', etc., etc. But in the sleepy, orderly Britain of the mid-twentieth century, Beatlemania truly did seem to verge on the psychotic. And it wasn't just the Mach-speed rise of the band's records in the charts, the multitudes who queued for their shows, the incessant shrieks that drowned out every song they played, the volleys of jelly babies that were flung at the stage or the rows of seats left drenched in female urine.

Prior to 1963, few Britons of either sex over 25 had any interest in pop, preferring the more adult spheres of jazz or folk. That now changed for ever. In any case, it was possible to like the Beatles without necessarily liking their music. Even the parents most jangled by their records and offended by their hair admitted to their personal charm, as revealed on radio and TV and, later, in their first feature film, *A Hard Day's Night*.

Their name became like a verbal virus, spread by screaming teens and drumming headlines, from which no stratum of society seemed immune. Politicians of every party hijacked it to gain publicity for their speeches, psychoanalysts invoked it to support theses about hysteria and mass-suggestibility, vicars linked it tenuously with the Scriptures to arouse Sunday-morning congregations. Pop music finally shed its blue collar as the middle class, the aristocracy and finally even the Royal Family became infected.

Thus, in February 1964, when they set out for America, everyone at home was rooting for them as fervently as for Neville Chamberlain on his flight to Munich three decades earlier. Now their remarkable luck and perfect timing kicked in as never before. For a nation still traumatised by the assassination of its beautiful young president, they proved the perfect diversion. European Beatlemania had nothing on their arrival in New York, forever enshrined on grainy black-and-white film: the demented crowds at JFK Airport; the perfectly pitched wise-cracking press conference; the siege of the Plaza Hotel; the appearance on *The Ed Sullivan Show* watched by a nationwide audience of 70 million during which, in all the city's five boroughs, crime came to a total standstill with not so much as a car hubcap reported stolen.

That October, Britain elected its first Labour government in 13 years, headed by Harold Wilson, MP for Merseyside's Huyton constituency (home of Paul's Auntie Gin). The wily, pipe-puffing Wilson had shamelessly harnessed Beatlemania to secure his narrow victory at the polls. Though actually a Yorkshireman, he milked his Liverpool connections to the utmost and got himself photographed with the Beatles quartet at a charity luncheon, smiling as beatifically as if they were his blood brothers. From then on, politicians of every stripe would attempt to curry favour with young voters by fawning over pop stars.

Labour's return to power had aroused fears of a return to postwar austerity and gloom. No one dreamed that, rather than food-rationing and chapped lips, Wilsonian socialism would usher in an era more colourful than the Roaring Twenties or the Naughty (Eighteen) Nineties, whose frivolity, creativity and style would resonate into the next century. Still less that Britain would once again enjoy an international prestige it thought it had lost back in the stale, threadbare 1950s: not derived from war and conquest this time around, but from four young musicians and their diffusion of pure happiness.

The Shadows apart, members of beat-groups in 1963 were an uninteresting lot whose most devout fans could seldom tell one from another. So after the Beatles' initial breakthrough, it took some time for 'the cute one's' identity to become generally known.

Even on their first album, *Please Please Me*, which topped the UK chart in May and remained there 30 weeks, many listeners were at first unable to distinguish between its four different singing voices. Of those, the highest, lightest one was most suggestive of energy and *joie de vivre*: its rousing 'One two three *faw!*' intro to 'I Saw Her Standing There'; its suppleness and sibilance on 'A Taste of Honey'; the harmonic lift it gave the self-pitying 'Misery'; its obvious joy in supplying the 'Bop-shoo-wop' backup vocals to 'Boys'.

Not until the third single, 'From Me to You' – like 'Please Please Me', a UK number one – was much made of the fact that it had been written by two band members, John Lennon and Paul McCartney. Most British pop musicians until then had used faux-American pseudonyms, so the two unusual genuine surnames struck a pleasingly unpretentious note.

Otherwise, what little was known about the four of them came from trade papers like the *New Musical Express*, whose 'Life Lines' feature subjected current hit-makers to a standard questionnaire. When the Beatles' 'Life Lines' appeared on 15 February, Paul gave his weight as 11 stone 4 pounds, his 'instruments played' as bass guitar, drums, piano and banjo, his hobbies as 'girls, songwriting, sleeping', his favourite singers as Ben E. King, Little Richard, Chuck Jackson and Larry Williams (same as John's), his favourite food as chicken Maryland, his favourite drink as milk, his favourite clothes as 'good suits, suede', his favourite composers as Goffin and King, his tastes in music as 'r&b, modern jazz', his 'professional ambition' as 'to popularise our sound' and his personal one 'to have my picture in *The Dandy*' (the comic book he'd read throughout his childhood).

Most of the Beatles' first broadcast interviews were on radio rather than television, notably with Brian Matthew, the host of two BBC live music shows, *Saturday Club* and *Easy Beat*. In an era when the cut-crystal 'BBC accent' still dictated elocutionary standards, the deep, curdled Liverpudlian of John, George and Ringo (heavily put on in middle-class John's case) came as rather a shock as well as making them sound much older than they were.

Paul had all the Scouse wit and plain-spokenness of the others but without John's sarcasm or George's dourness; he was always amusing, totally open (or so it seemed) and unfailingly polite, however asinine the question. And when the TV interviews began, he proved to be a natural. The camera loved that heart-shaped face between the Beatle fringe and the deep shirt-collar; those enormous, wide-set, button-deep eyes; that delicate mouth, slackened into what might have been called a pout if all its utterances weren't so down-to-earth and self-deprecating.

To begin with, before the full scale of his discovery became apparent, Brian Epstein remained based in Liverpool, with only a small office in London's West End. The Beatles would pay brief visits to the capital, usually to appear on the BBC, often returning that same day to rejoin whichever tour they happened to be on, occasionally staying overnight at some mid-priced hotel in the Bloomsbury area. It was to be their last taste of anonymity as they gazed into the windows of guitar-shops along Charing Cross Road, bought elastic-sided, Cuban-heeled boots (soon to be known as 'Beatle boots') at theatrical shoemakers Anello and Davide, or ogled the first girls in Vidal Sassoon's new 'geometric' bob and skirts ending an audacious inch or so above the knee.

NEMS Enterprises' London office, above a porno bookshop in Monmouth Street, Seven Dials, was set up principally for the Beatles' first full-time press officer, Tony Barrow. Twenty-seven-year-old Barrow was a Merseyside-born freelance journalist already settled in London, working for the Decca organisation as a writer of album liner-notes and contributing a record column to the *Liverpool Echo* which had given the Beatles several valuable early plugs. After a brief period when the band's press representative was Andrew Loog Oldham (who went on to discover the Rolling Stones), Barrow joined NEMS in May 1963.

When he first met the Beatles, in a West End pub, three of them were rather reserved and suspicious (John demanding bluntly, 'If you're not Jewish and not queer, why are you working for Brian?') but the fourth was 'Mr Geniality'. Barrow had brought his wife along, and Paul solicitously asked the couple what they'd like to drink, then took everyone else's bar order – a flourish only slightly marred by leaving Brian to settle the outsize bill.

One of Barrow's first pieces of advice to Brian, echoing George Martin's early instinct, was to rename the band 'Paul McCartney and the Beatles'. For Paul then seemed their driving force, a workaholic and perfectionist, whereas John was chronically laid-back, not to say lazy. Barrow later discovered that when they'd signed their management contract, Paul had told Brian that if the Beatles didn't work out, he was determined to become a star on his own.

In addition, as Barrow discovered, he had 'a natural flair for public relations' and in his tireless promotion of the band was a 'one-man Barnum & Bailey Beatle'. The Monmouth Street office also being the mailing address of the Beatles' national fan club, it was soon receiving two to three thousand letters per day requesting autographs and signed photos. Paul motivated the other three to carry out this irksome duty with cheerfulness; the poky office, in fact, possessed a romantic appeal for him, having previously been occupied by his easy-listening keyboard favourite, Joe 'Mr Piano' Henderson.

To the pop trade press, he was an interviewer's dream: no matter how many stood in line, he seemed to make a special effort for each one, and remembered the journalist's name on their next encounter weeks, months, even years ahead. Though these were days long before paparazzi, photographers could still pop up at inconvenient moments. Barrow remembers one early morning when the four were leaving their London hotel, gummy-eyed and hung-over, and a camera-flash waylaid them in the lobby. The others would have hustled straight through, but Paul rallied them to their duty, even setting up the photographer's shot: 'Come on, lads, pick up a case or something. Let's all be walking towards the door.'

Over the next six years, Barrow would realise that the inexhaustible geniality Paul showed the world was not always replicated in private, especially not to employees whom he found wanting. But the professional PR man had to acknowledge him 'a self-taught expert in an art we used to call gamesmanship, which was all about staying one step ahead of the competition'.

In disputes within the Beatles (i.e. with John) he would use subtlety and diplomacy to get his way, whereas John simply shouted. As a result, he always seemed to Barrow the one dictating the band's musical policy. '[And] unlike John (and Brian), Paul did not seem to have any half-concealed demons to deal with.'

He did have an unconcealed demon to deal with, however; one that was to put Tony Barrow's PR skills to an early test. On 8 April, John's wife, Cynthia, gave birth to a boy, John Charles Julian – always to be known as Julian – at Sefton General Hospital, Liverpool. The event went totally unnoticed by the national press, even though scores of local fans had got wind of it and staked out the hospital.

Two weeks later, with the *Please Please Me* album still topping the UK charts, the Beatles were allowed a brief holiday before starting their third nationwide tour in four months. Paul and George went to stay with their Hamburg friend Klaus Voormann at Klaus's family's house on Tenerife while John, instead of returning home to his wife and newborn son, jetted off on a ten-day trip to Spain alone with Brian Epstein.

That Spanish holiday has passed into legend as the moment when Brian finally declared his infatuation with John, and John, perhaps, reciprocated. Years later, he told a close friend he'd had sex, of some sort, with Brian, 'once to see what it was like, the second time to make sure I didn't like it'.

According to Bill Harry – Mersey Beat's founder/editor who knew them both equally well – Brian was simply following Tony Barrow's advice, in spirit if not actual name. 'He wanted to change [the Beatles] from John's group into Paul's group,' Harry says. 'So he took John away to Spain so that they could have some privacy while he explained the whole thing to him.'

Paul, for his part, has always viewed the holiday as evidence of John's 'gamesmanship'. 'John was a smart cookie. Brian was gay, and John saw his opportunity to impress on Mr Epstein who was boss of the group . . . He wanted Brian to know whom he should listen to.'

Once again, an uninquisitive popular press remained totally unaware of a story which nowadays would have splashed as 'SECRETLY WED BEATLE JOHN LEAVES WIFE AND NEW BABY FOR SPANISH TRYST WITH GAY MANAGER'. And once again in a John-centric episode, Paul might have been expected to take his accustomed 'back seat' with relief. But this time, he couldn't.

The eighteenth of June was his twenty-first birthday, an event which could be properly celebrated only in Liverpool. Encapsulating the two sides of his nature, there was a select cocktail party for him at the home of Brian Epstein's parents, then a traditional knees-up for his mates and wide family circle. To evade the fans now permanently besieging 20 Forthlin Road, this was held at the home of his Auntie Gin in Dinas Lane, Huyton, where a marquee had been erected in the back garden. All three of his fellow Beatles were present, along with fellow musicians like Gerry Marsden and Billy J. Kramer and new celebrity pals like Hank B. Marvin and Bruce Welch from the Shadows, who were currently appearing in a summer show at Blackpool.

The McCartneys' famous bumper servings of booze were, unfortunately, to lead to disaster. During the evening, Bob Wooler, the Cavern's notoriously sharp-tongued deejay, began teasing John about his Spanish 'honeymoon' with Brian. John by that time had drunk so much that his usual whipcrack repartee failed him; instead – with a fury that could equally have pointed to the barb's inaccuracy or accuracy – he began raining punches viciously on Wooler's head and body.

This was a story that undoubtedly *would* get into the newspapers, so Tony Barrow skilfully limited the damage by feeding it to a friendly showbiz columnist, the *Sunday Mirror*'s Don Short, dressed up as a remorseful confession: 'Guitarist John Lennon, leader of the Beatles pop group, said last night, "Why did I have to go and punch my best friend? . . . I can only hope [Bob] realises that I was too far gone to know what I was doing."' Wooler's silence was secured by an apologetic telegram from John (not a syllable of which he meant) and an *ex gratia* payment of £200.

Just then, as it happened, Paul was also in a spot of bother: four days before his twenty-first, he'd been pulled over in Wallasey for speeding. It being his third offence in a year, the police took him to court, where Beatlemania proved in short supply; he was banned from driving for 12 months, fined £25 and told by the presiding magistrate, Alderman W.O. Halstead, 'It's time you were taught a lesson.' Fortunately, the case wasn't reported outside Liverpool.

In August, with 'She Loves You' yeah-yeah-ing out of every transistor radio, he received his first press coverage in his own right. The *New Musical Express* published 'Close-Up on Paul McCartney – a Beatle', filed by its Beatles correspondent Alan Smith from the roof of London's Washington Hotel, where they were doing a photo-shoot. Smith summed him up as 'courteous but cheerful with it' and quoted some slightly double-edged chaff from the others:

> How do the rest of the Beatles get on with Paul? 'Oh, fine,'
> they laughed as we leaned against a chimney-stack. 'He hasn't
> changed a bit, you know. He's just the same old big-'ead we all
> got to know and love.' 'Funny habits?' said John. 'I'll say! Did
> you know he sleeps with his eyes open? We've actually watched
> him dozing there with the whites of his eyes showing.'

Actually, that had been John's frequent condition in Hamburg, when the amphetamines racketing around his body literally wouldn't allow his eyes to shut. But with Paul, it suggested un-sleeping ambition.

On 22 November, the day of President John F. Kennedy's assassination in Dallas, Parlophone released the band's second album, *With the Beatles*. Advance orders of half a million put it instantly at the top of the UK album charts, so finally ending the seven-month reign there of *Please Please Me*. It would eventually sell one million copies, more than any album previously released in Britain except the cast recording of Rodgers and Hammerstein's *South Pacific*.

With the Beatles brought a radical change of image, illustrating the vastly altered demographic of those who were now with them. On the *Please Please Me* album cover, four cheery, unabashedly working-class lads had grinned down a stairwell at EMI's Manchester Square headquarters, with Paul's good looks barely noticeable. Now they were shown as solemn, polo-necked faces half in shadow against a plain black background, less like pop musicians than a quartet of Parisian art students. It was an ambience which suited none of them better than Paul, that one-time art student manqué. The shadow seeping into the lit half of his face gave it an extra delicacy, pressing a groove above his top lip, sculpting a dimple in his chin, while his eyes gazed forth, as round and fathomlessly soulful as a bush-baby's.

The album featured seven Lennon–McCartney compositions, one by George Harrison ('Don't Bother Me') and six soul or R&B covers. On 10 of the 14 tracks John predominated, with Paul's harmonies acting as a kind of yeast, raising his partner's hardest, dourest vocal lead into the realm of good humour and fun. But two of his own three tracks were stand-outs: 'All My Loving' and 'Till There Was You'. All the rave reviews commented on the surprise of finding a Peggy Lee song cheek-by-jowl with Chuck Berry and Smokey Robinson, and praised Paul's interpretation set off by George's Latin-flavoured acoustic guitar.

Movie cameras are commonly said to 'love' certain personalities, but the relationship occurs less in the colder medium of television. How much the 1960s black and white TV camera loved Paul became increasingly obvious in the artier studio set-ups – heavily influenced by *With the Beatles* – that directors began to essay. It made his bushy head seem three-dimensional while the others' remained flat, put an extra twinkle in his eye and glow on his skin, etched every contour of the baby-face including the firm chin that most still cameras overlooked. Even when dutifully background-vocalling John, eyes demurely downcast over his bass fretboard, he stole every show.

The Beatles' first American visit, in February 1964, was technically not a tour but a promotional trip, taking in only New York, Washington DC and Miami. The vast audience who'd fallen for them on *The Ed Sullivan Show* had to wait until August, when they returned to give 30 concerts in 23 cities, each one to audiences of between 10,000 and 20,000.

This was a completely new concept of a tour – not just a series of random concerts but a kind of royal progress which at each stop called forth hysterical crowds and frantic media, threatened the fabric of huge arenas and tested the efficiency and patience of police forces and fire departments to the limit. It opened the door to an 'invasion' of America by other British bands and singers who never would have stood a chance without the Beatles' trailblazing; it created a method of parting young people from their money on a scale never before dreamed; it turned pop into rock, no longer merely music but a 'culture'; and changed the hairstyle of a generation, rendering the all-American crew cut as obsolete as the Model T Ford.

In the audience at Chicago's International Auditorium on 5 September was 13-year-old Glenn Frey, who would go on to co-found the Eagles, one of the biggest and best bands of the 1970s. That night when the Beatles ran onstage, there was no longer any doubt of 'the cute one's' identity. A girl who'd been standing on a seat in front of Frey fell backwards into his arms with a swooning cry of 'Paul!'

Longevity was something the Beatles never anticipated. From the moment they became famous, two questions were constantly thrown at them: 'How long do you think all this will last?' and 'What are you going to do when it's over?' For pop music's short history had seen the same pattern repeated time and again. Makers of hit records enjoyed only months, sometimes no more than weeks in the spotlight before their fickle young audience tired of them and their sound, and moved on to someone else. A lucky few managed to follow Elvis into conventional show business or films, but most sank back into the obscurity whence they had come.

Thus, after eight months as Britain's top pop group, the Beatles were starting to wonder if that might be it. Christmas 1963 seemed to bring an answer in the affirmative when they were knocked off the top of the UK singles chart by the Dave Clark Five's so-called 'Tottenham Sound' and were received with indifference on their first visit to France. It was just as the Paris press was calling them 'vedettes démodées' (yesterday's stars) that 'I Want to Hold Your Hand' reached number one in America.

Even after their conquest of America – and then the world – their management and record label continued milking their popularity as hard as possible before that inevitable day when the teat ran dry. As a result, they shouldered a horrendous workload. George

Martin at Parlophone demanded a new single every three months and a new album every six, which somehow had to be fitted in between touring Britain, America and Europe, making two feature films and doing innumerable interviews and photo-shoots. Only naturally tough Liverpudlians, schooled in sleeplessness by Hamburg, could have stayed the course. Looking at them in those days, ever fresh and chirpy, one never guessed how often they were worn ragged.

John and Paul were not the first British pop artistes to write their own material; their fellow Liverpudlian Billy Fury had released an album of self-penned songs in 1960. But they were first to arrive in the charts with a catalogue of more than 100 titles which grew larger and more valuable by the month. For both – as each declared publicly from mid-1963 – their insurance against a coming time when the world no longer wanted the Beatles was to become full-time songwriters. Even then, despite their impossibly crowded and frenetic schedule, they managed to be as prolific as if already doing it full time.

The Beatles' virtually non-stop life on the road meant they could write together just as they once had in Paul's front room at 20 Forthlin Road, each doing both words and music and grabbing inspiration from whatever was to hand. 'From Me to You', for example, was written on a tour-bus journey from Shrewsbury to York, its title suggested by the *New Musical Express*'s letters page, 'From You To Us'. 'In those days, the two of them turned out songs like a factory production-line,' Tony Bramwell remembers. 'They'd get an idea in the back of the bus and in about 20 minutes . . . bang, they'd finished it. People in other bands who'd started to write songs together, like Roger Greenaway and Roger Cook, couldn't believe how quick and easy it was for John and Paul.'

At the beginning of their partnership, every new composition would be listed in Paul's school exercise book as 'Another Original by Lennon and McCartney', irrespective of how much – or little – each had contributed to it. When the songs began to have value, they agreed that the dominant writer's name should come first, although it wasn't always the case: 'Love Me Do', largely Paul's work, was credited to Lennon–McCartney and 'Please Please Me', largely John's, to McCartney–Lennon (as were all the original tracks on their first album).

Thereafter, following the alphabetical precedent of most composing teams, it was fixed as Lennon–McCartney. By Paul's later account, the decision was taken by Brian and John; when he protested, not very strongly, they told him it wasn't set in stone but could be 'alternated' in the future. The byline could well have become a tripartite one, for record-producers in those days routinely got themselves listed as co-composers of original songs they recorded or demanded their own songs be used as B-sides. But George Martin, true gentleman that he was, asked no reward beyond shaping the raw songs into polished hits.

Initially, Lennon and McCartney's output was deliberately skewed to the Beatles' young female fans – the former Hamburg studs singing devoutly about holding girlfriends' hands. After 'Love Me Do', 'Please Please Me' and 'From Me to You', they developed almost a superstition that every hit had to have 'me' or 'you' in it; after 'She Loves You', they felt duty-bound always to throw in a 'yeah yeah yeah'. It brought the first breath of criticism from Paul's musician dad who'd loved everything up until then, the standards especially. 'Son, there are enough Americanisms around,' Jim McCartney protested. 'Couldn't you sing "Yes, yes, yes" for once?'

They also supplied material to the other Liverpool acts Brian Epstein was signing up and taking to Parlophone – the seemingly all-conquering 'Mersey Sound' – even though many posed a challenge to the Beatles in the charts. 'Do You Want to Know a Secret?' (from the *Please Please Me* album), 'Bad to Me' and 'I'll Keep You Satisfied' were consecutive UK number ones for Billy J. Kramer and the Dakotas. 'Love of the Loved' (from the Decca audition tape) launched the career of the Cavern's former cloakroom attendant, Cilla Black, while the Fourmost made the Top 20 twice, with 'Hello Little Girl', another Decca audition reject, and 'I'm in Love'.

In contrast with the hits he dashed off with John, Paul devoted much time and trouble to songs he wrote alone. 'All My Loving', that seemingly impromptu shout of joy, actually began as a piece of verse, for which the melody came as an afterthought. Early in Cilla's career, he gave her 'It's for You', an ambitiously complex ballad that would be one of her few brushes with subtlety.

Acts outside the Epstein 'family', too, benefited from Lennon and McCartney's seemingly infallible touch. 'Misery' was written for Helen Shapiro but, declined by her manager Norrie Paramor, was snapped up by Kenny Lynch, resulting in John and Paul's first cover version by a black artiste. 'I Saw Her Standing There', never issued as a Beatles single, went to a Larry Parnes artiste, Duffy Power. Most famously, 'I Wanna Be Your Man', shorn of Paul's airy harmonies and converted into raw R&B, was the number eight single that set the Rolling Stones on the path to becoming the Beatles' chief rivals.

In the early 1960s, the music-publisher's role was not only collecting royalties on cover versions and radio and TV plays but also issuing the songs as sheet music for live bands or Victorian-style home performance, with pictures of the artistes on the covers. The first Lennon–McCartney songs to reach this pinnacle, 'Love Me Do' and 'P.S. I Love You', went to Ardmore and Beechwood, an old-established London publishing firm on which Brian Epstein happened to stumble while still hawking round the Beatles' demo tape.

After Ardmore and Beechwood's lacklustre performance in support of their debut single, Brian decided to find a new publisher and sought advice from George Martin. Martin recommended Dick James, a former dance-band vocalist who had once himself recorded for Martin and, after years as a Tin Pan Alley song-plugger, had recently set up his own eponymous publishing company. As a quid pro quo for getting the Beatles onto an important TV pop show, *Thank Your Lucky Stars*, Dick James Music published 'Please Please Me' and its B-side, 'Ask Me Why'.

James's innovative idea was to set up an autonomous company

inside his organisation to deal exclusively with Lennon and McCartney's song output. It was given the sturdily plain-spoken name of Northern Songs and divided 50 per cent to James and his partner, Charles Silver; 20 per cent each to John and Paul; and 10 per cent to Brian. The arrangement would come in for criticism further down the line, but at the time it showed visionary faith in Lennon and McCartney's potential.

At first, Martin exercised a producer's absolute authority, backed up with the omniscience of a trained classical musician, conductor and performer. 'You can't do that,' he'd tell John and Paul, ahead of their song of that name, and they'd bow to his superior knowledge. Martin, however, soon realised that despite their lack of any formal training, both had an instinctive musicality, untrammelled by any rules or inhibitions. It was useless to tell them that something they wanted to do wouldn't 'work': when they tried it, more often than not it did.

For example, on the final 'yeah' of 'She Loves You', they'd un-wittingly used a major sixth. In vain did Martin protest that the Glenn Miller swing band had ended numbers that way time and again back in the 1940s and that it was 'corny'. Millions of other young Britons, who'd never heard of Glenn Miller or major sixths, screamed their disagreement through an entire summer. '[Martin] would give us parameters,' Paul remembers. 'Like "You mustn't double a third" or "It's corny to end with a sixth and a seventh is even cornier." It was a good thing we could override a lot of his so-called professional decisions with our innocence.'

Both Paul and John were still as euphoric at stumbling on a new chord-change as in their Quarrymen days – such as the more pensive middle eight of 'From Me to You'. Here, John later acknowl-edged, 'Paul was more advanced than me. He was always a couple of chords ahead, and his songs usually had more chords in them.'

Perceptions of pop music changed for all time in December 1963, when William Mann, classical music critic of *The Times* – then known as 'the top people's paper' – wrote an article naming Lennon and McCartney as 'the year's outstanding composers'.

In a detailed analysis of their songs, Mann discussed technical features of which the two had never been remotely aware: the 'octave ascent' in 'I Want to Hold Your Hand', the 'chains of pandiatonic clusters' in 'This Boy', 'the melismas with altered vowels' in 'She Loves You', the 'Aeolian cadence' at the end of 'Not a Second Time', whose chord-progression corresponded exactly with Mahler's 'Song of the Earth'. In the general paean of highbrow praise, Paul was singled out for his 'cool, easy and tasteful' cover of 'Till There Was You' and, indirectly, for 'a firm and purposeful bass-line with a musical life of its own'.

One aspect of this oft-quoted article tends to be overlooked. While *The Times*'s august critic extolled Lennon and McCartney's innate Britishness, after so many years of American-flavoured pop, he made no mention of their lyrics. The truth was that in 1963, these were mostly still at the 'you . . . true . . . things you do' level, though the odd native colloquialism sometimes crept in. Paul's original opening to 'I Saw Her Standing There', for instance, had been 'Well, she was just seventeen', followed by 'Never been a beauty queen', a memory of childhood visits to Butlin's holiday camps. In consultation with John, that second line changed to the more natural, and Liverpudlian, 'You know what I mean'.

July 1964 brought the soundtrack album to the Beatles' first feature film, *A Hard Day's Night*, newly-released to huge popular and critical acclaim in both Britain and America. The album was the first to dispense with cover versions and feature only Lennon–McCartney songs. John was its dominant presence with 10 out of the 13 tracks, while Paul had only 'Can't Buy Me Love', 'And I Love Her' and 'Things We Said Today'.

The last of those, while neat and catchy, was a somewhat throwaway McCartney Beatles track. But buried in it was a first hint of the particular Britishness he would bring to classics of the future:

> Someday when we're dreaming
> Deep in love, not a lot to say . . .

It's that 'not a lot' – which, in understated British vernacular, means 'nothing'. And that characteristically rosy view of the future: one-time lovers still together, perhaps when they're 64, sharing a fond, reminiscent silence.

13

'Changing my life with a wave of her hand'

Paul's relationship with Iris Caldwell had ended in early 1963. By that time, their cosy dating routine in Liverpool was long over and they saw each other only in brief interludes between his tours with the Beatles and her engagements as a cabaret dancer.

Lately, Iris had moved upmarket from seaside cancan shows to the chorus line at the swanky Edmundo Ros Club in London's Mayfair. Ros's calypso orchestra, broadcast every Sunday morning on the BBC Light Programme, was a cherished childhood memory of Paul's, so one evening he dropped by the club unannounced, bringing Ringo with him. 'They weren't allowed in,' Iris recalls. 'The doorman didn't think they were well enough dressed.'

Despite all the new diversions offered by London, breaking up with Iris wasn't easy for Paul. They'd been together for two years; besides, he remained hugely fond of Iris's eccentric mother, 'Violent Vi', and her brother, Rory Storm, who'd been top dog in the Liverpool music scene when Lennon and McCartney still fronted the Quarrymen. Somehow, Liverpool's 'Mister Showmanship' had been left behind by the national Mersey Beat craze which the Beatles had sparked off and which had brought recording deals to other city bands like Gerry and the Pacemakers, the Searchers, the Swinging Blue Jeans, the Fourmost, the Mojos, Faron's Flamingos and many more.

Unfortunately, no one had spotted Rory's potential as a glam rocker ahead of his time. Nor was he himself all-consumingly ambitious; still involved in athletics as much as music, he feared that going to London might stop him competing for his running club, Pembroke Harriers. So he settled for remaining a big fish in that small 'Pool', with a stage act now featuring a pet monkey in addition to his turquoise suits, gold lamé briefs and feats of indoor mountaineering.

On a visit home during the first throes of Beatlemania, Paul heard that Rory had been hospitalised for a cartilage operation, and decided to pay him a visit. It happened that Rory's selfless father was working in the same hospital as a volunteer porter. 'He came into the ward with his trolley and saw this crowd of nurses around my brother's bed, who couldn't believe it was Paul McCartney,' Iris remembers. 'Poor Dad had no idea that Paul was coming . . . he thought it was because of some medical emergency to do with Rory, like his heart stopping.'

In the end, she took the initiative and dumped Paul. 'It was on the day before my 19th birthday. My mum said I should have waited in case he'd got me a nice present.'

Wherever the Beatles were on Saturday nights, they always tried to watch *Juke Box Jury* on the BBC's single television channel, a 30-minute show in which a four-person panel listened to the newest pop releases, then voted each a 'Hit' or a 'Miss'. Most panellists were broadcasters or entertainers of the older generation who were still hostile to pop and there purely to be facetious at its expense. But in 1963, a newcomer, the actress Jane Asher, broke with tradition by being only 16, yet forthrightly articulate and intelligent.

Jane had been an actress since the age of five, appearing in British films like *Mandy* and *The Greengage Summer*, becoming the youngest-ever Wendy in London's traditional Christmas stage version of J.M. Barrie's *Peter Pan* and appearing on record in a dramatisation of Lewis Carroll's *Alice in Wonderland*. Following her success on *Juke Box Jury*, she was asked to commentate on a pop concert called Swinging Sound '63, and headlined by the Beatles, which the BBC staged at London's Royal Albert Hall on 18 April, two weeks before her seventeenth birthday. Part of her assignment was to interview the headliners backstage.

Seeing her on black and white television, the Beatles had thought Jane was blonde, but in real life her shoulder-length hair proved to be a rich Pre-Raphaelite red. Following their custom with any sophisticated 'southern bird', all four immediately proposed to her. At that stage, it was George ('the quiet one', always the most sexually forward) who seemed likeliest to score.

After the concert, Jane found herself hanging out with a group comprising all four Beatles, fellow performer Shane Fenton (whom, coincidentally, Iris Caldwell later married) and the pop journalist Chris Hutchins. They went to Hutchins's King's Road flat, where a drunk – and so, inevitably, malicious – John Lennon began plying Jane with questions designed to make her blush as red as her hair: 'What do girls do when they play with themselves?' and the like. She maintained her poise impressively, but was still forced to admit to being a virgin.

To rescue her from John, Paul led her into an adjacent bedroom amid knowing winks and nudges from the others. In fact, they spent the time sitting on the bed and discussing their favourite foods. Jane had been educated at Queen's College, one of London's most famous girls' schools, and was extremely well-read. One subject that came up was Chaucer's *The Canterbury Tales*, from which, thanks to his teacher 'Dusty' Durband, Paul could quote long passages from memory. As he would later recall, Jane seemed less impressed by his being a Beatle than his delivery of a line from 'The Prioress's Tale' in its original Middle English, 'ful semely hir wimpel pinched was' (which makes schoolboys snigger but only means 'her head-covering was neatly arranged').

Later, when the group headed off to party until dawn, Jane declined to go with them and asked to be dropped at her home. Paul saw her to her front door, taking the opportunity to get her telephone number.

Jane's father, Richard Asher, was one of Britain's most distinguished medical men, a specialist in haematology (blood) and endocrinology (glands and metabolism) who in 1951 had been the first to identify Munchausen's Syndrome, or attention-seeking by means of non-existent illness. Her mother, Margaret, was a classical oboe-player and a professor at the Royal Academy of Music, whose past pupils on the instrument included the Beatles' record producer, George Martin. Martin consequently had known Jane when she was a small child; as he observed when Paul introduced them, 'The last time I saw you, you were in the bath.' 'She didn't seem all that thrilled to hear it,' he recalled.

All the Ashers' three offspring, in fact, were child actors. Jane's bespectacled older brother, Peter, now studying philosophy at King's College, London, had also been in several British films and children's television programmes (once appearing alongside Jane in the *Robin Hood* series, whose theme-tune was sung by the Beatles' future music publisher, Dick James). Not to be outdone, their young sister, Clare, had landed a part in the BBC's famous radio soap *Mrs Dale's Diary* before leaving school.

The Ashers lived at 57 Wimpole Street, a six-floor Georgian terrace house on the edge of London's West End and in the heart of the district colonised by exclusive private doctors and clinics. If Wimpole doesn't have quite the professional cachet of nearby Harley Street, it is immortalised in a stage play, *The Barretts of Wimpole Street*, about the love affair between two great nineteenth-century poets; brash and breezy Robert Browning and the semi-invalid Elizabeth Barrett. Now another dashing young wordsmith came wooing a young woman almost as innocent and sheltered as Elizabeth.

Jane gave Paul instant access to all the refinement and culture his mother Mary could ever have wished for him. They spent their first dates mainly going to the theatre, spoilt for choice in the West End that was only a few minutes' walk from Jane's house. When she was first allowed to go away on holiday with him – to Athens – culture still predominated. Also on the trip were Ringo Starr and his soon-to-be wife, Liverpool hairdresser Maureen Cox, neither of whom had previously felt much fascination with Ancient Greece.

But inter-Beatle tolerance kicked in, as always: Ringo ruefully reported 'going round the Parthenon three times just to please Jane'.

Behind the Georgian fanlight of 57 Wimpole Street, life was very different from 20 Forthlin Road – the high rooms with moulded ceilings and the elegant staircase, all not in the very best repair; the constant comings and goings of Dr Asher's patients and Margaret's oboe-students; the scraps of classical music floating up from her tuition room in the basement. Not only the eminent specialist and the music professor but all three of their children seemed to have diaries permanently crammed with engagements; Paul, so he later said, had never known people 'who stuffed so much into a single day'.

The Ashers of Wimpole Street, though pillars of the establishment, were anything but conventional. Richard Asher was a maverick in his profession, a startlingly original thinker and writer whose articles in medical journals seldom failed to cause a sensation among his colleagues and in the wider world. For all his sober suits and suave consultant's manner, he was a one-off eccentric who'd taught himself to sign his name upside-down on the letters his secretary put in front of him, rather than waste time turning them right way up. During mealtimes, he liked to surprise his family by giving himself a (harmless) injection in the back of the neck. At night, he'd change into a blue boiler suit and occupy himself with ambitious if not always very skilful DIY jobs around the house until the early hours of the next morning.

Though the Asher household was like none Paul had ever known, he fitted into it quite naturally. Jane's family's addiction to intellectual word games made him bless those many times at Forthlin Road when his father sent him to look up a crossword conundrum in Chambers' dictionary. If he didn't understand a word, he'd say so frankly – then remember its meaning for always. Margaret Asher had a small sitting-room where she liked to serve afternoon tea to her children's friends and her students. At these gatherings, Paul would always be the soul of politeness, passing teacups and handing round plates of cakes.

It wasn't long before the Ashers met John, too – now on the best behaviour that, when he chose, could outshine even Paul's. Since the pair still had nowhere in London peaceful enough for their songwriting sessions, Margaret offered them her basement tuition room and piano.

It was there – 'playing into each other's noses', as John put it – that they got the idea for 'I Want to Hold Your Hand', the single which cracked America for the Beatles. Strange to think of its genesis in that high-priced medical quarter, where foreign potentates disembarked from Rolls-Royces for doctors' appointments, motorcycle couriers collected or delivered blood and urine samples and nurses and receptionists hurried to and from work.

When the Beatles first moved down to London permanently, Brian's plan was that they should live together like puppies in a basket. Accordingly, a flat was found for them at 57 Green Street, on the side of Mayfair nearest Hyde Park. Paul was last to view the accommodation – a rare instance of tardiness on his part – and found the others had already bagged the best bedrooms, leaving him a tiny, cramped one at the back.

For John, George and Ringo, the flat was merely somewhere to sleep, entertain their pick of the night's 'birds' and change clothes. All Paul's pleas to make it more homey, even buy basic necessities, such as a kettle, fell on deaf ears. As a result, it was hardly more comfortable or cheerful than the crash-pads they used to occupy together in Hamburg.

When John's wife, Cynthia, and baby son, Julian, followed him to London (not to his unalloyed pleasure) a family-sized flat was found for them in Emperor's Gate, Kensington, overlooking the old West London Air Terminal. George and Ringo moved to another part of Mayfair, William Mews, sharing a flat in the block where Brian himself lived. But for some time the fans who tracked the Beatles' every movement had no idea what had become of Paul.

In late 1963, returning from a holiday in Rome with Jane, he'd meant to drop her at 57 Wimpole Street, then go home to Liverpool.

But he missed his last connection, so the hospitable Margaret Asher invited him to stay the night. Rather as in George S. Kaufman and Moss Hart's play *The Man Who Came to Dinner*, that one night lengthened into weeks, months and finally years.

Jane's brother, Peter, had a large L-shaped bedroom at the top of the house, overlooking Wimpole Street. Paul occupied a former maid's room across the landing, overlooking Browning Mews (named after the poet) and right next to the bathroom. Jane slept on the floor below, but it was understood that there'd be no nocturnal creeping around. 'Jane had always slept in that room, and still had the nameplate on the door which had been put up when she was little,' recalls Barry Miles, another key figure in Paul's cultural education. 'For Paul, I think, it was like being in the world of Peter Pan.'

His room, in fact, was about the same size as the one he'd slept in since boyhood at Forthlin Road. There was space only for a narrow single bed and a heavy wooden wardrobe. A single shelf held guitar-picks, correspondence, a couple of drawings from Jean Cocteau's *Opium: The Diary of His Cure* and a constantly changing selection of improving books. Under the bed were a growing collection of Gold Discs and his MBE medal in a frame. With the Ashers' indulgence, he also managed to fit a piano into his tiny garret – a 'cabaret' model with a top low enough for its player to maintain smiling eye-contact with the audience.

His surroundings were so Spartan and his general lifestyle so modest that Peter Asher could almost forget that his music, and John's, virtually monopolised the international charts. Then one day he opened a drawer to reveal thousands of US dollars, still in the paper bands in which they'd come from the bank. He also showed Peter a letter he'd just received from the Beatles' accountant, Harry Pinsker. 'I thought you might like to know,' wrote Pinsker, 'that on paper you are now a millionaire.'

The Ashers regarded him as one of the family – all the more welcome now that so much of the world regarded him as a god. A few blocks from Wimpole Street, the Post Office's new 620-foot telecommunications tower was nearing completion. With the sublime self-assurance of London's old upper class, Richard Asher wrote to the Post Office that he, his wife and children would appreciate a guided tour of the miraculous structure before its official opening. This was granted – and Paul naturally went along, too.

After Jane, his closest relationship in the house was with her mother. Margaret Asher suffered from insomnia due to chronic migraine, and so was usually still up when Paul returned from gigs or nights out with fellow Beatles. No matter how late the hour, she would provide the warmest of welcomes, then cook him whatever he wanted to eat. She also did his laundry, never minding how many dirty tab-collared or long-collared or round-collared or button-down-collared shirts he presented her with. How could he not think of the mum whose last gift had been a pile of freshly-ironed shirts and towels?

For Peter Asher, having a Beatle in the house couldn't have been better timed. As a pupil at Westminster, the famous school in the shadow of Westminster Abbey, he had teamed with a fellow pupil named Gordon Waller to form a guitar-playing folk duo named Gordon and Peter. They had recently signed a recording contract with EMI, who had reversed the order of their names and were preparing to launch them as folk singers, though their producer, Norman Newell, said he would consider pop material, too, if they could find some.

Peter then remembered an unfinished song by Paul ('two verses, no bridge') that John had rejected as too soft for the Beatles and no one else seemed to want. This 'orphan' McCartney song, 'World Without Love', credited to Lennon–McCartney, became Peter and Gordon's debut single, reaching number one in the UK in April 1964 – displacing the Beatles' 'Can't Buy Me Love' – and in the US a month later.

'People often ask me, "How did Peter and Gordon get all those Beatles songs?"' Peter Asher says. 'It tends to be forgotten that in those days John and Paul were thinking of their future in terms of songwriting as much as performing. After "World Without Love" was a hit, they looked in the songwriters' manual, where it said "If you write a hit, for God's sake don't let anyone else write the follow-up." So then Paul came up with "Nobody I Know".'

Peter's new star status brought still more pop people into the Ashers' classical home. For a while, he dated the Jamaican singer Millie Small who, as plain Millie, scored a worldwide hit in 1964 with 'My Boy Lollipop'. The ever-surprising Richard Asher not only approved of their relationship but hoped Peter might marry Millie and so extinguish 'the family gene' that had given him his flamingly red-headed children.

Paul's cover among West End surgeons and urologists was eventually blown and fans formed a round-the-clock picket outside 57 Wimpole Street. He was deeply embarrassed that such a distinguished couple as Richard and Margaret Asher should run the risk of being mobbed whenever they left or entered their home. But the whole family took the squealing siege in stride. Jane might have stayed coldly aloof, if not shown open resentment, towards these deranged young women from all over the world who treated her boyfriend as their collective property. Yet she always took the trouble to be nice, even though envious kicks or yanks of her hair soon became an occupational hazard.

The nuisance intensified during the spring of 1965, when the Beatles were filming *Help!* Paul's fans wrote messages on the surrounding street signs, defaced Dr Asher's brass nameplate and, in their hunger for souvenirs, even managed to break off one of the two ornamental pineapples from the iron railings flanking the front steps. Instead of exploding with fury, as many a paterfamilias would have done, Jane's father gleefully rose to another DIY challenge, taking a cast of the remaining pineapple, then melting down various household utensils (many of them in crucial daily use) to fashion a new one.

The ever-inventive doctor also found a way for Paul to exit the house unseen that had echoes of prison-camp dramas in the Second World War. The next-door house, number 56, was also a residential property whose upper floors were occupied by an elderly retired military man. Donning his nocturnal blue boiler suit, Dr Asher climbed through the window of Paul's attic room and discovered a narrow parapet on which it was possible to inch along to his neighbour's top-floor windows. An arrangement was made with the bemused but obliging old military man whereby, if necessary, Paul would make the rather perilous journey along the connecting parapet, climb through number 56's open window, then exit from the rear via a house in Browning Mews, whose occupants also had to be brought into the Colditz-like plot. From there, it was just a couple of streets to the home of the Beatles' chauffeur, Alf Bicknell, in Devonshire Close.

The Browning Mews house belonged to a young married couple, who asked no recompense for having Paul make his way through their home at all hours. However, one day he noticed they didn't own a refrigerator, so he had one delivered to them.

The moment of falling for Jane is marked by a new tenderness and specificity in Paul's music. There's the naturalistic catch of breath in 'I've Just Seen a Face'; the unnamed presence in 'Here, There and Everywhere' – perhaps the most charming of all Beatles ballads – 'changing my life with a wave of her hand'; above all, the unqualified 'And I Love Her':

> A love like ours, will never die
> As long as I
> Have you near me.

He couldn't wait to show Jane off to his home city, as soon as his Beatle work schedule – and her packed engagement diary – permitted. They arrived at 20 Forthlin Road late at night, after Mike McCartney had gone to bed. Paul couldn't wait for him to get dressed, but brought Jane upstairs to meet him while he was still in his pyjamas. Mike, too, instantly fell for her – as, needless to say, did 'Gentleman Jim'. And the starched-aproned ghost of Mary seemed to smile down on this more-than-fulfilment of all her hopes.

Nor could Paul resist taking Jane to meet the Caldwells at the house their rock 'n' rolling son had renamed 'Stormsville'. Vi Caldwell's riotous ménage had now been further enlivened by Rory's pet monkey, which had fallen in love with Vi's husband and, like a Beatles fan in miniature, showed its hostility to her by dropping dinner-plates on her head.

'Violent Vi' bore Paul no ill will for already having found a successor to Iris. But she was determined he shouldn't still behave as he used to when he'd rely on his angel looks to get round people – smoking their cigarettes without ever buying his own – and she'd told him, only half-jokingly, 'You've got no heart, Paul.'

'My mum said that Jane could come in,' Iris remembers, 'but she sent Paul off to English's, our local shop, to get 20 cigarettes out of their machine. And when he came back, she was furious because he hadn't bought another 20 to give to her.'

At the same time, he was a Beatle, adored by millions of young women, many only too willing to turn adoration into positive action. To resist the temptation to be unfaithful to Jane that daily – hourly – came his way would have needed the superhuman self-control of some medieval saint.

Sex had always been pressingly on offer, whether on the Reeperbahn or outside the Cavern, when roadie Neil Aspinall and his hulking deputy, Mal Evans, would bring in willing females along with the takeaway fish and chips or chicken. After Brian arrived and the world touring began, it became part of room service. Among the Beatles' welcoming delegation at airports across America would usually be four high-priced, prepaid hookers to console them for being unable to set foot outside their hotels.

Not that it ever needed to be a commercial transaction, especially not for Paul. In any room he entered, he knew he could have his pick of the most beautiful young women there. During early Beatlemania, he would often act as a judge at bathing-beauty contests – as yet unchallenged by feminism – whose winners might then receive an extra prize along with a crown, a sash and a bouquet of roses.

Pop musicians with wives or steady girlfriends observed an un-written rule that 'sex on tour doesn't count', but for Paul it was more often a matter of *keeping* count. To his cousin, Mike Robbins, he once described a four-in-a-bed session in which he'd been the only male. The holiday camps where Robbins once worked used to be saturated in sex, but even he had to admit Butlin's had nothing on this.

The Beatles' on-the-road sexual activities were well-known to the large media contingent who travelled with them, at close quarters that today seem extraordinary. But no newspaper or TV reporter would have dreamed of dishing the dirt on the sacred Fab Four, any more than of delving into their murky Hamburg past. The media were as complicit in preserving the illusion as White House correspondents during the presidency of John F. Kennedy.

The same rule also held good when, as inevitably happened, figures from their past began to pop up, seeking a share of their supposedly unlimited wealth either for having contributed to their success or suffered wrongs at their hands. In this second category, the most potentially ruinous were from the ranks of young women they'd carelessly had sex with when they were nobodies.

Two of the earliest such claims involved Paul, threatening to unravel all the positive PR he had worked so hard to create. They came at the worst possible moment, both at the start of his idyllic relationship with Jane and the apogee of the Beatles' triumph as ambassadors for Britain and Liverpool.

The first was by a former Reeperbahn club waitress named Erika Hubers, who'd allegedly dated Paul throughout the Beatles' inter-mittent spells in Hamburg between 1960 and 1962. In January 1964, she came forward, claiming he was the father of her 14-month-old daughter, Bettina.

The story reached the London *Daily Mail* early in February, during the band's all-conquering first trip to America. The *Mail*'s New York bureau chief, David English, joined their media-packed train journey to Washington DC and, in a quiet moment, put the allegation to Paul. No clarification was forthcoming, however, and the *Mail* decided not to risk running the story.

Less easily suppressed was the case of Liverpudlian Anita Cochrane, a hardcore Beatles fan since their earliest days at the Cavern. Anita claimed to have had casual sex with Paul twice when she was 16 and still a virgin, and, as a result, to have given birth to a son in February 1964 – again while the band were conquering America. According to Anita, when she was four months pregnant she and her mother had visited Jim McCartney, telling him she was not seeking marriage or to damage Paul's public image, only some financial provision for the child. Jim, she said, had been 'really nice', given them 'a nice cup of tea', but told them 'Paul says he doesn't know you'.

They'd then gone to Brian Epstein, who was long familiar with such allegations against his 'boys' and had a policy of buying them off without trying to establish their truth or otherwise. Brian initially offered Anita the equivalent of £2.50 per week maintenance, then upped it to £5. When her lawyer threatened to call for blood-tests, Brian proposed a one-off payment of £5000 in exchange for signing a document promising 'not to make any allegations or statements to any person under any circumstances that or to the effect that Paul McCartney is the father of said child'. He seemed to regard Anita's claim as something more than the usual opportunism, for he visited her personally at her grandmother's house to make the offer. The money was then deducted from Paul's payments through NEMS.

Anita duly signed, but some of her family were outraged by the size of the settlement – and not bound by the same confidentiality agreement that she was. In July 1964, following the London premiere of *A Hard Day's Night*, the Beatles made an almost royal return to Liverpool, driving in via Speke – Paul's childhood home – to a civic reception by the Lord Mayor for them and their families. Afterwards, they appeared on the Town Hall balcony, waving to a cheering crowd estimated at 200,000.

As Brian looked proudly on, he learned that leaflets were being circulated among the crowd, denouncing Paul as 'a cad' for his alleged mistreatment of Anita Cochrane. A poem had also been circulated to local newspapers, written by her uncle as if in the voice of the baby she'd named Philip Paul, and referencing one of the alleged father's sunniest love songs: 'In spite of all her lovin', she got no thanks from him/ It seems he loved my mother just long enough to sin/ Besides his lust, she took his money to compensate a lie/ But Mr Paul McCartney, Dad, you make mother cry.'

Helped by his brother, Clive, Brian quietly put a stop to the leaflet-distribution and suppressed the poem. Neither Anita nor Erika Hubers had even dented the protective shield thrown around the Beatles by their manager. Alas, it was not to last for ever.

14

'Long life and happiness and lots of marzipan butties'

For 61 years, Jim McCartney's birthday had been marked by nothing more extravagant than a family tea-party, a cake with candles in petal-shaped holders, perhaps a little extra flutter on his beloved 'nags' if the *Liverpool Echo*'s racing tipster named a specially hot prospect.

But Jim's sixty-second – or, anyway, its eve – found him at the royal film premiere of *A Hard Day's Night* at the plushy London Pavilion cinema. He enjoyed the film hugely, even though its script unwittingly rubbed raw the heartbreak he and his sons had suffered eight years earlier. In the opening sequence, aboard the train, Alun Owen's script had John asking Paul why he'd been given the job of looking after his troublesome grandfather, played by Wilfrid Brambell. 'My mother asked me to,' he had to reply.

After the show there was a glittering reception at the Dorchester hotel, attended by Princess Margaret and her husband, Lord Snowdon, a royal couple as glamorous and popular in 1964 as William and Kate would be 50 years later. Jim was offered the chance to be presented to them but, with typical reticence, decided he'd rather not as he wouldn't know what to say.

As midnight signalled the official start of his birthday, Paul handed him a brown paper parcel which he unwrapped to reveal an oil painting of a racehorse. 'I said, "Very nice,"' he later recalled, 'but I'm thinking "What do I want with a picture of a horse?" Paul said, "It's not just a picture . . . I've bought the bloody horse. It's yours and it's running at Chester on Saturday."'

The horse was a gelding of impressive lineage named Drake's Drum. Paul had paid £1050 (£15,000 by today's values) for it and placed it with a leading Yorkshire trainer, Lieut. Col. Wilfred Lyde. The following Saturday, Jim and his two sons watched it run its first race at Chester – and finish second.

This very public display of Paul's affection for his father had a particular – and uncomfortable – resonance for John Lennon. For it happened that, actually during the filming of *A Hard Day's Night*, John had been reunited with his own father, Alfred Lennon, whom he hadn't seen since he was aged six. Alf, now known as Freddie and long out of the Merchant Navy, was leading a semi-itinerant life as an hotel kitchen-worker when colleagues pointed out that one of the Beatles had his surname.

In reality, despite his present lowly employment, Freddie was not the incorrigible wastrel his son had been brought up to believe. Nor had he simply absconded without a qualm just after the Second World War, leaving toddler John to be passed like a parcel around the family, ending up with his controlling Aunt Mimi. But Mimi's myth-making was too strong for John ever to feel easy in his long-lost father's company, or banish the suspicion that Freddie's only motive for resurfacing was a cut of the Beatles' riches.

By contrast, since Paul became famous Jim had never demanded anything in recompense for all his years of selfless single-parenthood. Drake's Drum therefore wasn't just a casual demonstration of a young millionaire's new wealth; it was payback beyond anything his dad would ever have asked, or dreamed.

A further sixty-second birthday present from Paul (which, Jim would always say, meant even more) was the leisure to enjoy his new life as a racehorse-owner to the full. Nineteen sixty-four had found him still employed by A. Hannay & Co., the cotton brokers he'd joined as a 14-year-old during the Great War, and at a weekly wage still hovering at only around £10. Now Paul said he should stop work three years before official retirement age, and he'd provide for him for the rest of his life. Attached though Jim was to the Cotton Exchange and Liverpool's dwindling commercial heart, he needed no persuasion.

He never envisaged spending his retirement anywhere but at 20 Forthlin Road, the tiny council house behind the police academy where he'd brought up his two boys – even though nowadays the police were now more usually out front, controlling mobs of hysterical young women.

Like all the other Beatles' families, Jim and Paul's brother Mike, who still lived with him, were unfailingly nice to the fans who besieged their home and deluged it with letters and gifts from all over the world. If the besiegers came from very far away, or looked specially weather-blown or forlorn, Jim would invite them inside and let them make a cup of tea in the tiny kitchen lined with Mike's pictures of John taking the battered tin kettle off the gas, or the master of the house himself, loading Paul's undies into the washing-machine.

But by 1964, the crowd situation at Forthlin Road was such that Paul could no longer come home, as he still liked to do. So he set about finding a new house for Jim in more secluded surroundings, which he himself could use as a base in the north-west whenever he needed one.

To any traditional Liverpudlian, the retirement dream was to move 'over the water' – i.e. the Mersey – to the leafy purlieus of Cheshire's Wirral peninsula. Paul found the ideal location in Heswall, a village at the Wirral's westerly tip, which he'd first got to know when the Quarrymen used to play at the Women's Institute hall. For the then sizeable sum of £8750, he bought his father a four-bedroom detached house with spectacular views across the River Dee to Wales.

The house had a name, 'Rembrandt', and was mock-Tudor in style – both features recalling John's childhood home in Woolton, which Paul used to consider so 'posh'. Though provided with only one bathroom, it had half an acre of garden, including good-sized greenhouses, where Jim could indulge the lifelong passion hitherto confined to little squares of grass behind council houses.

Paul paid for the house's renovation and for central heating and fitted carpets to be installed. As Jim's stepdaughter, Ruth McCartney, recalls, 'It was the first time he'd ever lived in a place where the carpet touched the walls.'

'Rembrandt' was also to be a home for Mike McCartney, who by now had also come into pop music albeit by a more roundabout route than the older brother he always called 'our kid'. After a period as a trainee ladies' hairdresser, Mike became an organiser of Merseyside's first arts festival, in 1962, and also took part in a sketch with the Liverpool poets Roger McGough and John Gorman. As a result, the three formed a vocal trio, specialising in old music-hall songs and children's playground chants and named, with Scouse gallows-humour, the Scaffold.

To avoid any accusation of piggybacking on 'our kid', Mike adopted the surname McGear – 'gear' in Liverpool slang being a noun for fashionable clothes or an adjective meaning cool. While the Scaffold were getting established, he received what he preferred to call a weekly covenant of £10 from Paul.

Jim himself could draw on a bank account held jointly with Paul, which at that time received a substantial part of his son's Beatle earnings. Having such wealth at his disposal went to Jim's head in only one respect: he became a wildly extravagant tipper. At the little tea room in Heswall, he would leave £1 extra on a bill for less than £2. On car journeys to and from Liverpool via the Mersey Tunnel, he'd even tip the man in the tollbooth.

In the eight years since Mary's death, what with the combined pressures of cotton and raising two sons, Jim had never shown any interest in women outside his circle of supportive sisters. His one innocent flirtation was with the Beatles' fan club organiser, Frieda Kelly, who called him 'Uncle Jim' and whom he'd take to Liverpool's Basnett oyster bar – a favourite haunt of Brian's – to teach her to appreciate wines and French cheeses she'd previously regarded as just 'smelly'.

After moving across the water, Jim seemed set on remaining a confirmed bachelor, with his sisters Millie and Gin still coming once a week to clean the house for him as they had since Mary's death. The only difference now was that he could send them home in a taxi.

He'd barely settled into 'Rembrandt', however, when romance struck him as suddenly as it first had with Mary in his mother's air-raid shelter. Through his niece, Bett Robbins, he met Angela Williams, a tiny 35-year-old in a modish beehive coiffure and spectacles with flyaway frames. Born in Hoylake, Angie had grown up in Norris Green (coincidentally where Jim met Mary) and had chummed up with Bett at a Butlin's holiday camp when they both entered a Holiday Princess beauty contest. Now she was recently widowed, with a four-year-old daughter named Ruth, living in a tiny flat on the Kirkby industrial estate and working for the Pure Chemical company.

If Jim was initially dismayed by the 27-year age gap between them, it never bothered Angie for a moment. 'The first time I went to the house and saw Jim standing at the front door,' she says, 'I knew I was going to marry him.' She was attractive, warm, lively and – the clincher for Jim – an accomplished pianist. On only her fourth or fifth visit to 'Rembrandt', he came up behind her while she was playing and put his hands on her shoulders. 'He said, "I want to ask you something,"' she recalls. 'Before he could go on, I said, "The answer's yes."'

The terms of the proposal indicated how the changing times had affected even 'Gentleman Jim'. Angie was offered the choice of becoming his resident housekeeper, living with him or marrying him. For the sake of her daughter, Ruth, she said it had better be marriage.

Jim went straight off to telephone Paul, whom Angie hadn't yet met but with whom, it became clear, he had already discussed the matter. 'I heard him say, "Yes, she is . . . yes, I have . . . yes, we are." Then he put me on to speak to Paul, who said, "Well, you sound very nice."'

Paul at the time was in London, but dropped everything and drove straight up to Cheshire in his Aston Martin. Following already established routine, his father opened the garage doors so he could drive in and enter the house through the kitchen, so avoiding any fans lurking around the front gate. Angie's daughter, Ruth, recalls being got out of bed and brought downstairs in her pyjamas to meet her future stepbrother. By then, the Beatles' faces were familiar even to four-year-olds. 'I remember the first thing I said to him – "my cousin's got you on the wallpaper in her Wendy house!"'

Always good with children, Paul sat her on his knee and took trouble to get acquainted with her. 'I'd had an operation to have a kidney removed not long before, so I lifted up my pyjama-jacket and showed him the scar. He told me Ringo had a big scar on his tummy [from childhood peritonitis] but not as good a one as mine.'

Next day, Angie summoned her elderly mother, Edie, to stay with her at 'Rembrandt' as a chaperone until the wedding. Paul had to drive back to London, so Edie – totally undaunted by his celebrity – offered to make him cheese sandwiches and a flask of tea for the journey. In Jim's unfamiliar fridge she found what she took to be cheese but in fact was a block of marzipan. 'A couple of hours after Paul left, we got a phone call from him somewhere in the Midlands,' Angie recalls. 'He was laughing over his marzipan sandwiches.'

Jim and Angie were married on 24 November, at a tiny chapel in Carrog, North Wales. TV commitments for the Beatles kept Paul in London and Mike was on tour with the Scaffold. The village gravedigger acted as Jim's best man, and the minister's wife as both matron-of-honour and organist. Paul's congratulatory telegram read 'Wishing you long life and happiness and lots of marzipan butties.'

Becoming stepmother to a deceased wife's sons can be full of problems but with Paul and Michael Angie seemed to avoid them all. The more likely source of tension was Michael, who returned from his Scaffold tour to the fait accompli of a new wife sharing 'Rembrandt' with his father and himself. However, both brothers were equally glad Jim had found such a vivacious companion for what might otherwise have been a lonely retirement. And Mike and Angie soon became as close as any real mother and son.

Paul seemed thrilled with this new extension to his family, so much so that at Christmas he invited Jim to bring Angie and Ruth down to London, stay in an hotel and join him for Christmas lunch with Jane's family at 57 Wimpole Street. To Angie and Ruth, the Ashers' home was 'like a dream' with its enormous Christmas tree and gold-wrapped presents. Also there for the festivities were Peter and Gordon and Peter Asher's latest girlfriend Betsy Doster, a publicist for the American group Sam the Sham and the Pharaohs. The McCartneys were made to feel thoroughly at home, Jim getting on especially well with Jane's father, who – primed by Paul – gave him the perfect gift of an *Oxford English Dictionary*.

On Boxing Day, Paul had a special treat for Ruth alone. Picking her up from the hotel in his Aston Martin, he took her to Kensington to meet a wide-smiling woman with a mass of curly hair whom he introduced as 'Alma'. She was Alma Cogan, Britain's biggest singing star of the pre-rock 'n' roll Fifties, known as 'the girl with the laugh in her voice' and for a gaggle of novelty numbers like '20 Tiny Fingers' and 'Never Do a Tango with an Eskimo'. Now in professional eclipse, she remained a hugely popular figure inside show business, and one of the most legendarily hospitable. All four Beatles – and Brian – were regular visitors to the mansion flat where she lived with her mother and kept open house literally around the clock for A-list celebrities up to Frank Sinatra, Cary Grant and Sammy Davis Jr.

Her sister, Sandra Caron, remembers how at Alma's gatherings Paul took the chance to meet every big star he could and learn what they could teach him. 'One time, he and George were in the kitchen and I went in and told them Noël Coward was in the next room. "Who's he?" George said. I said he was only one of the most famous playwrights and wits of the century. When I went into the sitting-room later, Paul was sitting at Noël Coward's feet.'

In those days, it was taken for granted that Angie looked after Jim and ran the house although, from long habit, he still did a large share of the cooking. Paul made them an annual allowance of £7000, from which Angie received £60 per week for housekeeping. Detailed accounts had to be kept and submitted to Paul's office of everything she spent ('Piano-tuner £3, TV aerial £7, Ruth dress £4'), right down to face-flannels and sweets.

Jim had never previously been able to afford a car, so had never learned to drive, and said it was too late now. Angie therefore became his chauffeur in the small car Paul provided, diligently noting down every gallon of petrol bought and every toll paid through the Mersey Tunnel on Jim's weekly trips into Liverpool to pay his bookmaker's account.

She also did her best to rein in his chronic overtipping. Early in 1965, they went on a belated honeymoon to the Bahamas where (for tax reasons) the Beatles were filming the climactic scenes of *Help!* One night at an open-air restaurant, a group of musicians came to the newly-weds' table and serenaded them with 'Yellow Bird'. Jim's tip was so munificent that for the rest of their stay the musicians pursued them with recitals of 'Yellow Bird', even following Angie to the toilet and playing it outside.

At home, he was forever distributing cash among his large family circle in Liverpool, who needed something or other but didn't like to ask Paul directly for it. He even tipped his doctor in Heswall £300 every Christmas. 'One year, this doctor said he wanted to buy a colour TV and so could he please have double the amount,' Angie recalls. 'So Jim just gave it to him.'

As Paul McCartney's stepmother, Angie had to get used to groups of excited figures waiting at the end of the drive at all hours of the day and night and in all weathers, nocturnal voices and scufflings in the garden and torchlight shining inquisitively up at her bedroom window. From time to time, the press would have to be let into the house, the furniture drastically rearranged to accommodate TV cameras and lights and endless relays of tea and refreshments served by her. Once, while she was in the kitchen, preparing yet another laden tray, an amorous hack sidled up and propositioned her.

Though 'Rembrandt' had been intended as a secret hideaway, fanmail for Paul soon began pouring through the letterbox. Among the piles stacked on the living-room table, Angie noticed several from the same person, with postmarks showing that the sender was getting nearer and nearer. Finally, one night, the Liverpool dock police contacted Jim to say they were holding a young woman who'd arrived as a stowaway on a freighter and claimed to have been 'invited to Paul McCartney's house'. Paul, who happened to be there, spoke to the stowaway, who, with typical McCartney hospitality, was then invited for tea and afterwards put up at an hotel in Liverpool until she could arrange her passage home.

It might well have caused tension with Paul and Mike when their father decided to adopt Angie's little daughter, Ruth, becoming 'Daddy' to her after half a lifetime of being 'Dad' to them. But both brothers saw it as a further happy sign of Jim going against the grain of retirement: growing younger rather than older. To Ruth, he appeared much as he had to them for all those years at 20 Forthlin Road – a quiet, methodical figure who never appeared at breakfast without a collar and tie, yet whose 'bubbling, underground sense of fun' ensured that in any tongue-pulling contest he always triumphed. Like Paul and Mike before her, Ruth would be sent to Chambers' dictionary to check the spelling of any arcane word in his crossword puzzle; like them, she learned his treasury of Scouse wisdom: 'Do it now'; 'The two most important "-ations" in life are "toler-" and "moder-"'; 'There's no hair on a seagull's chest'; 'Put it there if it weighs a ton'.

Paul always devoted time to Ruth on his visits, playing games with her in the garden, or showing her books about his favourite contemporary artists. It delighted him when she treated the surreal fantasies of Salvador Dalí as quite normal, remarking casually, 'Oh, look . . . a soft watch.'

Though never quite as close to his stepmother as Mike was, he liked Angie for her good humour and tireless hospitality to any friends he brought home; at whatever hour of the day or night, 'Ange' would go and put the kettle on. Her love of music and abilities as a pianist created a further bond, and her worship of Frank Sinatra became a family joke. Some time later, during a solo visit to America, Paul was offered a short-haul ride on Sinatra's private plane, not realising that Sinatra himself would also be aboard. During the trip, he couldn't help blurting out, 'Wait till my stepmother hears I've met *you*.'

Such gaucheness was completely untypical and he apologised at once. 'Don't worry,' Sinatra replied. 'I did exactly the same thing when I first met John Wayne.'

Other Beatles had been dismayed to find their parents and close relations treating them with reverence once they became household names. But when Paul came to stay, Jim treated him in the same way as always, never failing to ask if he was eating properly and his bowels were in good order, nor to suggest, with a twinkle, that his Beatle haircut must have served its purpose by now and might be changed to something a little less extreme.

Under Angie's influence, Jim had put aside his old, double-breasted pinstripe business suits and begun to wear more stylish leisure clothes, including trousers with the 'drainie' style he'd so detested in the late Fifties, when Paul was besotted by them. 'By this time, Paul and every other young bloke had taken to wearing flares,' Ruth McCartney says. 'So Daddy used to criticise those.'

Paul would often be accompanied by John or George, minus their respective wives, for a few days' relaxation very much in the spirit of the old Quarrymen. George loved Jim's cooking, especially his custard which was smooth, creamy and without any wrinkled skin on top. 'He was always asking for the recipe,' Angie remembers. 'But Jim wouldn't give it to him.'

John became a frequent house guest, developing a healthy respect for Angie when – with a touch of his Aunt Mimi – she reprimanded him for not saying 'Please'. He particularly enjoyed spending time with Ruth, in whom he showed an absorption that his own son, Julian, sadly never received. 'He taught me to ride a bicycle,' Ruth remembers. 'And he'd read to me, and make up stories about my Teddy bear.'

Once when John was visiting, he and Paul went on a shopping trip to nearby Chester by bus, disguised in old raincoats from Jim's greenhouse, plus trilby hats and dark glasses. Their purchases had to be delivered later by truck: for John, a large crucifix, a Bible, some candlesticks and books; for Paul, a pine-framed bed that turned out to be riddled with woodworm. On top of driving, shopping, cooking and endlessly putting the kettle on, his good-natured stepmother volunteered to get it fumigated for him.

John happened to be staying when Brian Epstein phoned 'Rembrandt' to tell Paul that the Beatles occupied all five top places in *Billboard*'s Hot 100 chart. 'They were chuffed,' Angie recalls.

Britain in 1965 as yet had nothing like America's burgeoning rock culture. The mark of the Beatles' success in their homeland was their acceptance into a catch-all showbiz world which hosted annual awards at formal luncheons regulated by scarlet-clad toastmasters, whose zenith was the annual Royal Variety Show and whose innermost in-crowd met at Alma Cogan's Sunday-night parties.

On 1 August, the band were to top the bill in a television spectacular called *Blackpool Night Out*, hosted by the comedians Mike and Bernie Winters. A few days beforehand, Paul telephoned his ex-girlfriend Iris Caldwell, with whom he'd remained on friendly terms. Iris knew how sensitive he could be, under that angelic smile. Yet she never dreamed how her mother Vi's half-playful jibe, 'You've got no heart, Paul', had been gnawing at him. 'Paul told me "Watch *Blackpool Night Out* and tell me if I've still got no heart . . ."' It was the first time he ever sang "Yesterday" on television.'

During the filming of *Help!*, he'd exasperated his fellow Beatles, not to mention their director, Richard Lester, by calling for a piano and continually tinkering with a little melody he said he'd dreamed one night in his unshared single bed in the attic of 57 Wimpole Street.

When he'd awoken, the melody was so complete in his head that he could play it almost instantaneously on his cabaret piano. So complete, indeed, that at first he couldn't believe it was original, but thought he must unconsciously be plagiarising some well-known song whose title and words he'd forgotten. For weeks afterwards, he kept trying it out on other people – John, George, Ringo, George Martin, Alma Cogan, passing grips on the *Help!* set – but the expected cry of recognition never came. 'It was like handing something in to the police,' he would recall. 'If no one claims it, I can have it.' This was long before pop's first great plagiarism case (against, fellow Beatle George) and few other songwriters would have been as scrupulous.

Meanwhile, he gave it only the jokey working title of 'Scrambled Eggs', to fit its three-note opening. 'Scrambled eggs', he took to singing in those endless demos, 'Oh my baby, how I love your legs': a very McCartney marriage of lechery with the cosiest of hot snacks.

In May, he and Jane went on holiday to Albufeira, on Portugal's Algarve coast, staying at a holiday villa owned by Bruce Welch of the Shadows. In those days, the Algarve's nearest international airport was at Lisbon, a five-hour drive away. In the back of their chauffeured car, while Jane slept, Paul started getting a lyric with the same scansion as 'Scrambled Eggs'.

'When the car arrived at my place, he jumped out and said, "Have you got a guitar?"' Bruce Welch remembers. They spent their first evening at the nearby villa of Muriel Young, a children's TV presenter who partnered an owl puppet named Ollie Beak. 'Paul had finished the song on my Martin guitar in the afternoon and he played it for us after dinner,' Welch says. 'We were the first to hear "Yesterday".'

By the time the Beatles met to record their *Help!* soundtrack album, a new anxiety was gnawing at Paul. The title 'Yesterday' sounded so familiar that maybe he'd unconsciously plagiarised that. But the nearest to it George Martin could call to mind was a Peggy Lee track from the 1950s called 'Yesterdays'. Stylistically there was an echo of Ray Charles's 'Georgia on My Mind', while Nat King Cole's 1954 hit 'Answer Me, My Love' had a similarly remorseful mood, similar line lengths, even the couplet 'You were mine yesterday/ I believed that love was here to stay'. Nonetheless, even the super-scrupulous Martin felt Paul was on safe ground.

How to record it was another matter. More like an Elizabethan love song than anything, it clearly wasn't suited to Ringo's drumming, George's lead guitar or John's acidic harmony, as all three readily conceded. Martin's initial idea was to release it under Paul's name only, but Brian Epstein wouldn't hear of it. 'Whatever we do,' he said, 'we are *not* splitting up the Beatles.'

To Martin, the setting Paul's vocal cried out for was a classical string quartet. He himself initially favoured something more experimental and toyed with the idea of using the BBC's Radiophonic Workshop, a pre-computer sound laboratory which created the effects for its sci-fi series *Doctor Who*. Strange to imagine that saddest and sweetest of elegies coming from the same dimension as a Dalek.

On 14 June 1965, four days before his twenty-third birthday, he recorded the vocal for 'Yesterday' at Abbey Road studios. Three days later, an all-male string quartet recorded the accompaniment to be overdubbed on the voice. As a trained classical musician, George Martin naturally did the arrangement, but so that all connection with the modern world shouldn't be lost, Paul asked that a seventh – what jazzers call a blue note – be inserted into the score. 'Bach would never have done that,' Martin demurred, but to no avail.

On the *Help!* album, 'Yesterday' was listed as by Lennon–McCartney and as having been performed by the Beatles. It was not used in the film – in fact, it was virtually buried in the home market. John, George and Ringo vetoed its release as a single by Parlophone lest it should damage their credibility as a rock band. Their American label, Capitol, could not be leaned on in the same way, and on 5 October (credited to Lennon and McCartney in the usual way) it reached number one in *Billboard*'s Hot 100, staying there for four weeks.

Among the Beatles' British peers, it was viewed as a disastrous step out of character that no one else wanted to follow by recording a cover version. It was offered to Billy J. Kramer, from Brian's NEMS stable, and to the R&B singer Chris Farlowe, but both turned it down as 'too soft'. Three months elapsed before it was covered by Matt Monro, a Sinatra-style crooner (and long-time associate of George Martin), and finally entered the UK Top 10, even then getting no higher than number eight.

The classiest cover was performed on British TV by Marianne Faithfull, accompanied by Paul himself. He admired Marianne's singing and virginal beauty but, more importantly, she was about to marry Peter Asher's friend John Dunbar, a Cambridge fine arts student, whose child she was already carrying. Paul began the song, strumming an acoustic guitar, then Marianne took it up with an orchestra and choir, and camera angles carefully designed to hide her pregnancy.

The song became part of the Beatles' stage act, for the short time they were still to have one. George would usually announce it, with a faintly snide parody of Britain's most famous amateur talent show – 'And now, for Paul McCartney of Liverpool . . . opportunity knocks' – and John would hand him a floral bouquet afterwards. When he performed it on America's *Ed Sullivan Show*, the audience was estimated at 73 million; as many as had watched the Beatles' legendary debut on the *Sullivan Show* in February 1964.

A Novello Award as 'the best song of 1965' was just the beginning of the superlatives destined to be heaped on 'Yesterday' tomorrow and tomorrow. By the end of the twentieth century, it would be calculated to have been played seven million times and to have inspired more than 2000 cover versions, challenging the record held for decades by Bing Crosby's 'White Christmas'. A poll of BBC radio listeners in 1999 would vote it 'the best song of the century', and *Rolling Stone* magazine and the MTV channel later jointly named it 'number one pop song of all time'.

Not bad for a 22-year-old remembering a dream.

15

'This is what a Beatle does in the evenings'

By 1965, the Beatles had transformed pop music – its sound, its look, its social status, its economics and its practices. The effect wasn't to make them less insecure, however, but vastly more so.

Formations of young men with guitars, bases and drums had come to dominate the British record charts, every one with Beatle fringes, skimpy Beatle suits and Cuban-heeled Beatle boots, playing with Beatle-esque energy and humour and singing in Lennon and McCartney-esque tough/tender harmony. Imitation may be the sincerest form of flattery but in this case it also created dozens of lookalike rivals whose chart-placings John and Paul were always comparing anxiously with their own.

When the Beatles started out, their Liverpool origins had been like a shaming caste-mark. Now, in the once snobbish, superior south, a Liverpudlian group was the very last word in chic. They had also opened the door to combos from other northern cities like Manchester, Newcastle and Sheffield – then points even further afield like Scotland, Northern Ireland, the West Country and East Anglia – whose birthplaces likewise no longer needed to be shamefacedly hidden, but could be positively flaunted.

The greatest barrier the Beatles had breached, greater even than Britain's class system or North–South Divide, had been the Atlantic ocean. In the wake of their monster American success came the so-called 'British invasion' of other UK bands – the Rolling Stones, Gerry and the Pacemakers, the Animals, the Searchers,

Wayne Fontana and the Mindbenders, Freddie and the Dreamers. America in effect declared a Year Zero for its pop music, rejecting almost all home-grown performers who'd been famous pre-1964; wanting only Beatle fringes, high-buttoning corduroy and British regional accents so thick that on TV they were often provided with subtitles.

A new kind of American pop group had emerged, looking like Beatles with their fringes, buttons and boots, using Beatle harmonies and instrumentation, often singing in faux-British or even faux-Liverpudlian accents, but drawing on the national heritage of blues, country and folk from which the invaders had borrowed. Back across the Atlantic, surreally, came hits by American musicians imitating British ones imitating American ones.

The Beatle-ishly named, and misspelt, Byrds created harmonies in a higher, sweeter register even than Paul's and a jangling guitar that knocked spots off George's in 'A Hard Day's Night'. The Lovin' Spoonful had a Lennon–McCartney-esque humour and lyricism and, in John Sebastian, a vocalist sharing some of Lennon's wolfish charm as well as his given name. The Beach Boys, previously known for their rather witless 'surfing' sound, suddenly revealed their leader, Brian Wilson, to be a T-shirted mini-Mozart. Bob Dylan, previously known as a folk singer in the Woody Guthrie mould, decided to 'go electric' at the 1965 Newport Folk Festival, thereby alienating the entire American Civil Rights movement, and proceeded to come out with one electrifying rock single after another. All of this wasn't just a tribute to the Beatles; it was a shaggy Hydra-headed challenge to keep going one better.

Even the offstage camaraderie that generally existed among bands had largely been dictated by their Liverpudlian mateyness and John and Paul's generosity in handing out their songs for cover versions (just in case they might one day have to subsist as songwriters only). The Rolling Stones were portrayed in the media as the Beatles' daggers-drawn rivals, Montagues to their Capulets, Sharks to their Jets; in reality, the two bands were good friends who participated anonymously in each other's recording sessions, timed their releases so as not to block each other's climb up the charts, at one point even considered merging their management operations.

The Beatles were just as friendly towards their American mirror-images, freely admitting that many possessed levels of musical expertise far beyond theirs. Even at their unparalleled level of stardom, they remained passionate music fans, always ready to talk up singers or bands they thought had potential, even if it might mean yet more competition for them.

None was keener than Paul, both to acknowledge and encourage new-rising talent. At various times during 1965, perhaps the greatest-ever year for pure joyous pop, he could be heard on radio unselfishly plugging the Lovin' Spoonful's 'Do You Believe in Magic?', the McCoys' 'Hang On Sloopy', the Beach Boys' 'Help Me Rhonda' and the Byrds' cover of Bob Dylan's 'Mr Tambourine Man' – while stressing that Dylan's own version, on *Bringing It All Back Home*, was even better.

He had first tried marijuana along with the other Beatles and Brian at the end of their second American tour, in August 1964. The place could hardly have been more public – a suite in New York's Delmonico Hotel with thousands of fans (and dozens of police) in the street below and a music industry reception going on in the next room.

The occasion was their first encounter with Bob Dylan, a performer in whom the similarities to John were already being noted. Dylan himself supplied the drug, assuming his hosts must already be familiar with a substance beloved by musicians since the jazz and ragtime era. He was amazed to find the Beatles had never tried any narcotic stronger than amphetamine uppers and the benzedrine wicks of nasal inhalers. It turned out he'd been deceived by their Liverpool accents on 'I Want to Hold Your Hand'; when they sang 'I can't hide, I can't hide', Dylan heard it as 'I get high, I get high!'

On John, George, Ringo and Brian, the effect of that first joint was uncontrollable giggles. Paul, by contrast, became convinced that all the secrets of life were suddenly being revealed to him, and made roadie Mal Evans follow him around with a pen and paper, taking them down at his dictation. Unfortunately, he could never find the bit of paper afterwards.

From then on, in their usual one-for-all-all-for-one spirit, pot became a central element in the band's collective life. And to begin with, little or no risk was involved. Early-Sixties Britain was a society virtually free of what would later be termed recreational drugs, although serious narcotics were available on prescription for medicinal purposes or sold over the counter as ingredients in products like cold-cures. Most British police officers in this era couldn't have identified either the sight or smell of marijuana. Any awkward questions were easily deflected by saying it was just 'a herbal cigarette'.

Paul regarded its effect as wholly positive, a view from which he could never deviate after medical opinion turned against it. For him, the sage-scented fumes were 'uplifting', though the effect on most people was to send them to sleep. He saw pot as a modern equivalent of the native American's pipe of peace, which reduced everyone to the same euphoric, amicable haze. 'Most people think his "Got to Get You into My Life" is a love song,' says Barry Miles. 'Actually, it was written about pot because he liked it so much.'

The Beatles made *Help!* mainly under its influence – 'a happy high', director Richard Lester would remember. On every tour it went into their luggage with minimal precautions: roadies Neil and Mal would buy cartons of 200 cigarettes in individual 20-packs, then extract the tobacco from each paper tube and force in the straggly, aromatic strands instead. The most blatant bravado – still without repercussions of any kind – surrounded their investiture as MBEs by the Queen at Buckingham Palace. John claimed that before meeting their sovereign, they had ducked into a palace washroom and taken a few nerve-steadying drags on a joint, though Paul now says they only shared a cigarette like naughty schoolboys behind the bike-shed.

When they were recording at Abbey Road, John would set off from his new home in Weybridge, Surrey, pick up Ringo from his house on the same estate, and both would pot-smoke the 20-odd miles to London. Usually by the time they arrived, the combination of fumes and the overheated car would have brought on travel sickness that turned them almost as green as their own grass.

In the studio, they didn't dare do it in front of the headmasterly George Martin, but would sneak off together to the gents' toilet or huddle down behind Ringo's drum-baffles out of view of the control room. Their producer remained equally unaware of the first drug reference John and Paul smuggled onto a track – 'turn me on when I get lonely' in Paul's 'She's a Woman'. Paul also was careful to keep his new pastime secret from his dad, although his little stepsister, Ruth, noticed that when he came to Heswall to stay, he and his musician friends spent inexplicably long, hilarious periods among the vines and tomatoes in Jim McCartney's greenhouse.

Among his Wimpole Street circle, he discovered, pot was nothing new. Peter Asher's friend John Dunbar had tried it – and much else besides – while hitch-hiking around America. Dunbar's bookseller friend Barry Miles possessed an encyclopaedic knowledge of creative people who had leaned on it, from the beat poets of the Fifties to the literary colossi of 1920s Paris. It was from Miles he learned about Alice B. Toklas, the lesbian lover of Gertrude Stein, whose eponymous cookbook, as famous as Stein's cryptic poems, included a recipe for hash brownies. 'I told Paul that my wife, Sue, was going to try out the Toklas recipe after getting it from Brion Gysin [the painter, writer and poet],' Miles recalls. 'When I got home later, I found him in the kitchen, sitting on the draining-board and talking to Sue. He'd called round to get the recipe. I don't think she was ever less pleased to see me.'

The one area that pot didn't invade – yet – was Lennon and Mc-Cartney's songwriting. Agreeing that it clouded their minds, they continued in the old way, giving themselves a maximum of three hours per song, then each writing out a fair copy of the finished lyric. Only if the song turned out well did they reward themselves by sharing a joint. After completing 'The Word' and getting the joint started, they didn't just write out the lyric but turned it into an illuminated manuscript, using coloured crayons belonging to John's son, Julian.

Certainly, their output through 1965 shows no evidence of clouded minds: the perfect balance of McCartney optimism and Lennon pessimism in 'We Can Work It Out'; the premature nostalgia of 'In My Life', that seemingly quintessential John track for which in fact Paul wrote most of the melody. Their surroundings might have changed to a Surrey mansion or a West End townhouse but the essential atmosphere remained that of 20 Forthlin Road circa 1957: cups of tea, normal 'ciggies', long chats about music and art, the occasional bit of schoolboy smut smuggled into a future million-seller, like 'She's a big [i.e. prick] teaser' in 'Day Tripper' or the background vocal to *Rubber Soul*'s 'Girl' that went 'tit-tit-tit-tit'.

They might have disagreements, even quite violent rows, but no real bad feeling ever lingered. One of Paul's fondest memories of John 'was when we were having some argument . . . and calling each other names. We let it settle for a second and then he lowered his glasses and he said "It's only me . . ." and put his glasses back on again. Those were the moments when I actually saw him without the façade . . . the John Lennon he was frightened to reveal to the world.'

Seemingly helped by constant communal puffs at droopy little cigarettes, that same amity pervaded the whole band, no matter what pressures were piled on them. 'They were the best example I ever saw of what Jerry Garcia from the Grateful Dead later called "the group mind",' says Barry Miles. 'They'd been together for so long that one only had to start playing for the others to know just what to do. Even with a 55,000 crowd at Shea Stadium, the biggest concert they'd ever done, they didn't decide on their running-order until they were in the dressing-room beforehand.'

The group mind entered another dimension that year when John, George and their consorts went to dinner with their dentist in London, and were puzzled to see a row of sugar cubes arranged

along the dining-room mantelpiece. After drinking coffee containing the sugar, as Cynthia Lennon would remember, 'it was as if
we suddenly found ourselves in the middle of a horror film'. Un-
beknownst to them, the cubes had been impregnated with LSD.

Lysergic acid diethylamide, popularly known as acid, arrived
in Britain from America rather like the Beatles had the other way
around – as the beginning of a new age. A manmade substance
processed from rye fungus, colourless and odourless, it did not
dull the senses like pot, but sharpened them to an unprecedented
degree, intensifying light, sound and colour and causing hallucina-
tions that could be exalting or terrifying. The visions experienced
on this so-called trip were known as psychedelic, from the Greek
words *psyche* for mind and *deloun* for manifestation.

Too new as a recreational drug to have been declared illegal, its
'mind-expanding' powers were openly preached like some latter-
day gospel by a Harvard professor named Timothy Leary. In the
summer of 1965, Leary's British associate, Michael Hollingshead,
arrived missionary-like in London and set up what he named the
World Psychedelic Centre in his Chelsea flat, offering LSD free to
all comers, sprinkled on fingers of bread.

Acid had an immediately divisive effect on the Beatles. Following that bumpy first trip, John and George both persevered with
it, quickly becoming converts as devout as any in Leary's flock. It
was the most social of drugs, recommended to be taken by groups
of friends who could comfort and support each other through bad
trips as well as sharing the rapture of good ones. It seemed to have
worked for John and George, bridging their previously awkward
two-year age gap and bringing them closer than in the band's
whole lifespan, before or after. Now they wanted Paul and Ringo
to share the new togetherness they'd found.

Ringo, as always, was prepared to go along with the others – but
not Paul. Though happy to smoke pot, he baulked at any suggestion of 'the hard stuff'. Nor was he any stranger to peer-pressure:
Richard Lester recalls watching 'an absolutely chilling exercise in
controlled evil' as two of the most beautiful young women he'd

ever seen deployed all their charms to try to get Paul to try heroin.

That Peter Asher's friend John Dunbar was well-acquainted with acid, and other sorts of 'hard stuff', only acted as a further deterrent. He had become a regular visitor to the flat in Lennox Gardens where Dunbar lived with his new wife, Marianne Faithfull, and their baby son, Nicholas. The flat presented a weird contrast, with baby-care going on at one end and Dunbar's druggy friends slumped at the other. Once when Paul was there, a fellow visitor had to be rushed to hospital after shooting up cocaine (then available on the National Health Service) using a length of red rubber tubing as a tourniquet. Red rubber tubes reminded Paul of unpleasant procedures his mother used to carry out in her midwife years, and were one further reason not to stray from harmless-seeming pot. Even a visit to the World Psychedelic Centre and the most persuasive of sells by John Dunbar couldn't change his mind.

The Beatles' 1965 American tour brought visions that LSD might have found hard to match – not only the 55,000 at Shea Stadium but an audience with Elvis Presley in Los Angeles. To add to Paul's emotion on meeting his hero of heroes, it turned out that the only Beatles song Presley seemed to know was 'I Saw Her Standing There'; he actually sang 'My heart went boom when I crossed that room . . .', thumbing an electric bass.

Yet for the hard-boiled John no less than Paul, there was a touch of sadness that they'd fulfilled Brian Epstein's once-preposterous prophecy and truly had become 'bigger than Elvis'. 'We never wanted to beat him,' Paul later explained. 'We wanted to *coexist* with him.'

In LA, Ringo took acid for the first time, in an empathetic crowd including David Crosby and Jim (later Roger) McGuinn of the Byrds, with Neil Aspinall as a hand-holding co-tripper. But Paul still held back. '[He] felt very left out,' George would remember. 'And we were all slightly cruel to him . . . "We're taking it and you're not."'

However, he refused to give in. 'It was the way I'd been brought up: "Beware of the demon drug."'

*

It has always irked Paul that posterity regards him as the tuneful, cosy, *safe* side of the Lennon–McCartney partnership and John as the rebel, experimenter and iconoclast. The casting had been decided in Liverpool, then Hamburg, where he'd always hung back, feeling himself a provincial outsider, while John hung out with the arty in-crowd. After the migration south John had had his usual shaggy head start, cast as the 'intelligent', 'clever' or 'deep' Beatle, as opposed to the merely 'cute' one.

In 1964, he'd become the first pop musician to publish a book and the only one ever to have it launched at a Foyle's bookshop literary lunch attended by the cream of the capital's intelligentsia. *John Lennon in His Own Write* was a collection of his cartoons and nonsense writings, with a deferential foreword by Paul, recollecting their first meeting at Woolton church fete (and characterising himself that day – unbelievably to millions of young women around the world – as 'a fat schoolboy'). The book was a massive bestseller and a critical triumph, its author hailed as a joint reincarnation of Edward Lear and James Joyce.

But by the mid-Sixties, the elastic-sided boot was firmly on the other foot. As Swinging London approached its zenith, McCartney was at the epicentre of its cultural avant-garde while Lennon rarely emerged from suburban Surrey. 'John was basically a lazy bastard,' their former assistant Tony Bramwell remembers. 'He was quite happy to stay down in Weybridge, doing fuck-all.'

If Paul owed his cultural education largely to the Asher family, he owed his counter-cultural one almost entirely to Barry Miles – known simply as Miles – the mildly-spoken but sharp-minded 22-year-old who, unusually, combined omniscience about modern art and literature with a love of all music, from rock 'n' roll to the wildest spheres of experimental jazz and *musique concrète*. Raised in genteel Cheltenham, Gloucestershire (where he hung out with future Rolling Stone Brian Jones), Miles had studied art, then gone to work for Better Books, London's innocuously-named centre of revolutionary writing. Better Books was a home from home for

American beat writers when they visited London, and Miles was on impressively friendly terms with Allen Ginsberg, Lawrence Ferlinghetti, Gregory Corso and many others.

His knowledge of avant-garde music was also encyclopaedic; from him Paul first learned about the free-form jazz of Ornette Coleman, the avant-garde saxophonist Albert Ayler and the composer/pianist Sun Ra, who believed himself to be the mouthpiece of an 'angel race' who'd come to earth from the planet Saturn. At Miles's flat in Hanson Street, Fitzrovia, sometimes smoking hash, sometimes eating Alice B. Toklas's hash brownies, he listened to John Cage's 'Indeterminacy', a sequence of 'sonic short stories'; and the world's first singing computer, an IBM 704, performing the Victorian music-hall song 'Daisy Bell'.

Away from Abbey Road studios, he and John had always used reel-to-reel tape recorders, both to develop their songs and unwind by acting out comic plays and poems with *Goon Show*-inspired sound effects. After the arrival of pocket-size cassette recorders in 1964, playing around with sound became a great deal easier. One day, while giving Barry Miles a ride in his Aston Martin DB 5, Paul flipped a switch on the dash and Miles heard what appeared to be an American radio station with frantic jingles, idents and commercial breaks, so unlike the stuffy BBC. In fact, it was a tape made by Paul, using some of the freebie records that were showered on him every week. The authentic-sounding deejay patter also featured impersonations of Al Jolson, Little Richard and a wickedly accurate one of the Beatles' good friend Mick Jagger.

Miles thereafter introduced him to experimental music, whose cutting edge was not Anglo-American but European and whose leading figures made his and John's audio adventures at Abbey Road seem tame indeed: the German Karlheinz Stockhausen, the Frenchmen Pierre Schaeffer and Edgard Varèse, and the Italians Ferruccio Busoni and Luciano Berio. He learned how, following on from IBM's model 740 computer, machines were turning into performers and magnetic tape into orchestras, cut up and re-ordered or played backwards or endlessly repeated on multilayered 'loops'.

Miles could also brief him on the growing number of American bands with no interest in becoming Beatle-clones, still less having hits or making money, who were pushing the boundaries of pop into art, beat poetry and radical politics. Many were eccentrics whom even Liverpool couldn't have conceived : from Frank Zappa, a chin-bearded devotee of Stravinsky who named his rock sidemen the Mothers of Invention, to the poets Ed Sanders and Tuli Kupferberg and their band the Fugs (named after what was then the only printable rendition of 'fuck').

Whenever Paul saw John, he'd be full of news from this esoteric new world: how the tape-loop maestro Luciano Berio was coming to Britain to teach a course at Dartington Hall; how Paul had written a fan letter to Stockhausen – quite a turnaround for a Beatle – and received a personal reply. 'God, man, I'm *so* jealous,' John would respond gloomily, but always left it at that.

Conversely, the most unlikely figures from the avant-garde now became bit-players in the Beatles story. Another friend Miles had made through Better Books was William S. Burroughs, the doyen of American beat writers (and a famously unrepenting heroin-user) whose third novel, *Naked Lunch*, had been taken to court under America's anti-sodomy laws. Burroughs would often hang out with Miles and John Dunbar at a flat in Montagu Square which actually belonged to Ringo but which Paul had commandeered to set up an experimental recording studio, using Burroughs's boyfriend, Ian Sommerville, as an occasional engineer.

'We were there one night, smoking pot and making free-form music – otherwise known as banging pots and pans – when Paul came by with an acetate of the Beatles' *Rubber Soul* album,' Miles recalls. 'Bill Burroughs was one of the first people he played it to.' Clearly awed by the great man, he said it had '14 flaws' that he'd been unable to rectify, though its billions of listeners since would be hard put to name even one.

Rubber Soul saw the further development of identifiable 'John' or 'Paul' songs, despite their continuing joint byline. From John came 'Girl', 'Norwegian Wood' and 'Nowhere Man', thinly-disguised self-portraits full of the restlessness and self-dislike first hinted at on 'Help!' Paul's most notable track, by contrast, seemed almost a brag about his sophisticated metropolitan life and smart new friends.

In fact, it owed much to a very old friend, Ivan Vaughan, who'd attended Liverpool Institute with Paul and introduced him to John at the Woolton parish church fete. 'Ivy' had gone on to read classics at University College, London, where he met his wife, Jan, a languages student. The couple now lived in Islington and often hung out with Paul and Jane, as they did with 'the nowhere man' down in Weybridge.

Jan Vaughan was a fluent French speaker and one day while she and Ivy were at Jane's house, Paul asked for her help on a song he was writing. 'He wanted a French girl's name and something that rhymed with it. I suggested "Michelle" and "ma belle". Then he wanted the French for "these are words that go together well", so I gave him *"sont des mots qui vont très bien ensemble"*.'

The previous September, Miles and John Dunbar had opened London's first bookshop cum art gallery dedicated to the visual and verbal avant-garde. When Marianne Faithfull declined to invest any of her pop earnings in her husband's project, Peter Asher provided the capital, lending Dunbar and Miles £600 each and putting in £600 himself, the three partners' surnames thereby giving birth to a company called MAD.

Premises were found in Mason's Yard, St James's, a tiny no-thoroughfare which happened already to be the location of the super-trendy Scotch of St James club. The ground-floor bookshop and basement gallery together were named Indica after one of the three types of marijuana plant.

Peter Asher's broad-minded family were as encouraging and supportive as always. For the Indica bookshop, his sister Jane contributed an old-fashioned money-drawer she'd played with as a child. As they'd already done for Paul, the Ashers introduced the MAD company to their own – and the Queen's – bankers, Coutts, where one's chequebook was brought on a silver tray by a uniformed footman.

No one worked so hard or so selflessly in converting and redecorating the Indica building as Paul. Drawing on DIY skills even his closest London friends had never suspected, he spent hours hammering, sawing, drilling and slapping on the 'green gunk' primer for the art gallery's de rigueur all-over white. He also made his pristine Aston Martin available for rough jobs like transporting the wood for the bookshop's shelves.

To the Beatles' press officer, Derek Taylor, he'd previously seemed the ultimate Swinging Sixties dandy 'who always knew how the crease at the back of his trousers was falling and how his jacket was hanging at the waist'. Taylor wasn't the only one to marvel at the ever-willing and cheerful navvy he became in the cause of helping out Jane's brother. One day, a female Japanese journalist arrived to interview Peter Asher, whose pop career with Peter and Gordon was still flourishing, helped by further songs from Paul under the Lennon–McCartney banner (and one under the pseudonym Bernard Webb). As the journalist sat with Peter in the unfinished gallery, she was amazed to see Paul in the distance, up a ladder, cigarette in mouth, knocking in a nail.

Other friends and acquaintances of Miles's and Dunbar's were also mobilised to help, among them an impecunious poet named Pete Brown, later to be the lyricist for supergroup Cream, and a Welshman known only as Taffy who claimed to be a bank-robbers' getaway driver. Taffy was given free use of the McCartney Aston Martin and would have run up a fortune in speeding fines had the police not waived prosecution on discovering who the car's owner was. Paul later learned that on a trip to collect Marianne Faithfull from Heathrow airport, it had been clocked at 128mph on the outward journey and 135mph on the return.

Early-arriving stock for the bookshop was stored in the Ashers' Wimpole Street basement, that space which had previously witnessed so many Margaret Asher recorder-lessons and Lennon–McCartney songwriting sessions. For Paul, this was like a private library: late at night, he'd come down from his attic bedsitting room and browse through the mint-fresh volumes, always scrupulously leaving a note of what he'd taken to be charged to his account.

A typical selection included *Peace Eye Poems* by Ed Sanders of the Fugs, Robert S. De Ropp's *Drugs and the Mind* and a biography of Alfred Jarry, the nineteenth-century French dramatist who wrote the first-ever surreal play, *Ubu Roi*, and conceived a philosophy 'beyond metaphysics' that he named pataphysics. Paul grasped Jarry's philosophy no better than anyone else (pataphysics having more than 100 different definitions, all equally long-winded and nebulous) but the adjective 'pataphysical' went into his mental word-bank, to turn up in a song-lyric, in a wildly different context, almost three years later.

Nor was his work for Indica solely manual; it also deployed the graphic flair that had no outlet when John was around. He helped put together the fliers that were circulated before the grand opening, and single-handedly designed the wrapping-paper for the bookshop. 'He worked on that for about two days, locked away in his room at Wimpole Street,' Miles remembers. 'We thought he must have a groupie in there.'

On the night of the opening, he roared up in his Aston with 2000 sheets of superfine paper he'd had made up in his design, showing Indica's name, address and telephone number in crosswise strips like one of the newly-modish Union flags. 'The care and thought he'd put in were amazing,' Miles says. 'He could easily just have given a rough design to a printer and had it typeset.'

The British press soon picked up on these un-Beatle-like new interests, giving him a foretaste of the incomprehension and mockery John was to attract for similar reasons much, much later. When Luciano Berio, the maestro of tape-manipulation, gave a rare performance in London, Paul turned up eagerly at the Italian Institute to see him. But the recital was ruined by press photographers with no interest whatsoever in the performer. This insult to Berio angered Paul in a way that little of his pop-star life ever could. 'All you do is destroy things,' he shouted at the jostling lenses. 'Why don't you create something?' The *Daily Mail*'s sarcastic headline next morning was 'THIS IS WHAT A BEATLE DOES IN THE EVENINGS'.

Not every outing with his avant-garde friends was quite so highbrow. One night, while sitting around with Miles and Dunbar, he read that Cliff Richard was currently appearing at the Talk of the Town, a garish new cabaret venue on the site of the old Hippodrome theatre in Charing Cross Road. Cliff had been Britain's nearest answer to Elvis back when the Quarrymen were still skiffling, but had since gone middle of the road as well as making a very public conversion to Christianity. 'Paul decided we had to go and see Cliff's show,' Miles recalls, 'so the three of us piled into his Aston and roared up to the West End. He just left the car outside the theatre, which he always seemed able to do anywhere without getting a ticket.

'As soon as the management saw who it was, we were ushered straight backstage to see Cliff. Outside his dressing-room, Paul was taking the piss out of the star that had been put on the door, like "Wow, look at that, lads! That's what it's *really* all about!" Cliff isn't a fool and knew we were only there as a piss-take, but he went along with it, and he and Paul got on very well. They ended up having a discussion about property.'

16

'It's a big one, 'cos I like big houses'

Just then, property was a subject much on Paul's mind. After almost three years as the Asher family's attic boarder, he'd finally decided to buy a home of his own, but the process was proving lengthy and troublesome.

This was because, at the outset, all he knew for certain was the kind he *didn't* want. He didn't want a modern bungalow with a psychedelic paint-job like George's, or a mock-Beverly Hills estate with a naff name ('Sunny Heights') like Ringo's, and especially not a faux Tudor mansion like the one where John lived, with wife Cynthia and three-year-old son Julian, in a growing fester of frustration and restlessness. In short, he didn't want anything picked out by Brian Epstein in Surrey's Stockbroker Belt, as the others' had been, with some quasi-paternal idea of keeping Brian's precious 'boys' all in one place and under his protective eye. What Paul had in mind was something altogether more complicated: peaceful and private yet still on the doorstep of Swinging London so he could keep what he called his 'antenna' constantly tuned to new developments in art and culture. And, most importantly, something not in any way identifiable with a nouveau riche pop star.

Since even this most particular, practical Beatle couldn't be expected to house-hunt for himself, Brian's personal assistant, Alistair Taylor, took on the job of poring over estate agents' catalogues and checking out promising entries. Taylor came up with a series of seemingly ideal properties, only to have them all rejected for what

Paul considered their showiness or vulgarity. 'He'd say, "This is the sort of place where Gerry Marsden [of Gerry and the Pacemakers] would live."'

The first to meet all his exacting criteria was in Chester Terrace, the longest of the John Nash facades bordering Regent's Park, whose illustrious tenants had ranged from H.G. Wells to Harold Pinter. However, the residents' association, led by theatrical impresario Jack Hylton, blackballed him on the grounds that screaming fans would create too much disturbance. (That Hylton had himself once been a popular dance-band leader, with his own clamorous fans, was conveniently forgotten.)

An ideal candidate then materialised in St John's Wood, a little to the north: the still verdant district where Victorian grandees used to hide away their mistresses. Number 7 Cavendish Avenue was on a quiet thoroughfare tucked away beside Lord's, the country's most prestigious and exclusive cricket ground. A substantial family home with a neoclassical portico, it stood back from the road, screened by a stout brick wall, and had a long rear garden ending in a grove of trees. Not only were the West End's theatres, galleries and clubs in easy reach but Abbey Road studios were just around the corner.

Paul bought the house, for £40,000, in April 1965 but, as it needed major refurbishment, didn't move in until March 1966. To compensate the Ashers for the wear and tear on 57 Wimpole Street by his fans, he had the exterior completely redecorated.

Other Beatle domiciles had received top-to-bottom makeovers by fashionable interior decorators, with little or no consultation of their owners. But for 7 Cavendish Avenue – henceforward known by him simply as 'Cavendish', just as 20 Forthlin Road was 'Forthlin' – Paul hired the relatively unknown husband-and-wife architectural team of John and Marina Adams. Marina was John Dunbar's older sister, and John Adams had designed Peter Asher's wood-panelled bedroom-cum-studio at Wimpole Street.

Paul's brief to the Adamses was the strangest they'd ever received, or ever would again; he said he wanted the kind of house where a smell of cabbage floated up from the basement. It clearly was his most elemental idea of comfort and security, deriving as much from the Asher household as from his old home in Allerton. He meant to spend only £5000 on the work – a mighty enough sum compared with redecorating 'Forthlin' with odds and ends of wallpaper and carpet all those years ago – but in the end paid £20,000.

Once installed, he gave a series of elaborate lunches and dinners to show off his new home to his fellow Beatles, Brian, George Martin, friends and relations. None was surprised to find it the same mixture of ultra-trendiness and ultra-tradition as Paul himself. Expensive finds from the Kensington and Chelsea antique-markets mingled with domestic fixtures to be found in humbler homes throughout the north. In the dining-room, an outsize clock, which had once hung outside the Army & Navy Stores in Victoria, loomed over a polished dining-table with an antique lace cloth. ('Very working-class posh', commented one metropolitan visitor.)

The living-room, where afternoon teas of home-made cakes and scones were served, had a coke-burning open fire with a brass coal-scuttle and coal-tongs in its grate. Outside, on the garden terrace, stood a human-size White Rabbit, Mad Hatter and other characters from *Alice in Wonderland*: a house-warming gift from his brother, Michael. To complement the pagoda-shaped red Victorian postbox that stood near the front gate, a wrought-iron street-lamp from the same era was installed in the front drive.

In fact, the house had no basement from which cosy cabbage-smells could waft to its upper storeys. But, as if in memory of 57 Wimpole Street, Paul's music room was in the former servants' quarters on the top floor, overlooking the front drive and the new black security gate – beyond which, from day one of his occupancy, a cluster of young women mounted guard around the clock.

All the very latest domestic technology was also there, including a colour television set and a prototype video-recorder, a gift from the BBC. In mid-Sixties Britain, electronic gadgetry still belonged to the realm of James Bond and in real life tended to be chronically unreliable. So it proved with many of the 007-style marvels Paul showed off to visitors. His bedroom curtains were supposed to open and close by remote control but seldom did, while his automated home cinema screen jammed so often it was quicker to unroll it laboriously by hand. His expensive stereo system continually broke down and knobs always seemed to be dropping off his professional Brenell tape-decks.

To complete the family atmosphere of his bachelor domain, he acquired four cats: one named Thisbe – after the character in Shakespeare's *A Midsummer Night's Dream* – the others, Jesus, Mary and Joseph. Fortunately, this mild bit of sacrilege never reached the Beatles' American public; otherwise he might have felt some of the godly wrath John was soon to suffer.

He also acquired an Old English shaggy dog puppy named Martha. The breed had become a minor style icon thanks to the perfectly-groomed specimen featured in glossy advertisements for Dulux paints in the chic Sunday newspaper colour supplements. Consciously or not, Martha was a further backward nod to the Peter Pan world of 57 Wimpole Street: in Barrie's story, when the Darling children fly with Peter to Neverland, their shaggydog-cum-nursemaid, Nana, goes with them.

Paul claimed he'd wanted a dog throughout his childhood but had been denied one because his family's house was too small (though plenty were always to be seen and heard in the police training school over the garden fence). When he introduced Martha to his ex-girlfriend Iris Caldwell, Iris was surprised by his devotion to the admittedly adorable puppy. She had no memory of him liking dogs; indeed, recalled his always being 'rather uncomfortable' around the Caldwells' boisterous family mutt, Toby.

In those same Sunday colour supplements one could read how, if traditional domestic servants might have no place in the egalitarian Sixties, wealthy young bachelors often employed a live-in married couple, usually Spanish, the husband combining the roles of butler and chauffeur, the wife cooking and keeping house. Paul started out at 7 Cavendish Avenue with just such a couple, albeit Irish rather than Spanish and with the reassuring Liverpool-echoey name of Kelly. When he hired them, he gave warning that his household would be anything but a conventional one, and defined their main role as just 'to fit in'.

He soon discovered the drawback in having domestic servants, as noted by writers like Harold Nicolson back in the Victorian country house era: there are always people standing around, eavesdropping on your conversations, obliging you to shut the toilet door (all the more irksome if you're fond of sitting there, playing guitar) and generally behave as if you're in an hotel rather than at home. Mr Kelly, evidently seeing himself as Jeeves to Paul's Bertie Wooster, would ceremonially lay out his young master's clothes for the day ahead until firmly dissuaded. Pop star pals who stayed overnight, and expected to be left comatose until after noon, would instead be briskly roused by Mr Kelly with early morning tea. On the big dining-room table, he placed a display of silverware whose highly-polished formality was too much even for Paul; to annoy them, he'd take out the ornate silver cruet and put a cheap plastic one in its place.

Cavendish saw the genesis of an art collection that was to be as eclectic as it was extensive. One of Indica gallery's first exhibitions was by the Greek sculptor Takis Vassilakis, whose angular metal shapes were embellished by flashing lights. Paul immediately bought a Takis, consisting of a long, spindly rod topped by a green light, and a matching, but shorter, rod topped by a red one. Seeing a resemblance to the singing duo that included Jane's diminutive, carrot-haired brother, he nicknamed it 'Peter and Gordon'.

At Indica's bookshop – where the wrapping-paper he'd designed was in daily use – he'd left a standing order that anything interesting which came in should automatically be sent to him, and also to the other Beatles in their suburban retreats. It wasn't long before John, that omnivorous reader, came up from Weybridge in his pot-fumed Rolls-Royce to check out the bookshop for himself. On his first visit, Miles steered him towards *The Psychedelic Experience*, Dr Timothy Leary's reworking of *The Tibetan Book of the Dead*, whose introduction commands 'When in doubt turn off your mind, relax and float downstream . . .' Waving away the McCartney wrapping-paper, John lay down on the couch in the centre of the shop and read the book from cover to cover.

Thereafter, he took to hanging out with John Dunbar, than whom few were better acquainted with the substance prescribed by Dr Leary for 'floating downstream'. Yet Paul still held out against trying LSD, the more so because Jane was vehemently against it. 'Socially speaking, Paul and I and the two Johns sort of went our separate ways,' Miles remembers. 'While they took acid together, we'd go with Jane and my wife, Sue, to interesting foreign films at the Academy cinema.'

But the greatest influence on Paul, as a connoisseur and collector, was the art dealer Robert Fraser, whom he met, fortuitously, at around the time of moving to Cavendish. Fraser was then London's foremost champion of the genre recently dubbed pop art, exhibiting Americans like Andy Warhol and Jim Dine, and Britons like Peter Blake, Richard Hamilton and Bridget Riley at his Duke Street gallery, despite an ever-present risk of police prosecution for 'indecency'.

Twenty-nine-year-old Fraser was himself a perfect picture of the Sixties' collapsing class and sexual barriers: the scion of an ancient Scottish clan, an old Etonian and former colonial army officer who dressed in immaculate brass-buttoned blazers, yet was openly gay, he revelled in the company of louche pop stars (he was already an intimate friend of the Rolling Stones) and took drugs on a scale of which even the louchest popstars didn't yet dream.

Paul would later call Robert Fraser the most important person he ever met after he became famous – even including Bob Dylan. It was from Fraser that he first learned of René Magritte, the Belgian surrealist who did not outrage but seduced the eye through images of bowler-hatted men with green apples for faces, and street-lamps shining among dark trees, with summer-blue sky overhead. Several Magrittes duly appeared at Cavendish, as did a work specially commissioned from Peter Blake. Paul had a sentimental weakness for 'The Monarch of the Glen', Sir Edwin Landseer's study of a

Scottish stag, expressing all the pride and bombast of the Victorian era, which had adorned many Liverpool parlour walls during his boyhood. Blake agreed (for who could tell Paul McCartney no?) to reproduce the monarch with an ironic pop art twist.

Fraser seemed to know everyone and his parties at his Duke Street flat always teemed with celebrities. At one, Paul met the Italian director Michelangelo Antonioni, who was currently shooting *Blow-Up*, the best film ever to be made about Swinging London, with David Hemmings and Vanessa Redgrave. Another night, Fraser visited Cavendish with Andy Warhol to give Paul a private showing of Warhol's new film, *Empire*. It proved to be a continuous shot of the Empire State building lasting eight hours, five minutes. Paul was bored to distraction but politely concealed the fact, helped by a good supply of mind-dulling pot.

Fraser's circle included several members of the aristocracy, who, Paul noted, were the greediest consumers of serious drugs, acid and even heroin, and the most insistent that he should try them, too: literal peer-pressure. Fraser himself was a heroin-addict and gave it its usual sell: how it didn't cloud the senses like pot, but sharpened them to a preternatural degree, and could be controlled if it were not injected but merely taken in tablet form or sniffed. Heroin was only a problem, he said, when one couldn't pay for it. In the end, Paul tried a sniff, but it did nothing for him and Fraser agreed never to offer it to him again.

When he finally gave in and took LSD, it was not with another Beatle but a young aristo, the Hon. Tara Browne. Tara's father was the Irish peer Lord Oranmore and Browne; his mother was Oonagh Guinness, heiress to the Guinness brewing fortune, whose family the British have always considered close to royal. To this most blessed member of Swinging London's elite Paul was 'the most intelligent man I've ever met'.

That first acid trip with Tara seems to have been an extremely mild one. Paul later remembered only that they took it in the toilet, sprinkled on some blotting-paper, and stayed up all night afterwards; that he felt 'quite spacey' and everything seemed 'more

sensitive'. Like the heroin-sniff, he regarded it as a one-off experiment and spoke little about it afterwards, although Iris Caldwell
now thinks she caught a reference during one of his conventional
trips back to Merseyside. 'He said, "I was combing my hair and
suddenly my mind went onto a different plane."' At the time, Iris
was baffled, though not as much as her mother, 'Violent Vi', who
once used to comb Paul's legs – and had always been famous for
getting the wrong end of the stick.

'What did he say?' queried Vi. 'He was combing his hair on a
plane?'

His main object in buying Cavendish was that he and Jane should
live together there. Even at this mid-point in the so-called 'permissive' era, few responsible British parents would have welcomed
such a move by their 20-year-old daughter. But Sir Richard and
Margaret Asher viewed Paul as a surrogate son who showed every
sign of turning into a son-in-law. He remained on close terms with
Margaret especially, regarding it as a huge compliment when she
used 'Yesterday' as an exercise for her recorder pupils. Among her
colleagues at the Guildhall School of Music, she had lately found
him a (male) piano-teacher, so that he could finally do as his father
had always urged and learn to play 'properly'.

In any case, so far as the unintrusive Sixties media were concerned, Paul occupied his impressive new property quite alone.
Soon after moving in, he gave an interview to BBC radio's Brian
Matthew in the soufflé-speak he had now perfected, seemingly
spontaneous and fulsome but actually revealing nothing. Jane
wasn't even mentioned.

MATTHEW: Right, let's get onto a, if we can, a kind of domestic
level, Paul. The other three boys, all being married, need or
choose to have large-ish houses. What about you for a pad.
What's your ideal? You've recently bought a house, haven't you?

PAUL: I've bought a house. Yeah, I love it. I love houses. I always

have. I always like going to visit people and seeing their houses
and things, because it's always the character of houses that gets
me. You go into a small house, and it's that kind of character
– it's still great. You go into a big house and it's completely
different and they are things on their own anyway. I like that.

MATTHEW: What sort of house have you bought?

PAUL: Um, a big one. 'Cos I like big houses. And it's an old one
because I like old houses.

MATTHEW: And it's in town, is it? Or near?

PAUL: It's near.

Jane seemed in every way his perfect partner with her Pre-
Raphaelite beauty, her natural poise, charm and lack of actressy
airs and graces – in short, her total dissimilarity from all his fellow
Beatles' chosen consorts. Even the eternal female pickets on their
doorstep, once so vocally and even physically hostile to Jane, had
been won over by her unfailing niceness and tolerance. Many,
indeed, now copied her clothes and grew their hair to similar
shoulder-length, pressing it with a warm iron on an ironing-board
before setting out on another day or night of Paul-stalking.

She seemed equally at ease wherever life as a Beatle's girlfriend
took her. When they visited racehorse-trainer Wilfred Lyde to buy
Drake's Drum for Jim McCartney, she charmed the beefy racecourse
types they met (not least by, at one point, innocently wandering
into the jockeys' changing-room). They stayed overnight with Lyde
and his wife, who later remembered them as the most gracious and
unassuming of guests. Not until after their departure did Beatlemania break out, the Lydes' domestic staff rushing into their room
and cutting their bedclothes into souvenir strips.

Jane also brought out a serious side of Paul, until now suppressed
by his Beatle duty to be chirpily non-committal on all subjects. It's
generally forgotten that throughout those so-envied Sixties, Western Europe lived under permanent threat of mutually-annihilating

nuclear war with Soviet Russia. America's 'anti-communist' war in Vietnam was also increasingly inflaming Britain's young people, even though – unlike in American foreign invasions of the early twenty-first century – the British government firmly withheld any support.

Thus, well before any talk of gurus or spiritual guides among the other Beatles, Paul and Jane sought an audience with Bertrand Russell, Britain's greatest twentieth-century philosopher and a founder of the Campaign for Nuclear Disarmament. The nonagenarian Russell listened to their concerns, then delivered advice of great wisdom: they should enjoy every minute to the full for as long as they could.

Their domestic life at Cavendish, amid the Magrittes and James Bond gadgets and 'working-class posh', was unpretentious in the extreme. Jane was an excellent cook and, in that pre-feminist era, accepted her role was to prepare meals and otherwise care for the man of the house. Several years before Paul's much-publicised renunciation of meat, the cuisine was largely if not entirely vegetarian.

She was likewise a gracious hostess when his relations came down from Merseyside to stay. A special red carpet was always rolled out for his beloved Auntie Gin, the matriarch of the McCartney clan. When Gin's visit coincided with the annual tennis championships at Wimbledon, Paul paid a small fortune to get her prime seats on Centre Court. But she preferred to stay home and watch the matches on his miraculous colour TV.

Jim McCartney was a frequent visitor, with his new wife Angie and his newly-adopted small daughter Ruth. Jane was especially kind and attentive to Ruth, teaching her to cook, sew and crochet. 'The two of them were always taking me on outings, like to Hamleys toyshop,' Ruth says. 'However relieved they may have been when it came time to give me back to my mum, they never showed it.'

Despite Jim's enormous pride in his son's new home, Ruth recalls, he could seem a little out of his depth there. 'One Christmas when we were visiting, Jane had commissioned family trees for Paul and herself. The Ashers dated back to the reign of King James, but the McCartneys only did to some late nineteenth century, dirt-poor farmer in Ireland.'

Jane was no Stepford wife, however, and there could be tensions when her independent-mindedness and plain-spokenness ran up against the reality of who her boyfriend really was. Modest and unaffected though Paul might seem, he was an enormous star, courted by the whole world and with a manager and support team dedicated to gratifying his every whim. Even at home, he generally had someone on standby to take care of whatever came into his head – one of the Beatles' two roadies, Neil Aspinall or Mal Evans, or Tony Bramwell from the NEMS office. And when-ever the sacred four congregated, to rehearse or record, the same northern-chauvinist rule applied as ever: 'No birds'.

At Wimpole Street, he and Jane had kept their social lives mainly separate. At Cavendish, she naturally wanted to entertain her thea-tre friends, and the mix of luvvies and rockers could sometimes be awkward. One evening when she had some fellow actors to dinner, Paul arrived home with John, who – whether the result of drink or pot or just plain Lennonness – was at his most maliciously provoc-ative. When one of the actresses at the table nervously requested an ashtray, he knelt beside her and facetiously offered one of his nostrils for the purpose. Jane, with her usual sangfroid, simply ex-tended a foot and pushed him over.

At the end of 1965, Jane had become a lead player in the Bristol Old Vic theatre company, which took her away for weeks, some-times months at a time. With her safely 200 miles away in the West Country, and no paparazzi yet to worry about, Paul could revert to being a singleton. While he sat in clubs, beautiful young women on the dance-floor would turn away from their partners and start miming a strip-tease just for him. His sexual antenna as keen as his cultural one, he could always tell in advance which one it would be.

The coast was also clear for pot-smoking, which usually happened in his top-floor music room, to keep the fumes away from Mr and Mrs Kelly. It was there that he claimed to have turned on Mick Jagger for the very first time. Nice to think of pop's foremost good boy sending its foremost bad boy thus off the rails.

In August 1966, at Candlestick Park, San Francisco, the Beatles gave their last-ever live concert from a conventional stage to a conventional audience. The four had been on the major league concert-circuit for only three years: an amazingly brief time compared with the Rolling Stones, who would still be performing as septuagenarians. But the wonder of it was that they hadn't quit long before then.

The breaking-point was a summer-long Far East and American tour which revealed how drastically the world had changed in those three years – and also how pitifully inadequate was the protection they took with them on the road. In Tokyo, they received death threats from Japanese nationalists who objected to the martial arts-sanctified Budokan Hall being used for a pop concert. In the Philippines, they were roughed up by police and airport staff after unwittingly 'insulting' the president, Ferdinand Marcos, by missing a photo-op with his narcissistic first lady, Imelda.

Then, in August, came the American tour whose advance publicity was the so-called 'butcher' album cover and John's observation that Christianity was fated to 'vanish' and the Beatles were 'probably more popular than Jesus now'.

The butcher cover enclosed a for-America-only compilation, *The Beatles – Yesterday and Today*, and showed the foursome looking like soulful art students no longer, but wearing white overalls and playing with bloody joints of meat, strings of raw sausages and dismembered plastic dolls (actually not such a far-fetched image, since George had once been a butcher's delivery boy and the Quarrymen had performed at an abattoir).

Their American label, Capitol, at first saw nothing amiss with this alleged 'pop art experiment'; only when people started gagging over the first store-deliveries were 75,000 copies hastily recalled for another picture to be pasted over them. Paul had favoured the drastic image-change as much as the others – even if it was linked to the most beguiling of his songs – and resented the censorship as much as they did.

John's 'more popular than Jesus' comment threatened to cause an actual bloodbath. It had, in fact, been made months earlier, in the London *Evening Standard,* without creating much comment, let alone controversy. Reprinted now in the American teen magazine *Datebook,* it caused outrage throughout the South's Bible Belt. Where Beatles shows had once provoked harmless rapture, they now provoked denunciatory sermons, boycotts, bonfires of their records and promises of vengeance by the Christian fundamentalist and racist Ku Klux Klan. In a moment of horrible prophecy, John said that they might as well pin a target on him there and then.

Long before this, playing live had become a joyless and sterile business. Thanks to the unceasing, mindless screams that assailed them on every continent, they hadn't been able to hear themselves onstage since late 1963. They could hit wrong notes, forget the simplest words (as even Paul did in 'A Hard Day's Night') and nobody would notice. At their historic Shea Stadium show, they'd been so out of tune and out of time that they later had to re-record or overdub the songs for its film documentary. A band that used to keep going all night in Hamburg was now onstage barely 15 minutes, and tried to reduce even that by galloping through the six or seven songs on the playlist.

The millions who so envied their collective public life little dreamed what it was really like on the inside. John would later sum it up as 'madness from morning to night with not one moment's peace . . . living with each other in a room for four years . . . being kicked, beaten up, walked into walls, pushed . . .'

Modern rock star egos may rival the nastier Roman emperors', but being a Beatle under Brian Epstein's aegis above all meant staying smiley and co-operative in the face of no matter what monstrous demand, discomfort or even danger. It meant uncomplainingly huddling on the back of a flatbed truck in the teeth of a Hong Kong monsoon, or preparing for a Barcelona show in a matadors' infirmary, complete with mortuary slabs. It meant being nice to endless relays of boring, bombastic local dignitaries, officious police chiefs and dumbstruck dumb-cluck journalists. It meant the front row of every arena consisting of children in wheelchairs, who would afterwards be brought backstage to touch them, as if the Liverpool lads had become endowed with the healing-power of Lourdes.

Both John and George had long since wearied of all this, but Paul seemed to thrive on it. When they were trapped in hotels by shrieking crowds, he often donned a disguise, including a false beard or moustache, slipped through the police-cordons and walked around, observing the craziness with the dispassion of some benign anthropologist. And whatever his private feelings, that look of angelic amiability never left his face. The band's press officer, Derek Taylor, remembered him looking through an air-craft window at some girls who'd invaded the tarmac, smiling and waving while simultaneously muttering 'Get them out of here' through lips as rigid as a ventriloquist's.

He hadn't lost his appetite for performing as the others had – nor would he ever. But he, too, accepted that the live shows had become intolerable and agreed that the recording studio offered infinitely more possibilities. As Lennon and McCartney's song-writing had grown more ambitious, so their producer, George Martin, had given them increasing freedom at Abbey Road, the former control-room autocrat using all his classical music training to put John's or Paul's Midas-touch whims into practice. Much of *Rubber Soul* therefore consisted of tracks impossible for them to play onstage in their usual guitar-bass-drums format.

Since then, their acolytes-turned-challengers across the Atlantic had given fresh impetus to their ambition in the studio. After hearing *Rubber Soul*, the Beach Boys held a spontaneous prayer-meeting to ask the Almighty's help in making an album even half as good. And the Almighty had facilitated the creation of *Pet Sounds*, on which the cool, blowsy harmonic genius of Brian Wilson reached its apotheosis.

The Beatles' riposte to *Pet Sounds* was their *Revolver* album, released in the summer of 1966, between their on-the-road ordeals in the Far East and America. Swinging London in full swing, England footballers victorious in the World Cup and unbroken glorious sunshine together produced a national mood of euphoria and self-congratulation. And, although there was a superabundance of great pop around (the Beach Boys' 'God Only Knows', the Kinks' 'Sunny Afternoon', the Lovin' Spoonful's 'Summer in the City', the Mamas and Papas' 'Monday Monday'), *Revolver*, above all, provided the soundtrack.

It was hailed, without undue surprise, as the Beatles' biggest creative leap forward to date. But even more notable was Paul's personal creative leap within it. His 'Good Day Sunshine' and 'Got To Get You Into My Life' both perfectly caught the moment: slick, soul-influenced anthems for the newly-popular discotheques, soaked in the atmosphere of London in that mythic season, its hot pavements, its wasp-striped minidresses, the mace-shaped, shimmering Post Office Tower symbolising how life for its young seemed to grow measurably better every day.

'Yellow Submarine', on the other hand, came out of nowhere; like 'Yesterday', Paul had thought of it in the zone between sleeping and waking when his mind took trips that needed no acid. Ostensibly a children's song, to fill Ringo's one-vocal-per-album quota, it was recorded like a latter-day *Goon Show*, with zany voices and maritime sound-effects like hooters, whistles and bells. At the end, the Beatles put down their instruments, took off their headphones and danced the conga, led by roadie Mal Evans banging a bass drum. So the studio could be more fun that the stage had ever been.

Paul's spectacular *Revolver* songs were not prompted by bursting confidence, as was generally assumed, but by the insecurity from which no one ever imagined he could suffer.

As he so often did, he'd been wondering what would happen when he reached the inconceivable age of 30; by which time the whole Beatles thing would presumably be over and all he'd have left would be songwriting. Picturing himself in middle-age, smoking a pipe and wearing a leather-elbowed tweed jacket – exactly like his father still did – he set himself to write the 'mature' kind of song he'd need to then if he didn't want to starve. And 'Eleanor Rigby' was the result.

Where inspiration strikes can be as interesting as why F. Scott Fitzgerald wrote much of his New York Jazz-age fable *The Great Gatsby* on the French Riviera, and James Joyce some of *Dubliners* while a hard-up language-teacher in Italy. So now a 24-year-old pop star in his St John's Wood mansion, in between nightclubbing and parties, imagined a lonely old woman, picking up rice from a church-floor after a wedding, and a threadbare priest as the only mourner at her funeral.

The name Eleanor Rigby was carved on a gravestone in the churchyard of St Peter's, Woolton, where Paul had first met John and where they'd often hung out as Quarrymen. But Paul has always been adamant that was never consciously in his mind. Originally he meant to call his melancholy church-sweeper Daisy Hawkins, and for a time sang the nonsense syllables 'Ola Na Tungee' when demo-ing the melody, like 'scrambled eggs' with 'Yesterday'. By his account, the Eleanor came from Eleanor Bron, the British comedy actress who'd appeared in *Help!* and with whom John had become infatuated. Then, on a visit to Bristol to see Jane in a play at the Old Vic, he'd passed the shop-front of a wine-importers named Rigby & Evans.

Personal to him though the vision was – suffused with the Irishness of his ancestors and the Catholicism into which he'd been born, although never practised – it evolved with traditional Beatle togetherness. Only the first verse was written in confessional solitude: the remainder took shape at John's house in Weybridge, with input from him, George, Ringo and even John's old school crony Pete Shotton. Paul had planned to call the melancholy priest Father

McCartney but, at Shotton's suggestion, substituted 'McKenzie' lest it be seen as a portrait of his dad, pathetically 'darning his socks in the night when there's nobody there' – a line supplied by Ringo. From George came the 'all the lonely people' refrain, which broadened the Joycean short story into a lament for the elderly and neglected everywhere.

At different stages, Paul tried it out on Donovan (who later remembered lyrics completely different from the final ones), on William S. Burroughs (who praised their conciseness, far from *Naked Lunch* though they were) and on his piano-teacher from the Guildhall School (who was indifferent).

For the recording session at Abbey Road, he requested the same classical string backing as on 'Yesterday', but this time asked that George Martin's score be in the more dramatic style of Vivaldi, to whose *Four Seasons* Jane had recently introduced him. As with 'Yesterday', none of the other Beatles contributed instrumentally, though John and George supplied backing vocals. The automatic Lennon–McCartney credit had more justification in this case: John later claimed to have written 'at least half' the lyric while always conceding the song to be 'Paul's baby'.

The single, issued a day ahead of *Revolver* (its quality making the old distinction of 'A' and 'B' sides irrelevant), paired 'Eleanor Rigby' with 'Yellow Submarine'. Though 'Eleanor Rigby' was much ad-mired – and almost all the album's tracks seemed like hit singles – it was 'Yellow Submarine' which caught the national zeitgeist on several levels, its intended appeal to children least among them. In the growing drug culture, its title was taken to be a sly reference to yellow barbiturates known as 'submarines' because they had to be dissolved in water (a charge its composers would always firmly deny). In the growing industrial strife that underlay Britain's Car-naby colours, marching strikers amended its chorus to 'We all live on bread and margarine'.

But the track that most excited critics was the final one on side two, John's 'Tomorrow Never Knows'. A bizarrely un-Beatle pro-duction it seemed, with its somnambulistic, one-dimensional beat, its squibbling, cawing background (created by multiple tape-loops) as John's voice, minus its usual sweet McCartney undertow – more like some religious chant or dirge – paraphrased Timothy Leary's precis of *The Tibetan Book of the Dead*: 'Turn off your mind, relax and float downstream . . .'

How typical of iconoclast John, they all said, and what a world away from Paul's homeliness and tunefulness. No one guessed who'd first turned him on to tape-loops and kept on at him to read *The Psychedelic Experience*.

17

'You might almost have said an alien had landed on the Mull'

Bands who have spent far less time on the road than the Beatles, and suffered far less pressure, usually end up loathing the sight of one another. But when John, Paul, George and Ringo gave up touring, they were still as close as ever and looking forward to the next phase in their collective career.

Those nightmare farewell shows in Japan, the Philippines and America through the summer of 1966 only strengthened the bond between them. At various tetchy press conferences across the US – so different from their first arrival in New York; could it be only two years earlier? – even Paul forgot his usual soufflé-speak to complain of how John's comments about Jesus had been 'misinterpreted'. The four then took only a token two-month break from one another before reconvening at Abbey Road to record what would become *Sgt. Pepper's Lonely Hearts Club Band*. John used the time to make his solo screen-acting debut in Richard Lester's *How I Won the War*, George immersed himself in Indian music and religion while Ringo spent his first real quality time with his wife, Maureen, and their two small sons.

For Paul, it was a further opportunity to prepare for the 'leather-patched sports jacket' years after he'd turned 30, when he still believed the Beatles would be forgotten and the only career open to him would be as a jobbing songwriter. At the end of 1966, he agreed to score a new British film comedy, *The Family Way*, adapted from a stage play by Bill Naughton and co-starring father and daughter John and Hayley Mills. Teeming with daring Sixties sex-jokes and double entendres ('in the family way' is old English slang for pregnant) its plot unconsciously echoed Paul's own recent situation with Jane at 57 Wimpole Street: a young man found himself inhibited from making love to his 20-year-old bride because her parents were under the same roof.

In practice, the actual scoring was done by George Martin, as was the performing with a specially-mustered eponymous orchestra. All that was required from Paul was a theme – 'a sweet little fragment of a waltz tune', Martin called it – to be reprised in different forms throughout the film. Though later released both as an album and a single (and the recipient of a Novello award), his music for *The Family Way* fails to qualify as the first solo Beatle project because Martin was the credited performer.

Of all the Beatles in this immediate post-touring period, Paul was the one who made most effort to return to a reasonably normal life. A few weeks after the band's return from America, he set off on a solo trip through France in his Aston Martin, wearing his favourite disguise of costume wig and false moustache and with a ciné-camera in his luggage, having arranged to meet roadie Mal Evans (for the off-road Beatles still needed roadies) two weeks later in Bordeaux.

To begin with, he enjoyed the feeling of being 'a little lonely poet on the road with my car', stopping and filming anything that caught his eye with a view to some later documentary, unrecognised by even the most avid young French Beatles fans. The novelty began to pall when he went to a small-town discotheque in his disguise, and was refused entry. Returning there later, minus disguise, he realised that awed adulation wasn't so bad after all.

Well before the Beatles stopped touring, he'd felt the need of a hideaway more private than Cavendish or even the house in Cheshire he'd bought for his father. As powerful a consideration as intrusive fans was the taxman, so bitterly invoked by George, with help from John, on *Revolver*. Under Harold Wilson's Labour government, top earners paid income tax as high as 98 per cent. If Paul didn't wish to become a tax exile – which he emphatically didn't – one of the few ways to reduce his liabilities was to acquire yet further property.

This time, obeying the call of the 'Mac' in his name, he decided it should be in Scotland. Jane, that born-and-bred Londoner, was all for his acquiring somewhere they could spend time together, away from nosey photographers and fans, and set about researching suitable properties.

One quickly materialised in Kintyre in the remote western Highlands, a narrow peninsula whose south-westerly tip is a savagely beautiful headland known as a 'Mull'. Seemingly beyond range of the hardiest Beatlemaniac, it also had a peculiar appropriateness for someone of Paul's mixed Scots and Irish ancestry. Many of the earliest migrants from Ulster to Britain had settled in and around Kintyre; and on a clear day at the Mull, the coast of County Donegal in the Irish Republic was distinctly visible.

In the spring of 1966, Kintyre residents Mr and Mrs J.S. Brown decided to sell their High Park Farm, having run a small dairy herd there for the past 19 years. The farm was situated five miles from the peninsula's only substantial settlement, Campbeltown, and 14 from the Mull. The price, for the three-bedroom farmhouse, outbuildings and 183 acres, was £35,000.

The Browns had already shown two prospective buyers the property when the Campbeltown solicitor handling the sale told them Paul McCartney would be flying up from London by charter plane to view it. He duly arrived in the Campbeltown taxi, accompanied by Jane; farmer's wife Janet Brown took them round and before they left cooked them a meal of ham and eggs. Mrs Brown later commented, with true Highland terseness, that 'You couldn't meet nicer'.

On 23 June, Kintyre's weekly paper, the *Campbeltown Courier*, confirmed the rumour that a Beatle had bought High Park Farm and gave a detailed reconstruction of Paul's visit 'in sunglasses', with Jane in a 'pyjama' (i.e. trouser) suit. Next to the story was a picture of Janet Brown at her stove, holding the same frying pan she had used to cook their ham and eggs.

It was, so Paul told the *Courier*, 'the most peaceful spot I've ever come across in the world'. The farm stood on a slope down to a gentle valley, with spectacular views over both land and water. In the foreground was a small loch; further away, a fringe of white dunes marked Machrihanish Bay, one of many vast, deserted, empty beaches in the vicinity. Of the five miles separating the property from Campbeltown, two consisted of a rutted, boulder-strewn track impassable to all but the ruggedest vehicles. There was no sign of other human habitation on any side; the nearest, another small farm, was three-quarters of a mile away.

As usual in the Highlands, the remote past remained very much part of everyday life. Above High Park Farm stretched a massive upland named Ranachan Hill, containing the remnants of an Iron Age fort. Paul's domain encompassed the Puball Burn, a natural spring that had given mountain-fresh water for thousands of years, and a 'standing stone', a Pictish monument predating the Roman conquest of Britain. This, too, was shown in the *Campbeltown Courier*, under the headline 'Something Old . . . Something Very New'. 'The arrival of a Beatle,' the paper said, 'provides just about the biggest imaginable contrast of ancient and modern.'

That arrival was by no means universally welcomed. Kintyre people were staunchly traditional churchgoers and Sabbath-observers, protected from the outside world by their peninsula and deeply suspicious of strangers. Even fellow Highland Scots who attempted to join the tight-knit community were known as 'white settlers'. 'We had no Swinging Sixties here,' recalls Campbeltown taxi-driver Reggie McManus, who was to become familiar with the rock-strewn road to High Park Farm in years to come. 'And a lot of people thought we were going to be invaded by hippies with all their drug-taking and free love. You might almost have said an alien had landed on the Mull.'

Fears of rock stars getting high at High Park Farm and stoned figures slumped under the standing stone were soon assuaged. The Browns didn't move out until the following November and it was several months more before Paul returned with Jane to spend their first night on the property. Thereafter, they often came for weekends, sometimes with friends but more usually by themselves. 'Everyone realised he was just looking for a place to escape to, where he could be himself,' Reggie McManus says, 'and that he only wanted to be left alone.'

The farm, in fact, was somewhat dilapidated, but for Paul – for the present – that seemed part of its appeal. So none but the most essential structural repairs were made to the farmhouse, and no chic interior decorator was turned loose inside it. He bought most of the furniture second-hand in nearby Campbeltown and installed a new electric stove for Jane to cook their (mostly vegetarian) meals. The handyman who'd always hidden inside the Beatle now came to the fore. He built a couch out of old wooden potato-boxes, and when the roof leaked, as it often did, would always find a way to fix the hole.

While revelling in this back-to-Nature existence, he was still as keen as always to be in London with his 'antenna out'. And now there was more than ever to keep it vibrating.

By 1966, the capital was moving away from its facile 'Swinging' phase of boutiques and discotheques. The in-crowd wore Beatle-inspired boots, corduroys and fringes no longer, but the robes, mystic amulets and shoulder-length hair of American hippies, the heirs of California's once-arty, elitist beatnik community. Nor was it preoccupied solely with clothes and 'sounds', but embraced a whole array of causes, grievances, philosophies and ideologies which British youth en masse had never bothered much about before.

Now too large and diverse merely to be an in-crowd, it was becoming known instead as 'the underground', a term historically signifying heroic resistance against tyranny, now denoting a general insurrection by young people against all manifestations of authority or convention. Equally redolent was it of London's actual Underground, with its many intersecting branches: pop (now more widely called rock) music, art, design, left-wing politics, peace activism, Eastern mysticism, sexual permissiveness, anti-censorship, the first stirrings of feminism. Pervading them all, as strongly as the Tube's own gritty winds, were the feeling of a revolution (even if most if its propagators were the most comfortable of capitalists) and the scent of drugs.

If this above-ground underground had any central marshalling-yard, it was John Dunbar and Barry Miles's Indica gallery and bookshop. And their friend Paul – that supposedly mainstream and 'safe' Beatle – was among its most important supporters and benefactors.

Though not financially interested in Indica, he was full of ideas for extending its scope and influence. One was a 'sound magazine' in vinyl disc form containing all the most notable current performances in the capital, not only music but drama, readings and lectures, to be funded by EMI Records together with Brian Epstein's NEMS organisation. This took shape in his studio at Ringo's Montagu Square flat, where he'd also recorded the demos and most of the effects for 'Eleanor Rigby', often with the great William S. Burroughs as an interested spectator.

The born journalist in him recognised the need to chronicle the underground's multifarious activities and give it a sense of community. The first attempt at this was a newsletter, named the *Global Moon-edition Long-Hair Times*, compiled by Barry Miles and John 'Hoppy' Hopkins (whose implausible previous occupation had been atomic scientist). Paul contributed anonymously, setting a readers' competition under the alias of a supposed 'Polish New Wave film director Ian Iachimoe' (the sound of 'Paul McCartney' backwards).

Out of the *Global Moon-edition Long-Hair Times* came London's first underground newspaper, the *International Times*, co-edited by Miles and Hopkins, with substantial financial backing from Paul.

On its appearance in October 1966, threats of legal action from the august daily *Times* forced the abbreviation of its name to *IT* – a term then without any connection with computers. True to pop art's worship of Hollywood movie icons, its mascot was the original 'it girl', Clara Bow (though the image on its masthead actually was of another silent-screen goddess, Theda Bara).

The paper's launch party, billed as 'a Pop/Op/Costume/Masque/Fantasy/Blowout/Drag Ball' took place at the Roundhouse, an old machinery-shed in north London that was to become the underground's equivalent of the Royal Albert Hall. Two thousand people attended, including Italy's coolest film director Michelangelo Antonioni and Marianne Faithfull – the latter wearing a nun's habit which barely covered her posterior – and music was provided by a then unknown Pink Floyd. The event mixed glamour and squalor in a way reminiscent of Liverpool's Cavern: the two available toilets soon overflowed and duckboards had to be laid so the beautiful people could waft around without getting their feet wet. Barely anyone noticed the figure in flowing Bedouin robes that were Paul's chosen costume-cum-disguise.

As well as backing the paper, he donated a long interview with Miles in hopes of drumming up advertising from the music industry. The interview frankly admitted the two had 'shared a joint' while it was going on. Paul, certainly, was in more expansive mood than at any soufflé-speaking press conference, even venturing into the territory where John had so recently been crucified. 'Everyone having realised there isn't such a thing as God and there's no such thing as a soul and when you die, you die . . .'

His profile as a patron of the avant-garde was so high that when the Japanese performance artist Yoko Ono had arrived in London that summer, he had been one of her first ports of call. Coincidentally, Yoko and her then husband, American film-maker Tony Cox, were living in the same north London district as himself – in fact, just the other side of Lord's cricket ground.

Yoko's projects at the time included assembling a collection of modern music manuscripts to give to the great musical adventurer

John Cage as a fiftieth birthday present. Hearing that Paul was an admirer of Cage's, she approached him to donate one of his manuscripts, but he declined. (He didn't possess such a thing in any case, being unable to read or write music.)

In November, John Dunbar gave Yoko her first London exhibition, Unfinished Paintings and Objects, at Indica. Since her overtures to Paul had come to nothing, Dunbar mentioned the event to John, who frequently dropped by the gallery to turn on with him. Rather than wait for the official private view, John walked into Indica on the night before, while Yoko was still arranging her exhibits.

Giving up life on the road, with its need constantly to close ranks against the world's worst hysterics, hustlers and bores, did not mean the end of the Beatles' 'group mind'. Quite the opposite in fact.

During the first stages of recording a follow-up to *Revolver*, Paul went to see his father in Cheshire, taking along his friend the brewing heir Tara Browne. For Jim McCartney, it must have been a moment of special unreality. All Jim's life, Guinness had been something kept in a crate out in the pantry: now it was sitting in his front room.

During the visit, Paul hired a couple of mopeds on which he whimsically suggested he and his fellow boy millionaire should ride into Liverpool to visit his cousin Bett. En route, while pointing out the Wirral scenery to Tara, he lost concentration and fell off his machine, hitting the pavement with his face so hard that a tooth came through his top lip. When he reached Bett's, she called in a doctor friend, who stitched the wound there and then without anaesthetic.

The rough-and-ready surgery left a scar that was barely noticeable – witness the promotional film for the Beatles' 'Rain', made in May 1966, in which he appeared in close-up. But he was painfully sensitive about this first serious physical flaw since his early teenage weight-gain and to hide it decided to grow a moustache.

Facial hair was unusual among young Britons at that time, and moustaches had not been generally worn since the Great War except by ex-military men and secretaries of golf clubs. Paul made his more exotic than the usual horizontal slab by turning down its ends: he later claimed his model had been 'Sancho Panza', though he probably meant Pancho, the Mexican sidekick of the Cisco Kid whose adventures he used to watch on 1950s television. When he unveiled it to his fellow Beatles, the group mind immediately produced a group upper lip. By the beginning of 1967, John, George and Ringo also sported moustaches in the same Mexican, or Zapata, style.

Perhaps the most surprising new mood among British young people was a sudden wave of nostalgia for their childhood – or, rather, for the Victorian artefacts and iconography that had surrounded them, unnoticed, throughout the 1950s. Pop art, largely through the unusually-bearded Peter Blake, fanned the craze for faded sepia photographs, tasselled lamps, button-back chaise-longues and enamel signs for Bovril, R. White's lemonade or Mazawattee Tea.

John and Paul had both independently picked up on this during the Beatles' brief furlough. When they returned to Abbey Road for the follow-up to *Revolver*, each had written a song which evoked his boyhood in the most abidingly Victorian of British cities. John's was 'Strawberry Fields Forever', commemorating an old Salvation Army orphanage near his Woolton home in whose grounds he and his lawless followers used to trespass. And Paul's was 'Penny Lane'.

Strictly speaking, this was predominantly Lennon territory. The winding lane on the fringe of Allerton and the modest district round about had numerous intimate family associations for John: his father, Freddy, had attended the nearby Bluecoat School while he himself had lived in Newcastle Road, a couple of turnings off the lane, until the age of five and later been sent to Dovedale primary school, which was even closer. His mother, Julia, once worked in a Penny Lane café and Julia's common-law husband, John Dykins – in a horrible reprise of her fate – was fatally injured in a car crash in the lane and died in the same hospital she had, Sefton General.

For Paul, Penny Lane was merely somewhere he'd passed through innumerable times at the Smithdown Place end, where it widened into a small shopping 'parade' and a confluence of bus-routes. Yet his memory was as clear as John's in 'Strawberry Fields' was fuzzy: in effect, a view from the top deck of a 1950s green Liverpool Corporation bus, possibly with George's dad at the wheel, while waiting for the conductor to ring the bell for departure.

There, in photographic detail, was Bioletti the barber, his front window displaying photographs of customers smirking proudly beneath outlaw Teddy boy coiffures. There was the traffic round-about with the shelter where the composer would sit on summer afternoons swapping cigarette-cards and marbles with school-mates, or on freezing winter nights with compliant girls. There, in the one direct autobiographical touch, was a glimpse of his mother Mary, the 'pretty nurse . . . selling poppies from a tray'.

Even on these most individual of their solo compositions, Lennon and McCartney remained a team, working on the final drafts together and helping each other unstintingly in the studio. Paul played the Mellotron intro to 'Strawberry Fields Forever', sounding like a creaky old harmonium in some dusty church hall of their boyhood. John donated lines to 'Penny Lane' – such as 'four of fish and finger pies', conflating fish-and-chip shop slang and smutty things they used to do with girls in the Smithdown Place bus-shelter.

The recording sessions illustrated not only what creative carte blanche the pair now enjoyed at Abbey Road, but also their very different ways of exercising it. Indolent as always, John left the orchestration of 'Strawberry Fields' to George Martin and was so indecisive about its two alternative versions that in the end Martin used both, making the first segue into the second. But Paul was always definite that 'Penny Lane' must have a 'clean' sound to match its clarity of recollection.

His growing interest in classical music, nurtured by Martin as well as by Margaret and Jane Asher, proved crucial in achieving that. In its original version, the track had a rather subdued instrumental passage of trumpet and woodwind that he never quite liked. Then on television he happened to see a performance of Bach's Brandenburg Concerto No. 2 featuring piccolo trumpet, an instrument half the size of a normal trumpet and pitched an octave higher. When he requested (which by now meant commanded) a piccolo trumpet for 'Penny Lane', Martin booked David Mason, the player he'd seen on television.

The arrangement scored by Martin – which would so perfectly conjure up those breezy, gritty 'blue suburban skies' – proved a severe test of Mason's virtuosity. 'Paul had no idea how damned difficult it was to play,' Martin recalled. 'David had to lip every note [i.e. control the pitch with only his lips and breath]. Paul's attitude was rather the same as to a plumber or electrician: "He's a piccolo-trumpeter . . . that's his job."'

Labouring over 'Strawberry Fields' and 'Penny Lane' for so long, the Beatles had missed the deadline for the second album they were contracted to deliver in 1966, and by the New Year it was still nowhere near completion. To appease their ravenous public, Martin put out the two tracks as a double A-sided single on 17 February.

The weight of brilliance and innovation packed onto one small 45 rpm disc had never been surpassed and probably never will be. Yet despite Lennon and McCartney's galvanic effect on Britain's pop musical taste, a large public still enjoyed the same easy-listening ballads it had back in the 1950s: 'Penny Lane'/'Strawberry Fields' was denied the number one slot in the UK by Engelbert Humperdinck's 'Release Me'.

18

Return of the Jim Mac Jazz Band

In any case, the album was no longer about Liverpool and childhood. The previous November, in another reconnecting-with-the-real-world exercise, Paul had gone on a safari holiday in Kenya, accompanied only by Mal Evans. During the flight home, he'd been thinking as always of the Beatles' American competition, especially the new West Coast psychedelic bands with ironically fanciful names – Jefferson Airplane, Quicksilver Messenger Service, Big Brother and the Holding Company – that were being embraced delightedly by the same people who'd once scoffed at 'Beatles'.

To while away the inflight hours, he thought up an imaginary addition to the genre, Sergeant Pepper's Lonely Hearts Club Band – a nod to the current fad for Victorian red military tunics – and began to put a song together around it. When 'Strawberry Fields Forever' and 'Penny Lane' were removed from the album-in-progress, the now fully-written (and abbreviated) 'Sgt. Pepper's Lonely Hearts Club Band' was among the little raw material remaining.

It was Neil Aspinall, that most intelligent of roadies, who later claimed most convincingly to have had the brainwave. Why not make the Pepper band alter egos of the Beatles in their new uniform whiskers, and devote the whole album to its exploits? Weary as they were of playing John, Paul, George and Ringo, all four concurred with enthusiasm; from then on, Martin recalled, 'it was as if Pepper had a life of its own'.

The idea that a pop album could be more than a random collection of tracks, but have the same cohesion as a classical symphony, was not new, or not quite. The Beach Boys' *Pet Sounds* and the Beatles' own *Revolver* had possessed such compulsive all-through listenability as to make each appear more than the sum of its parts. The first so-called 'concept' album had already come from the world of American experimental rock: in June 1966, Frank Zappa and the (all male) Mothers of Invention had released *Freak Out!*, a biting satire on American politics and culture, constructed in what were not tracks so much as movements or chapters. 'This is *our Freak Out!*' Paul often said during the *Sgt. Pepper* sessions, though he also had *Pet Sounds* repeatedly played at Abbey Road to remind the others, and himself, how high they were aiming.

Sgt. Pepper's Lonely Hearts Club Band is regarded as the ultimate concept album, but actually wasn't one at all. After the recording of Paul's signature song and a reprise to end side two, neither he nor John made any attempt to take the Sergeant Pepper theme any further; as Ringo later recalled, 'we just went back to doing tracks'. Almost every one of those tracks would acquire a subtext, real or imaginary, more fascinating to millions than anything a faux-Victorian NCO and three subordinates might conceivably get up to.

In many ways, the album carried on the childhood and Liverpool theme with its circus and fairground sound effects, its pervading atmosphere of the traditional northern music hall that was in both its main creators' blood. Yet in other places, it was grown-up to an unprecedented, indeed perilous, degree. It was at once sunnily optimistic and harrowingly bleak, fantastical yet down-to-earth, instantly accessible yet teasingly mysterious. Its superabundance reflected a conscious wish on the Beatles' part to make amends to their fans for their abandonment of touring. Clamped between headphones in a recording studio, they managed to put on a live show more exciting, more *intimate*, than any since they'd left the Cavern.

Sgt. Pepper certainly was John Lennon's *Freak Out!* The songs

he brought to it – one his masterpiece, 'A Day in the Life', another a close runner-up, 'Lucy in the Sky with Diamonds' – were
drenched in the LSD he now consumed in industrial quantities;
with his chronic shortsightedness added, the result could be imagery to dazzle Dalí. There was also a power-surge by George as
a songwriter and performer following his study of Indian music
and religion, which added sitars, tablas, a whiff of joss and a very
un-Liverpudlian earnestness.

In contrast, Paul's contributions all had the same 'clean' sound
as 'Penny Lane' (at one point making use of that unlikeliest pop
effect, a rippling harp) and were as firmly rooted in the everyday.
'Fixing a Hole' was a direct reference to DIY at High Park Farm.
'Lovely Rita (Meter Maid)' commemorated a female parking attendant who'd broken with tradition by giving him a ticket and
whose first name turned out to be Meta. 'When I'm Sixty-Four'
finally made use of the little music-hall ditty he'd started before
ever meeting John: of all its deft little domestic touches, perhaps
the best were the names of his imagined grandchildren, 'Vera,
Chuck and Dave'.

The harp introduced 'She's Leaving Home', another McCartney
'short story' song, destined always to be unfairly overshadowed by
'Penny Lane' and 'Eleanor Rigby'. The problem of young female
runaways was currently in the news, thanks to Jeremy Sandford's
milestone TV drama *Cathy Come Home*, which Paul had watched
with Jane at Cavendish. He'd been equally moved by the story of a
real-life runaway, 17-year-old Melanie Coe, whose distraught father
told the *Daily Mail*, 'I can't imagine why she would do it. She had
everything here.' He was never more sensitive and empathetic than
in this portrait of another 'Cathy', stealing away at daybreak for a
clearly ill-advised elopement with 'a man from the motor trade',
and her parents' bewilderment on discovering 'our baby's gone'.

That sensitivity could be less evident in his dealings with people
in the real world. After his forays into avant-garde music, he now
tended to regard the classically-trained George Martin as somewhat old-fashioned in refusing to rank the likes of John Cage and

Luciano Berio alongside Mozart or Brahms. One evening when Martin and his wife, Judy, were having dinner at Cavendish, Paul insisted on playing him a whole album by the experimental saxophonist Albert Ayler and – when that failed to convert him – started an argument about what did and did not constitute 'real music', citing numerous other names of whom Martin had never heard, and did not want to. The slightly embarrassing situation was lightened by Jane's deft switching of the subject to Gilbert and Sullivan.

So now, when 'She's Leaving Home' was mapped out to Paul's satisfaction, he asked George Martin to be at Abbey Road the next day to score the arrangement he'd worked out in his head. Martin was already booked for a session with Cilla Black and offered an alternative slot but Paul couldn't wait, so hired another musical director, Mike Leander. Breaking a matchless producer/artiste partnership for a single track, and snubbing that most invaluable as well as courteous of producers, meant nothing when he had the bit between his teeth.

Later, John would bitterly criticise the direction Paul's songs began to take on *Sgt. Pepper*. But at the time, far from lodging any objection, he provided a supporting vocal that hugely enhanced their atmosphere, swelling the plaintive 'Bye-bye' in 'She's Leaving Home', blissfully complicit with every cosy bourgeois image in 'When I'm Sixty-Four', its 'cottage in the Isle of Wight', its gardening, infant-dandling, Sunday driving and fireside sweater-knitting. On 'Lovely Rita', his trance-like counterpoint became the nearest the album had to a leitmotif, reinforcing the impression that a concept really was being pursued and a continuous story told.

Nor would its stunning climax, 'A Day in the Life', have been fully realised without an infusion of McCartney mundanity. John's epic, self-disgusted self-portrait was lacking a middle eight, so Paul supplied it with an unused song-fragment from his bottom drawer, about oversleeping and running for a bus. That little interlude of energy and positivity, amid its monumental inertia and melancholy, proved the song's finishing touch of genius.

Despite the size of John's LSD habit, he never let it interfere with work at Abbey Road, not even on this 'acid album', as he'd taken to calling it. 'There was only one time when I ever saw him incapacitated,' George Martin recalled, 'and at the time, of course, I had no idea why. I just thought he was looking a bit peculiar and sent him up to the roof for a breath of fresh air. After that, I left Paul to look after him.'

To be sure, kindly, caring nurse Mary McCartney seemed reborn in her son that night. Paul took John back to Cavendish, stayed up all night with him and, to keep him company, took acid for the first time since sampling it with Tara Browne. Tara had since died tragically, crashing his Lotus Elan sports car at more than 100mph while apparently on an acid trip and finding a posthumous niche in 'A Day in the Life' as 'the lucky man . . . who blew his mind out in a car'.

Sgt. Pepper's Lonely Hearts Club Band took five months to make, as against the single day needed for the Beatles' first album, and cost a jaw-dropping £25,000 as against *Please Please Me*'s £400. They were having such a good time that they stretched it out still further with costly but pointless sonic flourishes indicative of how Paul's taste for experimental music had entered the group mind. Not content with the thunderous chord that ended side two, they spent eight hours creating a chorus of gibberish to go on the record's playout groove, the usually silent bit where the playing-needle lifted off. Their final demand of EMI's sound-effect archives, after circus crowds, fairground carousels, crowing roosters, alarm clocks and fox-hunts in full cry, was a note at 20,000 hertz frequency that would be audible only to dogs.

The concept was always clear, at least, for what would become the most famous album cover of all time. While recording was still going on, Paul made a series of pen-and-ink sketches of the Beatles in Victorian military uniforms, holding brass band instruments and standing in front of a wall covered with images of their collective cultural heroes. Himself he depicted with an E-flat bass tuba like the one played by his grandfather, Joseph McCartney, in the band at Cope's tobacco works.

To art direct the cover, he brought in his gallery-owner friend Robert Fraser – just then awaiting trial for heroin possession after being busted along with Mick Jagger and Keith Richards of the Rolling Stones. Fraser in turn engaged Peter Blake, to develop Paul's rough sketch. With his then wife, Jann Haworth, Blake in effect built a stage set with the Beatles as psychedelic bandsmen, holding brass band instruments and standing around a bass drum bearing their alter egos' name. Subtract the psychedelia and they could have been Jim McCartney's Jim Mac Jazz Band 30 years earlier.

The collage of pop art icons ranged from Bob Dylan and Marlon Brando to Karl Marx, Mahatma Gandhi, Laurel and Hardy, Aleister Crowley and W.C. Fields. They were largely chosen by Blake, who crossed out Paul's nomination of Brigitte Bardot, the dream of his and John's teenage wanking sessions, and substituted a waxwork of the British 'blonde bombshell' Diana Dors.

The collage terrified EMI's lawyers, who believed those among its members who were still alive would sue for unauthorised use of their likenesses. The company's chairman, Sir Joseph Lockwood, personally went round to Paul's house to urge that the collage be dropped. Paul protested that 'They'll love it', but to no avail: EMI insisted that permissions were obtained from as many as possible and that the Beatles undertook to pay the costs of any legal trouble. Sir Joseph also insisted Gandhi be removed, so as not to imperil sales in the Indian subcontinent.

Another innovation, one they would have cause to regret, was that Lennon and McCartney's lyrics would be printed in full on the back cover. EMI were initially reluctant, fearing it would cut across sales of the songs in sheet music form, still then an important market. They also jibbed at the further expense of giving away cardboard moustaches and sergeants' chevrons with every album, and wanted to increase profit margins by manufacturing the cover from the cheapest possible cardboard. In each case, it was Paul who went to the company bean-counters and persuaded them not to compromise the quality that had gone into *Sgt. Pepper* at every other level – an argument one cannot imagine anybody winning today.

In the run-up to the album's release, Jane was in America with the Bristol Old Vic company and Paul, reverting as usual to a bachelor life, had two male friends staying with him at Cavendish and sharing his nightly clubbing. One was a young furniture designer named Dudley Edwards who, having decorated Paul's piano with psychedelic thunderflashes, was now painting little figures all over the William Morris wallpaper in his dining-room. The other was Prince Stanislaus Klossowski de Rola, otherwise known as 'Stash', a son of the French painter Balthus, who'd lately been busted along with Rolling Stone Brian Jones and consequently couldn't find a hotel in London that would take him.

On 17 May, with Jane still away, Paul was at the Bag O'Nails club, that favourite pop-star hangout, with Dudley Edwards and Stash to watch a set by Georgie Fame and the Blue Flames. There he bumped into the Animals, who were showing London to a friend just in from New York, a 25-year-old freelance photographer named Linda Eastman.

By a strange coincidence, Linda's true family name was also that of the Beatles' manager. Her father, Lee Eastman, had been born Leopold Epstein but had reinvented himself during his ascent from poor Russian-Jewish immigrant in the Bronx to high-level Manhattan lawyer. Her mother, Louise, was one of the Lindners, a prominent Jewish family from Cleveland, Ohio, who owned an old-established women's clothes store in the city.

Linda, born in September 1941 – nine months before Paul – was the second of the couple's four children. Under matrilineal law, she, her older brother John, and sisters Laura and Louise automatically took their mother's religion. But for Leopold-turned-Lee, it was too redolent of childhood poverty and obscurity and, with Louise senior's acquiescence, he excluded all Jewish observances and customs from their home. The children thus grew up as typical New York WASPS (White Anglo-Saxon Protestants), a disguise assisted in Linda's case by a rangy build and long pale-blonde hair.

Lee had many clients from the entertainment and art worlds, among them bandleader Tommy Dorsey, songwriters Harold Arlen and Jack Lawrence and painters Willem de Kooning and Mark Rothko. In 1947, Lawrence composed a ballad entitled 'Linda', dedicated to his attorney's six-year-old daughter, which was sung by Buddy Clarke with the Ray Noble orchestra and became a national hit.

Linda enjoyed a privileged upbringing, divided between the large family home in Scarsdale, Westchester, a beach house in East Hampton, Long Island and, later, a spacious apartment on Manhattan's Fifth Avenue. But her relationship with the self-made, dynamic Lee – an alpha male before the term existed – was often difficult. 'I was always a dreamer who liked just looking out of windows,' she would recall. 'My teachers told my parents I'd be watching the butterflies instead of looking at my books.' She was passionate about animals, especially horses, and would always say she only ever came properly alive on horseback.

After graduating from Scarsdale High School, she met Joseph Melville See, always known as 'Mel', a Princeton graduate whose mixture of scholarliness, athleticism and Hemingway-esque good looks impressed even her hypercritical father. When See received an offer to do postgraduate work in geology and cultural anthropology at the University of Arizona in Tucson, his birthplace, Linda went with him to study art history at the same university.

In 1962, her mother Louise was aboard an American Airlines plane, bound for Los Angeles, that crashed into the sea shortly after take-off from Idlewild, later JFK, airport, killing all its 87 passengers and eight crew. The tragedy precipitated Linda's marriage to Mel See and in 1963 she gave birth to a daughter, Heather.

Arizona, with its wide-open spaces and opportunities for horse-riding, suited Linda perfectly, and its awesome scenery prompted her to enrol on a photography course at Tucson Art Center. There she had the good luck to meet Hazel Larsen Archer, a famous name in the largely male-dominated photography world of the 1940s and 1950s, now confined to a wheelchair but as vigorous and unorthodox as ever. Leisurely Linda was galvanised by Archer's advice to forget theory but simply 'borrow a camera, buy a roll of film and get out and take photographs'. Her earliest subjects were landscapes in the Walker Evans style, the Arizona prairies and mountains she had come to love.

Then some students from Britain's Royal Academy of Dramatic Art happened to pass through Tucson on a Shakespeare tour of the US and were entertained by the university's English faculty. Linda became friendly with several of the company and offered to do publicity head-shots of them for nothing. As a result, the first pictures she had published appeared some time later in the British actors' directory, *Spotlight*.

At that stage, she seemed content with her role as a wife and mother, known only by her husband's Christian and surname. She became locally celebrated for her prowess as a cook, though with no sign of the vegetarianism she would one day preach so fervently. In 1965, the cookery page of the *Arizona Daily Star* ran a picture of 'Mrs Joseph Melville See' preparing her favourite recipe, meat loaf with cucumber mousse ('3 pounds of meat loaf mix, veal, beef or pork . . .'), wearing a vaguely cowgirl-looking outfit and watched by two-year-old Heather.

Unfortunately, Mel See regarded himself as an explorer/adventurer in the Victorian tradition, at liberty to take field trips to faraway places whenever he chose while his cowgirlie wife stayed home, caring for their child and making meat loaf. One such trip involved Mel's spending almost a year in Africa. Linda refused to accompany him and when he returned, he found she'd taken Heather back to New York and begun divorce proceedings.

With a young child to support, and unwilling to exist on handouts from her family, she had to find a career in short order. Her choice was photojournalism, a profession then at its apotheosis in the pages of mass-circulation glossy magazines like *Life* and *Look*. Her father urged her to study photography 'properly' – just as, thousands of miles away at about the same time, Jim McCartney was giving Paul the same advice concerning the piano – but Linda was no more receptive than he. In truth, becoming a photographer no longer required the training and technical dexterity it once had. With one of the modern single-lens reflex cameras, a Japanese Pentax or Nikon, all you really had to do was line up the image in the viewfinder and press a button.

She found a tiny apartment on Manhattan's Upper East Side and a job with *Town and Country*, a staid publication mainly read by WASPs rich enough to own homes in both localities. Linda worked on the reception desk, opening mail and making coffee, and had no visible ambitions to become anything more. Among her colleagues, she was said to be a descendant of George Eastman, inventor of the Eastman-Kodak photographic process, and as such the heiress to millions. Though Linda may not herself have originated the myth, she never went out of her way to deny it.

Another cause of friction with her father was her dislike of the *Town and Country* social set and preference for rock music clubs in the downtown quarter that was still considered dangerous and disreputable. But in one respect, she was as conventional as Lee Eastman could wish. However rackety her New York life might seem, her daughter Heather was scrupulously well cared for and always had a nanny looking after her while Mama was out on the town.

One night in 1966 at a club called The Scene on West 46th Street, she met a young photographer named David Dalton who was there covering a record company junket. Dalton specialised in rock singers and bands, not merely popping off a few shots in usual paparazzi style but posing his subjects in unusual locations and hanging out with them as friends. He later remembered 'a tall girl with long blonde hair [who] began asking me a lot of questions. Did I do this for a living? How does one get into this? Is it hard to learn? . . . She was dressed in a striped long-sleeved T-shirt and an A-line skirt down to the knees . . . this in the very heart of the Sixties [among] mini-skirts . . . silver-foil sheaths . . . Op Art . . . She dressed with the studied bad taste elite WASPs aspired to. It was a bizarre cult of exclusive dowdiness.'

The next day, Dalton was booked to photograph the Animals – currently America's favourite Brit band after the Beatles – against the gritty backdrop of New York's shipping piers. He invited Linda to come along, thinking she'd be merely an awestruck spectator. Instead, the band paid far more attention to her than to him and she ended up doing an intimate one-to-one shoot with lead singer Eric Burdon.

Soon afterwards, the Rolling Stones came to town to publicise their latest album, *Aftermath*, under the direction of their new American manager, Allen Klein. After 14 Manhattan hotels had turned the Stones away, fearing sex-and-drug orgies, Klein billeted them aboard a yacht, the *Sea Panther*, moored in the Hudson River, and invited the nation's media to interview them during a short cruise.

Normally, a publication like *Town and Country* would never have made the *Sea Panther*'s guest-list. But the magazine had recently published a flattering cover picture of the Stones by David Bailey, so was *persona grata* with the Allen Klein organisation. During her daily mail-opening duty, Linda came upon the invitation, pocketed it and went to the reception, camera in hand, posing as *T&C*'s official photographer.

So many reporters turned up to talk to the Stones that there wasn't space for the yacht to carry photographers too. But Linda managed to talk her way on board, and so had the band all to herself for the whole cruise. As a rule notoriously disobliging at photocalls, they did whatever she asked, sprawling around in louche attitudes with wide-apart legs and thrusting crotches. Afterwards, the reporters on board besieged her for pictures to accompany their articles, and she got a spread of her own in *Datebook* – the same magazine whose reprinting of John Lennon's 'more popular than Jesus' remarks had poisoned the Beatles' final US tour.

Her mentor David Dalton (who hadn't been asked to the *Sea Panther* reception) caught up with her at the Stones' after-cruise party, for which celebrities like Andy Warhol, Tom Wolfe and Baby Jane Holzer had likewise clamoured for invitations. 'Mick's just asked me for my phone number,' Linda told him. 'What should I do?' It was, Dalton recalls, 'a purely rhetorical question'.

On the strength of her Rolling Stones exclusive, she quit her job at *Town and Country* and turned freelance. She herself admitted she was 'too lazy' to bother overmuch about composition or even learn to use a light meter. But she possessed a superabundance of the photographer's most essential skill, the ability to gain access. At photocalls for new-in-town bands or singers, she had only to kneel in front of the media pack with what David Dalton called her 'leonine gawkiness' and the most ungracious and unco-operative became hers to command.

She became house photographer for New York's main rock venue, the Fillmore East, swelling her portfolio with the Doors, the Mamas and Papas, Simon and Garfunkel, Cream and Frank Zappa. Her detractors – of whom there were many, and would be many, many more – regarded her as a rarified form of groupie. After Mick Jagger, she had brief affairs or one-night stands with several more of her subjects (something considered quite normal for male photographers), among them the Doors' legendary singer and satyr Jim Morrison and the Hollywood star Warren Beatty, at that time a sexual icon as potent as any in rock.

She attended Beatty's press conference with a female colleague named Blair Sabol, who later recalled its outcome with vitriolic disgruntlement: 'I remember how impressed I was with her come-on talents as she sat in front of him in a mini-skirt and her legs in full wide-angle split for at least six rolls of Ektachrome. Warren ended up ushering me out of his Delmonico suite within 30 minutes and kept Linda for two days.'

In hindsight, she seems more like a genuine free spirit, already emancipated in most of the ways that the nascent feminist movement had only just begun to demand. She was also a busy and successful professional whose work appeared across a range of prestigious magazines from *Life* to *Rolling Stone*. No one who knew her then could have dreamed she would one day become a spectacular symbol of monogamy and domesticity – and give up cooking meat loaf for ever.

Despite having covered the Beatles' 1966 American tour and knowing several friends of theirs, Linda had never met any of them before she arrived in London in May 1967. Nor was she on a specifically Beatle-related assignment. She had been commissioned to take the pictures for a book entitled *Rock and Other Four Letter Words*, to be written by the music journalist J. Marks, and the first name on her British hit-list was Steve Winwood of Traffic.

Her share of the publishers' advance was only $1000 and, to her father's horror, she'd used almost all of it for her return air-fare. But Lee Eastman would later have to admit no money was ever better spent.

She had reunited with her first-ever photographic conquest, the Animals, and was with them at the Bag O'Nails club when Paul walked in, accompanied by Dudley Edwards and Prince Stanislaus Klossowski de Rola. The leonine gawkiness seemed to be doing its usual stuff when he asked her to accompany his party to another club, the Speakeasy. Once there, however, he seemed more interested in a new single the deejay was playing, Procol Harum's 'A Whiter Shade of Pale', and debating what its enigmatic lyrics might mean. Later, as limos were dropping everyone off, Linda briefly saw the interior of Cavendish and, she would recall, was 'impressed by all the Magrittes on the walls'.

Although she was not in London in pursuit of Beatles, professionally speaking, it clearly made sense to show her portfolio to her almost-namesake Brian Epstein. Brian being otherwise engaged, she was seen by his assistant, Peter Brown, just then deep in arrangements for the release of *Sgt. Pepper's Lonely Hearts Club Band* on 1 June. The Beatles were to do just one photocall for a dozen hand-picked photographers at Brian's house in Chapel Street, Belgravia. Impressed by Linda's work and even more by her connections, Brown added her to the list.

She turned up with her usual 'exclusive dowdy' look – striped blazer, too-long skirt, blonde hair not over-scrupulously brushed. The other photographers were hardened Fleet Street and agency men, experienced pushers and elbowers, not to mention unregenerate misogynists. Yet Linda, as always, won special access, lining the Beatles up in front of a marble fireplace with a copy of the album, then getting John to shake Paul's hand with a simultaneous jokey thumbs-up sign. A rival took some shots of her photographing Paul on his own, kneeling in front of him as he lounged in an armchair, and in an intimate huddle by the fireplace, staring deep into his eyes.

Afterwards, she took the initiative, charming his top-secret home phone number out of someone and calling the next evening – a Friday. However, she found he'd gone off to spend the weekend with his father in Cheshire, leaving Prince Stanislaus Klossowski de Rola alone at Cavendish. 'Stash' invited her over nonetheless. At that stage, there was no question of her being Paul's girlfriend, so his temporary lodger did not feel out of order.

A couple of days later, she returned to New York without having seen him again, and there the matter seemed to end.

19

'An irresponsible idiot'

The stupendous success of the album he had conceived, and done most to bring to fruition, ought to have brought Paul some sense of security at last. Instead, it was to usher in an era of upheaval and uncertainty that would destabilise even his carefully measured career path and have a catastrophic effect on his relationship with John.

In Britain, *Sgt. Pepper* sold a quarter of a million copies in its first week and stayed at number one in the album charts for more than six months, including over the Christmas holiday; in America, it spent 15 weeks at the top of *Billboard*'s Hot Hundred. Over the following decades, it would sell 32 million, make repeated returns to the charts and be cited time and again in newspaper and magazine polls as the most influential album of all time.

The heyday of mass album sales, between the late 1960s and early 1980s, would see other artistes shift more units, more quickly. But none would ever catch the zeitgeist more perfectly than the Beatles' blend of nostalgia, mysticism and faux naivety, nor cast so instant a spell over all races, ages, classes and intellects. At one end of the spectrum, the great drama critic Kenneth Tynan called it 'a decisive moment in the history of Western Civilization'; at the other, small children jigged up and down to it, wearing the paper moustaches and sergeants' stripes given away with every record. Untold numbers of the Sixties' young would always remember exactly where and in what circumstances they first heard it and how, more than anything else in that lucky decade, it seemed to transfigure and transform their lives.

As every rave reviewer agreed, it put the Beatles far ahead of even their strongest competitors. And the very strongest of those had to agree. During Paul's pre-release trip to America, he'd paid a social call on Brian Wilson, the Beach Boys' harmonic genius, who was currently at work on a new album called *Smile*, promising an even greater challenge to Lennon and McCartney than *Pet Sounds*. When Paul played an advance pressing of 'She's Leaving Home' to Wilson and his wife, the couple both burst into tears. So dented was the fragile Beach Boy's self-belief that he abandoned work on *Smile* soon afterwards; its disconnected fragments stayed on the shelf until finally being edited together and released in 2004.

Similar admiration came from the Beatles' musical peers across the board. In June 1967, London's most talked-about live performer was Jimi Hendrix, a beautiful young black man dressed like a gipsy Mad Hatter, whose blend of guitar virtuosity and blatantly sexual showmanship left Britain's native rock talents gaping. Three days after the album's release, Hendrix appeared at the Saville theatre in Shaftesbury Avenue, a venue lately acquired by Brian Epstein and partly used for Sunday-night rock concerts. The three-man Jimi Hendrix Experience's set opened with an acid-rock version of the formerly cosy *Sgt. Pepper* theme-song. Paul watched the performance, afterwards calling it 'one of the great honours of my career'.

With the Beatles' usual uncanny timing, *Sgt. Pepper's Lonely Hearts Club Band* appeared just as the hippy culture that had been growing in Britain and America turned into a visible and vociferous mass movement. The so-called 'flower children' with their creed of universal love and peace might have been expected to loathe any evocation of trumpety Victorian NCOs. Yet by some strange alchemy, Lennon and McCartney's cheery vaudeville show became absorbed into the hippies' manifesto for social, spiritual and sexual revolution – would indeed become the very touchstone for what they were proprietorially (but over-optimistically) billing as 'the Summer of Love'.

Ironically, musicians who'd given up live performance because they couldn't stand the hysteria now found themselves unleashing hysteria which made old-fashioned Beatlemania seem rational by comparison. For in the eyes of their hippy devotees, the Beatles were no longer just a band but a four-headed deity whose every song was invested with the power of Holy Writ.

John and Paul had always liked burying private jokes in their lyrics: initially bits of schoolboy smut, then underhand references to drugs. But on *Sgt. Pepper*, these were underhand no longer. John's 'Lucy in the Sky with Diamonds', a song drenched in acid-trip visions, formed the acronym 'LSD' – though he protested it was the innocent title of a painting his son, Julian, had done at school. 'With a Little Help from My Friends', a roughly equal John–Paul collaboration, spoke of getting 'high' and seemed a direct allusion to pushing and to acid's community spirit. In 'A Day in the Life', the long, wheedling chorus of 'I'd love to turn you o-o-on' was barefaced mischief, also with Paul's connivance, resulting in the first-ever banning of a Beatles track by the BBC.

But there was more; much more. The unprecedented printing of the lyrics on the album cover allowed them to be endlessly pored over and, in their readers' over-stimulated or beclouded minds, to yield up more hidden meanings than the Dead Sea Scrolls.

'A Day in the Life' on its own became a verbal archaeological site, what with the man who 'blew his mind out in a car' (Paul's friend and first acid-partner, Tara Browne), the '4,000 [needle?] holes in Blackburn, Lancashire', the 'smoke' Paul had on the top deck of his bus and the 'dream' that resulted. The chaotic orchestral passages, conducted by Paul, which John wanted to be 'a sound like the end of the world', were said to represent an addict's first 'rush', when the drug hits the system.

The Paul-originated *Pepper* songs were generally free of suspect subtexts, but that didn't stop people finding them. In 'She's Leaving Home', the 'man from the motor trade' with whom the runaway elopes was – and still is – thought to be fellow Liverpudlian Terry Doran, who co-owned a car-dealership with Brian Epstein, though Paul has always insisted he's pure fiction 'like the sea captain in "Yellow Submarine"'. 'Fixing a Hole' was taken as a metaphor for injecting heroin rather than DIY on a farm in the Scottish Highlands.

The hunt for hidden signs and meanings even extended to the brief jabber of speeded-up talk that had been put on the album's playout groove as a nod to Paul's interest in experimental music. One day in Cavendish Avenue, he was accosted by two boys who informed him that if the electronic gabble was played in reverse, it seemed to be saying 'Fuck me like a superman'. He invited the pair into his house, checked out their story on his own copy of *Sgt. Pepper* and was forced to admit they were right, although neither he nor any of his bandmates had been aware of it.

In Britain and America, hippies were most visible en masse at open-air rock concerts, now known as festivals or happenings and larger than had ever been known before. Their sanctification of *Sgt. Pepper* led to the first of many attempts to get the Beatles to play live again. Between 16 and 18 June, a giant festival was held in Monterey, California, co-organised by their former press officer, Derek Taylor, whose Anglo-American, multiracial roster – including Jefferson Airplane, The Who, Janis Joplin, Otis Redding and Ravi Shankar – almost all performed for free.

John Phillips of the Mamas and Papas flew to London to ask Paul if the Beatles would headline the festival. Paul himself was not averse but knew John and George would never agree, so suggested that Phillips should ask Jimi Hendrix instead. The result was Hendrix's breakthrough from cult club act to international superstar.

Hippies might be preparing to celebrate the Summer of Love, but Britain's law-enforcement agencies had other ideas. For months, there had been growing national unease about the spread of drug-use among young people, seemingly with the open encouragement of their favourite music stars. The police had been yearning to take reprisals on such figures but had been held back by their inexperience in spotting the various drugs – and also the fact that LSD was too new to fall within the scope of the UK's antiquated anti-drug laws. But at the end of 1966, it had finally been made illegal, untying the law's hands at last.

The first strike was against the nation's most infamous musical miscreants, the Rolling Stones. In February 1967, Mick Jagger and Keith Richards had been busted together for minuscule drug offences – neither involving acid – at Richards' Sussex cottage, where they'd gone after watching the Beatles complete 'A Day in the Life' at Abbey Road. Also netted in the raid was Paul's art dealer friend Robert Fraser, who at the time had 24 heroin tablets in his officer-style blazer-pocket. Photographer Michael Cooper, who'd shot the *Sgt. Pepper* cover, was present, too, but escaped any charges.

Next in line was *International Times*, the underground newspaper Paul had helped to fund and launch. *IT* was permanently under official fire for its open advocacy of marijuana – to say nothing of homosexuality and nudity – and had already been raided once, after publishing an interview with the black American comedian Dick Gregory which included the quote 'I say "fuck white folks".' On 1 June, the day of *Sgt. Pepper*'s release, a member of *IT*'s editorial board, John 'Hoppy' Hopkins, was sentenced to nine months' imprisonment for possessing a tiny amount of pot. Fearing this might presage a further, fatal police onslaught, the editorial team turned to Paul, who promised that if such a thing should happen, he'd hire the very best lawyers to defend them.

Yet for all the Beatles' open espousal of the drug culture, it seemed inconceivable that any of them personally might be targeted. George Harrison, in fact, had been among Keith Richards' house-party with his wife, Pattie, but they had left just minutes prior to the raid. Legend has it that the police waited for George to get clear before they went in, though in reality his escape was pure luck.

In this open season on British pop's top echelon, Paul was as vulnerable as anyone else. He was a habitual pot-smoker, had started on cocaine (thanks to Robert Fraser) and, during Jane's long absence in America, had taken to dropping acid. Jane would later recall her dismay when she returned to Cavendish, some time after *Sgt. Pepper's* release. 'Paul had changed so much. He was on LSD, which I knew nothing about. The house had changed and was full of stuff I didn't know about . . .'

Yet he seemed utterly confident that being a Beatle gave him immunity from what lesser figures in the musical and counter-cultural world were now suffering. For instance, neither he nor John ever thought of backing away from the two busted Rolling Stones despite the risk of attracting police attention. While awaiting trial, Jagger and Richards composed a sneering riposte to the authorities entitled 'We Love You', for which Lennon and McCartney provided (uncredited) backing vocals. Also present at the session was America's greatest beat poet, Allen Ginsberg, a friend of Barry Miles and regular contributor to *International Times*. Ginsberg later recalled John and Paul singing together, 'looking like Botticelli Graces', while he conducted them through the control room glass 'with Shiva beads and a Tibetan oracle ring'.

Paul was a steadfast friend to Jagger throughout these pretrial months when he could have expected further surprise visits from the forces of law and order at any moment. The Chief Stone was often to be found at Cavendish, together with Marianne Faithfull, whom he had wooed away from Indica gallery's co-owner John Dunbar – and who'd greeted the police raiders at Keith's cottage wearing nothing but a fur rug. During these hazardous demonstrations of solidarity, Paul little suspected that the Stones' new album-in-progress, *Their Satanic Majesties Request*, would turn out to be a shameless imitation of *Sgt. Pepper*, both in content and packaging.

He was similarly supportive of Brian Jones, also awaiting trial after a separate bust, and a far less well-protected and more psychologically vulnerable character than Mick. To distract Brian from his problems, Paul invited him to join a Beatles session at Abbey Road for a track that eventually became 'You Know My Name (Look Up

the Number)'. And Prince Stanislaus Klossowski de Rola, who had
been busted along with Brian – in his case, on non-existent evidence – was given sanctuary at Cavendish for as long as he needed.
'If they want to bust you again,' Paul said, 'they'll have to bust me
as well.' Which told 'Stash' there was no safer house.

The eve of his twenty-fifth birthday brought proof of just how
invulnerable he felt. This usual master of polite evasion and soufflé-speak became the first Beatle – in fact, the first major pop star
– to publicly admit taking LSD. It came about in an odd reprise
of John's 'more popular than Jesus' episode. Comments originally
made to a minor British publication and causing little reaction were
repeated by a major American one, unleashing a firestorm.

Some time previously, Paul had given an interview to *Queen*, a
tiny-circulation glossy magazine mainly covering London high society. To his prospective audience of duchesses and debutantes, he
not only owned up to having tried acid – before it became illegal of
course – but rhapsodised about the 'mind-expanding' effect. 'After
I took it, it opened my eyes. We only use one-tenth of our brains.
Just think what we'd accomplish if we could tap that hidden part. It
would be a whole new world.'

Then on 17 June, America's mighty *Life* magazine ran a post-*Sgt.
Pepper* article, headlined 'The Way-Out Beatles', which recycled
the quotes. In Britain, the resultant outcry was almost as great as
'more popular than Jesus' had caused in America. The Beatles' best
ambassador and PR man now found himself branded 'an irresponsible idiot' by the *Daily Mail*. A Labour Home Office minister, Alice
Bacon, declared herself 'horrified' by Paul's views and compared
him unfavourably with Lulu, one of various goody-goody popsters
to have spoken against the drug culture. 'What sort of society are
we going to create,' the minister mused clairvoyantly, 'if everyone
wants to escape from reality into a dream world?'

Two days later, Paul gave an interview to Independent Television
News in his garden at Cavendish in which he admitting taking acid
'about four times'. The reporter asked whether he didn't feel some

responsibility for making drugs alluring to the Beatles' millions of young followers. Deciding attack to be the best form of defence, he replied that he'd never wanted to 'spread the word' about acid: that was being done by ITN itself, and all the other news organisations currently at his heels. 'You're spreading it now at this moment . . . This is going into every home in Britain and I'd rather it didn't . . . If you'll shut up about it, I will.'

None of the other Beatles was caught up in the furore – though Brian Epstein loyally stood beside Paul, admitting to five acid-trips and insisting they'd caused him no harm whatsoever. John, above all, might have been expected to be sympathetic, but instead felt aggrieved that the band's last and most reluctant convert to acid had made himself the spokesman for it. Living at close quarters on the road, the two had never annoyed each other half as much as they now would as demigods.

Nobody in or out of the media imagined Paul's tripping had ended when LSD was outlawed. Yet he still was not considered to be in the slightest danger of being busted. Nor was the controversy allowed to interfere with the ultimate use of the Beatles as an advertisement for Britain. On 25 June, they starred in the BBC's first-ever live television transmission via satellite, performing 'All You Need Is Love', the hippies' mantra salted with Lennon sarcasm, to an audience of some 400 million people across five continents.

Mick Jagger and Keith Richards joined the Beatles and other pop VIPs in the television studio for this literally universal dissemination of the Summer of Love. Two days later, they stood in the dock at Chichester Quarter Sessions to answer for their microscopic drug offences the previous February. After the most grotesque of show trials (which also managed to smear the unaccused Marianne Faithfull) both Stones were found guilty and briefly incarcerated, but released on appeal. Robert Fraser, who was tried for heroin possession by the same court, received six months' imprisonment with hard labour, serving his time in full.

The Jagger–Richards case gave new impetus to the lobby calling for the legalisation of marijuana as a harmless recreational drug which did not lead to more serious use. On 16 July, a huge 'legalise pot' rally in Hyde Park gave London its first sight of flower children en masse and passed off peacefully, despite the heavy-handed intervention of police still clad in helmets and short-sleeved shirts rather than riot gear. The principal speaker was Allen Ginsberg, wearing a red sateen shirt covered with psychedelic patterns. The shirt was a gift from Paul, who'd hand-drawn the patterns himself.

Leading figures in the arts and science also rallied to the cause in an open letter to *The Times* (whose unexpected support had been mainly responsible for getting Mick Jagger off the hook). Since the letter was also to be a manifesto which couldn't risk being censored or cut, it would have to take the form of a paid display advertisement. Paul agreed to pay the necessary £5000 and to get the other Beatles and Brian to sign it.

The letter duly appeared in *The Times* of 24 July, headed 'The law against marijuana is immoral in principle and unworkable in practice'. In addition to John Lennon MBE, Paul McCartney MBE, George Harrison MBE, Richard Starkey MBE and Brian Epstein, its 64 signatories included Britain's greatest living novelist Graham Greene, the foremost drama critic of his generation Kenneth Tynan, the photographer David Bailey, the broadcaster David Dimbleby, a psychologist, a pharmacologist, a Labour MP and one of the two men who had discovered DNA.

However questionable its case that the risk of cannabis-smokers becoming heroin-addicts 'was less than of drinkers becoming alcoholics', the letter and background campaign had one positive long-term effect. Although pot was never to be legalised, the savage penalties for possession – up to ten years' imprisonment or a £1000 fine – would, over time, be drastically reduced.

But in other countries, no such liberalisation took place – as Paul would one day discover to his cost.

On 24 August, the hippies' four-headed deity found their own spiritual guide in Maharishi Mahesh Yogi and became converts to Transcendental Meditation. Soon afterwards, EMI's chairman

Sir Joseph Lockwood attended a reception hosted by the Queen at Buckingham Palace. He found Her Majesty disinclined to the usual polite small talk. 'The Beatles are turning awfully *funny*, aren't they?' she said.

Not so funny, perhaps. Young men who had achieved every possible and impossible success and tasted every conceivable material luxury by their mid-twenties might well become jaded by their so-envied lives and feel a yearning for some higher fulfilment.

Actually, only two of the four were in this susceptible state. George was already deeply immersed in Indian religion and music – hence the latter's influence on *Sgt. Pepper* – while John was open to any relief from his chronic insecurity and self-hatred. Paul was not conscious of any particular spiritual void, nor was the uncomplicated Ringo, but the group mind held its usual sway.

Indeed, this decision concerning their souls was taken even more quickly than the one to grow moustaches. Hearing (from George's wife, Pattie) that the Maharishi was to give a talk at London's Hilton hotel, John, George and Paul, accompanied by Pattie, Cynthia Lennon and Jane, turned up in their millionaire-hippy finery and sat at the front, experiencing the extreme novelty of a spotlight being turned on someone else.

Here it was monopolised by a diminutive Indian gentleman with straggly hair and black and white forked beard whose high-pitched voice seemed to quiver with perpetual mirth. But if his appearance was rather comical, his message was riveting. His Beatle listeners had heard of meditation as a way of calming the mind, but had always thought it involved self-discipline and patience aeons beyond their attention span. This transcendental variety, however, offered an inviting fast track, needing only 20 minutes per day to produce a state of perfect 'inner peace'.

After the lecture, John, Paul and George talked with the Maharishi and there and then signed up to his Spiritual Regeneration Movement, pledging to contribute a week's earnings apiece to its funds and to study meditation at the guru's ashram, or religious sanctuary, in India. Meantime, they agreed to join a ten-day induction course he was running at a college in Bangor, North Wales, starting the following August Bank Holiday weekend. With them went Mick Jagger and Marianne Faithfull, until then the Summer of Love's most notable casualties. But that distinction was about to be usurped.

At the end of the first day's indoctrination in Bangor, John, Paul and George held a joint press conference with the Maharishi to announce an early major benefit: they were giving up LSD. 'You cannot keep on taking drugs for ever,' Paul said. 'You get to the stage where you're taking 15 aspirins a day without a headache. We were looking for something more natural. This is it. It was an experience we went through. Now it's over and we don't need it any more.'

The next day, Sunday, as the cycle of spiritual chats with the Maharishi and press conferences continued, a telephone began ringing persistently inside the college's administration block. Paul said 'Someone had better answer that', and went off to do it. A few moments later, he was heard to shout 'Oh, Christ . . . *no!*'

20

'Everything was off the top of Paul's head'

Until that moment, Brian Epstein and the Beatles had seemed to be amicably but inexorably drifting apart.

At the age of only 32, Brian had become the biggest impresario the pop business had ever known. His NEMS company controlled a huge roster of young artistes, now from other locations as well as Liverpool, all of whom looked to him for the same seemingly magic touch that had launched John, Paul, George and Ringo. He had diversified into the theatre, his original passion, both as a producer and director, and even begun to emerge as a performer in his own right, presenting British segments of the American TV pop show *Hullabaloo*.

Yet all of it put together didn't mean as much as the first – and still the biggest – of his discoveries, those now-grown men he continued to call 'the boys'. The end of live shows might have liberated the Beatles, but it had been a heavy blow to Brian. For it meant he could no longer orchestrate and shield and fuss over them from morning to night as no pop manager ever had before, and none would again. 'What am I going to do now?' he asked a colleague sadly on the flight home from their final American tour. 'Shall I go back to school and learn something new?'

Despite the expansion of NEMS and the manifold demands for his attention, he kept the Beatles jealously under his wing – as he also did his second favourite NEMS artiste Cilla Black – dropping everything else if ever they needed him, knowing no greater pleasure or excitement than to be in their company. He was like a parent who couldn't acknowledge his children had flown the nest.

In common with royalty, the four never needed to carry money yet Brian still paid them the weekly cash wage he'd started when they first signed with him. Every Friday, £50 in £5 notes was sent to each of them in the same office wage-packets that other NEMS employees received. The money was delivered by Tony Bramwell, the NEMS assistant who nowadays worked mainly for Paul. One day at Cavendish, Paul asked Bramwell to fetch something from the safe he kept, unlocked, in his bedroom. 'Inside, there were dozens of these little pay packets from Brian that had never been opened,' Bramwell remembers.

In September 1967, the five-year management agreement Brian and the Beatles had signed in 1962 was due to expire. And lately there had been plenty of reasons to think it mightn't be renewed.

The situation was one that British pop, with its traditional six-month career spans, had never seen before, but which would be replayed by many other managers and artistes in the future. The deals Brian had made for the Beatles five years earlier when they were nobodies remained mostly still in place, looking laughably inadequate for the ultimate somebodies they'd become. And the once-naive, thrilled and grateful boys were now vastly more independent, discerning and worldly-wise; one of them in particular.

The most retrospectively ludicrous of those deals, at least, had been rectified. The 'penny-a-record' royalty rate the Beatles had received from EMI throughout their prodigious run of hit singles and albums had risen to a healthy 10 per cent in January 1967. But there was still no question of an advance against royalties, a practice the UK music industry was starting to pick up from America. It rankled that the Rolling Stones, their nearest rivals – and often shameless imitators – had received $1.25 million from Decca, thanks to the un-Brian-like strong-arm methods of their American manager, Allen Klein.

Other past misjudgements on Brian's part remained shrouded in mystery. When Beatlemania first hit America, for instance, the licensing of themed merchandise, wigs, plastic guitars and the like promised to generate fortunes on a Disney scale. But Brian had assigned the merchandising rights to a group of British businessmen on a 90–10 split in their favour (from which the Beatles stood to earn only 10 per cent of his 10 per cent) and the ensuing legal tangle had halted the bonanza in its tracks.

On a personal level, they felt they no longer needed the meticulous care and unerring instinct for the classy with which Brian had guided their career hitherto. Their supreme achievement, *Sgt. Pepper's Lonely Hearts Club Band*, had, after all, been conceived and carried through with only minimal input from him. A note he'd written about how the finished album should be packaged showed just how far he was out of the creative loop: 'Plain brown paper bags for Sergeant Pepper'.

'We'd always wanted to get the tools of the art into our own hands and at that point we were virtually managing ourselves,' Paul would later observe. 'So Brian had become a bit sidelined . . . and I'm sure it contributed to his unhappiness.'

There were many other contributors. As a gay man with years of secrecy and guilt behind him, Brian ought to have benefited from the Permissive Society, which reached its apogee in July 1967 when homosexual acts between consenting males over 21 were legalised in Britain. Unfortunately, his taste for rough trade and soliciting in public toilets left him still outside the law and a constant victim of violence or extortion by his pick-ups. To his lasting remorse, one such scrape had prevented him from seeing the Beatles' farewell live show in San Francisco.

He was also more hooked on drugs than any of his boys – pot and acid but mainly the amphetamines to which he'd been introduced at the Cavern, mixed with reckless quantities of alcohol. During most of the *Sgt. Pepper* recording sessions, he'd been an in-patient at The Priory, London's celebrity drying-out clinic: a cure that hadn't taken. The once immaculate businessman had turned into a tousled, ruffle-shirted would-be hippy who slept in until mid-afternoon and spent his nights importuning young Guardsmen from Knightsbridge Barracks or losing thousands on roulette at Mayfair gaming clubs.

His relationship with Paul had always seemed slightly uncomfortable, though no one could explain exactly why. Back in Liverpool, the gossip used to be that he felt guilty for becoming as fixated on John as much as he had, and was always trying to make amends to Paul without ever quite succeeding.

From the band's earliest days, Paul certainly had played the prima donna – as when preferring to soak in a bath rather than be on time for the first, crucial business meeting with Brian. *A Cellarful of Noise*, Brian's otherwise bland autobiography, said that Paul could be 'moody and temperamental and difficult to deal with', and tended not to listen to what he didn't want to hear.

He was never bothered by Brian's homosexuality, even at the very beginning when, as the prettiest Beatle, he might have expected himself rather than John to be a target. In fact, as he's since recalled, Brian always made determined efforts to be 'macho' around the Beatles. And other gay men had continually crossed his path, from Hamburg drag-queens to Robert Fraser, whom he often accompanied to Paris on art-buying expeditions. 'I was secure about my sexuality,' he would later reflect. 'I always felt "I can hang out with whoever I want."'

His independence and discernment having leapt far ahead of the other Beatles', he was inevitably the one most resistant to Brian's paternalism and keenly questioning of decisions taken on his behalf. Brian's last personal assistant, Joanne Newfield, later recalled how 'Paul would come in, doing his business-Beatle bit. There was never a row, but you could see Brian was uneasy while [he] was there . . . Whenever I saw him put down the phone really upset, he'd always been talking to Paul.'

At the same time, whenever anything needed fixing, smoothing out or covering up, Paul still turned to Brian as instinctively and with the same confidence as did the other three. One of EMI's conditions for using the *Sgt. Pepper* cover had been that all the figures in Peter Blake's 'heroes' collage still extant must give permission for their likenesses to be reproduced. Paul handed the onerous task of contacting agents all over Europe and America to Brian, who – without a murmur that 'plain brown paper bags' would have been easier – put his PA, Wendy Hanson, onto it full time.

His was likewise the only helpline when, during the Beatles' final world tour, the spectre of Paul's Hamburg sex-life raised its head again. Just prior to the West German concerts, former St Pauli bar-worker Erika Hubers had come forward with renewed claims that he was the father of her small daughter, Bettina. Brian quietly paid her off, forestalling a scandal that could have rivalled 'more popular than Jesus'.

In the months leading up to Brian's death, he and Paul seemed to become much closer. 'Paul was the only Beatle living in London, so the two of them socialised a lot, at receptions and first nights,' Tony Bramwell says. 'And Paul loved what Brian was doing with the rock shows at the Saville theatre.' This new bond was sealed when Brian publicly stood alongside Paul in the furore over his LSD-taking, became a signatory to *The Times*'s 'legalise pot' advertisement Paul had sponsored and made a substantial contribution to its cost.

It was never seriously on the cards that the Beatles would fire Brian outright when his management agreement expired in September. Nonetheless, he told several people, including fellow impresario Larry Parnes, that he was fully expecting it. Already he had almost lost Cilla Black, thanks to his seemingly loosening grip on NEMS. The best he hoped for was some kind of consultancy role with the Beatles and Cilla, at a reduced rate of commission.

He seemed to be preparing himself for this, deliberately standing back when, in July, the Beatles had the short-lived idea of buying a set of Greek islands on which to set up a communal home. 'I think it's a dotty idea,' he wrote to an associate. 'But they are no longer children and must have their own sweet way.'

Their discovery of Maharishi Mahesh Yogi seemed final confirmation of having found a replacement father figure. But Brian was classy to the last, refusing to join in the general chorus of incredulity that such a figure could have thus mesmerised them. Indeed, despite his Jewish faith, he, too, signed up to the Transcendental Meditation movement, promising to join the initiation course in Bangor as soon as he could get away from the office.

Instead, he died alone at his Belgravia home from an overdose of barbiturates chased with brandy. Although the verdict was accidental death, there were theories he might have been killed in a sex-game that went wrong, or even murdered. But Paul later talked to an employee who'd been in the house at the time, and was satisfied the inquest had got it right.

Amid the popping flashbulbs in Bangor, John was so stunned that he could barely get a word out. Paul, with Jane beside him, seemed quite composed, speaking of the 'terrible shock' of Brian's death and how 'very upset' he was. Years were to pass before he'd say what no young Englishman in 1967 yet could: that he'd 'loved the guy'.

Brian's autocratic rule at NEMS meant he had no natural successor inside the company. His younger brother, Clive, became managing director – promising 'a programme of vigorous expansion' – while his closest aide, Peter Brown, took over day-to-day attendance on the Beatles. A half-negotiated merger with the Australian manager Robert Stigwood, which had brought the Who, Cream and the Bee Gees into NEMS (and to which the Beatles strongly objected), was called off. Stigwood pocketed half a million pounds' compensation and formed his own company, going on to produce smash-hit films like *Saturday Night Fever* and *Grease*.

After their era-defining album, their telecast to 400 million, their elevation to hippy deities, their high-risk role in the LSD debate, their conversion to Transcendental Meditation and their loss of a manager now seen to have been irreplaceable, John, George and Ringo might have thought nothing more could possibly be crammed into the Summer of Love. But they were wrong.

A few days after Brian's death, Paul summoned them to a meeting at Cavendish. One of the first to know its purpose was Frieda Kelly, Brian's former secretary and still a trusted NEMS insider.

'Paul told the others that if they didn't find some way of working together again, *right now*, the Beatles would disintegrate.'

One of many questions Brian had left unresolved was that of their film career. *A Hard Day's Night* and *Help!* had both been huge critical as well as commercial successes, in which their ensemble comedy work had led more than one reviewer to dub them 'modern Marx Brothers'. Yet two years on from *Help!*, a follow-up had still to be announced.

The critics had not singled out Paul for special praise in the acting or comedy departments as they had John and, especially, Ringo. But he was the one most interested in film-making – as well as in insuring against that inevitable day when the public finally tired of Beatles music. He thus took the lead in seeking a new movie project, both in tandem with Brian and on his own.

Numerous producers had pitched ideas for developing the 'modern Marx Brothers' line. One was to feature the Beatles as D'Artagnan and the Three Musketeers in a zany updating of the Alexandre Dumas classic (a money-spinner time and again for others in the future). Another proposal cast them as a 'group mind' just like their real-life one, playing four different sides of a man's split personality.

A suggestion even came from the great philosopher and pacifist Bertrand Russell. At his meeting with Paul and Jane, Russell mentioned that the spy novelist Len Deighton had just bought the film rights to *Oh! What a Lovely War*, the celebrated theatrical satire on the carnage of 1914–18. An anti-war film in ironic military gear seemed the perfect Beatles vehicle, and Paul met with Deighton, its co-producer, to see if it could be so adapted. But the production was to consist entirely of songs from the Great War period, leaving no room for Lennon–McCartney.

Early in 1967, there was an attempt to team the Beatles with Joe Orton, the young working-class dramatist whose plays *Loot* and *Entertaining Mr Sloane*, with their mixture of sex and social anarchy, were the sensation of London's West End. Paul had much admired

Loot, so was in on Brian's meetings with Orton, whose original brief was merely to rewrite the split personality script. Instead, he came up with an original story called *Up Against It* which turned the Beatles into drag-wearing urban guerrillas who all ended up in bed with the same woman.

The script was rejected without comment – though Paul later blamed its heavy gay overtones. And the sequel was somehow entirely in character with the Summer of Love. A few days before Brian's body was found in Belgravia, Orton was bludgeoned to death by his lover, Kenneth Halliwell, in the Islington bed-sitting-room they shared.

The American United Artists Corporation, to which Brian had signed the Beatles in a three-picture deal, was waiting impatiently for the third in the trilogy. At the end of his life, he'd apparently despaired of putting them back on the screen in person, so had authorised a feature-length cartoon about them, based on Paul's 'Yellow Submarine', hoping that would clear the commitment to UA.

Thanks to Brian's poor deal-making, the Beatles had earned only a pittance from *A Hard Day's Night* and *Help!* Nor had they found either artistically satisfying. John voiced a general sentiment that, thanks to the number of scene-stealing British character actors involved, they were merely 'extras in our own film[s]'. Richard Lester, their director both times, further stirred the pot by opining that '[the Beatles] shouldn't be limited to the conventions of the professional film-maker. They should go on and develop their talents in this field and make a movie as they make their albums.'

Paul had long wanted them to make a film of their own devising and over which they had total artistic control, writing and directing and editing as well as acting and playing music. Andy Warhol productions like *Empire*, and his own travels with a cine-camera, had whetted his appetite for, as he put it, 'films that you sort of just make because you fancy making a film'.

In April 1967, while visiting Jane in America, he'd come up with a seemingly perfect theme. An essential feature of British seaside holidays in the 1950s was the mystery tour by motor coach to an unannounced, but seldom surprising, destination, with beer, fish and chips and sing-songs en route, ending with a cash-collection for the driver in his own peaked cap. Paul's idea was for the Beatles to take a 'magical' mystery tour in the same kind of vehicle and with the same lack of any preset destination, filming their adventures along the way.

As well as nostalgic–ironic in best McCartney style, the idea was also cool and cutting edge. In 1964, a group of proto-hippy performance artists known as the Merry Pranksters, including the novelist Ken Kesey, had crossed Middle America by psychedelically-painted school bus, handing out LSD diluted in the soft drink Kool-Aid to everyone they met. Tom Wolfe, father of so-called New Journalism, also joined the mischievous troupe, later chronicling their antics in his book *The Electric Kool-Aid Acid Test*.

Paul and John had written a title track, which the Beatles had recorded before the release of *Sgt. Pepper*, and Paul and Brian, in their latter, closer relationship, had discussed what the film might contain. Now, in the aftermath of Brian's death, Paul persuaded the others there was one sure way to show themselves still united and able to carry on without him. They should press ahead with the *Magical Mystery Tour*.

In Denis O'Dell, the ideal person was on hand to manage the project. O'Dell had been co-producer of *A Hard Day's Night* and producer of John's screen-acting debut, *How I Won the War*, as well as a classic Cold War thriller, *The Bedford Incident*. A passionate horse-racing enthusiast, he'd earned Paul's goodwill for arranging the purchase of Drake's Drum for Jim McCartney's sixty-second birthday. 'One day, I was having lunch with Dick Lester when I got a call from Paul and John,' he remembers. 'They said "Denis, come and run us."'

O'Dell's first act on coming aboard was to suggest a far simpler, more manageable format for the *Magical Mystery Tour* – the Beatles as Victorian music-hall artistes, performing at a giant picnic. But

Paul insisted they should stick to the Merry Prankster-ish road trip. He had taken overall command but – O'Dell soon realised – had little idea of what meticulous forward planning even the most spontaneous-seeming film requires. There was neither a script nor a shooting-schedule; only a circle he'd had drawn and marked off in segments to indicate different sequences, such as 'People on coach', 'dreams', 'stripper and band' and 'end-song'. 'Everything was off the top of Paul's head,' O'Dell recalls.

So, on 11 September 1967, in still-glorious Summer of Love weather, a customised yellow motor coach left London and headed for the West Country, carrying the Beatles together with hand-picked NEMS employees and their children, plus a selection of actors and old music-hall comedians chosen (mainly by Paul) from the *Spotlight* directory; a kind of *Sgt. Pepper* collage on wheels.

The four-day shoot quickly descended into chaos. No locations had been scouted in advance and none of the innumerable necessary permits and permissions necessary for filming along the way had been obtained, so problems and delays were continual. Cast and film crew alike grew increasingly confused and frustrated by the contradictory whims of their four different directors. An immense convoy of media vehicles preceded and followed the coach, causing traffic chaos and calling out retributionary police forces all the way to Devon and back.

The roadies Neil and Mal voiced the general sentiment as they struggled to cope with a more demanding and stressful road than ever. 'If only Brian was still around . . . Brian would never have let any of this happen.'

The circular diagram Paul called his 'scrupt' (for 'script' it certainly wasn't) also called for various interior sequences including an army recruiting-office, a wizards' laboratory and a ballroom with a Hollywood musical-size staircase. No one had thought to book time at a film studio to shoot these interiors and when Denis O'Dell tried, he found every major studio fully occupied on the requisite dates. The only large enough available space was a hangar on a disused airfield in West Malling, Kent, whose pitted runway also served for an impromptu car- and bus-chase.

Scattered through the action were songs for the new album the Beatles were obliged to put out even though *Sgt. Pepper* still topped the charts worldwide. Paul's 'The Fool on the Hill' featured him playing both recorder and penny whistle, as Jane's mother, Margaret, had taught him. For the accompanying film sequence he went off with a single cameraman and Mal Evans to a mountainside in the South of France, cavorting alone and adorably in a navy blue pea-jacket. He forgot to take his passport but, in a gleam of genuine magic, charmed both the British and French customs into letting him pass without it.

His other main contribution was 'Your Mother Should Know', a soft-shoe routine straight out of the Fred Astaire movies he'd adored as a child. For this, the four Beatles appeared as a chorus line in matching white tailsuits and red carnations – but still with hippy-length hair – descending a Hollywood-style staircase into the multitudes of extras, now augmented inexplicably by a squad of whirling ballroom dancers and a march-past of Air Training Corps cadets. The descent was accomplished without a slip, just about, but only Paul was rewarded with a floral bouquet.

Editing the ten hours of raw footage down to less than an hour took 11 weeks and was likewise a collective process, with the group mind anything but unanimous. 'Paul would come in in the morning and edit,' Tony Bramwell remembers. 'Then John would come in in the afternoon and re-edit what Paul had edited. Then Ringo would come in . . .'

Ahead of the film came a single destined not to be part of it, Paul's 'Hello, Goodbye', written in one day at Cavendish when NEMS executive Alistair Taylor asked him how he thought up his songs. Sitting down at his harmonium, he told Taylor to give the opposite of every word he called out. The resulting 'Hello-good-bye-yes-no-stop-go' became the lyric to a tune that came just as instantly. In this sphere, at least, the top of his head never put a foot wrong. 'Hello, Goodbye' was a monster Christmas hit, appearing to close the unnerving Maharishi episode and signal a return to lovely, sunny, normal *Sgt. Pepper*-land. Commented one British newspaper nannyishly: 'It's nice to see the roses back in the Beatles' cheeks again.'

Expectations for their first essay into film-making therefore couldn't have been higher. In America, two major television networks, ABC and NBC, were bidding for the privilege of screening its world premiere, an event confidently expected to top *The Ed Sullivan Show*'s 73 million audience in 1964. Paul, however, wanted it first shown on the BBC because of the Beatles' long-standing links with the Corporation.

It was duly snapped up by BBC1 for £9000 – a fraction of what America would have paid – and billed as the highlight of the channel's Christmas schedule. It had been shot in colour, with psychedelic special effects added, but as few British homes yet had colour TV sets, the majority of its guaranteed huge audience would see it in black and white.

It went out at 8.35 p.m. on Boxing Day, a time when Britons traditionally slump around their TV sets with their children and relations, bloated with Christmas food and drink and equal to only the most unchallenging 'family' entertainment. What this torpid mass had been expecting were the cuddly Beatles of *A Hard Day's Night* and *Help!* in something similarly slick, polished and charming. Instead, they got a rambling, disconnected narrative whose four heroes were only intermittently visible – 'extras' in their own film like never before.

In the entire 53 minutes, only Paul lived up to expectations with 'The Fool on the Hill', alone on his Côte d'Azur mountainside, making big eyes from inside his turned-up coat-collar. Against that was John's 'I Am the Walrus', a sequence like a Lennon cartoon featuring the Beatles in animal masks, big-footed policemen dancing hand-in-hand, the singer himself gowned and with a bandaged head like an escapee from some hospital, or psychiatric institution.

Most baffling was the instrumental 'Flying' sequence, when the tour bus supposedly left the everyday world and floated off into a psychedelic Nirvana. In black and white, the pulsating Dayglo clouds turned into a vague grey swirl which many viewers mistook for a breakdown in transmission.

In later years, *Magical Mystery Tour* would be seen as a pioneering piece which anticipated pop video and Monty Python free-form comedy, not to mention a time when anyone could make a movie on a mobile phone. But in technologically innocent 1967, it caused outrage. The *Daily Express*'s television critic received front-page space to declare that never in his career had he seen such 'blatant rubbish'. It was repeated after the Christmas holiday, this time in colour for BBC2's more intellectual audience, but provoked only the same mystification and mockery.

Today, a rock band making a flop movie wouldn't be such a big deal. But this was the Beatles' first miss in a line of hits that had seemed unbreakable and was as integral to Britain's national self-esteem and international prestige as the monarchy or Shakespeare. Especially so soon after their *Sgt. Pepper* triumph, it seemed a dereliction of duty that left millions feeling personally let down. And, with Brian no longer around to take all the flak, there was only one other candidate.

Paul accepted sole responsibility but insisted he remained proud of the film which, he said, ought to be viewed 'more like an abstract painting'. For him, just the Beatles playing 'I Am the Walrus' minus their animal heads, handling John's nonsense words and Marquis de Sade visuals – as, in the past, they'd handled Beatlemania, Hamburg and Litherland Town Hall – made the whole thing worthwhile.

Musically, it fared considerably better. In Britain, its six tracks had been released before Christmas as two old-style 'extended play' discs, together with a 28-page booklet and the lyrics in full. Because of the smaller disc format, it had to compete in the singles rather than album charts, but still reached number two (denied the top spot by 'Hello, Goodbye') and sold 600,000 copies by the New Year. In America, bulked out by 'Hello, Goodbye' and other recent singles, it became a full album which reached number one and was nominated for a Grammy.

In the aftermath of Brian's death, Paul and Jane had seemingly become close again. December found them alone in the peace and seclusion of Kintyre, and on Christmas Day – with Britain still looking forward to a Beatle TV treat the following night – they announced their engagement.

21

'A beautiful place where beautiful people can buy beautiful things'

Nineteen sixty-eight was the year when John and Paul got together with two women who, in widely different ways, would break the bond between them, so making the Beatles' break-up inevitable. Paradoxically, it happened against a backdrop of consolidation and diversification, intended to give them more longevity than they believed their music alone ever could.

During these past three years of ever more colossal success, there had been little attempt to shield their collective earnings from the UK's punitive top rate of income tax. Brian Epstein was at heart an old-fashioned provincial shopkeeper who regarded even quite legitimate tax-avoidance as unpatriotic. But in the last months of his life, a greater sum than ever before had been at stake. EMI Records owed the Beatles some £2 million of back royalties which was to be paid over in a single instalment. The only way to avoid handing almost the whole sum to the taxman, their accountants advised, was for them to put it into a business.

In 1963, they had become equal partners in a limited company, The Beatles Ltd, whose tax advantages had been minimal. In April 1967, this was replaced by a more complex partnership structure, Beatles & Co., 80 per cent of which was to be owned by a corporation receiving all the band's earnings, bar those from songwriting. It meant they would now be paying only corporation tax, a fraction of the personal tax rate; moreover, by contracting their services to the new corporation, each received a whopping cash windfall of £200,000.

Under the Beatles & Co. umbrella appeared a nest of companies pursuing activities in which they were already involved – recording, music publishing and film-making. The corporation's overall name was Apple, suggesting simplicity, freshness, innocence – a Garden of Eden even – and its branding couldn't have been classier. One day, the art dealer Robert Fraser called at Cavendish with a 1966 work by René Magritte which Fraser felt sure Paul would wish to add to the other Magrittes on his walls. Entitled *Le Jeu de Mourre* (The Guessing Game) it showed a pristine green apple with '*Au revoir*' written slantwise across it. Paul was filming out in the back garden so, rather than interrupt him – in a display of cool guaranteed to clinch its sale – Fraser simply left the painting propped on the dining-room table.

The Apple logo, a version of the Magritte image minus '*Au revoir*', made its first, inconspicuous appearance on the back of the *Sgt. Pepper* cover. The name was also copyrighted in some 30 countries – a move which would pay off incalculably a quarter of a century later.

After Brian's death, Apple continued to evolve in the Beatles' group mind. At the suggestion of his brother, Clive, following the example of the Epstein family's own original business, they decided to go into retailing, a huge Swinging London growth area headed by Terence Conran's Habitat stores and Barbara Hulanicki's Biba boutique. Paul was particularly excited by the prospect, visualising a department store in which everything would be white – furniture, clothes, pianos, even domestic pets.

With all four Beatles throwing in ideas, and no authority figure to restrain them, what had started out as the plain fruit of financial wisdom took on a candy coating of hippy idealism. Across the multisegmented corporation – now punningly named Apple Corps, pronounced 'core' – profitability was to be a secondary motive. The Beatles would not be bosses but philanthropists, using their wealth and influence to give young people opportunities which they felt they themselves had once been denied by a grey and grudging older generation. (Actually, for most of their career, they had received extraordinary encouragement and indulgence from their elders: Brian, George Martin, Dick James and others.) Above all, Apple would have a spirit of freedom, democracy, fairness and fun never known in conventional business. Paul coined various oxymoronic mission statements for it: 'An underground company above ground'; 'A kind of Western Communism'; and 'a controlled weirdness'.

Among the assets Brian had acquired on their behalf was a corner building at 94 Baker Street, a thoroughfare immortalised by the mythical detective Sherlock Holmes. The ground floor of this now became a boutique named Apple, with the corporation's – initially modest – offices above it.

The job of creating the boutique went to a Dutch hippy design collective known as The Fool, who had made the Beatles' clothes for their 'All You Need Is Love' telecast and as a result become couturiers to London's rock elite. The Fool received a budget of £100,000 – £1 million-plus by today's values – to decorate the boutique and make the garments it was to sell. Their plan involved the total transformation of the early Victorian corner-site with a giant psychedelic mural covering both walls: the figure of a sloe-eyed goddess or genii juggling with suns and moons. For such radical defacement of a historic building, permission had to be obtained from the local planning authority. This was refused, but the designers still went ahead, employing a team of art students to finish the mural in time for the boutique's opening on 7 December 1967.

In the public mind, the project seemed more suggestive of Paul than any other Beatle; it was from him, naturally, that the media sought a *raison d'être* for the boutique, and were rewarded with 'A beautiful place where beautiful people can buy beautiful things'. But at the glittering inaugural party, as celebrities like Cilla Black and Ken Tynan munched apples and drank apple juice and The Fool performed tinkly pipe-and-bells music, John and George were the only Beatles present. Paul was with Jane in Scotland, prior to announcing their engagement.

Soon the cramped upstairs rooms could no longer contain all Apple's blossoming branches and the organisation moved to a suite of offices at 94 Wigmore Street, just round the corner from Paul's former billet with the Asher family. A press and publicity department was established by Derek Taylor, who'd done the same job under Brian a few years earlier and had since been based in California, representing the Byrds and helping organise the Monterey Festival.

Jobs were given to Beatle friends and cronies, regardless of qualifications or experience. Apple Publishing was run by Terry Doran, Brian's former partner in a car-dealership, forever tagged the 'man from the motor trade' in 'She's Leaving Home'. The boutique was managed by John's old school crony Pete Shotton, whose only previous retail experience had been running a supermarket in Hampshire that John had bought, while its sales staff were headed by George's fashion model sister-in-law, Jenny Boyd.

With Denis O'Dell already in place as head of Apple Films, the most pressing task was to set up the record label that would be the company's centrepiece. To head it, Peter Asher recalls, the Beatles wanted 'a big, impressive American record guy', so they chose Ron Kass, chief executive of the prestigious Liberty label.

During the first flush of Paul-written hits for Peter and Gordon, Asher had become interested in record production, and had gone on to produce a solo single for Manfred Mann's Paul Jones. 'I asked Paul [McCartney] to play drums on one track because I always thought he was a great, underrated drummer. When the Apple label was being put together, he asked me if I'd like to produce some things for it. Then, somehow, it turned into my becoming head of A&R.'

One of the first recipients of Apple's largesse was a blond young Greek named Ianni, or Alex, Mardas. He was always viewed as a John protégé, but actually had Paul – or rather Paul's eclectic artistic taste – to thank for his entrée to the Beatles' inner circle. He was currently lodging with the recently-divorced John Dunbar, from whose Indica gallery Paul had acquired so many pieces. Dunbar had met him through the wife of the Greek sculptor Takis Vassilikis, one of whose spindly metal-rod constructions had pride of place at Cavendish.

Twenty-one-year-old Mardas was good-looking and charming and, despite his unexalted work as a TV engineer, claimed to be the scion of a wealthy Greek family whose social circle included the Queen's Greek-born husband, Prince Philip. He'd got to know the Beatles, fortuitously, when they were thinking of buying a string of Greek islands as a communal home, and needed a negotiator with the country's newly-installed fascist military government. Mardas had accompanied them on a reconnaissance cruise in the summer of 1967, a maritime acid trip which ended without the purchase of a single island.

His real appeal, however, was as an electronics 'wizard' with a vision far beyond the TV sets he repaired for a living. Some of his ideas foreshadowed soon-to-be developments in telecommunications – such as phones that dialled automatically and displayed the numbers of incoming calls – but others belonged more to the realm of science fiction. John, a technophobe who couldn't even change a light-bulb, was dazzled by Mardas's plans for an 'X-Ray camera', a force-field of coloured smoke to replace conventional burglar-alarms, and a house that could be made to hover a short way above the ground. He named the young Greek 'Magic Alex' and took him into the most top-secret band-meetings, introducing him as 'my new guru'.

The reclusive, paranoid George was equally smitten by Mardas's many projected devices for keeping unwanted intruders at bay. But practically-minded Paul, to begin with anyway, seemed just as impressed. The result was another new division, Apple Electronics, with premises in Bayswater and Magic Alex assigned a hefty budget to design revolutionary new forms of lighting for the Apple boutique.

The Beatles seemed unable to start a business without giving it as many tracks as one of their albums. Plans were further announced for an Apple bespoke tailoring shop on Chelsea's King's Road and an Apple Foundation for the Arts to fund youthful talent in every creative medium. There was even to be an Apple school, run on hippy principles and bearing no resemblance to the rigorous (and excellent) academies the Beatles themselves had attended. Its head was to be Ivan Vaughan, who'd once lived over the garden wall from John, been Paul's classmate at Liverpool Institute and brought the two together at St Peter's church fete. After gaining a degree in classics, 'Ivy' had become a primary school teacher – the career that had once beckoned strongly to Paul also.

Since the previous August, the band had made no further statement about Maharishi Mahesh Yogi or their conversion to Transcendental Meditation. But they had kept in touch with the Maharishi and steered several celebrity friends into the TM movement. Now, just as the public were adjusting to the idea of them as businessmen, and with all their new companies barely up and running, they put Mammon firmly behind them, departing for a three-month course of study with the guru in Rishikesh, north India.

Lennon and McCartney were not too immersed in spirituality to leave behind a single to hold the charts in their absence. This was Paul's 'Lady Madonna', a piano-pounding ode to a homeless and chaotic single mother, depicted with a realism that didn't flinch even from the 'baby at your breast'. It was equally a feast of McCartney wordplay echoing the nursery rhyme 'Three Blind Mice', its chorus of 'See how they run!' becoming a comment on the subject's laddered stockings.

Recorded at the same time, but not destined for release until 19 months later, was John's 'Across the Universe', melding the sweetest and loneliest of his lyrics ('Thoughts meander like a restless wind inside a letter box . . .') with the mantra he'd soon be chanting in the Himalayas. He wanted a female chorus totally without artifice so, rather than professional backing singers, it was decided to use two of the fans permanently on watch outside Abbey Road studios. Paul was deputed to fetch them, and picked out a pair he recognised from his own front gate in Cavendish Avenue.

The girls' awestruck voices created just the right effect for 'Across the Universe', although their wavery chorus – 'Nothing's gonna change my world' – would prove as untrue in Paul's case as in John's.

It was in effect a Meditational Mystery Tour which arrived at Rishikesh in the spring-like warmth of a north Indian February. With the Beatles, their three wives and one fiancée were their roadie-in-perpetuity Mal Evans and Magic Alex Mardas, who was to apply his electronic wizardry to building the Maharishi a radio station that could reach all round the world. Several other star converts were on the same study course: folk singer Donovan, actress Mia Farrow with her sister, Prudence, and Mike Love from the Beach Boys.

Although situated in the foothills of Asia's remotest mountain-range, the ashram offered the comforts of an hotel or, at least, superior youth hostel – individual cabins with carpets, hot and cold water and reliable plumbing. The vegetarian cuisine was good and plentiful. The guru himself spent long periods meditating alone inside his impressive detached residence, but his deputy and a staff of 30 were always on hand to minister to VIP disciples. An (initially) enraptured John dubbed it 'a recluse holiday camp' and 'the Butlin's of Bliss'.

Paul adjusted easily to the vaguely school-like routine he later recalled as 'eating, sleeping and meditating, with the occasional little lecture from Maharishi thrown in'. He set himself the target of sticking it out for a month, but soon found himself no longer counting the days until the end of term.

It was in fact the first complete rest the Beatles had ever had: a Club Med with mantras and mountains instead of a Med. The world's media, which had trekked after them en masse, were kept at a distance throughout. Snapshots taken by fellow inmates show them evidently relaxed and content in locally-made tunics and flower-garlands, with Jane, Cynthia Lennon, Pattie Harrison and Maureen Starkey (Starr) all looking beautiful and tranquil in the soft sunshine.

Their aide Tony Bramwell, based at a luxury hotel in Delhi, paid frequent visits, bringing mail and updates about the manifold developments at Apple. Bramwell also kept them supplied with non-spiritual comforts like cigarettes, records, music trade papers and film for the movie camera Paul was seldom seen without. Even 'behind the wire', as John put it, a handful of two-rupee notes could buy anything, from alcohol to superior grades of pot.

Lennon and McCartney made use of the time to write songs for the album the Beatles had to record when they returned home – the first to be released on their Apple label. George, the Maharishi's most serious student, protested that they weren't here to think about making albums. But Paul couldn't stop composing, however hard he tried to focus on higher things. One evening, the group walked to a nearby village for an open-air cinema show where the entire population watched a four-hour Hindi-language epic projected onto a white sheet. Paul, as usual, had his guitar with him: on the way back through the jungle, amid exotic bird-calls and chattering monkeys, he suddenly thought of 'Desmond has a barrow in the marketplace', the first line to what would become 'Ob-La-Di, Ob-La-Da'.

Ringo went home after two weeks; his stomach, weakened by childhood surgery, couldn't deal with even that mildly-spiced vegetarian food, and Maureen hated the flies. Into their cabin moved two members of the Apple team, Neil Aspinall and Denis O'Dell, who'd arrived from London. O'Dell was there to discuss John's idea for a documentary about the Maharishi and the hard-headed Aspinall to make sure it never got off the ground.

O'Dell brought with him what he considered the best idea for the Beatles' next feature film since the Joe Orton script. This was J.R.R. Tolkien's fantastical trilogy *The Lord of the Rings*, already an enormous hit on American college campuses but still relatively unknown in Britain. Consequently, neither Paul or John had ever

encountered Tolkien's world of hobbits, elves and wizards which –
so their film 'guru' said – offered plum screen-acting roles for them.

Knowing that no Beatle could be expected to plough through a
1000-plus-page trilogy, O'Dell gave the three remaining medita-
tors a volume each, subconsciously maintaining their usual order
of precedence: John was to read the first in the sequence, *The Fellowship of the Ring*; Paul was to read the second, *The Two Towers*; and
George the last, *The Return of the King*.

Paul and Jane stayed on for a further three weeks, leaving just as
John's infatuation with the Maharishi was turning to disillusion and
resentment. He had expected to be given the Secret of Life in one
quick hit, like a pill or a tab of acid, but it hadn't happened. The guru
fell under suspicion of exploiting his famous disciples for personal
publicity; there were also rumours that he'd made sexual advances
to Mia Farrow's sister, Prudence. The transformative spiritual pilgrimage thus ended on a note of smutty character-assassination
more suited to some backstage on Hamburg's Reeperbahn.

The expedition left its deepest mark on George, who came home
convinced the Maharishi had taught him to levitate, and remained
a loyal TM practitioner and propagandist for the rest of his life,
leaving behind most of his sense of humour in the process. But
Paul, too, felt the guru's influence overall had been beneficial and,
more discreetly, continued to practise what he had taught.

Already in his back garden at Cavendish he had a 'meditation
chapel' – a glass geodesic dome with a floor that could be raised to
bring the meditator closer to Heaven. There in years to come, he
would continue to practise what he'd learned in the Himalayas, the
spiritual ambience only slightly marred by a gift he received from
the rock-horror star Alice Cooper – a circular bed that had once
belonged to Groucho Marx.

22

'It was the *coup de foudre* the French speak of in hushed tones'

Paul's engagement to Jane Asher had in fact marked the beginning of the end of their relationship. And after their return from India, where they'd looked so happy and at peace together, the end came quickly.

He would later say that throughout the two years they had lived together, for all their seemingly perfect domestic harmony, he'd never really felt that Jane was the woman for him. 'I liked her a lot and we got on very well. She was a very intelligent and very interesting person, but I just never clicked. One of those indefinable things about love is some people you click with and some people, who maybe you should click with, you don't.'

Much of the problem – paradoxically in those 'classless' Sixties – was the huge difference in their backgrounds. As sophisticated and civilised as Paul had become on the journey from Liverpool, his attitude to women still had more than a touch of traditional northern male chauvinism. Once the novelty of dating a posh young actress had worn off, he began to resent it that Jane had an independent and flourishing career of her own, which she continued to pursue energetically rather than focusing all her attention on him.

In their early days, he could sometimes treat her with a macho roughness more suited to Merseyside dance-halls: 'trying to beat her down' was his own candid – but slightly troubling – term for it in one of the few joint interviews they ever gave. Despite her air of almost child-like innocence, Jane was not one to be beaten down. The occasional sour note in Paul's music reflected rows in which he himself had ended up feeling out-manoeuvred and hard-done-by: 'The day breaks, your mind aches' in 'For No One', or the almost-furious 'I'm looking through you – but *you're nowhere!*'

Over time, they had come to lead almost separate lives, Paul with his musician and underground friends, Jane with her theatrical ones. She stood firm in her refusal to take drugs – even though many in her own profession now did – and was scathing in her disapproval of those who fostered Paul's various habits, and of their adverse effects on him.

He hadn't wanted her to join the Bristol Old Vic theatre company and her decision to put this major career step above his wishes created a distance more than merely geographical. In Bristol for long periods during play-runs, Jane had been seeing someone else and word had got back to Paul. Thus the world's most adored young man had to deal with his first-ever dose of rejection.

Yet breaking up was a prospect from which both of them shrank. Paul was still close to Jane's family, especially her mother, and had embarked on an already fruitful working relationship with her brother Peter, Apple Records' Head of A&R. All of Paul's family adored Jane, Jim McCartney especially. After some initial unease, Jim now regularly played host at 'Rembrandt' to Dr Richard Asher, in whom he discovered a fellow dictionary addict. 'They'd sit in the garden together, doing crosswords,' Paul's stepsister, Ruth McCartney, remembers.

There was also the wider reaction to be considered. The announcement of Paul's engagement at Christmas, when the Queen traditionally broadcasts to the nation, had an inescapable symbolism. And indeed, the betrothal of so adored a young prince to so eminently suitable a consort had sent a wave of goodwill through Britain and around the world, wiping out unfortunate recent memories of LSD and unmagical mystery tours. PR of that near-royal quality was not to be lightly cast aside.

So, rather like a dutiful young royal couple, he and Jane put on a public show of unity and affection while privately feeling growing coldness and estrangement. Ostensibly still sharing the same roof, they lived mostly apart, getting together only when neither had anything else in the diary, as a rule for holidays on the ski-slopes or in the sun.

On significant Beatle occasions, Jane always would be seen at Paul's side, as loyally and unassertively as Cynthia was at John's, Pattie was at George's and Maureen at Ringo's. Despite her hatred of drugs, she had joined Magic Alex's pot-wreathed shopping-expedition for Greek islands; she had been with Paul for the first encounter with the Maharishi at the London Hilton, with him at Bangor when news of Brian's death came through and for all nine weeks of meditating in the Himalayas. The sharpest-eyed of the Beatle media pack never suspected anything amiss between them.

Jane had always had to live with the knowledge that half the young, and not so young, women in the world wanted to sleep with Paul and that for him accepting the sexual opportunities which endlessly came his way counted as only a step beyond signing an autograph. What she didn't know, and never would, was that for almost the whole time they'd lived together at Cavendish he was having a parallel affair with an actress and model named Maggie McGivern.

In 1966, 20-year-old Maggie had been hired by John Dunbar and Marianne Faithfull as a nanny for their six-month-old son, Nicholas. 'One day, John was out, Marianne was entertaining some of her girlfriends and I was cooking a casserole for their lunch,' she recalls. 'The front-door buzzer went and a voice said, "It's Paul McCartney to see John." John wasn't there but – who can blame me? – I still said, "Come up."

'Marianne never showed and while her friends stayed in the sitting-room, Paul and I sat at the kitchen table, ate the casserole and talked. It felt completely comfortable, as if we'd known each other all our lives. At that time, I was in a relationship I wanted to get out of, so I told Paul about that, and from what he said I gathered he was in a similar situation.'

Thereafter, he took to visiting the Dunbars' rather more often, and talking to their beautiful, unintimidated young nanny as much as to them. Then he started calling when they were out and Maggie was alone in the flat with Nicholas. 'He'd always phone up first, to make sure no one else was there,' she remembers. 'He'd sit and talk to me while I got on with looking after Nicholas. He seemed to enjoy just watching that.'

They spent their first night together, chastely, at the flat while John and Marianne were away in Paris. 'Before Paul arrived, I'd smoked some pot, which had a really bad effect on me. All sorts of traumatic memories were going through my mind, and I was crying and jumping around. I remember Paul holding me, saying, "I gotta go, I gotta go . . ." When I woke the next morning, I felt perfectly fine again. I turned round and there he was, lying beside me.'

The affair remained totally secret, even from her employers. Paul warned her especially not to confide in the gossipy, mischievous Marianne. 'I realised how insecure he was – and not just about his private life getting into the papers. As loved as he was by everyone, he was still always looking for approval. That went for his music as well, even though he'd been told for years how brilliant it was. I remember him playing me some of the tracks from the *Revolver* album and being really anxious . . . asking, "Do you think it's OK?"'

After Maggie left the Dunbars' employment to do film-extra and modelling work, more elaborate measures had to be taken to preserve their cover. They would arrange to meet at furniture auctions in Chelsea or Fulham, pretending to bump into each other accidentally at the presale viewing. 'I often had to go away on jobs, and Paul would lose sight of me for a week or so. I used to wonder if I'd hear from him again . . . but he always sent Neil Aspinall out to find me.'

Paul allowed them to be seen together only very occasionally, when no telltale photographers or fans would be around. 'We once went out for a drive in the country in his Aston Martin. Ike and Tina Turner's "River Deep, Mountain High" was blasting out of the speakers, and it gave him the idea for "Good Day Sunshine". He started beating out the rhythm on the dashboard. He was like a sponge. Whatever was going on around him, he'd soak up and turn into a song.'

Though Maggie had already tried pot, and would later experiment with LSD, she never took drugs with Paul. 'I remember him showing me what looked like an ordinary tin of Benson & Hedges tipped [cigarettes] but with marijuana in them instead of tobacco. He carried them around in his pocket, not seeming at all scared of being busted. The feeling in those days was that because of what they were doing for British exports, the Beatles were untouchable.'

Paul never tried to hide her existence from the other Beatles or from Brian Epstein – another mark of their closeness at the end of Brian's life. Her most ambitious outing with him was a trip to Paris in company with John and Brian; each travelled separately, meeting up at the Plaza Athénée hotel. 'We all shared a suite and when Brian came in, he handed me a beautiful bouquet of red roses. "I like 'er," John kept telling Paul. As we walked along Avenue Montaigne, I was getting a lot of looks from Frenchmen, so John made me go in front so that the two of them wouldn't be noticed.'

As time passed, Paul grew more relaxed about being seen with Maggie. He even sent her an invitation to travel on the *Magical Mystery Tour* bus, but she was abroad at the time. A few weeks later, as he and the other Beatles watched the first rough cut in a Soho editing-suite, Maggie sat unobtrusively in a corner, doing a crossword puzzle.

To avoid the fans outside, they had to leave by a back door; John, George and Ringo bolting in one direction, Paul and Maggie in the other. 'We managed to stop a cab but as we got in, one of the fans managed to slip in as well. She was sitting there between us, looking almost as shocked as we were. Paul stopped the cab and told her very politely that she'd have to get out. He was always very nice to the girls who pursued him, but very firm.'

She even spent the occasional night at Cavendish, once cooking breakfast for Paul and his brother, Michael, who by then was in on the secret. Paul's live-in domestic couple, the Kellys, had left his employment in January 1967, after Mrs Kelly talked out of turn to an Australian newspaper, though he still hand-wrote her a reference calling her 'efficient and trustworthy'. After trying another couple, the Millses, he found Rose Martin (no relation to George), an unflappable, unshockable woman who would serve him with irreproachable loyalty and discretion for many years to come. However, Rose was fiercely loyal to Jane, so treated Maggie with barely restrained hostility.

On one visit, Paul took her into the back garden to show her his meditation chapel. Maggie, it so happened, had learned Transcendental Meditation from a friend some time before the Maharishi taught it to the Beatles. But the technology that assisted Paul's meditations came as a shock. 'We were standing there, looking at the stars – then he touched a switch and the whole floor started to rise.'

Latterly, while still seeing Maggie McGivern, he'd begun another affair which, likewise, never got back to Jane. But in contrast to the discretion he exercised with Maggie, all his new colleagues and employees at Apple knew of his involvement with Francie Schwartz.

Francie was a 24-year-old New Yorker, striking rather than pretty, with a brisk manner and a head of tight black corkscrew curls. She had come over to London in April 1968, and – following the growing trend – made her way straight to Apple's new offices in Wigmore Street. An aspiring film-maker, she hoped to pitch a script about a New York street entertainer she believed would make a perfect role for Paul.

At first, she was just one of the crowd haunting Apple's reception area in hopes of a Beatle cash jackpot. Then one day, Paul walked by and noticed her. Taking her into a side room, he began questioning her about herself and her aims in life, then suggested a stroll along Wigmore Street. 'He always did like Jewish girls from New York,' says Barry Miles. 'And always would . . .' Francie never got to pitch her script idea but, instead, was offered a job in Derek Taylor's press office.

At the end of April, Paul went back to Scotland with Jane, hoping to recapture the feeling that had made him propose four months earlier. But High Park Farm failed to exert its usual spell, and on his return to London he took up with Francie Schwartz.

On 11 May, he and John flew to New York to launch Apple Corps in the US, accompanied by Mal and Neil, Derek Taylor and Magic Alex Mardas. Unlike their first arrival in 1964, they landed at JFK Airport to be greeted by only a token 200–300 fans; Paul stayed at the apartment of Brian's old associate, Nat Weiss, the others at an un-beleaguered St Regis hotel.

During the four-day visit, they held a business meeting with Apple Records' new head, Ron Kass, sailing round New York harbour aboard a Chinese junk, and made a wisecracking TV appearance with the actress Tallulah Bankhead on Johnny Carson's *Tonight* show. Most of the media interviews took place at the St Regis but on the final day there was a press conference at a different hotel, the Americana. The massed photographers included a rangy young woman with unkempt blonde hair and clothes of studied unfashionability, whom Paul had last seen at the *Sgt. Pepper* photo-shoot in London almost a year previously: Linda Eastman.

The American media were most keen to hear about the Beatles' recent Indian pilgrimage, and by what rope-trick yesterday's converts to Transcendental Meditation had become today's would-be business tycoons. Despite himself having no quarrel with the Maharishi, Paul loyally echoed John's line that they'd simply been hoodwinked. 'We made a mistake. We thought there was more to him than there was. He's human. We thought at first that he wasn't.'

Surprisingly, most of the Apple sales-talk came from John. 'We're in the happy position of not really needing any more money,' he began – a statement inconceivable from any modern rock star, and one that would soon come back to haunt him. 'So for the first time the bosses aren't in it for the profit. We've already bought all our dreams, so now we want to share that possibility with others.'

Paul's strangely subdued air, he later said, came from a drugs-hangover and an atypical dose of stage-fright. For the first time in years of plumbing uncharted waters, he felt the Beatles were getting out of their depth. 'We were talking to media like *Forbes* magazine and they were interviewing us as a serious economic force, which we weren't. We hadn't done any of the business planning . . . we were just goofing off and having fun.'

At a time when headlines in America were consistently grim – race riots, student revolt against the Vietnam War, Dr Martin Luther King assassinated just a month previously, Bobby Kennedy to suffer the same fate a month later – he hoped Apple's new approach to business would at least strike a positive note, maybe even spread a little happiness. Was he himself happy, someone asked. The unexpected question received a totally unexpected downbeat answer: 'Not completely happy, no. I'd be a fool to say I was.'

Since he'd last seen Linda Eastman, her photojournalistic career had continued to flourish; that very week, she'd become the first woman to shoot a *Rolling Stone* magazine cover with her portrait of Eric Clapton. She was in her usual centre-sightline position and after the press conference she and Paul picked up the conversation they'd begun 11 months earlier next to the fireplace at Brian Epstein's house. When Neil signalled it was time to leave, Paul asked for her phone number. Having nothing else to hand, she scribbled it on the back of a blank cheque.

He phoned her later to say he wanted to see her but hadn't a free moment before his return to London the following day. So as not to miss her altogether, he asked her to ride with him in the limo to JFK Airport, a journey that could take up to two hours if the traffic was bad.

She did so, sitting between Paul and John with her camera-bag on her lap. After a few moments alone together in the Pan Am first-class lounge, and a couple more quick pictures, Paul's flight was called and Linda returned in the limo with Neil Aspinall and Nat Weiss.

Having turned acquaintanceship into romance, Apple brought it to fruition a month later. On 20 June, Paul flew to Los Angeles for the sales convention of the Capitol record label which, like EMI in Britain, was to manufacture and distribute Apple's records. During a brief stopover at JFK, he phoned the number Linda had given him to ask if she'd meet up with him in LA.

She wasn't at home, so he had to leave a message with her answering-service – the laborious precursor to voicemail – then travelled on, unsure whether she'd even receive the invitation, let alone accept it. He was staying at the Beverly Hills Hotel, whose premier guests occupy luxurious poolside bungalows set among groves of jasmine and orange blossom. This time, John and even the omnipresent roadies Mal and Neil had been left behind; the only others on the trip were Tony Bramwell, now deputy head of Apple Films, and Paul's old Liverpool friend Ivan Vaughan, principal of the still-germinating Apple school.

Bramwell's memoir *Magical Mystery Tours: My Life with the Beatles* gives a rollicking account of the initial 24 hours in their shared bungalow, literally inundated with gorgeous young women competing for Paul's attention. At that stage, the front runner seemed to be Winona Williams, a spectacular African-American model who'd previously dated Jimi Hendrix and would later move on to David Bowie. But when the night's partying was over and a day's work lay ahead, Bramwell noted, Paul cleared every female from the place 'like sweeping away the ashes with a broom'.

He spent the following day conscientiously with Bramwell and Ron Kass at the Capitol convention, announcing the manufacturing and distribution deal with Apple and charming executives. When he returned to the bungalow, he found it once again full of females, Linda now among them. Rather than return his phone call in the expectation of being bought a plane ticket, she had paid her own way. To ensure her welcome, she'd brought along a draw-string bag full of the pot she smoked along with all her rock-star subjects. 'She was waiting for [Paul] radiantly, totally spaced out,' Bramwell writes. 'She had a joint in her hand and a beatific smile on her face.'

Suddenly, all the other, more obvious beauties crowding the bungalow, ringing its phones or stalking through the orange and jasmine groves became a severe embarrassment. 'Like a poacher caught with a string of salmon,' Bramwell continues, 'Paul pretended they were not his catch. "They're all with Tony and Ivan," he said.' Vaughan, the ultra-respectable married schoolteacher, must have found this a specially surreal moment.

'Then Paul detached himself from the circus surrounding him and took Linda aside. As I looked across the room, I suddenly saw something happen. Right before my eyes, they fell in love. It was like the thunderbolt the Sicilians speak of, the *coup de foudre* the French speak of in hushed tones, that once-in-a-lifetime feeling.' Or, to use his own term, he finally 'clicked'.

Later, at LA's famous star hangout the Whisky à Go-Go, he and Linda sat in a secluded corner booth with Bramwell and Vaughan forming a hedge against inquisitive eyes. Coincidentally, the next booth was occupied by Eric Burdon of the Animals, Linda's first-ever photographic conquest, and Georgie Fame, who'd been playing London's Bag O'Nails club the night she met Paul there. After a ritual hour or so in the celebrity darkness, he took her back to the bungalow, leaving his two co-occupants to party on tactfully until dawn.

The next morning, Bramwell received instructions to refuse all social invitations, even one to a 'toga party', twentieth-century Hollywood's version of a Roman orgy. Winona Williams quickly realised the score and withdrew with dignity but, alas, was not the only one to believe she had a special pass to Paul. There was also Peggy Lipton, an 18-year-old model and TV actress he'd been seeing in America for the past couple of years – even been photographed with hand-in-hand. Knowing nothing of the developments with Linda, she called up Tony Bramwell repeatedly, asking when she and Paul would be getting together.

For most of that day, he remained in seclusion with Linda and her little drawstring bag of pot. Finally, the hundreds of fans outside among the jasmine and orange blossom recalled him to his duty; he emerged, bare-chested, with his guitar, sat on the bungalow steps and played them a just-written song, 'Blackbird'.

The one social engagement he was loath to break was an invitation from the theatre director Mike Nichols to sail to Catalina Island in Nichols's yacht. Also aboard would be Dustin Hoffman, the lauded young star of Nichols's recent film-directorial debut, *The Graduate*, which Paul had hugely admired. He wanted Linda invited, too, but felt queasy about revealing their secret just yet; Nichols and Hoffman, therefore, were led to believe she was merely shadowing him for a photographic assignment.

Unfortunately, Peggy Lipton learned of the trip and met the party at the hotel entrance, still convinced she was Paul's preferred escort. 'I had to tell her in the nicest possible way that it was a private party, while Linda stood quietly to one side, pretending she wasn't with us,' writes Tony Bramwell. 'Peggy was very upset and got very argumentative . . . We drove off fast, leaving [her] standing on the hotel-steps in tears.'

That evening found Paul and Linda sharing another ride to an airport before flying off in different directions, he back to London, she to New York. '[They] were like Siamese twins,' writes Bramwell, 'holding hands and gazing into each other's eyes.'

As they awaited their respective flights at LAX, a security alert was announced and squads of armed officers began searching departing passengers' hand luggage. According to Bramwell, the remains of Linda's pot supply were in a vanity case, which she'd put under her seat. As the searchers approached, she gave the case a surreptitious backward kick, sending it sliding across the floor and under a neighbouring row of empty seats, where – because unattended luggage as yet caused no alarm – it lay completely unnoticed.

Twelve years later, as man and wife at Tokyo airport, they wouldn't be so lucky.

In July 1968, Apple Corps moved its headquarters to 3 Savile Row, the select Mayfair street traditionally devoted to London's bespoke tailoring trade. Number three was a classic plain-fronted Georgian townhouse, five storeys high, fronted by iron railings, with a flight of stone steps up to its entrance. Ironically, it had formerly been the headquarters of Jack Hylton, the bandleader-turned-impresario who, three years earlier, had blocked Paul's attempt to become his neighbour in Regent's Park.

The building was purchased outright for half a million pounds – a bargain even then – and refurbished to the highest standard, its interior repainted white, its corridors, stairs and reception area carpeted in apple green. The senior executives were allowed to choose the décor and furnishings of their elegant panelled offices. On the second floor was a kitchen, staffed by two debutantes warranted to cook to cordon bleu standard. The grandest front ground-floor room was provided with a ten-foot oak conference table with a gold-bordered leather top, and four carefully unmatched but equally costly and comfortable armchairs. Here, the idea was John, Paul, George and Ringo would direct their great business project in the ultimate manifestation of the group mind.

Although Regent Street and the West End were only yards away, security in the modern sense was completely absent. It consisted of a single doorman in a dove-grey tailcoat, with orders to let in only authorised visitors (a task in which he would prove sadly deficient) and control the cluster of fans at the bottom of the steps. Some were foreign tourists but most were the young women to be found stationed patiently outside Beatle recording studios and homes at all hours and in all weathers. From now on, they had a nickname, coined by George at one of his least charming moments – Apple Scruffs.

Three Savile Row was primarily to be the home of Apple Records, with everything the label needed housed under its

200-year-old roof. Peter Asher's A&R department settled in on the top floor while work began on converting the basement into a recording studio. John's electronics 'guru', Magic Alex Mardas, was commissioned to design and install facilities, including a 72-track recording-desk, which would make Abbey Road look like something from the Stone Age.

Asher remembers the hard work Paul put into setting up Apple Records and the genuine idealism he brought to the project. 'For months beforehand, he had plans and charts spread out at his house. His idea was to completely change the rules under which record companies had operated. For all the time the Beatles had been making records, their idea of a record company boss had been Sir Joseph Lockwood [the chairman of EMI]. Paul wanted to create a label that totally believed in the people it signed and did everything possible to encourage and develop them. "Artiste-friendly" was what it came to be called. And in the future, every company would be like that.'

Paul had announced the label's *raison d'être* with a large display advertisement – conceived, art-directed and written by himself – which appeared in the *New Musical Express* and other leading trade publications the previous April. It showed his aide Alistair Taylor playing a guitar and singing with a bass drum on his back and a pile of brass band instruments round his feet, under the headline 'This man has talent'.

> One day, he sang his songs into a tape recorder (borrowed
> from the man next door). In his neatest handwriting he wrote
> an explanatory note (giving his name and address) and,
> remembering to enclose a picture of himself, sent the tape,
> letter and photograph to *apple* music, 94 Baker Street, London
> W.1. If you were thinking of doing the same thing yourself,
> do it now. **This man now owns a Bentley.**

In years to come, nationwide appeals from TV pop talent shows would produce competent – often gifted – candidates by the thousand. But in 1968, pop stardom wasn't yet a career for which most British boys and girls seemed to spend their whole adolescence rehearsing. The wording of Paul's invitation implicitly limited it to males, and merely asking for tapes, rather than holding live auditions, virtually guaranteed the main response would come from the solitary, the sad and the delusional. Sacks full of cassette tapes, lyric sheets, letters and photographs poured in to 94 Baker Street and kept coming after Apple moved to Wigmore Street, then Savile Row. Peter Asher received the job of sifting through them, helped by a couple of secretaries. 'In the whole lot, we found nothing,' he is still incredulous to recall. *'Nothing.'*

Talent had to find its way to the label by more roundabout means. Asher's first discovery was a lanky North Carolinan teenager named James Taylor, lately with a New York band named the Flying Machine whose leader, Danny Kortchmar, used to back Peter and Gordon on their American tours. Taylor was a solo singer/songwriter – a genre that had become all but extinct since the Beatles' rise – with the quiet, yearning style of some long-haired young monk. After hearing a selection of his early work, including 'Knocking Round the Zoo' and 'Something's Wrong', Paul and George gave Asher carte blanche to make an album with him at Trident Studios in Soho. There, a few weeks later, he recorded his classic 'Carolina in My Mind', with Paul on bass.

Another major find came through the unlikely medium of *Opportunity Knocks*, then British TV's only talent show, whose contestants were traditionally incurable amateurs, achingly devoid of originality or charisma. But in May 1968, the audience's vote (registered on a device called a 'Clapometer') was overwhelmingly for Mary Hopkin from Pontardawe, South Wales, an 18-year-old with shoulder-length hair and no smidgen of sexuality, who strummed a guitar and sang in a soprano as clear and unnuanced as a choirboy's.

A fellow member of Swinging London's elite, the model Twiggy, saw her in the show's finals and recommended her to Paul. A few days later, she received a telegram asking her to phone Apple, and was put through to 'a bloke with a Liverpool accent' she didn't immediately recognise as Paul himself. He sent a car to bring her to London to audition, with her mother as chaperone, and afterwards took the two of them for lunch at an Angus Steak House (a tactful choice, for a posh restaurant might have intimidated them). The last thing on his mind when he devised his 'one-man band' advertisement had been a folk-singing Welsh madonna. 'But he instinctively knew what Mary should record as her debut single,' Peter Asher says. 'To me, it was a bit of real genius.'

'Those Were the Days' was an old Russian ballad which had been given its English title and lyrics by the American novelist and folk singer Gene Raskin. Paul had seen Raskin and his wife, Francesca, perform the song at London's Blue Angel club somewhere around 1965, and thought it might suit Donovan or the Moody Blues. Now he presented it to Mary Hopkin in an arrangement counterpointing her sweet soprano with vaguely louche, vodka-flavoured instrumentation. True to his 'do everything' philosophy, he not only produced her recording session but also played acoustic guitar on it.

John, George and Ringo were all impressed by their new Mayfair mansion, and had various personal projects and interests among its multifarious activities. But they tended to come in separately and hang out in the offices of their favourite executives, Neil Aspinall or Peter Brown. The ground-floor salon, where they were to have directed operations around that ten-foot leather-topped table, remained permanently empty.

Paul, however, acted as resident managing director in addition to talent scout, producer and session-musician. He kept office hours, arriving each day around 10.30 and staying until 6 p.m. or later. Often, he didn't bother with his chauffeur-driven limo or stable of traffic warden-proof cars, but simply took a bus in from St John's Wood.

An already indispensable member of Apple's staff was Peter Asher's secretary, Chris O'Dell (no relation to Apple Films' head, Denis O'Dell), a tranquil, ringletty-haired 20-year-old whom press

officer Derek Taylor had met in California. 'Paul had real management skills,' she recalls. 'He cared about his employees and what
they thought. He had a suggestion box installed in the office. Or
you could talk directly to him, and he'd always listen.'

He involved himself in the minutiae of every department, from
vetting the press releases that went out from Taylor's office (frequently correcting their spelling and grammar) to designing the
office Christmas card. 'I can remember a meeting with him about
whether there should be paper towels or cloth ones in the bath-
rooms,' Chris O'Dell says.

With junior female staff, secretaries and receptionists, he was
unfailingly polite and appreciative. Once, after O'Dell had organised something quite routine for him, he sent her a large bunch
of flowers. But middle-rank executives grew accustomed to the
bollockings he could deliver without slackening his smile, and his
way of emphasising points with jocular, but still not quite pleasant,
pokes of a forefinger. 'That McCartney is so charming,' one was
heard confiding to a colleague. 'He calls me a cunt, you know. He
told me I was more clever with words than he was, and then he
tells me I should take a vacation and then he pokes me in the ribs
and starts pulling all those cute chipmunk faces he's got, and then
you can't help but *like* him.'

The one executive not to feel the constant pressure of Paul's interest was Denis O'Dell at Apple Films. It seemed as if the critical
mauling given to *Magical Mystery Tour* had killed his interest in the
medium that used to fascinate him.

In 1968, the only film released under the Apple emblem was
Yellow Submarine, the cartoon fantasy inspired by Paul's *Revolver*
track, which Brian Epstein had authorised shortly before his death.
The Beatles' cartoon figures were voiced by actors and they took
little interest in the production: their only involvement was a handful of consciously substandard songs (including Paul's 'All Together
Now') and a brief on-screen appearance in the flesh with the closing credits. For all their apathy, *Yellow Submarine* turned out to be a
pop art masterpiece which gave a boost to British animation after

decades of Disney-dominance and massively influenced a future TV comedy classic, *Monty Python's Flying Circus*.

Nothing came of the film idea Denis O'Dell had brought out to India so excitedly: the Beatles in J.R.R. Tolkien's *The Lord of the Rings*. At the Maharishi's ashram, it had been provisionally agreed that Paul would play the hobbit Frodo Baggins, John the slithery humanoid Gollum, George the wizard Gandalf and Ringo Frodo's sidekick, Sam. 'John told me he could write a double album to go with it,' O'Dell remembers.

To direct, O'Dell approached the great Stanley Kubrick, then fresh from what many consider his supreme cinematic achievement, *2001: A Space Odyssey*. Even the reclusive Kubrick was not proof against an opportunity to meet the Beatles: he had lunch with John and Paul, was comprehensively charmed, but could see no way of making the picture. Without Paul's shoulder behind it, the project lapsed: not for three decades would others turn Tolkien's books into a multi-billion-dollar movie franchise.

Latterly, there had been an approach from the French director Jean-Luc Godard, a figure revered by John since his student days and Paul since his pretend-student ones. In the combustible political climate of early 1968, Godard embarked on a film about revolution and urban mayhem, part feature, part documentary, to be shot in London and include footage of the Beatles in the recording studio.

Denis O'Dell read the script, was much impressed, then passed it over to Paul. 'Jean-Luc Godard and the Beatles – an amazing combination! I thought Paul would love it and get the others on board in about five minutes.'

A few days later, he called at O'Dell's house in Pimlico, beside the Thames. 'He had tea and a big piece of cake. Then he brought out the Godard script and said it was a "no" because George didn't want to do it. When I tried to persuade him, he just threw the script into the river.

'So Godard used the Rolling Stones instead, and from then on I never had another serious conversation with Paul about films.'

23

'You have found her, now go and get her'

The journalists of all nations who flocked to the Beatles' apple-carpeted ashram on Savile Row never suspected that the sacred foursome had now become five. Nor, for some little time, did Paul, George and Ringo.

After meeting John in 1966 at the Indica gallery, Yoko Ono had not returned home to New York, but settled in London and become a bit-player in its teeming pop cultural pageant. She appeared in the newspapers now and then for attention-grabbing stunts, not yet recognised as 'performance art', such as wrapping the stone lions in Trafalgar Square in white canvas, and making a film named *Bottoms* which was indeed entirely composed of disembodied, naked arses.

The few press pictures of her showed a diminutive Japanese woman in all-over shapeless black whose unsmiling face, half-hidden by untamed black hair, belied the apparent pointlessness and absurdity of her projects. Her art also embraced sculpture, film-making, poetry and music, all in forms very different from their normal ones, and similarly designed to challenge and provoke. At 35, she was eight years older than John, and looked every bit of it. No one further from the instantly accessible, super-chic, sunshiny Beatles could be imagined.

Yoko had fascinated John at their first meeting but – after an initial, clumsy seduction attempt – he made no move to get to know her further for the next two years. Both of them were married,

Yoko to her second husband, the American film-maker Tony Cox, and the thought of the potential scandal scared this supposedly most reckless, unconventional Beatle witless.

Instead, through the eras of *Sgt. Pepper*, the Maharishi and setting up Apple, Yoko had remained tantalisingly in John's peripheral vision. Next to his bed, he kept a copy of her book, *Grapefruit*, a collection of what she called 'instructional poems' and meant to be obeyed as literally as notes in a musical score, e.g. 'Steal a moon on the water with a bucket' or 'Draw a map to get lost'.

When she put together an exhibition called the Half a Wind Show – comprising halves of domestic objects like a table, a chair and a bed – she asked and received funding from John, though he was still too timid to let his name appear as co-sponsor. During his Indian retreat, she sent him a stream of postcards with cryptic messages like 'Look for me, I'm a cloud in the sky', which Tony Bramwell would relay to him at Rishikesh in plain brown envelopes so that his wife, Cynthia, wouldn't see them.

They had finally got together in May 1968, fittingly just after John's Apple-promotion trip to New York with Paul – and Paul's rediscovery of Linda Eastman. While Cynthia was away on holiday, he invited Yoko to his faux-Tudor mansion in Surrey. Cynthia returned home to find the two of them there together and a pair of Japanese slippers outside her bedroom-door.

John's experience with Yoko, in fact, had been exactly Paul's with Linda: after years with a never quite satisfactory or sympathetic partner, he finally 'clicked'. A decade later, that epiphany would still be fresh in his mind. 'My God [I thought] this is different from anything before. This is more than a hit record. It's more than gold. It's more than anything.'

He immediately left Cynthia and their five-year-old son, Julian, and Yoko left her husband, Tony Cox, and daughter, Kyoko. Following the protocol of Liverpudlian 'best mates', Paul was first to hear about it from John: the intention was less to put him in the picture than to warn him off, in case he had any designs on Yoko.

Not for John and Yoko the discretion Paul had always exercised

She Loves Them Yeah! Yeah! Yeah! At Buckingham Palace after receiving their MBEs from the Queen, 26 October 1965.

Rampant Beatlemania, held in check by the tolerant British bobbies of yesteryear.

Gentleman-guru: Sgt. Pepper-era Paul in the studio with the Beatles' producer, George Martin, who turned his increasingly ambitious concepts into reality.

Paul and Jane: the classy young actress introduced him to a sophisticated new world of classical music and West End first nights.

Above and below left Always patient with fans and ready to sign autographs – even when one fan waylays him outside the Ashers' home in Wimpole Street.

Above right The hippy look takes hold. Back then, no pop idol minded being seen with a 'ciggie'.

Right 1967: Paul is cornered by an American photographer named Linda Eastman.

Far right The short-lived Apple boutique with the mural that outraged its Baker Street neighbours.

Left The Beatles film
their second clip for
'Hello, Goodbye' at the
Saville Theatre on 10
November 1967 during a
filming session for the
Magical Mystery Tour.

Below left With his
cartoon self in the *Yellow
Submarine* film.

Right Paul with Martha,
his Old English sheepdog.

Below Paul and Jane,
almost like a young royal
couple – though he said
they never really 'clicked'.

With John and Derek Taylor at the launch of Apple Corps. Paul says he already knew they were out of their depth.

A bit of clowning to try to hide the unstoppable drift apart.

over his amours; from the beginning, theirs was a performance art partnership as much as a romance. They announced both at the same moment by ceremonially burying two acorns near Coventry Cathedral, one facing west and one east to symbolise their respective cultures. Yoko immediately replaced Cynthia at John's public appearances, like the opening of Apple's new bespoke tailoring shop in Chelsea and the first night of a play based on his comic drawings and writing, *The John Lennon Play: In His Own Write*, at the National Theatre.

John had always fantasised about what he naively termed 'exotic Orientals' and Yoko, despite her fondness for shapeless black and seeming abhorrence of hairdressers, did possess a powerful sexual magnetism. But she had other, more potent attractions. She was a 'real' artist, a species he had always revered and secretly yearned to join. Perhaps the greatest aphrodisiac for him was her fearlessness: she simply did not give a shit what people thought of her work or of her. The life she'd made for herself was the antithesis of John's controlled, constricted, compulsorily smiley Beatle existence, and it electrified him with envy and longing.

At Yoko's prompting, he put aside the little cartoons that had filled two best-selling books, and began seeking recognition as a conceptual artist in the same challenging mode. Apple's arrival in Savile Row coincided with his first exhibition, at the nearby Robert Fraser Gallery; titled 'You Are Here', it featured an array of charity collection-boxes, a rusty bicycle and the release over London of hundreds of white balloons saying 'You are here'. Although Yoko was the show's driving force, John might never have met London's most adventurous gallery-owner in the first place but for Paul.

The full implications of the new partnership didn't become clear until the Beatles finally got down to work on their next album. More than a year had passed since the release of *Sgt. Pepper's Lonely Hearts Club Band* and a huge amount of Lennon-McCartney material had built up, largely thanks to their stay in India. It was therefore decided to use the novel double disc format already pioneered by

Bob Dylan's *Blonde on Blonde* and Frank Zappa's *Freak Out!*, which would accommodate around 30 tracks compared to the usual 12-15.

When they reconvened in Abbey Road's Studio 2, John had Yoko with him. A woman entering a monastery or some antediluvian Oxbridge college would hardly have caused greater shock. 'Northern blokes just didn't take their wives and girlfriends to work,' says Tony Bramwell. 'Right from the start, the rule had always been "no women in the studio". Pattie might drop by occasionally to pick up George or Maureen to meet Ringo if they were going on to a club somewhere, but that was it.'

Fully aware of the enormity, John implied it was just a one-off visit, because Yoko had been depressed and needed cheering up. 'I had no idea what he'd told the others,' she would remember. 'I couldn't understand why they kept asking me if I was feeling better.' It being unthinkable for Lennon to enjoy a privilege that McCartney didn't, Jane Asher soon afterwards found herself invited to her first Beatles recording session in five years with Paul. As his relationship with Jane began to peter out, he took to bringing along Francie Schwartz, the New Yorker working in Apple's press office who'd recently caught his eye.

A studio snapshot shows Francie sitting on the floor, watching him sing and play a new song he'd written after visiting his father and stepmother, Angie, in Cheshire. Angie's mother, Edie – she who had once innocently made 'marzipan butties' for Paul instead of cheese – was staying at the house after an illness. Edie was finding it hard to sleep at night, she told him, but found solace in the song of a blackbird outside her window which seemed unaware that the day was over. Paul tape-recorded the sound and, within a few minutes, had a song to go with it.

His recent transfiguring encounter with Linda Eastman in LA did not stop him beginning an affair with Francie Schwartz, and after things ended with Jane he asked Francie to move into Cavendish with him, again not bothering to keep it a secret from his colleagues at Apple. Peter Asher's secretary, Chris O'Dell, took over Francie's old flat in Chelsea.

He was also still seeing his undemanding 'secret' girlfriend, Maggie McGivern. 'One day while we were out in his car, he suddenly got an inspiration for a song and needed a piano to try it out,' she recalls. 'So we stopped by Alma Cogan's flat in Kensington. Alma had died by then [of cancer in 1966] but her sister, Sandra, knew Paul, too, and was very welcoming. That was how I became the first person ever to hear "The Long and Winding Road".'

Yoko, meanwhile, proved to be no mere day tripper to Abbey Road. She came in with John every evening and sat beside him on a stool for every minute. When he wanted to talk about something he was singing or playing, it was no longer to Paul or George Martin that he turned first, but to her. They never separated for a moment; even when John visited the men's toilet Yoko would follow him, not just to the door but all the way inside.

It has gone down in history as the ultimate example of her pushiness and determination that no one else should have a moment alone with him. According to Yoko, she was merely indulging his almost pathological jealousy and possessiveness. 'He *made* me go into the toilet with him. He was afraid that if I stayed in the studio by myself even for a few minutes, Paul or one of the other Beatles might make a move on me.'

Unbeknown to the others, John had decided she should become a fifth Beatle; something in which Yoko saw nothing strange whatsoever. Although she knew nothing about pop music – claiming never even to have heard of the Beatles before first meeting John – she didn't hesitate to offer criticisms of the tracks they were working on and to pontificate about their place in contemporary culture. Thinking her just another passing Lennon fad, the other three were extraordinarily tolerant, refraining from even the faintest Scouse sarkiness to her face. It grated with Paul that when speaking of the band, she called them 'Beatles' without a definite article: 'Beatles mean this' or 'Beatles should do that'. 'It's *the* Beatles actually, love,' he longed to say but never did.

Recording and mixing took five months, almost as long as *Sgt. Pepper* but in very different conditions. George Martin had tired of being a grossly underpaid and undervalued EMI employee and left to set up his own independent studio. Working now as a hired-in freelance, he was no longer on tap whenever Paul, in particular, felt the creative urge.

As time passed, it had increasingly seemed to Martin that he was no longer working with a group mind but with three soloists, each with a different and competitive agenda. Once Yoko had broken into the magic circle, others soon followed. To play on his (suddenly) impressive song 'While My Guitar Gently Weeps', George passed over the Beatles' two highly competent alternative lead guitarists and brought in his friend, Eric Clapton. Time was spent on an inferior Lennon track entitled 'What's the New Mary Jane?', half-written (so John later claimed) by Magic Alex Mardas. Of the double album's eventual 30 tracks, only 16 would feature all four Beatles together.

Gone was the happy atmosphere of all their previous recording sessions back to 'Love Me Do', which had always made itself felt in the music. George Martin was appalled by Yoko's presence, and the interventions and distractions from her that repeatedly took John's mind off the business at hand; though he was too much of a gentleman to say anything outright, the chill from the control room was palpable. Work periodically ground to a halt when someone went on holiday without forewarning the others – a sign of indifference of which even the usually punctilious Martin was guilty.

The only one to stay totally committed and focused was Paul, and what was seen as his schoolmasterly bossiness and badgering caused strife with George and John – or, rather, the two-headed entity John had become – that even their worst pressures on the road never could. We were all fed up of being sidemen for Paul', John would later observe, though in fairness Paul was just as often a sideman for him.

The bad atmosphere finally even got to studio engineer Geoff Emerick, who'd been on every session since 'Love Me Do', and made many important contributions along the way. Unable to stand the three's 'arguing among themselves and swearing at each other', Emerick quit in the middle of the sessions for Paul's 'Ob-La-Di, Ob-La-Da'.

The unravelling of the group mind was perhaps best illustrated by 'Revolution 9'. This had started out as the finale to John's 'Revolution', but had been extended by him and Yoko into a separate track heavy with the influence of Karlheinz Stockhausen. Eight minutes long, it was a melange of random sound effects and squibbling tape-loops, punctuated by spoken interjections from John – and George – and Yoko's voice repeating, for no discernible reason, 'You become naked'. It was recorded while Paul was away in America, and finished by the time he returned.

His own appreciation of experimental music (and reverence for Stockhausen) far predated John's; he had in fact instigated a not dissimilar piece during the 'Penny Lane' sessions two years earlier, which was premiered (on tape) at the Roundhouse under the title 'Carnival of Light'. But until now, surrealistic sound effects had appeared on Beatles tracks only in tightly-controlled portions. Backed by Martin, he argued that putting 'Revolution 9' on the album was a piece of self-indulgence that would leave most listeners totally baffled. But John, backed by Yoko and George, insisted on its inclusion. The most avant-garde Beatle thus found himself cast as a play-safe reactionary, standing in the way of experimentation and adventure.

Ironically, the worst upset was precipitated by the band's least demanding member: the drummer so resigned to his eternal back seat that he'd used the hours of *Sgt. Pepper* sessions not involving him to learn to play chess. Halfway through work on 'Back in the USSR', Ringo fluffed a tom-tom fill and received one of Paul's little lectures, followed by a demonstration of how it *really* should be done. His response was to fling down his sticks and exit in an unprecedented huff, saying that his playing clearly was no longer good enough and he felt like the odd man out. (When he mentioned the latter to John and Paul in turn, each replied that he thought *he* was the odd man out.) The real reason, George Martin says, was that he couldn't take any more bickering.

His defection – to Sardinia, to stay on his movie friend Peter Sellers's yacht – was hardly catastrophic. Paul took over as drummer on 'Back in the USSR' and on John's 'Dear Prudence'. But it made his bandmates feel like warring parents who suddenly notice a child looking miserably down through the banisters. A contrite telegram from all three was immediately dispatched ('You're the best rock 'n' roll drummer in the world . . . we love you'), and when Ringo returned to Abbey Road, a couple of weeks later, he found welcome back posters all round the studio and his drum-kit covered in flowers.

If only the other problems ahead could have been resolved so simply.

Yoko's affair with John transformed her from marginal eccentric to the most hated and reviled woman in Britain. The media portrayed her with one voice as a ruthless hustler who'd set out to snare a Beatle solely to use his wealth and fame to advance her own infinitely less worthwhile career. Enduring anger over Japan's brutality to Allied prisoners in the Second World War – and enduring, unchecked racism – also came into play. Leaving his nice English wife and child for someone whom it was totally acceptable to call a 'Jap' seemed the ultimate example of Lennon waywardness, only now no longer amusing or endearing.

There was equal unanimity from John's female fans, every one of whom had considered herself next in line should the day ever come when he was no longer with Cynthia. Wherever Yoko appeared publicly at his side, she was greeted with cries of 'Jap!', 'Chink!', 'Yellow!' and 'River Kwai!', jostled, kicked, spat at and yanked by the hair. One day, a group of girls offered her a bunch of yellow roses the wrong way round so that the thorns would tear her hands when she accepted them.

Whatever Paul's reservations about Yoko, there was no question but that he'd be there for John amid these hurricanes of hate. The pair were living like fugitives – albeit with the cushion of John's wealth and the Apple support system – crashing at friends' flats, then moving on before the press could trace them. Paul offered sanctuary at Cavendish, where they stayed a month in company with his just-moved-in girlfriend, Francie Schwartz. Though few women got along with Yoko, fellow New Yorker Francie did; she would later fondly recall how John 'liked his cornflakes' and the three of them trying opium together.

John and Yoko were by no means the only negative Beatles headlines that summer. On 3 July, the Apple boutique in Baker Street closed down after barely six months' trading. The garments made by its Dutch design group, The Fool, had proved too weird and far too expensive for its hoped-for mainstream clientele, while the fatal combination of semi-darkness and amateurish staff had created a shoplifters' heaven. Not that Paul admitted any of that when questioned about the decision; it was simply, he said with Napoleonic loftiness, that 'the Beatles are tired of being shopkeepers'.

The four and their inner circle had first pick of the remaining merchandise, then the doors were thrown open for the public to help themselves. Scenes of plunder and tug of war ensued that even Harrods' New Year sale could not have matched. One middle-aged businessman was seen to emerge wearing a multicoloured jump-suit so constricting that he could only hop.

On 17 July, John once again showed off Yoko – now no longer dressed in shapeless black but tailored white – at the London premiere of *Yellow Submarine*. That evening, very noticeably, Paul had no Jane doing her usual royal duty beside him.

Three days later, on the BBC's *Dee Time* programme, she told host Simon Dee she was no longer engaged to Paul and that their five-year relationship was over. 'I haven't broken it off but it's broken off, finished,' she said. 'I know it sounds corny, but we still see each other and love each other . . . but it hasn't worked out. Perhaps we'll be childhood sweethearts and meet again and get married when we're about 70.'

Paul himself would only ever volunteer that he'd 'got cold feet' – a normal enough thing for a young man of 26, even if the refrigeration process wasn't quite as sudden as it appeared. Jane, on her side, refused all offers from Fleet Street to sell her story – and throughout her subsequent career as successful actress and author would maintain the same dignified silence.

In the press, there was regret that as one lead Beatle acquired a consort so grotesquely unsuitable, the other should part with one who'd seemed so eminently suitable. Even the female pickets who haunted Paul's gate admitted how nice Jane had always been and how perfect he and she had looked together. But among the Apple Scruffs there was no hiding the jubilation: he was *available* again.

In reality, the break-up wasn't quite as clean and civilised as it appeared. Not long after her *Dee Time* announcement, Jane paid a surprise return visit to Cavendish, evidently having been told that Paul now had Francie Schwartz living there and seeking to verify the story for herself. The girls at the front gate saw her coming and rang the entryphone to warn him, but he wouldn't believe them and as a result he was caught in bed with Francie.

Later, too, there was an uncomfortable encounter with Jane's mother – who'd once been nearly as much to him – when Margaret Asher arrived to take away her daughter's remaining possessions. In the same spirit, Jane's brother, Peter, to whom she'd always been specially close, might have been expected to resign, or be fired, from his job as Apple Records' A&R head. But he and Paul managed to preserve their friendship and go on developing the label as fruitfully as ever. 'I can't remember ever waking up in the morning and thinking "Oh shit, I don't want to go into work today,"' Asher says.

Paul's loyalty to John, though absolute, was far from unconditional. After six years of marriage, Cynthia Lennon had found herself expelled from his life with extraordinary cruelty and ruthlessness. Pending their divorce, she was still living at their Weybridge mansion, shunned by everyone in the Beatles' circle she'd formerly considered her friends, like Pattie Harrison and Maureen Starkey. Only Paul, who had always liked and sympathised with Cynthia, refused to join in the boycott. Regardless of how John might react, he drove down to see her in Weybridge, presented her with a single red rose and joked, 'Well, how about it, Cyn? Why don't you and I get married now?'

The worst aspect of the affair for Paul was John's abandonment of his five-year-old son, Julian, even though the trauma of being given away by his own father at the same age had never left him – and never would. The hurt was compounded by his easy acceptance of Yoko's daughter, Kyoko, an unruly six-year-old, to whom she was given occasional access by her husband, Tony Cox. Then, to make Julian's rejection complete, Yoko fell pregnant.

Paul had always been good with children and, over the years, had taken more interest in Julian – certainly played with him more often – than John ever had. During the boat trip around the Greek islands, John had watched the two of them have a riotous game of cowboys, then taken Paul aside and asked, 'How do you *do* that?'

'Paul was really close to Julian,' Maggie McGivern recalls. 'I'd seen them playing together for hours in the pool at John and Cynthia's house. He thought it was really awful that John should be doing to his son just what his own dad had to him.'

On the drive down to see Cynthia, he'd begun writing a song for Julian, intended to be both a message of comfort and an exhortation not to give up hope. It began with the lightly-fictionalised title 'Hey Jules', but then metamorphosed into 'Hey Jude', an echo of Thomas Hardy's tragic novel *Jude the Obscure*. As well as consoling advice to Julian, it was an oblique criticism of John that ended up lasting seven minutes; a prodigious length for a 1968 pop song. John, however, missed the point completely, seizing on the line 'You have found her, now go and get her' as support for his affair with Yoko.

Even here, the Lennon–McCartney symbiosis couldn't stop working. One verse still lacked a final rhyme and Paul was singing nonsense words, 'the movement you need is on your shoulder', until he could think of proper ones. But John told him it was the best line in the song, so he left it as it was. In years to come, playing it alone to seas of rapturous faces, the memory of that moment would always bring a lump to his throat.

'Hey Jude' owed its first public performance to Paul's parallel careers as Apple Records' talent scout and producer and independent freelance composer (always thinking ahead to those 'leather elbow' years after he passed 30, when the Beatles were no more). Recently, he had somehow found time to write theme music for a Yorkshire Television sitcom called *Thingumybob*, starring the great character actor Stanley Holloway. His score was intended for a northern brass band such as he'd loved since boyhood, the kind traditionally formed by workers in collieries or factories.

To perform it – and also record it for Apple – he chose the century-old, multi-award-winning Black Dyke Mills Band, originating from John Foster and Son's cloth mill in Queensbury, near Bradford. Seeking the most authentic sound possible, he recorded them in a church hall in Saltaire, near Shipley, making the 200-mile journey north by road with Peter Asher, Tony Bramwell, Derek Taylor, music journalist Alan Smith and Martha, the sheepdog.

The Black Dyke Mills Band instantly fell under the dual spell of McCartney charm and professionalism, and the taping of 'Thingumybob', plus an instrumental version of 'Yellow Submarine', went off without a hitch. But the spell-creating wasn't over yet. On their return journey to London, the Apple party decided to stop for dinner in rural Bedfordshire and turned off the main road at a signpost to Harrold simply because they liked the name.

Harrold turned out to be an almost impossibly perfect village of thatched cottages and riotous gardens, bathed in evening sun. What happened there would be recalled by Derek Taylor in his 1974 memoir *As Time Goes By*, as if it had been a midsummer night's acid trip:

> We found ourselves in [the local dentist's] house, below dipping oak beams, a banquet provided for us, hams and pies and salads, new bread and cakes, chicken and fruit and wine, and the dentist's wife, a jolly lady, still young beyond her maddest

fantasies, bringing out her finest fare. Paul McCartney was at her table in the village of Harrold.

Hiding at a turn on the crooked staircase stood a little girl, shy and disbelieving. But she had brought a right-handed guitar, and landed it in Paul's (left-handed) hands, but the wizards were producing this play by now and floating with the splendour of this, the strangest Happening since Harrold was born, the dentist and his wife, and the neighbours as they crowded the windows and the parlour, and the children, all caught their breath as Paul began to play the song he'd written that week . . . which went 'Hey Jude, don't make it bad, take a sad song and make it better . . .'

Afterwards, they all adjourned to the village pub, which had been kept open after hours in Paul's honour. True son of Jim Mac that he was, he played the bar piano, sang and led community singing until 3 a.m.

When a woman from the village gave a rendition of 'The Fool on the Hill', it wasn't until midway through that he realised she was on crutches. He went over, danced a couple of gentle steps with her, kissed her on the cheek, then returned to the piano and struck up again.

On 30 August, the Apple label released its first four titles simultaneously in the UK: the Beatles' 'Hey Jude', Mary Hopkin's 'Those Were the Days', 'Thingumybob' by the Black Dyke Mills Band and 'Sour Milk Sea' by Jackie Lomax. The last-named, formerly vocalist with Liverpool band the Undertakers, was a protégé of George Harrison's, singing a George song; otherwise, everything had been either written, vocalised, discovered or produced by Paul.

A special presentation edition in a shiny black box, labelled 'Our First Four', was hand-delivered to each of the British establishment's first four: the Queen at Buckingham Palace, the Queen Mother at Clarence House, Princess Margaret at Kensington Palace and Prime Minister Harold Wilson at 10 Downing Street. The music business had never seen a record company take such patent pride in its artistes, nor aim so high.

'Hey Jude' was paired with John's 'Revolution' but marketed as the A-side for pragmatic commercial reasons, not least its greater acceptability to America, where real revolution currently seemed very close. (It clearly would also go down much better with the inhabitants of Buckingham Palace, Clarence House, Kensington Palace and 10 Downing Street.) John wasn't happy with the decision but, having larger matters than the Beatles now on his mind, accepted it.

In America, it spent nine weeks at number one, the longest-ever run for a Beatles single, having 'gone gold' with sales of a million copies after only two. In Britain, it had just two weeks in the top spot before being displaced by 'Those Were the Days', which in turn was displaced by Joe Cocker's cover of 'With a Little Help from My Friends' from the *Sgt. Pepper* album.

'Hey Jude' received its British TV premiere on the *David Frost Show*, in a seemingly live performance to a large studio audience. Though actually pre-recorded, it was still the Beatles' first public recital since 1966 and as such attracted a colossal viewership. Coincidentally, John and Yoko had been Frost's guests two weeks earlier, promoting a piece of Yoko performance art called 'Hammer a Nail In'. Audience members took turns to hammer a nail into a block of wood and then describe the emotions it caused them. Even the fawning host, when asked to try it himself, could not pretend to have found it illuminating.

But for the 'Hey Jude' broadcast, to palpable general relief, Yoko was nowhere in sight, and even John chose to take an atypically low profile. It was virtually a solo turn by Paul at the piano in red velvet, brown eyes heartbroken above the mic as the singalong power of that four-minute-long 'Na na na nanana na' coda was unleashed for the very first time.

He could never resist a promotional opportunity, however small. Since closing down, the Apple boutique had stood empty and forlorn in Baker Street, its formerly riotous display windows

blotted out by white paint. Unwilling to waste such a prime location, Paul paid it a visit, accompanied by Francie Schwartz and
Alistair Taylor, and scratched 'Hey Jude' on the whitened glass. Unfortunately, it was mistaken for the anti-Semitic slogan *Juden Raus*
(Jews Out) that used to be daubed on Jewish-owned premises in
Nazi Germany. An outraged passer-by smashed the window and a
local Jewish shopkeeper telephoned Paul and threatened him with
physical violence.

By now, he had tired of Francie and was cursing himself for
having moved her into Cavendish. Though she didn't realise she'd
worn out her welcome, her Apple colleagues did – some hearing
it directly from Paul himself. 'I remember being with him at the
house one day,' Chris O'Dell says. 'Francie was in the next room,
and he was going, "How can I get rid of her?"'

Soon afterwards, Chris left the country temporarily. She had
come from California to work at Apple without the necessary work
permit, and the Home Office ruled she could only apply for one
outside Britain. 'I went to Ireland to get the permit, which took
longer than I expected and I ended up being there for about three
weeks. When I got back, Francie wasn't around any more.'

With that problem tidied away, Paul turned back to someone
with whom he'd always felt comfortable and who never asked
anything from him. 'Out of the blue, he rang me up,' Maggie
McGivern remembers. 'He told me to pack my bags because we
were off to the sun tomorrow. I told him I hadn't got a passport.
"Don't worry," he said. "You won't need one."'

The next day, a car collected Maggie from her Chelsea flat,
then stopped to pick up Paul in St John's Wood. As he came out,
one of the girls who haunted his gate realised he was going on
holiday and offered him an Instamatic camera, which he accepted.
'At the airport, we met up with one of Paul's Liverpool cousins
[Uncle Jack's son, John] and his American girlfriend. Paul had chartered a private jet. I still didn't know where we were going.'

They flew to Sardinia, spending five days in a beach-side hotel
and living in swimsuits, T-shirts and flip-flops. Looking back to

illicit drives in his Aston Martin with Maggie, Paul started a song called 'In the Back Seat of My Car', too late for the now double album – and in fact never destined to be released by the Beatles.

'We met this English couple on the beach who invited us to dinner and seemed so nice that Paul accepted,' Maggie recalls. 'We turned up in our shorts and T-shirts, only to find it was a formal banquet with women in long dresses, covered with expensive jewellery. Paul was complaining that he couldn't get drunk any more, because the Beatles had got so used to every kind of booze, so the waiter started bringing us a local concoction called a Sardinia that was absolutely lethal.

'We were in a big room with wooden rafters, and after a few Sardinias, he jumped up and started swinging from one of the overhead beams. I expected all these women in their jewels and finery to be shocked, but several of them got up and started swinging beside him.

'One day when we were coming out of the sea, Paul said, "What would you think about getting married?" I gave some flip answer like "You never know what may happen." That was how casual and jokey our relationship was.'

They weren't spotted by the media until their last day, when a photographer snapped them walking through the town. The following Sunday, after they'd returned to London and gone their separate ways, the picture appeared in Britain's *Sunday People* with a story about 'Paul McCartney's new girlfriend'.

'I phoned him up and said, "If anyone asks me if it's true, what shall I say?"' Maggie remembers. 'He said, "Tell the truth."' With that, he faded out of her life once again.

Chris O'Dell, too, recalls how he seemed 'a little lost' at this point, and compensated by devoting even more of his energies to Apple. He had launched a subsidiary of Apple Records called Zapple, to be run by his old Indica bookshop friend Barry Miles and devoted to the spoken word. Miles was to start with a series featuring top contemporary writers from Allen Ginsberg and Lawrence

Ferlinghetti to Charles Bukowski, Michael McClure and Richard Brautigan; later, world leaders like China's Mao Zedong and India's prime minister Indira Gandhi were to be invited to expound their political philosophies. No one doubted that, for Paul McCartney, they would all form an orderly queue.

Although he remained as meticulous and micromanagerial at 3 Savile Row as ever – even designing a uniform cover for Zapple's intended 'paperback records' – his out-of-office life now became atypically confused and chaotic. His former skill at disentangling himself from one-night stands seemed to disappear: at one point, he had three women at once living at Cavendish. 'They *argue*,' he complained to Barry Miles. When one of the trio remained stubbornly deaf to hints that her time was up, he threw her suitcase over the wall into Cavendish Avenue.

Not until late September did he realise the message of 'Hey Jude' that John had so taken to heart – 'you have found her, now go and get her' – applied equally to himself. He phoned Linda Eastman in New York and asked her to return to London without delay. She instantly agreed.

When she arrived, Paul was at Abbey Road with the Beatles, so Mal Evans met her at the airport and took her to Cavendish, where she was to wait for him. She was a little disconcerted by the squalor into which the house had descended since she'd last seen it. Previously, what had struck her were the paintings on the walls; now it was that, among all the state-of-the-art electronic gadgets, 'nothing worked'. In the refrigerator, she found only a mouldering bottle of milk and a wedge of ancient cheese.

When Paul finally returned, he brought a tape of the song the Beatles had recorded that night. It wasn't one of his, but John's 'Happiness Is a Warm Gun' – a horribly prophetic title if ever there was one. He still insisted on playing it to Linda before they fell into bed.

These comings and goings had, of course, been witnessed by the knot of his female fans who kept watch outside the front gate around the clock. On this balmy September night, their patience brought a rare reward: the sound of Paul singing 'Blackbird' through the open music-room window.

He was welcoming Linda into his world of perpetual song but the girls, eavesdropping 'in the dead of night', preferred to think it was for them.

PART THREE

Home, Family, Love

24

'You've been playing on the roof again and your Mommy doesn't like it'

The arrival of the Beatles' double album, on 22 November 1968, was an event like none in pop music before. Yes, there had been huge anticipatory audiences for other records, other long lines waiting for record stores to open, other dashes home to audio equipment like the diarrhoea-smitten to toilets. But never quite such hunger to possess, such prestige in ownership, such kudos in being first to know a tracklist by heart.

The packaging was as different as it could be from the dazzle and pomp and fun of *Sgt. Pepper's Lonely Hearts Club Band*. In place of Peter Blake's psychedelic pantheon was a plain white front cover showing only the artistes' name, in small, off-centre type, and a serial number. Created by a different, more cerebral pop artist, Richard Hamilton, it suggested some limited-edition print rather than a gramophone record mass-produced by the million. Its official title was THE BEATLES, though it would be known for ever afterwards as the White Album.

George Martin had felt the 30 tracks spread over four sides included many that were only average and some even rather poor (to say nothing of 'Revolution 9'). Until the very last minute, he'd urged that the two discs should be edited down to just one, sardine-packed with quality in the tradition of *Sgt. Pepper* and *Revolver*. But neither John nor Paul would consider cutting anything. Now their 'more is more' approach seemed triumphantly vindicated. In the UK, the White Album spent seven weeks at number one and a total of 24 weeks in the Top 20. In the US, it sold 3.3 million in four days and was number one for nine weeks. It would ultimately be certified America's tenth best-selling album of all time, having gone platinum (for one million-plus sales) 19 times over.

Yet the reviews seldom touched the same rhapsodic heights as *Sgt. Pepper*'s. Critics complained that the tracks seemed to have no unifying theme or concept and that their prevailing mood of gentle whimsy had little relevance to the political and social upheavals of the time. (In later years, when Paul and John individually sought to make their music more politically engaged, they would be censured just as severely.)

The now traditional moment of highbrow hyperbole came from the British TV director Tony Palmer. Writing in the *Observer*, Palmer called Lennon and McCartney 'the greatest songwriters since Schubert' and predicted the White Album would 'surely see the last vestiges of cultural snobbery and bourgeois prejudice swept away'. Since few pop record-buyers realised Schubert had been a songwriter, this in itself was cultural snobbery of a high order.

The album was certainly remarkable in its efforts to raise its audience's aesthetic sights. But the number of evergreen Beatles favourites it proved to contain would be even smaller than George Martin's estimate; no more than half a dozen tracks of the 30. Ironically, too, after all his efforts to keep it on course and bring it home, Paul's presence is nothing like as strong as the seemingly indolent and wayward John's.

Under the stimulus of his affair with Yoko and his new sense of liberation, John travels through a remarkable creative spectrum, from the visceral 'Yer Blues' and the taunting 'Sexy Sadie', a coded swipe at the Maharishi, through the delicate and subtle 'Dear Prudence' to 'Julia', his lighter-than-air mourning fragment about his dead mother.

Paul, at the same time, was distracted by Apple, emotionally adrift after parting from Jane yet still not quite ready to commit to Linda. The result, for the most part, are songs in smiley masks: 'Honey Pie', a pastiche of 1930s Hollywood musicals; 'Rocky Raccoon', halfway between cod-Western and strip-cartoon; 'Why Don't We Do It in the Road?', suggested by the sight of copulating monkeys in India; 'Martha My Dear', named after his Old English sheepdog. Only in 'Blackbird' does his talent fully show its glossy wings and golden beak; Bach on an acoustic guitar, and what sounds like a memo to self, finally putting aside those doubts about commitment:

> All your life . . .
> You were only waiting for this moment to arise.

The most joyous moments, as always, are where Lennon and McCartney co-operate, still with no hint of a sundering presence between them. Paul's 'Back in the USSR' (minus an unmissed Ringo) revives their old talent for close-harmony mimicry with an expert take-off of the Beach Boys. John may have fulminated against 'Ob-La-Di, Ob-La-Da' in retrospect but on the day of its recording he turned up at Abbey Road in high spirits, sat straight down at the piano and played its honky-tonk intro with all the brio at his command.

The pair's ability to switch identities was never more remarkable. John's 'Good Night' seemed pure Paul in its evocation of 1950s BBC *Children's Hour*, glowing Magicoal fires and warm Ovaltine. Paul's 'Helter Skelter' (a conscious effort to be louder than the Who's 'I Can See for Miles') was a heavy metal onslaught that made 'Revolution' seem almost decorous.

For now, John could still be indulgent to those who gleaned hidden messages and prophecies from his lyrics. 'Glass Onion' referred back to 'Strawberry Fields Forever' and then 'I Am the Walrus', supposedly offering a key to that most impenetrable of his nonsense verses: 'Well, here's a clue for you all . . . the Walrus was Paul'. Later, after it had taken on the darkest of interpretations, he would protest that he'd merely wanted to 'say something nice to

Paul' after their recent stresses while signalling in the gentlest way possible that their partnership was moving to a close.

In fact, 'Glass Onion' was almost all about Paul – and in an unequivocally positive way. Three McCartney songs were mentioned by name: 'The Fool on the Hill' (with Paul adding a sliver of his original recorder-solo), 'Lady Madonna' and 'Fixing a Hole'. There was even a reference to the Cast Iron Shore, the metal-strewn Mersey beach near the McCartneys' old home in Speke where he was robbed of his wristwatch as a ten-year-old.

Even at the best of times, John had never been lavish in his praise of Paul's work, so to receive a tribute from him on this scale, at this particular moment, was extraordinary. All the more so in view of the mud-slinging with which he would follow it.

Paul's personal retinue at Apple all liked Linda from the beginning and recognised her beneficial effect on him. 'I thought she was lovely,' Tony Bramwell says. 'And she tidied him up a bit. Since Jane went, no one had been looking after him. I don't know what his housekeeper was doing. The house had turned into a bachelor dump. Martha [the sheepdog] was crapping all over the floor and nobody bothered to clear it up.'

Other areas of his life were less easily tidied. During Linda's first days at Cavendish, there was a stream of phone calls from unidentified women who knew nothing about her arrival. One was Maggie McGivern, who hadn't heard from Paul since their Sardinian holiday, when he'd seemed on the verge of proposing to her. 'I rang up one day – one of only two times I ever did – and an American voice answered that must have been Linda,' Maggie remembers. 'Paul grabbed the phone away from her and we talked for a while. But he didn't explain anything, just said, "I don't know what the scene is."'

As Linda was already known to the other Beatles, Paul's introduction of her into their inner circle caused none of the shock waves John had with Yoko. 'She just stayed in the background and let Paul get on with what he had to do,' Bramwell says. 'She'd usually be taking photographs, but she did it so quietly that people hardly seemed to notice.' She didn't attempt to publish any of these intimate studies, despite having magazine contacts in New York who were begging for them. Every so often, her friend Danny Fields, the editor of *Datebook*, would receive a postcard from her bearing the single word 'Wow!'

Nevertheless, her presence brought a new tension to the directors' quarters at 3 Savile Row. Despite both being from New York, and each having a small daughter, she and Yoko found little common ground. And although John had seemed to like her well enough in their previous encounters, he now visibly cooled towards her, mistaking her understated manner for impoliteness, even hostility, to Yoko.

Yoko had grown up in one of Japan's four wealthiest families, with 30 domestic servants who entered her presence on their knees and exited on their knees backwards. Even the doting John once said of her that she viewed all men 'as assistants'. At the office, he expected her commands to be executed as promptly as his own, and remained fiercely watchful for any sign of less than total enthusiasm and dedication on the part of the doer. Linda, by contrast, was always politeness itself to Paul's employees and seemed embarrassed to ask even the smallest service of them. 'She'd never send the office-boy out to buy her Tampax like the Japanese one,' Tony Bramwell says.

Mal Evans drove her around, and fellow American Chris O'Dell, from the A&R department, was on call to help her make the major cultural adjustment of settling in London. Chris had grown up in Tucson, Arizona, where Linda had lived during her marriage to Mel See, and the two women soon became good friends. 'She asked for very little,' Chris recalls. 'Just things like the name of a good shop where she could order camera equipment.'

In mid-October, Paul accompanied Linda to New York to bring her six-year-old daughter, Heather, back to live with them at Cavendish. Linda prepared the ground by telling Heather about Paul on the phone – not as a Beatle but 'this guy I really like' – then putting him on to introduce himself. As so often, he was nowhere near as chirpily self-assured as he seemed. '[I was thinking] "Oh my God, if she hates me, this could be very very difficult,"' he recalled, 'So I was slightly over-friendly probably. I said, "Will you marry me?" She said, "I can't, you're too old" . . . but that broke the ice and I said, "Oh, yes, of course. I forgot that. Well, maybe I should marry your mummy."'

They spent ten days in New York, staying at Linda's tiny Upper East Side apartment, which proved not much more than a single room with a fold-down bed. Paul had grown a beard – of surprising blackness and bushiness – from the shelter of which he saw Manhattan for the very first time, walking, taking yellow cabs, even riding the Subway, rather than cowering deep inside a limo with his fellow Beatles as faces flattened against the windows and bodies spreadeagled themselves across the roof.

He paid his first-ever visits to Chinatown and Little Italy, checked out music venues like the Fillmore East and Max's Kansas City, even finally made it to black music's most famous venue, the Apollo Theater in the then no-go area of Harlem. He went to Greenwich Village to visit Bob Dylan, who still lived there, and Linda photographed them together with Dylan's wife, Sara, and baby son, Jesse. But most of the time, it was just Linda and himself, being left miraculously alone. The occasional eye pieced together the delicate features beneath the piratical whiskers and widened in disbelief, but there was not one single mindless scream nor scuffle of pursuing feet.

In New York, their usual roles were reversed, Paul usually having time on his hands while Linda followed a busy routine centred on Heather. 'It was one of the things that impressed me about her – she seriously looked after her daughter,' he later recalled. 'It all seemed very organised . . . in a slightly dishevelled way.' For the first time, he became aware of a quality in Linda he could only define as 'womanliness', something on a profounder level than the dolly-bird prettiness on which he'd always feasted; something whose only other incarnation in his whole life had been his mother.

One day, while strolling along Mott Street in Chinatown, they saw a Buddhist temple advertising weddings. Paul grabbed Linda's arm and half-jokingly suggested they go in and get married there and then. 'I really didn't want to,' Linda later recalled. 'I was so newly not married again, so I went, "No, no, no." And we kept walking, and it was like it was never said.'

Towards the end of the visit, Linda introduced him to her father, Lee Eastman, the Manhattan entertainment lawyer who, by the strangest coincidence, had been born Leopold Epstein. Now 58 and married to a second wife, Monique, Eastman remained very much the alpha male whose disapproval of Linda's bohemian ways wasn't much mitigated by the celebrity boyfriend she'd now landed. He went out of his way not to show deference to Paul, ignoring the subject of the Beatles and, instead, making provocative remarks about Britain's 'sinking' economic state. Paul remained smilingly unruffled, and once Eastman realised he couldn't be bullied or needled, the two got on well.

So, having gone to New York with his girlfriend, Paul returned to Cavendish with a family. His first act was to suggest they should visit the remote Scottish farm he'd originally bought for Jane and hadn't visited since their break-up. As he later admitted, he thought the Kintyre peninsula would have little appeal to a WASP-y New York photojournalist. 'I said, "I know you won't like it . . . but let's just go up there."'

Actually, Linda was more a child of nature than she'd ever been of skyscrapers and yellow cabs. She instantly fell as much in love as Paul first had with Kintyre's wildness and remoteness, the looming mountains and white-duned bays, the Pictish standing stones and thousand-year-old springs, the eternal, inviolable silence. 'It was like nothing I'd ever lived in before,' she would recall. 'The most beautiful land you have ever seen . . . way at the end of nowhere.'

During that brief visit, an 18-year-old local freelance journalist named Freddy Gillies saw them together and realised he had a world scoop. Paul allowed Gillies to interview and photograph them – using Linda's own Nikon camera – but on condition he wouldn't sell the story to the national and international press. So it went no further than the Scottish *Daily Express*.

High Park Farm had never been a luxurious habitation and now seemed to Linda 'not much more than a building-site . . . a three-room house, with rats in the wall and no hot water'. Yet on that first camping-out visit together, she said something that resolved any lingering doubts Paul may have had about commitment and monogamy:

'I could make a nice home here.'

While Paul revolutionised his life thus secretly, John and Yoko continued to live theirs in banner headlines. On 18 October, while borrowing Ringo's flat in Montagu Square, they were raided by the police and charged with possessing 219 grains of cannabis. Though John maintained the drug had been planted on him by the arresting officer, he pleaded guilty and took sole responsibility (thus saving Yoko from possible deportation) and was fined £150 with £20 costs. So ended the golden age when Beatles had been considered untouchable by Scotland Yard's drugs squad; from here on, they would be busted just as gleefully as anyone else – with John by no means the record-holder.

The fact that Yoko was five months pregnant did not inhibit outraged fans from viciously jostling her and pulling her hair as the couple emerged from court together. Subsequently – perhaps a direct result of the stress she had suffered – her pregnancy developed complications and on 21 November, the day before the White Album's release, she suffered a miscarriage at Queen Charlotte's Hospital in London. Refusing to leave her for a moment, John donned pyjamas and climbed into the next bed; when it was needed for another patient, he slept on the floor.

He had already presented Apple Records with an album by the two of them, instructing that it should be packaged and promoted no less lavishly than the White Album. Titled *Unfinished Music No. 1: Two Virgins*, it contained the experimental tapes they'd made during their first night together the previous May – a project so absorbing, according to John, that they didn't get around to having sex until sunrise.

He also supplied an image for the front cover that was as different as it could be from Richard Hamilton's chaste white-out. Taken by John himself on a time-lapse camera, it showed the two alleged virgins full-frontally nude with an arm wrapped around each other. A back cover picture, taken by the same method, was a reprise of Yoko's *Bottoms* film, with the pair looking coyly over their shoulders.

It was all a horrendous clash with the record label Paul had built up so carefully with Ron Kass and Peter Asher; from the Black Dyke Mills Band to surreal electronic wailing, from sweet, virginal Mary Hopkin to exposed nipples and unabashed pubic hair. However, matters quickly moved beyond a row between Paul and John. EMI, who manufactured and distributed Apple's records, wanted nothing to do with visuals which, in 1968, could have brought a prosecution for disseminating pornography. The company's chairman, Sir Joseph Lockwood, personally pleaded with John to choose a different image. 'Why not put Paul on the cover . . . he's much prettier,' the covertly gay Lockwood suggested. 'Or a statue from one of the parks.'

In the end, an untidy compromise was reached: *Two Virgins* came out on the Apple label but EMI's role was confined to manufacturing the record. Its distribution in the UK was handled by the Who's Track record company and in America by an obscure agency named Tetragrammaton. When it reached the stores, the John–Yoko cover was inside a plain brown paper wrapper, an ironic nod to pornography's traditional camouflage. The album sold only a minuscule quantity but, as expected, unleashed a fresh wave of angry disappointment in John and mystification at his choice of nude playmate.

With all this John-and-Yoko scandal to feast on, the media were slow to pick up on Paul's new girlfriend. But the fans who haunted Paul's front gate knew all about Linda, or thought they did, and already hated her every bit as much as they did Yoko. In his case, in fact, even greater offence was taken that, with all the world's beautiful women at his disposal, he should have picked one so very far from conventional prettiness, whose blonde hair usually looked as if it could do with a good brushing and whose clothes were so determinedly unfashionable, not to say dowdy. And Linda's shyness was interpreted as aloofness, mixed with smug exultation at her undeserved prize.

John had always been recognised as an uncontrollable maverick, but being a Paul fan involved a strong feeling of proprietorship. Like so many tut-tutting aunts, the gate pickets now observed the change from his former dandified, fastidious self; the bushy black beard, the perceptible weight-gain, the baggy tweed overcoat he seemed to wear all the time.

To the fans, it signified how 'she' had got her hooks into him; what it actually signified was that he was happy.

His personal life thus replenished and stabilised, he now turned his attention to replenishing and stabilising the Beatles after their ordeal with the White Album. That they were already beyond help by any quick fixes never crossed his mind. Despite having been entirely studio-based for more than two years, they had never officially announced they'd given up live shows, and thus were still considered the world's premier concert attraction. For every rock festival that came along, they were the dream headliners; in the music press, a week seldom passed without some fresh speculation about when and where they would retake the stage.

Paul, of course, had never really given up live shows: as the Bedfordshire village of Harrold knew, he was ready to perform for any size of audience anytime, anywhere. And he now believed all their problems as a band would disappear if they descended from their four-seat Olympus and started performing to real people again.

His first proposal, that they should simply play some surprise club dates under an alias, was far too extreme for the others. But in principle, the idea was no longer totally unthinkable. They'd enjoyed their appearance on David Frost's television show, before a studio audience who, while greeting them rapturously, had listened to their music with an attention and appreciation they hadn't experienced since the Cavern. John's appetite for performing had been further revived by the shock therapy of partnering Yoko. Ringo was becoming increasingly involved in film acting, but would conform with the group mind, as always. Only George, who had hated Beatlemania worst of all, remained to be won over.

Paul therefore came up with an alternative plan for the Beatles to get back to the milieu they had once dominated – and in the process revive the film company that had lain dormant since *Magical Mystery Tour*. They would give a one-off stage show, to be filmed and marketed worldwide by Apple. Released in tandem with this would be a documentary of the band in rehearsal, much like Jean-Luc Godard's *One Plus One*, which had starred the Rolling Stones after the Beatles turned it down.

Initially, Paul suggested the director might be Yoko: a typically subtle stratagem for giving her the respect John demanded while also ungluing her from his side. But Yoko had no interest in conventional film-making – indeed, felt insulted by the very idea – so the job went to 28-year-old Michael Lindsay-Hogg, who'd directed several Beatles promo-films, most recently those for 'Hey Jude' and 'Revolution', as well as the documentary-length *Rolling Stones Rock and Roll Circus*.

The original idea was to film the concert at the Roundhouse in north London, a venue well-known to Paul through his underground connections, which would have given the Beatles huge credibility with the hippy acid-rock crowd. The Roundhouse was booked for 18 January 1969, but then deemed too ordinary for an event so momentous. Various other locations were put forward, each more grandiose and implausible than the last, from the Egyptian Pyramids to the deck of a passenger-liner in mid-ocean.

On 2 January, only 11 weeks after finishing the White Album, the Beatles reconvened for the in-rehearsal documentary that was to be a companion piece or trailer to their concert film. This was scheduled to last two weeks and take place in a single location, a vacant sound stage at Twickenham Film Studios in west London. The studios promised security from intrusive fans and media, and had good associations for the band: they'd made their revivifying *David Frost Show* appearance there and, in earlier, happier times, had trodden the sound-stages in both *A Hard Day's Night* and *Help!*

It proved a disastrous choice. The sound stage in midwinter was icy-cold as well as bleak and comfortless; in addition, they were expected to keep film studio rather than recording studio hours, which meant clocking in at nine sharp each morning rather than drifting comfortably into Abbey Road in the early evening. There was no shooting-script nor structure of any kind: Michael Lindsay-Hogg's brief was simply to film everything that happened as the Beatles assembled a tracklist for their grand comeback concert, in whatever location it should eventually take place.

Although no more enamoured of the conditions than anyone else, Paul characteristically made the best of them, turning up bang on time every day in his baggy tweed greatcoat, setting the agenda of numbers to be rehearsed and conferring with Lindsay-Hogg about set-ups and camera angles. He was both producer and musical director by default: neither George nor Ringo showed any interest in the project, while John had just been introduced to heroin by Yoko and as a result was often barely coherent.

The documentary is celebrated as an amazing exercise in honesty – some might say masochism – which destroyed any remaining illusions that being in the Beatles was the greatest fun on earth. But it also contains a great deal of harmony and humour against the odds, along with some moments of musical magic comparable with any hitherto.

They still don't seem to mind Yoko's being in their midst, once again acting as a backing group as she exercises a vocal style modelled on the shrieks and moans of servant women she used to overhear giving birth during her childhood in Tokyo. Paul gets into the avant-garde spirit by jabbing his live bass against his amplifier fabric to create a wail of Jimi Hendrix-style feedback.

Most interesting is the evolution of Paul's 'Get Back', whose title sums up the spirit of the whole enterprise. From a few basic riffs, it turns first into heavy metal, then an upbeat country ballad about 'Jojo [leaving] his home in Tucson, Arizona'. Tucson was the home of Linda's ex-husband, Joseph Melville See, who'd recently been so accommodating over the custody of Heather, but Paul would always insist that was pure coincidence.

The original lyric also has a political agenda, mockingly echoing the recent fulminations of Tory MP Enoch Powell against Britain's immigrant Pakistani community. That verse is jettisoned – wisely since it sounds rather racist in itself. With bitter hindsight, John would say that each time Paul sang 'Get back to where you once belonged', he seemed to be looking directly at Yoko.

But on the film, the two often seem to be working together with much of their old relish. There's real warmth in their performance of Paul's 'Two of Us', actually about Linda and himself, but now a seeming tribute to a staggering joint career: 'You and I have memories longer than the road that stretches out ahead.' They even revive 'One After 909', which they wrote together for the Quarrymen in the skiffle era when no subject matter was more glamorous than a train. To the composer of 'Eleanor Rigby', that chorus of 'Move over once/ Move over twice/ Come on baby don't be cold as ice' has always been profoundly embarrassing; now he kind of admires it.

But there was also a lot of apathy and ragged playing, and in the end even Paul's resolution began to waver. 'I don't see why none of you is interested, get yourselves into this,' he told the others. 'What's it for? It can't be for the money. Why are you here? I'm here because I want to do a show, but I really don't feel an awful lot of support . . . There's only two choices. We're gonna do it or we're not gonna do it. And I want a decision. Because I'm not interested in spending my fucking days farting around here while everyone makes up their mind whether they want to do it or not.'

Finally, on the eighth day of filming, Lindsay-Hogg's camera homed in on an exchange between George and Paul. George had just played a riff which Paul thought could be played better, and was demonstrating how with a downward sweep of one arm.

> PAUL You see, it's got to come down like this. There shouldn't
> be any recognisable jumps. It helps if you sing it. Like this:
> 'waw-waw-waw . . .'

Nobody said 'cut' and, in an instant, Beatles were clashing on
camera, one like a bearded young teacher trying to enthuse a slug-
gish student, the other exuding resentment over the top of his red
polo neck.

> PAUL I always hear myself annoying you. Look, I'm not trying
> to *get* you. I'm just saying, 'Look, lads . . . the band. Shall we do
> it like this?'

> GEORGE Look, I'll play whatever it is you want me to play. Or
> I won't play at all. Whatever it is that'll please you, I'll do it.

In truth, there was a history of this kind of thing: during the
recording of George's song 'Taxman' for *Revolver*, Paul had also repeatedly criticised his guitar solo and finally wrested it away from
him. He had accepted it then but now walked off the sound stage
and, seemingly, out of the Beatles, his only farewell a curt 'See you
around the clubs.'

John and Paul agreed that what John called 'the festering wound'
within the band might be past healing and that if George didn't
return by the following Friday the Beatles would effectively have
broken up. In the event, Press Officer Derek Taylor, to whom he'd
always been especially close, persuaded him to attend a business
meeting at Apple two days before the expiry of the deadline. But,
he made clear, he would return to the ranks only on condition that
Paul stopped bossing him around and the McCartney master-plan
was jettisoned forthwith. They must forget all those grandiose
ideas of comeback concerts in exotic places and concentrate on
making the next album.

Paul offered no objection, being as weary as the others of conditions at Twickenham. It was agreed to take a short break, then transfer operations to the recording studio in the basement at 3 Savile Row, which Magic Alex Mardas had supposedly been installing for most of the past year. The fracas actually helped determine the character of the new album, which, they only got as far as agreeing, must be totally unlike their recent, overwrought double-disc blockbuster.

It was the continuing anomaly of George's life that while being a second division Beatle, permanently overshadowed by Lennon and McCartney, he was held in the highest esteem by first-rank musicians like Eric Clapton, Bob Dylan and Dylan's virtuoso sidemen, the Band. He had recently returned from America, enthusing about the Band's album *Music from Big Pink*, in which the quintet had explored their country and hillbilly roots with largely acoustic instruments, creating an intricate, quiet masterpiece. Rather than White, the Beatles decided, they should now be thinking Pink.

The title of the song Paul had developed at Twickenham Studios defined this new objective as well as it had the previous one. Rather than getting back to live concerts, they would emulate the Band and get back to their roots. Since in their case their only roots were themselves, this meant recapturing the simplicity of their music when there had been just the four of them, blasting out raw soul and R&B in Liverpool and Hamburg; before the arrival of French horns, harps, piccolo trumpets, cacophony orchestras in false noses, backwards-fairground-carousels, sitars and tape-loops.

In that spirit, Paul decided to use the instrument most redolent of those exuberant, uncomplicated years, his Hofner violin bass. Actually, he owned two, the first bought in Hamburg and played through a thousand and one sweaty Reeperbahn and Cavern nights; the second, improved model given to him by the Hofner company in 1963 after he'd made the brand internationally famous. For maximum rootsiness, he brought both to the recording sessions.

George Martin was called in to produce and briefed by John in terms which as good as dismissed Martin's incalculable contribution to the Beatles over the previous six years. What they wanted, said John, was an 'honest' album, with 'none of that production crap'.

Martin had been led to believe he would be working in a studio where Magic Alex's technological marvels would make Abbey Road seem prehistoric. On his first visit to 3 Savile Row's basement, however, he found no useable recording facilities yet in place, months after the studio had been commissioned. (Mardas later claimed not to have been working there at all, but constructing a mock-up of the layout at another address.) There were not even feed-holes through the walls for electric cables, Martin found, and an adjacent central-heating plant created an intrusive din which would somehow have to be muffled. The only way he could start work at once, as required, was by importing a mountain of equipment from poor old outdated EMI.

The opening session for an album with the working title of *Get Back* took place on 22 January 1969. Assisting George Martin was Glyn Johns, long-time engineer and producer to the Rolling Stones. Michael Lindsay-Hogg's cameras continued filming everything that happened – though with what ulterior purpose Lindsay-Hogg was no longer sure.

There was also an addition to the Beatles' line-up: the first ever for the duration of a whole album and a symptom of the fraught atmosphere between them. This was the black American singer and organist Billy Preston, whom they'd got to know in the early Sixties when he was with Little Richard's band. George asked him to play on *Get Back*, not just for his keyboard skills but because rows would be less likely with an outsider present.

Martin's task was, in effect, to produce an album of live Beatles performances, without overdubs or editing of any kind. Their very first album, *Please Please Me* in 1963, had been just that – made by four boys whose hunger and passion, not to mention awe of their new record-boss, enabled them to power through it in a single day.

To underline their purpose, they had a cover prepared just like that of *Please Please Me*, with a picture of their present-day, lank-haired selves by the same photographer, Angus McBean, looking down the same stairwell at EMI's Manchester Square headquarters.

Now they were no longer boys but gods, no longer hungry but sated a thousand times over, no longer passionate but weary beyond imagining – and no longer amenable to being driven by anyone on earth. Sticking doggedly to the no-editing-and-overdubs rule, they would stop at every mistake and start all over again. They'd sometimes do as many as 60 takes, leaving George Martin at a loss as to whether the sixtieth had been any improvement on the fifty-ninth. 'Then you're no fookin' good, are you,' John snapped at him on one occasion. Martin was still too much a gentleman to reply in kind, but increasingly turned over the production to Glyn Johns.

For much of the time they simply jammed, wandering back through the vast repertoire of rock 'n' roll and R&B they'd accumulated before they were famous and still knew by heart. Paul gave up all attempts to maintain discipline and focus and went along with the others. Around 100 tracks ended up in the can, most of them self-indulgent, slipshod rambles; a few – like Paul's 'The Long and Winding Road' and John's 'Don't Let Me Down' – touched a wholly new level of brilliance. But by now no one could tell the difference. To lower Paul's spirits still further, somewhere between Twickenham and Savile Row the older of his two violin basses, the one he'd bought in Hamburg and played until halfway through Beatlemania, was stolen.

Director Michael Lindsay-Hogg had envisaged filming the Beatles' comeback concert at sunrise in a 2000-year-old Roman amphitheatre in Tunisia with their music ringing out like a muezzin, summoning the faithful by the ten thousand. In the end, the only live performance Lindsay-Hogg got to film was from an improvised stage on the roof of 3 Savile Row, watched by a sprinkling of Apple employees and a few bemused onlookers from neighbouring buildings. It lasted only 42 minutes before being brought to a halt by the police, following complaints about the noise from businesses in the area. Half-hearted compromise though it was, it would become one of the most famous moments in Beatle history – and create an essential ritual for any rock band seeking credibility as urban guerrillas. In years to come, countless others would clamber onto roofs with film-crews and start blasting, their ears hopefully cocked for the wail of police-sirens.

In its familiar edited form, the Apple rooftop concert looks like a continuous performance, but actually was more like a rehearsal-cum-jam session. It began with Paul singing two consecutive versions of 'Get Back' in his rather parsonical black suit and pale shirt, his beard blown back by the winter wind. He was singing it for a third time when the police appeared – and waited politely until he'd finished. 'You've been playing on the roof again and you know your Mommy doesn't like it,' he ad-libbed. 'She's gonna have you arrested . . .'

And, of course, it was no comeback concert but the Beatles' formal farewell to the world: not needed just yet, so put away for later.

25

'Fuck you, money!'

With that metal din booming above Savile Row's tailoring establishments and across London, the Apple house might have been
giving voice to the conflict and confusion which now gripped it.
Somehow, each new attempt to bring a semblance of rationality to
the Beatles' business only seemed to make things worse.

Apple has passed into legend as an unmitigated fiasco which saw
the band comprehensively ripped off by con-artists and freeload-
ers as a prelude to their painful demise. Yet by the end of its first
year, the company had notched up achievements of which its four
owners – and one above all – could be proud. With Paul behind
them as talent-spotter, writer, producer and session-musician, Ron
Kass and Peter Asher had built Apple Records into an unarguably
dynamic and innovative independent label. Not that it was viewed
as what would later be called an 'indie': if the Beatles started a
record company, people naturally expected it to compete on equal
terms with all the giants.

Apple Records, at least, had kept faith with the company's mis-
sion to sponsor unknown young talent. After Mary Hopkin and
Jackie Lomax, it had signed the Iveys, a Welsh band discovered by
Mal Evans, and the Scots songwriting duo Benny Gallagher and
Graham Lyle. The allure of the Beatles was not limited to un-
knowns, however: established names on both sides of the Atlantic
soon began putting out feelers to join Apple, notably Fleetwood
Mac and the new supergroup Crosby, Stills & Nash.

The eclectic spirit implanted by Paul with the Black Dyke Mills Band remained integral to the label. Through Ron Kass, it signed the Modern Jazz Quartet – the nearest there had been to rock stars before rock – to make two albums, one including a cover of 'Yesterday'. The MJQ were a ferociously cool and solemn-looking foursome whose leader, John Lewis, made them play in immaculate suits and ties, like Epstein-era Beatles. 'But whenever Lewis was out of the way,' Peter Asher remembers, 'the jackets were taken off, the ties were loosened and the joints came out.'

And Apple records were selling. In March 1969, Mary Hopkin's second single, 'Goodbye', went to number two in the UK and thirteen in America. As well as writing the song (still under the Lennon–McCartney credit), Paul demo-recorded it for Hopkin, produced it and played bass, acoustic guitar and drums with additional percussion. The following month, 'Get Back' was released as a Beatles single together with John's 'Don't Let Me Down', instantly going to number one in Britain – so denying the top spot to 'Goodbye' – and topping the charts in America and around the world.

Apple was always meant to be about more than just music, and to discover and support struggling young creators across all the performing and visual arts. At the time, it seemed the vast sums that were doled out had not fostered a single original talent – but in the longer term, one notable one would reveal itself. This was 18-year-old Richard Branson who came to 3 Savile Row seeking support for his first business venture, a national newspaper for university students. Branson's protuberant eyes took in everything he saw; a decade later, Apple's concept of 'an underground company above ground' would be artfully synthesised in his multidivision, money-spinning Virgin organisation.

The house in itself had a diplomatic function as important as any conventional embassy's. Derek Taylor's second-floor press office fielded an incessant flood of requests from newspapers, magazines and broadcasting organisations all over the world for interviews or photo-sessions with the Beatles, together or individually. The room was kept in semi-darkness, with a psychedelic light show casting wriggling spermatozoa shapes across one wall. Taylor directed his three secretaries from a wicker armchair with a huge scalloped back; journalists waiting to see him moved along a line of velvet sofas until they finally gained his ear. A small ante-room dispensed brimming tumblers of Scotch and Coke, to visitors and press officers alike, and was stacked like a bullion-vault with cartons of Benson & Hedges Gold cigarettes.

As Barry Miles recalls, the charming, hospitable Taylor and his department served as a substitute for the Beatles in the flesh. 'Any time a big American act like the Mamas and Papas came through London, they naturally expected to see Paul or John, but Paul and John didn't necessarily want to see them. So they'd come in to Apple, talk to Derek, be given a drink and a joint and go away happy.'

Miles also notes that by far the greatest extravagance was that of the Beatles themselves. Whenever John and Yoko were expected, Beluga caviar had to be fetched from Fortnum & Mason in Piccadilly. On one occasion, when the pair failed to arrive as scheduled, the two in-house cordon bleu cooks spread the entire contents of a pot on a single round of toast and ate it themselves.

During a trip to California, George met a troupe of Hell's Angels and invited them to London, promising them the hospitality of 3 Savile Row. They duly arrived on their motorbikes, and terrorised the house for a week, consuming its food and drink in epic quantities and sexually harassing its secretaries, all under the inviolable protection of their Beatle host. The climax to the Angels' visit, ironically enough, was their gatecrashing and wrecking of a Christmas party for Apple employees' children, presided over by John and Yoko dressed as 'Father and Mother Christmas'.

That extravagance inevitably filtered down to employees who believed the Beatles' coffers to be bottomless. Travel was always first-class, limos were always ordered in preference to taxis and all meals at the company's expense taken at the best restaurants.

One small example sums up the general climate: a certain brand of vodka popular with Apple senior executives was available only at a restaurant in Knightsbridge which refused to sell it as a takeaway. So two underlings would be sent there to eat lunch and bring back the prized bottle, their food, wine and return taxi-fares having roughly quadrupled its cost.

Of all the Beatles, only Paul ever showed any concern about Apple's outgoings. 'He'd look at the budgets for the various departments,' Chris O'Dell recalls, 'and try to curb any waste he found.' The press office worried him especially, with its numerous secretaries, flowing booze and atmosphere of a psychedelic rave. He had never got along that well with Derek Taylor, who was closest to John and George. 'I had a good lunch with Paul today,' Taylor would confide indiscreetly to the next journalist in line to see him. 'We just about got through it without a row.'

At one stage, mindful of Savile Row police station only a couple of hundred yards away, Paul banned all drug-taking on the premises. It made little difference to the press office, where secretaries took turns to bring in batches of home-baked hash brownies and a deranged-looking boy known only as Stocky squatted on top of a filing-cabinet every day, stoned on acid, drawing endless pictures of genitalia.

The nearest Apple had had to a financial watchdog thus far was Brian's old accountant, Harry Pinsker – the man who'd written to Paul at Wimpole Street to tell him he was now a millionaire. Pinsker sat on the board of directors with the aim of keeping an eye on expenditure, but increasingly had found it a hopeless task. When John and Yoko appeared nude on their *Two Virgins* album, he resigned in protest but, fearing the worst, assigned a junior member of his firm named Stephen Maltz to conduct a detailed survey of the company's books.

Maltz spent several weeks on the task, then sent each of the Beatles a five-page letter outlining his grim findings. In less than a year, Apple had spent the whole of the £2 million set aside as a tax write-off, plus an additional £400,000, the first instalment of their collective payment for selling their services to their own company. In addition, each had overdrawn his partnership account – Paul the most heavily at £66,988 – and each faced income tax liabilities of around £600,000.

'As far as you were aware,' Maltz wrote, 'you only had to sign a bill and pick up a phone and payment was made. You were never concerned where the money came from or how it was being spent, and were living under the idea that you had millions at your disposal . . . Each of you has houses and cars . . . you also have tax cases pending. Your personal finances are in a mess. Apple is in a mess.'

It was a bitter pill for the Beatles to swallow. Their attempt to run their own affairs – into which Paul above all had poured such energy and dedication – had failed utterly. They had sworn never to have another manager after Brian, but that was just what they needed desperately at this moment: somebody to sort out the mess at Apple and also the psychological mess they'd got into as a band. And needed in double-quick time, before any more of their money and creative vitality haemorrhaged away.

There was one obvious internal candidate. Neil Aspinall had discharged most of the duties of a manager for years while still technically only their roadie, and was trusted and respected equally by all four. 'Come on, you may as well have the 20 per cent,' John urged him. But Neil, that seemingly quintessential Liverpool hard man, lacked the confidence to take on the job officially. So a saviour would have to be brought in from outside.

The search began at a level more suggestive of a troubled nationalised industry than a spendthrift pop group. John made contact with Lord Beeching who, as Dr Richard Beeching a few years earlier, had 'rationalised' Britain's state-owned railway network by closing down huge swathes of it. After looking over Apple's figures, Beeching offered a similar remedy – they should axe unproductive branch-lines like Apple Electronics and Apple Tailoring and concentrate on the high-volume Pullman-class business, i.e. Apple Records.

Paul, typically, chose a more upmarket route. From Sir Joseph Lockwood at EMI he obtained an introduction to Lord Poole, chairman of the exclusive Lazard's merchant bank and a personal financial adviser to the Queen. For all Poole's eminence, he proved a friendly, sympathetic man who took off his tie to make his pop star visitor feel more at ease. 'He offered to sort out the Beatles and, what was more, he offered to do it for nothing,' Lockwood was to remember. 'But they never followed up on it.'

This was because Paul had found another potential solution much closer to home. Linda's father, the New York entertainment lawyer Lee Eastman, had decades of experience in managing the finances of major figures in the show business and art worlds. Her older brother, John, was also a lawyer and a partner in the family firm of Eastman & Eastman which Lee had set up in 1965.

Although only 28, John Eastman possessed a talent for untangling the complex contractual problems from which young pop artistes, above all, tend to suffer. Already to his credit was a deal whereby the American band Chicago merely leased their record masters to Columbia Records rather than the label owning them outright. He would go on to act for Andrew Lloyd-Webber in curbing unauthorised performances of Lloyd-Webber's first musical, *Jesus Christ Superstar*.

Paul therefore put forward Eastman & Eastman as the Beatles' 'new broom'. Because of his special expertise – and as a passionate and knowledgeable Beatles fan – John Eastman rather than his father came to London, at his firm's expense, to look into the situation at Apple.

He arrived just before Christmas 1968, registering, impressively, at Claridge's. 'I had the cheapest room in the place,' he recalls, 'and the whole time I was there, I didn't order so much as a Coke on room service. It was just to show that [Eastman & Eastman] were at the best hotel in town, so we were serious.'

Among Paul's fellow Beatles, John especially, there was some initial frostiness because Linda's father hadn't come in person but sent what they, mistakenly, took to be an inexperienced junior.

Eastman's immaculately conventional appearance, in contrast to his sister's, also raised some eyebrows to the hippy hairline. 'In those days I figured that if I couldn't think like a lawyer I could at least dress like a lawyer, so I always wore a suit.'

Once they had got used to his suits, the Beatles were 'generally welcoming'. Not so Apple's senior executives, who were appalled by this young American interloper and the threat to their jobs he represented. (They hadn't seen anything yet!) 'I didn't get any help from any of them,' Eastman recalls. 'Every door was closed.'

At 3 Savile Row, he found 'a company that was bleeding money'. But far more serious to his mind was the way Apple had been structured with an eye to capital gains more than to protecting the Beatles' brand and securing their copyrights in the long term. 'There was no understanding of the value of great creativity. It was as if their career was still expected to come to an end at any moment.'

As it happened, a chance had just arisen to put the emphasis where John Eastman believed it should be. Two years on from Brian Epstein's death, his old NEMS management company, now renamed Nemperor Holdings, continued to receive all the Beatles' income (except that from songwriting) and deduct commission of 25 per cent. Brian's successor, his less dynamic younger brother Clive, had initially promised 'vigorous expansion' for the company, but hated being a pop impresario and now longed to return to his former quiet life in Liverpool.

Clive and his widowed mother, Queenie, the major shareholder, had lately received an offer to sell to a London merchant bank named Triumph Investment Trust. But they felt that as NEMS/ Nemperor's foundation and greatest asset – and for old times' sake – the Beatles should be given first refusal.

Buying the company made sound financial sense, at a time when little else did. At a stroke, they could increase their income by a quarter – and in the process also acquire the 7.5 per cent stake Brian had owned in their publishing company, Northern Songs. Sir Joseph Lockwood at EMI agreed to advance the whole purchase

price out of their future royalties, offering to write John Eastman
a cheque for £1.4 million there and then. Properly impressed, all
four signed a letter authorising Eastman to negotiate the deal
for them.

Clearly, it was a moment for extreme discretion where the media
were concerned. Unfortunately, John Lennon recognised no such
moments. In mid-January 1969, during the chilly *Get Back* sessions
at Twickenham Studios, he gave an interview to Ray Coleman,
editor of *Disc and Music Echo* and usually a safe pair of hands where
Beatles coverage was concerned. Still in shock over Stephen Maltz's
revelations, John couldn't help blurting it all out: 'We haven't got
half the money people think we have. It's been pie in the sky from
the start. Apple's losing money every week because it needs close
running by a big businessman. If it carries on like this, all of us
will be broke in six months. Apple needs a new broom and a lot of
people there will have to go.'

Disc and Music Echo's headline that week, 'JOHN LENNON
SAYS BEATLES IN CASH CRISIS', if anything caused even
greater worldwide shock, consternation and disillusionment than
'JOHN LENNON SAYS BEATLES MORE POPULAR THAN
JESUS'. The notion of a Beatle without unlimited gold in his pocket
was as unthinkable as that of an archangel with halitosis. John
himself made no effort to backtrack, causing redoubled horror by
telling *Rolling Stone* he was 'down to my last fifty thousand' (which
was rather like someone nowadays complaining of being down to
their last million).

Among Apple's management, there was despair that John should
have broadcast the company's predicament just as active measures
were being taken to remedy it. Only Paul spared a thought for its
rank and file, the secretaries and clerks who did not squander the
Beatles' money, in fact worked long hours for average wages without perks, yet still felt included in John's denunciation and threat
of mass firings.

A few days later, he met Ray Coleman on the stairs at 3 Savile
Row and gave him a furious bollocking for having run the original

story. 'This is only a small company and you're trying to wreck it,' he shouted. 'You *know* John shoots his mouth off and doesn't mean it.'

He also sent round a morale-boosting staff memo, inviting anyone who felt worried about developments at Apple to write to him directly. 'There's no need to be formal. Just say it. Incidentally, things are going well, so thanks – love Paul.'

On 28 January, John and Yoko had a top-secret private meeting at the Dorchester Hotel with the Rolling Stones' manager, Allen Klein. Afterwards, John wrote a note to Sir Joseph Lockwood which in effect was the Beatles' execution warrant. 'Dear Sir Joe,' it read. 'From now on, Allen Klein handles all my stuff.'

Thirty-eight-year-old Klein could claim, in his way, to have revolutionised pop music as completely as the Beatles had. Before his advent, recording artistes thought it a privilege to be with a major label and accepted minuscule royalty-rates and sclerotically slow payment as the inevitable price. Klein ended this age-old scam by forcing record companies to pay his protégés large sums upfront rather than peanuts years in arrears. Power thus shifted from the label to the artiste, and the money involved shot into the stratosphere.

Born into dire poverty in New Jersey and raised in a Jewish orphanage, Klein had started out as an accountant with a niche all of his own. Thanks to the record companies' opaque and often devious bookkeeping practices, many top names were owed large sums in back royalties of which they were totally unaware. Klein would go in like a sniffer dog and, more often than not, find thousands, or hundreds of thousands of dollars due to them. As a result, he became known as 'the Robin Hood of Pop', a man who could conjure fortunes literally from thin air. Squat, oily-haired and un-couth, he cultivated the persona of a street-fighter with a touch of mobster. His ruthlessness and rudeness were as spectacular as his results.

Though he had made a first clumsy bid for the Beatles in 1964,

Klein owed his entrée into UK pop to the Stones, for whom he secured their astounding $1.25 million advance on renewing their contract with the Decca label in 1965. The Beatles had never received any advance from EMI and two years later, when Brian Epstein renegotiated their contract, were still not thought to merit one.

Paul had been particularly envious of the Stones' Decca deal, and – ironically in view of what was to come – suggested that Brian find a way of bringing Klein into the Beatles' management. There were rumours of a merger between NEMS and Klein's New York-based company, ABKCO Industries, before Brian managed to see off the threat. Since then, Klein had acquired a string of other big-in-America British acts including Donovan, Herman's Hermits and the Animals, while all the time making no secret of his ultimate ambition. Now, 'JOHN LENNON SAYS BEATLES IN CASH CRISIS' brought it suddenly within reach.

At their secret rendezvous at the Dorchester, Klein handled John with consummate skill, introducing himself first and foremost as a besotted fan who knew every Lennon song and could recite all their lyrics word-perfectly. He further had the wisdom to declare himself an admirer of Yoko's art, expressed shocked disbelief that there had never been a major exhibition of her work and promised to arrange one, however this present discussion might turn out.

Having studied John in advance, Klein knew just which cards to play, and played them expertly: his impoverished childhood, his fostering by an aunt (just like John), his indomitable rise to the top of his profession in the face of snobbery and prejudice, his crusading triumphs against music-business crookery whose beneficiaries had included one of the Beatles' great soul idols, Sam Cooke. From there, it was the smoothest segue into observing that no Beatle, especially not this one, should ever be down to his last fifty thousand.

A few days later, in the Apple boardroom, John introduced Klein to the other three as the answer to all their problems. The meeting went on so long that Paul upped and left, saying there was more to life than sitting round a table. George and Ringo stayed on, and both were won over by Klein in their turn.

Like John, they warmed to his down-to-earth manner and sharp wit, and were amused, yet reassured, by his determinedly un-rock 'n' roll appearance (George thought he looked like Barney Rubble from *The Flintstones*). Most of all they warmed to his promise to make them wealthy beyond their dreams, expressed in a salty acronym: 'You shouldn't even have to think about whether you can afford something or not. You should be able to say FYM – Fuck you, money.'

Paul learned of their adoption of Klein when he arrived at Apple the next day. He clearly couldn't agree, having already asked Linda's father and brother to do the same job and brought the latter across the Atlantic to make a start on it. Besides, everything about Klein that appealed to John, George and Ringo was calculated to appal him: greasy hair, nylon polo necks, a pipe belching smoke that smelled of prunes and custard.

With the Eastmans' aid, Paul also learned that in New York Klein's reputation was currently in the toilet. He had recently bought an almost defunct label named Cameo-Parkway (which had once made millions with Chubby Checker's 'Let's Twist Again') and then apparently tried to inflate its value by spreading false rumours that various wealthy music companies, including Britain's Chappell & Co., were in hot competition to acquire it. As a result, dealing in Cameo-Parkway shares had been suspended by the New York Stock Exchange and Klein was facing investigation by its regulatory body, the Securities and Exchange Commission. If that were not enough, his ABKCO company was embroiled in around 50 lawsuits while he personally was in trouble with the Internal Revenue Service for serial failures to file income tax returns.

But sharing this information with John, George and Ringo proved of no use whatsoever. If anything, they felt it a plus for Klein to be so notorious on his home turf, a confirmation that he truly was the tough guy they needed. Rumours that he might actually be involved with the Mafia (which he himself encouraged, although devoutly Jewish, with no known underworld affiliations) only increased his appeal, especially to John.

There was one powerful anti-Klein voice on which Paul could call for support and which, he thought, even John would be unable to ignore. The Rolling Stones, once the stars of Klein's stable, had grown increasingly discontented with his management and even now were secretly plotting to get rid of him. By the end of 1969, thanks to his peculiar remunerative methods, the whole band would find themselves owing such huge amounts in UK income tax that their only alternative to bankruptcy was emigration to France. The Stones' 'Lennon and McCartney', Mick Jagger and Keith Richards, would also discover that Klein owned the copyrights on their biggest hits, like 'Satisfaction', 'Get Off of My Cloud' and '19th Nervous Breakdown', which he'd secretly bought years earlier from their previous manager, Andrew Oldham.

Paul had heard about the Stones' Klein problems from Mick Jagger and, at his request, Jagger called at Apple to tell the other Beatles (walking there from the Stones' office, off Piccadilly, which by contrast was a model of efficiency and frugality). He'd expected to meet John, George and Ringo privately but found Klein sitting round the boardroom table with them; never one for confrontation, he pretended it was just a social call and left after a few minutes. Later, he phoned John at home and urged him not to make 'the biggest mistake of your life'. But John refused to listen.

On 3 February, the Beatles authorised Klein to conduct his own audit of their finances. Paul strongly opposed the idea but went along with it when he was outvoted. As he would explain in a High Court deposition two years later: 'I was most anxious not to stand out against the wishes of the other three except on proper grounds. I therefore thought it right to take part in discussions concerning the possible appointment of Klein, though I did not in the least want him as my manager.'

The original idea was that the two rival new brooms would work as a team. As Klein embarked on his audit, John, George and Ringo agreed to a proposal from Paul that Lee and John Eastman be appointed general counsel to Apple and themselves. Accountants and lawyers fulfil totally different functions and their servicing of the same client is standard practice from which the client normally benefits.

But there was never any chance of Klein and John Eastman working as mutually helpful colleagues. 'We were in opposition right from the beginning,' Eastman says, though he denies the stories of them trading insults and obscenities in rallies worthy of Wimbledon's Centre Court. 'I'm a pretty patient sort of guy. In all our arguments, I never raised my voice once.'

Eastman, by now, was finalising the seemingly straightforward deal for the Beatles, through Apple, to acquire Brian Epstein's NEMS management company, latterly renamed Nemperor Holdings. 'The Epstein family said that Brian had always wanted the boys to end up owning NEMS, so there was no question of them choosing the rival bidder [Triumph Investment Trust] instead of Apple. The situation was that there was around half a million pounds in Nemperor that the Epsteins couldn't take out without losing most of it in tax. We were going to give them that half-million for the company.'

But Klein pooh-poohed Eastman's terms, claiming to have a strategy of his own to acquire Nemperor 'for nothing'. The negotiations stalled, and the goodwill of the cash-strapped Epstein family evaporated. In February 1969, Clive Epstein sold to the Triumph Investment Trust for a mixture of cash and stock. Klein immediately made a threatening phone call to Triumph's chief executive, Leonard Richenberg, claiming that NEMS/Nemperor owed the Beatles large sums in unpaid back fees, which would be pursued in the courts unless Triumph waived its right to 25 per cent of their income. He also instructed Sir Joseph Lockwood at EMI not to make the Beatles' next royalty payment, of around £1.3 million, to Nemperor Holdings, but directly to Apple.

After an initial skirmish before a High Court judge, Richenberg elected to settle the matter out of court, with Nemperor giving up its quarter-share of the Beatles' income in exchange for £800,000 plus a quarter of the £1.3 million. 'It was an absolutely disastrous outcome for the Beatles,' says John Eastman, 'when they could have got the company for half a million.'

Klein, however, managed to dress it up as a victory, and early in March a band meeting was called to vote for his appointment as business manager. Paul refused to attend, instead sending along his solicitor, Charles Corman, to register a token 'No'. 'I was very nervous about how the Beatles would react to me,' Corman remembers. 'But John Lennon just looked at me and said, "Where's yer bass guitar then?"'

Though 'business manager' was not quite the totalitarian title Klein sought, it gave him a mandate to sort out Apple as he had promised. All the peripheral branches, however dear they had once seemed to this or that individual Beatle, were instantly lopped off. It soon became clear that Klein was as intent on axing potential rivals as reducing waste. So Apple Records suffered a drastic pruning despite its success, and the two men who'd made up Paul's winning team left 3 Savile Row without any intercession from him. Label boss Ron Kass received a lavish golden handshake and took an identical job with MGM Records in Los Angeles. Peter Asher went with him as head of A&R, then became the manager of Apple's first signing, James Taylor, and enjoyed a spectacular career as an independent producer for Linda Ronstadt and other major names in the 1970s.

Being a close mate of John or Paul – or even John *and* Paul – proved no help now that Klein was in charge. After spending a year on developing the Apple school, their old Liverpool friend Ivan Vaughan was told the idea had been dropped. Likewise, Paul made no protest when the Zapple 'spoken-word' label was shut down, leaving Barry Miles stranded in New York midway through a recording session with Allen Ginsberg. Like the other Beatles, he felt he had to grit his teeth and take the medicine, however repugnant it – and the nurse administering it – might be.

Among Klein's first firings was Alistair Taylor, who'd been Brian's assistant back in the Liverpool days, and had done everything conceivable for Paul from house-hunting to posing as the 'one-man band' in his first Apple advertisement. But when Taylor phoned Cavendish to plead for his job, Paul preferred not to come to the phone.

26

'Go on, cry! You'll be in the paper'

On 11 March 1969, Apple's press office issued a brief announcement that Paul McCartney was to marry Linda Eastman in a civil ceremony at Marylebone Register Office the next day. They had decided on it only a week earlier and chosen the quickest, simplest way – although Paul was still enough of a traditionalist to contact Linda's father and formally 'ask for her hand'.

Even after the date was set, Linda continued to have serious doubts about trying matrimony a second time. Their relationship in those early days, Paul would remember, was 'very up and down', sometimes 'crazy'; and on the wedding-eve they had a furious row and almost called it off.

Paul spent the day in the studio with George and Jackie Lomax, working on a single to follow Lomax's surprisingly unsuccessful 'Sour Milk Sea'. When the session ended late that night, he did not return to Cavendish but turned up at the Chelsea apartment of his long-time secret girlfriend Maggie McGivern; the first she'd seen of him since Linda's arrival.

'There was no car, no cab, so he must have walked,' Maggie recalls. 'He was scruffy, unshaven and in a terrible state – he couldn't even talk, just held on to me. I was trying to ask what was wrong but not to make a noise because my teenage brother was staying with me and was asleep in the same room. After about an hour, he just left. I looked out of the window and saw him walking down the street, somehow knowing I'd never see him again.'

The scenes outside Marylebone Register Office next day were like nothing seen in London since mid-season Beatlemania. Heavy rain made a fitting accompaniment to the hundreds of young women weeping with the desolation of those bereaved – or, rather, jilted. Press photographers went round snapping the most lachrymose specimens and urging the dry-eyed, 'Go on, cry! You'll be in the paper.'

Paul, in a dark suit, pink shirt and yellow tie, looked oddly youthful beside Linda, who wore a fitted coat of egg-yolk yellow and, in some photo-ops, cuddled a tabby kitten. The bride was four months pregnant (a fact already known to the Cavendish Avenue pickets from the chemist's prescriptions they'd seen arriving at the house). Six-year-old Heather attended her as bridesmaid.

None of the other Beatles was present, as Paul had been on all their wedding days. Ringo was filming *The Magic Christian* with Peter Sellers and John had taken Yoko to meet his Aunt Mimi for the very first time. George was working in the recording studio but had promised to come to the reception with Pattie. Their absence 'didn't seem important', Paul would remember. 'It was mainly just the two of us.'

Peter Brown and Mal Evans acted as witnesses and the best man was Mike McCartney, who had to travel by rail from the north where he was touring with the Scaffold. Mike's train developed problems and he arrived at nearby Euston station an hour late thinking he'd missed the ceremony, but Paul had insisted on waiting for him. 'We just sort of giggled our way through it,' his older brother would remember. 'All that "I promise" stuff . . . Linda was breaking up.'

Afterwards came a (totally serious) service of blessing at St John's Wood Parish Church, next to Lord's cricket ground, and a further photo session at Cavendish, where Paul performed the ancient ritual of carrying his bride over the threshold. Then, friends and musician cronies were invited to a reception at the Ritz hotel in Piccadilly. The Harrisons arrived late following a police raid on their home in which a sniffer dog named Yogi (after the cartoon bear, not the Indian mystic) had discovered 57 grams of cannabis.

At the Ritz, the newly-weds were interviewed together by Independent Television News. Paul gave his usual good value, answering the banal questions with earnest politeness in between larking around with Heather to stop her from feeling left out. But Linda made little attempt to win over the several million viewers for whom this would be their first sight and sound of her:

Q: What prompted [your decision to marry]?
PAUL: Just, you know, we decided to do it instead of talking about it.
Q: Linda, how do you feel about it? You're obviously terribly happy. How are you feeling this morning?
LINDA (barely audible): Very happy. Unquote.

When they returned home that evening, there was still a large crowd outside Cavendish, its mood now decidedly uglier. Linda was greeted with boos, catcalls and spittle and after a wad of burning newspaper was pushed through the letterbox, the police had to be called. Paul came to the front gate to appeal to reason – a tactic that had always worked in the past, but signally failed now. 'Look girls,' he almost pleaded, 'I had to get married *sometime.*' The comforting fiction could therefore circulate that he was doing it somehow against his will.

The first that Maggie McGivern knew of the wedding was a news bill in Chelsea's King's Road. In shock, she found her way to 48 Cheyne Walk where Marianne Faithfull, for whom she used to work as a nanny, now lived with Mick Jagger. 'Marianne couldn't believe it when I told her and when Mick heard, he went, "*Wha-a-at?*" He said he'd had a fling with Linda in New York during the great power blackout of 1965.'

As the unfavourable stories about his new wife piled up, Paul, that media-handler par excellence, took a personal hand in trying to secure her a better press. At his request, Derek Taylor arranged for Linda to be interviewed by the Beatles' favourite pop correspondent, Don Short of the *Daily Mirror*. Although Short's interview with Linda was the softest imaginable, her shyness and unease were painfully obvious. She was giving it, she said, only to rebut the story that had followed her from New York (and lately appeared in *The Times* as fact): that she was one of the Kodak Eastmans. 'I don't know how that mistake came about, except through the name and the fact that I'm a photographer.' It hardly mattered any more; her surname now was bigger than any mere American brand except, perhaps, Coca-Cola.

Paul's father hadn't yet met Linda, but was unable to do so at the wedding. In recent years, Jim McCartney had suffered increasingly from arthritis, and the condition was now so severe that a journey from the north-west down to London would have been too great an ordeal for him. Instead, Paul took Linda and Heather to stay with Jim and his wife, Angie, in Cheshire before flying off for a three-week honeymoon in America.

Jim, in fact, had two debilitating forms of the complaint, osteo-arthritis and rheumatoid arthritis, which mainly attacked his knees and ankles and which a series of remedies – from calcium to gold – barely alleviated. Semi-invalid as he'd become, 'Rembrandt', the dream home in Heswall that Paul had bought him, was now full of inconveniences, especially the long staircase from the front hall up to the bedrooms. As this had too many turns to accommodate a conventional stairlift, Paul proposed installing a hotel-style Otis elevator on the outside of the house. But Jim would not hear of such expense and simply moved his and Angie's room down to the ground floor.

As Angie McCartney recalls, they were both nervous about meeting Linda. 'We were expecting this very exotic person from America, who we wouldn't have anything in common with and wouldn't understand us. That ended for me as soon as Linda walked into the kitchen and I realised how much she loved cooking. Jim took to her immediately as well. He was just so happy to see Paul become a happy family man at last.'

To complete the bonding, Heather and Angie's nine-year-old

daughter, Ruth, instantly became friends. 'There was three years between them and they were completely different characters,' Angie recalls. 'Ruth was mad about dancing and Heather was mad about animals. But they'd spend hours in Ruth's bedroom, dressing up and doing girlie things.' Jim had adopted Ruth when he married Angie; Paul now hoped to do the same with Heather.

His aunts, uncles and cousins across the water in Liverpool naturally wanted to meet Linda, too, and he dutifully took her around them all. But there was no big McCartney clan-gathering, as in the old days when he and his father would take turns at the piano. 'We all had too many concerns about Jim's health,' Angie says. 'So it wasn't party time.'

Whenever Paul visited, he and Jim had always had long heart-to-heart talks while pacing to and fro over the back lawn. Now, with Jim's mobility reduced, they spent their private time together in the little lower garden which caught the most sun and where Paul – that ever-versatile handyman – had built a flight of stone steps. 'Jim would sit in a deck-chair, with Paul beside him, both smoking their ciggies,' Angie recalls. 'I know he talked to his dad about the problems he was going through at Apple, but none of it was ever mentioned to the rest of us.'

The onward journey to stay with Linda's family in New York ran into an unforeseen hitch. At Manchester Airport, Paul discovered he'd forgotten his passport; a phone call had to be made to Peter Brown at Apple, and a minion deputed to drive up from London with the missing document. The world had moved on since 1967, when he'd made his 'Fool on the Hill' film and charmed his way to the Côte d'Azur and back without a passport.

Eight days after Paul's wedding, in the copycat spirit that had always characterised their relationship, John married Yoko on the Rock of Gibraltar. She, too, was a reluctant bride, and had accepted him as her third husband only on condition that their wedding wouldn't be 'a media circus like the McCartneys'.

Instead, after the quietest of ceremonies in a sleepy British colony, the Lennons turned their honeymoon into a media circus that made the recent scenes outside Marylebone Register Office seem positively Garbo-esque. In a luxury suite at Amsterdam's Hilton hotel, they staged what they called 'a commercial for peace', spending a week side-by-side in a kingsize bed, voicing anti-war sentiments to non-stop relays of international media, most of whom had expected to witness them having sex. Such was the storm of ridicule they unleashed that the new Mrs Paul McCartney quite vanished from sight.

Paul and John were both still on honeymoon when, without warning, the final piece of the world Brian Epstein had constructed around them crumbled away. Northern Songs, the company which had published their music since 1963, became the target of a hostile takeover bid.

Northern Songs was the creation of Dick James, the dance-band crooner turned music publisher into whose lap the Beatles had fallen just before the release of 'Please Please Me'. Presciently recognising the potential of Lennon and McCartney's songwriting, James had set up a company solely to handle their publishing rights, of which 50 per cent was owned by him and his business partner, Charles Silver, 20 per cent each by John and Paul and 10 per cent by Brian. So rich and extensive did the catalogue soon become that in 1965 Northern Songs became the first music publishers ever floated as a public company on the London Stock Exchange. After the flotation James and Silver held 37.5 per cent and John and Paul now only 15 per cent each but the balance of power remained with them as Brian's company, NEMS, held 7.5 per cent and George and Ringo together a token 1.6 per cent.

James had the good sense never to try to influence what Lennon and McCartney wrote, although Northern Songs always earned most, through cover versions and sheet music, from tuneful Mc-Cartney compositions like 'Michelle' and 'Yesterday'. To John and Paul, he was a joke figure with his bald head, desperate sideburns and cheesy Tin Pan Alley bonhomie, but they understood that Brian had found them a publisher as different from the norm as

George Martin, who believed in quality and was essentially honest.

However, as time passed a familiar syndrome had set in. A deal that had seemed so bountiful to impressionable boys in 1963 looked somewhat different after six years as the entertainers of the century. And James had undeniably grown wealthy on their backs, not only as managing director and a major shareholder in Northern Songs but also through his separate organisation, Dick James Music, which handled the catalogues of numerous other successful young songwriters and now even had its own independent record label.

After Brian's death, one of John and Paul's first 'self-management' initiatives had been to seek a new deal from Northern Songs. They were not overly polite about it, suggesting that their meeting with James should be filmed like some police interrogation. James had declined to revise the existing arrangements and since then relations between the two sides had been chilly.

In any case, James also bore the responsibility of heading a public company and safeguarding the interests of its shareholders. To begin with, Beatlemania had kept Northern's stock at a perpetual high. But latterly, as John's behaviour had become more and more erratic – and especially since he'd teamed up with Yoko – it had begun to fluctuate alarmingly, to the severe detriment of Dick James's nerves.

The *Two Virgins* album cover followed by the Amsterdam Bed-In finally proved too much for James and his associate, Charles Silver, and on 28 March they sold their 37.5 per cent of Northern Songs to Associated Television for just under £2 million. At the same moment, ATV's chairman, Lew Grade, announced he was seeking overall control of the company and was prepared to spend up to £9 million to acquire it.

Neither John nor Paul received any prior warning of the sale from Dick James. To add insult to injury, the organisation now intent on gobbling up their catalogue had nothing to do with the pop business but was the commercial TV franchise holder for the Midland region, best-known for a cheapo teatime soap called

Crossroads. Grade himself was the archetype of the cigar-chewing showbiz moguls who'd spent the last decade denigrating pop music as just a passing fad. The Beatles' competing advisers, Allen Klein and Lee and John Eastman – now Paul's father- and brother-in-law – were thus forced back into alliance, to prevent ATV from taking over Northern Songs by increasing John and Paul's own stake to beyond 50 per cent.

As Northern was a public company, some of the requisite extra shares could be bought up piecemeal from private investors. But a crucial block belonged to a City investment group known only as 'the Consortium', and amounted to around 14 per cent – exactly what each side needed to gain control. The Consortium by no means regarded the Beatles as automatic heirs to the company, for all that they were its *raison d'être*, and intended to consider both bids on equal terms.

Meanwhile, John had returned from his trans-European nuptial odyssey with a new song which temporarily drove everything else from his mind. Titled 'The Ballad of John and Yoko', it was a piece of musical reportage chronicling the search for a wedding-venue that had first taken the couple to Southampton and Paris, their eventual nuptials in Gibraltar, their Amsterdam Bed-In and subsequent trip to Vienna, where they'd given a press conference with bags over their heads. It was clever, witty and self-mocking: in fact, everything that people thought John Lennon had forgotten how to be.

His proposal to make it the Beatles' next single – so confirming Yoko's election to the band – looked like yet another guaranteed source of dissent. However, both George and Ringo happened to be out of London when he was ready to record it. And, despite their recent battles over the management question, he still instinctively turned to Paul to bring it to fruition. On 14 April, they completed it together at Cavendish, then went round to Abbey Road and recorded it on their own with George Martin, assisted by Geoff Emerick, the gifted engineer whom their bickering had driven away from the White Album.

To Paul, the song was about everything that spelt disaster for the Beatles, while its chorus of 'Christ, you know it ain't easy', and references to John's being 'crucified', threatened to drag them into another more-popular-than-Jesus furore. Yet he gave it his all, playing bass, drums, piano and maracas, adding his sweet top-line harmony to 'bag', 'drag' and 'crucify me'. The two hadn't played as a duo since appearing as the Nerk Twins at Paul's cousin's pub, and they joked around as if the intervening years and mobs and millions had never been. 'Go a bit slower, Ringo,' John quipped as Paul laid down his drum-part. 'Okay, George,' came the answer.

'The Ballad of John and Yoko', credited to Lennon and McCartney, became the Beatles' eighteenth and last UK number one single. In America, where it reached number eight, a picture cover showed the band as a quintet, with Yoko in rock 'n' roll black leather and blue denim. But by then, a second 'Bed-In for Peace', this time in Montreal, Canada, had shown beyond any doubt what the next verse would be.

So important was the battle with ATV for control of Northern Songs that Lee Eastman flew to London to take over the lead from his son. Coincidentally, the same moment to cross the Atlantic was chosen by Allen Klein's long-standing notoriety in New York.

On 13 April, the *Sunday Times*'s famous Insight investigative team published the first detailed survey of Klein's business methods to appear in the British press. Headlined 'The Toughest Wheeler-Dealer in the Pop Jungle', it examined his alleged shady share-dealing over the Cameo-Parkway record label, the many and varied litigants currently ranged against his ABKCO company and his mounting problems with the Internal Revenue Service. The juiciest revelation concerned his most famous exploit as a scourge of record companies and miracle-worker for his clients – the $1.25 million advance he had secured for the Rolling Stones from Decca Records in 1965. According to Insight, that mythic sum had never found its way into the Stones' pockets, but gone straight into their manager's.

Lee Eastman thus arrived at this first face-to-face meeting with the Beatles and Klein primed with new ammunition against his rival. But Klein struck first. He had discovered that Lee came from a Jewish immigrant background as humble as his own and had started life with the surname of Epstein, the same as the manager whom the band were having such a hard job to replace. This might have seemed a recommendation, but was held up by Klein as evidence that Lee was 'a phoney'.

The usually calm, measured celebrity lawyer lost his cool – though not because of the Epstein taunt, his son John believes. 'I wasn't there, but I know my dad would never have been bothered by something like that. It was more likely because Klein was criticising me behind my back.' The meeting ended with Lee shouting at Klein while John threw petrol on the flames by addressing him as 'Mister Epstein' and Paul looked on in an embarrassment that can only be guessed at.

Paradoxically, there was no disagreement between the rival advisers on how to save Northern Songs from takeover by Lew Grade. The Beatles would offer £2 million to the investment group known as the Consortium for the crucial 14 per cent shareholding that would give them control, so turning the public company back into a private one. The money was to be borrowed from a merchant bank, Henry Ansbacher & Co., on collateral provided by Apple shares, plus John's entire holding of 644,000 shares in Northern Songs.

But this last detail caused an even worse scene at a second meeting with Lee Eastman, on 18 April. Klein suggested that Paul, too, should put up his Northern shares as collateral for the bank loan, but Lee told him not to think of it. Klein then revealed that Paul had recently substantially increased his holding without telling any of his fellow Beatles. At this, their aide Peter Brown later recalled, John 'flew into a rage' and seemed about to attack Paul physically.

Lee's visit to London, as he himself recognised, had been a disaster. Afterwards, he received a letter signed by John, George and Ringo, terminating his appointment as the band's general counsel

– but acknowledging that Eastman & Eastman in the person of John Eastman would continue to represent Paul alone. Again, Paul's embarrassment can only be guessed.

Those recent boardroom scenes might have been expected to kill off any remaining creative spark between Lennon and Mc-Cartney. But on both of them, as 'The Ballad of John and Yoko' had shown, music acted as a kind of healing amnesia. On 30 April, they were back in the studio together, finishing off 'You Know My Name (Look Up the Number)', a comedy track that had been hanging around since 1967. It had no commercial potential whatsoever, and went nowhere beyond repeating the title in a series of funny voices, yet they still devoted hours to it, singing into a single microphone, coughing, spluttering and doing *Goon Show* accents, for all the world like the teenage pals and co-conspirators of long ago in Liverpool. Paul would later remember it as his favourite Beatles session of all.

Outside the studio, as before, rapprochement melted away. Having seen off Lee Eastman, Allen Klein was ready to claim his prize and he now drafted a three-year management agreement beween the Beatles and his company, ABKCO Industries. This would give him 20 per cent of their earnings, as opposed to Brian's 25 per cent (and Colonel Tom Parker's 50 per cent of Elvis Presley). Record royalties were excluded unless he negotiated a higher rate, in which case he would receive only a percentage of the increase.

The agreement assumed the Beatles would stay together, putting out singles and albums on the cycle they had been locked into since 1963. That they might fall apart at the very moment he won them was something Klein didn't allow himself to think. In those days, no one imagined that the break-up of a band might not necessarily be the end of it.

On 9 May, the Beatles met at Olympic Studios in Barnes. The ostensible reason was to talk to producer Glyn Johns about the formless mass of tapes, recorded the previous January, which Johns had been tasked with moulding into an album called *Get Back*. But that discussion did not progress far.

John, George and Ringo had already signed Klein's management agreement and wanted Paul to follow suit there and then. He did not refuse outright, but said they ought to negotiate further, perhaps offering a lower commission than 20 per cent (just as, years earlier, they'd tried to beat Brian down from 25 to 20). The others said there was no time: Klein was flying back to New York that night to have the agreement ratified by his board at ABKCO.

Paul alone recognised this as a ploy to rush them. Klein's company consisted solely of Klein and his wife, Betty (as could be read from its initials), and had no 'board'. He further pointed out that, today being Friday, nothing further was likely to happen with the agreement until after the weekend. The others told him in unison to 'fuck off', then did so themselves.

Glyn Johns at the time was producing an album for the American Steve Miller Band, whose leader Paul knew and liked. After John, George and Ringo's exit, he found Miller working alone on a track and volunteered to sit in on drums – a providential way of giving vent to his feelings – for which he'd later be credited, under his Silver Beatles alias of 'Paul Ramon'. The song's title, for him, was to prove only too fitting: 'My Dark Hour'.

In mid-June, George Martin received a surprise phone call from Paul. It wasn't the bad news about the Beatles that Martin expected, however, but a plea for further healing amnesia.

Six months after the band had finished recording their *Get Back* album, Paul said, there still were no plans for its release. Glyn Johns had put together a 16-song version, leaving in all their false starts, fluffs and ad-libs – 'us with our trousers down', as John called it – which all four were unanimous in rejecting. But, far from terminally sickening them of albums, it had made them want to go back into the studio to make a whole new one from scratch. And they wanted Martin to work with them, as Paul put it, 'the way we used to do it'.

Martin had no wish to return to the fraught atmosphere of Twickenham Studios the previous January, and of the White

Album before that. 'If the album's going to be the way it used to be,' he replied with a touch of his old schoolmasterly sternness, 'then all of you have got to be the way you used to be' – meaning hard-working, focused, good-humoured; above all, friends with each other. Paul promised that they would be. And, incredibly enough, they were.

On the sunny morning of 8 August, the four met in Abbey Road, that tree-lined north London boulevard whose name had long been usurped by their recording studio and now would be all over again by the album nearing completion. They were there to pose for a cover picture sketched out in advance by Paul: in that department, at least, his views still carried weight.

A few metres south of EMI's studios was a black and white pedestrian crossing to the junction with Grove Road. Photographer Iain Macmillan positioned a small stepladder in the middle of Abbey Road and from that slight elevation took several shots of the Beatles walking over the crossing in single file, both from right to left and left to right.

Every one showed them in the same order: John first, then Ringo, Paul and George, in a military 'quick march' in which only Paul was out of step. His dress was similarly nonconformist – a double-breasted dark blue pinstripe suit just like the ones his father used to wear to work at Liverpool Cotton Exchange throughout the Forties and Fifties. Undercutting this period formality were an open-necked shirt, a cigarette, thongy sandals without socks and – in some shots, including the one chosen for the album cover – bare feet.

The image could hardly have been more mundane. Yet in years to come, any other band aspiring to greatness would replicate that four-figure tableau marching over similar broad black and white bars. And each day in Abbey Road, there wouldn't be a moment when the crossing was without a quartet of pilgrims strung across it, risking the highly dangerous traffic to be photographed à la Beatles – one of them barefoot and carefully out of step with his companions.

27

'Paul is still with us'

The three most notable celebrations of 1960s youth culture all took place in the golden summer of the decade's final year, almost as if responding to a mass desire to squeeze the very most out of its every remaining minute.

On 5 July, a crowd of 250,000 watched the Rolling Stones memorialise their late guitarist, Brian Jones, with a free concert in London's Hyde Park. Between 15 and 19 August, 500,000 spectators swamped a muddy pasture near Woodstock, New York, for a 32-act programme that included Joan Baez, Santana, Jefferson Airplane, the Who and Jimi Hendrix. Two weeks later, a different half-million descended on the sleepy Isle of Wight, off England's south coast, for another three-day Anglo-American rock marathon, culminating in Bob Dylan's first performance since his near-fatal motorcycle accident in 1966.

At each event, communing with the elite of contemporary rock in the open air meant extreme discomfort, overcrowding, bad sanitation, hunger and thirst, yet at all three the audience remained overwhelmingly law-abiding and good-humoured. This recurrent phenomenon of young people congregating in vast numbers, without violence or disorder, could not but impress even their bitterest critics among the older generation. For a hallucinatory moment, the hippy credo of love and peace truly seemed to have become a force capable of changing the world for the better.

Sadly, the musicians who had done most to create this mood of freedom and goodwill were nowadays locked up in endless acrimonious business meetings. Compared with Mick Jagger gyrating in a frilly dress under Hyde Park's oaks, or Jimi Hendrix playing an ironic 'Star-Spangled Banner' at Woodstock, the Beatles even seemed a touch passé. Yet, as so often before, it was they who created the quintessential summer sounds, albeit late in the season and with a hint of chill autumn to come.

The *Abbey Road* album, released in Britain on 26 September, seemed to banish all the recent rumours of their imminent disintegration. After the sprawling, fragmented White Album, it was a return to the top form of *Revolver* and *Sgt. Pepper*; a one-disc collection whose every track was an indispensable gem. A new step forward, indeed, as it contained two songs by George that were the equal of any from John or Paul ('Here Comes the Sun' and 'Something') plus one by Ringo ('Octopus's Garden'). Most reassuring of all were vocal harmonies sweeter and closer than any since 'This Boy' or 'Here, There and Everywhere'. What George said on one of his two surprise tours de force really seemed true: 'Here comes the sun . . . it's all right'.

Paul's pledge of good behaviour to George Martin on the others' behalf had been kept way beyond Martin's expectations. They had succeeded in forgetting their business differences and turned back into musicians who still knew no better company than one another. In the boardroom they might be drifting irretrievably apart, but this last time together in the studio they'd never seemed more united. The poignancy that underscores every track – smiles hiding tears, polish masking pain, a seeming fresh start that's really a dead end – would ultimately make *Abbey Road* the best-selling Beatles album ever.

There was inevitably the odd lapse. Some of the material had already featured in the *Get Back* sessions, so carried a legacy of boredom and impatience born of vainly striving for perfection in a single take. Paul's 'Maxwell's Silver Hammer', in particular, had been tried so many times under its composer's relentless cosh that John refused to work on it any further.

Nor did 'going back to the way they used to do it' mean excluding Yoko. On the contrary, the *Abbey Road* sessions included a bed-in right there on the studio floor. Before reporting for work, John had taken Yoko on a car-trip through the Scottish Highlands – his attachment to which long predated Paul's – accompanied by his son Julian and her daughter Kyoko. A chronically bad driver, he had landed their hire-car in a ditch, badly gashing his face and injuring Yoko's back to the extent that walking and even sitting were still painful for her. Rather than be without her in the studio, he had a double bed delivered from Harrods department store. There she lay, propped up by pillows, with a microphone rigged above her head to allow her to comment on the proceedings at will. Amazingly, the ceasefire still held.

For once, none of Paul's contributions had 'hit single' tattooed on it. 'Oh, Darling' was a pastiche of overwrought soul singers like Jackie ('Reet Petite') Wilson; an early example of the 1950s nostalgia soon to flavour most British pop. 'Maxwell's Silver Hammer', recorded sans John, began in familiarly cute, homey McCartney style with a character named Joan studying 'pataphysical science' – the term he'd picked up in his days of hanging out with underground intellectuals at the Indica bookshop. Inside the pretty wrappings, a serial-killer medical student, Maxwell Edison, mutely stalked and bludgeoned his inoffensive victims with a cheery 'Bang-Bang!' to '[make] sure [they were] dead'. Giving him a silver hammer was meant to dilute the sick humour (just as putting 'Silver' in front of 'Beatles' had once seemed to bestow more glamour). But even for the charts of 1969, whimsical mass-murder was way too strong.

So the double A-side single taken from the album was John's 'Come Together' – a blatant double entendre which no longer held any risk – coupled with George's 'Something'. Yet, far from creating further tension, 'Come Together' revived the old unselfish creative interplay of Lennon and McCartney at their best. In John's original version, Paul noticed the opening line slightly resembled Chuck Berry's 'You Can't Catch Me'. To forestall any charge of plagiarism, he suggested giving it a different arrangement that he envisioned

as 'swampy'. Hence its somnambulistic, bass-heavy beat, suggestive of tropical night, croaking frogs and sex under mosquito-nets.

There, alas, creative interplay hit the buffers. Although 'Come
Together' seemed made for a live Lennon–McCartney harmony,
John opted for vocal overdubs, done solely by him. Paul would
later remember hoping the two of them would share a microphone
again, but being 'too embarrassed to ask'. It was, perhaps, the saddest measure of the gulf now separating them.

Side two of the album had the strongest air of innovation
rather than valediction. For some time past, George Martin had
been urging John and Paul to take their music to a higher level
by writing in symphonies and movements rather than just the
three- or four-minute flurries of a pop track. Now, as an extended
finale to *Abbey Road*, he suggested they each root out fragments
of unfinished or unrecorded songs from their bottom drawers, to
be arranged into a classical-style suite. 'Paul went for the idea at
once,' Martin remembers. 'John grumbled a lot at first, but then he
started coming in and saying, "'Ere, I've found another bit for the
medley."'

John's 'bits' were very obvious leftovers with *Sgt. Pepper*-y titles,
ribald lyrics and lapses into Scouse dialect, like poltergeists of his
pre-Yoko self. Paul's, by contrast, formed a complex mosaic revealing more of his private feelings and emotions than his music ever
had before. Indeed, all the reassurance the album had built up so
carefully was undermined in its final few minutes, thanks to the
Beatles' one-time consummate PR man.

'You Never Give Me Your Money' was an unmistakable reference to Allen Klein's promises of fabulous wealth, which so far had
produced only 'funny paper' like the management contract Paul
alone had held out against signing. Outvoted and marginalised, his
'one sweet dream' was for himself and Linda to be 'out of here . . .
step on the gas and wipe that tear away'.

'She Came In Through the Bathroom Window' recalled his chaotic bachelor existence, just before Linda, when one eager groupie
actually had entered Cavendish by that route. 'Golden Slumbers'

derived from a setting of 'Cradle Song', by the Elizabethan pamphleteer Thomas Dekker, which Paul's nine-year-old stepsister, Ruth, happened to have been learning on the piano. A passionate lullaby, from a soon-to-be father, turned into an anthemic chorus that was an uncannily accurate glimpse into his own future: 'Boy, you're gonna carry that weight . . . a long time!'

Here, at least, he had the last word – or, rather, two. In 'The End', the others really were just 'sidemen for Paul' as he pronounced their collective epitaph: 'The love you take/ is equal to the love you make'. Then, when the album seemed over, as if to make up for all that grousing, came 'Her Majesty', a fragment of his old cheeky charm apparently calling Britain's sovereign 'a pretty nice girl'. He'd actually decided to cut it, but the studio engineers didn't dare.

It was to promote *Abbey Road* that the Beatles had done their last-ever photo-shoot together, a melancholy occasion at John and Yoko's new country mansion, Tittenhurst Park, on 22 August. They wore virtually the same clothes as on the album cover – save that John sported a wide-brimmed black hat like a Quaker elder – and seemed as awkward and withdrawn as four strangers.

It was hard to equate those cold, indifferent men with the boys who'd survived the Liverpool Cavern, Hamburg, Beatlemania and even crazier post-Beatlemania together, sustained by laughter, passion, optimism and, above all, a friendship that seemed indestructible. The love they'd made had been infinitely greater than any they could take – and this was the heaviest price of all.

Paul never did sign Allen Klein's management agreement: John, George and Ringo's majority vote had been sufficient to swing the appointment. His contractual obligations to the Beatles' partnership and Apple meant he was now stuck with a manager he'd never wanted and could not stand.

Klein, for his part, assumed the lofty air of a man on a mission far more important than petty personality-clashes. '[Paul] was obligated into Apple for a considerable number of years,' he told a TV interviewer in the stilted legal-ese he employed in public, 'so his disassociating from me has really no effect.' Privately, his ironclad self-belief persuaded him Paul would come over to him in the end.

Paul's own skills as a politician, for once, had failed him completely. George, he guessed, could not be dissuaded from backing John over Klein. But the commonsensical, fair-minded Ringo might still be amenable to reason. So in July, Ringo and his wife, Maureen, received a rare invitation to dinner at Cavendish. After a sumptuous meal cooked by Linda, Paul reopened the case against Klein. As Ringo would later recall, he felt he was being emotionally blackmailed; whenever he volunteered something in Klein's favour, Linda dissolved into tears and said, 'They've got you, too.'

After the *Abbey Road* thaw, Paul was seen less and less at the Apple house in Savile Row where he'd once been a daily, omnipotent presence. 'He'd only come in for business meetings that he absolutely had to,' Tony Bramwell recalls, 'though he was still on the phone all the time, asking me to do things.'

Admittedly, life now held other interests. On 28 August, at the Avenue Clinic in St John's Wood, Linda had given birth to a girl. Paul was with her throughout the confinement; while the midwifery stuff he remembered so well was going on, he stared fixedly at a Picasso print on the wall. 'It showed a guitar being played with only two fingers,' he was to remember, 'so I thought I'd try to write a song around the same chord.'

He watched his daughter arrive, six pounds eight ounces and perfect, later describing it as 'the first time I'd really seen magic taking place in front of my eyes'. She was named Mary, after the mother whom he'd lost when he was 14 but who had never really left him.

Actually, he now had two daughters, having decided to adopt Linda's daughter, Heather, just like his father had adopted his stepmother Angie's daughter, Ruth. But unlike Ruth's, Heather's biological father, Joseph Melville See, was still very much alive in Tucson, Arizona.

In the years since his divorce from Linda, See had had little contact with Heather and had raised no objection to her being brought from New York to London to live with Paul. Even so, he could have created all kinds of legal obstacles to the adoption plan, maybe thwarted it altogether. He decided not to do so, he told his subsequent partner, Beverly Wilk, 'because Heather will have a better life as a McCartney'.

Despite the distractions of double fatherhood, the chunky spectre of Allen Klein continued to haunt Paul, and what Klein had done and was still doing to Apple only compounded his feelings of betrayal, rejection and impotence.

If the company's vast expenditure and waste had been curbed, there was no longer any sense of pioneering or mould-breaking at 3 Savile Row – only fear of where the axe would fall next. Klein's relentless firing of the useful along with the useless had continued unabated, finally even reaching the Beatles' two most trusted aides, Neil Aspinall and Peter Brown (though both were immediately reprieved by John and George). All that survived from the Paul era were the press office and the 'Apple Scruffs', clustered around the front steps, who already sensed what had been done to their darling and greeted Klein's arrivals and departures with shouts of 'Mafia!'

The front ground-floor office had been commandeered by John and Yoko as headquarters for the peace campaign their two bed-ins had initiated. It also housed a new company, Bag Productions, named after their fondness for wearing bags over their heads and set up to handle their joint music and film enterprises. Apple staff were expected to work for Bag Productions on projects such as collecting acorns to be sent as peace-tokens to world leaders, like China's mass-murderous Mao Zedong. The press office, meanwhile, was called on to publicise *Self-Portrait*, a 20-minute film of John's penis slowly achieving partial erection. A bit of a change from virginal Welsh sopranos and Yorkshire brass bands.

At the Montreal bed-in, John had recorded his campaign anthem, 'Give Peace a Chance', with Yoko and a choir made up of celebrities and media people who happened to be there at the time. It gave him the idea for a rock band consisting, not of a shackled-together

four like the Beatles, nor even necessarily of musicians, but an impromptu ensemble with as many or as few members as happened
to be on hand and which would keep changing size and shape like
an amoeba.

For 'Give Peace a Chance', he therefore coined the name the
Plastic Ono Band, putting Yoko firmly in the foreground and com-
missioning four perspex towers full of audio equipment as its only
other permanent constituents. But although Paul was not involved
at any point, the song still bore the Lennon–McCartney byline.
John was later to regret feeling 'guilty enough to give McCartney
credit on my first independent single instead of . . . Yoko, who
wrote it with me'.

The Apple record label continued to acquire and develop new
artistes, but with few of the lavish resources Paul used to pour into
it. George mainly took over the driving-seat, signing the American
soul singer Doris Troy and the Radha Krishna Temple singers,
whose orange-robed troupe was a familiar chanting, bell-clashing
sight up and down Oxford Street. (As a result, the newest catch-
phrase among 3 Savile Row's tense and paranoid workforce was
'Hare Krishna'.) Crosby, Stills & Nash auditioned with a gorgeous
version of 'Blackbird', but were rejected.

Paul's final producing job for Apple was with Mal Evans's Welsh
band the Iveys, now renamed Badfinger ('Bad Finger Boogie' had
been an early title of 'With a Little Help from My Friends'). During
a pause in the Abbey Road sessions, he decided which of the quartet
should be lead singer and instructed them exactly how to perform
his song 'Come and Get It'. The track was intended for Ringo's
film *The Magic Christian*, but sounded like a send-up of Klein and
his almost coercive promises of wealth there for the taking: 'If you
want it, here it is, come and get it, make your mind up fast/ Did I
hear you say that there must be a catch?/ Will you walk away from
a fool and his money?'

But there could be no walking away from Klein for the moment,
immersed as he was in a project that had Paul's full consent. This
was the fight to save Northern Songs from the clutches of Lew

Grade's Associated Television, which by now had been dragging on for almost four months.

The situation was still exactly as it had been back in May: a group of City investors held the block of shares both the Beatles and Grade needed for overall control, but still coyly refused to sell to either side. Initially, this consortium had felt it only right for Lennon and McCartney to own the publishing company which administered their back catalogue. The leading members had been wooed by meetings with John and Yoko in person – but the strategy had misfired when John lost patience with all the schmoozing and declared he was 'tired of being fucked about by men in suits sitting on their fat arses in the City'.

The real problem, however, was Klein, whose chequered CV had recently been laid out in detail by the *Sunday Times* Insight team. The Consortium felt an old-fashioned sense of responsibility for the future of Northern Songs and feared that if the Beatles won control, 'the toughest wheeler-dealer in the pop jungle' would end up as its chief executive.

Apple hastily offered reassurances that Klein would not be involved with Northern in any way if the Beatles' bid were to succeed. There were also strenuous efforts to counter all the recent stories of disunity and instability at 3 Savile Row. To emphasise the company's bright future under Lennon and McCartney, the two offered to extend their contractual commitment as songwriters beyond the present expiry date of 1973. Paul even posed for a photograph by Linda of Klein and himself joking around, apparently after the signing of what looked like an important contract but in reality was just another 'funny paper'.

Early in September, Klein sensed the Consortium might be swinging back his way and, to his credit, brought John Eastman over from New York so that Paul's interests would be properly represented. But on the 19th, as the Beatles prematurely celebrated victory – with yet another office wrangle, this time about who should sit on Northern's board of directors – they heard that the vital block of shares had been sold to ATV after all.

In another small rapprochement, John and Paul agreed they wanted no part of a Northern Songs headed by Lew Grade. Keeping their minority stake would have maintained their connection with their own work, perhaps even encouraged them to mount a further takeover bid at some later date. Instead, they let Klein broker a deal to sell Grade their combined holding for £3.5 million.

They would continue to receive royalties from their songs: a dividend on a scale unimaginable in 1969. But that prodigious body of work, from 'Please Please Me', 'Can't Buy Me Love' and 'Help!' to 'Penny Lane', 'Lucy in the Sky with Diamonds', 'All You Need Is Love' and 'Hey Jude' – the bottled joy and optimism of a whole decade – was now owned by others.

A week earlier, John and the first incarnation of the Plastic Ono Band – Yoko, Eric Clapton, bassist Klaus Voormann and drummer Alan White – had made a surprise appearance at a one-day rock 'n' roll festival in Toronto. Their set was barely rehearsed and shambolic, but it cured John of a paralysing superstition. For years, he'd believed himself incapable of going onstage with any musicians not named Paul, George and Ringo. In his euphoria, he told Ray Connolly of the *London Evening Standard* that he was quitting the Beatles – but made Connolly promise not to use the story for the present. On the flight home, he also told Allen Klein.

For Klein, this was appalling news. Just days earlier, he had finalised a deal that was to have wiped away the failings over NEMS and Northern Songs and established him, even with Paul, as the saviour the Beatles had sought. He had negotiated a new contract with their American record label, Capitol, under which their per-unit royalty would rise from 17.5 per cent of wholesale price to an unheard-of 25 per cent. Their part was to guarantee two albums and three singles per year for the next six years.

When other top bands had lost important members – Brian Jones of the Rolling Stones, John Sebastian of the Lovin' Spoonful, Paul Jones of Manfred Mann, Graham Nash of the Hollies – they'd simply found replacements and carried on. But there could never be any question of replacing John: if he walked, it was the end of the Capitol contract – and of the Beatles.

On 20 September, the day after the loss of Northern Songs, they met at 3 Savile Row to sign the Capitol contract. Only Klein and Yoko knew of John's decision. Klein had asked him to say nothing until after the contract was safely signed, and he had agreed. It was an occasion with somewhat less of the usual tension between the two opposing factions. Klein had represented Paul along with the other three in the Capitol negotiations and, after his people had gone over every syllable of the contract, he admitted being impressed by the new royalty rate. 'If you're screwing us, I can't see that you are,' he told Klein.

The meeting began somewhat like a family therapy session, with John grumbling about the way Paul had bossed the band since Brian Epstein's death, his tireless productivity, his 'hogging' of space on albums and his 'granny music' like 'Ob-La-Di, Ob-La-Da' and 'Maxwell's Silver Hammer'. George was also dragged in, in the character of neglected child. The quality of 'Something' and 'Here Comes the Sun' on *Abbey Road* had finally given John some respect for 'that bloody kid', and he now seemed to be blaming Paul for the years George had spent in Lennon and McCartney's shadow.

Paul might have countered that on the Beatles' current international hit single, 'Come Together/Something', the glory all belonged to John and George while he himself was nowhere in evidence. Most of John's grievances were wholly unreasonable, the consequence of his own insecurity and chronic laziness. Even so, Paul's replies were low-key, conciliatory, once even a little sad as he questioned whether their professional life really had become such unmitigated hell. 'When we get into a studio, even on a bad day, I'm still playing bass, Ringo's still drumming . . . we're still *there*, you know.'

Still, the fact that John had turned up to sign a six-year contract seemed to indicate he saw some future for the four of them. Under this misapprehension Paul began talking about a possible return to live shows, reviving his former idea of incognito appearances in small clubs. 'You don't understand,' John broke in. 'I'm leaving. I want a divorce, like my divorce from Cynthia.'

The immediate question was whether the band should sign a contract they now had little chance of honouring. Klein favoured going ahead and John Eastman, for Paul, did not object. 'We signed in a bit of a daze,' Paul was to remember, 'not really knowing why we'd done it.'

Paul and Klein briefly became allies, together persuading John to continue to keep his defection under wraps. The object wasn't only to prevent alarm-bells ringing at Capitol. *Abbey Road* was about to be released and – according to the wisdom of 1969 – the thought of a dying band might put people off it.

Although John managed to keep his vow of silence, he couldn't hide his increasing detachment from the others. For him, the band had become 'they' rather than 'we', and represented things he no longer wanted any part of. 'The Beatles can go on appealing to a wide audience,' he told one interviewer in this objective vein, 'as long as they make nice albums like *Abbey Road* with nice little folk songs like "Maxwell's Silver Hammer"[!] for the grannies to dig.' During a later radio appearance, he made a scathing reference to 'The Beatles, so-called'.

Most significant was his absorption in a different music ensemble, one of them his wife and four of them perspex towers. In October, he reassembled the Plastic Ono Band – this time with Ringo on drums – to record 'Cold Turkey', his searing recreation of his and Yoko's recent struggle to get off heroin. Uninvolved though Paul had been, either in the heroin or the recording, it should have carried the Lennon–McCartney credit, but bore John's name only.

Paul, on his side, was worn down by 'days of arguing about money, arguing with the other Beatles, so [that] something that had once been full of artistic freedom had become a nightmare'. Even on the most resiliently youthful of the four, it was all taking a physical as well as mental toll. 'I swear I got my first grey hairs . . .' he was to recall. 'I looked in the mirror and thought, "I can see you! You're all coming now. Welcome."'

London, too, was starting to get him down as the former man-about-town and culture-vulture had not dreamed it ever could. The hostility of his fans towards Linda, far from wearing off as he'd expected, seemed to grow more virulent. The front wall of Cavendish was repeatedly daubed with graffiti hate-messages. One hot afternoon, as Linda returned home alone, a member of the front gate pickets pushed an iced chocolate dessert into her face. A moment later, a furious Paul rushed out and demanded, 'Who just threw a choc-ice at Linda?' '*Actually*,' the assailant corrected him pedantically, 'it was a chocolate mousse.'

The pickets had long been able to get into the house while he was out, but hitherto had always crept about as respectfully as if it were a holy shrine, disturbing nothing, carrying off only flowers out of vases or sheets of toilet paper as souvenirs. Their most prized trophy had been a pair of Paul's trousers which a group of fans took turns to wear, shortening or lengthening them according to the size of the wearer.

Now there were regular thefts of clothes, Linda's photographic prints, even money. Rather than involve the police, Paul decided to catch the thief or thieves red-handed. He and Linda made an ostentatious exit from the house, then stopped their limo a little way down the road, crept back on foot into their opposite neighbour's front garden and mounted surveillance from behind the hedge.

Unfortunately, it was the moment chosen by one of the most honest and respectful picketers to nudge open Cavendish's ineffectual security gate and leave a bunch of flowers outside the front door. To her horror, the object of her adoration suddenly pounced on her, shouting 'It's you! It's you!', and began to shake her. Seeing the flowers and realising his mistake, he stopped shaking and instead began remorsefully stroking her hair.

That 20 September confrontation with John was the final straw for Paul. He decided, in his word, to 'boycott' Apple and seek refuge with Linda in their remote Scottish Highland hideaway. 'We took the kids, we took the dogs, we took everything we had, a guitar on top and a potty for the baby.'

All at once, the most public Beatle, the band's formerly tireless ambassador and PR, became the Invisible Man. In that era of communications limited to the telephone, telegrams and letters, it truly was possible for someone to vanish into a remote part of the country and remain incommunicado indefinitely. None but his family and closest Apple associates knew about the Kintyre Peninsula and High Park Farm, and even they heard little or nothing from him and had no idea how long he intended to be there. The fans, who normally possessed almost psychic knowledge of his whereabouts, had to confess themselves utterly baffled.

Beatle death-rumours were nothing new. Paul had already been the subject of a good many, started by people trying to make money from newspapers or simply discover where he lived. A telephone-caller to his office would say he'd been killed in Manchester or Glasgow, hoping to be told he was alive and well at home in St John's Wood. Now, after his disappearance had lasted several weeks and still no explanation was forthcoming, a student newspaper at Drake University, Iowa, published a spoof report that he was dead.

Long before the age of the Internet or Twitter, the story went viral. The Drake students' spoof was taken seriously, first by radio stations across the Midwest, then by fan-mags and scandal sheets, then television and the serious press, along the way acquiring a fully-developed storyline. It was that Paul had died in a road accident in 1966 but for the sake of the Beatles' career his death had been hushed up and a double in the person of an actor named William Campbell hired to take his place.

The story was pounced on by analysts and interpreters of Beatles lyrics – always at their most obsessive in America – who hadn't had anything really to get their teeth into since *Sgt. Pepper*. Now it was said that Paul's bandmates, seemingly racked with guilt over his death, had scattered concealed references to it through their musical output ever since.

The hunt for and dissemination of these so-called 'clues' kept the rumour on the boil for almost two months. In 'Revolution 9', an unidentified voice supposedly intoned 'Turn me on, dead man'. In the last section of 'Strawberry Fields Forever', John was said to sing 'I buried Paul', though he himself always maintained the words were 'cranberry sauce'. On the *Sgt. Pepper* album cover, the blue-uniformed Paul figure allegedly confessed its own bogusness with an armband lettered OPD, for 'Officially Pronounced Dead' (actually OPP, for Ontario Provincial Police). So it also had in the *Magical Mystery Tour* film by wearing a black carnation while the other Beatles wore red ones.

Attention focused most of all on the *Abbey Road* album cover, which had never been intended to mean anything whatsoever. Now the four ill-matched figures marching over the crossing were recast as a funeral procession, with white-clad, bewhiskered John as the priest, Ringo in his formal black suit as the mortician, blue-denimed George as the gravedigger and Paul's bare feet symbolising his role as the deceased. A car parked in the background was said to add the clinching detail: a Volkswagen 'Beetle', part of whose number plate read 28 IF, or Paul's age *if* he had lived until the autumn of 1969 (though actually he would still have been 27).

By November, there was an inundation of 'Paul is dead' singles ('Brother Paul' by Billy Shears and the All-Americans, 'Saint Paul' by Terry Knight, 'So Long Paul' by Werbley Finster aka José Feliciano, 'We're All Paul Bearers' by Zacherias and his Tree People) and Apple's press office was having to deny the rumour dozens of times a day to media organisations all over the world. A few managed to get through to Jim McCartney in Cheshire, who did the same. But as no one was willing to say where Paul was at present, the necrophilic fever refused to abate.

Finally, America's *Life* magazine did what had occurred to no British publication, ferreting out the existence of High Park Farm and dispatching a writer and photographer there. They arrived early one morning, while Paul was still in bed. At first, he was furious at the intrusion, and flung a bucketful of kitchen slops at them. Then, realising this had been caught on camera, the PR man in him took over: he agreed to an interview on condition the slop-throwing shot was 'killed'. *Life*'s 7 November cover showed him, tousled and unshaven, holding baby Mary, with Linda beside him and six-year-old Heather gripping a shepherd's crook. 'Paul is still with us,' said the cover line.

Quoting Mark Twain, he joked that 'the rumours of my death have been greatly exaggerated . . . Perhaps the rumour started because I haven't been in the press much lately. I have done enough press for a lifetime, and I don't have anything to say these days. I am happy to be with my family and I will work when I work. I was switched on for ten years and I never switched off. Now I am switching off whenever I can. I would rather be a little less famous these days.'

Buried in the diplomatic soufflé-speak was a momentous statement which at the time went completely unnoticed: 'The Beatle thing is over. It has been exploded . . .'

As the Sixties ran out, the spotlight switched back to John – and stayed there. On 25 November, he returned his MBE decoration to the Queen as a protest against the British government's support of America in the Vietnam War, its failure to alleviate the current famine in Biafra and (undercutting all seriousness) the fact that 'Cold Turkey' was slipping down the UK charts. This perceived slight against Paul's 'pretty nice girl' caused almost as much of an outcry as giving the Beatles MBEs had four years earlier.

In December, Badfinger's 'Come and Get It' – every detail of which Paul had dictated, despite the stress he was under – reached number four in the UK and seven in America. Reviewers remarked how much it sounded like the Beatles with him lead-vocalling in younger, happier days.

Just before the holidays, a series of enormous black and white billboards appeared in the centres of 12 major cities throughout the world, including New York's Times Square. Each one read:

WAR IS OVER!
IF YOU WANT IT
Happy Christmas from John & Yoko

No billboards announced the end of Paul's Scottish self-exile; yet again, John was making him take a back seat, though he didn't intend to stay there for long. He returned quietly to London with Linda and the children and began work on a solo album.

28

'It was a barrelling, empty feeling that just rolled across my soul'

And 'solo' really meant what it said. The whole thing was taped at Cavendish between December 1969 and January 1970 on a single four-track Studer machine set up in the living-room. Paul was his own producer and engineer, and played every instrument: bass, drums, lead, rhythm and steel guitar, piano, maracas, bongos, tambourine, Mellotron cowbell, wine glasses, xylophone and what would be listed as 'bow and arrow'. His only helper was Linda on backing vocals.

The contents were a mixture of new songs, written in Scotland, and bottom drawer ones, like 'Teddy Boy' and 'Junk', which had already been tried out with the Beatles but fallen victim to the others' indifference or impatience. There was even a relic of the Quarrymen era, 'Hot as Sun'. Paul wanted the no-frills immediacy and informality which he'd intended for the Beatles' *Get Back*, but which had somehow got lost along the way. So there was to be no tricksy editing, overdubbing or post-production; some of the tracks would be as brief as in the *Abbey Road* medley, some made up on the spot, some not even fully finished.

More important still, he wanted to tell the world of his new-found domestic bliss. The first thing he taped – intending simply to test the equipment – was a 45-second fragment called 'The Lovely Linda', which had noises from Linda in the background and ended with an involuntary giggle from them both as if they could hardly believe their own nerve. It would stay on the album, giggle and all.

One cannot but feel some sympathy for Allen Klein at this point. Klein had fought with every weapon at his disposal to win his all-time dream clients, only to have John quit on him and the break-up of the others guaranteed as a result. The only card he held was John's promise of secrecy pro tem; a few months, maybe even weeks, to wring the maximum out of the Beatles that could be wrung.

Among their unexploited assets, he had found the band-in-rehearsal TV documentary, made by Michael Lindsay-Hogg more than a year earlier as a companion piece to the filmed performance that never was. Klein saw himself as a film mogul as much as a pop music one, and now instructed Lindsay-Hogg to expand the documentary to feature-length for cinema release. The problem was that much of the live performance captured at Twickenham Studios and in the Apple basement was not of sufficient quality for a film soundtrack and would have to be re-recorded.

Thus, on 3 January 1970, Paul found himself back at Abbey Road with Ringo and George to cut a new version of George's song 'I Me Mine' – an unwitting acknowledgement of the death of the 'group mind' – on which he played bass, electric piano and Hammond organ and sang backup vocals. John and Yoko were away in Denmark, trying to give up smoking and having their identical long hair identically cropped; nonetheless, the session would pass into history as the last time the Beatles ever worked together on new material.

Klein's most urgent need was for the band to keep putting out records, thereby triggering the munificent new royalty rate he'd negotiated with Capitol – and his own 20 per cent of it. So far, all Capitol had been given in return was a compilation album of past hits and B-sides, cobbled together by one of his ABKCO minions; from 'Can't Buy Me Love' and 'I Should Have Known Better' to 'Rain', 'Lady Madonna' and 'The Ballad of John and Yoko'. To add to Paul's feelings of alienation and impotence, its title track was 'Hey Jude'.

Klein was now making all the Beatles' creative decisions, with the distracted air of a man watching sand run out in an hourglass. And the next one was to bring the worst affront Paul suffered under his regime.

The documentary which Michael Lindsay-Hogg was expanding to cinema-length clearly would need a soundtrack album to be released alongside it. And this could only come from the mass of tapes that was once supposed to become *Get Back*. Over the past year, the Rolling Stones producer Glyn Johns had heroically sifted through it and submitted two separate edits to the Beatles, but had both rejected without comment.

It was a musical slush-pile everyone tried to forget; the Beatles' own equivalent of the amateur demos and cassettes that had once poured into Apple at Paul's invitation. Yet buried in it were two future McCartney classics, 'Let It Be' and 'The Long and Winding Road'.

'Let it be' was a saying he'd often heard from his mother, the sweet-natured but wise and practical district nurse, when she counselled him not to brood about some boyhood quarrel or griev-ance. At one of the many recent low points with the Beatles, he'd dreamed that 'Mother Mary' had come back to him, speaking such 'words of wisdom'. 'I saw my mum,' he would recall. 'It was so wonderful for me, and she was very reassuring. In the dream, she said, "It'll be all right." I'm not sure if she used the words "let it be" but that was the gist.'

The resulting song was like a hymn to the blessed presence that had gone out of his life when he was 14, now transmuted into an almost saintly visitant. Working with George Martin, he had since prepared a finished version in which church organ chords segued into soft rock without spoiling the devotional mood. He also employed the Liverpool accent his mother so wanted him to lose, singing 'times of trooble' rather than 'trouble'.

It was also a first for Linda, whom Paul discovered to possess a sweet singing voice, instantly at home in the song's fluid harmonies. He had therefore added her to the backing choir, initiating a career that had never previously crossed her mind.

'Let It Be' was released as a Beatles single, credited to Lennon–McCartney, on 6 March, coupled with 'You Know My Name (Look Up the Number)', the last time Paul and John had ever had fun together in a studio. The soft-rock hymn reached number one in America but only two in Britain – further proof to Paul of how the world had turned against him.

Although their creative partnership was plainly over, he and John still spoke at regular intervals, often with flashes of their old empathy. They could even joke about being boardroom adversaries and the way their respective courtiers sought to curry favour by bad-mouthing one to the other. 'Do they try to set you against me?' John once asked, 'the way they try to set me against you?'

In March, Paul finally let John in on the secret of what he'd been up to all these weeks at home. 'I'm doing what you and Yoko are doing. I'm putting out an album – and I'm leaving the group, too.'

'Good,' John replied. 'That makes two of us who have accepted it mentally.'

John was in uncharacteristically buoyant mood, having just seen 'Instant Karma', his latest song for the Plastic Ono Band (now including George Harrison and Billy Preston) reach number three in America. To produce the session, he'd coaxed out of retirement the great Phil Spector, whose 'Wall of Sound' technique had revolutionised early-Sixties American pop. Though preceded by a fearsome reputation as a paranoid semi-hoodlum, Spector had behaved impeccably and contrived a brilliant single that would make John the first solo Beatle to sell a million.

Spector was also to produce the Ono Band's first album that summer but, meanwhile, having such a maestro around seemed too good an opportunity to miss. So, on John's recommendation, Allen Klein hired him to salvage the *Get Back* album – now, like its accompanying film, renamed *Let It Be.*

By this time, Paul's album, simply titled *McCartney*, was nearing completion, still shrouded in secrecy. For some of the taping and mixing, he used the tiny Morgan Studios in Willesden, north London, booking in under the name 'Billy Martin'. Linda, baby Mary and Heather went with him each day, strewing the place with baby paraphernalia, toys and picnic food. Only for the final stages did he use Abbey Road, keeping his Billy Martin alias – though he can hardly have gone unrecognised there. John Eastman then sought out New York's most state-of-the-art studios and delivered the masters personally for a final tweak.

When Allen Klein finally learned of the project, he attempted to stop it in its tracks, afraid that it might jeopardise the Beatles' Capitol Records contract. 'He wrote to the president of Capitol, Sal Iannucci, saying Paul was contracted to the Beatles, so he wasn't allowed to put out a solo album,' Eastman recalls. 'I talked to Iannucci and told him, "*McCartney* comes out on Capitol in five weeks or we go straight to Clive Davis at Columbia."

'Iannucci threatened to sue and I said, "So sue, it'll be a great case and terrific publicity for the record." "You can't talk to me like that," he said, "I went to Harvard Law School." I said, "Well, I went to Stanford, so just go and fuck yourself."' Nonetheless, the risk of losing Paul to a rival label hit home, and the *McCartney* album's release went ahead.

Paul was not the only Beatle with a solo album about to come out on Apple. Ringo, too, was breaking the mould with *Sentimental Journey*, a collection of standards, aimed primarily at pleasing his mum in Liverpool, which had elicited no objections from Klein and been scheduled for release on 27 March. Paul was given a release-date of 10 April for *McCartney*, but agreed to a one-week postponement to allow Ringo a little longer in the limelight.

However, it transpired that Phil Spector had worked so hard on his doctoring of the *Let It Be* tapes that a finished album could be ready for release on 24 April, a week ahead of the film's world premiere in New York. The problem was that if *McCartney* came out as scheduled on 17 April, the two albums would be competing with each other. And to those now in power at Apple, there was no question which was the more important.

After his recent tussle with John Eastman, Klein was careful to stay out of the picture, leaving John and George to handle things in their capacity as Apple directors. John wrote to Apple Records' distributors, EMI, that releasing two albums so close together 'would not be in the best interests of the company' and therefore *McCartney* was to be put back to 4 June. George then wrote to notify Paul of what had been done behind his back, signing off with a weak stab at affection and humour: 'We're sorry it turned out like this – it's nothing personal. Love John & George. Hare Krishna. A Mantra A Day Keeps [Hindu goddess] Maya Away.'

In a last, heavy-handed attempt at conciliation, the letter was addressed 'From Us To You' – echoing the Beatles' second UK number one – then left in Apple reception to be collected by a messenger. There it was spotted by Ringo, who introduced the first touch of sensitivity into the proceedings. Thinking it wrong for Paul to be handed such a missive by just 'an office lad', he volunteered to deliver it personally.

No good turn ever goes unpunished. Having read the letter and gathered that Ringo agreed with John and George, Paul launched a furious attack on the messenger. 'He went crazy,' Ringo would recall. 'He was out of control, shouting and prodding his finger towards my face, saying "I'll finish you all now" and "You'll pay" . . . he told me to get my coat on and get out.' Subsequently, George received a phone call in which '[Paul] came on like Attila the Hun . . . shouting so loud that I had to hold the receiver away from my ear'.

Paul would never deny his outburst nor that, in the well-meaning Ringo, he had picked totally the wrong target. 'I got really angry . . . I said, in effect, "This is the last straw and if you drag me down, I'll drag you down." I had to do something to assert myself because I was just sinking.'

Instinctively he turned for support to his old ally Sir Joseph Lockwood at EMI, but Lockwood was no longer the final arbiter concerning Beatles records, so had no choice but to accept John and George's (and Klein's) ruling. In the end, it was Apple's unlucky Mister Postman who saved the day. Knowing now just how much *McCartney* meant to Paul – and feeling a twinge of compassion for one who'd never before invited such an emotion – Ringo talked the others into reinstating its 17 April release. It was Paul's first victory in the Savile Row wars, but one almost immediately poisoned.

Phil Spector had professed himself a devoted Beatles fan who would handle their material as sensitively and respectfully as fine china. In remixing the *Let It Be* album, he had therefore been given a totally free hand, authorised to bring in extra musicians and arrangers as he saw fit, and left to get on with it unsupervised.

It was never likely that a man once known as 'Pop Music's First Svengali' would settle for a self-effacing editorial role like George Martin or Glyn Johns. And, sure enough, the demo Spector turned in with such impressive speed reeked of his conviction that he alone knew what was best for the Beatles and that even their most musically-gifted member lacked his transforming touch. Thus, he'd revamped the original version of 'Let It Be' by Paul and George Martin (which by then had been an international hit), inserting a seam of brass and juggling the guitar breaks, all to no effect but the coarsening of its sweet, prayerful mood. But that was minor compared with his treatment of 'The Long and Winding Road'.

Paul had recorded the song as a simple piano ballad in the style of Ray Charles, accompanied only by the other Beatles and Billy Preston. (John had taken over on bass, fluffing so many notes that he'd later be suspected of deliberate sabotage.) Though not prompted by a dream like 'Let It Be', it had a similar heart-aching confessional feel with its references to being 'full of tears' and 'crying for the day'. Onto this, Spector had superimposed a massive orchestra, including 18 violins, and a 14-strong female chorus, so turning a perfectly-mixed dry Martini into an over-sugared milk shake. As an extra unkind cut, the arranger was Richard Hewson, who had created the perfect setting for Paul on Mary Hopkin's 'Those Were the Days'.

John, George and Ringo approved the demo immediately, thankful that the shaming, shambolic *Get Back* had been turned into a releaseable product at last. To John especially, Phil Spector was, and would always be, a hero on a par with Hercules in the Augean Stables. 'He was given the shittiest load of badly-recorded shit with a lousy feel to it ever, and he made something of it.' Posterity would feel that on two tracks, at least, it was the other way round.

Not since the earliest days with George Martin had anyone challenged, let alone changed, Paul's work. As everyone at Apple well knew, his reaction was likely to make the contretemps with Ringo look mild. However, the album's production deadline was now so tight that altering any of the tracks would be impossible. And, seemingly, no great haste was made in sending a copy of the Spector demo to him at Cavendish.

Absorbed as he was by the final stages of *McCartney*, Paul put off listening to it for several days. When he finally got around to it, he immediately called 3 Savile Row and asked to speak to Allen Klein. On being told Klein was out, he dictated a letter over the phone, demanding that his version of 'The Long and Winding Road' be used on the album and that his music should never be tampered with again. But it was, as he realised, a futile gesture.

An interview with the *Evening Standard*'s Ray Connolly offered a perfect opportunity to vent his feelings. But he still stuck to soufflé-speak, insisting that he didn't dislike Klein personally and making only vague reference to the 'Long and Winding Road' issue. 'I don't blame Phil Spector for doing it, but it just goes to show it's no good me sitting here, thinking I'm in control, because obviously I'm not. I've sent Klein a letter, asking for some things to be altered, but I haven't received an answer yet.'

In places, the interview felt almost like an appeal to the other Beatles to make peace. 'We are beginning now only to call each other when we have bad news . . . There's no one to blame, we were fools to get ourselves into this situation . . .' However, it contained a second unmistakable public warning: 'The party's over, but none of us wants to admit it.'

Just as he'd sung and played every note on *McCartney*, so – in consultation with his photographer wife – he oversaw every detail of its packaging. The front cover was an image of cherries scattered on a white counter around a bowl of, possibly, wild cherry soup; the reverse showed a stubble-faced Paul in the Scottish wilds with baby Mary peeping out from inside his sheepskin coat. A gatefold opened to reveal 21 colour snapshots by Linda of the new McCartney family.

Marketing and publicity were organised from 3 Savile Row, without any of the input Paul was wont to lavish on Beatles albums. In the press advertisements, he discovered a further affront: the Apple logo, once his pride and joy, was now subtitled 'An ABKCO-managed company'. To remove even that tiny shadow of Allen Klein, he commissioned a set of new ads at his own expense that made no mention of ABKCO or Apple.

He did not release a single from the album and refused all requests for interviews. 'Whenever I'd meet a journalist, they always floored me with one question,' he would later explain. 'They'd say "Are you happy?" [i.e. professionally] and it almost made me cry. I just could not say "Yes, I'm happy" and lie through my teeth.'

Instead, the UK edition came with a sheet of dialogue confected between Apple's Peter Brown and himself, answering the questions every interviewer would have put. As a public relations gambit, it was familiar enough – but this was no longer PR man Paul. Bypassing the media he had always played with such consummate skill, he'd decided to come clean directly to his public:

Q. Are all songs by Paul McCartney alone?

A. Yes, sir.

Q. Will they be so credited: McCartney?

A. It's a bit daft for them to be Lennon–McCartney-credited, so McCartney it is.

Q. Did you enjoy working as a solo?

A. Very much. I only had me to ask for a decision and I agreed with me. Remember Linda's on it, too, so it's really a double act.

Q. What is Linda's contribution?

A. Strictly speaking she harmonises but of course it's more than that because she's a shoulder to lean on, a second opinion and a photographer of renown. More than all this, she believes in me – constantly . . .

Q. The album was not known about until it was nearly completed. Was this deliberate?

A. Yes, because normally an album is old before it ever comes out (aside) Witness *Get Back*.

Q. Are you able to describe the texture or feel of the album in a few words?

A. Home. Family. Love.

Q. Will Linda be heard on all future records?

A. Could be. We both love singing together and have plenty of opportunity for practice.

Q. Will Paul and Linda become a John and Yoko?

A. No, they will become Paul and Linda.

Q. Is it true that neither Allen Klein nor ABKCO have been nor will be involved in any way with the production, manufacturing, distribution or promotion of this new album?

A. Not if I can help it.

Q. Did you miss the other Beatles and George Martin? Was there a moment when you thought 'I wish Ringo were here for this break?'

A. No.

Q. Assuming this is a very big hit album, will you do another?

A. Even if it isn't, I will continue to do what I want, when I want.

Q. Are you planning a new album or single by the Beatles?

A. No.

Q. Is this album a break away from the Beatles or the start of a solo career?

A. Time will tell. Being a solo album means it's the start of a solo career and not being done with the Beatles means it's a rest. So it's both.

Q. Is your break with the Beatles temporary or permanent, due to personal differences or musical ones?

A. Personal differences, business differences, musical differences, but most of all because I have a better time with my family. Temporary or permanent? I don't really know.

Q. Do you foresee a time when Lennon–McCartney will become an active songwriting partnership again?

A. No.

Q. What do you feel about John's peace effort? The Plastic Ono Band? Yoko's influence? Yoko?

A. I love John and respect what he does. It doesn't really give me any pleasure.

Q. What is your relationship with Klein?

A. It isn't. I am not in contact with him and he does not represent me in any way.

Q. What are you planning now? A holiday? A musical? A movie? Retirement?

A. My only plan is to grow up.

The *Daily Mirror* got hold of an advance copy and splashed the story on 10 April: 'PAUL IS QUITTING THE BEATLES'. So 12 years, nine months and four days after he'd played 'Twenty Flight Rock' to John in St Peter's Church Hall, it was all over.

Despite the uproar of corroborative banner headlines and news-flashes around the world, there was an odd sense of anticlimax – almost relief that the months of uncertainty were finally at an end. The Beatles were dissolving in sync with the Sixties: to their followers, it felt like waking from a blissful dream with nothing but bleary hangover to be discerned in the new decade stretching ahead.

In London, there was a vigil around the front steps of the Apple house like those traditionally held outside Buckingham Palace on the passing of monarchs. Among the 'Apple Scruffs' interviewed on camera, the consensus was that it was all Linda's fault. 'Technically, she's supposed to be Paul's wife,' one of them explained to a BBC reporter. 'But she's his ruler, his guardian . . . she says "jump", he jumps. A genius like that . . . you can't let a woman do that to a man.'

Paul defended himself vigorously against the charges of wilful destruction from every side. 'I didn't leave the Beatles,' he protested. 'The Beatles have left the Beatles, but no one wanted to be the one to say the party's over.' It made little difference: the media almost unanimously accused him of overweening egotism, selfishness – and ruthlessness in pegging the terrible moment to the release of his first solo album. For even the best-informed commentators knew nothing about the ostracism, marginalisation, back-stabbing and humiliation within the band that he'd endured over the past months, yet still gone on trying to hold it together.

John meanwhile erupted in fury to think how he'd been talked into delaying his own resignation for the common good six months earlier. Now here was Paul, stealing the grand exit that ought to have been his. When asked for a reaction, he had plenty to say, albeit with a hefty dose of amnesia: 'It's a simple fact that [Paul] can't have his own way so he's causing chaos. I put out four albums last year, and I didn't say a fucking word about quitting.'

After the momentous event it had signalled, *McCartney*, too, came as something of an anticlimax. Listeners expecting the ambition and finesse of 'Penny Lane' or 'Eleanor Rigby', and the tightness and cohesion of *Sgt. Pepper* or *Revolver*, were disconcerted, if not disappointed, by its home-made, often half-finished quality. Most of the new songs – 'Teddy Boy', 'Junk', 'Every Night' – were in Paul's softest, blandest manner, and there was a puzzling emphasis on guitar-led instrumentals whose underlying message seemed to be 'Anything George can do, I can do better.' The Quarrymen number, 'Hot as Sun', sounded like nothing so much as Hamburg lounge-music, and segued into a fragment called 'Glasses' lasting only seconds but a glaring waste of space nonetheless. Even Paul

McCartney on musical wine glasses sounded no different from anyone else.

Two tracks only strayed from the overall atmosphere of having fun at home. 'Suicide' – which, bizarrely, Paul had once hoped Frank Sinatra might cover – came from the same well of chirpy sick humour as 'Maxwell's Silver Hammer'. And the Linda-inspired 'Maybe I'm Amazed' did not sound in the least home-made: a soaring ballad whose unspoken eroticism matched the best of Cole Porter.

Reviews were mixed, although every one singled out 'Maybe I'm Amazed' as outstanding. Richard Williams in *Melody Maker* attacked the album's 'sheer banality', calling the faux-hillbilly 'Man We Was Lonely' 'the worst example of [Paul's] music-hall style'. But to the *NME*'s Alan Smith, it was all 'like hearing a man's personal contentment committed to the sound of music . . . Excitement is not a word to use for this album. Warmth and happiness are.'

Whatever the critics might say, the supposed beady calculation of *McCartney*'s release more than paid off: it spent three weeks at number one in *Billboard*'s Hot Hundred, reached number two in Britain and topped charts all around the world.

Despite everything, the reaction which meant most to Paul was that of his now ex-bandmates. George, wrapping cattiness in a tone of affected concern, regretted how he had 'isolated' himself from musicians of his own calibre, so that 'the only person he's got to tell him if a song's good or bad is Linda'. There was nothing, however, from the person who'd been a sounding-board for his music since he was a schoolboy and whose rare approval had always meant most to him. Actually, John hated the album to the point of apoplexy but – for the moment – held his peace.

On 13 May, the *Let It Be* film received its world premiere in New York, followed later by grand openings in London and Liverpool. The Beatles were present only on a poster showing their four faces rigorously fenced off from each other by borders of thick black; in truth, these were not galas but wakes.

There finally, projected onto a big screen in unsparing close-up, were the chilly rehearsal-sessions at Twickenham Film Studios 16 months earlier for an album that was never to be, with Paul so much like some obsessive young schoolteacher struggling to motivate a reluctant class. There was George, dourly answering teacher back ('Look, I'll play whatever it is you want me to play. Or I won't play at all. Whatever it is that'll please you, I'll do it . . .') before his own, unrecorded, walk-out. Counting Ringo's brief defection during the White Album, *everyone* else had walked before Paul.

There, climactically, was the Apple rooftop concert, the four's last-ever live performance together, at noon on a winter weekday, rounded off by Paul with 'Get Back' while polite police invaders waited for him to finish. There was the horribly final sound of plugs being pulled, and the sardonic ad-lib from John: 'I'd like to say thank you very much from the group and ourselves and I hope we passed the audition.'

The film was generally panned. *Billboard*, whose chart the Beatles had once almost owned, felt no regret at the exit of 'four moppet dolls who, for the good part of a decade, have danced and squealed as the creative playthings of a great mass who built an economy around their pleasant music'. The *Sunday Telegraph* noted how in the rehearsal sequences 'Paul chatters incessantly . . . even when, it seems, none of the others is listening'.

The album also attracted widespread criticism, not least because lavish packaging pushed its price to almost double the cost of a standard LP. The *NME*'s Alan Smith, so long a staunch ally, called it 'a cheapskate epitaph . . . a sad and tatty end to a fusion which wiped clean and drew again the face of pop music'. But without those disillusioning film-sequences, enough of the old magic remained for it to go to number one almost everywhere, as instantly as when the Beatles used to be happy.

No one seemed to care that neither of Paul's two main contributions was as perfect as he'd intended. 'The Long and Winding Road', in its over-produced, chocolate-boxy version, became the band's last number one single in the US, selling 1.2 million copies in two days, while 'Let It Be', however reconfigured, won him a large measure of forgiveness for his defection. The same comfort 'Mother Mary' had given him, he now seemed to be offering the world at this most monumental 'time of trooble'. On the record, John tried to spoil the mood by introducing it in a comic child-voice as "ark the Herald Angels Come'.

The album later won the Beatles their only Oscar for 'Best Original Song Score' in a film. As proof of their indifference, none showed up at the awards ceremony and the statuette was collected on their behalf by the night's musical director, Quincy Jones.

That summer of 1970, John submitted himself to the American psychotherapist Dr Arthur Janov for a course of so-called Primal Therapy designed to exorcise the demons of his childhood. Paul might have no childhood demons to exorcise, but his concurrent psychological state was hardly less fragile.

Years later, when the baby peeping from inside his coat was a grown woman, he would confess to her how parting from the Beatles left him feeling 'very insecure, very paranoid, very out of work, very useless . . . I nearly had a breakdown, I suppose . . . [from] the hurt of it all and the disappointment . . . the sorrow of losing that great band . . . those great friends'. The poor reviews for his solo album debut fuelled a conviction – aged 27 – that 'I'd outlived my usefulness'.

He recalled how, taking refuge in Scotland once again, he developed 'all the classic symptoms of the unemployed, the redundant man', too depressed to get up in the mornings, no longer troubling to shave or change clothes. He began to chain-smoke, both legal and illegal cigarettes, and turned to whisky – his father's favourite tipple – reaching for the bottle as soon as he awoke.

The dreams that once had given him 'Yesterday' and 'Let It Be' became haunted by Allen Klein in the guise of a demonic dentist, trying to plunge a hypodermic into him; as his song 'Every Night' on *McCartney* had revealed, he would lie in bed shaking uncontrollably, his head too heavy to raise from the pillow. Hard drugs also began to beckon. He would recall how 'a friend' (gallery-owner and smack-addict Robert Fraser) had told him. '"You'll be all right. You wrote 'Yesterday', so you'll always be able to pay for your heroin," and for half a second I almost listened.'

It was, in any case, a tense time for Linda, with two young children to care for in the primitive conditions of High Park Farm. Having known Paul only as an all-powerful, all-conquering pop god, she found the change in him – as she later admitted – 'scary beyond belief'. 'I was impossible . . . I don't know how anyone could have lived with me,' he would recall. 'I was on the scrapheap in my own eyes . . . it was a barrelling, empty feeling that just rolled across my soul.'

Yet through the darkest of these days, Linda remained imperturbably calm and unshakably supportive, never hinting at the anxiety she felt, merely telling him in her laid-back hippy way not to let it all make him too crazy. Unlike John, he did not turn himself over to some modish therapist, but toughed it out, 'hiding in the Scottish mists', his only medications 'home, family and love'. 'She just sort of eased me out of it,' he would remember with lifelong gratitude.

Aside from Linda and the children, and the miraculous peace of Kintyre's hills and lochs, his main therapy was the DIY for which he'd always had so surprising an aptitude. Clad in his favourite indigo velvet trousers and rubber boots, he single-handedly tackled High Park Farm's most urgent needs, laying a new concrete floor in the kitchen and scaling a ladder to plug the ever-recurring holes in the roof.

Linda had become an expert horsewoman during her years in Arizona. The last time Paul had sat on a horse, not very comfortably, was for the 'Penny Lane' video in 1967, but now he began to learn how in earnest, rediscovering the love of horses he'd felt as a small boy, watching the stately police mounts exercise in the field behind 20 Forthlin Road. Soon he was skilled enough to join Linda in cowboy-style control of the sheep, both their own and their neighbours', which covered the surrounding hills. 'Paul's a great rider,' Linda said in a rare radio interview. 'We round up the

sheep on the horses and cook 'em ourselves.' Vegetarianism was
still some way off yet.

Back in London, however, hard realities needed to be faced; the
kind Paul had avoided for most of his adult life. No longer was
he surrounded by an organisation dedicated to shielding him and
smoothing his path, with minions at his beck and call around the
clock. 'It was just Paul, Linda and me,' John Eastman says. Against
the combined forces of Apple and ABKCO, 'I only had the sweat
of my brow. I was terrified that my client was going to get pulled
under.

'Paul said John wanted a meeting, so late one night we went
along to see him and Klein, who was staying in the Harlequin Suite
at the Dorchester. When we walked in, the place was full of their
lawyers – but there were just three of us and I knew we were going
to get slaughtered. Playing for time, I went into the bathroom,
where I noticed this big blue glass jar full of suppositories. I took it
out into the suite and said. "Who do these belong to?" "Oh, they're
mine," Klein said. "Allen," I said, "I always thought you were a perfect asshole" – and we got out of there as fast as the Road Runner.'

The gold-spinning youth who'd been a millionaire at 23 was
even starting to have money worries. Under the Beatles' ten-year
partnership agreement, binding until 1977, all proceeds from
projects by individual band members automatically went into the
communal coffers. Klein had refused Eastman's repeated request
for Paul to have a separate income stream: his earnings from *Mc-
Cartney* were thus locked away as securely as his Beatle ones, and
he and Linda were having to live on her savings.

Right at the beginning, John Eastman says, he'd told Klein that
Paul would be happy to walk away from the Beatles with his 25 per
cent of their fortune. 'Klein agreed to that, but afterwards I could
never pin him down to talk about it any further.'

Now Paul wrote to John, pleading that they should 'let each
other out of the trap'. John's response was a postcard of Yoko and
himself, with a hand-drawn bubble saying 'How and why?' 'How?
By dissolving our partnership,' Paul wrote back. 'Why? Because

there is no partnership.' John replied that if George and Ringo were also in favour, he'd think about it, but there the correspondence ended.

When it was clear that no informal settlement could be reached, John Eastman and his wife, Jodie, went to stay with Paul and Linda in Scotland, and Eastman set out the legal options. Paul wanted to sue Allen Klein, but as his brother-in-law pointed out, Klein had not been party to any of the Apple agreements which were tying him down. The only viable course, Eastman said, was a lawsuit to dissolve the partnership. 'I told him it had to be in the British High Court, framed as Paul McCartney versus John Lennon, George Harrison and Ringo Starr. It was a terrible step for him to take against people he'd been friends with since he was a kid.'

He took a few days to think it over while his lawyer made doubly sure there was no alternative. 'A week later, I went back and he asked me if it really was the only way,' Eastman recalls. 'I said, "Yes – or you lose everything."

'"Okay," he said, "pull the trigger." And from then on, he never wavered.'

29

'It was almost as if I was committing an unholy act'

Paul's legal action was launched on New Year's Eve 1970, in the Chancery division of the High Court in London. A writ issued in his name against the other three Beatles and Apple Corps sought 'a declaration that the partnership business carried on by the plaintiff and the defendants under the name of the Beatles and Co., and constituted by a deed of partnership dated 19 April, 1967, ought to be dissolved and that accordingly the same be dissolved'.

In an accompanying personal affidavit, Paul said he'd been 'driven to make this application because (a) the Beatles have long since ceased to perform as a group, (b) the defendants have sought to impose on me a manager who is unacceptable to me, (c) my artistic freedom is liable to be interfered with as long as the partnership continues and (d) no partnership accounts have been prepared since the Deed of Partnership was entered into'.

His writ further sought the appointment of an official receiver – a measure normally adopted in bankruptcy cases – to take charge of the Beatles' finances pending a final resolution of the case. The implication, therefore, was that Apple was insolvent and Allen Klein unfit to handle the Beatles' finances. 'It was the only way to get the money out of Klein's hands,' John Eastman says. 'Dissolving the partnership, I knew, would be pretty straightforward, but getting a receiver in a case like that was a very rare and extreme measure. At the beginning, no British lawyer I approached would take the case.'

Eastman rose to the challenge, feeling more than his brother-in-law's finances to be at stake. 'I knew that if I failed, it would be the end of my career . . . this preppy journeyman lawyer from New York had been seen off by the British establishment. So I set out to get us the imprimatur of the British establishment.'

Though Paul's resources at this point were anything but bottomless, Eastman persuaded one of the City of London's most powerful and exclusive merchant banks, N.M. Rothschild, to act as his bankers in the case. 'They agreed to do it on the basis of £1.5 million in loan stock Paul held that wasn't due to mature for five years.' With that unbeatable imprimatur, Eastman began to assemble a legal team headed by a newly-qualified Queen's Counsel, or 'silk', named David Hirst, a libel specialist who'd never taken on a commercial brief before.

The six months the case took to prepare seemed to confirm that the Beatles' creative partnership was no more. In that time, each of the others released an album under his own name which seemed as much a declaration of independence as *McCartney* had been – but enjoyed notably greater critical success.

September had brought Ringo's second solo album, *Beaucoups of Blues*, actually a collection of country songs which one American critic ranked with Bob Dylan's *Nashville Skyline*. In November came George's monumental triple-disc *All Things Must Pass*, marrying Indian mysticism with cool mainstream rock, which, like its single, 'My Sweet Lord', became a global, multifaith hit.

'All things must pass' might have been a comment on the transience of earthly fame, even a thankful farewell to the ordeals of Beatledom, but actually had an earthier connotation. George himself compared it to recovering from constipation after years of having his songs clog up inside him while Lennon and McCartney's enjoyed perpetual motion.

Then, in December, came *John Lennon/Plastic Ono Band* – produced by Phil Spector with not a mushy violin to be heard – in which John employed the techniques of his recent Primal Therapy to howl out his childhood insecurities, his final repudiation of the middle-class world into which he'd been born and his absolute commitment to Yoko. The track simply called 'God', which listed all that he now rejected and detested, provided yet further ammunition to John Eastman's legal team. 'I don't believe in *Bea-tles . . .*' he sang, almost retching on the name (and omitting its definite article as Yoko so much annoyed Paul by doing).

Not content with that, he gave a marathon interview to *Rolling Stone*, excoriating his former life as a Beatle and the others for their treatment of Yoko, the first instalment of which appeared just as Paul's High Court action was launched. *Time* magazine combined the two stories under a headline echoing Wagner's epic opera about the twilight of the gods: 'Beatledammerung'. Compared with the spleen he vented throughout the rest of the interview, John's references to Paul were strangely muted. His belated verdict on the *McCartney* album adopted the tone of a master sadly watching a former pupil go astray: 'I was surprised it was so poor . . . I expected just a little more because if Paul and I are sort of disagreeing and I feel weak, I think he must feel strong . . . Not that we've had much physical disagreement.'

According to John, the errant pupil's best hope was that the Plastic Ono Band's album would 'scare him into doing something decent and then he'll scare me into doing something decent . . . I think he's capable of great work'. After all the complaints about digs at Yoko, Linda came in for one over her family snapshots on the *McCartney* cover – an idea John said had been copied from Yoko and himself. 'They do exactly what I do, a year or so later . . . They're imitators, you know.'

Paul did not respond to the interview, publicly or privately, but Linda wrote John a protest letter on behalf of them both. He replied with six handwritten pages, pointedly addressed to 'Linda and Paul', saying that his remarks had been mild compared to the 'shit you and the rest of my kind, unselfish friends laid on Yoko and me', and railing against what he called Linda's 'petty little perversion of a mind' and the 'petty shit from your insane family [Lee and John Eastman] . . . In spite of it all', he concluded, 'love to you both from us two', then added an angry PS because Linda's letter hadn't been addressed jointly to Yoko and him.

Calmly resolute though Paul seemed on the outside, he felt a permanent knot of anxiety in his stomach at the thought of the legal machinery he'd set in motion. 'Not only were the Beatles, that fabbest of groups and those nicest of people, breaking up but the other three Beatles, those truest of friends of mine, were now my enemies overnight,' he would remember. 'I'd grown up in this group, they were my school, my family, my life . . . I was just trying to . . . keep it low-key but I couldn't. It was either that or letting Klein have the whole thing.'

To shut out the anxiety as much as possible, he'd begun work on a new album with which he was determined to win the unqualified praise *McCartney* had been denied. This one was to see Linda credited jointly with him: she had collaborated on around half the tracks and was to sing harmonies throughout.

Responding to the criticisms of *McCartney* as too rough and home-obsessed, he decided to begin the recording in New York, using the best session musicians the city could provide. Rather than fly, he and Linda crossed the Atlantic on Cunard's new liner, the *QE2*, taking Mary and Heather with them. Throughout their five-day crossing, Paul was never seen without dark glasses – a sure way of attracting notice he might otherwise have avoided in the crowded seaborne hotel. It earned him what was supposed to be a withering rebuke from a female table-neighbour in the swanky Columbia Restaurant.

'Elizabeth Taylor's on this boat and *she* doesn't wear them,' the woman said.

'I'm not Elizabeth Taylor,' Paul pointed out.

In New York, he and Linda advertised for session musicians without giving their names or the nature of the work. Six-foot-two Denny Seiwell, one of the city's top drummers, answered a call to make 'a demo' at an address on the West Side. 'It was at this brownstone house that looked as if it was about to be demolished,' Seiwell remembers. 'I went down into the basement, thinking I was going to get mugged at any moment, and there was Paul McCartney.'

Seiwell got the gig, along with guitarist David Spinozza (who'd later also appear on John's *Mind Games* album), and the sessions duly took place at the Columbia and A&R recording studios, with supernumeraries that would include the New York Philharmonic Orchestra. Nobody would be able to say this one sounded like Paul had made it in his living-room.

The 11-day hearing of McCartney vs. Lennon, Harrison, Starkey and Apple Corps opened on 19 February 1971 at the Royal Courts of Justice in the Strand, before Mr Justice Stamp. The British pop business had engendered other legal battles but none that riveted the nation's attention as this one did. Every newspaper carried daily reports, even *The Times* – though still clinging to its archaic formula of calling the participants 'Mr McCartney', 'Mr Lennon' or 'Mr Starkey'.

This being a civil action not a trial, the leading players weren't required to give evidence other than in statements read out by their lawyers, or even to attend court. But on John Eastman's advice, Paul turned up every morning with Linda, who was now pregnant again, and sat attentively through the whole day's proceedings. None of the other Beatles ever put in an appearance. 'The message was clear,' Eastman says. 'He was the only one who cared enough to be there in person.'

His brother-in-law gave him another piece of advice he also followed scrupulously. 'I said, "This is going to be theatre, so you have to treat it like theatre. Wear a suit."' He chose the dark blue double-breasted pinstripe of the *Abbey Road* cover, but didn't wear a tie for fear of looking too deliberately conformist. It would have been obscured, anyway, by the heavy black beard which he had regrown.

He would later recall how on his first day in court, surveying his bewigged and gowned counsel, David Hirst QC, and a three-foot-high pile of supporting documents, he found himself wondering all over again if he really was doing the right thing. 'Anyone else suing the Beatles would have been immoral, but for one of the Beatles to sue them . . . it was almost as if I was committing an unholy act.'

Allen Klein was not named in the action, but essentially it was all about his management – and himself. He, too, was in court every day, seated a few feet from Paul; the bogeyman dentist of so many recent nightmares, now reduced to podgy life-size, and wearing one of his trademark grubby turtlenecks. The two never exchanged a word.

Born performer that Paul was, he knew he had Mr Justice Stamp's attention from the beginning. Whenever a statement was made that he particularly disagreed with, he gave a little shake of his head, certain it had registered with the bench. Klein was later to remark bitterly that 'the judge got Beatlemania'.

His QC David Hirst's opening address expanded on his three main complaints against Klein. Under the head of interference with his artistic freedom, there had been the remixing of 'The Long and Winding Road' and the attempt to block the *McCartney* album on the grounds that it breached the Beatles' partnership agreement. In fact, Hirst said, the agreement allowed for solo albums, prohibiting only solo *appearances* – a clause John had many times disregarded, first in live performances with Yoko, then fronting the Plastic Ono Band.

Over and above his affidavit, Paul accused Klein of financial malpractice, made possible by Apple's chaotic business affairs. In the four years since the Beatles' partnership had come into being, he said, he'd never once seen a copy of its accounts. As a result, his advisers were warning the Beatles might not have enough in their collective coffers to meet an imminent tax bill of between half and three-quarters of a million. Latterly, when he'd tried to investigate Apple's financial position, he said, Klein had instructed the company's accountants not to give him information. However, he'd gleaned sufficient to accuse Klein of deducting excessive management commission, to the tune of some half a million pounds.

David Hirst attacked Klein as 'a man of bad commercial reputation', citing his multifarious exploits across the Atlantic. And during the trial, still more evidence came to hand. 'We heard that, from sheer stupidity and negligence, he'd been convicted on 10 charges of failing to file tax returns in New York District Federal Court,' John Eastman recalls. 'David knew that Justice Stamp always adjourned at one o'clock sharp. So I got a certified copy of the judgement in Klein's tax case and at 12.55 David handed it up to the judge to read during lunch. He came up with this great line: "Mr Klein has as little respect for the British Inland Revenue as for the US Internal Revenue Service."'

Klein mounted an aggressive defence, albeit by proxy. Apple's counsel, Morris Finer QC, read an affidavit from a senior accountant saying that in two years under ABKCO's management the Beatles' assets had increased from just over £1 million to £6.5 million and that Apple was now solvent and fully able to meet its tax liabilities.

Finer stoically went on to read a 46-page statement from Klein himself, justifying everything he had done since May 1969. The failure to produce accounts for the Beatles' partnership back to 1967 he blamed on 'obstruction' from Lee and John Eastman – i.e. it had been Paul's fault. Far from taking more commission than his entitlement, he claimed often to have taken less. He also pointed out the benefits Paul enjoyed under the partnership agreement, especially now that another solo Beatle was so strongly outshining him. Under its royalty-pooling system, he got 25 per cent of George's global blockbuster *All Things Must Pass* – by implication, a lot more worth having than George's quarter-share of the *McCartney* album.

John, George and Ringo were each heard from in statements whose stilted language, read in a posh lawyer's voice, sounded bizarrely unlike them. John's gave Klein back some points for clearing the 'spongers and hustlers' out of Apple. It also downplayed

Paul's grievances, saying that there'd always been conflict within the Beatles but that, far from undermining them, it had made them stronger:

> From our earliest days in Liverpool, George and I on the one hand and Paul on the other had different musical tastes. Paul preferred 'pop type' music and we preferred what is now called 'underground'. This may have led to arguments, particularly between Paul and George, but the contrasts in our tastes, I am sure, did more good than harm musically speaking and contributed to our success.

When it came to Klein's appointment against Paul's wishes, John uttered a blatant untruth – that, historically, band decisions had often been taken on a majority vote. As he knew better than anyone, the pre-Klein Beatles had been an unshakable democracy: nothing was done without the consent of all four. He ended by accusing Paul of behaving 'selfishly and unreasonably'.

George's and Ringo's statements, too, spoke of their previous ability to resolve their internal problems. George described how his own walk-out during the *Let It Be* sessions – the result of 'the superior attitude which for years past Paul has shown towards me musically' – had quickly been patched up. 'Since the row, Paul has treated me more as a musical equal. I think this whole episode shows how a disagreement could be worked out so that we all benefited.'

Ringo instanced the even worse contretemps when he'd delivered the news that *McCartney*'s release was to be postponed so as not to clash with *Let It Be*, and Paul had ordered him out of the house, jabbing fingers at his face. He still felt that the band's disagreements 'contributed to really great products' and that 'all four of us together could even yet work out everything satisfactorily'.

Paul's statement was read last. It recalled how Klein had been brought in by John after the Beatles' apparent acceptance of Lee and John Eastman as managers, and how despite his misgivings

– borne out by Klein's derailing of the NEMS purchase deal – he'd initially gone along with the majority vote. He recalled how Klein had tried to win his favour by belittling John, at one point confiding, 'You know why John's angry with you, don't you? It's because you came off better than he did in *Let It Be*.' And at another: 'The real problem is Yoko. *She's* the one with ambition.'

David Hirst had remained impressively on the ball, picking up pointers to the partnership's disintegration from *All Things Must Pass* as well as *John Lennon/Plastic Ono Band*. 'One has only to look at recent recordings by John or George,' Paul's deposition continued, 'to see that neither thinks of himself as a Beatle.' He ended by rejecting John's assertion that band decisions had ever been carried by a majority vote: 'I know of [none] taken on a three-to-one basis.'

With the evidence all in, and only lawyers' closing submissions to come, there was no further point in attending court, so Paul and Linda returned to America to complete their joint album, now transferring operations from New York to Sound Recorders studios in Los Angeles.

But the stress of the case seemed to have impaired Paul's usual focus and the work dragged on indecisively. 'I tried getting him together with Jim Guercio, who produced and managed my first big music clients, Chicago, and had just won a Grammy for his work with Blood, Sweat and Tears,' John Eastman recalls. 'Jim was so keen to work with Paul that he put off his honeymoon.'

Together they laid down a track called 'Dear Boy', which both chided and thanked Linda's former husband, Mel See, for not holding on to her. However, even the turbocharged Guercio seemed unable to galvanise Paul back into his old efficiency: he would block-book the studio, not turn up until evening and then only want to smoke a joint and jam. Recording 'Dear Boy' alone took five separate sessions. 'After about three days, I got a call from each of them, saying it wasn't working,' Eastman remembers.

The McCartneys were still in LA when, on 12 March, after a week of deliberation, Mr Justice Stamp delivered his verdict in the Court of Chancery. The judge found in Paul's favour on every count, ruling that the Beatles had 'long since ceased to perform as a group', that Apple was not 'a Frankenstein set up to control the individual partners' and that the situation with regard to the partnership accounts was 'quite intolerable'.

Allen Klein incurred withering personal condemnation for having taken commission 'grossly in excess' of what he was entitled to. His claim to have taken less than his due, the judge added, was 'like the irresponsible patter of a second-rate salesman'. Since neither the Beatles' manager nor anyone else around them seemed competent to handle their finances, Paul's application for an official receiver would be granted.

Four days later, at the annual Grammys ceremony in Hollywood, *Let It Be* won the award for Best Movie Soundtrack. John, Paul and George were named joint recipients, but only Paul went onstage to collect all three statuettes, firmly leading three-months-pregnant Linda by the hand. Neither of them had bothered to dress up for the occasion; indeed, they looked oddly like a pair of runaways, a brighter-coloured version of John and Yoko two years earlier.

Paul responded to the half-mourning applause with just a 'Thank you! Goodnight!' and they vanished into the darkness again. The accidental symbolism was impossible to miss. And also that his true triumph had lain in *not* letting it be.

The moment Judge Stamp's verdict was announced, Morris Finer QC lodged an appeal on John, George and Ringo's behalf. But on 26 April, it was withdrawn. As Finer explained to the Court of Appeal, 'My clients now consider, in the unhappy circumstances which have arisen, that it is in the common interest to explore . . . a means whereby the plaintiff may disengage himself from the partnership by agreement.'

Paul was effectively free of Apple, his one-time passion, other than in an obligation to release his records through Apple Music until 1975. And the Beatles were officially no more. 'When we heard we'd won, we didn't yell and throw our hats in the air,' John Eastman recalls. 'We just looked at each other and sort of went "uh!" After that, I think I slept for 36 hours.'

*

While the case was still going on, Paul had put out his first solo single, 'Another Day', written and unsuccessfully tried out with the Beatles and finally recorded with Linda in New York the previous January.

It was another of his 'short story' songs, about a lonely woman trapped in a soulless office job and living for the occasional visits of a feckless lover – in fact, very much how the protagonist of 'She's Leaving Home' might have ended up with her 'man from the motor trade'. This one had even deeper empathy with the implicitly ageing, faded figure who 'takes a morning bath and wets her hair . . . slipping into stockings, slipping into shoes, dipping in the pockets of her raincoat'.

Although Paul's name alone appeared on the single, it came in a picture cover showing him and Linda together and she was credited as his co-writer. For all that, it seemed a throwback to the Beatles, even using the sound effects of voices and laughter so familiar from *Sgt. Pepper* and 'Revolution 9'. Just then, record-buyers wanted nothing more than a throwback to the Beatles, so it easily jumped to number two in Britain and five in America.

The signs thus could not have been better for the album credited to Paul and Linda McCartney which followed on 17 May. At High Park Farm, they now had a flock of 200 Highland blackface sheep whose wool was sold commercially. Ever-practical Paul had become adept at shearing, handling even the aggressive rams with their dangerous downturned horns.

One day, driving north from Glasgow with Linda, he decided *Ram* was a perfect title for their album because 'it was strong and male . . . and succinct. Once you heard it, you weren't going to forget it. Then there was the idea of ramming . . . pushing ahead strongly.' The front cover was taken from a Linda photograph of him straddling one of the beasts in question and gripping its horns as if taking part in some non-equine rodeo.

'Another Day' did not appear on *Ram*, but the single taken from the album for US release only, 'Uncle Albert/Admiral Halsey', employed its Beatle carry-over formula with even greater success. This was a medley of *Abbey Road*-style song-fragments, built around Paul's own Uncle Albert and full of 'Yellow Submarine'-style comic voices – ringing telephones, bird-calls, rain-showers and thunder-storms. It reached number one on the *Billboard* chart, sold a million copies and later won Paul a Grammy for Best Arrangement Accompanying Vocalists.

The album was likewise a commercial smash, reaching number one in the UK and two in America. But it was slaughtered by the critics whose approval Paul so desperately sought. *Rolling Stone* called it 'incredibly inconsequential', 'monumentally irrelevant' and 'emotionally vacuous', noting how John Lennon had 'always held the reins in on McCartney's cutesey-pie, florid attempts at pure rock Muzak'. The *Village Voice* called it 'a classic form/content mismatch'. *Playboy* accused Paul of 'substitut[ing] facility for substance' and likened the effect to 'watching someone juggle five guitars . . . it's fairly impressive but you keep wondering why he bothers'.

Worse consequences were to follow. The track called 'Too Many People' contained several references to John, albeit so oblique that they went unnoticed in the media. 'Too many people preaching practices' meant the Yoko-inspired peace campaign and all the other attention-seeking crusades which Paul thought 'a little bit hypocritical'. 'You took your lucky break/ And broke it in two' (toned down from '*Yoko* took your lucky break . . .') reproached John for giving over his life to someone who didn't even say '*the* Beatles'. In the repeated phrase 'piece of cake', the first two words were slurred into 'piss off'. The very album-artwork featured its own little sidelong, symbolic dig, a back-cover picture of two bee-tles copulating. Translation: *You tried to fuck me over and look what happened.*

Even allowing that his and John's relationship had always been based on such schoolboyish stuff, it's hard to reconcile with the subtle intelligence of 'Another Day'. And, coming so soon after his High Court victory, it was obviously asking for trouble.

In fact, John not only picked up every slur on Yoko and himself, and himself singly in 'Too Many People', but others on different tracks that Paul had never intended. 'Dear Boy', the song about Linda's ex-husband, he decided was all about him even though it contained not a single line that could be so interpreted. Also on the list were '3 Legs' ('Well, I thought you was my friend . . .'), 'Smile Away' ('Man, I can smell your breath a mile away . . .') and 'The Back Seat of My Car', a song actually dating from Paul's pre-Linda affair with Maggie McGivern ('We believe we can't be wrong').

John at the time was making his first solo album without the Plastic Ono Band, whose title track was a plea to 'imagine all the people, living life in peace'. To this he now added a venomous 'answer' song entitled 'How Do You Sleep?', with help on the lyrics from Yoko, and even Allen Klein, and George, that other disgruntled co-litigant, playing slide guitar.

The title was nonsensical; Paul had done nothing to lose sleep over. But fairness was not on John's agenda. With withering contempt, intensified by faux-blues diction, he lampooned his old friend for 'liv[ing] with straights' and 'jump [ing] when your momma [Linda] tell you anything'. Some of the barbs were unintentionally self-revealing. A whiff of envy of Paul's looks accompanied the dismissal of his solo career with 'A pretty face may last a year or two/ But pretty soon they'll see what you can do'. Rancour over his recent hit single surfaced in 'Since you're gone you're just another day'.

Ringo was also around during the song's gestation, feeling more and more uncomfortable as John's rant lost any touch with reality: 'Those freaks was right when they said you was dead' (i.e. in the rumour-epidemic of 1969), 'The sound you make is Muzak to my ears' and, most monstrously, 'The only thing you done was Yesterday'. This last was meant to be followed by a scream of 'You prob'ly pinched that bitch, anyway!' but Klein ordered it to be cut, fearing Paul might sue for libel.

The nuclearly disproportionate tit-for-tat also included an answer to the copulating beetles on *Ram*'s back cover. Inside John's *Imagine* album was a postcard on which he parodied Paul's parody-rodeo pose with the blackface ram, but wrestling a pig instead.

Far from having second thoughts about what he'd done, he positively gloried in it, publicly thanking Allen Klein for contributing the 'just another day' jibe. 'Some people don't see the funny side of it,' he complained in a self-review for *Crawdaddy* magazine. 'It's what you might call an angry letter – sung. Get it?'

Paul responded in an interview with *Melody Maker*'s Chris Charlesworth, prefacing most of his answers with 'Don't print this' but still plainly on the record throughout. 'Everyone thinks I'm the aggressor but I'm not, you know. I just want out . . . I just want the four of us to get together somewhere and sign a piece of paper saying it's all over and we want to divide the money four ways. No one else would be involved, not even Linda or Yoko or Allen Klein. We'd just sign the paper and hand it to the business people and let them sort it out . . . but John won't do it.

'"How Do You Sleep?" I think it's silly. So what if I live with straights? I like straights. I have straight babies . . . He says the only thing I did was "Yesterday". He knows that's wrong. I used to sit in the studio and play, and he'd really dig some of the stuff I played to him. He can't say all I did was "Yesterday" because he knows and I know it's not true.'

At one point, the mild, conciliatory tone gave way to a defiant twirl of the matador's cape. 'John and Yoko are not cool in what they are doing. I saw them on television the other night, and thought that what they're saying about what they want to do together is basically the same as what Linda and I want to do.'

John demanded equal space in the *MM* to reply, and did so in a letter addressed to 'Paul, Linda et all the wee McCartneys', from which a section had to be cut for fear of libel.

'It's all very well playing "simple ole honest Paul" in *Melody Maker*, but you know damn well we can't just sign a piece of paper. You say "John won't do it", but I will if you indemnify us against the Tax man.

'If YOU'RE not the aggressor (as you claim) who the hell took us to court and shat all over us in public? . . . As I've said before, have you ever thought that you might POSSIBLY be wrong about something? Your conceit about us and Klein is incredible. You say . . . "we secretly feel that you're right" [about Klein]. Good God! You must know we're secretly right about Eastman.

'. . . Wanna put your photo on the [album cover] like uncool John and Yoko, do ya? (Ain't ya got no shame?) If we're not cool, WHAT DOES THAT MAKE YOU?

'No hard feelings to you either. I know basically we want the same . . . whenever you want to meet, all you have to do is call.'

But Paul didn't.

That summer of 1971, two of the New York session musicians who'd played on *Ram*, drummer Denny Seiwell and guitarist Hugh McCracken, were invited to visit him and Linda in Scotland. Thinking they'd merely been offered a holiday, Seiwell and McCracken brought along their respective wives, Monique and Holly.

The two couples were put up at Campbeltown's best hotel, the Argyll Arms, and given a tour of High Park Farm, where Paul's latest DIY project had been to turn its tumbledown outbuilding into a recording studio with a four-track machine sent up from London by EMI. He called it Rude Studio, which it certainly was, though the word was meant in the reggae sense of cockily rebellious.

As the visitors were leaving, Linda took Seiwell and McCracken aside and asked if they'd return the following day without their wives 'to play some music'. Only then did they realise why they were there.

The idea had come to Paul in between sheep-shearing or mowing fields on the tractor Linda had given him. 'Instead of thinking "After the Beatles, it's got to be important . . . super musicians . . . let's just find ourselves" . . . One night, I said to Linda, "I'm going to form a band, do you want to be in it?" [and] with some trepidation, she said, "Er, yes". . . . She and I knew she was a novice while I was a veteran . . . But I liked the tone of her voice [because] I'd never sung with a woman before. All my harmonies to that date had been with males.'

The musical chemistry with Seiwell and McCracken proved just as immediate with real rams ripping at grass and covering ewes just a few yards away. Unfortunately, Monique Seiwell and Holly McCracken chafed at being left to their own devices at the Argyll Arms, where the food was poor and the rooms were so cold they needed hot-water bottles in their beds even in June.

In any case, this particular line-up was never going to work. McCracken had two small children by his previous wife back in America and couldn't contemplate moving to Britain permanently. After a few days, he decided to return to New York. Denny Seiwell also left, to visit Monique's family in France, but offered to return when Paul found another guitarist.

This he soon did in Denny Laine, formerly of the Moody Blues, who'd voiced the Birmingham band's huge 1964 single 'Go Now'. The 'Moodies' had often supported the Beatles on tours, including their last UK one in 1965, and known them well socially. A talented guitarist and keyboard-player, Laine had gone on to play with Ginger Baker's Air Force, and had written several successful songs, notably 'Say You Don't Mind' for Colin Blunstone.

It was significant that Paul should have chosen someone with established form in every area where he'd lately enjoyed autonomy: singing, soloing and songwriting. Since 1957, he'd been accustomed to working with a strong, stimulating musical partner; even though Linda had officially succeeded to that role, he also felt he needed something by way of a John-substitute.

Denny Laine just then happened to be at a low ebb, without a regular band and reduced to sleeping in his manager's office. 'Paul phoned me up out of the blue and said, "Hey, man, what are you up to now?"' he recalls. 'I said, "Nothing." "Why don't you come up to Scotland then?" Paul said. "We'll just jam around and see what happens."'

The two Dennys, Laine and Seiwell, were each put on a weekly retainer of £70, and rehearsals in Rude Studio began. As an old friend of Paul's, Laine stayed at High Park while the Seiwells rented a farmhouse with its own 300 acres at Kilkenzie-by-Campbeltown. 'We started with old rock 'n' roll numbers, Buddy Holly, Elvis and them, and it all just felt right,' Laine recalls. 'Nobody knew we were there, and no one around there knew who we were. There was no publicity . . . no pressure.'

Linda – by now heavily pregnant – had been having piano lessons from a neighbour in Cavendish Avenue. 'Now and then Paul would show her something on the organ, but Denny and I had no idea that she was going to be *in* the band,' says Laine. 'She just organised him and the two kids and did the cooking.'

In August, George Harrison mobilised friends like Ringo Starr, Bob Dylan, Eric Clapton and Leon Russell to join him onstage at New York's Madison Square Garden in a benefit concert for the victims of famine, flood and genocide in newly-created Bangladesh. (Paul was invited to appear but declined, fearing it would make the event look like a Beatles reunion.) With the Concert for Bangladesh added to *All Things Must Pass* and 'My Sweet Lord', George found himself not only rock's biggest performer of the new decade but also its first saint.

Meanwhile, in a shed on a sheep-dotted hillside in Kintyre, eight tracks had been laid down – five of them in a single take – by a band which as yet had no name. Denny Seiwell tried to persuade Paul to bring in a keyboard-player named Paul Harris, who'd backed top-notch names like ex-Lovin' Spoonful John Sebastian. 'That's when he told me he was going to teach Linda how to play. I was used to working with the best in the world, and here I am working with *the* best in the world, and suddenly we're going to have an amateur on keyboards. But what could I say?'

The band still lacked a name in early September, when Paul and Linda returned to London for the birth of their second child. On the 13th, Linda went into labour and was taken to King's College Hospital. There she was found to be suffering from placenta previa, a condition in which the placenta is situated too close to the uterus, complicating the delivery process and causing heavy bleeding.

An emergency Caesarian section had to be performed and, for a time, both mother and baby were in serious danger. Paul later recalled 'praying like mad', and being answered by a further vision from his midwife mum that named his band before his new – and perfectly healthy – daughter, Stella Nina.

As if angels hovered around Mother Mary, he seemed to see a multitude of golden, spreading . . . wings.

30

'Hell, we've really blown it here'

At around noon on 9 February 1972, Elaine Woodhams, social secretary of the Nottingham University students' union, was drinking with friends in the union bar when two unfamiliar, un-collegiate-looking young men approached her. 'They said "We're with Paul McCartney and his band, Wings,"' she recalls. '"We're on the road and looking for places to play. Would you like them to do a show here?"'

'I went outside with them, thinking it was all a joke and my mates would all be there laughing or I'd have buckets of water chucked over me. A van was parked in the road, the window rolled down and there in the driving-seat was Paul McCartney, with his family and two dogs in the back.'

A succession of other British provincial universities were to have the same unreal experience – a pop giant turning up unannounced with wife, children and pets in tow and asking, rather humbly, if he and his new band could play for the students. Paul's way of breaking in Wings was to do the surprise live gigs he'd once seen as the Beatles' salvation. Only now he was out to prove he still had what it took as a stage performer by starting from even below Square One.

There was also an element of back-pedalling from Wings' ex-travagant launch the previous November. To introduce them and their first album, *Wild Life*, Paul had hired the Empire ballroom in London's Leicester Square and invited 800 guests including some of the fellow musicians he most hoped to impress: Elton John, Keith Moon, Ronnie Wood and Led Zeppelin's Jimmy Page.

Wild Life consisted of the eight tracks he'd rehearsed in Scotland with Linda, Denny Laine and Denny Seiwell, supplemented by leftovers from the *Ram* sessions and mostly sounding even more home-made than *McCartney*. 'We weren't trying to be too clever, just trying to find a couple of grooves,' Laine says. 'A bit like Bob Dylan's *Basement Tapes*, if you like.'

The title track was not about a rock star's existence but about real wild animals and their mistreatment – an issue that would become increasingly important to Linda and Paul. Unfortunately, it revealed that while he could write devastatingly about small human detail, broad-brush campaigning in the John Lennon mode reduced him to banality ('What's gonna happen to . . . the animals in the zoo?').

Only here and there was a track not redolent of long-haired blokes jamming in a pine shack in the Scottish Highlands. 'Love Is Strange' was a catchy reggae version of Mickey and Sylvia's 1950s hit, later covered by the Everly Brothers and Buddy Holly. And 'Dear Friend', as opposed to 'Dear Boy', was a message of real love and regret to John ('Dear friend, what's the time?/ Is this the borderline?') which, if Paul had included it on *Ram* as he'd originally intended, might have spared him an awful lot of Lennon bile.

The album reached number ten on the *Billboard* chart and eleven in the UK, but received a critical mauling even worse than *Ram*'s. *Rolling Stone* wondered whether, for some unfathomable reason, it might be 'deliberately second-rate'. British critics variously derided it as rushed, defensive, badly-timed and over-publicised, the *NME* saying it showed Paul's songwriting 'at an absolute nadir just when he needed a little respect'. As usual, he pretended to ignore the reviews, but later admitted thinking, 'Hell, we've really blown it here.'

The University Tour, as it would become known, was to be more than just a boot camp for Wings. Approaching his thirtieth birthday, Paul was determined to connect with a new generation of pop fans whose idols resembled nothing the Beatles had ever been. Reacting against hippy drabness and psychedelic faux naivety, so-called Glam Rock bands like Slade and T-Rex now wore sparkly clothes, tinted highlights in their hair, even donned lipstick, rouge and eyeliner, while playing the same macho rock as ever (and still seeking no higher accolade than 'new Beatles').

To this end, when choosing a post-Apple publicist, he opted for Tony Brainsby, who represented a slew of cutting-edge bands like Curved Air and Thin Lizzy and whose bumptious manner could not have been more unlike Derek Taylor's discreet charm. Fuelled by pot and amphetamines, Brainsby worked virtually around the clock for his clients but, to begin with, found Paul and Wings a tough sell. All the UK media wanted to know about any ex-Beatle was when he'd be getting back with the others.

Fellow publicist Keith Altham, whose clientele included the Who, T-Rex's Marc Bolan and the post-Denny Laine Moody Blues, had offices on the top floor of Brainsby's house in Pimlico. 'Tony was an intelligent choice for Paul at that time,' Altham says, 'and both of them did like their pot. I remember once when he and Linda came in, the fumes wafting up the stairs were so strong that you didn't need a joint to get high.'

In January, as another firm break with Beatle precedent, the line-up had increased to five. Henry McCullough, who'd pre-viously been with Joe Cocker's Grease Band, was brought in to alternate with Denny Laine on lead guitar. As with Paul, the 'Mc' prefix did not denote Scottish but Irish origins, in this case the British province of Northern Ireland. And coincidentally soon after McCullough's arrival, Wings became embroiled in the incendiary politics of his homeland.

The early Seventies had brought a steep escalation in North-ern Ireland's long-festering sectarian troubles following the British army's deployment to protect its minority Catholic and republican-minded population from the rabidly loyalist Protestant majority. That mission dissolved into sick irony on 30 January 1972 – forever afterwards known as Bloody Sunday – when men of the Parachute Regiment shot dead 13 Catholic civil rights demonstrators, three teenagers among them, in the Bogside district of Londonderry.

Although McCullough was a Protestant from County Derry, he'd been on the road with rock bands too long to feel much religious or political zealotry. But, despite having no ancestral connection with Northern Ireland, Paul was moved to write a song calling for Britain's 300-year rule of the province to end and for it to receive the same independence as the south.

'Give Ireland Back to the Irish' magnified the weakness with big themes revealed by 'Wild Life'. Leaving aside the simplistic message, its screamy rock treatment was quite unsuitable and its tone oddly ingratiating: 'Great Britain, you are tremendous/ As nobody knows like me/ But really, what are you doin'/ In the land across the sea?'

Despite having all the rabble-rousing potential of a party squeaker, the single instantly went onto the BBC's 'banned' list, joining such politically controversial ditties as Noël Coward's 'Don't Let's Be Beastly to the Germans' and the Goons' 'A Russian Love Song'. It still reached number 16 in the UK and number one in the Irish Republic – and also hotly republican Spain.

Interviewed about the furore by America's ABC TV, Paul insisted his Irish blood had not been his main motivation. 'I'm British, and I was brought up to be proud of things like the British Empire. I don't want my army going round shooting my Irish brothers.' At one point, he seemed almost to side with the Irish Republican Army whose terror tactics included murdering unarmed police officers and Protestant loyalists, often in front of their children, and 'kneecapping' recalcitrant members of their own community. 'I don't dig it, but if people shoot at [the IRA], they have to shoot back.'

As the newly-augmented Wings prepared to launch themselves into university-land, it was made clear that their stage repertoire would not include any Beatles songs. Indeed, no one in the new band was even supposed to mention the B-word. 'I'd sometimes

say to Paul I liked one of their old tracks, like "Michelle",' Denny
Laine remembers. 'He'd go "Oh, yeah", then change the subject.
He wanted his own identity, not just to be a tribute band doing
Beatles stuff.'

Preparations were minimal. There were two roadies, brothers-
in-law Ian Horn and Trevor Jones (who had first recommended
Henry McCullough to Paul); a 12-seat Transit van for the Mc-
Cartneys, their band, children and dogs; and a white trailer, rented
from Avis, for the equipment. 'On the day we left, I showed up at
Cavendish, leaving my wife, Monique, at home in bed,' Denny Seiwell recalls. 'Then Paul goes, "Where's Monique? She's supposed
to come along, too." It was going to be a real family thing.'

No route was planned, no hotels were booked in advance: they
simply took off northward on the M1. In the Midlands, Paul was
amused by a signpost to Ashby de la Zouch, and asked the roadies
to see if it had a college, which was how they stumbled on Nottingham University.

The show for the students' union was at lunch-time – like hundreds he had played with the Beatles at the Liverpool Cavern – with
tickets priced at 40p. Word quickly spread through the campus and
800 students packed into the Portland Building's ballroom, many
cutting tutorials or leaving them halfway, in some cases followed
by their tutors. Paul took the stage in denim dungarees and a red-
and-white-striped shirt, explaining that Wings were just starting
out and apologising in advance if the sound was a little rough.
Linda, making her stage debut on keyboards, wore a shapeless
floral dress and trainers, and kept Heather, Mary and baby Stella
all within reach in an impromptu crèche.

Wings' performance included only four of their own tracks,
mixed with old rock 'n' roll favourites like 'Long Tall Sally' and
'Lucille', allowing Paul to bring his Little Richard scream out
of mothballs. Even so, Denny Seiwell remembers, they had to
do 'Give Ireland Back to the Irish' twice over to make a full set.
The students loved it but, in this era of cerebral singer/songwrit-
ers, bopping around to music had become passé. Linda, whose

audience-pleasing technique still needed some work, asked her nearest spectators why they hadn't brought their knitting.

There were ten further shows, on this same cold-calling basis, at universities throughout the north, then down south in Oxford and westward in Swansea. Everywhere, admission cost 40 or 50p, with the band receiving their share in small change on the spot. Paul later remembered being in a constant state of 'sheer panic . . . Quite a few times [Linda and I] looked at each other and said, "Oh, God! What have we bitten off?"' At Newcastle University, Linda completely forgot the opening chords to 'Wild Life'; when Paul rushed protectively over to rescue her, he realised he'd forgotten them, too.

His plan was for Wings to follow *Wild Life* with a double album (he had that many new songs to hand), begun in Los Angeles, then transferring to Olympic Studios in Barnes, south London, with Glyn Johns as producer. Olympic had bad memories for Paul; it was where John and George had tried to railroad him into signing Allen Klein's management contract. But if he wanted the sought-after Johns, whom he saw as his best hope of changing the critics' minds, there was no other choice.

Johns had his own bad memories of compiling serial versions of the Beatles' *Get Back* album only to have each one curtly rejected. And now that he had the whip-hand, he didn't spare it. Accustomed to producing the likes of the Stones, the Who and Led Zeppelin, he decided early on that Wings' sidemen were nowhere near the same league, just 'a bunch of guys hanging round Paul . . . up his bottom most of the time'. At sessions, he would sit in his control room reading a newspaper, refusing to roll tape until they came up with something that interested him. There were acrimonious scenes and in mid-April Johns bowed out.

With the album stalled, Paul chose to release a single at the furthest possible extreme from 'Give Ireland Back to the Irish' and one which would take Wings' credibility as a rock band to rock bottom: a singalong version of 'Mary Had a Little Lamb'.

At the time, recording this prissiest of nursery rhymes was seen as his sardonic riposte to being banned as too politically controversial by the BBC. Actually, the idea had predated 'Give Ireland Back to the Irish' and was simply an attempt to create a song for small children, like his own three, whom pop music usually overlooked (and at High Park Farm, his daughter, Mary, really did have a pet lamb). The one, faint, protest from his musicians was voiced by Denny Laine. 'I said, "Hold on, I didn't sign up for this, Paul,"' Laine remembers. But in Wings, now and throughout its life, two against three counted as a majority.

Unlike most nursery rhymes, this had a known author, the nineteenth-century American poet Sarah Josepha Hale. Paul's arrangement also used Hale's lesser-known second and third verses, adding a lengthy 'La-la' chorus in which both Mary and her half-sister, Heather, joined. The single reached number nine in Britain but in America, where many radio stations preferred the B-side, 'Little Woman Love', it didn't even make the Top 20.

All the deejays who played it took much the same heavily ironic line: 'Once, Paul McCartney wrote and recorded songs like "Michelle", "Eleanor Rigby" and "Penny Lane". Now here he is with "Mary Had a Little Lamb".'

Paul's father had been profoundly upset by the Beatles' break-up. To Jim McCartney, John and George were still the lads who used to practise in his tiny living-room in Forthlin Road and devour his cooking, and he couldn't understand how their old camaraderie could have turned into such hatred.

While the High Court action was in progress, the chronic discomfort of Jim's rheumatoid arthritis and osteoarthritis had been exacerbated by a severe attack of shingles. His wife, Angie, tried to keep him from watching TV news reports on the case for fear they'd make the condition even worse.

Though none of the remedies and treatments Jim tried could check the spread of his arthritis he refused to let it spoil his enjoyment of life. He adored having three granddaughters from Paul and a further three from Michael McCartney, who had married local girl Angela Fishwick in 1968, with 'our kid' as best man. Like Paul and Mike before them, the little girls were initiated into Jim's 'bubbling underground sense of fun', his nonsense Scouse-isms ('There's no hair on a seagull's chest'; 'It's imposausigable!') and unbeatable prowess at sticking out his tongue. 'It often used to hurt him when they all climbed on his knees,' remembers his adopted daughter, Ruth, 'but he never showed it.'

Next to his family, the pride of Jim's life was Drake's Drum, the racehorse Paul had bought him as a birthday gift in 1964. Since then, the gelding had won several important races, usually with a conscientiously-besuited and binocular-wearing Paul or Mike there to watch their proud dad lead him around the winners' enclosure. The climax of Jim's career as an owner was to see him run at Aintree, Liverpool's world-famous steeplechase course, on the same card as the Grand National. Drake's Drum won the race immediately before it, the Hylton Plate.

Between race-meetings, Jim loved to visit Wilfred Lyde's stables in Middleham, Yorkshire, where the horse was in training. As his racing career declined – and long journeys grew more trying for his owner – Paul had him moved to Crossley's stables in Heswall, just a mile or so from Jim and Angie's home. At least once a week, Angie would drive Jim to Crossley's to feed him sugar-lumps in his stall or watch him exercising on the nearby beach.

Despite Jim's decreasing mobility, he still paid regular visits to Paul and Linda at Cavendish, generally at Christmas when one, or both, of his favourite sisters, Gin and Millie, might also be there. Paul always laid on some spectacular treat like afternoon tea at the Ritz hotel, a starchily formal ritual for which he dutifully donned suit and tie and reprimanded nine-year-old Heather, the unruliest of his girls, for dancing on her chair.

Now and again, Jim even made the 300-mile car journey to High Park Farm, enduring its spartan conditions with unfailing good humour. 'Here we go on the long and winding road,' he'd say to Angie as they set off.

'Once when we arrived, Paul proudly told us he'd done up the garage for us,' Angie recalls. 'We slept on a mattress on the floor. The girls were inside the house, on bunk beds with horse-blankets for covers.'

Linda had come to be loved by Jim and Angie, although her possessiveness with Paul caused the occasional raised eyebrow. If he was driving them somewhere, she automatically got into the front passenger seat beside him, unaware – or else not caring – that in northern family pecking-order it should have been his father's place. But her affectionate manner and spontaneity were disarming: on the spur of the moment at High Park, she might ask Heather and Mary 'Shall we go see Grandpa?', order two taxis from Campbeltown, stash them and the dogs inside and hit the long and winding road down to Cheshire.

Angie McCartney remembers the front doorbell once ringing after midnight, mingled with a sound of clucking. En route from Kintyre to London with Paul, Linda had managed to buy some chickens which she planned to keep in the back garden at Cavendish. The agitated birds were kept overnight in a downstairs cloakroom where, despite newspaper on the floor and only dry food to eat, they managed to spatter droppings everywhere. 'When we opened the door next morning, it looked like a scene from an Oliver Stone war movie,' Angie recalls.

If Linda was Paul's main source of strength and reassurance in navigating the unknown waters of a solo career, her family – or, rather, family *firm* – was of critical importance. Indeed, having his father-in-law and brother-in-law, Lee and John Eastman, as his lawyers, which had been such an embarrassment with the Beatles, proved of lasting benefit now.

Of the two, he was closer to John since their journey from seeming hopelessness to victory in the High Court. Each summer, the McCartney family would exchange the austerity of Kintyre for East Hampton, Long Island, where John, a passionate sailor, and his wife, Jodie, had a home. 'They virtually lived in our house,' he recalls. 'Our kids got along great and virtually grew up together.'

Lee also had a home in East Hampton, as did Eastman &

Eastman's most illustrious artist-client, the great abstract expressionist painter Willem de Kooning. Paul revered de Kooning, so was hugely impressed that the Eastmans called him 'Bill' and knew him well enough to ask him to do a drawing of the family as a sixtieth birthday gift for Lee.

Between Paul and Lee things were trickier, for even now that Linda was married to one of the world's most famous men, her father still tended to treat her like a wayward teenager. Once at his New York apartment, when he was haranguing her over the dinner-table, Paul quietly chipped in, 'I'd rather you didn't do that.'

'[Lee] looked at me like "Who are you?" and I said, "I'm her husband and I'd really prefer you didn't do that,"' he later recalled. 'It was like throwing a grenade into the middle of the table. I just took her hand and said, "Right. Good night everyone. Pleasant evening. Thank you very much," and we left.' Significantly, Linda did not leap to her father's defence, as many daughters would have, but went unresistingly.

But as an attorney-cum-business manager, no one suited this particular client better. Having been rejected by the Beatles to run Apple, Lee was to help Paul build a business organisation that would never suffer Apple's problems – and ultimately be even more profitable than his music.

Back in February 1969, before the Beatles' break-up was anything like a reality, he had bought a small company called Adagrove Ltd, renaming it Paul McCartney Productions and basing it in a one-room office in Greek Street, Soho. To be managing director, he hired 32-year-old Brian Brolly, a film and television producer who had presciently encouraged Andrew Lloyd-Webber and Tim Rice to create their first stage musical, *Jesus Christ Superstar*. Brolly would also act as Paul's personal manager, though in this case the title brought with it rather less power and influence than normal.

In April 1970, Paul McCartney Productions had announced as its first project a cartoon film based on Alfred Bestall's Rupert Bear strip in the *Daily Express*. As with most post-war British children, the adventures of check-trousered Rupert and his friends Bill Badger and Pong-Ping the Pekinese had been a staple of Paul's boyhood. He still possessed a Rupert Christmas annual he had been given aged ten and it was proudly inscribed with his name and address (12 Ardwick Road, Speke). Before a frame of animation was drawn for the film, he'd completed a song for its soundtrack, 'Little Lamb Dragonfly'.

Over time, however, it would not be films but Lee Eastman's knowledge of American music publishing that ensured the success of Paul McCartney Productions, later known as McCartney Productions Ltd, then MPL. Paul might have been helpless to prevent the copyrights of his Beatles songs being bought up by Lew Grade's ATV. But with his father-in-law's guidance there would be some solace, as well as great profit, in buying up other great songwriters' back catalogues in his turn.

Wings' second exploratory flap as a live band was a continental tour between July and August of 1972, somewhat grandiosely billed as Wings Over Europe although its 28 small-venue dates were concentrated in France, Belgium, Switzerland, West Germany, Norway, Denmark, Sweden and Finland. Once again, Paul and Linda took their children with them.

McCartneys and musicians travelled together in a personalised London double-decker bus, its top deck open, its lower one fitted with aircraft-style seats, a kitchenette and bunk beds for Heather and Mary. In a nod to the *Magical Mystery Tour*, its usual red paintwork was covered by psychedelic cartoons. The party flew to Marseilles to pick up the vehicle, which had been driven overland from London. As the roadies loaded the gear on board, the painters were still putting the final touches to its decoration.

Actually, the atmosphere would turn out to be closer to Cliff Richard's *Summer Holiday*, with bare-torsoed musicians sunning themselves on mattresses on the open top deck amid guitars, plastic toys, potties and ten-month-old Stella's playpen. That one-class democratic spirit also applied to the venues, where everyone shared the same dressing-room, even on occasion the same washing facilities.

'Most nights, I used to see baby Stella put to bed on a pillow inside a drawer,' Denny Seiwell says. 'Paul and Linda didn't alter their lives for their kids: the kids had to fit in with them. But there was never a time when those girls didn't have someone looking out for them, something to eat and something to do. I'd never seen such great parents before, and I never have since.'

In Paris, time had also been booked at EMI's Pathé Marconi Studios for Wings to record the first full song Linda had written, the reggae-flavoured 'Seaside Woman'. Paul was in sufficiently high spirits to risk re-igniting the row with John by introducing her to the French media as 'Yoko'.

Early-Seventies rock musicians on tour lived an orgiastic life unmatched since the days of the nastier Roman emperors, gorging food and drink on bottomless tabs and competing with each other in sheer, mindless waste. The Rolling Stones – who were travelling across America this very same month – would order tray after tray of high-priced cocktails simply for the infantile pleasure of throwing them out of the window, trays and all. Led Zeppelin were famous for having once stayed at a hotel overlooking the Pacific and fished for sharks from their suite, using costly room service steaks as bait.

But Paul had learned his lesson from Apple – and from Beatles tours long before that. His sidemen were booked into the same luxury hotels as Linda and himself, but with only bed and breakfast paid for. Bar- and room-service bills were their responsibility. Since all three were still on the same £70 per week salary, the tour ate up everything they earned.

Wings were now unequivocally a Glam Rock band, with Paul in a sparkly top, open almost to the navel, and Linda more glammed up than ever in her life before, with tumbling blonde hair, sheer backless dresses and crimson suede knee-boots.

In fact, this first exposure to paying audiences, rather than starstruck college students, had terrified her. Before the opening show, at Châteauvallon, near Arles, she wept with stage-fright on Denny Seiwell's shoulder. 'I tried to tell her everything would be okay,' he recalls, 'and when we got out there, she did a pretty good job.'

She also acted as Paul's chief protector, putting herself in harm's way rather than leave him exposed. 'On the French Riviera, we were at a dinner after the show,' Seiwell remembers, 'when this guy comes up to Paul and says he's got a gun in his pocket. Linda would have taken the bullet no question, but suddenly this little French security man sitting at our table makes a move – and the guy is gone.'

Her protectiveness was needed on many levels. For public and committed family man though Paul now was, almost every woman who crossed his path still shamelessly came on to him. And the Beatles had virtually invented the old rock musicians' adage that 'it doesn't count on the road'.

Denny's wife, Monique, was no threat, frequently acting as a babysitter to the McCartney children. Such could not be said for Joanne – alias Jo Jo – La Patrie, a 20-year-old model and would-be pop singer from Boston, USA, who talked her way backstage after the Juan-les-Pins show. While waiting for either couture- or chart-stardom, Jo Jo had notched up an impressive record as a groupie, losing her virginity to Jimi Hendrix at the Woodstock festival, moving on to Jim Morrison, then Rod Stewart who, she claimed, had written 'You Wear It Well' for her.

She now set methodically to work on Wings, first seducing one of the roadies, which allowed her to hitch a ride aboard the equipment bus following the double-decker and make eyes at Denny Laine whenever the two vehicles drew level. Having hooked Laine and won a seat on the band-bus, she revealed that, as a 17-year-old Beatles fan, she'd bombarded Paul with passionate letters and had first come to Britain with the sole object of meeting and marrying him. Finally, an embarrassed Laine had to tell her that 'Paul and Linda are very uptight about you being around'. But unlike the one in 'Get Back', Jo Jo refused to get back to where she once belonged.

'We weren't a druggy band, any more than we were a drinking band,' Denny Seiwell says, 'but in Sweden, Linda said she'd like a little grass. I knew a guy in London, so I got him to drop off some at the office for them to mail it to me at the hotel where we were staying in Gothenburg. When we came into town, Paul and Linda stopped off at the hotel to pick it up so that we could all have a little at the gig.

'The customs form said the package contained cassettes, but someone at the hotel must have noticed that it felt squishy. During the show that night at the Scandinavian Hall, the place suddenly gets full of armed police. The encores kept going on, so they tried to stop us by chopping through a 20,000-watt PA cable, which could have killed someone. Backstage, I'm arrested, put in a police car and taken to police headquarters. Then a few minutes later, they also bring in Paul and Linda.'

Threatened with charges of trafficking, the McCartneys protested that the grass had been sent to them as a gift by fans, and that they'd had no idea what was in the package when they picked it up. They were believed, and the group got off with a collective fine of £1000.

The following day, they gave an interview to the *Daily Mail*, repeating the same story. But Paul didn't deny that they used grass, nor feel any need to apologise. 'We smoke [it] and we like it, and that's why someone sent it to us in an envelope. At the end of the day, most people go home and have a whisky. Well, we play a gig and we're exhausted, and Linda and I prefer to put our kids to bed, sit down together and smoke a joint. That doesn't mean we're heavily into drugs or anything. You can't expect us to pretend we don't smoke for the sake of our fans. But now that I've been caught, I'll say "Yeah, it's true."'

'We had to sign a written promise not to use marijuana again while we were in Sweden,' Seiwell says. 'But the next day, a guy from Holland gave us some and we shared it from a paper plate inside the bus with all the press and the fans right outside.'

*

Back in Britain, further trouble of the same kind was waiting – this time in the place where Paul had always felt most private and able to do as he liked. And yet again the postal service would take the rap.

On 19 September, a uniformed officer of the Campbeltown police, PC Norman McPhee, paid an unannounced visit to High Park Farm. Paul and Linda were in London, just back from Wings Over Europe, and no one else was at the property. McPhee later claimed merely to have been carrying out a routine security check. But just a few days previously he'd been away on a drug-awareness course in Glasgow, learning how to recognise illegal substances, both artificial and natural. Nor could he have been unaware of the *Daily Mail*'s 'WHY I SMOKE POT – BY PAUL' headline, and of feelings among Kintyre's predominant conservative, God-fearing element. It's even possible he was acting on a tip-off from one of Paul's less-enamoured neighbours.

The spot- or, rather, pot-check yielded rich dividends. In the farm's tumbledown greenhouse were growing five of the distinctive spikey-leaved plants PC McPhee now knew to harbour cannabis resin. He took one away for analysis and, the results proving positive, returned with a search-warrant and seven colleagues to seek further drugs in the farmhouse, Rude Studio and other outbuildings. But the five cannabis plants proved the extent of it.

Next day, Paul was charged with three counts of growing and possessing cannabis, a crime far graver in 1972 than nowadays and usually punished by imprisonment. As Scotland's legal system differs radically from England's, a Glasgow-based solicitor, Len Murray, was engaged to represent him. Murray entered a plea of not guilty to all three charges by letter and the case was set for trial at Campbeltown Sheriff Court the following March.

With that cheerless prospect ahead, Paul took Wings back into the recording studio to finish the album that had been interrupted the previous spring, only now as a single one rather than the double he'd first intended. Guitarist Henry McCullough took credit for persuading him it would be better shorter – something that George Martin had so signally failed to do with the Beatles' White Album. After the problems with Glyn Johns, he decided to produce the remainder of it himself.

Midway through the sessions, as it happened, the Beatles' old producer offered him a commission only someone with his talent for multitasking could have accepted. Martin had been asked to score the eighth James Bond film, *Live and Let Die*, and had persuaded its producers that the title song – invariably a hit in the pop charts – should be written by Paul and recorded by Wings.

Stimulated as always by composing to order, he speed-read Ian Fleming's novel, then set to work, calling on Linda for help yet again. Like a famous co-composition with John, the song ended up in two distinct halves, its soft, pensive opening by Paul, its perky reggae middle by Linda. As arranger and producer, George Martin brought in percussionist Ray Cooper, and added 'Day in the Life'-like symphonic effects as explosive as a Bond car chase. With that kick from 007, Wings really rocked for the very first time.

The problem was that Bond movie songs had previously been recorded by solo artistes, usually female ones. When the franchise's co-producer, Harry Salzman, heard Wings' track, he assumed it was merely a demo. 'That's great – now who do we get to make the record?' he asked Martin. 'Whaddaya think of Thelma Houston?' Only with great misgivings was he persuaded that Paul McCartney's new band was the better bet.

With Wings' new album – now titled *Red Rose Speedway* – still not ready for the Christmas market, Paul released their third single in 1972, the rock-boogie 'Hi Hi Hi'. It earned him his second BBC ban of the year, both for its blatant drug-references ('We're gonna get hi hi hi') and crude, not to say chauvinistic, sexual sentiments like 'Get ready for my body-gun', which he rather implausibly claimed was a mishearing of 'polygon'.

It reached number five in the UK and ten in America, but was the unwisest possible prelude to appearing before Campbeltown Sheriff Court.

*

Paul's trial, on 8 March 1973, brought the world's media to Kintyre and caused telescopic camera lenses to be trained for the first time from the slopes above High Park Farm. But the outcome was better than he'd dared to hope.

Just before the case came to court, his barrister, John McCluskey QC – a future Solicitor-General for Scotland – spotted procedural errors in two of the three charges against him. McCluskey and so-licitor Len Murray sought a private meeting with Campbeltown's Procurator Fiscal, or prosecutor, Iain Stewart, who conceded both errors and agreed to accept a not guilty plea on two of the charges in question if Paul would plead guilty to the third. The McCartney legal team could not but feel a twinge of sympathy for the Procura-tor as he lamented that he'd practised law for 30 years in obscurity and now that the eyes of the world were about to be on him, he'd botched his case.

For his court-appearance, Paul exchanged the persona of local sheep-farmer for that of international superstar, flying up from London with Linda in a private jet. At Machrihanish airport, they were met by Murray and McCluskey and driven in the solicitor's Jaguar to Campbeltown's granite Victorian courthouse. Paul was told that two of the charges would be dropped if he admitted the third one and (according to Murray) replied 'Yes, let's go with that and get it over with' while Linda 'sat quietly, sipping an orange juice'.

The case lasted barely 25 minutes. In mitigation, McCluskey told Sheriff Donald J. McDairmid that his client had had 'an interest in horticulture for many years' – causing an involuntary spasm of mirth among the assembled journalists – and that fans often sent him gifts of seeds by post, which he planted in his greenhouse without necessarily knowing what they were. Those five spikey-leaved culprits were just such an innocent modern version of 'Jack and the Beanstalk'.

McCluskey added that the matter was already potentially dam-aging to Paul since America's immigration authorities refused admission to drug-offenders on principle even where the offence was, as in this case, purely technical.

Sheriff McDairmid's summing-up suggested a swingeing penalty. 'I take into account that the seeds were sent to you as a gift,' he told Paul, 'but I also take into account that you are a public figure of considerable interest to young people and I must deal with you accordingly.' A fine of just £100 was then imposed. As if pleading for some penniless vagrant hauled up for urinating in public, his counsel requested time for him to pay off the £100, and the court granted a month.

Outside the courthouse, Paul gave an impromptu press conference with Linda clinging to his arm and jokily wearing John McCluskey's bowler hat. As many a hack noted, she was 'in high spirits' – whether assisted by seeds received in the post would never be known – and seemed to be treating the occasion with less than due seriousness.

A totally serious Paul was at his diplomatic best as he paid tribute to the Sheriff as 'a great guy' and said he bore his prosecutors no ill will. 'You have to be careful, like [with] Prohibition in the olden days . . . I think the law should be changed. I don't think cannabis is as dangerous as drink. But I'm dead against hard drugs, though.'

His case would have received greater media attention but for the conflict for which his solution had been 'Give Ireland Back to the Irish'. That same day, an IRA bomb exploded at London's Old Bailey law courts, killing one person and injuring 125. The following morning's front pages were full of blood-soaked lawyers and court officials rather than cannabis-cultivating pop stars.

But one exchange with a BBC reporter was horribly prophetic of a similar, far less lucky experience, seven years in the future:

PAUL: 'Well, I'm glad to have got off like this y'know. I'm glad it wasn't jail.'

BBC man: 'Did you think it might have been?'

PAUL: 'I thought it might have been, but I would have been OK as long as I could have taken my guitar in with me.'

31

'Screw you, I'll make an album you'll wish you'd been on'

On 16 April 1973, America's ABC TV network broadcast a one-hour special entitled *James Paul McCartney*. Its aim was to restore a public image dented by two recent drugs-busts, two singles that had been the subject of broadcasting bans and a third that many radio stations had refused to play; it also acted as a substitute for a getting-to-know-Wings tour. Unimpressed that Paul's Scottish drug offence had been adjudged merely technical, the US Immigration Service had revoked his visa.

The special's British makers were Associated Television, the same organisation which had bought up Lennon and McCartney's back catalogue with Northern Songs four years earlier. As much as Paul might hanker for an hour's prime-time exposure on ATV's national network and syndication to American ABC, the company's chairman, now Sir Lew Grade, was ordinarily the last person for whom he'd want to work.

That he did so now was a result of his determination to make Linda his musical equal. Although he and John had lost the copyrights in their entire Beatles *oeuvre*, Northern Songs continued to have them under exclusive contract as composers and to expect further Lennon–McCartney works yielding the same rich rewards as in the past. Instead, Paul was providing songs credited jointly to Linda and himself, of which Northern could therefore claim only 50 per cent.

The result was a lawsuit from Northern's US subsidiary Maclen, claiming back $1 million in royalties. Maclen (i.e. McCartney–Lennon) had originally been set up as a conduit for Paul's music with John; he was thus being sued by a company bearing half his own surname. In the wake of his High Court victory, more tortuous litigation threatened, with an outcome by no means as assured. Then Sir Lew, that consummate deal-maker, offered a solution: he'd drop the lawsuit if Paul would make the TV special (and also write theme music for an ATV drama series, *The Zoo Gang*).

As part of the peace settlement, Paul's company, McCartney Music, entered into a seven-year co-publishing agreement with ATV Music for the songs he wrote with Linda. In return, a number of his post-Beatles song-copyrights, which had automatically gone to Northern Songs, would revert to McCartney Music at the expiry of the agreement in 1980.

Normally in television specials dedicated to a single entertainer, the star brings on guests to share duets or take part in comedy sketches. But *James Paul McCartney* dispensed with this formula: the whole hour was purely Paul, assisted by Linda and Wings, in film- and studio-sequences aimed at pleasing absolutely *everyone*.

So here he was with Wings playing 'Big Barn Bed' in front of a bank of TV monitors, then by himself perched on a stool, stroking a left-hand guitar and humming 'Blackbird' as Linda knelt in front of him with her camera, adding the occasional diffident harmony. Here he was now out of doors, defiantly reprising 'Mary Had a Little Lamb' with Wings, a largeish flock of sheep nudging his piano and Linda in a Victorian gown and picture-hat, seated on a swing and playing a tambourine.

Here he was now indoors again, playing 'My Love' from *Red Rose Speedway*, another ode to Linda, like 'Maybe I'm Amazed', so far beyond his usual Wingspan that the dream-voices which had whispered 'Yesterday' and 'Let It Be' into his ear might have returned.

In an early example of pop video, here was 'Uncle Albert' (minus the 'Admiral Halsey' section) with Paul as a mustachioed business executive, attended by Linda as a bespectacled PA, ringing up a whole harem of Uncle Alberts. Cut to a tribute to his roots: a filmed sequence of Liverpool docks and terraced streets and a pub reunion of the extensive McCartney clan with Paul leading a sing-song of old favourites – his no less than theirs – like 'April Showers' and 'California Here I Come'. Here were the show's only guest stars, his dad and his two favourite aunts, Gin and Millie.

'Are there any celebrities here?' another aunt asked him, showing how in Liverpool even the biggest star can never feel too big-headed.

'Gerry Marsden's here,' Paul answered without a blink.

Next came a big-production pastiche of a 1930s Hollywood musical with Paul, mustachioed again, leading a Busby Berkeley tap-routine in a pink tail suit; a CinemaScope version of 'Your Mother Should Know' in *Magical Mystery Tour*. 'Learn to tap-dance' had been advice given to the Beatles, and most Sixties pop names, as insurance against the day when their music blew over, but no one else had followed it so diligently.

Nineteen-thirties camp gave way to scenes from the new James Bond film, *Live and Let Die*, and Wings performing its title song with special effects untroubled by any health and safety considerations. At the end, Paul's grand piano was made to explode, with the unforeseen result of knocking guitarist Henry McCullough flat on his back and raining chips of blazing wood on the studio audience.

Only one part of the extravaganza featured songs from the Beatles years. A selection of ordinary Britons in the street, shoppers, van-drivers, mums with small children and the like, sang half-remembered, mostly out-of-tune versions of 'Can't Buy Me Love', 'Yellow Submarine' and 'When I'm Sixty-Four'. It proved their universality but also belittled them, relegating them to the same pub-singalong past as 'April Showers' and 'You Are My Sunshine'.

The reviews were worse than for any of Paul's solo albums to date. *Melody Maker* voiced a general sentiment in calling the special 'overblown and silly'. The most extreme hatchet-job appeared in *New York Sunday News* under the byline of Lillian Roxon, who'd once been a close friend of Linda's but felt she'd been dropped when Paul came along. Roxon particularly hated the pub-singalong sequence, which Linda hadn't wanted Paul to do, and in which she'd certainly looked ill-at-ease among the pints of ale and overloaded ashtrays. The Roxon review portrayed Paul in the bosom of his family as 'sweaty, pudgy and slack-mouthed' and Linda as 'catatonic with horror at having to mingle with ordinary people . . . disdainful if not downright bored . . . her teeth relentlessly clamped in a Scarsdale lockjaw . . . incredibly cold and arrogant'.

In May, Paul took Wings on their first UK tour, to promote the *Red Rose Speedway* album and the single 'Live and Let Die' (not included on it) which was to be released to coincide with the Bond film's London premiere. On the tour, as on the album, their billing now became 'Paul McCartney and Wings', in case anyone out there still didn't get who their front man was.

Everything possible was done to kill any Beatle echoes and suggest the cutting-edge of contemporary rock. Before setting out, Wings made a one-off appearance at London's trendiest new venue, the Hard Rock Cafe, in aid of the drugs charity Release. There Paul saw a young band named Brinsley Schwarz, who'd weathered an over-hyped launch to reveal genuine talent, notably in vocalist Nick Lowe. Realising how they would enhance the image he wanted for Wings, he hired them as a support act.

The tour was Britain's first close look at the woman who'd presumed to take John Lennon's place. At that time, females in rock bands were still a rarity, female keyboard-players still more so, and wives playing in their husband's bands totally unknown. No one who saw Linda onstage with Wings doubted she was there under the falsest of pretences and at her own egotistical insistence. And unfortunately her quiet, oblique charm failed to work outside a radius of about three feet. Although Paul introduced her to audiences in homey style as 'Our Lin', she came across as aloof, unsmiling, even resentful at having to share him with so many others.

Everywhere Wings went, she was criticised and mocked with

a bile that once had been reserved for Yoko Ono. Pop reviewers – in these days largely male and unfettered by feminism – poured scorn on her wispy vocals and the careful way her limitations as a keyboard-player were camouflaged by Wings' *real* musicians.

Like Paul, she now sported the ubiquitous early-Seventies 'mullet' hairstyle of spiky topknot and long, dangly bits at the back. Added to her blonde hair, high forehead and prominent cheek-bones, it gave her somewhat the look of David Bowie's alter ego, Ziggy Stardust. Glam Rock ethos was outraged by her fondness for lumpy quilted jackets and Argyll socks in unmatching tartans, and her admission that she didn't shave her legs or armpits. A cruel chauvinistic riddle went around: 'What do you call a dog with Wings? Linda McCartney.'

In her rare interviews, she was far from 'cold and arrogant', but disarmingly honest about her musical shortcomings. 'I think [the criticism] was justified. I didn't have any training and I was still learning piano when we started. Now I do know chords and I have a feel for music and I really love it, so I don't think they'll get me so much.' Some hopes.

On 18 May, Wings reached Liverpool and played a sold-out show at the Empire Theatre. By now, the city's once-booming docks had grown deathly quiet, great transatlantic liners no longer glided up the Mersey (bringing American rock 'n' roll among their cargoes) and Jim McCartney's beloved cotton trade had all but unravelled in the face of cut-price competition from the Far East.

The Cavern club, where Paul had sweated out his musical apprenticeship, was scheduled to close down a few days after his Empire show. The dank vault, on whose matchwood stage pure magic had been born, would then be bulldozed as part of construction work on the new Merseyrail metro system. Although many of its old habitués protested (Paul not among them), there was no effort to save what in years to come would have been a precious-beyond-price heritage site. Liverpool seemed to be suffering the same amnesia about the Beatles as did the Beatles themselves.

★

But if Paul could dismiss them from his thoughts, the rest of the world had more trouble doing so. It was the reason why, after three years and a string of hit singles and albums, his solo career still wasn't regarded as a success. Too many people were waiting for him to see sense and get back with John, George and Ringo. They little guessed that he himself still remained unsure he'd done the right thing in going it alone.

Publicly, he took every opportunity to stress what a weight off his mind – and soul – the Beatles' break-up had been. 'I take life much more simply,' he told a Leicester radio station during the UK tour. 'I wake up each morning and I think "Ah, I'm alive. Great! What do we do today?"'

Behind the chirpy smile and unruffled tone was a self-confessed 'born worrier' who more usually woke up feeling 'a ten-ton weight' on his shoulders because Wings still hadn't reached the level of musicianship nor received the critical recognition he wanted. It scarcely counted with him that 'Live and Let Die' had become the most successful Bond theme to date, spending two weeks at number one in the *Billboard* chart. Nor that *Red Rose Speedway* had reached number one in the US and five in Britain and 'My Love' been hailed as an instant classic. He now hated everything he'd done on the album, believing he'd been trying too hard. Even Linda, usually the staunch defender of every note he sang and played, thought it 'a non-confident record'.

The very fecundity of his talent brought nagging insecurity. What if he should wake up one morning and find his extraordinary facility with music and words had flown away in the night? As insurance against that awful day, he constantly worked the incomprehensible mechanism in his head, never passing a piano without sitting down and trying out yet another idea.

During a pre-tour holiday with Linda and the children in Montego Bay, Jamaica, he'd hung out with the Hollywood stars Dustin Hoffman and Steve McQueen, who were on location filming *Papillon*. One evening, Hoffman challenged him to come up with a song there and then about the recent demise of Pablo Picasso, whose dying words had reportedly been an exhortation to drink to his health. As a result, 'Picasso's Last Words' (a country number, of all things) was waiting to be used somewhere.

Wings were due to make a new album in the late summer (just as the Beatles used to) to catch the Christmas market. Feeling he'd exhausted the possibilities of British and American studios, Paul decided to make it in some more interesting, out-of-the-way place and asked EMI for a list of their recording facilities around the world. It turned out that they had one in Nigeria's capital, Lagos. He booked Wings in there for most of September, visualising 'gorgeous African music, African culture . . . lie on the beach all day, then breeze into the studio to record'.

Rehearsals took place throughout August in Scotland, where Wings had begun, though now in surroundings more spacious than Rude Studio. Paul had recently purchased nearby Low Ranachan Farm from its retiring owner, Archie Revie, so adding to the seclusion of High Park Farm as well as its very basic amenities. Low Ranachan had a large barn where the band could rehearse – hence 'Big Barn Bed' – and a grey stone cottage where they could live. It was just over the hill from High Park, so Paul and Linda could come to rehearsals on horseback.

The Wings crèche was about to expand still further. Following their European tour, Denny Laine had married the 20-year-old 'supergroupie' Jo Jo La Patrie, who was now pregnant and installed in the cottage at Low Ranachan. The baby was due to arrive at around the time Wings departed for Nigeria, but Denny still intended to go with them.

The Low Ranachan barn sessions began on an optimistic note. 'Paul had written some great new songs for the album,' drummer Denny Seiwell recalls, 'and we were sounding really tight as a band.'

But tensions soon developed between Paul and lead guitarist Henry McCullough. The bony Ulsterman was the most wayward member of the line-up, the only one besides Paul to have been busted for drug-possession, in his case while touring Canada with the Animals. A more immediate problem was his heavy drinking and the embarrassing scenes to which it could lead. At the McCartney family reunion shown in *James Paul McCartney*, he'd had a boozy altercation with his girlfriend, Sheila, then spent the rest of the night wandering the Liverpool streets barefoot in a rhinestone-studded jacket. And during a performance of 'My Love' on BBC1's *Top of the Pops* show, he'd spoiled the rhapsodic mood by throwing up.

For some time, McCullough had been chafing at the way Wings' much-touted family atmosphere could be broken at any time by some authoritarian gesture from Paul. After a one-off guest appearance at a London club with jazz singer Carol Grimes, he'd been carpeted and tersely informed that Wings members played *only* with Wings. One week, he opened his (still) £70 pay packet to find that £40 had been deducted, without consultation or warning, for the hire of an extra amplifier.

But the real bone of contention was Paul's insistence that all Wings' guitar breaks must be meticulously planned in advance while McCullough, still a bluesman at heart, played his best when improvising. On the 'My Love' session, for example, he'd departed from the script to extemporise one of the great slow rock solos. Paul couldn't help but pardon him then, but made it clear that he shouldn't make a habit of it.

The final breaking-point came two weeks before the band's departure to Nigeria. 'We were in the barn,' Denny Seiwell remembers. 'Paul wanted Henry to play something a certain way, and Henry didn't want to do it. Both of them were just having a real bad day.' Finally, there was an angry exchange which ended with Paul storming out, mounting his horse and riding home. Realising it was the rock 'n' roll equivalent of being left alone with a loaded revolver, McCullough got in his car and drove away, never to return.

Seiwell, too, had grown unhappy about the way Paul ran Wings, in particular his apparent reluctance to divvy up the proceeds of their recording and performing successes. 'At the start, it was understood that we'd all be part-owners of the band, and share in its rewards, but there was never a contract. It was all done on a handshake – on trust.'

Yet after two years, Seiwell was receiving the same flat salary of £70 per week when, as a top New York session-drummer, he used to earn $2000. 'The European tour had sold out every night, but Paul said he'd still lost money on it. Things had gotten so bad with me financially that to pay off my American Express card, I'd have to go back to New York and do a few quick sessions.'

For his £70, he was expected to be on call 24 hours a day and do whatever was asked of him, however loosely music-related. During the European tour, Paul had simultaneously been working on a film about a cartoon character named Bruce McMouse who lived under Wings' stage and interacted with them like Jerry from Tom and Jerry dancing with Gene Kelly in *Anchors Aweigh*. The human characters were filmed first at Elstree Studios, with the cartoon one superimposed afterwards. Hence the tough 6' 2" Seiwell was required to converse with an imaginary talking mouse on his out-stretched hand.

He also felt that Paul should not have let a talented guitarist like Henry McCullough go so readily. 'The band's musicianship really deteriorated after Henry left. Denny Laine was an okay guitarist, but nowhere near the same league. And without him, it was going to be that much harder to hide Linda's mistakes.'

A few days before the band's scheduled departure to Lagos, Jo Jo Laine gave birth to a son, to whom she and his father also gave the Christian name Laine. 'I heard from Denny that when the baby was born, Paul and Linda hadn't sent flowers or even a card. That got to me for some reason,' Seiwell recalls, 'and the night before we were to leave for Africa, I phoned Paul and told him I was quitting.'

This eleventh-hour loss of two key sidemen would have made most people call off the Nigeria venture, or postpone it until suit-able replacements could be found. Denny Laine – still on for the trip despite his newborn son – thought it a fatal blow. 'They were both such brilliant musicians. And Henry's Irish sense of humour and Denny's New York one made such a great combination. They were my kind of people.'

But Paul decided to go ahead anyway, if nothing else to show the defectors they weren't as important as they believed. 'I thought "Screw you",' he would remember. '"I'll make an album you'll wish you'd been on."'

So a severely clipped Wings consisting of Paul, Linda and Denny Laine, plus the McCartneys' three children, departed for Lagos on 29 August. At the airport, Laine half-expected Denny Seiwell to have had second thoughts and be waiting to rejoin them, but he hadn't and wasn't.

Nowadays many Western rock bands go to Africa to make albums but in 1973 Paul was a pioneer. And, as with many pioneers, what he found was not what he'd expected. He'd visualised Nigeria in terms of 'gorgeous African music [and] African culture', a riot of sound and colour that would make Glam Rock seem drab by comparison. He hadn't visualised arriving as a VIP observer on the aircraft's flight deck and realising that neither the pilot nor co-pilot seemed able to find the runway of Lagos airport among the misty tracts of jungle beneath. He hadn't expected it to be monsoon season, when every afternoon brought ferocious rainstorms in drops the size of wet crowbars.

Nor had his concept of 'African culture' included the repressive military regime of President Yakubu ('Jack') Gowon, which membership of the British Commonwealth did little to restrain. It was only three years since Gowon had ruthlessly crushed the country's would-be breakaway state of Biafra, causing a million deaths from genocide and famine – and providing one of John's reasons for returning his MBE decoration to the Queen.

Also in the Wings party was Geoff Emerick, the Abbey Road sound-engineer who'd worked with the Beatles almost throughout their recording career and whom Paul had hired to sort out possible technical glitches in the month of recording ahead. For the quiet, suburban Emerick, downtown Lagos came as a stupefying culture shock. As the group's minibus wove through nightmare traffic, Denny Laine reported seeing a man knocked off his bicycle and apparently killed, all without the slightest reaction from passers-by. Noticing quantities of white-sheeted figures among the crowds, Emerick asked the bus-driver who they were. 'Lepers,' came the casual reply.

EMI's studio was located in Wharf Road in the port area of Apapa, facing the Atlantic, a link with Liverpool in more ways than one. Paul's uncle Will Stapleton – the only member of his family thus far to do time in prison – had been serving on a merchant ship called the SS *Apapa*, bound for West Africa, when he'd pilfered £500 from a cargo of banknotes, and had come ashore in Lagos to spend some of the loot.

Paul's instinct about bringing along Geoff Emerick was one he soon had cause to bless. The studio possessed only the most basic taping and mixing equipment and had no soundproof recording booths. An adjacent lean-to served as a record-pressing plant, whose operatives currently worked ankle-deep in rainwater.

Emerick set to work on making the control desk fit for purpose while Paul charmed the studio manager and tape-operator – whose names turned out to be Innocent and Monday – and persuaded them to bring in carpenters to build soundproof cubicles. When their labours seemed to be flagging, he picked up a hammer and joined in himself.

The trio then began laying down the tracks that had been rehearsed by a quintet at Low Ranachan – Denny Laine on guitar, Linda on keyboards, Paul on bass, drums and everything else. The atmosphere, Laine recalls, wasn't that of a band but of two producer-musicians putting an album together. Paul never mentioned Henry McCullough or Denny Seiwell, and Laine surmised that he shouldn't either.

They stayed in the upmarket suburb of Ikeja, occupying two rented villas – Paul and family in one, Laine and Emerick sharing the other – on a private estate with walls and round-the-clock security. Heather, Mary and little Stella quickly adapted to their new surroundings, catching multicoloured, befrilled lizards in the exotic garden, giving them names and keeping them as pets like the lambs at home in Kintyre.

Not so poor Geoff Emerick, who was terrified by the outsize spiders and other creepy-crawlies that shared his living quarters. Fun-loving Denny took pleasure in collecting the largest, least attractive specimens killed during the day and leaving them on his housemate's pillow like hairier versions of the bedtime mints distributed by luxury hotels. Unable to stand this rock 'n' roll prankishness any longer, Emerick moved into a local hotel, whose cockroaches proved hardly less intimidating.

Ikeja's many hangovers from British rule included a country club where Paul took out a membership so that they could all use the pool and relax between recording sessions. One pleasant discovery among the many unnerving ones was that no one objected even to the most overt smoking of marijuana.

Every expat they met stressed the need for perpetual vigilance in what was one of Africa's most impoverished and crime-ridden cities and cautioned against going anywhere on foot after sunset, even in the protected environment in which they were staying. Thinking this couldn't possibly apply to the short distance between the two villas, Paul and Linda decided to walk back to theirs one evening after a discussion of the day's work at Denny and Emerick's.

They had gone only a few yards when a car pulled up beside them and the driver called out, 'Are you travellers?' Mistaking it for the offer of a lift, Paul politely replied that they were all right, thanks. The car moved ahead, then stopped and five men got out, including 'a little squat one' holding a knife.

Linda, as always, put herself in harm's way to protect Paul, shielding him from the knifeman and screaming, 'Leave him alone! He's a *musician*!' Paul handed over the bag he was carrying, exercised his charm to the utmost, and the gang allowed them to go on their way. 'Later, the people at the studio told us how lucky we'd been,' he was to recall. 'In Nigeria, robbery carried a death sentence, so thieves often killed their victims to stop themselves being identified. If we'd have been locals, we would have had it.'

The stolen bag contained lyric-sheets and cassette demos of album tracks rehearsed in Scotland that he'd intended to use as guides to the made-in-Africa finished versions. However, during his early songwriting days with John, he'd acquired the habit of memorising everything he wrote, both words and arrangements, so the loss was delaying but not disastrous.

Between visits to street markets with the children and looning around palm trees for Linda's camera, he worked his two-person band relentlessly inside the rickety studio on Wharf Road. At times, the opening words of what would be his title track seemed only too apposite: 'Stuck inside these four walls . . . sent inside for ever . . . if we ever get out of here'. And, at regular intervals, 'the rain exploded with a mighty crash'.

One day, in mid-vocal, he suddenly turned pale and began to gasp for breath. Stumbling outside for air, he received the full blast of African midday heat and collapsed unconscious into Linda's arms. 'I laid him on the ground,' she later recalled. 'I thought he was dead.' Rushed to hospital in the studio manager's car, he was found only to have suffered a 'bronchial spasm' due to excessive smoking of the conventional sort.

Nigeria's own pop music in 1973 was teemingly creative, though as yet little known outside the African continent. Its pre-eminent figure, Fela Ransome Kuti, combined the role of performer, composer and broadcaster with that of political activist and fierce opponent of the Gowon regime. He had lately exchanged his 'slave-name' Ransome for Anikulapo ('he who carries death in his pouch') and declared the commune of musicians and followers he'd founded in central Lagos an independent republic named Kalakuta.

Kuti also operated Lagos's foremost music club, the Shrine, where he appeared with his band, Africa 70. Paul persuaded Linda and Denny Laine to accompany him to the Shrine, expecting to be feted the way he was in clubs everywhere. Instead, some of the house musicians began questioning him with a palpable lack of hero-worship about the Wharf Road recording sessions. The next day, Kuti went on the radio to accuse him of 'stealing' Nigerian music and culture.

The situation was potentially every bit as unpleasant as that encounter with the five muggers. Paul's typically diplomatic solution was to invite Kuti to the studio to listen to what Wings had in the can so far. After doing so, 'He who carries death in his pouch' conceded there was no trace of stolen Nigerian culture.

An equally tricky musical encounter was with Ginger Baker, formerly drummer with Cream – and rock's most famous 'wild man' – who'd emigrated to Nigeria and set up a recording studio in partnership with Fela Kuti. Denny Laine had once played with Ginger Baker's band, Air Force, and Jo Jo Laine had also crossed his path, leading him to observe later that 'no sane man would ever go near her'.

Baker was known to be deeply offended because Wings weren't using his ARC studio. To forestall possible trouble (which with him tended to take extreme physical forms), Paul agreed to record one track, 'Picasso's Last Words', at ARC. The passing of the twentieth century's greatest artist was thus commemorated in hillbilly style as the monsoon lashed the roof and a red-bearded drummer, famous for launching sticks like guided missiles, provided the softest percussion of his life with a can full of pebbles.

The McCartneys said goodbye to their Nigerian colleagues and friends by hosting a beach barbecue – still no sign of militant vegetarianism – then returned to London to finish off the album at George Martin's AIR studios with orchestral arrangements by Tony Visconti. Waiting for Paul at Cavendish was a letter from EMI's group director, Len Wood, saying that on no account should he think of going to Lagos because of an outbreak of cholera.

His idea of himself and Linda as refugees or escapees crystallised in the album's title, *Band on the Run*. One could argue that actually two-thirds of the band had gone on the run from *them*. However, they had indubitably broken out of the confines of normal recording and made a courageous journey through unfriendly territory with disaster often snapping, bloodhound-like, at their heels.

And despite all the problems and technical limitations, the end result was the one Paul had sought. In Lagos, he'd found a new style for Wings that put his transition from the Sixties to the Seventies beyond any doubt. The album's title track and the one that followed it, 'Jet', both had a sound big, glossy and grandiose enough for the Glam Rock era, perfect to be performed in giant arenas, set off by video-screens and flashing lights as seas of punching forearms kept time.

His overall aim seemed to be a concept album like *Sgt. Pepper's Lonely Hearts Club Band*, where the Beatles had adopted musical alter egos whose recital unfolded an epic saga. *Band on the Run's* cover had a feel of *Pepper's* with its role-playing principals and supporting cast of camp icons. Paul, Linda and Denny Laine were shown in convict garb, caught in a prison spotlight together with six celebrity co-escapees: chat show host Michael Parkinson, singer Kenny Lynch, Liverpool boxer John Conteh, movie actors James Coburn and Christopher Lee, and chef and Liberal MP Clement Freud.

In reality, *Band on the Run* was no *Sgt. Pepper* for the Seventies. The title song seemed to start telling a story, but soon dissolved into cartoony surrealism, its 'Jailer Man' joining forces with a 'Sailor Sam' evidently left on the beach since 'Yellow Submarine'. The remainder consisted of snapshots from Paul's home life, not one mentioning a band or a need to escape.

'Jet', despite having all the drive and euphoria of a mass jailbreak, was simply the name of his Labrador dog. 'Let Me Roll It' was a send-up of, or homage to, John and the Plastic Ono Band. 'Mamunia' commemorated the grand hotel in Marrakesh where Lord Grade had offered the deal leading to the *James Paul McCartney* TV special. 'No Words' was the first song Denny Laine had written for Wings, though (shades of Lennon–McCartney!) he'd needed Paul to help him finish it. 'Helen Wheels', i.e. Hell on wheels, was what Paul called his Land Rover in Scotland.

In another nod to *Sgt. Pepper*, overture numbers were reprised in softer, nostalgic versions at the end, 'Picasso's Last Words' morphing from country song to dramatic orchestral piece, then French radio broadcast and finally pub sing-song. Keeping faith with Fela Kuti to the last, there was not the smallest murmur of Nigeria.

Band on the Run was released in December 1973, to reviews as ecstatic as those of Paul's previous albums' had been dismissive. All the major rock critics who'd previously considered him a spent force now competed to praise him to the skies. Those who'd poured most scorn on his musical partnership with Linda were most vocal in applauding and empathising with it. In *Rolling Stone*, Jon Landau described it as 'a carefully composed, intricately designed personal statement that will make it impossible to classify McCartney as a mere stylist again'.

Best of all was the comparison with the two fellow Beatles whose solo work had up to then been rated far above Paul's. Indeed, the qualities usually cited as marks of his inferiority were the very ones singled out by Landau for special praise – his 'healthy propensity for playfulness and nonsense', as against John's and George's 'high-minded and overbearing seriousness'.

Paradoxically, the album made a slower chart ascent than any of its predecessors, taking seven months to reach number one in the UK – but then staying in the charts for 124 weeks. In America it reached number one on three separate occasions, eventually going triple platinum. It would be the best-selling album in Britain in 1974 and by the end of that year would have sold six million copies worldwide. The two singles taken from it also became hits, 'Band on the Run' reaching number one in the US and selling a million while 'Jet' peaked at seven both there and in the UK.

So, after three years of work, worry and self-doubt, Paul finally had everything he wanted. And did it satisfy him?

32

'An old estranged fiancé of mine called Paul'

With the Seventies' halfway point in sight, there were still peri-
odic rumours of the Beatles getting back together. These were
invariably based on the thinnest of evidence: George and Ringo
had attended the same film premiere or Paul been seen entering a
lawyer's office John had just left. Yet they never failed to create a
hen-house flutter in media around the world. All the multifarious
'new Beatles', from Slade, T. Rex and the Jackson 5 to the Partridge
Family, the Bay City Rollers and the Osmonds, seemingly couldn't
stop the pining for the old ones.

Between Lennon and McCartney, if there was not yet exactly
peace there was at least quiet. After the release of John's *Imagine*
album in 1971, he and Yoko had left Tittenhurst Park and moved to
New York, ostensibly seeking sanctuary from the relentless abuse
and mockery they'd suffered in Britain. Instead, they'd become
figureheads for the extreme leftist politics which now permeated
American rock culture and were, if anything, more conspicuous
and controversial than before.

Since John's unreasoning rant in 'How Do You Sleep?' his anger
against Paul had cooled. Nowadays he no longer bit the heads off
people, like his American assistant, Dan Richter, who urged him
to seek some kind of reconciliation. 'I kept saying, "You guys had
your divorce, so put it behind you,"' Richter remembers. '"You did
so much wonderful stuff together . . . you should at least be talking
again."'

By 1972, they were. Early that year, Paul visited John at the small apartment in the West Village where he and Yoko held court, often in bed, to a constant stream of political activists, journalists and street-performers, handing out money and support like a pared-down Apple. The two agreed that slagging one another off, on albums or through the music press, was stupid and childish.

After that, whenever Paul visited New York he'd usually telephone John, who by then had moved with Yoko to a Gothic apartment building called the Dakota on Central Park West. But, as he later recalled, he never knew what to expect; John would sometimes be friendly, sometimes hostile, sometimes 'very frightening'. As ever, Yoko's voice would be audible in the background, and he'd hang up thinking, 'Thank God they're not in my life any more.'

Once when he called, the deep Scouse voice he'd known since he was a teenager started going 'Yeah? Yeah? Whaddaya want?' like a natural-born New Yorker. To Paul, it sounded as bogus as the bald Greek cop in the TV series who went around sucking lollipops. 'Oh, fuck off, Kojak!' he retorted, and slammed the phone down.

The softening of John's attitude towards Paul had much to do with his hardening one towards the manager who had caused their final, fatal rift. He was beginning to wonder if Paul hadn't been right about Allen Klein.

For both George and John, disenchantment with their one-time financial saviour had begun to set in during 1971's two-part Concert for Bangladesh, which Klein had helped organise and which had seen George and Ringo perform together, albeit in a phalanx of fellow superstars like Eric Clapton and Bob Dylan. John had been invited to take part but had declined for the same reason as Paul: each was afraid that the other would also walk onstage, so turning the event into the Beatles reunion the whole world kept plaguing them for.

However, while avoiding that ghastly possibility himself, John had been deeply offended because Yoko wasn't asked to appear on her own, and blamed Klein for the snub. George, for his part, had developed serious misgivings over Klein's handling of the concerts and their accompanying triple album and film, specifically just how much of the $8–10 million proceeds had actually reached the famine and flood victims of Bangladesh.

On 2 April 1973, Klein's ABKCO company issued a statement announcing the severance of all links between himself, his three ex-Beatle clients and Apple. John confirmed that he, George and Ringo had 'separated ourselves' from Klein, adding the closest to a public apology their old bandmate would ever receive: 'Let's say possibly Paul's suspicions were right and the time was right.'

A major opportunity for a Lennon–McCartney rapprochement arose that spring when Ringo recorded his eponymous third album in Los Angeles. Both John and George contributed to the sessions, in company with Billy Preston, Klaus Voormann and T. Rex's Marc Bolan. Paul, too, agreed to take part with Linda, but by that time was banned from the US for his Scottish drug conviction, so had to do his track separately in London. Nonetheless, the *Ringo* album sparked the strongest Beatles reunion rumour yet.

While Paul was excluded from America, John had effectively become a prisoner there. Thanks to his political activities in New York, in particular his friendship with the radical demagogues Jerry Rubin and Abbie Hoffman, he had been placed under surveillance by both the FBI and the CIA, and was fighting efforts to deport him by the Immigration and Naturalization Service. He dared not leave the country for fear of not being allowed to return.

Nor was persecution by the US government his only problem. After seven years of spending every minute of every day with him, Yoko had begun to weary of his haunting insecurity, obsessive jealousy and unending, sexually-tinged obsession with his long-dead mother. The breaking-point came at a party where he had noisy casual sex with a young woman while Yoko was in the next room. So in September 1973 she kicked him out of the Dakota, packing him off to LA with a 22-year-old Chinese-American assistant named May Pang to act as both his PA and bedfellow.

The idea was that Yoko should be as sexually liberated as John.

Instead, she returned to London and, surprisingly, turned up at Paul's door, as he later recalled: 'a little diminutive, sad figure in black'. She had never confided in him before, still less in Linda, but now told them she already missed John and wanted a reconciliation.

Paul, by rights, should have felt little concern for the relationship which had started the Beatles on the downward slope. Still, he offered to play Cupid and deliver a message from Yoko the next time he saw John, although with his present visa situation there was no telling when that might be. Yoko then set out the conditions John had to observe if they were to start over: 'He would have to come back to New York. He can't live with me immediately. He'd have to court me, he'd have to ask me out again. He'd have to send me flowers.'

In the end, John spent 14 months in LA on what he afterwards called his lost weekend, boozing and taking drugs in blithe disregard of his FBI 'tails' and his parlous immigration-status, egged on by Ringo, Keith Moon of the Who and the alcoholic singer-songwriter Harry Nilsson. One night he was thrown out of the super-chic Troubadour club for drunkenly heckling the cabaret; on another, he took his seat in the packed VIP section with a Kotex sanitary-towel stuck to his forehead.

Even in his most unhinged moods, however, he kept to the pact he'd made with Paul and wrote no more lyrics like 'How Do You Sleep?' He let it be known he'd enjoyed the *James Paul McCartney* TV special, although its pub sing-song sequence made him 'squirm a bit'. He was even nicer about *Band on the Run*, whose 'Let Me Roll It' track sounded so Lennon-esque, there were rumours that he'd actually played on it. It was, he said, 'a great album', though he stopped short of mentioning Linda. 'Wings keep changing all the time. It doesn't matter who's playing. You can call them Wings but it's Paul McCartney's music and it's good stuff.'

In the spring of 1974, Paul's American visa was restored to him for a probationary period of a year. He was thus able to go to LA in March for the Oscars ceremony, where 'Live and Let Die' had been nominated for Best Original Song. He had become bearded once again, now sporting a thick turned-down moustache with a dark blob on his chin like Frank Zappa.

John at the time was supposed to be making an album of rock 'n' roll oldies – the kind that had first brought Paul and him together – with Phil Spector as producer. But the project had lapsed after the combustibly paranoid Spector fired a handgun in the studio, then absconded with the tapes of everything recorded so far. John therefore turned to producing an album by his hell-raising crony Harry Nilsson, with the unlikely title of *Pussy Cats*.

'Live and Let Die' didn't win an Oscar, losing out to Barbra Streisand's 'The Way We Were', written by another husband-and-wife team, Alan and Marilyn Bergman, with music by Marvin Hamlisch. The Bergmans' tearful lyrics were soon to take on extra meaning for Paul: 'Memories may be beautiful and yet/ What's too painful to remember we simply choose to forget'.

On the evening of 28 March, he and Linda paid a spur-of-the-moment visit to Burbank Studios, where John was working on *Pussy Cats* with Nilsson, the Rolling Stones' saxophonist Bobby Keys and guitarist Jesse Ed Davis. Ringo, too, had been playing on the album, but happened not to be there at that moment; otherwise, another Beatles-back-together story would doubtless have burned up the wires.

Cocaine was heavily in evidence and May Pang, John's Yoko-appointed girlfriend, who largely bore the brunt of his excesses, feared the worst when the unexpected visitors appeared. Instead, Pang would later recall, he and Paul started chatting as if there'd never been a cross word between them. The atmosphere was so benign that a jam session soon started, with John and Nilsson on vocals, Linda on keyboards, Paul playing the absent Ringo's drums and Pang beating a tambourine. The supporting line-up of Bobby Keys on sax and Jesse Ed Davis on guitar might have seemed un-improvable, but it wasn't. Stevie Wonder, Motown Records' boy prodigy, who happened to be working next door, came in to play keyboards along with Linda.

And this room full of virtuosity created . . . nothing. Everyone was too overwhelmed by the momentous melodic reunion they were witnessing. 'There were about 50 people playing,' John later recalled, 'and they were just watching me and Paul.'

The jam session eventually saw the light as a bootleg album whose title, *A Toot and a Snore in '74*, pretty much describes it. John's speaking voice predominates, slurred by 'toots' of cocaine and griping monotonously about the microphones. There's a version of Little Richard's 'Lucille', far inferior to the one the boy Beatles used to play in Hamburg while all of them were paralytic. Then John goes into Ben E. King's 'Stand By Me', announcing 'McCartney's doin' harmony on drums'. But they can only sing in counterpoint to each other: their matchless sweet-and-sour fusion has gone.

That Sunday, 31 March, Paul and Linda were invited to the beach house in Santa Monica where President John F. Kennedy had once taken his mistresses, including Marilyn Monroe, and which John was now sharing, at some cost to its fabric, with Ringo, Nilsson, Klaus Voormann and Keith Moon. Though it was early afternoon when the McCartneys arrived, he still hadn't got up. 'He was a teenager again,' Paul would remember. 'He was being his old Liverpool self, just a wild, wild boy.'

While the visitors waited, they were offered something called 'elephant tranquilliser' by Nilsson, then sat by the pool chatting to Moon who, when not destroying hotel suites, was the most urbanely charming of companions. When John finally surfaced he seemed to be 'in a mellow mood', so at a suitable moment Paul took him to one side and relayed Yoko's message from the year before, which was essentially 'She loves you'.

Throughout the Beatles' performing years they had had a perfect, unalterable line-up. But finding a merely workable one for Wings, with its peculiar blend of the familial and autocratic, was proving harder than Paul ever anticipated.

Having winged it, as it were, as a trio on *Band on the Run*, he set about recruiting a lead guitar to replace Henry McCullough and a drummer to replace Denny Seiwell. McCullough had originally been recommended by Wings' roadie Ian Horn, and in a bizarre coincidence Horn now steered Paul to a guitarist named McCulloch, though now Scottish instead of Irish. This was 20-year-old, Glasgow-born Jimmy McCulloch, who'd played on Thunderclap Newman's 'Something in the Air' aged only 15, then graduated to Stone the Crows after their lead guitar accidentally electrocuted himself onstage.

The elfinly pretty McCulloch was first hired to play on Mike McCartney's solo album, *McGear*, produced by Paul, and acquitted himself so impressively that an invitation to join Wings soon followed. With extraordinary candour he warned his new chief he could be subject to mood swings, but was taken on nonetheless.

Auditions for the drummer's spot took place at a London theatre, the Albery, and attracted some 50 applicants. Among them was Mitch Mitchell, formerly of the Jimi Hendrix Experience, who hadn't found a satisfactory niche since Hendrix's tragic death in 1970. Mitchell's playing was spectacular but it turned out that if he joined Wings, he'd expect to be treated like a star. There was, of course, room for only one of those.

The job finally went to 31-year-old Geoff Britton, a tough-looking Londoner who'd previously been with a black-leather rock 'n' roll outfit called the Wild Angels. Despite that Gene Vincent (and early Beatles) image, Britton did not drink, smoke or use drugs, and was a member of Great Britain's amateur karate team. His entry-ticket to Wings was a ferocious technique, using thicker sticks than ever Ginger Baker could handle. 'He has a Black Belt,' Paul said when introducing him to the press. 'I feel that with those credentials he'll be able to lick the band into shape.'

In June 1974, the new line-up set off for six weeks' intensive licking into shape, though not by Geoff Britton, in America's country music capital, Nashville, Tennessee. Paul had always loved country – it had been the inspiration for one of his earliest songs, 'In Spite of All the Danger' – and its latter fusion with rock, through bands like the Eagles and Poco, was another dimension he wanted to give Wings Mk. 2. As usual, the children went, too.

It happened that his father-in-law Lee Eastman's other music clients included Kevin Killen, a leading Nashville engineer and producer. Killen agreed to act as host and fixer for Wings and arranged for them to stay on a farm belonging to songwriter Curly Putman, Jr. (author of maudlin country classics like 'Green Green Grass of Home' and 'D.I.V.O.R.C.E.') in rural Wilson County.

The elite of Nashville's musical community opened their arms to Paul. At the Putman farm, he was visited by the great Roy Orbison, whose drowning-out on a 1963 tour had been one of the earliest signs of Beatlemania. He met the country 'picking' virtuoso Chet Atkins and pianist Floyd Cramer, whose 'On the Rebound' had thrilled him with its cross-handed chords in 1961. He and Linda were received by country's reigning king and queen, Johnny Cash and June Carter, a husband-and-wife performing act to which nobody ever objected.

Top of his list of places to visit was the Grand Ole Opry, otherwise known as the Ryman Auditorium, a chapel-like hall in downtown Nashville where most of the country music greats had gotten their first break. To his disappointment, the Opry had now been replaced by a modern entertainment complex called Opryland, but his host/fixer Kevin Killen assured him there were still great things to be seen there.

Naively, Killen did not arrange VIP access in advance but simply turned up at Opryland with Paul, his wife, children and band, and bought tickets at the gate. When the staid country fans saw who it was, they reacted as hysterically as any old-time Beatlemaniacs. Killen was deeply impressed by the measured way Paul ushered the whole party through the crush. 'When I was a Beatle, I learned that if you stay calm, you're OK,' he said, 'but if you bolt and run, they'll tear you apart.'

After the show, Killen suggested they hang out at his house, stopping on the way to pick up a supply of Kentucky Fried Chicken. It proved a heroic exercise in Southern hospitality, for Paul and Linda made no effort to restrain five-year-old Mary and three-year-old Stella as they used their host's pristine white leather sofas as a trampoline and streaked the walls with their greasy fingers.

As soon as politeness allowed, Killen suggested a sightseeing drive around Nashville. He was just setting his security-alarm when Stella realised she'd left her shoes behind, ran back inside the house and careered into a plate-glass door. The bottom half shattered and the top half slid down, badly cutting her on the arms and legs. Linda staunched the blood with towels and she was rushed to the hospital in nearby Donelson. 'Later on, I told Paul a couple dozen people died at the hospital that night,' Killen would recall. 'Because all the doctors were watching you.'

Much as Paul loved country music, Nashville's greatest allure was its part in the birth of rock 'n' roll. As a thirty-second birthday present, Linda bought him the stand-up bass used by Bill Black when Elvis Presley recorded 'Heartbreak Hotel' at the city's RCA studios. Playing pool in a bar one night, he bumped into Waylon Jennings, who'd almost taken the same charter flight that killed Buddy Holly in 1959.

He and Linda also wrote both sides of a new single which Wings recorded at Soundstop Studios on Music Row. The A-side, 'Junior's Farm', was suggested by Curly Putman, with a nod to Dylan's 'Maggie's Farm', but actually was a rousing rocker that would be Paul's last-ever appearance on Apple (and a US number three by the end of the year). However, the B-side, 'Sally G.', composed in a local bar, was pure country, extolling 'the friendly state of Tennessee' and featuring two of Nashville's most renowned session musicians, Johnny Gimble on fiddle and Lloyd Green on pedal steel.

Unfortunately, the new line-up's immersion in 'Music City USA' had not welded them together as Paul had intended. Geoff Britton, it had become plain, was a different animal from the others with his mouthy Cockney manner, his devotion to physical fitness and distaste for alcohol, cigarettes and pot. A visceral rock drummer, he found himself struggling with quasi-symphonic Wings numbers like 'Band on the Run' and 'Live and Let Die', especially on the 'poxy' kit that had been provided for him. And his devotion to karate was continually mocked by his exertion-averse bandmates.

'Are you gonna play those drums or chop 'em in two?' Denny Laine liked to quip.

Least of all had Britton bonded with his fellow new recruit, the ten-years-younger Jimmy McCulloch, whose slightness and prettiness belied a large appetite for everything the drummer considered unhealthy, as well as a true Glaswegian acid tongue. One day in the studio – when, according to Britton, 'everyone else was stoned' – he and McCulloch almost came to blows after the latter made a remark about Linda's musicianship that reduced her to tears. Paul blamed Britton for the fracas and said he needed to 'reassess the situation', which Britton interpreted as being fired and angrily walked out. The miniature Ringo-moment passed, however, and he was persuaded to return the next day.

The mood swings about which McCulloch had warned Paul were also kicking in with a vengeance. Some mornings, the boy-wonder guitarist would be sweetness itself, creating what he thought 'some of the best music I've ever laid down in my life'; on others, hung-over from booze or grass, he'd be dour and scowly, muttering about Britton and Linda and the sloppiness of Denny Laine's tuning. Once, in response to a minor quibble about his playing, he picked up an empty bottle and hurled it through the control room glass.

The two new recruits had expected their Nashville stay to include the signing of long-term contracts with Wings. Instead, they learned that Paul wanted them only on a piecemeal basis, paying them per recording session or stage performance. All his persuasiveness was needed to convince them the arrangement would be to their advantage, allowing them to play in other bands (something forbidden to Wings Mk. 1) and so potentially earn far more than mere staffers.

Denny Laine didn't particularly want a contract, having signed too many injudicious ones in the past. But after six weeks, even his usual blind willingness to follow Paul's lead was starting to waver. 'At one point, I thought "I don't know what we've come here for. We should be at home, gigging,"' he recalls. Weary of acting as a buffer between his band-boss and the fractious recruits, he, too, talked about quitting, though never seriously, he insists. 'It's not like these things had never been said before . . . You're walking out, but the next minute you can be walking back.'

In mid-July, the expedition came to a premature end when Jimmy McCulloch was charged with drink driving. Had the case reached court, it doubtless would have uncovered the fact that Wings were in America without work permits, so putting Paul's probationary visa in jeopardy. However, Kevin Killen was able to get the charges dropped on condition McCulloch left 'the friendly state of Tennessee' forthwith.

Word of the problems in Nashville, in particular the Britton/ McCulloch issue, had already leaked back to Britain. When Paul arrived home on 17 July, it was to find a *New Musical Express* story headlined 'WINGS UPHEAVAL' and suggesting they were breaking up over their two newest members' terms of employment.

Through his PR, Tony Brainsby, he issued an immediate 'clarification': 'Wings members are free to pursue their own musical careers. This will enable them to develop working relationships free of contractual ties. Wings will have a fluid concept, which will be adapted to suit current and future projects.' The *NME* also republished Brainsby's rebuttal of its scoop, expressed rather less diplomatically: 'It is wrong to say that Wings are no more because Wings are Paul and Linda McCartney.'

Having rehearsed the new line-up, Paul now needed to know how they'd look together onstage. He therefore decided to have a film made of them in rehearsal, using the new medium of videotape. To direct, he turned to David Litchfield, a graphic designer/ editor then running a small art magazine called *The Image* – later co-founder, with David Bailey, of *Ritz*, London's answer to Andy Warhol's *Interview*.

Litchfield had run some of Linda's rock star photographs in *The Image* but had never made a film before. 'Paul said that was OK because the documentary wasn't meant for anyone but him, Linda and the band,' he recalls. '*The Image* was just about to go bust, so it saved my life.'

As new to the world of rock-megastardom as to that of film-making, Litchfield went to see Paul's manager, Brian Brolly, at McCartney Productions' one-room office in Greek Street, Soho. There, among other things, he learned what being Paul's manager entailed nowadays. 'While I was sitting there, Brian was being torn off a terrible strip on the phone by Linda. He'd had to order some mayonnaise to be sent to her at the house, and had got the wrong size. While she was going on at him, he said to me, "You'd better listen to this, to give you an idea what to expect," and switched on the speakerphone.'

Litchfield also received a briefing from Paul's chief roadie and factotum, Alan Crowder, in what amounted to a set of command-ments wrought by long experience: 'If Paul says he'll be somewhere at nine in the morning, he won't turn up until two in the afternoon . . . Any woman you introduce to him who promises she won't come on to him is lying . . .'

Litchfield's home-cum-office was in St John's Wood, and he became a frequent visitor to Cavendish to discuss the Wings-in-rehearsal documentary. 'The first time Paul took me there, his housekeeper, Rose, greeted him with the words "That fucking bitch has been in my kitchen again." It turned out she often talked about Linda that way, though they were good friends, and Paul seemed quite used to it. "Why don't you go and watch TV with the kids," he said to me, "while I sort this out." I think he liked having a ballsy person like Rose around when most people were so reverential to him.'

Filming was to take place entirely at Abbey Road, where Paul had booked a studio around the clock. Despite his huge standing there, and the money he was spending, Litchfield remembers, he still had to obey the same rules and regulations as in the days with 'headmaster' George Martin. 'The canteen closed at five in the afternoon – and there were no extensions. Linda wasn't even allowed into its kitchen to prepare anything for the band.'

Although not destined to be released or broadcast, the documentary was given a title, *One Hand Clapping*, and included a voice-over by Paul. In it he confessed that what he really enjoyed was playing every instrument himself, as on the *McCartney* album, 'just like an old professor in a laboratory'. Still, he dutifully pushed Wings' new members' charter: 'My ideal is to get a steady group . . . with enough looseness so that any of us at any time can go off and do what he wants to do.'

Jimmy McCulloch continued to be a problem, feuding with Geoff Britton and sniping at Linda, his mood swings fuelled now by more than alcohol and grass. 'Two Italian girls were always coming to see him and slipping him envelopes,' Litchfield recalls. 'And what was inside was harder than cocaine.'

Wings' filmed run-through of 'Live and Let Die' was augmented by the London Symphony Orchestra in full evening dress – an echo of the famous 'Day in the Life', similarly never meant to be broadcast. Also on hand were a cohort of top session musicians including saxophonist Howie Casey, whom Paul had known since they were in rival Liverpool bands on Hamburg's Reeperbahn. Times had changed, however, since they played all night to gangsters and strippers, fuelled by foamy oceans of beer. When Casey was asked what he'd like to drink, he replied 'A beer' and was served with just the one bottle.

'Paul didn't do his vocal until late in the day, after I'd had a few gins, and I couldn't stop myself bursting out laughing,' David Litchfield remembers. 'He stopped and said, "Is there something funny?" I said, "I'm sorry, but you look just like Shirley Bassey." She'd sung a James Bond song before ['Goldfinger'] and Paul had got all the moves. He didn't laugh and I realised I'd gone too far.

'There was a cello solo, which the LSO musician kept getting wrong. I realised why: it was ten to five and after five he'd be on overtime. Finally, Paul went to this bloke and said, "To help you, I'll sing it for you." Then he sang the whole cello solo, using the names of the chords as words, so that the bloke couldn't help but get it right. It was a brilliant piece of musicianship and at the end the whole orchestra stood up and applauded him.'

As John and Paul started communicating again, so their once-implacable business differences gradually melted away. By the end of 1974 they seemed to have nothing left to quarrel about.

The previous year had officially terminated their contract with Northern Songs, the last remaining thing – apart from their past – that yoked them together. Each now controlled the publishing rights in his solo output although, gallingly, their joint Beatles *oeuvre* belonged to others.

Apple continued as a company still owned by all four ex-Beatles but reduced from a Georgian mansion to a single office run by Neil Aspinall, their faithful one-time roadie. Aspinall was said to be mainly occupied in amassing film footage for a marathon documentary looking back over their career. There was no inkling yet of their phenomenal future afterlife, still less of the golden windfalls to come simply from their company's name.

Above all, the issue that had divided Paul and John most bitterly and turned Paul into an outcast inside the Beatles – damaging him more than the others knew or ever would know – had worked itself out, to his complete vindication. On 2 November 1974, John, George and Ringo filed suit against Allen Klein for 'misrepresentation', a charge of special gravity where a manager was concerned. Klein immediately countersued, claiming allegedly unpaid fees, commissions and expenses totalling around $19 million.

John by now had wearied of his lost weekend in LA and returned to New York, although he hadn't yet found the nerve to attempt a reconciliation with Yoko. Unknown to all but a few musician friends, he and May Pang were living in a small apartment on East 52nd Street. Paul and Linda were among those let into the secret and allowed to call on him there.

It was two years since John's last live performance. He was convinced he'd built up too much stage-fright ever to do another one, especially without Yoko, and had firmly resisted all attempts to coax him back on the boards. His resolve weakened, however, with his fifth solo album, *Walls and Bridges*, one of whose tracks, 'Whatever Gets You Thru the Night', featured harmonies by his friend and devoted fan Elton John. When it was released as a single, Elton made him promise that if it made number one, they would perform it onstage together.

In late November, to John's amazement, 'Whatever Gets You Thru the Night' went to the top of both the *Billboard* and *Cashbox* charts, giving him the only American solo number one single he would have in his lifetime. True to his word, though with huge misgivings, he agreed to make a guest appearance during Elton's concert at Madison Square Garden on the 28th, Thanksgiving night.

This selflessly generous gesture by Elton showed what a vast reservoir of affection still remained for Beatle John – and not only John. As their third and climactic duet, he announced 'a number by an old estranged fiancé of mine called Paul. This one I never sang. It's an old Beatle number and we just about know it.' It was 'I Saw Her Standing There', which had kicked off Beatlemania with that old estranged fiancé's rousing cry of 'One, two, three, *faw!*' and it brought the house down. Thus their reconciliation was made public.

Yoko attended the show escorted by a new companion of her own, Paul's former session-guitarist David Spinozza (who might easily have ended up in Wings). Backstage, she and John almost fell into each other's arms and he began to woo her afresh, following the conditions she'd laid out to Paul – asking her on dates, sending her flowers. By early 1975, they would be back together again.

In December, the legal process Paul had set in motion in the British High Court nearly four years earlier finally reached an end with the legal dissolution of the Beatles' business partnership. This necessitated a reunion of sorts in New York, where the papers had to be signed. There was a sad symmetry in the city which had given them their greatest and happiest triumph, in 1964, now becoming the last stop in their divorce exactly ten years later.

George was in town at the end of an American tour to promote his latest album, *Dark Horse*, supported by his musical guru Ravi Shankar and a sitar ensemble as well as a backup band. The album-title was an ironic allusion to his years of being overshadowed by John and Paul and his latter emergence as a surprise winner. Actually, it was becoming clear that whatever talent George possessed had largely rubbed off them and, without their stimulus, was already fading fast. His tour had been derided for its poor presentation and long, preachy mystical interludes: 'Transcendental Mediocrity', *Rolling Stone* called it.

There was much else currently on George's mind: his wife, Pattie, had run off with his best friend, Eric Clapton, and his globally-revered single, 'My Sweet Lord', stood accused of plagiarising 'He's So Fine', a 1963 hit for a black female group, the Chiffons. Yet he still seethed over Paul's treatment of him in the recording studio, and lost no chance to hit back when asked if the Beatles could ever conceivably reunite. 'I'd join a band with John any day,' he told one interviewer, 'but I couldn't join a band with Paul McCartney.'

The signing of the papers dissolving the partnership was set for 19 December at the Plaza Hotel, where the Beatles had laughingly holed up before conquering the continent on *The Ed Sullivan Show*. Now there weren't screaming, heaving crowds to be faced; just stacks of documents more suited to some armistice ceremony after a world war.

At the appointed time, only Paul, George and Ringo had turned up. John was known to be at the Dakota Building, just across Central Park, but there was a lengthy wait, then a gofor brought word that he wouldn't be coming; Yoko's astrologer had advised against it. Instead, he sent a balloon with a message saying 'Listen to this balloon'. He would sign a few days later while visiting Disney World in Florida; by his lights, a fitting enough conclusion.

The deed three-quarters done, Paul and Linda went to Madison Square Garden to see George wind up his *Dark Horse* tour. Both disguised themselves with Afro wigs and Paul wore a false moustache. He was recognised nonetheless, setting off a fresh rumour that the Beatles could be getting back together . . .

33

'Man, if I was Paul McCartney, I'd buy the road'

During the first years of his marriage to Linda, Paul's life had struck a seemingly perfect balance between his farm in the Scottish wilds and his London home in St John's Wood, with culture and sophistication near at hand whenever he needed a restorative draught of one or the other, and Abbey Road studios just around the corner. But with Wings' accelerating success, and the resultant touring and recording schedule, it was no longer as easy as it once had been to bury himself in Kintyre for weeks, even months on end. At the same time, 7 Cavendish Avenue was starting to feel the strain of the household he now headed.

Thanks to Linda, that former elegant bachelor establishment had taken on the look of an urban farm. The back garden contained rabbits, ducks and chickens with a cockerel whose crowing, not confined to sunrise, could be heard by Test Match crowds at nearby Lord's cricket ground. Beside the geodesic glass meditation temple, with the circular bed that had once belonged to Groucho Marx, stretched a large vegetable-patch. The old stabling at the bottom had been restored to accommodate four horses, for Sunday-morning rides up to Primrose Hill and Hampstead.

The McCartneys' animals were allowed the same free rein as their children. One night when Paul accidentally left a window of his Rolls-Royce open, some chickens gained entry and did £6000-worth of damage. 'And there was a duck named Quacky that used to be allowed in the house,' David Litchfield remembers. 'It used to sit on the sofa with the kids.'

In addition, a pack of dogs created a constant uproar like the one he'd grown up with from the police dog training school over his garden fence. Martha the Old English sheepdog had been joined by Jet the black Labrador commemorated on *Band on the Run*, a yellow Labrador named Poppy and a Dalmatian named Lucky. When Martha, rather late in life, found romance in Scotland and gave birth to a litter of mongrel puppies, Linda insisted on keeping them all.

The incessant barking endeared Paul even less to other Cavendish Avenue residents than the eternal traffic of fans to his front gate. One of his neighbours, a Mrs Griswold, went so far as to complain to the Royal Society for the Prevention of Cruelty to Animals that the dogs were left alone in the house when he and Linda went away. However, an RSPCA investigation found that Paul's housekeeper, Rose Martin, was always there and regularly employed some of the better-behaved fan-pickets to walk the dogs on Hampstead Heath.

The episode underlined his need of a weekend bolt-hole from London where he, Linda and the children could enjoy the same freedom and privacy they did in Scotland without having to trek all the way up there. So in June 1973, he had paid £42,000 for a property named Waterfall Cottage in Peasmarsh, East Sussex.

The location could hardly have been more suitable. Situated three miles to the north-west of Rye and close to the Sussex–Kent border, Peasmarsh was a postcard-perfect village dominated by the Norman church of St Peter and St Paul (a fortuitous combination of Paul's name and that of the Merseyside church where he and John first met). True to the Rye area's strong literary heritage, it had once been home to the Very Reverend H.G. Liddell whose daughter, Alice, inspired Lewis Carroll's *Alice's Adventures in Wonderland*.

Waterfall Cottage was situated just outside the village, at the end of a long unmarked track called Starvecrow Lane. The house itself was a modest two-bedroom affair dating only from the 1930s with a circular shape recalling the oast houses, or hop-drying kilns, to be found throughout neighbouring Kent. But with it came approximately 100 acres of woodland mapped with ancient names like Four Acre Wood, Dinglesden Wood, Sluts Wood and Waterfall Wood, in which could be found the stream tumbling over perpendicular rocks that gave the property its name.

Surrounded by protective armies of trees, it was almost as remote and secluded as High Park Farm. Yet London was only an hour away by road and Lydd Airport, with its access to Paris and the Continent, just 25 minutes. But for now, Waterfall Cottage would be used only for spur-of-the-moment weekend breaks. Paul's main home and first love continued to be Kintyre, as he showed by repeatedly purchasing large tracts of it.

This expansion stemmed from his discovery that High Park was not as impregnably private as it had seemed. The first fan to run him to earth there was a young Mormon woman from Utah who'd already been tenaciously doorstepping him in London for about three years. In 1971, she was found to be camped with a female friend in a small wood on the slope above the farm, both of them spying on it through binoculars. Paul drove up to confront them in person and, recognising his long-time persecutor from Cavendish, made little of his usual effort to be nice. The Mormon later went to Campbeltown police claiming that he'd struck her across the face, but he denied it and no formal charge was ever brought.

To stop others camping in the wood, he purchased it outright and from then on began systematically acquiring other properties and land around High Park to create one vast, continuous McCartney exclusion-zone. Low Ranachan Farm, bought on the retirement of his neighbour Archie Revie, added a further 304 acres to his domain, as well as the barn where Wings rehearsed *Band on the Run* and the cottage where Jo Jo Laine went into labour. The addition of Low Park Farm, also known as Skeroblinraid, with its similar acreage, completed the circle; now one could not even see High Park without trespassing on Paul's land.

His ownership had an immediate beneficial effect on the

environment, something for which conventional farmers in those days cared little. At Linda's prompting, most of the walls and fences which had formerly divided the properties were removed, effectively creating a nature reserve where fauna and flora flourished as never before. The Highland red deer which had largely deserted the area – fearful of stalkers of their own – returned in abundance.

All the satellite farmhouses and cottages were in a poor state of repair when Paul acquired them, and needed extensive modernisation which he oversaw with his usual practical flair and restrained good taste. Yet, strangely, no such effort and expense went into the heart of his empire. He seemed to prefer High Park looking half-finished, with stacks of timber and corrugated iron lying around everywhere but never used. His daughter, Mary, would recall playing with her sisters in what seemed like 'one big lumber-yard'.

Linda in Scotland was unrecognisable as the reluctantly glammed-up figure who accompanied Paul in Wings, still attracting almost universal hostility and ridicule. 'Mother and wife is *it* for me,' she admitted in a complete U-turn from the feminism she'd once pioneered. 'And riding my horse and animals is *it* for me.'

One of the locals who got to know her best was Campbeltown taxi-driver Reggie McManus, who regularly drove the family to and from the airport and ferried Linda and the children down to Cheshire to visit Paul's father. McManus remembers a woman utterly devoid of the airs and graces one would expect from a rock megastar's wife. 'Both she and Paul always called me "Mr McManus", which I used to appreciate,' he recalls. 'Paul was very likeable, but I think he was always holding back a little bit. With Linda, well, she wore her heart on her sleeve.'

After all the stories of Beatle millions he'd read, the McCartneys' simple lifestyle came as a revelation. 'Every so often, I would go to Glasgow to pick up a parcel of clothes Linda had ordered, mostly for the children. There was never any of this designer stuff – just the kind of wee dresses you could get in Woolworths back in those days. Simple kids' stuff.'

Linda's great pride, McManus recalls, was her vegetable-patch. 'One day when I was there with my wife, she asked if we'd like some vegetables to take home. The next thing, she was down on her hands and knees pulling up carrots, then she asked if we'd like some potatoes and before you could stop her she had both hands deep in the soil. I said, "Stop, use a fork," but she was having none of it and as she clawed at the soil she said, "This is the best way, Mr McManus." Her hands were filthy but she didn't care.'

Here, too, she had time for photography, her first love and undisputed talent, finding subjects very different from the rock stars and backstage courtiers who used to be her main material.

At Low Ranachan Cottage, Paul set up the first real studio she'd ever had. But she preferred to wander the streets of Campbeltown snapping local characters like the colloquy of elderly men in flat caps, known locally as 'the Mill Dam Midges', who always gathered on the same street-corner, putting the world to rights. Her other favourite subjects were small children in prams or strollers. Years later, leafing through her various books of photographs, adult Campbeltonians would come upon their infant faces juxtaposed with Jim Morrison or Mick Jagger.

Her adoration of animals became a local legend. When one of Martha's mongrel puppies was kicked by a horse and suffered a broken leg, it was taken by taxi for treatment at Glasgow Veterinary Hospital, a round-trip of 280 miles. By the time the pup was returned to High Park, Paul and Linda had departed for London, so it was then flown down to join them. On an even more famous occasion, the Campbeltown vet found himself called to High Park Farm to treat a duck with a broken leg.

Despite Linda's pride in her home-grown veg, the cuisine at High Park still remained largely meat-based. But there were already signs of wavering. One Christmas time, she asked Reggie McManus to go to Glasgow and collect a goose she'd ordered as a change from turkey for the festive meal. McManus expected the bird to be already plucked and dressed but found it very much alive, in a crate so large that he had to lash it to the taxi roof.

On the return journey to Kintyre, he ran into high winds and lashing rain such as only the Scottish Highlands can produce. Fearing that the goose mightn't survive the journey – and so rob Paul and Linda of the experience of butchering their own Christmas dinner – he made frequent stops amid the tempest to check it was still alive. Furious hisses and wing-beatings confirmed this to be so.

However, its destiny was not to be carved by Paul at the head of a table decorated with crackers and tinsel. When McManus called at High Park some weeks later, Linda took him into the backyard, and there was his former outside passenger waddling around at the head of a flock of goslings. They hadn't had the heart to kill it, Linda said. 'It was now part of the family, raising its own family.'

Vegetarianism did not have much of a following in Britain at this time. Most people regarded it as a rather pitiable eccentricity practised by joyless characters who wore sandals and made their own clothes, and summed up in the drab phrase 'nut cutlet'. Most vegetarian restaurants were gloomy places still redolent of the hippy era. The name of London's most successful one, Cranks, wryly acknowledged the overwhelming public view of its clientele.

Paul had grown up an enthusiastic carnivore whose favourite meal, before he discovered more sophisticated fare, was lamb chop and chips (though at 20 Forthlin Road, his father's catering sometimes included 'pea sandwiches'). Though he'd tried vegetarianism with Jane Asher, he'd rather back-slid with Linda, whose earliest taste of fame had been with a meat loaf recipe ('take three pounds of mixed veal, beef or pork . . .') in the *Arizona Daily Star*. 'When they came to my house, Linda would go into the kitchen and make BLTs,' David Litchfield remembers. 'And I can hear her now asking me. "Do you fancy a burger?"'

Neither had ever felt anything contradictory in loving the lambs that were born by the hundred at High Park early each spring, giving the cutest ones names, letting the children bottle-feed the weaklings and then, a few weeks later, seeing them herded into trucks to be taken to Campbeltown livestock market. But one sunny Sunday noontime, realisation suddenly dawned.

'We were having lunch and looking out the window at all these little lambs jumping around, full of life,' Paul would remember. 'Then we realised we were eating leg of lamb. We looked at each other and had the same thought: "Maybe we should find a way of *not* doing this."'

For Wings' fourth album – their first after leaving the Apple label – Paul continued his policy of recording in hopefully inspirational foreign places and took them to New Orleans. Despite the magnetic pull of the city's jazz and blues heritage, he'd been there only once before, as a Beatle. All he remembered from that hermetically-sealed visit was the heat, the vibrator bed in the motel, and meeting Fats Domino.

The Wings troupe arrived on 5 January 1975, unaware that the city's Mardi Gras festival was in full swing. Venturing out to explore, they found themselves engulfed by fancy dress parades and marching Dixieland bands. Always glad of a chance to dress up, Paul and Linda joined the festivities disguised as circus clowns. But the chalk-white face and red nose fooled no one. 'Hi, Paul,' one after another fellow reveller greeted him.

Sea-Saint Studios, where the band were booked to record, also had an inspirational purpose. The studios' co-owner, songwriter and producer Allen Toussaint, was one of the most influential figures in New Orleans R&B, the composer of seminal early-Sixties hits like Ernie K-Doe's 'Mother-in-Law' and Lee Dorsey's 'Working in the Coal Mine'. Toussaint himself was to play backup piano for Paul in support of Linda's keyboards.

There was no current rumour of a Beatles reunion but the ravenous media had recently missed the strongest prospect yet. At their meeting in LA the previous summer, Paul had invited John to New Orleans to play on Wings' album and John had said he'd think about it. Later, according to his then companion, May Pang, he'd talked seriously about writing with Paul again and, at Pang's urging, decided to accept the New Orleans invitation. But the very week he was due to go, Yoko finally agreed to a reconciliation: he cancelled his flight and settled down with her in the Dakota Building to have a child and, in Yoko's poignant words, 'grow old together'.

It had been over a year since the release of *Band on the Run* and expectations for Wing's follow-up were almost as great as for the successor to *Sgt. Pepper's Lonely Hearts Club Band*. Paul had planned a formula similar to his 1973 smash – and his 1967 one – with songs linked together and reprised to create a seemingly coherent narrative. Holidaying in Jamaica prior to the trip, he'd set out all the tracks on a paper scroll 'almost as long as the room', continually changing their running-order to get the right balance of light and shade. The only other time he'd done that was with his medley at the end of *Abbey Road*.

Sea-Saint Studios and the New Orleans vibe did not disappoint. Allen Toussaint was a courtly host and a consummate professional who submerged his own highly individual piano style to do whatever Paul wanted. A succession of local legends dropped by to meet the McCartneys and jam, including the two great pedagogues of Southern blues, Professor Longhair and Dr John, and Sea-Saint's famous house band, the Meters. At a press reception aboard a Mississippi riverboat, Paul was evasive about the album's name, but Linda let it out: '*Venus and Mars*.'

In contrast with this positive creative atmosphere, there was still unrest in Wings' ranks. After six months, drummer Geoff Britton remained at loggerheads with lead guitar Jimmy McCulloch and noticeably isolated from the others. His problem was the same as Pete Best's long ago in the baby Beatles: neither his playing nor his face seemed to fit. And a fortnight into the *Venus and Mars* sessions, Paul fired him, making him the third Wingsman to fall to earth in less than two years.

Luckily, this was a part of the world where high-grade musicians grew as plentifully as watermelons. As a temporary stand-in, Paul hired 26-year-old Joe English, a migrant from Syracuse, New York, who'd been playing with a band called the Tall Dogs Orchestra in Macon, Georgia. Besides being an excellent drummer, he had a good singing voice and an easy-going manner, and was soon offered a permanent place in the line-up – by his own account, 'the greatest thing that's ever happened to me since my first Communion'.

In March, Paul and Linda returned to LA to finish off the album at the Wally Heider Studios and attend the Grammys for a double triumph. With sales now at five million, *Band on the Run* received the award for Best Pop Vocal Performance by a Group. It was also named Best-Produced Non-Classical Album, finally recompensing its engineer, Geoff Emerick, for his ordeals with Nigeria's insect life.

The evening also brought the kind of embarrassing moment usually associated with the Oscars. To present the award for Record of the Year, host Andy Williams introduced 'two of the most prolific talents of this or any other musical generation . . . They have both recently parted from respective partners of whom you may have heard. Now they're alone and adrift in the sea of rocky royalties.' It was John and Paul, though in this case the latter's surname was Simon.

The new, domesticated John was a strange-looking figure with shoulder-length hair, a black beret and an orchid corsage, all vaguely reminiscent of his Aunt Mimi back home in Britain. In a front seat sat Yoko, on guard against any further signals that he might get back to writing with Paul.

The co-presenters recited a slightly bitchy script that cannot but have soured *Band on the Run*'s achievement a little: 'Hello. I'm John and I used to play with my partner, Paul.' . . . 'Hello, I'm Paul and I used to play with my partner, Art [Garfunkel].' The award went to 'I Honestly Love You' by Olivia Newton-John, but was collected for her by Garfunkel, to Simon's obvious discomfiture.

'Are you guys getting back together?' Simon took the opportunity to ask John on behalf of the assembled industry bigwigs.

'Are *you* guys getting back together?' John quipped – then, in a mischievous aside to Garfunkel: 'Where's Linda?'

The answer was: taking the heat for Paul as usual. Late one night, they were driving along Santa Monica Boulevard with the three children asleep in the back when he accidentally ran a red light and was pulled over by the police. Smelling a telltale fragrance, the officers searched their car, to find 17 grammes of marijuana in Linda's bag and a still-smouldering joint under a passenger seat.

To protect Paul's visa, and thinking the cops might go easier on an American citizen, Linda claimed sole responsibility for the stash. She was taken in and booked for possession, with a further charge of 'contributing to the delinquency of a minor' because Heather, Mary and Stella had been in the car at the time.

Paul drove the girls back to their hotel, then hurried to the police station to find Linda's bail had been set at $500. Though he'd long since given up his royal/Beatle habit of carrying no money, there was still only $200 in his wallet. Luckily, his old Apple factotum, Peter Brown, was staying at the Beverly Hills Hotel and rushed over to make good the deficit. The LAPD proving more tolerant than Campbeltown Constabulary, both charges against Linda were later dropped.

The album wrapped with a party aboard the great Cunard liner *Queen Mary*, now retired from transatlantic service and moored at Long Beach as a tourist attraction and hotel. Three hundred and fifty guests, including Bob Dylan, Marvin Gaye, Joni Mitchell, Jimmy Page, Robert Plant and Cher, watched performances by Paul's new New Orleans friends, Lee Dorsey, Ernie K-Doe, Professor Longhair and the Meters.

John and Yoko had returned to New York by then, but George turned up with his new partner, Olivia Arias. It was his first public appearance with Paul for almost four years, and in no time another Beatles reunion rumour went flashing around the world.

Venus and Mars was released in May, with a cover on which a red and a gold orb hung in an indigo void like a couple of soft-boiled billiard balls. An accompanying TV ad showed the band skylarking around a billiard table, watched by Linda in a curly blonde wig.

When the ball she potted failed to reach its pocket, Paul inflated his cheeks and blew it in for her.

The music press was generally underwhelmed, none more so than *Rolling Stone* which, 18 months earlier, had hailed *Band on the Run* as his solo breakthrough and Linda's musical emancipation. Reviewer Paul Nelson drew the kind of disparaging parallels with John and Yoko's Plastic Ono Band that Paul hoped to have left far behind. 'The ghost of [John's] sincerity not only haunts but accentuates the cool calculation of the McCartney project,' Nelson wrote, 'and a jarring primal scream or two might make me feel less enraged by Paul and Linda's chic, unconvincing and blatant bid to be enshrined as pop music's Romeo and Juliet.'

The punters did not agree: *Venus and Mars* reached number one in Britain and America, was quickly certified gold and would go on to sell ten million. Just as *Band on the Run* had shown no trace of Nigeria, so *Venus and Mars* showed none of New Orleans, Mardi Gras, the French Quarter, shrimp gumbo or Tennessee Williams. Allen Toussaint's contribution was all but buried. From the bravura opening title track and its segue into 'Rockshow', everything was customised for the Glam Rock stage. The printed lyrics contained a lapse from Paul's usual punctiliousness; Venus and Mars were said to be 'alright tonight'. The Liverpool Institute schoolboy of yore, with his dad's dictionary behind him, would never have been guilty of such a slip.

The album's runaway hit single was 'Listen to What the Man Said', a buoyant love song with an almost gospel tinge (i.e. 'the Man Upstairs') that went to number one in America but only six in ungodly Britain. Rock authors Roy Carr and Tony Tyler later cited it as an example of how 'artful and sensitive production [could] elevate what had originally been a piece of inconsequential whimsy into what can only be called High Pop'.

In Britain, the main target of critical ire was a track where Paul's desire to be young and Glam-Rocky seemed to go out of the window. As the finale to side two, Wings played the theme music to *Crossroads*, the famously cheap but hugely popular early-evening soap broadcast four times a week by Associated Television. The fact that ATV had made off with the copyrights to all his Beatles songs made this identification with cardboard sets, wooden acting and wonky screen-graphics all the more mystifying. It seemed yet another symptom of the craving for universal acceptance that pushed Wings into areas like 'Mary Had a Little Lamb' and their recent commercial for Mother's Pride sliced bread, for which he'd written a special 60-second song.

Paul responded that it was simply a joke, although one not without relevance since the preceding track, 'Treat Her Gently', about lonely old people, must apply to a large section of *Crossroads'* 15 million audience. Joke or not, it played over the soap's closing credits, heightening one ludicrous cliffhanger over another, until the show was taken off the air in the mid-1980s.

Actually, *Crossroads* wasn't such a bad metaphor for Paul and Wings in the summer of 1975. 'We'd come from very small beginnings, after the hugeness of the Beatles,' he would later reflect. 'We'd wanted to start something up, just to continue playing music. Then we'd wanted it to be something cool that was us, that allowed us to be free and experiment. Then we'd wanted to practise and get a really good group. So we'd finally done all those things. Now, here we were poised to take it out and show off a bit.'

So, after Wings Over Kintyre, Wings Over Universities, Wings Over Britain and Wings Over Europe, there was to be Wings Over the World, a year-long tour beginning in September with the UK and Australia, continuing through 1976 with Europe, North America, then Europe again, a total of 66 shows winding up at London's Empire Pool arena in October. The guitarist Jerry Reed, whom Paul had got to know in Nashville, expressed astonishment that he still felt a need to go on the road: 'Man, if I was Paul McCartney, I'd buy the road.'

The itinerary was also to have included Japan. But early in November, as Paul was starting its Australian leg in Melbourne, the Japanese government refused him entry because of his Scottish drug conviction three years earlier. Though he'd already received a visa from the Japanese Consulate in London, it had been rescinded on direct instructions from the country's Minister of Justice.

Paul protested that neither Australia nor America had sought to exclude him on those grounds, but the Minister remained immovable. Instead, his Japanese fans had to make do with a TV documentary of Wings' Melbourne show and a filmed greeting from him, Linda and the band, squashed together matily on a couch, performing a snatch of 'Bluebird'.

'We'll see you next time,' he promised – rashly, it would prove. 'Sayonara.'

34

'They'd saved themselves for him'

The fourth track on *Venus and Mars*, 'You Gave Me the Answer', was not merely a nod to the vogue for 1930s pastiche epitomised by London's Biba superstore and vocal groups like Manhattan Transfer. It was also the most pointed of many musical tributes over the years which Paul, consciously or subconsciously, had paid to his father.

From the moment he found his own voice on record, there had been constant reminders of the modestly extrovert cotton salesman who'd been his first – and only – music teacher, banging away on the old upright piano at 20 Forthlin Road. It was to 'Gentleman Jim' McCartney that he owed his enduring love of the traditional and sentimental, of northern brass bands, sonorous Anglican hymns and old Hollywood show tunes, that helped to lift his songs so many miles above any competitor's, bar one.

So now with Wings, his drive to reinvent himself, and surpass everything he'd done in the Beatles, often gave way to a rather touching desire to please his father. Along with his *Ram* album in 1971, he'd made an instrumental version under the pseudonym 'Percy Thrillington', recorded in big-band style with easy-listening vocal accompaniment by the Mike Sammes Singers. The Thrillington character was modelled on high-society bandleaders like Harry Roy and Lew Stone who'd been the pop idols of Jim's youth, just as 'You Gave Me the Answer' was a tight-lipped Mayfair love song in the style of Jack Buchanan or Noël Coward.

Jim was now in his seventies and in rapidly declining health due to rheumatoid arthritis and osteoarthritis and bronchial problems caused by a lifetime of smoking. He still lived on the Cheshire Wirral with his 28-years-younger second wife, Angie. But his severely reduced mobility had made it impossible for him to remain at 'Rembrandt', the house in Heswall Paul had given him on his retirement. Paul had therefore bought back 'Rembrandt', enabling Jim and Angie to afford a more convenient bungalow in Beverley Drive in the nearby village of Gayton.

Now that Jim could no longer get to Scotland, Paul always called in on him during the long drive there from London or back. On one return journey, he arrived wearing shoes still caked in mud from High Park Farm. Outraged that he could go around looking so scruffy, Jim insisted on lending him more presentable footwear, a pair of deeply square suede Hush Puppies. Next day when he met David Litchfield at Abbey Road, he still had on the Hush Puppies. 'It amused him to be wearing his dad's shoes,' Litchfield recalls. '"You watch," he said to me, "by tomorrow, everyone around here will be in Hush Puppies, too." And they were.'

Jim had always thought Paul couldn't ever give him a more thrilling present than his racehorse, Drake's Drum – but the summer of 1974 proved him wrong. During his years of leading the Jim Mac Jazz Band, he'd composed a tune for himself to play on the piano entitled 'Eloise'. His family knew about this sole excursion into composing, though with typical modesty Jim always refused to say he'd 'written' it, believing himself disqualified from the company of Cole Porter or Rodgers and Hart by being unable to read or write music. Even after his son had flouted that rule dozens of times over, all he would ever say about 'Eloise' was that he'd 'made it up'.

Paul had heard the tune often enough for it to be engraved on his memory like a pianola-roll. And during Wings' rehearsal-sessions in Nashville, he recorded it as a part-country, part-jazz instrumental with an ad hoc group called the Country Hams, including Chet Atkins on guitar and Floyd Cramer on piano. Since a song named

'Eloise' had already been released by Barry Ryan, he renamed it 'Walking in the Park with Eloise'.

Proving to Jim that he truly had 'written' a number which Nashville's two greatest instrumentalists were happy to perform would be a memory to treasure. So would his dad's delight, as ever imperfectly concealed by a dig in the ribs and a murmur of 'You daft buggcr'.

At the beginning of 1976, Jim's condition took a sharp turn for the worse. Until then, Angie had been his only carer, helped by her teenage daughter, Ruth, whom Jim had adopted on their marriage. When he could no longer leave his bed, his sisters Gin and Millie and other Liverpool relatives told Angie he should go into a care home, assuring her that 'Paul will pay for everything'. But Jim had made her promise long before that he'd die in his own bed, and both Paul and Mike wanted the same.

Thereafter, she and Ruth took turns in giving him round-the-clock care. 'There was nothing wrong with his mind,' Ruth McCartney recalls. 'He'd often sit up in bed in the middle of the night and say he fancied a boiled onion or a tin of Crosse and Black-well barley soup. Whatever it was, either Mum or I would be there to get it for him.'

Paul drove up to see him early in March, just before setting off for Europe with Wings. 'He brought a new photograph of himself with Linda and the children, which Jim put beside his bed,' his stepmother remembers. 'As he was leaving, he put his arms around me and said, "I'll never forget what you've done for my dad, Angie. You'll never want for anything again."'

On 18 March, Jim died of bronchial pneumonia. His last thoughts were of the gentle, refined Irish wife he'd lost to breast cancer exactly 20 years earlier. 'I'll be with Mary soon,' he whispered to Angie.

As a 14-year-old, Paul had coped with the trauma of his mother's death by 'putting a shell around me' – and now seemed to do the same again. The day after Jim's passing, he went ahead with Wings' scheduled pre-tour press conference, outwardly his usual chirpy, jokey self, then departed for the opening shows in Copenhagen.

Jim's funeral took place at Landican Crematorium, near Birkenhead, on 22 March. Paul was in Copenhagen and did not return home for the ceremony although Wings had no show that day and the journey by private jet would have been an easy one. '[He] would never face that kind of thing,' Mike McCartney later commented.

His Wings sidemen were not told of his bereavement. Even Denny Laine, who had known and liked Jim, only found out by accident later that month during a French television interview with Paul, the American teen-idol David Cassidy and himself. When the interviewer asked Paul about his parents, he simply replied that they were both dead, in a tone that discouraged any further inquiry. 'I was physically shocked on camera,' Laine would recall. 'But one thing you have to remember about Paul, he's a very, very private guy. He doesn't like to share certain things. He takes them on his own shoulders . . . He has to be out there looking like he's Paul McCartney, happy-go-lucky and not bothering the world with his problems.'

Angie continued to live at the bungalow in Gayton that Paul had enabled Jim and herself to buy, but her relationship with the McCartney family soon began to deteriorate. Jim's Liverpool relatives took it amiss that straight after the funeral she and Ruth had gone off on holiday to Spain – understandable enough after their months of arduous round-the-clock caring. Paul shared that disapproval and, despite his promise that his stepmother would 'never want for anything again', a rift opened up between them.

Angie, now widowed for the second time, was still only in her late forties, and needed to make a new life for herself. After Jim's death, she entered on what she now admits was an ill-advised business venture, a partnership in a theatrical agency. It was a failure, and when Paul declined to rescue it, she lost everything including the Gayton bungalow, which she'd mortgaged to fund the agency.

She and Ruth moved to London, where they did a total of five low-paid jobs between them, and a burglary of their rented flat took most of their remaining valuables. Desperately short of money, Angie sold her story to the *Sun* newspaper which, without her permission, headlined it 'THE MEAN SIDE OF PAUL McCARTNEY'. Several of Jim's family souvenirs had passed to her and a few years later. Paul was angered to read that she'd sold his birth certificate to an American memorabilia-collector – though in fact it was only a copy.

His stepsister Ruth, who'd taken up music with his encouragement, achieved some success as a singer-songwriter, signing with Jupiter/BMG records and releasing an album entitled *I Will Always Remember You* (in memory of Jim) which sold well outside the UK and reached number one in Russia. Angie never remarried, and mother and daughter stayed together, living in Germany, Australia and latterly on America's West Coast, launching a multimedia company with Ruth's third husband, producer Martin Nethercutt.

Now an octogenarian, Paul's stepmother remains a vivacious, energetic figure with her own line of 'Mrs McCartney' organic teas and a daily blog. They haven't communicated since the mid-1970s but, watching him from afar, Angie's constant thought is that 'Jimmy Mac', her pet name for his dad, would be proud of him.

Wings arrived in America in 1976 exactly a decade after the Beatles' last tour there, and with no guarantee of even moderate success. Despite Paul's latter *Billboard* chart-toppers, he knew he was taking a huge chance in performing without John, George and Ringo in the land where Beatlemania lingered on most stubbornly. American cinemas were currently showing a film comprising footage of the Beatles in the early and mid-Sixties, whose lines around the block rivalled those for *A Hard Day's Night* or *Help!* Whenever Paul's mop-topped face appeared on-screen, the squeals were as demented as ever.

Stateside Beatles-reunion rumours were always at their biggest and brassiest. In February, a Los Angeles promoter named Bill Sargent had offered a guaranteed $50 million for a single performance back together, anywhere in the world they cared to name, to be shown on closed-circuit television. Sargent was said to be 'in talks' with George's lawyer while John – supposedly the immovable obstacle to all such ideas – privately told Apple's managing director Neil Aspinall, 'I'd stand on my head in the corner for that kind of money.'

Since then, Mike Matthews, head of the Electro-Harmonix guitar-accessory company, had placed a rival bid of $3 million down with a percentage of the TV syndication that could have taken the Beatles' share to around $30 million. Again, no outright refusal came from three of them; only Paul's lawyers, Eastman & Eastman, responded that neither Matthews' nor Sargent's offer was even being considered.

Midway through Wings Over America Paul would turn 34, an age once thought inconceivable for a rock star. On the tour's Australian leg in late 1975, a tactless newsman had asked if he wasn't getting a bit old for all this. 'Ancient,' he answered through gritted teeth. 'Just come along and see the show and then tell me if you still think I'm past it.'

With all these pressures weighing, he prepared Wings for America with four months' intensive rehearsal in between the tour's UK, European and Australian legs. He also boosted their line-up with a four-man horn section comprising his old Liverpool and Hamburg friend Howie Casey and three top session-players from Sea-Saint Studios in New Orleans. There was a dress rehearsal at Elstree film studios in front of an invited audience including Ringo and Harry Nilsson – kept a total secret in case Ringo's presence set off another reunion story.

Among Paul and Linda's 20-strong entourage were their housekeeper, Rose Martin, to look after Mary and Stella, and a tutor for 13-year-old Heather. There would also be the first 'artist-in-residence' ever taken on a rock tour, a young painter named Humphrey Ocean to whom it would hardly be a novelty. Ocean also played bass in Kilburn and the High Roads, a new London band led by a then unknown Ian Dury, whom Paul particularly rated.

To soften up the US market, there was a new studio album,

Wings at the Speed of Sound – for which Humphrey Ocean had designed the inner sleeve – and a single, 'Silly Love Songs', Paul's riposte to critics who complained his music was too lightweight: 'Some people want to fill the world with silly love songs . . . and what's wrong with that I'd like to know?' Nothing apparently: it spent five weeks at the top of the *Billboard* chart and would be his biggest-ever American hit.

In the end, all this meticulous pre-planning was derailed by Jimmy McCulloch, ever the loose cannon of Wings' line-up. During February's European leg, he had a boozy scuffle with another angelic-looking popster, David Cassidy, in a Paris hotel bar, sustaining a broken finger that left him unable to play his guitar. Departure for the US therefore had to be put back a month. The media were told Jimmy had slipped on a wet marble floor while getting out of his hotel bath.

America at the time was gearing up for a presidential election that would see Republican incumbent Gerald Ford (a stopgap after Richard Nixon had left office, disgraced by the Watergate scandal), pitted against a dizzy-looking peanut farmer from Georgia named Jimmy Carter. 'But none of it impinged on us,' Humphrey Ocean remembers. 'Wherever we went in the country, the only big story in the papers or on TV was Paul.'

To spare the children the boredom of travelling huge distances between shows, the McCartneys had rented four comfortable family homes, in Dallas, New York, Chicago and LA, basing the girls at each one in turn, flying out to gigs in a customised jet hired from Braniff Airlines, then returning the same night. The equipment and crew went by road in a convoy of giant white trucks, equipped with state-of-the-art citizen-band radios, the leading truck with 'WINGS' in vertical red letters along its roof, the second with 'OVER' and the third, 'AMERICA'.

The two youngest children were always around; angelic blonde Stella carried in her father's arms during meet-and-greets with fans; dark Mary, beaming minus one milk tooth from the rear window of a limo; both of them noisily rushing around, pretending to be aeroplanes, during pre-performance soundchecks. In those less fearful days, the only security watching over them was a fair-haired young giant in platform boots and flares known as Billy and said by Paul to have 'a heart of gold'.

He and Linda still attracted criticism for taking such little ones on the road, depriving them of childhood's normal, healthy routines and exposing them to the myriad horrid habits associated with rock stars. However, Mary McCartney recalls how she and her sister were always put to bed at the proper time, despite their pleas to stay up. 'Yes, there were parties,' Paul himself admits, 'but they were more *family* parties.'

In any case, Wings in their downtime were the healthiest, most outdoorsy rock band around, less likely to be found skulking in shuttered motel rooms than out on horseback with their leader. Denny Laine had learned to ride in Scotland and Jimmy McCulloch, too, proved adept at it. Galloping behind Paul and Linda, the uptight boy maestro visibly relaxed, his puckered, never-to-age face becoming as clear and uncomplicated as an extra child's.

The American shows were their most spectacular yet, with lasers, billowing smoke, exploding 'flash-pots', slow- and fast-motion effects and constantly changing back-projections including a film of the *Band on the Run* cover photo-shoot, with Clement Freud and Christopher Lee, and a homage to American *Marvel* comic books by David Hockney.

In a performance lasting almost two hours (as against the 30 minutes tops the Beatles used to do) Paul worked his way through *Wings at the Speed of Sound*, *Venus and Mars* and *Band on the Run*, as well as pre-Wings highlights like 'Maybe I'm Amazed'. There was also 'Let 'Em In', a soon-to-be-released second single from *Wings at the Speed of Sound* that carried another poignant memory of his father. At McCartney family gatherings in Liverpool, a constantly chiming doorbell used to announce relays of new partygoers while Jim tirelessly thumped away on the piano. On the record, an identical door-chime introduced fanciful guests, like 'Martin Luther' and 'Phil and Don' (Everly), along with true-life relatives Brother Michael, Uncle Albert and Auntie Gin.

Out of all Wings' many line-ups, Paul was always to consider this the best ever. His newest appointment, Joe English, was not only a fine drummer and a good harmony singer but a force for unity, hitting it off equally well with Denny Laine and the volatile Jimmy McCulloch. Best of all, the woman he loved and depended on for everything else was no longer regarded as the band's weakest link.

For years, Linda had struggled with the basic keyboard-chords he showed her, exasperating the highly skilled musicians in the band, feeding resentments and triggering rows, sometimes even exhausting Paul's patience. Once he'd blurted out that he could have had Billy Preston instead of her, but then instantly regretted it and apologised. Always she had been the first to admit: 'I'm not here because I'm the greatest keyboard-player. I'm here because we love each other.' Now she was a competent, if not brilliant, musician who no longer had to be hidden away at one side of the stage but could be placed on a high plinth behind him.

And with that, her deep discomfort – stage-embarrassment rather than stage-fright – had vanished. The great black arena spaces full of judgemental eyes that used to appal her now seemed positively welcoming. 'I find big stadiums really intimate,' she told one interviewer. 'I don't ever want to go back to the little ones.'

Throughout the show came reminders that Wings shouldn't be regarded as just a one-man band. Laine got to sing his 'Go Now', the Moody Blues' mega-hit from 1964, with Paul and Linda on backing vocals; Jimmy McCulloch sang his co-composition 'Medicine Jar'; and drummer Joe English took the lead vocal on 'Must Do Something About It'.

The interlude where Paul, Linda, Denny and Jimmy sat in a row playing 'Bluebird' seemed as intimate, harmonious and egalitarian as rock musicians could ever be. However, as the tour's artist-in-residence, Humphrey Ocean, had soon learned, democracy had its limits. 'Paul and Linda were always very friendly and open, but there was a moment when one had to step back,' he remembers.

'And after every show, they got in their limo and went off to their house, whichever one it was, and the band went to hotels.'

For the first time, Wings' set list included a selection of Paul's Beatles' songs: 'I've Just Seen a Face', 'Lady Madonna', 'Blackbird', 'Yesterday' and 'The Long and Winding Road'. To begin with, he introduced each one almost apologetically, as 'an old one you may remember'. Always a kind of muted tidal wave through the vast indoor darkness confirmed that indeed they did.

Unfortunately, the effect was to re-ignite questions from the media at every stop about a possible Beatles reunion for one or other of the multimillion-dollar paydays on offer. For a good two-thirds of the tour, the B-word ran through Paul's every interview:

Q. Have you seen the Beatles lately?
A. We run into each other and stuff. We're just good friends.
Q. Is Wings really a logical development from the Beatles?
A. Well, I've always written songs, but with the Beatles we only ever rehearsed for three days at the most. With this band, we rehearse a lot.
Q. Will Wings ever become as big as the Beatles?
A. I think it could be, funnily enough.
Q. How different is Wings from the Beatles?
A. They scream at our concerts, but they don't scream as much. People used to come and scream and didn't hear any of the music. Now they can.
Q. Do you want to bring back the Beatles?

Heedless of the answer, American TV news reporters, with their walrus moustaches and hideously striped shirts, went away and filed the stories their editors wanted: 'Tonight, maybe – just *maybe* – the four Beatles could be back onstage together. And if it happens, you'll know about it first on Eyewitness News.' In the end, Paul became so exasperated, he made up a little poem like those the world heavyweight boxing champion Muhammad Ali (whom he'd met on the Beatles' first American trip in 1964) was wont to deliver to taunt his opponent and predict his own victory:

The Beatles split in Sixty-nine and since then they've been doin' fine. And if that question doesn't cease, ain't no one gonna get no peace. And if you ask it just once more, I think I'm gonna break your jaw.

But by the time Wings Over America reached Seattle on 10 June, the tide had turned. An audience of 67,000 at the Kingdome broke the national attendance record at an indoor event. Paul was on the cover of *Time* ('McCartney Comes Back') and a slew of other magazines including *People* and *Creem*. 'McCartney has returned to the US victorious,' began a typical report. 'Alone of the ex-Beatles, he has formed a new band and it's that band that provides the popular music event of the year . . . making the same impact the Beatles made a decade ago, but with a new sound for a new generation.'

The tour would later be turned into a chart-topping triple live album and a cinema documentary, *Rockshow*, which was among the first productions distributed by Harvey Weinstein's Miramax company. Weinstein found a lucrative market on American college campuses, so taking Wings to audiences too young to mourn the Beatles – and giving Paul a US 'university tour' to bookend his modest British one of 1971.

After Seattle, the scenes of welcome were as wild as any in the Beatles years – but now for only one, not four. Tour artist Humphrey Ocean was on his way to filling eight sketchbooks, largely with portraits of individual audience-members reacting to Paul. 'The girls all had the same look on their faces,' Ocean recalls. 'They'd saved themselves for him, even though they all knew perfectly well he was already married.'

In his euphoria, Paul could even overlook another of Jimmy McCulloch's inexplicable mood swings after a show when the audience was roaring for an encore but McCulloch, for some reason, didn't want to do one. Instead of acting the big star boss, Paul simply grabbed him and bundled him back onstage where, with typical contrariness, he played his best all evening.

On 18 June, that much-dreaded thirty-fourth birthday, the tour personnel gave their star a surprise party featuring a Mexican mariachi band that Jim McCartney would have loved. There was also a piñata, a dangling papier mâché animal filled with sweets and toys that a blindfolded Paul had to break apart with a long stick. After a couple of wild flails, he caught it squarely and multicoloured goodies rained down. Not unlike Wings Over America in fact.

Three nights later at Inglewood Forum, Ringo suddenly jumped onstage, presented him with a bouquet and they hugged – both gestures utterly alien to young men in Liverpool when they were growing up. After the show, Ringo came backstage, pretending to be frog-marched with one arm pinned behind his back. But there was no mistaking the rekindled affection between them, nor Paul's pleasure when Ringo conceded that the show 'wasn't *so* bad . . . eight out of ten'.

His best birthday present of all was the TV reporter overheard doing a piece to camera against the noise of '20,000 people on their seats . . . Onstage there's no John Lennon, no George Harrison, no Ringo Starr – just Paul McCartney and Wings. And for everyone here tonight, that seems to be plenty.'

The Apple rooftop concert, January 1969. Destined to be imitated by other bands down the decades . . .

Above Tap your troubles away: the 1973 TV special *James Paul McCartney* featured Paul in a Busby Berkeley routine.

Right Woolly sentiment: performing 'Mary Had A Little Lamb' with sheep back-up.

Left Hiding out in Scotland with Linda, Martha and a beard after his brutal sidelining by John, George and Ringo.

Cover of the Wings album that finally won over the critics.

Wings' fourth line-up: Paul, Linda, Denny Laine, Jimmy McCulloch and Geoff Britton.

Country life: Paul and Linda with Heather, Mary and baby Stella. Thanks to Linda, all their children grew up in the saddle.

Magical Mystery Tour revisited: psychedelic transport for Wings Over Europe.

The McCartneys with some of their menagerie. Vets were regularly called to treat ducks with broken legs.

On the road again: Paul and Linda attracted much criticism for taking their children on tour.

Toyko bust: *(above)* Paul under arrest in Tokyo, 1980. *(below)* The culprit suitcase is put on display.

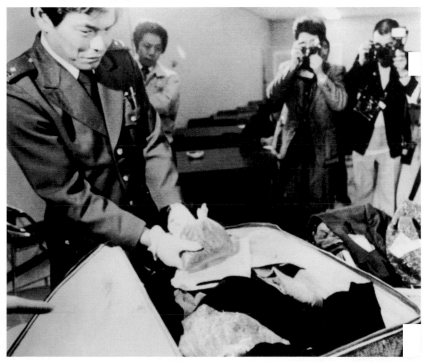

'What do you call a dog with Wings?' ran the cruel sexist jibe when Paul first put Linda into the band. But she gradually won over her critics and became a competent musician.

Paul with conductor Carl Davis after the premiere of his *Liverpool Oratorio* in Liverpool Cathedral, 1991. Years before, he'd been rejected for its choir.

35

'Oi, Paul, you know that Mull of Kintyre? It's fakking great!'

After 20 years, thanks largely to the Beatles – and one of them in particular – pop music appeared to have civilised itself. But in 1976–77, the process was violently thrown into reverse.

Britain by then had come a long way from the Swinging Sixties' world-enchanting sounds and styles and the youthful optimism so perfectly caught in Paul songs like 'I'll Follow the Sun' or 'Getting Better' or 'We Can Work It Out' or 'Good Day Sunshine'. Under James Callaghan's impotent Labour government, the country was plagued by runaway inflation and despotic trade unions whose incessant strikes – sanctimoniously renamed 'industrial action' – paralysed public transport, put the sick and vulnerable at risk without compunction and left mountains of uncollected garbage rotting in the streets.

Unlike the pampered, adulated children of the Sixties, young Britons in the Seventies grew up with pessimism and cynicism, feeling alienated from a society which seemed to have little to offer them but the dole-queue. And pop music, always hitherto the voice and solace of youth, became part of their alienation. In truth it didn't seem to belong to them at all, but stayed firmly in the grip of the Sixties generation, now 30 years old and more. Britain's biggest star bands in the mid-Seventies were exponents of so-called 'symphonic' – or pomp – rock, like Yes and Emerson, Lake &

Palmer, whose immensely long and earnest concept albums, the distant offspring of *Sgt. Pepper*, had titles such as *Tales from Topographic Oceans* and *Brain Salad Surgery* and whose drum solos alone could go on as long as 20 minutes. The singles charts, meanwhile, were clogged with twee novelty songs and knee-jerk rock 'n' roll pastiche.

Hence punk rock, a genre born a few years earlier in bohemian downtown New York, but now reshaped – or, rather, unshaped – to reflect the aggression and nihilism of late-Seventies British youth. Its founding band, the Sex Pistols, made their debut in October 1976 with a single entitled 'Anarchy in the UK' whose first words, in the shockingly unmusical voice of lead singer John Lydon – aka Johnny Rotten – were 'I am the Antichrist!'

The Pistols sent a wave of revulsion through Britain like nothing since the arrival of rock 'n' roll 20 years earlier. In December, they ensured the loathing of the media and the adoration of their followers by using four-letter words on an early-evening TV chat show. After being dropped by the Beatles' old record company, EMI, and getting kicked off another mainstream company, A&M, after just one week, they were signed by the fledgling Virgin label whose owner, Richard Branson, used to loiter so observantly around the Apple house.

Pop music changed overnight – and fashion, too, for punk rock brought with it a fully-evolved aesthetic created by the Pistols' manager Malcolm McLaren and his designer girlfriend Vivienne Westwood mixing affected poverty with the taboo concepts of sexual fetishism and self-mutilation.

The long-lingering tailored Sixties look, another legacy from the Beatles, was obliterated, as were distinctions between male and female. Both sexes wore the same shaven heads with Mohican crests dyed fluorescent red or orange, the same torn T-shirts and jeans, army-style boots, S&M chains and spiked wristbands or neck-collars. In the first-ever recorded outbreak of mass masochism, boys and girls alike had metal ornamentation implanted in the tenderest areas of their flesh: rings through their noses, lips, nipples and navels, studs in their tongues and eyebrows and out-size safety-pins hanging from their cheeks.

Punk bands sprang up all over the country, needing as little to get started as the skiffle groups of Lennon and McCartney's boyhood. The atmosphere was somewhat like the fall of the Bastille; the pomp rockers hiding in their mansions, with their redundant synthesisers and strobes, listening for the sound of the tumbril.

Early in 1977, the Sex Pistol's bass guitarist, Glen Matlock, was sacked for having musical aspirations: he admired the Beatles and sought to model his bass style on Paul McCartney's. In his place came 19-year-old John Ritchie, aka Sid Vicious, who couldn't play a note and became as great a draw as Johnny Rotten, chiefly by stripping down to grubby underpants to reveal a torso striped with self-inflicted knife cuts and physically assaulting members of his audience.

Paul might have been expected to feel most threatened by punk rock's Year Zero, yet he refused to join the chorus of revulsion and contempt. The antics of Johnny Rotten and Sid Vicious were nothing he hadn't seen from that proto-punk John Lennon during the Beatles' Hamburg era. Besides, he recalled only too well the hostility of older 'professional' musicians in the mid-Fifties towards untutored boys like himself who wanted to play rock 'n' roll.

He and Linda took to using punk names: 'Noxious Fumes' and 'Vile Lin'. When 13-year-old Heather started playing the Damned, Mum and Dad had to listen too, and Linda was later heard singing 'Neat Neat Neat' ('No crime if there ain't no law/ No more cops left to mess you around'). Paul wrote a joke punk song for Heather entitled 'Boil Crisis', about 'a kid named Sid' who gets 'scarred with a rod in a pyramid', though it had rather too much content and rhymed too exactly to carry real conviction.

Anarchy in the UK music business there might be but in Paul's personal music business there was steady, methodical expansion and diversification.

In 1977, Paul McCartney Productions Ltd, now known as MPL, moved from its one-room office in Greek Street to Soho Square, the small green oasis separating Soho from the clamour of Oxford Street. The new premises were a six-storey Edwardian building on the north-west side of the square – not as elegant as the eighteenth-century houses that adjoined it but enjoying the McCartneyesque distinction of being number one.

Its interior was extensively renovated and decorated in art deco style by the designers of the Biba superstore in Kensington. The ground floor acquired a dark brown façade with an under-stated *mpl* and two curved plate-glass windows reminiscent of an old-fashioned shop, though showing no trace of the valuable merchandise within.

Paul's office was on the second floor, a large, airy room with oak panelling and dark blue carpet and upholstery patterned with musical notes. In one corner stood a rainbow-hued Wurlitzer juke-box, stocked with classic rock 'n' roll hits. Round the walls hung a selection of Linda's rock star photographs and two paintings by her father's client and friend, Willem de Kooning. An arched window overlooked the square's small central park with its faux-Tudor chalet and constant crowd of shopworkers, tourists, drug-dealers and meths-drinkers. Paul had always got his best song-ideas from simply looking out of windows, and the scene below promised plenty.

As head of his own company, he put into practice all the lessons he'd learned the hard way from Apple. One Soho Square would have none of the mad extravagance and parasitic hangers-on that had done for 3 Savile Row. Under managing director Brian Brolly, a small team, dealing both with Wings and MPL's ever-accumulating other interests, was kept continually at full stretch. The most friv-olous activity was the running of Wings' fan club – known as 'the Wings Fun Club' to underline its family appeal. Its organiser, Sue Cavanaugh, sent out a newsletter called *Club Sandwich* that included a punningly-named letters page, 'Sue's Lettuce', and a crossword compiled by Paul's cousin, Bert Danher. Wings' juvenile fans were encouraged to improve their word power just as he'd once been by his father and cousin Bert.

John, George and Ringo had by now finally rid themselves of Allen Klein, paying $4.2 million of the almost $19 million severance package Klein had sought. Paul played no part in the long drawn-out and costly legal process; when its conclusion was announced, he gave an interview to the *Daily Express*, reflecting with justifiable smugness on his foresight in 1969 and pooh-poohing the idea that Klein had made him a fortune along with his fellow Beatles. Merely between 1974 and 1976, he claimed to have earned more from Wings 'than in all those other so-called boom years'.

Even so, deals that Klein had done for the future release of Beatles music added significantly to the income rolling into 1 Soho Square. In 1973, EMI issued two compilation albums, one covering the years 1962–66, the other 1967–70 – known as the red and blue albums because of their covers – that topped the UK and American charts and would continue selling for the rest of the decade.

Further additional revenue derived from ATV/Northern Songs' marketing of Lennon–McCartney compositions. In 1974, Liverpool playwright Willy Russell, who'd seen the Beatles at the Cavern as a schoolboy, scored a West End hit with *John, Paul, George, Ringo . . . and Bert*. The last-named was a fictitious member of the Quarrymen, seen in later life attending a Wings concert and fondly reflecting on the Fab Four's career. Beatles music was licensed to the production, though performed by a single vocalist, Barbara Dickson.

Russell's play had depicted the break-up accurately but a segment shown on television that Christmas was edited in such a way that Paul appeared solely responsible and blameworthy. He was highly incensed, and Russell's assurance that the play had been misrepresented could not completely placate him. Later, when a film version was mooted, he used his influence with ATV to stop it.

In 1977, a show called *Beatlemania*, with Lennon–McCartney music licensed by ATV's American division, became a Broadway smash hit. Paul greatly disliked the production and there were meetings between his lawyer and father-in-law, Lee Eastman, and ATV's New York chief, Sam Trust, that seemed to foreshadow a withdrawal of his work. In the end, however, the 'fabulous' royalties accruing to MPL persuaded him to let the show run and run.

His own songs for the Beatles might not belong to him, but by now he owned an impressive collection of other people's. Under the guidance of Lee Eastman, he had been steadily buying up American music-publishing companies, most of them controlling the old standards and show tunes his father had so loved. Classics of songwriting and musical theatre were little valued in the Seventies, so they could be had at bargain prices and also brought substantial tax advantages to the buyer.

The most satisfying such acquisition resulted from a chance meeting between his brother-in-law, John Eastman, and a lawyer friend on a New York bus. The friend mentioned he was in the process of selling the Nor-Va-Jak company, which published the songs of Paul's teenage hero, Buddy Holly.

Nor-Va-Jak already had a prospective buyer, John Eastman's friend said, but he was being exasperatingly slow to close the deal. His name: Allen Klein. Eastman recognised the typical Klein delaying tactics and jumped at this chance to score off his old adversary. 'I said, "MPL will buy the company and if you come over to my office right now, we'll sign the papers." Paul got it for $150,000, which it soon earned back several times over every year.'

He thus came to own the songs which had most inspired him to perform and write, among them 'That'll Be the Day', the Beatles' first wobbly little recording together. So elated was he that in September 1976 he inaugurated a 'Buddy Holly Week' in London, to coincide with what would have been Holly's fortieth birthday, inviting the subject's former manager and producer, Norman Petty, over from New Mexico as guest of honour. At a welcome lunch, attended by music-biz VIPs and the media, Petty presented him with a slightly sick souvenir – the cufflinks Buddy had been wearing on that fatal plane trip with Ritchie Valens and the Big Bopper in February 1959.

*

The first of what would be Paul's only two record releases in 1977 seemed as far as he could possibly get from the punk pandemonium. In April, he finally put out *Thrillington*, the easy-listening instrumental version of the *Ram* album he'd produced six years previously, largely to please his father, but then shelved because of the formation of Wings. *Thrillington* sold only a handful of copies and the media were baffled as to why he should devote such effort to a project so removed from the screeching cockatoo-crested, nipple-pierced zeitgeist. Had he completely lost touch with popular taste, many commentators wondered – or just become too grand to pay it any heed?

Early in the year, he'd taken Wings back to Abbey Road to start the follow-up to *Venus and Mars*. But it soon became clear that everyone – himself included – was still drained by the Wings Over the World tour. Linda, now pregnant with their third child, had special need of rest and recreation. He therefore resumed the practice of recording in sunny foreign parts, this time choosing the American Virgin Islands on the recommendation of engineer Geoff Emerick, who'd recently worked there with another band. Denny Laine, who loved boats, persuaded him the album should be made actually at sea.

A large yacht, the *Fair Carol*, was chartered and a five-strong technical team, led by Emerick, flown out to convert its stern into a studio with a 24-track desk. Two support vessels were also engaged: the *Samala*, a converted minesweeper, to accommodate the band, roadies and catering facilities, and a trimaran, the *El Toro*, for Paul, Linda and the children. No other wives or girlfriends were invited.

For several weeks, the flotilla cruised around the islands of St Croix, St John and St Thomas, dropping anchor in pre-selected idyllic bays. The days were spent sunbathing, swimming, snorkelling and petting the dolphins who swam up to watch with the wondering eyes of old-time Beatles fans. Recording took place in the evenings, followed by drinking and jamming on the open decks in the velvety night. Paul wrote a mini-musical for Mary and Stella entitled 'The Two Little Fairies', which they performed with his piano accompaniment, to general rapture. Reflecting this family seaside holiday atmosphere, the album was provisionally named *Water Wings*.

It wasn't all plain sailing, however: the improvised aquatic studio created numerous technical problems and a series of mishaps dogged Paul's crew. Alan Crowder, his invaluable fixer and factotum, slipped down a companionway, broke a foot and had to hobble around on crutches. Denny Laine got severe sunstroke, Jimmy McCulloch went temporarily deaf, and the dangerous proximity of seawater and power cables resulted in Geoff Emerick receiving a nasty electric shock in one leg. Paul himself, attempting a too-ambitous jump from one vessel, landed badly and was lucky not to break something.

The crew had brought along a liberal cargo of marijuana, thinking it could be smoked at sea in perfect privacy and safety, forgetting that the island paradise was an outpost of the United States where greater rather than lesser caution in such things ought to be exercised.

Jamming at anchor in the harbour at St John, Wings breached noise regulations that forbade even the playing of transistor radios and, within minutes, the *Fair Carol* found herself being boarded by paramilitary rangers from the island's national park. Discovering the culprits to be rock musicians, they made a cursory search for drugs but found none and departed after levying a $15 spot fine. They contacted their colleagues in the US Customs Service, who subsequently visited all three vessels, again finding nothing illegal but issuing a stern warning that they might return.

The episode worsened relations between Paul and the skipper of the *El Toro*, who had smelt marijuana smoke wafting from the McCartneys' cabin – and for whom a drugs-offence would mean professional ruin. After an angry confrontation, Paul moved his family living-quarters to another trimaran, *Wanderlust*. It would all go into a song of that name, destined not to be released for five years, by which time it would seem small stuff indeed.

In June, Queen Elizabeth II reached the twenty-fifth anniversary of her Coronation – the event which had brought 11-year-old Paul his first public writing award. All over Britain, the Silver Jubilee was celebrated in a manner barely changed from Victorian times, with flags, bunting, street parties and commemorative china mugs.

Only one thing marred the tributes to a sovereign whose unchangingness in a growingly insecure world was suddenly noticed and marvelled at. This was the Sex Pistols' second single, a shrieking parody of the National Anthem whose lyric rhymed 'queen' with 'fascist regime' and whose cover showed Her Majesty with a punk safety-pin through her cheek. Virgin Records' boss, Richard Branson, released it on Jubilee Day, 4 June, and held its launch party on a Thames riverboat moored beside the Houses of Parliament.

The single was banned by the BBC and almost every commercial radio station, but still went to number two. Some music papers refused to print its name or that of the Sex Pistols, simply leaving their place in the Top 10 a blank. On the Pistols' subsequent 'Anarchy in the UK' tour, so many shows were cancelled by outraged theatre-managements or local authorities that the destination sign on the front of the band's bus read 'Nowhere'.

Wings by now had returned to the McCartneys' Scottish estate to continue work in the barn-studio now known as Spirit of Ranachan. Linda's baby was due in September and Paul wanted the final weeks of her pregnancy to be as unstressful as possible.

They would hardly be that. Among the community dispersed around the estate were Denny Laine's wife, Jo Jo, and their children, Laine and Heidi. Jo Jo deeply resented her exclusion from the Virgin Isles trip and complained incessantly about the accommodation at Low Ranachan cottage, which she later described as 'a couple of old chairs and some ragged pee-stained mattresses'.

Lead guitarist Jimmy McCulloch was even less in a mood to be exiled to Scotland for an indefinite period. He had been deeply unsettled by the punk explosion which labelled him a 'dinosaur' at the age of only 24. Under Wings' new moonlighting charter, he was simultaneously playing in a trio named White Line with his drummer brother Jack. White Line signed with EMI at the same time as the Sex Pistols, and one day the two bands had found themselves in the same pub near the company's Manchester Square headquarters. Jimmy shouted at the Pistols that they were crap and, in the altercation that followed, physically attacked one of them, whose name he took pride in not knowing.

He, too, disliked his quarters with the roadies at Low Ranachan, which he referred to as 'the bunker'. One night, in the grip of boredom as much as booze or drugs, he invaded the storeroom where Linda kept the eggs from her hens meticulously arranged, helped himself to a dozen or so and began hurling them against the living-room wall. This wanton waste reduced Linda to tears and a furious Paul ordered him off the premises.

A few days later, Steve Marriott telephoned from London to say that Jimmy would be joining a relaunched version of Marriott's band, the Small Faces. He himself then came on the line to confirm his resignation from Wings.

Paul shed no tears over the loss of a sideman who, although brilliant, had caused havoc within the band, not least by his continual sniping at Linda's musicianship. 'It's a pity he's leaving, but problems have been building up for quite a while now and the rest of us are happy to carry on without him.' Jimmy's valedictory statement said they'd 'had some good times' and – still provokingly – that 'although Linda doesn't know much about music, she's a nice chick'.

Although Wings was never really the right band for Jimmy McCulloch, it proved the apogee of his career. The Small Faces relaunch came to nothing and he moved on to form another trio, Wild Horses, with his brother Jack, then abandoned that for an unremembered band named the Dukes. In 1979, he was to die of a heart attack after a heroin overdose, aged 26.

Without a lead guitarist, Wings' album was temporarily stalled – but Paul never could stop working. Things with Jo Jo at Low

Ranachan being what they were, Denny Laine had fallen into the habit of walking over to High Park Farm each morning to have breakfast with the McCartneys. One day when Denny arrived, Paul already had a guitar out and was strumming the chorus of a song which he said had been in his mind for the past couple of years.

He had noticed how long it had been since any composer or poet came up with a Scottish anthem in the super-patriotic genre of 'Scotland the Brave' and 'The Hundred Pipers'. He'd therefore decided to write one – an ambitious, not to say audacious idea for a non-Scot, albeit of Scottish ancestry filtered through Ireland and Liverpool. Its theme was the beauty of this lonely peninsula and the peace and seclusion he had found here, epitomised by the gaunt, spray-lashed headland just a mile or so down the road; its title was 'Mull of Kintyre'. Denny picked up another guitar and, with the help of a bottle of whisky, they finished the song together.

It was based on only two chords, A and D, yet inside them there was a lot going on. The lyric was a direct address to the Mull and its 'mists rolling in from the sea' – the classical poetic device called apostrophe, which could have sounded absurd to modern ears, but never did. 'Kintyre' provided most of the bang-on rhymes, some of them artfully engineered, like its coupling with 'sea', 'my *desire*' and 'always to *be* here'. And the tempo that seemed as sonorous and measured as a hymn or psalm was actually a waltz.

To complete its atmosphere, Paul decided that the arrangement must include bagpipes. And for once when gearing up to record at High Park, he didn't have to send down to London. Campbeltown had its own amateur pipe-and-drum band, which turned out for civic festivals in traditional uniform of tall bearskin hats and kilts. The commander, or pipe-major, Tony Wilson, was an impressive figure who had formerly played with the band of the Scots Guards and the city of Glasgow.

Paul invited Wilson to High Park, played and sang the song to him and asked if he could score a section for his pipers. This needed some work since pentatonic bagpipe-notation bears no resemblance to rock chords and pipers hold notes whereas guitarists bend or stop them.

The recording took place on a hot evening in August. Geoff Emerick came from London to do the engineering and the pipers turned up in a minibus, wearing full ceremonial rig of bearskins and kilts. 'We're thinking "Where is he . . . is this a joke after all?"' piper John Lang remembers, 'and just then he comes round the corner and says, "Are you ma pipers?" What really impressed me was that he got Tony to introduce him to every one of us and shook all our hands.'

The instrumental track was laid down outside in the long-lingering twilight, with Paul counting the pipers in after the third verse. 'We got it in the first take,' Lang recalls. 'After we'd finished, Paul came along with a wheelbarrow full of cans of beer and all of us partied long into the night.' Linda, now heavily pregnant, served food and was 'sweet to everyone'.

Kintyre's magic was not infallible, however. The song that would immortalise it was barely in the can when Wings' drummer, Joe English, announced he felt homesick and was quitting the band to return to Macon, Georgia. So for the second time Paul had lost a drummer and lead guitarist together.

English was later to suggest that, like his predecessor-but-one, Denny Seiwell, he'd become disillusioned by his leader's reluctance to share out Wings' rewards. But in a testimony on a religious website many years later, he would admit being able to afford 'two Porsches and 200 acres' on his drummer's pay, as well as 'living a first-class lifestyle'. 'Both Joe and Jimmy made money from the band,' Denny Laine says. 'Same as I did.'

The real problem was that, behind Wings' fun-family façade, English had acquired a heroin habit even worse than Jimmy Mc-Culloch's and spent most of his earnings on it. By his own later admission, he overdosed two or three times, once stayed unconscious for 24 hours and grew accustomed to waking up with no idea where he was.

Early in September, the McCartneys returned to London for Linda to have her baby at St John's Wood's Avenue Clinic. They had agreed this should be their last child and both hoped for a son, which Paul became convinced it would be after finding an unexplained blue bootee in a pocket of an old overcoat. If so, he was to be called James, after his father and grandfather, and Louis after Linda's maternal grandfather.

Sure enough, on 12 September, Linda gave birth to a healthy boy. Paul hugged her nurse, then rushed off to phone Heather, Mary and Stella, all of whom had been longing for a little brother.

'Mull of Kintyre' was released on 11 November, two weeks after the Sex Pistols' first, and only, studio album, *Never Mind the Bollocks – Here's the Sex Pistols*. The word 'bollocks', Cockney slang for balls or nonsense, made it unmentionable in print or on the air and rendered its cover liable to prosecution under British obscenity laws. One Virgin record store-manager was actually put on trial for displaying it, but acquitted when his lawyer persuaded the judge that 'bollock' was an Old English word originally not meaning testicle but priest. All of which guaranteed a turbocharged rise to number one in charts that dared not mention its name.

Up until the last minute, Paul felt qualms over sending a waltz about Scottish scenery out into such an environment, rather than 'something thrashy, fast and loud'. He was doing so mainly at the behest of the Campbeltown pipers, who assured him it would be bought by homesick Scots all over the world. Hedging his bets, he balanced it in a double A-side with 'Girls' School', another collaboration with Denny Laine, featuring lyrics about drug-taking and sexual deviancy in a Catholic convent that might give him some credibility with the new order.

A few days after 'Mull of Kintyre's' release, he phoned MPL to check on progress and was told it was selling 30,000 copies a day. 'I said, "Don't get back to me until it's selling 100,000 a day,"' he would recall. 'And by the next week, it was.'

His instinct had been right. Despite all these decades of change and upheaval in popular music, there was still nothing that appealed to the British quite so much as a stirring, sentimental song about the Scottish 'Heelands' amid the wail of bagpipes.

In what amounted to a quiet rebellion against punk rock – a rallying-cry for tunefulness, tradition and safety-pins stuck into kilts rather than faces – it spent nine weeks at number one, becoming the first UK single to sell two million on release and the country's most successful one ever. (To add a final pinch of porridge-salt to Paul's triumph, that record had previously been held by the Beatles' 'She Loves You'.)

It went on to be a hit around the world except, oddly, in America – usually second to none in romanticising Scotland – where it failed to make any pop Top 20 chart, reaching only the lower rungs of easy-listening charts. 'Girls' School' received more airplay.

In the process it made the Kintyre peninsula internationally famous, increasing annual visitor numbers by around 20 per cent, to the inevitable detriment of the peace and seclusion Paul had hymned, but with huge benefits to the local economy. It also prompted a surge of interest in bagpipes from the most unlikely quarters. Several Middle Eastern Gulf states subsequently added the instrument to their military bands, competing to recruit Scottish pipe-majors on huge salaries as instructors.

The Campbeltown pipers, whose usual engagements were local parades and sports-fixtures, now found themselves accompanying Paul and Wings on BBC television's *Top of the Pops*. Their appearance was on a weekday, so pipe-major Wilson had to ask schoolboy John Lang's head teacher to give him time off.

The TV studio had been decorated to resemble Scotland and, as the pipers awaited their cue, 'mists rolling in from the sea' were supplied in the form of billowing dry ice. 'We were just taking big lungfuls of air to inflate our pipes,' Lang recalls, 'and all that chemical at the back of our throats nearly finished us off.'

Their most-watched television appearance was on impressionist Mike Yarwood's Christmas show, Paul, Denny Laine and Linda seated on a row of stools – revealing Wings to be reduced to a trio again – and the pipers marching out of a thicket of silvery

Christmas trees. 'Paul was very protective of us,' says Lang. 'We were put up in a good hotel and he made sure we had food and drink and were well looked after.'

Nor were rock's Bastille-stormers totally hostile. One day as Paul and Linda were driving through central London, they found themselves stuck in traffic next to a pavement gathering of ferocious-looking punks. Paul flipped down the sun-visors and the two *ancien régime* aristos sank low in their seats, hoping not to be recognised.

However, a male member of the group spotted Paul, signalled him to wind down the car-window a few inches, then stuck a lip-ringed, eyebrow-studded, safety-pinned face into the crack. 'Oi, Paul,' he said, 'you know that Mull of Kintyre? It's fakking great!'

36

'McCartneyesque whimsy on punk steroids'

After 1978, Paul and Linda's main home was their estate in Peasmarsh, East Sussex. What had started out as a weekend retreat became the place where they decided to bring up their children, rather than remote Kintyre or urban St John's Wood.

There was a particular reason for the move. Paul's daughter Heather, now a teenager, had never really settled down at any of her expensive north London private schools. She did not shine academically and was teased for her American accent and the dreamy nonconformity she'd inherited from Linda. Even having so famous a father turned into an embarrassment. The cynical rich kids who were her classmates soon winkled out the fact that she was adopted and told her if she ever had any 'trouble' with Paul, she should go straight to the press about it.

He later admitted not having given Heather the best advice on how to fit in. 'I said, "Don't try and make friends with everyone, just sit in a corner reading a book and they'll eventually come to you." [Later] she said, "They never did, Dad." . . . She wasn't desperate or anything, she was just a little sad.'

Hoping she might do better in the egalitarian atmosphere of state education, Paul and Linda began looking for comprehensive schools in East Sussex and were recommended to the Thomas Peacocke in Rye. An interview with headmaster Roy Sooke impressed them both, and their exodus from London followed almost immediately.

Just as Paul's Scottish domain had done, the original 100-acre Peasmarsh estate began to expand its borders dramatically. Two neighbouring properties, accessed by the same secretive forest-tracks, happened to come onto the market at about the same time and were snapped up by him: 159-acre Lower Gate Farm, to which he restored its old name of Blossom Wood, and East Gate Farm, which came with less land but stood on higher ground with consequently better views.

Waterfall Cottage, ideal as a weekend hideout, was too small to be a permanent home for a family of six. The McCartneys therefore moved up the hill to East Gate, whose farmhouse was backed by a pair of windmill-shaped oast houses, or hop-drying kilns. Rather than restoring the derelict house, Paul decided to demolish it and build a new one.

He could have commissioned the world's finest architects to create a state-of-the-art dream home hidden there in the forest. Instead, just as he'd been wont to do with album covers, he designed the new house himself. It was no rock-star mansion or folly but a bog-standard four-bedroom structure in red brick with a steeply pitched roof, somewhat like an enlarged version of 20 Forthlin Road, Allerton. Planning permission for the build was easily obtained, but it turned out that an ancient public right of way ran right through East Gate Farm, passing only inches from the new house's front door. A lengthy legal process was necessary to move it 150 yards away.

Various new ancillary buildings sprang up round about: a stable block and Wild West-style corral for Linda's horses. A few yards from the main house arose a 65-foot observation tower which, in conjunction with the six-foot wire perimeter fence, looked like something from a German prison camp in the Second World War. Peasmarsh residents were at first mystified and perturbed by what British newspapers gleefully dubbed 'Paulditz'. The McCartneys hastily issued reassurances: the fence was merely to protect the woodland's wild life and the tower to allow them to look over the treetops to the sea.

The house was as unpretentious inside as out. The décor was Linda's usual style of comfortable verging on shabby – soft, neutral-coloured fabrics, stained and scuffed by kids and their innumerable, seldom-house-trained pets. All the ground-floor rooms interconnected – just like 20 Forthlin Road's – their hub a large kitchen with a stone floor where all family meals were eaten and visitors entertained. Upstairs were a master bedroom with a sundeck for Paul and Linda and three bedrooms divided among the four children but, pointedly, no guest-accommodation.

Linda became a familiar figure in Peasmarsh village, using its simple shops and becoming a regular at the hairdressing salon, where her fashion sense caused much comment. 'All that money, yet she still goes round in gym-shoes,' a fellow client was once heard to marvel. 'And she doesn't even bother to do up the laces.'

Early in their relationship she had told Paul how, as a little girl, she used to wake each Christmas morning hoping Santa had left her a horse with a bow around its neck, but always being disappointed. Since then, he'd never minded how many she bought or adopted. Even Drake's Drum, the racehorse he'd given his father, was now one of her Scottish string, enjoying a happy retirement among the domesticated geese and safe-from-slaughter sheep.

Nothing was too good for Linda's horses; in fact, the new stable block at Peasmarsh had a modernity and opulence the house never did. One winter day, David Litchfield was there with Paul, looking at two Native American Pinto ponies, newly brought over from Arizona.

'I said, "Hey, Paul, aren't they going to feel the cold a bit after where they've come from?" "Shut the fuck up," he said out of the corner of his mouth, "the paddock's got underfloor heating."'

In March 1978, the Wings album recorded the year before in the American Virgin Islands was released under the surprising title of *London Town*. Despite the contribution of the two departed band members, Jimmy McCulloch and Joe English, neither appeared on its cover; just Paul, Linda and Denny Laine outlined against a wintry image of Tower Bridge.

London Town spun off an American number one single in 'With a Little Luck', a gentle sing-along radiating McCartney optimism and touched with McCartney literariness ('together' rhymed with 'inclement weather'). The album peaked at number two in America and four in the UK, but received generally dismissive reviews. For *Rolling Stone*, so recently among Wings' chief enthusiasts, it was 'an irritating melange of lyric fragments, squandered melodies and clever but half-assed arrangements, the whole unrealised mess packaged with a slick, unctuous flair that would have reduced an idea like "Eleanor Rigby" to a two-line roundelay'.

Its British media launch took place aboard a Thames riverboat cruising to Tower Bridge. Alas, the media showed little interest in the album or photo-ops of Paul, Linda and Denny showing London-ness by eating fish and chips from traditional newspaper wrappings. For everyone, the big story was *All You Need Is Cash*, a spoof TV documentary about the Beatles – thinly disguised as a quartet named the Rutles – by Eric Idle from the Monty Python comedy team and Neil Innes, formerly of the Bonzo Dog Doo-Dah Band, which aired that same week on BBC2.

Idle's and Innes's wickedly accurate parody of this so-called 'Prefab Four' included cameo appearances by real-life rock stars like Mick Jagger and Ronnie Wood, plus a genuine Beatle, the one usually least known for his sense of humour. George played a television correspondent reporting from outside the band's business HQ, 'Rutle Corps', as behind him a stream of looters ran from the building with photocopiers, TV sets and potted plants.

Innes was the John character, 'Nasty', while Idle satirised Paul as 'Dirk McQuickly', a moon-faced manipulator who turned out glib tunes without effort and peddled them without shame. 'Any old slag he'd sell a song to,' said Jagger of McQuickly – an unkind cut since the Rolling Stones had owed their first chart success to Lennon and McCartney.

Paul admired the Python pranksters and knew Innes well,

having co-produced the Bonzo Dog Band's only hit single, 'Urban Spaceman', under the pseudonym Apollo C. Vermouth. Asked jokey questions about 'Rutlemania' at the *London Town* press launch, he expressed the requisite tolerant amusement. In reality, *All You Need Is Cash* touched rather too many raw nerves, especially with its cracks about 'Rutle Corps' and the band's American manager, 'Ron Decline'. And after 15 years' incessant adoration and admiration, it was a sobering experience to be mocked.

He'd decided not to keep Wings' trio format – well though it had worked in the past – but to recruit a third lead guitarist and a fourth drummer for the follow-up to *London Town* and subsequent live shows. In contrast with the previous pairings of problematic American with hard-drinking Scot, both new arrivals were English and, for both, Paul had Denny Laine to thank.

Twenty-three-year-old drummer Steve Holley happened to live in the Surrey village of Laleham, where Laine had recently bought a home. Holley attended the Laines' house-warming party, joined a jam session with Denny and Paul, then was auditioned at MPL and offered the gig on the spot. He was also being headhunted by Elton John, and his own band, Vapour Trails, had recently signed to Warner Brothers, but he turned his back on both prospects without a qualm.

Then, on a David Essex TV special, Laine talent-spotted session-guitarist Laurence Juber, a darkly handsome 26-year-old somewhat like Paul's teenage hero, Don Everly. London-born Juber, impressively, had studied music theory at London University, played in the National Youth Jazz Orchestra and, to round off his CV to perfection, was a strict vegetarian.

To forestall the arguments over money that had bedevilled previous Wings line-ups, both recruits were flown to New York and taken to the East Hampton home of Paul's father-in-law and lawyer, Lee Eastman. There – 'sitting on a blanket, drinking lemonade', as Steve Holley remembers – they were offered a yearly salary considerably higher than any of their predecessors', and guaranteed, however much or little Paul used their services.

In June, he took them to Scotland, to rehearse with Linda and Denny Laine and start on an album he'd provisionally named *We're Open Tonight*. Then Linda, that assiduous hen-keeper, came up with a title suggesting a more fundamental fresh start, *Back to the Egg*. Each side had an egg-related subtitle, 'Sunny Side Up' and 'Over Easy'.

Having risen above punk and every other contemporary pop style, like disco and new wave, the previous year, Paul was now determined to embrace as many of them as possible. On *Back to the Egg*, therefore, he sacrificed his usual total control, working with an outside producer for the first time since the abortive experiment with Glyn Johns.

His appointee, 31-year-old Chris Thomas, was a former assistant to George Martin who'd supervised some of the Beatles' White Album sessions when Martin could stand no more of their bickering. Thomas had gone on to work with top bands like Procol Harum, Pink Floyd and Roxy Music, but most famously had produced *Never Mind the Bollocks – Here's the Sex Pistols*. No other symbol of old-school rock was so willing to learn new tricks.

Making *Back to the Egg* would take seven months, in part thanks to Paul's fondness for unusual locations. In September, work transferred from the Spirit of Ranachan studio to Lympne Castle in Kent, a medieval pile not far from Peasmarsh. Recording took place in the castle's great hall, with Steve Holley's drums set up in front of the enormous fireplace; Paul and Laurence Juber recorded guitar-parts in an echoing stairwell, and books from the castle library provided spoken inserts that were read by the owners, Harold and Deirdre Margary, and overdubbed in the kitchen.

After a break lasting the whole of August, work resumed in Abbey Road's Studio 2. There Paul convened what he dubbed his Rockestra, a symphony-sized ensemble of super-sidemen to perform a catchy but slight instrumental of the same name. The massed talent included David Gilmour from Pink Floyd, John Bonham and John Paul Jones from Led Zeppelin, Pete Townshend from the Who and Hank B. Marvin from the Shadows, plus younger virtuosi like Bruce Thomas, bass-player with Elvis Costello's Attractions, and James Honeyman-Scott, guitarist with the Pretenders. The drummers were to have included Keith Moon from the Who, but 'Moon the Loon' had died of a drugs overdose a few days earlier.

In December, with dubbing still unfinished, Studio 2 was needed for other artistes, notably EMI's new chart-topper Kate Bush (whose unearthly wail made Yoko's vocal efforts of yore seem positively normal). Paul therefore moved to the basement at 1 Soho Square, bringing in equipment identical to Abbey Road's and naming it 'Replica Studio'. To further the illusion, and hopefully catch a magic vibe, one wall had a huge photograph of the view from the real Studio 2's control room.

Much was riding on *Back to the Egg*. Paul had become dissatisfied with Capitol Records, particularly over the promotion of *London Town*, and when his contract expired in 1978 had signed with Capitol's arch-rival, Columbia. The label had shelled out an advance of $22.5 million which, with an unheard-of 20 per cent royalty, made him the world's highest-paid recording artiste. In addition, Columbia's parent company, CBS, made him a present of one of its choicer publishing subsidiaries, the Frank Music Corporation, founded by the great Broadway songwriter Frank Loesser. He thus acquired the song-copyrights of Loesser's *Guys and Dolls* and other classics of American musical theatre such as *Damned Yankees*, *The Pajama Game* and *The Music Man*, the source of 'Till There Was You' which he'd sung countless times with the early Beatles. As a final sweetener, he was to have use of the company's private jet.

Columbia's CEO, Walter Yetnikoff, had every reason to feel bullish about this epic investment. In March 1979, Wings scored a number five single in America and the UK with the disco-flavoured 'Goodnight Tonight', recorded during the *Back to the Egg* sessions but not to be included on the album. The accompanying video showed Paul and his Wingsmen in 1930s dinner jackets, with slicked-down, shiny hair – yet another reincarnation of the Jim Mac

Jazz Band – and Linda in a purple tea-gown, coquettishly fluttering a fan.

In May, Paul, George and Ringo were guests at Eric Clapton's wedding to George's former wife, Pattie. Though George had apparently not minded his best friend's theft of his wife, the occasion could still have been a sticky one. Sexual buccaneer that he was under that dour mystical exterior, he'd since admitted a covert affair with Ringo's wife, Maureen, explaining it away as 'incest'.

However, no grudges, ancient or modern, marred the happy event at Clapton's Surrey mansion, Hurtwood Edge. Paul took the marquee stage and made a gracious speech, name-checking George and Ringo as 'old flames'. John rang up from New York to congratulate the newly-weds and say he would have come to the party if he'd known about it.

Later, as champagne and other stimulants flowed, Paul, George and Ringo got up onstage with Clapton for a jam session that included a couple of *Sgt. Pepper* songs done karaoke-style. Denny Laine later described their performance as 'absolute rubbish' and said it was lucky no one had made a tape.

Back to the Egg was released in Britain on 8 June 1979, with a colossal publicity budget behind it. For the press launch at Abbey Road, Studio 2 was draped in black to suggest the inside of a frying pan and the guests sat at tables under parasols resembling fried eggs.

A minute-long TV commercial, transmitted in prime time, eulogised 'a timeless rock 'n' roll flight through twelve superbly produced songs on an album that really is perfect'. With it came seven different promotional videos, mostly shot at Lympne Castle, to be shown individually on pop music programmes, then combined in a half-hour special. The sequence for 'Winter Rose' had entailed spraying white foam over a large tract of the castle's beautifully-manicured grounds, which left it as brown as the Serengeti afterwards.

The album reached number six in Britain and eight in America, where it sold more than a million. But as a return on Columbia's investment it was considered a failure, compounded when none of its four singles even made the Top 20 on either side of the Atlantic. Its most successful track was the Rockestra theme, which later won the first-ever Grammy for a pop instrumental. For most critics, Paul's attempt to give Wings an edgy modernity was an embarrassing mismatch; 'McCartneyesque whimsy on punk steroids' jeered one reviewer.

His morale received a boost in August when Allen Klein stood trial in New York for tax evasion and was sentenced to two years' imprisonment (with all but two months suspended) plus a $5000 fine. The triviality of the charge was in stark contrast to the millions that had passed through Klein's hands with the Beatles and Rolling Stones. He had neglected to declare a few illicit dollars made by selling what should have been free promotional copies of *The Concert for Bangladesh* album.

Paul, however, refused to gloat. 'I feel sorry for [Klein] now. I was caught in his net once and that panicked me. I really wanted to do everything to get him. I was contemplating going to where he lives and walking outside his house with placards. I was really crazy at that time . . . but it all turned out OK.'

The Clash's new single, 'London Calling', bellowed that 'phoney Beatlemania has bitten the dust', but in the case of Beatlemania's chief inspiration it had a hollow ring. The 1979 edition of the *Guinness Book of Records* listed Paul McCartney as 'the most successful composer of all time', for having written or co-written 43 songs that sold a million records or more, and accounted for 100 million sales in singles and the same number of albums.

The great and good of London's music business gathered at the Savoy Hotel to see him receive an award of a rhodium-plated disc from the book's co-founder, Norris McWhirter. He replied to their applause with a double thumbs-up – a gesture of infallible cheery optimism that was replacing a violin-shaped bass as his trademark.

At the end of November, Wings Mk. 6 received their first outing with a two-week UK tour, but playing mostly theatres rather than the arenas the previous line-up had been used to. The opening shows were in Liverpool, not at the Empire Theatre but the more intimate Royal Court. On the first night, Paul reserved front-stall seats for a large contingent of his relatives led by Auntie Gin of 'Let 'Em In' fame. His two new sidemen could not believe how jittery he was about playing to his own family.

There was an additional free matinee for his old school, Liverpool Institute, both the boys and the girls from their once out-of-bounds enclave across the road. The headmaster in Paul's time, J.R. ('the Baz') Edwards, had since retired and been succeeded by the former geography teacher, B.L. ('Blip') Parker. But whereas the Baz had led the onslaught on rock 'n' roll, Blip came to the show with his pupils and cheered and clapped as loudly as anyone.

Holley and Juber were both outstanding musicians who got along well with each other and seemed unconcerned by the band's tricky internal politics. Yet while Paul gave his all onstage, as ever, there was a noticeable lack of afterglow. Steve Holley recalls these early signs of waning enthusiasm for the whole Wings project, though he didn't recognise them as such. 'We'd come offstage and I'd say, "Wasn't that great?" Paul would just go, "Yeah, it was OK." At the time, I just thought "Hey, what do I know? This guy played with the *Beatles*."'

After a sold-out week at the Hammersmith Odeon, the final two dates were in Scotland, reflecting Paul's new persona as a latter-day Robbie Burns. At the Glasgow Apollo on 17 December, the Campbeltown pipers were waiting in a side-alley and, during 'Mull of Kintyre', clattered up the fire escape for a surprise march-on.

And to seal the recovery, he was back in the UK singles charts. Following the lead of John and Yoko in 1971, he had released a Christmas song, under his own name and in 'mad professor' mode, playing bass, guitar, keyboards, drums and percussion. Compared with the sombre, admonitory 'Happy Xmas (War Is Over)', his 'Wonderful Christmastime' was as insubstantial as tinsel, yet it reached number six and would be played throughout the holiday season for evermore, generating an estimated $15 million and inspiring numerous covers.

As Britain gave way to pre-Christmas hysteria, the news media were full of the crisis in Cambodia, now renamed Kampuchea, where thousands of refugees were trying to escape the country's homicidal ruler, Pol Pot, and disease and starvation were endemic. Fresh off the road, Paul was contacted by no less a figure than the Secretary-General of the United Nations, Kurt Waldheim. To aid the UN's Kampuchean relief effort, Waldheim asked if he'd give a benefit concert taking advantage of the so-called season of good-will. Despite the absurdly short notice, he agreed at once.

The initial plan for a one-off Wings gig quickly developed into the British rock community's first-ever display of collective social conscience. Under Paul's aegis, there would be four Concerts for Kampuchea at the Hammersmith Odeon, starting on the day after Christmas and featuring an impressive mix of old and new talent: Queen, the Who, the Specials, the Pretenders, the Clash, Ian Dury and the Blockheads and Elvis Costello.

At once, rumours began circulating that the final concert on 29 December, headlined by Wings, might finally bring the Beatles back onstage together. George and Ringo agreed to take part on condition that they'd be playing with other musicians as well as Paul. But although John was now free to break his exile in New York, he would have nothing to do with the project, refusing to change his mind even after a personal plea from Kurt Waldheim. Then when the media learned of George's and Ringo's involvement, both of them pulled out.

As it was, Paul closed the final show with Wings and his 30 Rockestra sidemen, all – except the reliably-bolshie Pete Townshend – resplendent in silver tail suits and top hats. A rumour persisted that John had relented and was secretly watching the show from the side. During Wings' set, a little clockwork robot walked onstage, set off by some japester among the road crew. 'It's not John Lennon,' Paul quipped to the audience.

He thus ended the year, and the decade, on a top note of public esteem and personal dignity. And 1980 already looked full of promise. McCartney Productions Ltd had a new managing director, a go-getting young Australian named Steve Shrimpton, formerly the head of EMI Music Australia. As defined by his predecessor, Brian Brolly, Shrimpton's role combined running the office at 1 Soho Square with all the duties of a personal manager, save, in any way, shape or form, trying to tell Paul what to do.

The New Year was to bring Shrimpton's first major test – a far greater one than he could ever have foreseen. After months of patient diplomacy by Japanese concert promoters Udo Music, their government had agreed to lift the ban on Paul for his 1973 drug conviction, which had prevented Wings 2's intended visit in 1975. He was to be allowed back into the country before the end of his seven-year exclusion, for a two-week tour with Wings 6, starting on 16 January.

Eleven shows were scheduled, including several at Tokyo's Budokan Hall, where the Beatles had appeared in 1966 during the chaotic Far East tour that had helped finally sicken them of live performances. Wings' record-sales were massive in Japan and after the long wait to see Paul in the flesh there was huge excitement among his fans there, with all the 100,000 tickets already sold.

The Japanese tour was to take Steve Holley and Laurence Juber another step above previous Wings sidemen. As a mark of Paul's appreciation for their work over the previous year, they would each receive a small percentage of the profits. 'The trouble was,' Juber reflects wryly, 'there weren't going to *be* any profits from the Japanese tour.'

A precondition of the tour had been that Paul signed an affidavit saying he no longer used cannabis; nevertheless, he and his musicians clearly could expect rigorous attention from Japanese customs on their arrival. Wings' sidemen and the accompanying horn section were sternly warned by Alan Crowder not to take any illegal substances with them and to check their suitcases, their pockets, even under their fingernails for any incriminating fragments.

Before they departed, there was a final run-through at Peas-marsh, with a film camera running as usual. 'Hello, people of Japan,' Paul greeted his waiting audience light-heartedly. 'This is Paul McCartney here . . . we're just rehearsing.' He then cued 'Got to Get You into My Life', singing words soon to come horribly true: 'I was alone, I took a ride, I didn't know what I would find there . . .'

37

Japanese Jailbird

The tour party that arrived at Tokyo's Narita International Airport on the afternoon of 16 January 1980 was split into two contingents on separate flights. One came from London with the band and road crew, the other from New York with Paul, Linda and their children, plus lead guitarist Laurence Juber who'd been taking a pre-tour break in Los Angeles. Since both planes were scheduled to land at around the same time, the party were to meet up at the airport and be bussed to their hotel together.

When the band and roadies disembarked from the London flight, they were surprised not to receive the strenuous going-over from customs officials they'd been warned to expect. Drummer Steve Holley and his wife, Sharon, were with Denny Laine, who had feared being targeted because of the drugs-bust on his own record (when he'd taken the rap for Jo Jo). Everybody went through without a problem, however, and climbed aboard the tour bus outside to wait for the McCartney contingent.

Paul's Pan Am flight from New York touched down about half an hour later. There was a brief VIP moment outside the Arrivals entrance as he posed for TV cameras, holding his toddler son, James, in his arms and cheerily saying 'Hello, Tokyo'. It would be his last experience of VIP-ness for some time.

Laurence Juber, who'd been on the same flight, was standing beside him at the moment which Juber says 'will be seared on my memory for ever'. During what struck the guitarist as only a 'cursory' search of Paul's luggage, the surgical-gloved customs officer lifted up a jacket to reveal a transparent plastic bag containing a large wedge of what was clearly marijuana.

'When the fellow pulled it out of the suitcase, he looked more embarrassed than me,' Paul would later remember. 'I think he just wanted to put it back and forget the whole thing.' Instead, the officer ploughed on, discovering a further, smaller amount of the same substance in a toilet-bag.

With that, Juber says, 'alarms started going off, doors opened and people came running from every direction'. Both he and Paul were marched away to separate side rooms for questioning. Juber's interrogators were specially interested in a Les Paul guitar he'd bought in New York, which they suspected of harbouring further drugs. Only after proving it was 'clean' by dismantling it with a screwdriver was he released.

'I went and got on the bus, and we all sat there for a while, hoping the whole thing might blow over and Paul would come out and join us,' he recalls. 'Then Alan Crowder [the tour-manager] told us there was still a problem and we were to go ahead to the hotel.'

This was the splendiferous Hotel Okura, coincidentally the place where John and Yoko stayed on visits to Yoko's Tokyo family. An entire floor had been reserved for the Wings party and Paul and Linda were to have the Presidential Suite, which the Lennons always occupied – though for Paul, somewhat different accommodation lay ahead.

Having checked in, Steve and Sharon Holley retired to rest after their 18-hour flight. Holley was woken by a phone call from Linda. 'She was screaming that Paul had been arrested and locked up. Thinking it was a joke, I said, "Yeah, nice one, Linda. See you downstairs in the restaurant." Then when we went down, the elevator-doors opened on a lobby full of TV lights and photographers.'

Paul, meanwhile, was alone and had taken a ride to Metropolitan Police Headquarters in central Tokyo, not knowing what he'd find there. It proved to be five hours of gruelling interrogation by a group of drug squad officers with only a smattering of English between them. The total weight of the marijuana in his case was 7.7 ounces, enough to suggest it was meant for more than just personal use and invite charges of smuggling or even peddling. He protested that he'd got it from some friends, solely for his own use, and signed a confession, drafted by his interrogators, that 'I brought some hemp for my smoking'.

Nevertheless, despite the immensity of his fame and the major national event that Wings' tour represented, prosecution proceedings were set in motion. A person facing such charges in Europe or America could expect to be given bail, but Japan had no such system; pending a further investigation of the evidence against him, he would be held in custody.

Rather than checking into the Hotel Okura's Presidential Suite, he was taken to a holding wing which, ironically, shared a building with one of the radio stations that had earlier reported Wings' arrival. After handing over all his personal effects, including his wedding ring, he was shown to a tiny, bare cell with a thin mat in place of a bed.

The only time he'd even been in such a situation before was as an 18-year-old in Hamburg, when he and Pete Best had been briefly banged up for allegedly trying to burn down a porno cinema with a lighted condom. This was an infinitely worse experience: all alone, denied any contact with Linda and the children, racked by a blinding headache and by fears absent from his earlier, brief incarceration at St Pauli's police station. He didn't sleep a wink but spent all night sitting on the floor with his back against the wall, terrified of being raped.

Linda was similarly in torment, besieged by ravenous media at the Okura with no idea what was going on or where it would end. For the sake of Heather, Mary, Stella and little James – who kept asking 'Where's Daddy?' – she did her best to put on a brave face. 'It's really very silly,' she told one TV camera. 'People are so different over here. They take [grass] so very seriously. Paul is now in some kind of detention place and I haven't been allowed to see him.

As soon as they get someone nice like Paul, they seem to make a field-day of it. I'll never come back to Japan again. This is my first visit and my last.'

Secretly, haunted by memories of Japanese prisoner-of-war movies, she was afraid he might be subjected to torture. At this moment when he needed her protection like never before, she was unable to give it.

The immediate question for MPL in its chief's absence was whether to abort the tour – but that decision proved to have been taken already. 'When we'd come in from the airport, we'd seen posters for our concerts about every 50 yards,' Steve Holley remembers. 'Next morning, there wasn't one anywhere, and all Wings music had disappeared from the radio.'

They could all only watch the TV news reports that second day as Paul was delivered to the Tokyo police's Narcotics Control Department by three tough-looking plain-clothes officers, handcuffed and with a rope around his neck – 'like a dog', as he later said. Despite having already made a full confession and apology, he was subjected to six more hours' interrogation led by the drug squad's renowned chief investigator, Koyoshi Kobayashi.

'I had to go through my life story . . . school, father's name, income,' he would recall. 'They would say, highly curious, "You are MBE?" And I would say "Yeah", hoping that would carry weight. And it sort of did. Then they said, even more curious, "You live at Queen's palace?" I said, "Well no, not actually . . . well yes, quite near." I was hoping they'd let me off if I lived near the Queen's house. They said, "You smoke marijuana?" I said, "Hardly." They said, "Makes you hear music better?" I thought "God, I wonder if that's a trap . . ."'

When the interrogators had finished, he was allowed a brief meeting with Linda, then remanded back to custody at Metro Police Headquarters. As his escort brought him out by a rear door, they were surrounded by around 200 young women, weeping hysterically and calling his name – the Japanese difficulty with the letter 'l' somehow lending it extra anguish: 'Paur! *Paur!*' The melee became so uncontrollable that riot police had to be called. 'It was like Beatlemania,' he would remember. 'Only instead of going to a gig, I was going to a cell.'

By now, his lawyer and brother-in-law John Eastman had hurried from New York and his new manager Steve Shrimpton from London to organise his defence and shield Linda and the children from the media storm at the Okura. An English-speaking Tokyo lawyer, Tasuku Matsuo, was engaged to represent him at the interrogations and whatever might follow.

So far, his only visitor had been Donald Warren-Knott, an official from Tokyo's British Embassy, which happened to be located next door to his custody block. Warren-Knott found him calm and in reasonable spirits, though full of anxiety about Linda and the children. He said he was being well-treated and didn't seek any special privileges beyond asking for a vegetarian diet including some fruit, which Warren-Knott duly requested on his behalf. His jailers agreed to supply apples and oranges but not bananas because of the risk of an unwary guard slipping on one of the skins.

The next day, 18 January, he was brought to the District Prosecutor's office for yet further interrogation, hustled in by a back door because weeping, 'Paur'-ing fans were blocking the front. Under Japan's draconian anti-drug laws, he learned, he faced a possible seven years' imprisonment with hard labour in a penal system widely criticised for human rights violations. And no one yet could give him any firm assurances that it wouldn't happen. 'I was looking at bringing the kids up in Japan,' he would later admit.

That afternoon, he was questioned by district judge Haruo Matsumoto, who then granted the prosecutor's application to keep him behind bars for up to ten further days' investigation. Now transferred from police custody to that of the Justice Department, he was taken to central Tokyo's grim nineteenth-century Kosuge Prison. There he was to spend a week in company with some of Japan's most hardened criminals, and be treated little differently.

Meanwhile, his case had aroused shock and disbelief around the world, with politicians and public figures of all sorts expressing concern on his behalf and calling on the Japanese government to take things no further. While Donald Warren-Knott from the British Embassy was discussing the case with investigator Kobayashi in the latter's office, a phone call came through from Washington DC. It was Senator Edward Kennedy, last surviving brother of President John F. Kennedy; he'd heard Wings were scheduled to tour America the following summer and was concerned Paul might not be at liberty to take part.

George sent a message from himself and his wife, Olivia: 'Thinking of you. Keep your spirits high.' But the other two former Beatles expressed neither support nor sympathy for a friend who had always shared their drugs travails: Ringo merely observed cagily that Paul had been 'unlucky' while John made no comment.

There was also much hilarity over the size of the marijuana-stash. American chat show king Johnny Carson quipped that after Paul landed at Narita, his suitcase had remained in a holding pattern for another four hours. Less amusingly, a deranged Beatles fan named Kenneth Lambert – a species later to become horribly familiar – turned up at Miami airport announcing he meant to fly to Tokyo and 'free Paul', despite having neither a plane ticket nor money. During an altercation with airline staff, Lambert pulled out a toy gun and a police officer shot him dead.

To begin with, Paul found conditions at the Kosuge Prison 'barbaric'. He was allotted a cell measuring only 10 feet by 14, with just a thin mat to sleep on. Normally hyper-fastidious about his wardrobe and personal hygiene, he still wore the same green suit he had on when he was arrested.

The day began at 6 a.m. with roll-call, when history's most successful songwriter sat cross-legged on the floor among his fellow inmates, replying to his prison-number, 22, with a ritual shout of 'Hai!' The double estate-owner and employer of multiple domestics then had to clean his tiny domain, using a miniature dustpan and reed brush pushed through a hole in the door, and fold up his sleeping-mat.

Inspection was followed by breakfast, a bowl of seaweed-and-onion soup ('not the greatest thing in the morning if you're used to cornflakes'). Lunch was soybean soup and bread and supper a bowl of rice with dessert of an apple or orange, if he was lucky, but no banana. He was in virtual solitary confinement, allowed neither books nor writing materials. Lights-out was at 8 p.m.

The routine was broken by further trips to the prosecutor's office, with mobs of shrieking girls at both ends. At the prison-gate, 19-year-old Minako Shitega was one of many holding a personal vigil for, as she put it, 'the greatest fellow ever to live on earth'. A petition for his release was organised outside the Budokan Hall, where the Beatles had played in 1966 and Wings were to have given their main shows.

Such an ordeal could have broken a far more physically robust man. Paul's salvation was the competitiveness that the other ex-Beatles knew so well, allied to the practicality of a one-time badge-accumulating Boy Scout. 'After a few days, I became like Steve McQueen in *The Great Escape*,' he would remember. 'My natural survival instinct and sense of humour started to kick in. [I thought] "Right, I'm going to be the first up when the light goes on, the first with his room cleaned, the first who gets to wash and do his teeth."'

Similarly, he was undaunted by the fact that almost no one around him spoke a word of English and he no word of Japanese beyond 'Sayonara' and 'Konnichiwa' (hello). He communicated with the tenants of neighbouring cells by shouting out Japanese brand-names: 'Toyota!', 'Kawasaki!', 'Datsun!', and that of Britain's prime export cigarette, 'John Player Special!' They responded 'Johnnie Walker!', the name of the Scotch whisky they most fantasised about, and the ice was broken.

The inmates socialised only for a short period each morning when they smoked their daily two-cigarette ration sitting around a tin can, into which they tapped their ash. Here Paul learned to put faces and names to his fellow inmates' numbers, for instance his next-door neighbour, a Marxist student, also on a drugs charge, who spoke some English.

Four cells away dwelt a huge man doing time for murder whose tattooed back identified him as a yakuza or Japanese mafioso. Through an interpreter, this terrifying individual asked Paul what he was in for, then held up seven fingers to indicate his likely sentence. 'No, ten,' Paul replied, making the yakuza roar with laughter. Later, he heard a shout from the yakuza's cell of 'Yesterday, please', a request with which it was clearly wise to comply. Their guard shouted for silence but didn't enforce it as he was listening, too, and instinctively responding even to this small audience, Paul acappella-ed three more songs.

He became quite the life and soul of those smoke-wreathed gatherings around the tin can, introducing the others to a game the Beatles used to play during their own spells of confinement in hotel-rooms or at Abbey Road. It was called Touching the Highest Place on the Wall because everyone in turn jumped up and tried to touch the highest place on the wall. Since Paul towered above his slightly-built competitors, he usually won.

As time passed, the harsh regime softened somewhat: his request for a guitar met with firm refusal but members of his entourage were allowed to bring him clean clothes, hot food and blankets. His fear of rape receded, so much so that when offered a bath in private he elected to use the communal showers. There he led a sing-song of old standards his father had loved, like 'When the Red Red Robin Comes Bob-Bob-Bobbin' Along'.

After so many years of limitless power and free will – and the stresses, both external and self-inflicted, that went with them – he found himself almost relishing the bleak simplicity, solitude and utter powerlessness of his prison life. 'Suddenly,' he would remember, 'I didn't have to do the job any more.' Far from a penance, it came as a relief to lose all the myriad trappings of being Paul McCartney – even his very name – and revert to his status long, long ago when he'd first known John and George, as 'just one of the lads'.

Among his musicians initial shock and sympathy were giving way to resentment. Laurence Juber and Steve Holley weren't alone in expecting a share of the tour profits: the horn section, including Paul's old Liverpool colleague Howie Casey, had each stood to make around $1000 per day in Japan, many times more than they'd ever previously earned on the road.

They had also counted on further lucrative work from the American tour in the summer. But after this new (and worst-of-all) drug offence, who could doubt that Paul's US visa would be withdrawn yet again? Nor could anyone understand why he'd bothered to bring grass to Japan in the first place. Before the troupe left home, they'd been told it would be easily available via American military bases.

All the band had also been questioned by the police – as had Linda – and were now under 24-hour surveillance. To forestall any further trouble they took a trip to Kyoto, hoping that in their absence the problem would be resolved and the tour still able to happen. However, Paul's defence team thought it wisest for them to leave the country, which they did on 21 January. Holley and Juber had been provided with first-class round-the-world air tickets, allowing them to go anywhere they liked; Holley opted to visit family in Australia while Juber returned to Los Angeles.

On his sixth day in the Kosuge, Paul was finally permitted a half-hour visit from Linda, although not the children. She brought him a cheese sandwich and some sci-fi paperbacks, and they conversed through a metal grille with guards looking on to ensure there was no physical contact. Linda was surprised, and not best pleased, by how institutionalised he'd become.

By now it was clear that despite the ferocious pretrial routine he was being put through, the Japanese government did not want the embarrassment of actually bringing him to court. Representations from the British Foreign Office through Donald Warren-Knott also played their part and on Paul's ninth day of captivity, all proceedings against him were dropped. The reasons cited were that he'd made a full confession, had shown 'repentance' and, by his time in custody, had already suffered 'social punishment'. He was therefore to be released and immediately deported.

If oddly redemptive spiritually, the episode cost him dear financially. The aborted tour's Japanese promoters, Udo Music, had to be compensated to the tune of around £184,000 for reimbursing 100,000 disappointed ticket-holders and the advertising and promotion costs. And keeping his family and retinue at the Hotel Okura while he was in his prison cell brought a bill for around £10,000 per day.

Regaining his freedom almost 'with a sigh' like Byron's Prisoner of Chillon, he signed autographs for his former guards, then was given back the personal effects he'd had to check in on his arrival. One thing was missing, presumably stolen – his wedding ring. There being no time to make a complaint, he begged a paper-clip from the prison office to wear in its place.

He was driven straight to Narita airport to be put on the first available flight, a Japan Airlines one to Amsterdam. Linda and the children were already on the plane. Before boarding, as some recompense for all those cancelled shows, he grabbed an acoustic guitar and sang a few bars of 'Yesterday' – then, with a final thumbs-up, he was gone.

Paul has never really explained what made him forget all the warnings he'd been given and pack those two hunks of hemp, not even at the bottom of his suitcase but near the top. 'How could Linda, who was so much smarter than me, let me do it?' he reflected in a TV interview with his daughter Mary in 2000. 'I must have said, "Oh baby, don't worry, it'll be all right." There are times in your life when you think to yourself "OK, you're an idiot" and that's one of them. I was an idiot.'

But the truth was that he'd always taken reckless chances with drugs, and got away with it so often that he may well have thought himself invulnerable. And Linda was widely suspected of abetting him; indeed, after the Tokyo bust rumour had it the stuff had actually been found in her bag and Paul had taken the blame.

For the media-hordes awaiting him in Amsterdam, then London, he had a ready explanation. He'd been caught off-guard as a result of his pre-tour stay in New York, where pot-smoking was now so widespread and overt as to seem virtually decriminalised. The large residue of the stuff he'd enjoyed there being 'too good to flush down the toilet', he'd packed it 'still [with] the American attitude that cannabis isn't all that bad'.

He blamed no one but himself, made light of his experiences in the Japanese penal system ('It wasn't exactly *The Bridge on the River Kwai*') and slipped in a little proselytising for the legalise-pot lobby he'd supported since the mid-Sixties. To help while away the time in his cell, he said, he'd made a mental list of all the dangerous drugs that were legal. 'Society thinks alcohol is terrific, yet it kills. Cigarettes can kill. What about all those little old ladies on Valium? They are worse than marijuana. Think of aspirin's danger to the stomach.'

Nonetheless, he promised he'd learned his lesson, offering a sizeable hostage to fortune in an interview with the *Sun* headlined 'I'LL NEVER SMOKE POT AGAIN, SAYS PAUL'.

In Britain, the chorus of 'How could he be so silly?' was all the more virulent because his children had been involved. One censure that stung particularly came from 'Blip' Parker, headmaster of his old school, Liverpool Institute, to whose pupils he'd given a free show before turning Tokyo-wards. 'It is hard enough nowadays to keep youngsters away from drugs without having people they look up to involved in something like this,' said Blip – and who could disagree?

Paul would even ask himself whether, at some subconscious level, he had known just what he was doing. His enthusiasm for Wings had waned to such an extent – so he reasoned – that possibly he seized this chance to sabotage the Japanese tour in a way calculated to damage the band beyond repair. 'It was almost,' he told Mary, 'as if I *wanted* to get busted.'

For Laurence Juber and Steve Holley, it was a bitter blow after having been Wingsmen such a short time. As well as losing their promised percentage of the Japanese gigs, they felt cheated of the opportunity to show what they could contribute as musicians.

'We'd only done about 22 Wings appearances, on the UK tour and at the Concert for Kampuchea,' Holley says. 'That's not really enough time for a new line-up to settle down together. By the time we went to Japan, we were just starting to sound like something.'

Paul on his side felt they and Denny Laine had deserted him in his hour of need, unaware that they'd been ordered to leave Tokyo by the tour's managers. It rankled especially that Laine had flown directly to the MIDEM music festival in the South of France to negotiate himself a solo album.

Although no formal break-up was announced – yet – recrimination and disunity pulsed in the air. Urgently needing money for income tax arrears, Laine put together a band with his wife, Jo Jo, on vocals and Steve Holley, and went out on tour. His album, when it came out in December, would bring a faint, but unignorable, echo of John's 'How Do You Sleep?' diatribe, in 1971. The title, a reference to young women weeping inconsolably for a no-show 'Paur', was *Japanese Tears*.

Paul, meantime, had been assembling a solo album since mid-1979, a sign of growing boredom with Wings that he'd carefully kept under wraps. This was released in May 1980 as *McCartney II* and – like *McCartney*, a decade earlier – consisted of himself singing and playing everything with Linda his only backup. Not at all harmed by his recent notoriety, it reached number one in Britain and three in America.

McCartney II's most popular track proved to be a buoyantly trite electronic dance tune called 'Coming Up' which became a British number two. It had featured in Wings' stage show during the pre-Japan UK tour and for the American market Columbia preferred to release their live version, recorded in Glasgow in November 1979. When it reached number one, Paul was miffed that his studio version hadn't been used and, instead, Wings seemed to be getting a new lease of life.

On his return home, he had recorded a video message to be shown on Japanese television, apologising to his tearful fans for his 'mistake' and giving a thumbs-up to his former guards. He had also written a 20,000-word account of his ordeal – a considerable feat for someone conditioned to turning out song-lyrics a couple of dozen words long in a few minutes – which sold more copies than the biggest best-selling author.

In fact, he'd always wanted to write a book – like John back in the Beatle years – but never thought he had it in him. He titled it *Japanese Jailbird*, had one copy privately printed for himself, then locked the manuscript away, intending to give it to his children when they grew older and sought an explanation of the traumatic scenes they'd witnessed. 'One day when we're old and my son's a great big 30-year-old . . . I'll be able to say, "There you are. Read that."'

However, the *McCartney II* album raised doubts about just how seriously he viewed the episode and how contrite he really was. Linda's cover picture showed him in head shot wearing a white T-shirt, like a prison ID but with a jokey 'ouch' expression. And one of the tracks, a synthesiser instrumental, was called 'Frozen Jap'. Although few Westerners then had any problem with 'Jap', it felt less like a thumbs-up than a thumbed nose.

The track actually dated from summer 1979, well before the Japanese nightmare: Paul had meant his instrumental to suggest the iconic traditional scene of snow on Mount Fuji, and 'Frozen Jap' was just a rough working title that had stuck. On albums exported to the Far East, it was changed to 'Frozen Japanese'. But, as he admitted, his late hosts still thought it 'an incredible slur'. The fans whose response to his trouble had been anything but 'frozen' doubtless most of all.

At any event, here he was safely back at Peasmarsh with Linda and the children, surrounded by protecting woods and water-falls, lulled by the comfortable whinny of horses in their heated paddock. And after all he'd been through, what else could 1980 possibly throw at him?

38

'It put everyone in a daze for the rest of their life'

John's fight against deportation from America had ended in 1975 when the US Court of Appeals ruled that his single drug conviction, in London seven years earlier, had been unfair and he thus posed no threat to the nation's moral fabric. Accordingly, a halt was called to his surveillance by the FBI and harassment by the immigration service and a year later he received the green card that granted him permanent residence.

On his thirty-fifth birthday, 9 October 1975, Yoko gave birth to a son, Sean Taro. His recording contract with EMI/Capitol having expired, John decided to retire from music and devote himself to raising Sean while Yoko looked after their business affairs. The former radical sloganeer, junkie, drunk and hell-raiser took on the role of house-husband at their seventh-floor apartment in the Dakota Building, gave up drugs, alcohol and cigarettes and learned how to change nappies, cook, even bake bread.

He did not become a recluse, as would later be widely believed, but was often seen in Central Park or around the secure-seeming Upper West Side. He continued to have ideas for songs and make demos on his determinedly archaic home equipment. And, careless and chaotic though he'd always seemed, he was as meticulous as Paul in preserving relics of his past. A corner room of the apartment contained every piece of clothing he'd ever worn onstage and off, right back to his Quarry Bank school blazer, hanging on rows of circular racks like some ghostly boutique.

A salutary moment for John was the death of Elvis Presley in 1977, aged only 42. 'The King' by then was a pathetic figure, bloated by prescription drugs and junk food and trapped on a treadmill of kitsch cabaret shows in Las Vegas. John had feared ending up in a similar predicament, so had no doubt that getting out of the rock rat-race had saved his life.

His contacts with his fellow ex-Beatles – 'the in-laws', Yoko drily termed them – became more and more infrequent as George and Ringo pursued dwindling solo careers and Paul's soared into the stratosphere with Wings. Paul made the most effort to stay in touch; when passing through New York, as he often did, he'd speak to John on the phone or sometimes just show up with Linda at the Dakota.

Nowadays, John's uncertain temper often came from the pressures of childcare, something which he'd never known with his first son, Julian – and which Paul had taken in his stride three times over. 'Look, do you mind ringin' first?' he once grumbled to his unexpected visitor. 'I've just had a hard day with the baby. I'm worn out and you're walkin' in with a damned guitar.'

Other encounters were perfectly pleasant: if the two no longer had the rapport that used to illuminate their music, their presence together still made magic. One night, they went with Yoko and Linda to Elaine's, the East 88th Street restaurant beloved of literary VIPs like Woody Allen, Tom Wolfe and Norman Mailer. Its usually ferocious patronne, Elaine Kaufman, was so captivated that when they could find nothing they fancied on the menu, she allowed them to send out for pizza.

At regular intervals, yet another American promoter would publicly offer still more millions of dollars for a single Beatles reunion concert. In 1976, the producer of the satirical TV show *Saturday Night Live*, Lorne Michaels, appeared on-screen with his own tongue-in-cheek bid of $3000 for three songs performed live on his programme. All four ex-Beatles happened to be in the country at the time and John and Paul were watching the show together at the Dakota. They were on the point of calling a cab to the SNL studios and collecting the money, but then decided they were too tired.

Yet despite John's conviction of having grown up at last, his old juvenile competitiveness with Paul remained as keen as ever. It galled him, for instance, that whenever he walked into the Plaza Hotel's Palm Court to have tea, the string quartet struck up 'Yesterday', which, despite its Lennon–McCartney credit, he'd had no hand whatsoever in writing.

He listened to every new Wings album and single, initially to check for more concealed insults to Yoko and himself, but then often with approval – even admiration – and watched the band's repeated ascents of the American charts with unconcealed envy. That envy peaked in 1978, when Paul received $22.5 million for signing with CBS Records. 'I'll never have that kind of money,' John lamented to Yoko. 'We haven't got Daddy Eastman behind us the way he has.'

Yoko, who came from a great financial dynasty (her great-grandfather had been the Emperor of Japan's personal banker), undertook to make an equal amount within two years, and did so by skilful investment in real estate and herds of valuable Holstein dairy cattle.

Ironically, an idea Paul had had in 1967 was to bring vastly bigger sums into the Beatles' collective coffers although, sadly, John would not be around to see it. Personal computers were becoming noticeable in the world and in 1978 it emerged that a young electronics whizz-kid in California named Steve Jobs had named his new computer company Apple. A hardcore Beatles fan, Jobs later admitted he'd taken the name from the company which they'd created, and which Paul had named after his favourite Magritte painting.

Apple Corps was still very much alive, if only as a conduit for the four's residual earnings, and its managing director, the faithful Neil Aspinall, immediately filed suit for infringement of copyright. A settlement was reached which allowed Jobs to continue using the

Apple name on condition his computers had no musical content – a notion which then seemed impossible.

There were times when John talked to Yoko about Paul with almost parental pride as one of the two great discoveries he'd made – the other being her. In one of his last television appearances before 'retiring', he was asked which Beatles tracks he thought likeliest to stand the test of time. The two he named were both Paul's: 'Eleanor Rigby' and 'Hey Jude'.

Often, however, his rampaging insecurity would keep him awake into the small hours, sitting in the Dakota apartment's huge white kitchen with his three pet cats, brooding about the multitude of cover versions his old partner's songs generated. 'They always cover Paul's songs,' he'd say wistfully to Yoko. 'They never cover mine.' She would try to reassure him, as work like 'Lucy in the Sky with Diamonds', 'A Day in the Life' and 'I Am the Walrus' apparently could not: 'You're a good songwriter. It's not just June-with-spoon that you write.'

When Paul stopped off in New York with Linda en route to Japan, he had phoned the Dakota to see if they could come over, but been told by Yoko (by now heavily reliant on astrologers) that it wasn't a good time.

John followed the Tokyo drama on television, as amazed as everyone by Paul's carelessness – though sure it betrayed a secret longing to be thought 'a bad boy'. 'If he really needed weed, surely there's enough people who can carry it for him. You're a Beatle, boy – a *Beatle*! Your face is in every corner of the planet. How could you be so stupid?'

Later, after it had been eclipsed by an infinitely larger tragedy, there was an attempt to blame the bust on Yoko. According to her former assistant, Fred Seaman, she was incensed that Paul and Linda had booked the Hotel Okura's Presidential Suite – thus spoiling John's and her 'hotel karma' – and had used high-level connections in Tokyo to arrange the search of Paul's bag. Yoko herself denied it and, despite their often rocky relationship over the years, Paul has never given the story any credence.

In the spring of 1980, with John's fortieth birthday looming, he ended his retirement as abruptly as he'd begun it. His competitiveness with Paul had proved too strong, especially after Wings' live version of 'Coming Up' spent three weeks at number one on the *Billboard* chart that April.

The result was a John–Yoko album, named *Double Fantasy* after his favourite freesia blooms, half consisting of newly-written Lennon songs and half Yoko tracks with his accompaniment. Made in double-quick time, it was offered to record companies for $22.5 million, the same advance Paul had been paid by CBS. Ahead of it, on 24 October, came John's first single for five years, aptly entitled '(Just Like) Starting Over'. In contrast with his former angry agit-prop, it was a mild love song pastiching the early Sixties American pop that had nourished the Beatles before he and Paul found their combined voice.

The album that followed a month later offered a full portrait of this new John Lennon, seemingly purged of his old demons and obsessions, happy in his new-found domesticity and at ease with himself. Its themes were the very ones for which he used to deride Paul – home, family love. Indeed, 'Woman', dedicated to Yoko, and 'Beautiful Boy', dedicated to Sean, were hymns to marital and parental joy that Paul could hardly have matched.

An intensive round of media interviews dispelled the recent rumours of a Howard Hughes-style hermit who'd gone totally bald and eroded the septum of his nose with cocaine. John was in better physical shape than in his whole life, slim and suntanned, and still as funny and bluntly honest as ever. Beside him at every minute still sat Yoko, proclaiming the longevity of a relationship the whole world had once spat on.

Significantly, too, he had ceased to be in denial about his Beatle years. For a long interview with *Playboy* magazine, he went through most of the Lennon–McCartney catalogue, identifying which songs were his and which Paul's and where and to what extent they'd collaborated. A bit of denial remained, however. 'I don't follow Wings,' he told an interviewer from *Newsweek*. 'I don't give a shit what Wings are doing.'

He was full of an optimism and positivity no one recalled in glum, apostle-bearded Sixties John, and looking forward to testing the old adage 'life begins at 40'. Yoko's astrologers having forecast 1981 would be a good year, he was planning a return to Britain to see his Aunt Mimi and take Sean to Liverpool, sailing up the Mersey on the liner *QE2*.

The last time Paul spoke to him was by phone just before *Double Fantasy* came out, when his house-husband duties were still uppermost. 'Oh God, I'm like Aunt Mimi, padding around in me dressing-gown,' he'd joked. 'This housewife wants a career.'

They'd ended the conversation on good terms, something for which Paul was always to be grateful. 'It could easily have been one of the other calls when we blew up at each other and slammed the phone down.'

Early on the morning of 9 December, Steve Shrimpton phoned him at Peasmarsh with the news that John had been shot outside the Dakota at around midnight New York time and had died soon afterwards at Roosevelt Hospital. Linda happened to be out, driving Mary and Stella to school, so Paul was alone in the house. When she returned, she found him standing in the front drive. 'I could tell by looking at him there was something absolutely wrong,' she would recall. 'I'd never seen him like that before. Desperate, you know . . . tears.'

His first reaction was to telephone his brother Michael, whose forthcoming book, *Thank U Very Much*, included Mike's photos of John at 20 Forthlin Road, writing songs with Paul in their facing armchairs, secure enough even to wear his hated horn-rimmed glasses. Mike, always closer to John in temperament than 'our kid', was equally devastated.

Paul that day was scheduled to be at George Martin's AIR studios in London, to record a track called 'Rainclouds' with Paddy Moloney from the Chieftains. Several top session musicians had been booked, including Denny Laine, and Moloney was flying over specially from Dublin; after discussing it with Linda, he decided not to cancel the session.

The story led every TV and radio news bulletin in Britain, as all over the world. John's killer, 25-year-old Mark David Chapman, was a Beatles fan for whom he had signed an album some hours earlier. When he and Yoko returned home from a late-night recording session, the waiting Chapman had pumped five shots from a handgun into his back, then leaned against the wall to wait for the police, nonchalantly reading a copy of J.D. Salinger's *The Catcher in the Rye*.

The shock of John's death in such a manner recalled the assassination of President John F. Kennedy 17 years earlier – but on a far more personal level. Millions in many lands and languages mourned the loss of one whom they felt they'd known like a friend and whose wayward, often exasperating behaviour was far outweighed by his humanity, honesty and wit. The world was suddenly poorer not only in music but laughter. Grief-stricken mass vigils were held outside the Dakota, around St George's Hall in Liverpool and in many other places. Special memorial issues of newspapers and magazines were rushed into production and instantly sold out.

At AIR studios, Paul, George Martin and the other musicians went through 9 December 'like robots', Paul later would recall, as they finished off a track for the Rupert Bear film ironically called 'We All Stand Together'. Rupert inevitably awoke memories of his and John's 1950s childhood, when the world had seemed so safe and assassination was something that happened only to be-medalled potentates in countries far away.

During the afternoon, Paul received a phone call from Yoko which he took in private, returning with tears in his eyes. 'John was really fond of you,' she had told him. He later recalled how the songwriting mechanism in his mind kept replaying the same phrase for Mark David Chapman – 'the jerk of all jerks'. There was a stomach-churning moment when he and Denny Laine were gazing numbly through the window at passing traffic and saw a van from a company named Lennon's Furnishings.

AIR studios were on Oxford Street, then in the throes of pre-Christmas shopping fever. When Paul emerged, it was through the front entrance, straight into a thicket of TV cameras. There was no time, as he usually did in moments of tragedy, to 'put a shell around me'. The familiar puckish face was gaunt and waxy, as if all his cuteness had been siphoned away. Yet his reflex was still to pause and answer television news's perennial, asinine query of 'How do you feel?'

'It's terrible news,' he answered. 'We're all very shocked.' Although nothing else needed to be said, he stayed for further laboured questions, answering briefly between chews of gum. Who had told him the news? 'A friend of mine.' What had he been doing at AIR? 'Just listening to some stuff.' On such a day, why hadn't he stayed home? 'I didn't feel like it.' When the questioner finally dried, he added, 'It's a drag, isn't it? OK, cheers,' then ducked into his waiting car.

The remark made headlines for its apparent flippancy, indifference even. Paul excused himself as being 'no good at public grief', rightly pointing out that neither George nor Ringo 'came up with any big comment either'. George said he had been awoken by the news, then gone back to sleep, 'and when I woke up it was still true', adding the mechanical cliché 'I'm shocked and stunned.' Ringo, who'd been in Barbados, said nothing but did something, immediately chartering a private plane and flying to New York accompanied by his soon-to-be wife, Barbara Bach, to condole with Yoko.

Paul, usually so good at soundbites, beat himself up over the faux-pas more than anyone imagined. He'd been doing the same since he was 14, over his first response to his mother's death; while his father and brother were engulfed in tears, he'd pragmatically asked how they would get by without her midwife's salary. Then, at least, the unguarded words had been said only once; now they were endlessly repeated on news bulletins and front pages. As he would later observe, 'You can't take the print back and say, "Look, let me just rub that in shit and pee on it and then cry over it for three weeks, then you'll see what I meant when I said . . . it was a drag."' Later, back at Peasmarsh, there certainly was no flippancy. 'We just sat looking at the news on the telly and we sat with all the kids, just crying all evening.'

An irreproachably-worded public statement via MPL soon followed: 'I can't take it in at the moment. John will be remembered for his unique contribution to art, music and world peace.' Paul seemed back in control, though that impression could not have been more misleading. On 10 December, there happened to be a pheasant shoot in the woods around Peasmarsh. The sound of guns going off so spooked him that Linda had to ask the shooting party to move away. 'For months afterwards,' he would recall, 'any mention of the word "gun", "rifle", "pistol" just shocked me, sent a wave of reverberation through me like a little echo of [Chapman's] pistol-shot.'

John's Aunt Mimi, now living in a bungalow he had bought her in Poole, Dorset, first heard the news on her radio. Neil Aspinall subsequently telephoned her, but none of the surviving ex-Beatles did. Paul might have been expected to be first in line even though in the old days Mimi hadn't been that nice to him, calling him John's 'little friend' and considering him forever socially tarnished for once having lived in the blue-collar suburb of Speke.

He shirked the duty, however, explaining later that he wouldn't have known what to say. But in years to come, he would more than make up for it. 'Paul is the only one of them who stays in touch,' Mimi told an interviewer shortly before her own death in 1991. 'He always asks how I am and do I need anything.'

As for Yoko, her worst enemy couldn't have wished on her the horror of seeing John shot down in front of her. And with that, the resentment and ridicule that had pursued her from the Sixties disappeared; there was only sympathy, heightened by the tragedy of her son, Sean, who'd been robbed of a doting dad aged only five.

Likewise, it was assumed the other ex-Beatles must have put any old resentments aside and be rallying round her in their common grief. However, when asked a few weeks later how supportive they had been, she pointedly answered 'No comment', which was unfair on both Ringo in the short term and Paul in the longer one.

Prior to John's death, Paul had been on not at all bad terms with Yoko but in the aftermath he made a conscious effort to get to know her better. He discovered a woman even more adept than himself at donning a protective shell, who initially bristled at his overtures saying she didn't want to be treated like 'the widow of the year'. 'At first, I felt rebuffed and thought "Oh well, great, sod you then,"' he would recall. 'But then I thought, she's had the tragedy of a lifetime here and I'm being crazy and insensitive to say "well if you're not going to be nice to me, I'm not going to be nice to you".'

The ice cracked, at least a little, one day when he and Linda were visiting the Dakota apartment and Yoko offered them something to eat. They settled on caviar, which she and John used to gorge by the Fortnum & Mason potful at the Apple house. When a tin of it arrived from the kitchen, all but a tiny morsel had been scoffed by her employees. Then she offered wine but when her only bottle was sent for, that too had been almost emptied by the staff. 'We were all just hysterical,' Paul remembered. 'And the relief was indescribable.'

It meant a huge amount to him to hear from Yoko that despite their conflicts, John had always liked him and, more importantly, had admired his songs and often replayed them. In the Beatles, there had seldom been time to pass judgement on each other's work before the world went crazy over it, and John had been particularly sparing with praise. 'If you ever got a speck of it, a crumb of it, you were quite grateful.'

Back in the era when Stu Sutcliffe was still a Beatle, they'd loved messing around with seances and Ouija-boards and agreed the first one to die would try to get a message to the others. Stu had been first, but no message had come. Now with John, Paul kept an ear half-cocked to the afterlife for years.

In truth, the world would never recover from John Lennon's

death. Aside from the senseless eradication of one unique, irreplaceable talent, it ushered in an era when psychopathic nerds in the Mark David Chapman mould increasingly turned to murder – and then mass-murder – for their Andy Warhol-prescribed '15 minutes of fame'. Certainly, no one in John's personal orbit ever fully recovered. 'It put everyone in a daze for the rest of their life,' Linda was to observe. 'It'll never make sense.'

From here on, Paul would have to live with a perception of his and John's character that seemed unalterable – Lennon the avant-garde, the experimenter and risk-taker, McCartney the tuneful, the sentimental, the safe. He'd learn to be philosophical about all the times he'd taken a back seat to John or seen John given credit for something he'd initiated, like getting into *musique concrète* or reading Tibetan religious books or growing a moustache.

He came to realise he'd 'always quite enjoyed being second' in the context of a completely different group; when he'd go out with other people on horseback, the lead rider always had to cope with the tricky job of opening gates for the others. 'Whoever's second, which is damned close to first, just waltzes through and has an easy life. But you're still up with number one. Number one still needs you as his companion.'

In time, to friends like the designer David Litchfield – usually when he was drunk – he could even joke that in the contest they'd always waged, John's death had been a final act of oneupmanship. 'He died a legend and I'm going to die an old man. Typical John!'

PART FOUR

Carrying That Weight

PART FOUR

39

'Give me back my babies, Lew'

In the Eighties, Paul would cease to be known solely by the Christian name that occupied an immovable place after 'John' and before 'George and Ringo'. He also regained the schoolboy nickname of Maca, that very Liverpudlian abbreviation of McCartney he'd once shared with his brother, only now given exclusivity by a double 'c'. But whereas 'Paul' had a sigh of female adoration built into it, 'Macca' would mainly be used by males and suggest a more nuanced view.

Far from disbanding Wings after the Japan debacle, as expected, he maintained the illusion they were still a going concern for the rest of 1980. In the autumn, they returned to the studio apparently to start a new album and were filmed by BBC1's *Nationwide* programme rehearsing in a rented barn in the village of Tenterton, near Peasmarsh. But drummer Steve Holley felt he was just going through the motions: 'I could see the band unravelling in front of my eyes.'

John's murder at the hands of a seemingly devoted fan had terrified all other major rock stars and made them vastly increase their personal security, especially at live shows. On the Rolling Stones' 1981–82 American tour, a veritable army of yellow T-shirted thugs guarded the stage while the band themselves were watched over by a seven-foot-high giant and an entire martial arts academy.

It was no time to be taking young children on the road but, in truth, the McCartneys and Linda had already decided to scale down that side of Wings. 'Touring wasn't gelling with where they were in their lives,' recalls Laurence Juber. 'Linda had four children who needed to be at school; she had no more energy for travelling round the world and Paul didn't want to do it without her.'

Juber had already been hived off from Wings to accompany the couple to France and join them on Ringo's new album, *Stop and Smell the Roses*. This last-ever potential Beatles reunion once again saw three ex-members rallying round the abandoned 'child' of their divorce to try to keep his career alive. As well as singing backup vocals with Linda, Paul wrote and produced two tracks and George wrote and produced another. The summer before his death, John too had promised to take part and given Ringo a song that might be used, poignantly entitled 'Life Begins at 40'.

Paul had seemingly found a successor to Denny Laine: another noted vocalist and songwriter – and additionally someone almost as angelic-looking as himself – who was willing to be his sideman. Fellow northerner Eric Stewart had been in Wayne Fontana's backing group, the Mindbenders, then gone on to 10cc, one of the most original British bands of the Seventies, co-writing and performing their massively successful single 'I'm Not in Love'.

Following the Apple model, 10cc had started a fruit-themed independent studio, Strawberry, in Stockport, Lancashire, later opening a southern branch in Dorking, Surrey, only a few miles from Peasmarsh, which was what brought Stewart into Paul's orbit. He was in fact hospitalised after a serious car crash when Paul telephoned and suggested they work together.

In February 1981, a fully-recovered Stewart joined the personnel on what would be Paul's fourth solo album, *Tug of War*, recorded at George Martin's newly-opened AIR studios on the West Indies island of Montserrat, with Martin back in the producer's chair, as politely authoritative as ever. Although Wings were theoretically still in existence, only Linda and Denny Laine took part. The rest were VIP session musicians like Eric Stewart and American drummer Steve Gadd, plus two guest artistes whom Paul held in sufficient reverence to share lead vocals with them.

The first was Carl Perkins, the Fifties rockabilly legend who'd written and first recorded 'Blue Suede Shoes' and whose equally infectious 'Matchbox' and 'Honey Don't' used to be staples of the Beatles' stage act. A gentle, unassuming man who'd never grown that rich from his songbook, Perkins arrived on Montserrat without an entourage, in fact all alone. Strangely, Paul chose to waste him on an underpowered oddment called 'Get It' which, judging by his strained laughter at the end, Perkins didn't.

The album's other spectacular guest turn was Stevie Wonder, with whom Paul had only ever worked in the shambolic LA studio-session with John that became *A Toot and a Snore in '74*. Now there was no 'tooting' and certainly no snoring as they duetted 'Ebony and Ivory', Paul's plea for interracial harmony like the black and white keys on a piano. Stevie was his match in ruthless perfectionism, at one point pulling him up for handclaps that weren't quite in beat.

Three months on from John's death, he seemed fully recovered – but actually so many self-defence mechanisms had been in play that the enormity of it was only now sinking in. One day in the studio with Eric Stewart, he suddenly stopped work, overwhelmed by the realisation that the hilarious, irascible, cruel, kindly, haunted boy for whom he played 'Twenty Flight Rock' at St Peter's church fete was no longer in the world.

He had released no kind of 'tribute' song to John – further evidence to many of coldness or indifference. Now on *Tug of War* there would be 'Here Today', a direct address to an unnamed John, reflecting on the vast differences between them and the essential bond that had lasted almost to the end: 'Didn't understand a thing/ But we could always sing'. 'Here Today' wasn't released as a single or drawn attention to on the album, so most of the media never noticed it.

The doom of Wings was finally sealed by Denny Laine, who had survived all the band's personnel-changes and internal politics through the Seventies, but now wanted out if there was to be no more touring. Paul announced the break-up in April 1981, without forewarning drummer Steve Holley. 'The first I knew about it was a story in the *Evening Standard*,' Holley recalls. 'So I rang Paul and he said, "Oh, yeah . . . I meant to tell you."'

Despite Laine's finger-pointing *Japanese Tears* album, there seemed to have been no personal rancour in his departure. A month later, he joined Paul and Linda in overdubbing vocals for 'All Those Years Ago', a tribute to John by George which grabbed all the attention that should have gone to 'Here Today'. It was a three-quarter-Beatles reunion, the first time the survivors had recorded together since 'I Me Mine' in 1970. Mainly for that reason – the song itself being a feeble effort, previously offered to Ringo with different words – 'All Those Years Ago' spent three weeks at number two on the *Billboard* chart.

After that, Laine 'just kind of drifted away' from Paul. 'The next time I saw him was on the video for "Ebony and Ivory".'

Five pistol-shots outside the Dakota Building had shattered the decade-long hope that someday the Beatles might come back again. The result was a new wave of Beatlemania, far surpassing the 1963 version and this time destined never to subside.

Inevitably, the main focus was John. His last album, *Double Fantasy*, which had sold only moderately on its release in November 1980, became a posthumous global hit, as did '(Just Like) Starting Over' and the other singles taken from it. Three months after his death, he had sold two million records in the US alone. Even that was dwarfed by demand for the Beatles' 11 landmark albums, the compilations issued since their break-up and the new ones now being rushed into production. Everything they had ever recorded became of priceless value, back to the old jazz chestnuts they'd played as Tony Sheridan's backing band on the Polydor label and the amateur tapings of them drunk onstage at the Hamburg Star-Club.

Apart from the record companies, the main beneficiary of this international listening frenzy was Northern Songs, the publishing company created for Lennon and McCartney's output, which they'd lost to Lew Grade's ATV organisation in 1969. All Paul's success with Wings hadn't erased the nagging sense of injustice that he didn't own his Beatles songs. And now, with those songs at a greater premium than ever before, he suddenly had a chance to get them back.

Seventy-four-year-old Grade, recently elevated to the House of Lords, was in a financial hole comparable to the Beatles' when he'd snapped up Northern 12 years earlier. Moving from television to feature films, he had produced *Raise the Titanic*, an epic about salvaging the sunken liner which ended up so expensive and unprofitable that he remarked 'it would have been cheaper to lower the Atlantic'. With shares in his Associated Communications Corporation in freefall and his funding from City bankers terminated, he had no choice but to sell off parts of his entertainment and real estate empire.

Late in 1981, he approached Paul's lawyer, Lee Eastman, offering ATV Music, the division that included Northern Songs, for $30 million. Paul had maintained good relations with Grade and requested a personal meeting at which he asked if Northern might be for sale as the separate entity Grade had originally bought. By Paul's later account, Grade said yes, naming a price of £20 million. This was almost three times what he'd paid but, if new Beatlemania continued at its present pace, the money would very quickly be earned back.

The negotiations required Paul to join forces with Yoko, who now had sole, and beady-eyed, control of John's estate. She was content to let him take the lead but thought Grade's asking price far too high and – according to Paul – suggested offering only £5 million. Reports in the UK business press suggested he was putting up between £20 and £25 million but that Grade wasn't interested in separating Northern Songs from ATV Music: it had to be the whole publishing division or nothing.

A deal between Paul and Grade was said to be 'in its final stages' when four other potential purchasers appeared, among them CBS, the label on which Paul recorded. He and Yoko then jointly announced they were to sue ATV 'for breach of trust over past

Beatles sales and royalties'. Actually it was a revival of litigation over royalty payments begun in 1969 and since in limbo, and was widely seen as an attempt to spoil the impending auction of ATV Music.

Early in 1982, Paul gave an interview about the matter to *The Times* in a tone that could only offend an old-school showbiz type like Grade – in fact, an early manifestation of Macca. 'He should not screw me for what he could get for someone else. I'm not interested in buying the whole company. Give me back my babies, Lew.'

Initially, teaming with Yoko seemed to create a bond between them, so much so that Paul felt their past conflicts had come purely from 'misunderstanding'. 'Nobody understood John and Yoko,' he added in his *Times* interview. 'I didn't, to my everlasting sorrow.'

But as the affair dragged on, and their respective accounts of it began to differ, there was an abrupt mutual cooling. Meanwhile, an Australian industrial and media tycoon with the medieval-sounding name of Robert Holmes à Court was quietly buying up shares in Grade's overall company, Associated Communications Corporation, until by the end of 1982 he held 51 per cent. Holmes à Court, a devout Beatles fan, was not interested in offloading Northern Songs. From that point, the Paul and Yoko coolness became a deep freeze.

If he still didn't own that five-star chunk of his past work, Paul's control of the works of other composers continued to widen and diversify. Indeed, his MPL organisation's acquisition of publishing companies and copyrights had a luck and timing reminiscent of the Beatles in their heyday. For example, MPL hoovered up the music from three hit Broadway shows, *Grease*, *A Chorus Line* and *Annie*, each just a year before it became a huge-grossing Hollywood film. And while he mightn't have got back 'Eleanor Rigby', 'Penny Lane' or 'Hey Jude', there was some satisfaction in staking his claim to an original song so old that it had escaped the Lennon–McCartney branding-iron.

In July 1958, when the Beatles were still the Quarrymen, they'd scraped together a few shillings to make a record and so hopefully give themselves more credibility with Liverpool dance promoters. Cut at Percy Phillips's tiny home-studio, one side was a cover of the Crickets' 'That'll Be the Day' and the other an original Paul composition, 'In Spite of All the Danger',

Unable to afford a copy each, the five Quarrymen had to share one ten-inch acetate disc, keeping it for a week at a time, then passing it along. It thus came into the possession of Paul's school friend John Duff Lowe, who'd recently joined on a casual basis playing piano. At the end of his week, Lowe somehow forgot to pass on the disc, no one else asked for it and soon afterwards he drifted away from the band still with it in his possession.

In late 1981, with even the most mass-produced Beatles memorabilia booming in value, Lowe remembered the Percy Phillips recording session 23 years earlier and the solitary disc that had resulted and was still lying in a drawer at his parents' home. Having no idea what it might be worth, he decided to put it up for auction at Sotheby's. The London *Sunday Times* subsequently reported that the earliest known recording of John Lennon and Paul McCartney performing together was about to come onto the market and was expected to fetch a five-figure sum.

The story brought Lowe a warning letter from Clintons, a London law firm with a large rock star clientele. This forbade any auction of the disc because one of its two tracks, 'In Spite of All the Danger', was by Paul McCartney and his copyright would thereby be infringed. (In fact, the song had been jointly credited to Paul and George.) A phone number was given on which Lowe could reach Paul to discuss a possible private sale. The number proved to connect directly with Peasmarsh. Linda took Lowe's call, saying that Paul was out at present and adding, vis-à-vis the Sotheby's story, 'He's not pleased.'

When the two old school-friends did speak, Paul initially seemed to suggest Lowe had no right to the disc and should just hand it over: 'Come on, Duff, you're not supposed to have hung on to it . . .' But Lowe stuck to his guns that possession was nine-tenths of the law and a price, evidently in the low five figures, was agreed, subject to the authenticity of the merchandise being verified.

This was done rather in the style of a James Bond film with a Wings soundtrack. Paul's manager, Steve Shrimpton, and a Clintons lawyer travelled to Bristol where Lowe now worked; he fetched the disc from the bank-vault in which it had been kept in a briefcase, the authenticating features (ten-inch shellac disc, yellow label saying 'Kensington', handwritten credits) were checked and the money was handed over.

During their phone conversation, Paul had suggested Lowe should come to London after the business side was concluded and they'd have a nostalgic night out together. About a week later, he rang Peasmarsh again on the number he'd been given. But it had been disconnected.

Without a band to keep them on the run, Paul and Linda settled more deeply into Sussex, making it a place to work as well as live. Paul had further extended the Peasmarsh estate by buying Hog Hill Mill, a converted windmill in the nearby village of Icklesham, becoming only the mill's sixth owner since its construction exactly two centuries earlier. Here he installed a 48-track recording studio where he could make albums without the bother of journeying to Abbey Road.

Despite all the land and real estate they owned in the area, the McCartneys' personal lifestyle remained as unpretentious and unobtrusive as ever. Their younger daughters, Mary and Stella, both attended local state schools, first Peasmarsh C of E (Church of England) primary, then following Heather to Thomas Peacocke, the large comprehensive in Rye. As Stella would later acknowledge, it was the best possible antidote to being the children of a megacelebrity. 'You didn't boast about stuff, otherwise you'd get beaten up. It was healthy to see how most people in the world lived.'

One morning when Paul took the girls to school, he found the teachers on strike and picketing the front gate. They explained their grievances to him, expecting sympathy from someone with such well-publicised northern working-class roots. Instead, he snapped,

'*My* teachers never went on strike. You'll get no sympathy from me.' An amateur paparazzo took a photograph of him striding off across the playground in evident displeasure; the following week, it appeared on the front page of the *Times Educational Supplement*.

Thirteen-year-old Mary had inherited the dark, aquiline Irish beauty of her namesake, the mother Paul lost when he was 14. He'd told her about her grandmother's career as a nurse and midwife, and saw in her some of that same caring spirit which had been cut off so tragically early. Mary decided to become a nurse in her turn, until a tonsillectomy operation showed what horrendously hard work it was; after that, her interest moved to the camera her mother never stopped pointing and clicking, whatever else was going on.

But 11-year-old 'Stell', small, fair, and angel-faced, never had any doubt where she was headed. As a toddler, she would watch old Technicolor Hollywood movies, fascinated by the wardrobes of the female stars, especially when they had a tomboy look, like Doris Day's buckskins and army cap in *Calamity Jane*. Unknown to her parents, she'd sit for hours inside their shared walk-in clothes closet, gazing at both the 'his' and 'hers' racks. As a result, both Linda's thrown-together preppy look and Paul's carefully-calculated dapperness would one day contribute to groundbreaking couture.

Stella had a directness and sassiness that gentle Mary lacked. She resented it, for instance, that everyone she met knew everything about her mother and father, yet would have been horrified at any invasion of their own parents' privacy. 'And who are *your* mum and dad?' she always wanted to ask.

Heather, now 19, had passed a confusing adolescence, half in the hippy-organic atmosphere of home, half in the punky clamour of her comprehensive school, and was – she would later recall – 'the most clumsy, chaotic teenager'. As Paul's adopted daughter, she had never been made to feel any less loved and valued than his biological ones, to both of whom she was extremely close, as she was to her five-year-old brother, James.

Former Apple stalwart Tony Bramwell had observed the family

from the inside since Paul brought Heather from America, and knew of the problems in adjusting to her new life that had largely brought about the move to Sussex. Bramwell recalls that while never showing her overt favouritism, Linda always kept her 'sort of separate' from the others as if in special need of protection and nurturing.

For a time, she seemed set on following in her mother's footsteps: she took a photography course at the London College of Printing and in 1981 won an award for her portrait of American drummer Steve Gadd during the *Tug of War* sessions on Montserrat. Then, deciding she couldn't compete with Linda, she took up printing at the Photographers Workshop in Covent Garden, winning an award as Young Black and White Printer of the Year with a study of the waterfall at Peasmarsh.

All three of Paul's daughters shared his and Linda's strict vegetarianism, now developing into an interest in the growing animal rights movement. All shared their mother's passion for horses and had become accomplished riders, though inevitably there were occasional spills. Heather suffered a particularly bad fall and had to be rushed to the Royal East Sussex Hospital, where she was found to have a broken arm and collarbone. A grim-faced Paul later told journalists that the family had been 'struck down by bad luck' but refused to go into detail about the accident.

Awkwardly for the McCartneys, riding in the Peasmarsh area was inextricably bound up with fox hunting. The East Sussex and Romney Marsh Hunt was a regular winter spectacle, pursuing its quarry over neighbouring fields in a swirl of red coats, braying horns and yelping hounds. In recent years, the hunt had been disrupted by saboteurs from animal rights groups, using increasingly extreme tactics. Paul and Linda abhorred hunting but, as they had to live here, did not publicly align themselves with the 'sabs'.

During one particularly violent confrontation, the huntsman, Tony Percy – the official in charge of the 140 foxhounds – was attacked with a pickaxe-handle and pulled off his horse, suffering a back injury that ended his riding career. Percy later opened the Old

House Saddlery in Peasmarsh High Street, selling high-class riding tack made by in-house craftsman Keith Lovejoy. The McCartneys – whose animal rights stance did not yet outlaw leather – became frequent customers. Percy's daughter, Natalie, then aged 12, recalls Linda ordering a bridle of Havana leather with cut-out diamond shapes for Paul.

To Natalie, he was a deity to whom she seldom spoke directly but who was unfailingly benign. Her best friend, Lucy, lived beside Hog Hill and the girls would often creep up to the mill and eavesdrop on the sounds coming from its studio, whose guest musicians could be anyone from Eric Clapton to Roger Daltrey of the Who. One day, as she was riding along School Lane to a horse-show, Paul suddenly appeared behind her at the wheel of a blue Mercedes so wide that it barely fitted the lane. He didn't try to pass or show any sign of impatience, but slowed down to her horse's pace, switching on his hazard lights to warn other traffic, in effect watching over her until she reached her turning.

While Linda's commitment to her children was absolute, protecting Paul always remained her primary concern – if not from physical harm, then from being taken advantage of. 'People were always trying to do that,' his designer friend David Litchfield remembers. 'Often the very last people in the world that you'd expect.

'One time, their Lamborghini had been brought back to MPL after having something minor done to it. Paul wouldn't accept it until Linda checked it out. We heard a lot of shouting in reception and found her giving the delivery guy hell. She'd discovered that while it was at the garage, someone had nicked its new tyres and put four half-worn ones in their place.

'I said to Paul later, "If anyone tried to hurt you, Linda would tear his ears off, wouldn't she?" He laughed and said, "Yeah, you're right."'

40

'About as close as you can get to a non-movie'

Paul turned 40 in June 1982. The sombre milestone was marked by two major lifestyle changes: he gave up smoking (tobacco, that's to say) and took up painting.

He was always the most actively artistic Beatle – for a long time much more so than John – using his flair for drawing and design in numerous ways, from sketching the band's earliest stage-suits to conceiving the covers for *Sgt. Pepper, Abbey Road* and every Wings album. But his view of painting remained as it had been back when John was the art student and he just a cartoon-drawing schoolboy: he thought it something one couldn't do without having gone to college.

That lingering superstition was dispelled by meeting America's greatest modern painter, Willem de Kooning, the Eastman family's friend and East Hampton neighbour. 'Bill' was the most unpretentious of men, working in just a pair of old shorts in his huge, airy studio. Unlike most abstract painters, he didn't at all mind being questioned about the 'meaning' of his works, and seldom gave very complicated answers. One day, Paul plucked up the courage to ask what a certain purple silhouette might represent.

De Kooning peered at it, then replied, 'I dunno. Looks like a couch, huh?'

Then came a summer when the McCartneys rented a house of their own on Long Island and found its owners had removed all the pictures, leaving walls dotted with unsightly hooks. To conceal them, Paul bought some oil paints and dashed off a set of largely monochrome canvases. Having never used oils, he didn't realise how long they took to dry; when the rental ended two weeks later, his canvases were still wet and he had to have a special case made to transport them home.

Willem de Kooning gave the spur to his painting that Buddy Holly and Elvis once had to his music. He bought his paint and brushes at the same art-store de Kooning used and set up his easel on a porch looking towards de Kooning's house. Like all who take up the pastime, he found it hugely relaxing and refreshing, though the workaholic never let up: replicating de Kooning's expansive brush-strokes, he turned out abstracts and landscapes almost as quickly as he wrote songs. One night while Linda was watching television, he started a portrait of her which taught him that skin wasn't just one colour, as he'd always thought, but demanded many shades of pink, blue, red and black.

For Linda – who turned 40 nine months before Paul – 1982 brought the first serious attention as a photographer she had received outside America. A selection of her work over the past decade and a half, simply entitled *Photographs*, was published in a lavish coffee-table book and formed a travelling exhibition which opened in Liverpool, then moved to London, Jarrow, West Germany and Australia.

The work was an eclectic mix ranging from her mid-Sixties studies of rock icons like Jim Morrison and Jimi Hendrix and snap-shots of the Beatles making the White Album – including some touching ones of John and Yoko – through numerous portraits of Paul and the children to Bill de Kooning, her beloved Appaloosa stallion, Lucky Strike, and sheep. Her toddler son James appeared, unnamed, urinating on London's Thames Embankment rather like the Manneken Pis statue in Brussels.

The book received respectful coverage and the exhibition drew crowds wherever it went. The plaudit that meant most to Linda came from the great French photographer, 88-year-old Jacques-Henri Lartigue. A shot of a little Scottish boy running across wasteland so impressed Lartigue that, without knowing who the photographer was, he requested a copy to pin up in his Paris studio.

Linda did a full round of interviews – her first without Paul at her side – from BBC radio's *Woman's Hour* to Channel 4's *The Tube*, sounding more relaxed and forthcoming than she ever had before. In every one she insisted she had no ambition other than to be with her family and friends. 'I like truth,' she told *The Tube*'s Paula Yates. 'I like being ordinary.'

Wings were already becoming a distant memory. 'Ebony and Ivory', Paul's duet with Stevie Wonder, released in April 1982, spent seven weeks at number one on the *Billboard* singles chart – his twenty-eighth song to be logged there – en route to a Novello award as International Hit of the Year. *Tug of War*, the album on which it appeared, was number one in both the US and the UK and sold massively all over the world, particularly in Japan.

Another ebony-and-ivory duet was on its way – this time with a colour-contrast rather less pronounced. On Christmas Day 1980 at Peasmarsh, he had received a surprise transatlantic phone call. 'Hi, Paul,' said a fragile falsetto voice. 'It's Michael Jackson. Do you wanna make some hits?'

By now, the former child singer in Motown's 'black Beatles' had more than fulfilled that long managerial fantasy of an act rivalling the real ones. With his corkscrew curls, Sgt. Pepper-ish scarlet jacket, single white glove and magic feet, Jackson was the most original, insanely successful presence in pop since fringed hair and violin basses. He was a huge admirer of the real Beatles, especially Paul, who had contributed a song named 'Girlfriend' to his first solo album, *Off the Wall*. As their respective record-labels, CBS and Epic, had the same parent company, there were no contractual difficulties in their teaming up.

They began work together in London in the autumn of 1981. Jackson had already begun the course of plastic surgery that would increasingly seem more like self-mutilation; a condition called vitiligo had drained the pigmentation from his skin, making him look strangely raceless as well as sexless.

A showbusiness pro since the age of six, he had been denied any normal childhood and consequently was a child manqué, obsessed by J.M. Barrie's story of Peter Pan, 'the little boy who never grew up', and only really happy in the company of the very young. Though in the early Eighties this did not excite much comment, it would increasingly overshadow his short, sad life.

A top secret session had been booked at George Martin's AIR Studios to develop a McCartney/Jackson co-composition called 'Say Say Say'. No one else was allowed to be present but Linda and little James McCartney, with whom Jackson played on the floor like a fellow five-year-old.

The collaboration went so well that Paul invited him down to Peasmarsh to see another side of growing up in the rock business. He was wistfully envious of Mary and Stella's idyllic world of pets and horses, though he declined an invitation to go on a ride with them, explaining, 'I'm not allowed to get dirty.' To Paul he confided that he now identified with Peter Pan so closely, he even shared Peter's ability to fly.

Despite all his years in the business, Jackson seemed strangely naive about its financial workings, so one evening over dinner – as he later recalled – his host showed him 'a little book with MPL printed on the cover . . . It contained a full list of all the songs Paul owned – and he'd been buying rights to songs for a long time. I had never given the idea of buying songs any thought before.'

'This is the way to make big money,' Paul explained, a little like the teacher he'd so nearly become. 'Every time someone records one of the songs, I get paid. Every time someone plays one of the songs on the radio, I get paid. And the other important thing is to make some really good videos.' He would later wish the lesson hadn't sunk in quite so well.

In April 1982, he rejoined Jackson in Los Angeles to complete 'Say Say Say' and record two more duets, 'The Man' and 'The Girl Is Mine', featuring the pair in the implausible role of rival suitors, complete with some twee dialogue between them. The three tracks were then shared, 'Say Say Say' and 'The Man' going to Paul and 'The Girl Is Mine' appearing on Jackson's *Thriller*, the most successful album of all time with 65 million ultimately sold.

Those LA sessions, so musically productive, were awkward on a personal level. For Jackson's producer, Quincy Jones, was married to the actress Peggy Lipton, a former girlfriend of Paul's whom he'd unceremoniously ditched, along with several others, when he met Linda. To show there were no hard feelings, Jones proposed the four of them should have dinner. It was a rather sticky encounter nonetheless, hardly helped by Paul's insistence on calling Peggy 'Mrs Jones'.

The success of MPL's music publishing arm had not lessened Paul's wish for it to be equally significant in film production, as was shown in its recent name-change to MPL Communications. And the autumn of 1982 brought a seemingly perfect way to make that happen.

The company had already put out two highly successful documentaries about Wings tours, *Wings Over America* and *Rockshow*. But simply having cameras pointed at him, though never unwelcome, wasn't enough for Paul. He wanted to make 'real' movies and be involved at every level in a creative process which had always fascinated him. He'd tried it once, with the Beatles' *Magical Mystery Tour*, and engineered a monumental flop – but he was older and wiser now and MPL wasn't Apple.

He'd always wanted to make a film based on the *Band on the Run* album and in 1974 had asked the great science fiction writer Isaac Azimov to develop a 'sci-fi movie musical' in which a rock band discovered they were being impersonated by extraterrestrials, but nothing ever came of it. Ten years later, he still felt the idea had potential, so commissioned the Liverpool playwright Willy Russell, author of *John, Paul, George, Ringo . . . and Bert* to come up with a different story and write a full script. Suddenly cooling on the project – exactly why, Russell never discovered – he sent an appeal for new scripts around the film companies that were his Soho neighbours, but found nothing else that caught his fancy.

Then one day, stuck in traffic in the back of his chauffeured limo, he'd started jotting down a script of his own. Its hero was a rock star bearing a strong resemblance to himself – named Paul in fact – whose career was thrown into crisis when someone stole the only tapes of his latest recording session. Real-life Paul had suffered that very misfortune while making *Band on the Run* in Nigeria. But whereas he'd simply re-recorded the pilfered tapes from memory, he launched his alter ego on a quest to recover them.

Its title came from a news item that Broad Street station, a Victorian railway terminus in the City of London, was scheduled for closure and redevelopment as offices. For pun-loving Paul, the location echoed one of his father's favourite old songs, George M. Cohan's 'Give My Regards to Broadway'. So, in a spirit of John Betjeman-esque nostalgia – though he'd barely been aware of the station hitherto – he titled his script *Give My Regards to Broad Street*.

Among his wide circle of powerful friends outside music was the producer David Puttnam, whose *Chariots of Fire* had won the Oscar for Best Picture in 1981. In his search for film projects, he'd become accustomed to bouncing ideas off Puttnam; so much so that the producer was starting to feel a bit like a squash court. One thing Puttnam had impressed on him above all was that making a movie wasn't like making an album, which could be stopped and re-started as the mood took him, but would demand at least two years of solid commitment.

Give My Regards to Broad Street thus started out as a less demanding vehicle, a one-hour TV film that would be part whodunnit, part documentary and part musical, showcasing present and past songs by Paul with A-list session musicians including Eric Stewart. As such, it did not call for a movie director but a television one who, because of the subject matter, had best be British. On Puttnam's recommendation, Paul chose 40-year-old Peter Webb, then considered Britain's top director of TV commercials but ripe to move into features like Alan Parker and Hugh Hudson before him.

Shooting began at Elstree Studios, in a convivial atmosphere of old friends and colleagues meeting up again, with plenty of in-jokes to savour. George had declined to take part but Ringo joined the backing musicians while his wife Barbara played a journalist; George Martin was musical director and also appeared as himself, as did engineer Geoff Emerick. The Australian actor Bryan Brown was cast as on-screen Paul's manager, Steve, acting very much like real Paul's real-life Australian manager, Steve Shrimpton.

The main object, Paul announced, was for everyone to have fun and, to begin with, he seemed to be having plenty himself. He relished the role of leading man which, unlike that of lead rock musician, meant relays of people titivating him each time he had to perform. 'If someone wants to come and brush my hair, I must admit I like it,' he told Melvyn Bragg, whose TV arts programme, *The South Bank Show*, was following the shoot. He also enjoyed working with George Martin to compose incidental music for a whole film rather than just bits of them as he had previously.

Linda, who had various cameo – though non-speaking – roles, was on hand every day in her role of shield and people-filter. But her vigilance could slip. At the musician auditions, sax-player Mel Collins brought along his wife, the former Maggie McGivern, once the most secret of all Paul's clandestine girlfriends, who hadn't seen him since he turned up on her doorstep, seemingly distraught, on the night before his wedding.

Maggie had kept in touch with Neil Aspinall, hence this invitation. Thanks to her presence, Mel Collins became the only auditionee whom Paul invited to lunch. 'There were only the three of us and Cubby Broccoli [producer of the Bond films],' she remembers. 'Paul and I just talked and talked. Afterwards, Mel said to me, "it was just like you were coming home". I saw Paul's son, James, and his brother, Mike, but Linda didn't appear until we were leaving.' She feels it may not have been just coincidence that Mel subsequently didn't get into the film.

The only person conspicuously not having fun was the film's director, Peter Webb, to whom every day seemed to bring a fresh, dismaying revelation. The first was that he had to film Paul's script, which covered only 22 pages (one page usually equals a minute of screen-time) and which, because it was Paul, had gone through none of the customary rewriting, rethinking and re-rewriting. Still more dismaying was the discovery that, while totally at ease as his real self in front of still or television cameras, Paul was oddly stiff and self-conscious when acting the part of himself – and he was the centre of virtually every scene.

As he later admitted, he felt the role of jivey rock star 'Paul', for whom life held nothing worse than missing tapes, was really too young for him. One day, watching George Martin give a flawless portrayal of George Martin, he realised he was now six years older than Martin had been when the Beatles first came to Abbey Road and they used to consider him so elderly.

While a director normally enjoys total autonomy on the set, Webb felt his function become more like a record producer in the 'enabling' George Martin style; there simply to listen to what Paul wanted, then make it happen. Nonetheless, with an impressive professional supporting cast, a bunch of excellent musicians and a top-drawer crew and technical team, Webb felt he had the ingredients for a memorable hour of television.

But then, with shooting well under way, everything changed. Lee Eastman took the project to Harvey Weinstein, the American rock-promoter-turned-movie mogul whose Miramax company had distributed MPL's *Rockshow* documentary. Without reading the script, Weinstein took it to 20th Century Fox, still the most prestigious of the old-time Hollywood studios, whose executives (without reading the script) scented a Beatle screen musical to rival *A Hard Day's Night*. Fox added £4.4 million in funding to MPL's original £500,000 and scheduled *Give My Regards to Broad Street* as a virtually guaranteed box-office smash in 1984. Despite never having directed a big-budget film, Peter Webb was kept in post, feeling that 'the carpet had been pulled from under my feet'.

Filming continued into 1983, by now absorbing so much of Paul's attention (as David Puttnam had warned) that he had no time to record the new album he would have expected to release later in the year. Instead, a selection of leftovers from *Tug of War* came out under the title *Pipes of Peace*, topped off by 'Say Say Say' and 'The Man', his two duets with Michael Jackson. The title track – with its resonance of John – was accompanied by a video recreating the First World War's famous Christmas truce. A British and a German soldier were shown emerging from their trenches and crossing a shell-blasted No Man's Land to shake hands, both of them played by Paul in different moustaches.

In April and May, the memoirs of Jo Jo Laine, who had split from Denny the previous year, were serialised by the tabloid *Sunday People* in excerpts headlined 'My Galaxy of Rock Star Lovers', 'Lust at First Sight' and, climactically, 'Inside the Strange World of Paul McCartney'.

Jo Jo's relations with Linda in the Wings era had always been difficult – by her account, because Paul always fancied her. Although not suggesting he had been among her galaxy of rock star lovers, she waxed eloquent on the McCartneys' rustic lifestyle and fondness for dope. Linda came across as a controlling hausfrau and Paul as a bit of a wimp who 'enjoys Big Mama . . . running the show'.

There were some things from which Linda couldn't protect him. 'He was giving me a lift one day and told me to move a sack of letters from the front passenger seat to the back,' David Litchfield remembers. '"Go ahead and read one,"' he said, "they're all the same." Every one was from a woman, claiming he'd slept with her in the past and she'd had a child by him.

'"Some of them are really impressive," Paul said. '"They come with lawyers' letters and exact details of when and where, and I start racking my brains and thinking to myself 'Maybe I *did* once have sex with her'."'

Often such allegations were what a later era would term 'historical'. In 1983, Erika Hubers went before a Berlin judge, claiming that Paul had fathered her daughter, Bettina, during the Beatles' visits to Hamburg in the early 1960s. The former Reeperbahn waitress had first made the allegation in 1964 in the midst of the band's first American tour. But the British press, fearful of damaging the nation's darlings at their moment of supreme triumph, had refused to touch the story.

Resurfacing in an age increasingly hungry for celebrity sex-scandals, Hubers claimed £1.75 million on behalf of the now-adult Bettina and herself. Paul denied the allegation but the Berlin judge found it sufficiently plausible to order him to take a blood test. When the result exonerated him, Hubers alleged that he'd used a stand-in and he was ordered to retake it, meantime paying Bettina maintenance of £175 per month. The second test also proving in his favour, he magnanimously saved Hubers from financial ruin by settling her legal costs.

Nearer home, Liverpudlian Anita Cochrane openly claimed that her 19-year-old son, Philip, had been fathered by Paul, whom she'd first met at the Cavern when she was 16 and still a virgin. That charge, too, had first surfaced in 1964, as the Beatles basked in their carefully-constructed image of cuddly moptops. Anita herself had accepted a once-and-for-all pay-off from Brian Epstein and sought nothing further from Paul, but her outraged relatives had taken to the streets, handing out leaflets about 'Paul the cad' to crowds at the Beatles' civic welcome home by the Lord Mayor.

The Anita Cochrane story was finally revealed in 1983 by Peter Brown, that formerly loyal and discreet Beatles aide, in a memoir entitled *The Love You Make* – a quotation from Paul's finale to the *Abbey Road* album. Paul made no public response, any more than he had to Jo Jo Laine's *Sunday People* extravaganza. Privately, he was outraged and ceremonially burned a copy of Brown's book while Linda took photographs.

George Orwell's chilling post-war novel of the same name had made 1984 a year to dread. But its arrival found Britain suffering none of the post-nuclear totalitarian horrors Orwell had predicted: no Communist-style police state, no cowed, impoverished populace and (with neither mobile phones nor e-mail yet) no uncontrolled, indiscriminate mass surveillance.

Instead, under Margaret Thatcher's Conservative government,

there was rampant capitalism, wholesale privatisation of publicly-owned utilities and a war against trade unions culminating in the brutal suppression of a miners' strike. There was much of the same frivolity and hedonism against a grim background as in the Sixties; there was bisexual pop music, postmodernist architecture, breakfast-time television, alternative comedy, outsize shoulder pads for women and a vogue among both sexes and all ages for the same virulent shade of jade green.

In 1984, too, the renaissance in British films sparked by David Puttnam's *Chariots of Fire* reached new heights with David Lean's *A Passage to India*, Hugh Hudson's *Greystoke*, Neil Jordan's *The Company of Wolves*, Puttnam's own *The Killing Fields* and *A Private Function*, co-produced by none other than George Harrison – but not, alas, with Paul McCartney's *Give My Regards to Broad Street*.

The year started badly enough for Paul. In January, he and Linda were in Barbados, enjoying a quiet evening with Eric Stewart, Stewart's wife Gloria and some pot, when a squad of police burst in. Although cannabis was technically illegal on the island, it was widely used and sold openly on the beach in front of the McCartneys' rented villa, so they had considered themselves quite safe. It turned out that one of their temporary domestics had snitched on them, forcing the law to act.

The next day, they appeared in court in nearby Holetown and were fined $100 each. Their holiday ruined, they flew home at once, landing at Heathrow, then switching to a private plane. When their baggage appeared from the Barbados flight, one of Linda's suitcases was missing. It had been intercepted and opened and a tiny amount of weed – less than .02 of an ounce – had been found. A large media contingent was present, so once again Paul found himself being busted on TV, though this time, at least, no prison cell awaited him.

'Can we get one thing straight?' he said, now very much Macca. 'This substance, cannabis, is a lot less harmful than rum punch, whisky, nicotine or glue, all of which are perfectly legal.' Would he be using it again, someone asked. 'No, never again.'

Linda took sole responsibility and later appeared at Uxbridge Magistrates' Court, where all Heathrow malefactors end up. In view of the tiny quantity involved, she escaped with a fine of £75, telling the press it had been 'much ado about nothing'. Paul's last album gave Fleet Street a perfect headline: 'PIPES OF POT'.

The timing could not have been worse for still more embarrassing revelations from a formerly intimate and trusted associate. Since the end of Wings, Denny Laine's solo career had not prospered and his financial difficulties had multiplied to the point where he'd sold his equity as co-writer of 'Mull of Kintyre' back to Paul for £135,000. Now, following his ex-wife's example, his memoirs of the Wings era were all over a British tabloid, in this case the far nastier and more widely-read *Sun*.

The series was titled 'The Real McCartney' and its opening instalment bore the strapline 'I saw Paul smuggle pot in his son's coat'. According to Laine, Paul and Linda smoked pot on a daily basis, so much so that Paul's records suffered chronically from delay and lack of focus. Referring back to the Tokyo episode, he said they derived a perverse thrill from trying to get illegal substances past customs officials. He also reiterated Jo Jo's view of their relationship, but more woundingly: '[Paul's] a mummy's boy who didn't have a mummy after his mother died when he was 14. He would be lost without Linda now.'

For Peter Webb, directing a major Hollywood movie instead of the originally-planned one-hour TV special had turned into 'a nightmare scenario'. By now he was editing *Give My Regards to Broad Street* in London and driving down to Sussex to let Paul and Linda edit his edit. These viewings at Hog Hill Mill became increasingly fraught; Webb sensed that Paul regretted hiring him and longed to turn the project over to Richard Lester, who had directed *A Hard Day's Night* and *Help!*

When a rough cut was finally agreed, Webb flew to Los Angeles to show it to 20th Century Fox. Its plot remained the paper-thin one of Paul trying to track down his stolen album-tapes as a succession of distinguished British actors struggled to provide plausibility. Sir

Ralph Richardson, perhaps the greatest Shakespearian actor of his generation, had a minuscule role as a pub landlord feeding a pet monkey. That ignominious cameo proved Richardson's last screen appearance: he had died soon after completing his part.

Broad Street railway station, supposedly the film's nostalgic *raison d'être*, appeared only at the end as the place where the tape-snaffler had inexplicably gone to hide out and then got locked in a lavatory. Bleak and charmless, it suggested no reason why Paul or anyone else should give it their regards. The final moments showed him busking 'Yesterday' on a platform, then awakening in the back of his limo and realising it had all been a dream.

The only substance – or, indeed, sense – was in the music. Between bouts of tape-hunting, Paul and a star-studded new Rockestra played Wings material like 'Silly Love Songs' and 'Wanderlust' and a handful of his Beatles songs, including 'For No One', 'Here, There and Everywhere', 'The Long and Winding Road' and 'Eleanor Rigby', the last of which he'd never previously performed in public.

Thanks to his Hollywood budget, he didn't just perform it – on the stage of an empty Royal Albert Hall – but expanded it into a lengthy Victorian fantasy sequence starring himself, which began like Manet's *Le Déjeuner sur l'herbe* with Linda, Ringo and Barbara, and ended with him on his own, prowling nocturnal streets in a top hat and cloak like some angel-faced Jack the Ripper. At one point, for no discernible reason, the scene changed to a snowy Highgate Cemetery and a vision – horribly sad in retrospect – of a ghost-like Linda on a white horse.

All this totally baffled the 20th Century Fox executives, who had been expecting a latter-day *Hard Day's Night* but been presented with what one of them called 'Paul McCartney's home movie'. Yet because of their investment, and because it was Paul, the release-process ground into gear nonetheless. By now, the stress had become too much for Peter Webb and he was hospitalised suffering from extreme nervous exhaustion. A remorseful Paul inundated him with so many flowers 'I thought someone had died'. He would later say it took him two years to recover.

Give My Regards to Broad Street opened in October 1984 with a huge fanfare, premiering in Los Angeles and New York, then Liverpool and London. This return to his home city had double significance for Paul as Liverpool Council (not without some internal opposition) had recently voted to give all four former Beatles the freedom of the city. Before the film premiere at the Odeon cinema, he accepted his award in the Picton Library – the same place where he'd received his prize for his Coronation essay as an 11-year-old in 1953.

The film's reviews made those for *Magical Mystery Tour*, 17 years earlier, seem positively benign. *Variety* found it 'characterless, bloodless [and] pointless' while to the *Washington Post* it had 'the kind of smothering tedium that leaves you screaming for air'. The *Chicago Sun-Times*'s influential, and scrupulously fair, Roger Ebert, while praising the music, called it 'about as close to a non-movie as you can get', adding that 'the parts that try to do something are the worst'.

At the starry London premiere at Leicester Square's Empire cinema, it was greeted by an embarrassed silence, as Eric Stewart remembers. 'People were looking at each other, saying, "What *was* that?"' The next edition of *Spitting Image*, ITV's satirical puppet-show, featured a steroid-eyed Paul figure at a restaurant table, being served a film can on a plate. 'Your turkey, sir,' leered his waiter.

The soundtrack album, however, was a huge hit, as was its lead single, 'No More Lonely Nights', with a video of Paul on a now romantically dark and rainy Broad Street platform, and a yearning guitar solo by Pink Floyd's David Gilmour.

When *Give My Regards to Broad Street* went on general release, it was accompanied by another MPL film in the old-fashioned role of 'second feature' which audiences could applaud unreservedly. This was *Rupert and the Frog Song*, a 13-minute sample of the feature-length Rupert Bear cartoon Paul had been planning since 1969.

Animator Geoff Dunbar had created a Disney-standard vignette of Rupert stumbling on a choir of frogs said to convene only once every 200 years. Their song, 'We All Stand Together', was the one on which work had been stopped by the news of John Lennon's death. Paul was the voice of Rupert and his friend, Bill Badger. The imperturbable Mr Bear in tweed plus-fours, working in his garden, was yet another involuntary echo of Gentleman Jim McCartney.

'We All Stand Together' became a UK number two single and the film won a BAFTA award in the 'animated short' category. But, although it ended with a teasing 'That's all for now', there was to be no sequel. Another producer had acquired the Rupert rights and insisted the feature-length version could only be made by his company and MPL in partnership. With that, the project quickly withered away.

But at least there was now in existence a movie with a story and script by Paul, and with Paul playing the lead, that indisputably worked.

41

'I bought your songs, Paul'

In July 1985, a devastating famine in Ethiopia prompted Live Aid, to this day the biggest charity pop concert ever staged. Simultaneous outdoor shows in Britain and America, featuring a multitude of top names – among them Queen, Bob Dylan, Madonna, Mick Jagger, Duran Duran, Elton John, U2, Led Zeppelin, Phil Collins, Spandau Ballet, the Who, Elvis Costello, Eric Clapton, the Beach Boys and Tina Turner – were watched live by almost 200,000 people and televised to an estimated 1.9 billion in 150 countries. With glorious weather at both venues, it was like a rebirth of 'All You Need Is Love'.

Because of the five-hour time difference, the marathon opened with a British segment from London's Wembley Stadium, which then linked up with the American one at Philadelphia's John F. Kennedy Stadium. Despite formidable younger competition, the only possible choice for the British finale, just before 10 p.m., was Paul, alone at a white piano singing 'Let It Be'.

He suffered sound problems from the beginning, so was forced to give a rather souped-up version of his mother's dream-hymn. Over-the-shoulder videoing allowed millions to share his view of Wembley's huge, living darkness, from which faint boos signalled that many people couldn't hear. Towards the end, David Bowie, Pete Townshend, Alison Moyet and Live Aid's organiser, Bob Geldof, joined him as impromptu backup singers. Afterwards, when the other UK artistes congregated onstage, he and

Townshend saluted Geldof's achievement by hoisting him onto their shoulders.

Only later would the full story emerge of what ego-clashes and back-stabbing had gone on behind Live Aid's seeming altruism and unanimity. As if for old times' sake, there was even a breath of historic Beatle rancour. Originally Paul wanted George to join him in 'Let It Be', a nice thought for the man whose Concert for Bangladesh had first motivated rock stars to unite for good causes. But to George, the song was too redolent of his bruised ego in the Beatle wars of 1969–70. Paul hadn't wanted him to sing on it 16 years ago, he responded when Geldof made the request, so why would he want to now?

After the *Give My Regards to Broad Street* disaster, Paul had sought refuge in his new windmill studio on Hog Hill and his fifteenth album since leaving the Beatles. Rather than draw on his banks of existing material, he wanted to write a complete new set of songs with a new collaborator would also be a co-producer.

The perfect candidate seemed to be his VIP sideman Eric Stewart, who'd had extensive production experience at 10cc's Strawberry Studio and whose major composing credits included 'I'm Not In Love' and 'The Things We Do for Love'. Accordingly, Stewart was asked down to Peasmarsh as co-writer and co-producer of the album that would become *Press to Play*. 'Bring your acoustic round and we'll have a plonk,' was how Paul would remember the invitation.

But when Stewart arrived at Hog Hill Mill, he found he wasn't the only one to have received the call. In the eternal quest for con-temporaneity, Paul had also recruited Hugh Padgham, a young producer currently enjoying great success with Genesis, Peter Gabriel and the Human League.

The two rival co-producers did not fall out – that, indeed, was the trouble. Early in the sessions, Stewart felt that one of Paul's vocals wasn't as good as it could be, so he switched on the intercom and said so. When Paul asked Hugh Padgham's opinion, Padgham was at first reluctant to criticise such a colossus but, under pressure, admitted that he agreed with Stewart. 'Hugh, when did you last make a number one record?' Paul inquired coldly.

Yet that autocratic Macca could always be replaced by democratic Paul, whose accessibility and informality seemed too good to be true – but weren't. At Christmas time, he was a familiar sight at Hamleys toyshop in Oxford Street, standing in line like anyone else with armfuls of purchases for his children. One day when travelling into London by train, he saw an elderly woman on the platform struggling with a heavy bag and insisted on carrying it for her.

His thoughtfulness, and sheer sweetness, could be overwhelming, as his designer–editor friend David Litchfield discovered when leaving for a holiday in France. As a goodbye gift – though the trip was only for two weeks – Paul composed and recorded a short instrumental piece, with seabird sound effects, and gave Litchfield the tape, as he said, 'so that you won't forget me'. The tape later got mislaid in a house move, but Litchfield recalls: 'It was a lovely, haunting tune, rather like the theme to the *Deer Hunter*. He called it Seabird or Seadance, probably because I was working on a movie script called Seadance at the time.'

If that was pure Paul, the circumstances of its recording were even more so. He'd been at Abbey Road studios one day, testing some amps, and got talking to a delivery-driver who was a classical violinist on the side. At Paul's invitation, the man had fetched his violin from his truck, Paul sat down at the piano and the two had made the track together.

Little of the same sweetness was to be felt by the young co-producer/engineer of *Press to Play*. There was only one now since Eric Stewart – shocked by Macca's frigid put-down of Hugh Padgham – had bowed out of the album a few days later, so ending an otherwise happy and fruitful relationship extending over five years. Padgham soldiered on alone with a growing feeling of being able to do nothing right.

As a forty-third birthday present, he'd given Paul the Trivial Pursuit board game, not thinking that its pop music section was bound to feature questions on the Beatles. Paul was incensed to find one of them was about his mother's death.

The month after Live Aid, he received some news that drove all thought of album-making from his mind and turned up the Macca-control even higher. His erstwhile collaborator Michael Jackson had bought ATV Music and so now owned the Lennon–McCartney song catalogue. As Padgham – relieved not to be the offender for once – would later recall, 'The air turned blue.'

Since his failed attempt to buy ATV Music with Yoko in 1981–82, Paul had seemed as intent as ever on getting back his 'babies'. An additional spur was discovering that he couldn't sing 'Yesterday' and the other Lennon–McCartney songs in *Give My Regards to Broad Street* without first clearing the rights with ATV. The fact that he and John's estate took a share of the copyright-fees didn't make it any less galling.

Lord Lew Grade had by this time been ousted as boss of ATV Music's parent company, Associated Communications Corporation, by its Australian majority shareholder, Robert Holmes à Court. And in 1983, Paul had approached Holmes à Court with another bid to regain control of his songbook. This time, there was no mention of any partnership with Yoko: he believed her interventions had stymied the previous attempt – just as she believed his had – and they were no longer in contact.

Forty years Grade's junior, Holmes à Court had grown up with the Beatles and was thrilled by the prospect of negotiating with Paul. He seemed refreshingly simple and approachable, although Lee Eastman recognised this as a favourite pose among predatory tycoons and urged caution. Nonetheless the two got on well, so much so that Holmes à Court cherished hopes of Paul hosting a charity telethon on the TV channel he owned in his native Perth.

Yoko was also turning the charm on ATV's new boss, with no obvious purpose other than perhaps to disrupt Paul's dealings with him. She invited Holmes à Court and his wife, Janet, to the Dakota and gave them a guided tour, ending at the white piano on which John had played 'Imagine'. So moved was Janet Holmes à Court that she arranged for ATV to make Yoko a gift of the song's copyright.

Those 1983 manoeuvrings came to nothing, however: Holmes à Court was committed to halting Lord Grade's previous asset-stripping and in any case Paul still wasn't interested in buying the whole of ATV Music, only the Northern Songs company inside it.

By 1985, Holmes à Court had been unable to reverse Associated Communications Corporation's losses and was regretting his involvement in the British music industry with its culture of small exertion and vast expense accounts. To shore up ACC, he had no choice but to follow Grade's example and put its one reliably profitable (through Lennon and McCartney) division ATV Music up for auction yet again.

Initially, there were three main prospective bidders: EMI's publishing arm, EMI Music; the Swedish producer Stig Anderson, whose records with Abba had outsold the Beatles during the Seventies; and the Japanese pop mogul Shoo Kasauno. But Paul was widely expected to weigh in alongside them, possibly in an alliance with his new best friend Michael Jackson.

His little lecture to Jackson on the joys of owning song-copyrights could not have been better – or worse – timed. Soon after Jackson's visit to Peasmarsh, the *Thriller* album (on which Paul had appeared) made him stupendously rich, with around $100 million to play with. At Columbia, the record company he and Paul then shared, he'd been strongly advised to invest his new wealth in publishing and was now doing so under the guidance of its president, Walter Yetnikoff (last seen signing Paul for $22.5 million, plus the *Guys and Dolls* catalogue as a welcome-aboard gift).

When Jackson heard ATV Music was up for sale again, he instructed his lawyers to go after it, but not – he later insisted – before contacting Paul and Yoko in turn to check that neither was in the running. Yoko allegedly replied that for her to pursue Northern Songs would create too many issues with the former Beatles, while John Eastman said it promised to be 'too pricey' for Paul.

Jackson would also claim to have personally forewarned Paul of his intentions.

In the end, the King of Pop was the only bidder for pop's Crown Jewels. The thought of the *Thriller* millions made Holmes à Court continually raise the price and at one point Jackson backed away, allowing another would-be buyer briefly to enter the frame: none other than that former Apple loiterer Richard Branson. The deal was eventually done with Jackson for $47.5 million. By then, Northern Songs' catalogue was light two titles – not just 'Imagine' but also one of Paul's undisputed masterpieces. Holmes à Court kept back 'Penny Lane' because his daughter's name was Penny.

To Paul, all this felt like a betrayal by someone he'd considered a friend, although Columbia's president Walter Yentikoff, who'd been as close to the transaction as anyone, maintained that Jackson had acted squarely and above board with him throughout. 'Paul had the resources to buy back the songs,' Yentikoff commented later. 'He simply chose not to.'

But in time he saw the funny side of having his good advice rebound on him so monumentally. He'd tell the story with a spot-on impersonation of Jackson's child-falsetto, saying, 'I love your songs, Paul' on one day and on the next, 'I bought your songs, Paul.'

His dissatisfaction with Columbia had been simmering for some time before his record company seemed to side with Michael Jackson against him, and with the *Press to Play* album he returned to the Beatles' old home, Capitol/EMI.

After Eric Stewart's departure, a starrier-than-ever throng of sidemen had been invited to Hog Hill Mill, among them Pete Townshend, Phil Collins, Split Enz's keyboard-player Eddie Rayner and Carlos Alomar, the Puerto Rican guitarist–producer best-known for his work with David Bowie, who spent a week as the McCartneys' house guest. Alomar would later recall being welcomed by Paul with 'a nice big spliff' but then spending bucolic times together, flying kites or drinking warm draught beer at village pubs. All in all, he thought, Paul's lifestyle seemed less like that of an international megastar than a local farmer.

Press to Play was released in August 1986, its cover a silvery black and white portrait of Paul and Linda like a still from a 1940s film noir. It reached number eight in Britain but failed to make the American Top 20 and, at fewer than a million copies, was the poorest-selling McCartney solo album to date.

The only notable single from it was 'Press', described by the *Los Angeles Times* as 'one of the most playful, positive songs about the joy of sex ever written'. The video showed Paul at his most endearing; white-trousered and feathery-haired, riding a London Tube train among a crowd of unsuspecting real-life passengers – a situation with which he was anyway quite familiar – charming astonished females of all ages, tipping buskers in the sympathetic spirit of one essentially in the same game, at one point even giving directions to a lost tourist, before disappearing up the long, lamp-lined escalator at St John's Wood station.

Paul-ness also permeated MPL's next film release, a documentary about his teenage idol Buddy Holly, intended to counteract Hollywood's risible 1978 biopic starring Gary Busey. This first serious investigation of Holly's brief life was a quality product with contributions from everyone of significance to it: his older brothers, Larry and Travis, his fellow Crickets Jerry Allison and Joe B. Mauldin, his widow, Maria Elena, his close friends Don and Phil Everly and guitarist Tommy Allsup, who'd almost taken the same charter flight that killed him.

Holly's influence on the early Beatles was commemorated by a few bars from their version of 'That'll Be the Day' on the 1958 home recording Paul had bought from John Duff Lowe. But he himself appeared only in the – completely convincing – role of still-faithful fan, seated with a guitar on a bale of straw in one of his barns, replicating the magical Holly hiccups that had first got John and him started.

He now had another new manager, the last he would ever employ. On the recommendation of his lawyer/brother-in-law John

Eastman, he'd hired 37-year-old Richard Ogden, formerly British head of Polydor, the German record label on which the Beatles had first recorded.

Ogden took over at a moment when Paul's reputation had been eroded by flops like *Give My Regards to Broad Street* and *Press to Play* and a new generation of British solo singers like Phil Collins and George Michael were cornering the international market. His advice to his new boss was not to bank on stored-up Beatles and Wings goodwill but to get out and promote himself with interviews and photocalls as aggressively as any of those young rivals.

Paul agreed, with the stipulation that he must own the rights to all photographs taken of him. This soon proved unworkable: during a promotional visit to Spain he landed at Barcelona airport to find around 5000 people, including dozens of photographers, blocking his way to his limo and virtually no security to shield him. As he struggled through the crowd, one man kept hitting him on the back of the head with an acoustic guitar, and saying, 'Sign my guitar, Paul.' Afterwards, Richard Ogden prepared himself to be fired, but instead found Paul glowing with exhilaration.

With no new product at hand, Ogden persuaded EMI to issue a compilation album, *Paul McCartney: All the Best*, a thumbs-up of a title, featuring tracks with and without Wings back to 1970, including 'Mull of Kintyre', 'Say Say Say' with Michael Jackson and Rupert Bear's 'Frog Song'. Released in late 1987, it peaked at number two in Britain, denied the top spot by George Michael's *Faith*, and eventually went double platinum. It would have sold more had Lee Eastman not initially blocked its release in America, maintaining that compilation albums signified that a performer's career was over.

Ogden had been hired to manage Linda alongside Paul, specifically the photography career she pursued in an on-off fashion. In this he felt slightly redundant since she already had a first-class photography agent in Robbie Montgomery, a London-based New Yorker who represented many of Britain's leading photographers including David Bailey and Clive Arrowsmith. Montgomery worked hard to get her assignments on their level, but was often thwarted by her reluctance to stray far from Peasmarsh and her animals.

Yet when her passion for animal rights or the environment was stirred, she could produce an image every bit as eye-catching as her studies of Jimi Hendrix and Jim Morrison in the old days. She contributed to an illustrated book from the Council for the Preservation of Rural England, along with Bailey, Don McCullin and Lord Snowdon, and to Lynx, the campaign against the use of animal fur in haute couture. Lynx employed visual shock tactics which for a time all but wiped out the British fur trade. Linda's poster was a prime example, headlined 'Rich Bitch, Poor Bitch' and juxtaposing a fur-clad model with the mangled body of a fox.

Robbie Montgomery's greatest coup was to secure her an exhibition at the Royal Photographic Society's prestigious gallery in Bath. To publicise its opening, Montgomery hired a young PR man named John Gibb with whom she'd worked on the Council for the Preservation of Rural England book and who now came up with a stunt worthy of the Sixties and *Sgt. Pepper*. Beside the M4 motorway between London and the West Country lies the enormous Queen Mother Reservoir whose grass embankment is plainly visible to passing traffic. On this Gibb proposed spelling out 'Linda McCartney' in flowers, with an arrow pointing westward towards Bath.

Paul loved the idea and, as always when Paul loved an idea, money was no object. Gibb and a team armed with 25,000 flowers worked all night to create Linda's outsize byline, miraculously unobserved by police cars or highway maintenance gangs. Next morning, rush-hour traffic on the M4 came to a standstill as drivers of every kind of vehicle stopped to view the display. 'People even arrived on buses to look at it,' Gibb recalls. 'Finally, the police told me I'd be arrested if I didn't get it covered up.'

There was somewhat less spousal support, however, when Linda decided to write an autobiography. It was to be called *Mac the Wife* and ghosted by Lesley-Ann Jones, a young journalist who had interviewed her, sympathetically, for the *Daily Mail*. They met again when Linda visited Great Ormond Street Hospital to open a new wing for terminally ill children and Jones was sent to cover the event despite being heavily pregnant. Spotting her and realising her delicate condition, Linda beckoned her out of the media scrum and they went around the new wing together.

The autobiography was contracted to a British publisher, Arlington Books, and Jones began interviewing Linda at Peasmarsh, often taking her baby daughter, Mia, along with her. However, Paul seemed hostile to the project for the light it promised to shed on his marriage. Once, she recalls, 'he thumped the table and said, "There's only one effing star in this family!"' Soon afterwards, the project was cancelled.

From the late Eighties, many of Linda's pictures featured the terrain which originally inspired her to take up photography. Paul had further enlarged his enormous property portfolio by buying an estate near Tucson, Arizona, where she'd lived with her first husband, Joseph Melville See, fallen under the spell of the seminal photojournalist Hazel Larsen Archer and appeared in the *Arizona Daily Star* with her very meaty recipe for meat loaf.

This fourth McCartney home was located in Pima County, about 45 miles north-east of Tucson in the foothills of the Rincon Mountains; a classic Wild West landscape of mesquite bushes and giant cacti where rattlesnakes, gophers and scorpions lurked and coyotes howled after dark. It comprised 150 acres of private desert and a modest stone house which Paul had repainted in 1930s-ish pink and turquoise but otherwise did little to alter. Backing onto it was the Tanque Verde dude ranch – i.e. for city dwellers seeking a taste of frontier life – whose stabling Linda could use for her horses.

Mel See had never left Arizona, and now lived in the Tucson Mountains, a few miles to the west. He had not remarried but in 1985 had entered into a 'permanent engagement' with a former beautician named Beverly Wilk, a divorcee like himself, who shared his passion for geology, archaeology, architecture and collecting ethnic art.

Since he had allowed Paul to adopt his daughter, Heather, contact between them had been rare, and it did not greatly increase after the McCartneys acquired their Tanque Verde property. 'We visited them a couple of times and Paul once came to our house,' Beverly recalls. 'Heather still hardly knew her father, and there wasn't a lot of warmth toward Mel from Linda. I got the feeling she would have liked it if he disappeared.'

Paul had never socialised much with his neighbours around Peasmarsh, preferring to entertain consignments of friends from London and overseas or of his Liverpool relatives. But that changed in 1987 when Spike Milligan came to live in the nearby village of Udimore.

Back before rock 'n' roll, Milligan's lunatic *Goon Show* on BBC radio, co-starring Peter Sellers and Harry Secombe, had given a generation of British schoolboys their first heady sniff of anarchy. The Goons were a bond between Paul and John as strong as Elvis or Buddy Holly and were at the heart of the Beatles' early stage act. Part of the band's great luck was meeting George Martin, who had once made comedy albums with the Goons and so instantly recognised their musical equivalent.

Since the end of the *Goon Show* in 1960, Paul had followed Milligan's solo career as a playwright, poet and children's author with equal admiration. Indeed, it was a Milligan *pensée* – 'black notes, white notes/ and you need the two to make harmony, folks' – that triggered the only really successful 'big-issue' McCartney song, 'Ebony and Ivory'.

Now nearing 70, Milligan – like Paul – had fled London to escape bothersome fans and found refuge with his third wife, Shelagh, in an Udimore byway called Dumbwoman's Lane. Rural life had not quenched his misanthropic comic spirit: he proclaimed his 1960s-built home to be 'the ugliest house in the world' and had changed its name from Carpenter's Meadow to The Blind Architect.

Paul approached him as a devoted fan and the inheritor of an equally bizarre address in Peasmarsh, Starvecrow Lane. Linda, of course, knew little about the *Goon Show*, but was won over by a sign in the Milligan kitchen reading 'Vegetarians are nice to meat'.

They became regular visitors to 'The Blind Architect', whose cluttered interior displayed gifts from other, equally admiring Beatles – a 'Love and Peace' banner from George, a book on trauma therapy autographed by John and Yoko. Paul enjoyed playing a rare Broadwood grand piano, dating from 1883, which Milligan had rescued from a London building-site. Soon he had a standing invitation to let himself into the house and use the Broadwood if the Milligans were away or even just sleeping late.

After Milligan's death, his effects were found to include a handwritten poem by Paul dedicated to 'The Poet of Dumbwoman's Lane'. With it was a caricature subtitled 'the Nutters of Starvecrow Lane', a male and a fair-haired female both giving self-identifying thumbs-up signs:

> The voice of the poet of Dumbwoman's Lane
> Can be heard across vallies [sic] of sugar-burned cane
> And nostrils that sleep through the wildest of nights
> Will be twitching to gain aromatic delights . . .

The welcome could be less warm if Milligan was in one of his frequent depressed moods or absorbed in composing some new piece of Goonery. One morning, he answered an unexpected ring at his front door to find Paul accompanied by George and Ringo, who were visiting Peasmarsh and both equally keen to pay their respects.

'Not today, I'm busy,' he said, shutting the door in their faces.

No longer did Paul regard his Beatle years as a war zone from which he'd only just escaped with his life and never wanted to think about again. These days, he would recall them in any detail an interviewer liked, even exploit them in the perpetual struggle to keep himself at the top of the charts.

Writing the title song for *Spies Like Us*, a Hollywood film comedy co-starring Dan Aykroyd and Chevy Chase – which made number seven in America – might seem to have given little scope for this. Yet its video was like Trivial Pursuit for advanced Beatlemaniacs, with a nod to Wings.

Paul was shown arriving at Abbey Road studios on a bicycle, disguised by a hooded duffel-coat, bifocals and a droopy ginger moustache; then arriving all over again by taxi, wearing a trilby hat and a moustache now horizontal and black. Clips from the movie barely interrupted a sequence of him alone in a studio playing drums as well as guitar, just as on 'The Ballad of John and Yoko'. The closing shot pastiched both the *Abbey Road* and *Band on the Run* album covers, with Aykroyd, Chase and Paul on the famous zebra crossing like escapees caught in a prison searchlight.

Reconciled to his Beatle past he might be, but reconciliation with his fellow participants was still apt to falter. Since he had taken the lead in the British High Court, they had all sued each other so often that litigation no longer seemed a noteworthy event. 'George phoned me the other day and said, "I'm suing you,"' Ringo told a chat show host around this time. 'I told him, "OK, but I still love you."'

In January 1988, the Beatles were to be inducted into the Rock and Roll Hall of Fame in only the third such ceremony ever held. Paul had accepted an invitation to the event at New York's Waldorf Astoria hotel and had rounded up George and Ringo to appear alongside him. But it had since emerged that under his new Capitol/ EMI contract, he would receive an extra one per cent from Beatles backlist sales. As a result, he was being sued jointly by the two of them and Yoko. His response was to issue a statement that he'd be boycotting the Rock and Roll Hall of Fame investiture: 'After 20 years, the Beatles and I still have some business differences which I had hoped would be settled by now. Unfortunately, they haven't been, so I would feel like a complete hypocrite, waving and smiling with them at a fake reunion.'

The induction ceremony was performed by Mick Jagger, and

watched by most of the great names from the Anglo-American rock fraternity who had the Beatles to thank for their careers. An unusually forthright and heartfelt Jagger confessed how Lennon and McCartney had motivated Keith Richards and himself to try songwriting one long-ago afternoon in Soho by casually knocking off the Rolling Stones' breakthrough single, 'I Wanna Be Your Man'.

George, Ringo and Yoko were joined onstage by John's two sons, 25-year-old Julian – now a recording artiste engineered to sound uncannily like his father – and 13-year-old Sean. After a few woozy words from Ringo, George made a formal acceptance speech giving no hint of the litigation hovering in the background: 'It's unfortunate Paul's not here because he's the one who had the speech in his pocket. Well, we all know why John can't be here and I'm sure he would be and it's hard to stand here supposedly representing the Beatles. It's what's left, I'm afraid. But we all loved him so much and we all love Paul very much.'

Still, the feeling of an angel-faced elephant in the room was inescapable. George thanked the Rock and Roll Hall of fame by quoting the 'Paul' song that had kicked off *Sgt. Pepper's Lonely Hearts Club Band*: 'It's wonderful to be here . . . it's certainly a thrill'. And the silver-clad Yoko, who spoke next, didn't bother with diplomacy. 'I wish John was here,' she began. 'He would have been here, you know. *He* would have come.'

The evening ended with a superstar jam of near-Live Aid dimensions featuring, among others, Jagger, Bob Dylan, Elton John, Bruce Springsteen, Neil Young, the Beach Boys, Little Richard, Billy Joel and Mary Wilson of the Supremes. Included in the ten-song set were Dylan's 'All Along the Watchtower', the Stones' 'Satisfaction', the Beach Boys' 'Barbara Ann' and the Supremes' 'Stop! In The Name of Love'. But the show-stopper was Paul's 'I Saw Her Standing There', with Jagger, Joel and Springsteen sharing the vocal.

The stage was so crowded with guitarists and stand-up vocalists that Elton John at the piano could scarcely be seen. As he pounded away in obscurity, Elton's thoughts must have gone back to his

Thanksgiving concert at Madison Square Garden in 1974, when John had sung 'I Saw Her Standing There' in caustic tribute to 'an old estranged fiancé of mine called Paul'.

Now he was estranged again, and here again was 'Well, my heart went boom as I crossed that room' – naturally known by heart by three of the world's greatest performers – as potent, as joyous, as ever.

42

'You're such a lovely audience'

Linda had always been too wrapped up in Paul, her family and her animals to have many outside friends, particularly female ones. But during the late Eighties, she acquired two who would bring great changes into her rather isolated life: the television comedy writer Carla Lane and Chrissie Hynde of the Pretenders.

Hynde was one of rock's most distinctive talents, combining as she did the macho swagger of her male bandmates with the sultriest singing voice since Marlene Dietrich. Like Linda, she was an American living with a British pop legend – in her case, Ray Davies of the Kinks. And like Linda, she was a vegetarian and a passionate believer in animal rights who had yet to find an outlet. In 1987, she invited some like-minded women friends to her London flat to discuss what collective action they might take. The group included Linda and Carla Lane, who had never previously met although they lived only a few miles from each other in Sussex.

Liverpool-born Lane had written a string of hugely successful BBC comedy series often deploying the scabrous wit of her home city. Her first, *The Liver Birds*, portrayed the flat-sharing life of two girls who might have been plucked from a lunch-time queue outside the Cavern. Her latest, *Bread*, the saga of an unruly Liverpool Catholic family named the Boswells, had a weekly audience running into millions.

At the Chrissie Hynde meeting, she didn't recognise Linda or even particularly notice her until their hostess knelt on the floor in

front of them, explaining how much the animal kingdom needed
their protection. With the Pretenders' vocalist in full flight in that
smoke-and-honey voice, everyone listened raptly – except Linda.
'You are talking about animals and their plight,' she broke in, 'but
I see you are wearing a leather skirt.'

From that moment, she and Carla Lane – in Lane's words – were
'friendship-struck ... We were like identical twins [dedicated] to
trying to make the animal people in the country break out and lead
the world in animal rights.'

The success of Lane's television work had allowed her to settle
near Haywards Heath, only 36 miles from Peasmarsh, where she
owned a sixteenth-century house named Broadhurst Manor and
a 25-acre estate which she'd converted into an animal sanctuary.
The house itself was so huge and rambling that she didn't know
exactly how many rooms it contained. One day, she opened what
she thought was a cupboard and found a passageway to nine more
she'd never known were there, one of them 45 feet long.

Linda became a frequent visitor to Broadhurst Manor, where
Lane ran an animal-rescue service called Animaline, pledged never
to turn away any creature in need. The two women were somewhat alike with their blonde hair and hippy-floaty manner, though
Lane was five years older as well as a head taller.

Peasmarsh soon turned into an overspill area for Animaline's
rescuees, either maltreated domestic pets or injured wild creatures
needing to be nursed back to health, then released. Often, the liber-
ating was done by the duo in person, using Linda's bright pink Mini
(which reminded Lane of 'a sweet') or, for larger passengers such
as deer, a horsebox or closed truck from Peasmarsh. Using Lane's
verbal skills and Linda's painfully acquired keyboard ones, they
also decided to have a shot at some animal-rights protest songs.

Carla Lane had always regarded herself as the most hardcore
animal-lover and non-meat-eater, but Linda easily surpassed her.
At Peasmarsh, even the livestock were kept on a vegetarian diet,
every animal was spared neutering and allowed to die of old age,
huge veterinary bills were incurred to succour ailing cows, ducks

or chickens, and the most unlikely candidates became beloved fixtures. Among them was a bullock which Paul had found wandering in the lane, bought from the farmer who'd been about to send it to market and christened Ferdinand.

Paul was all for this new friendship of Linda's. He had loved *The Liver Birds* – originally the name of Merseyside's first all-female rock band – and was a huge fan of *Bread* with its matriarchal Nellie Boswell and her shiftless, finagling brood, so different from any Liverpool relatives he'd ever known. He welcomed Lane as 'our Carla', made a donation to her animal sanctuary and sent a consignment of straw for its inhabitants. She even persuaded him to make a guest appearance in *Bread* with Linda, playing themselves, in October 1988. The episode showed Linda setting up an animal shelter near the Boswell home and Paul arriving to collect her as she took tea with Nellie, who of course totally failed to recognise him. 'Has your chap got a job?' she asked. 'Yes, sort of,' Linda replied.

If Carla Lane was a soulmate for Linda, Peter Cox – whom she likewise met through Chrissie Hynde – opened the way to a new career that was to transform her public persona. Cox was a former advertising man who'd become chief executive of the Vegetarian Society, then gone on to publish *Why You Don't Need Meat*, an exposé of the livestock industry which put him onto every TV and radio talk show and became a national bestseller. Chrissie felt he was someone the McCartneys urgently needed to meet, so took him along on one of her regular visits to Peasmarsh.

'When the Land Rover brought us from Rye station, Paul and Linda met us on horseback,' he recalls. 'I thought I'd never seen such an amazingly beautiful couple. Then Paul jumped down off his horse and said, "'Ere, you're Peter Cox! I saw you on the Wogan [TV] show, talking about your book. I've got to get your autograph."'

As was often his way, he immediately treated Cox like the most intimate friend, suggesting they take a walk around the garden on their own. 'He talked about John a lot – but the strange thing was that it was in the present tense, "John says this" or "John thinks that". At one point, he asked me, "Have you ever thought what power the Beatles could have had if we'd been evil . . . if we'd gone over to the dark side?" Hearing something like that after only knowing him for about five minutes sort of freaked me out.'

In Britain, the Eighties had brought a steep rise in vegetarianism, boosted by health concerns over red meat and revulsion at the factory farming methods Cox had exposed. Vegetarian staples like tofu and beansprouts and meat substitutes like Quorn, once available only from health food shops, were now routinely stocked by supermarkets. Yet, as far as Cox knew, there was not a single cookbook aimed at what had become a mass market. 'Thousands of families included a vegetarian, usually one of the kids, who always had to be given special food. I couldn't see why there shouldn't be a vegetarian cookbook with dishes the whole family would enjoy.'

Over the years, Linda had evolved a vegetarian cuisine all her own, mostly meatless facsimiles of the traditional British dishes Paul preferred. One of her earliest creations was a 'bird' made of pasta so that he'd still have something to carve at the Christmas dinner-table. 'She did what I'd call truck-driver food,' Cox recalls. 'Sausage-and-mash and shepherd's pie that no one would ever know were vegetarian.' That was her one weakness for her friend Carla Lane, who saw no point in condemning meat, then eating facsimiles of it.

Cox felt that Linda's recipes were ideal to fill the gap in the publishing market, and suggested she should produce a cookbook with his help. At first, she was reluctant to put her head above the parapet again after all the insults she'd received with Wings. He persuaded her by stressing the value of such a book to the animal rights cause. '"If it makes any money," she told me, "I want it all to go to the animals."'

Despite the McCartney name and Cox's recent bestseller, all the main London publishers turned down the project. 'I went to see one woman who was supposedly a legend in the industry – and who always wore white gloves to the office. She told me a vegetarian cookbook couldn't possibly sell unless it had some chicken in it.'

The only offer came from the new Bloomsbury imprint at number 2 Soho Square, next door to MPL (which, coincidentally, had just published a picture book about John with a foreword by Yoko). 'I don't think even Bloomsbury thought it would sell,' Cox recalls. 'I suspect the intention was to get an in with Paul, so that at some later stage they could set up an authorised biography of him.' The deal was done through MPL Communications, with Linda and Cox splitting the proceeds 50–50. 'At MPL, it wasn't taken very seriously either. It was just seen as a little side project for Linda.'

Throughout 1988, Cox made regular trips to Peasmarsh to choose the recipes with Linda. He was then living in Hampstead, north London; early on the appointed days, a chauffeur-driven car would collect him, then make a huge detour to the East End to pick up Paul's cleaning-lady before heading for Sussex. 'Yes, he could have found any number of cleaning-ladies around Peasmarsh, but he happened to like that one. It was my first taste of the Paul way of doing things.'

Compiling the recipes proved a laborious process, for Linda was an instinctive cook who never bothered to measure things out. And, conscious of the critics who'd be lying in wait for her, Cox insisted on testing each one several times over to ensure it would work for anyone, and enlisted a celebrity panel including Ringo and Twiggy to try it out for themselves.

Nor were the dishes she made for Paul and the children shining examples of healthy eating. 'She used tons of butter and double cream, and seemed never to have heard of cholesterol. A lot of the meat substitutes she used came from America and were often kosher; there was some terrible stuff called Bolono, non-meat Bologna sausage. I tried to tone it down by only putting two pints of cream into a cheese omelette where she would have used three. But still having to eat all that dairy so many times every day left my stomach in such a state that I could only stand plain boiled rice afterwards. In the end, it made me become a vegan.'

Linda felt no great compulsion to complete the book, often saying, 'Let's not bother to work today. Let's just sit out in the garden and have a cup of tea.' But Cox was a hard-up freelance for whom it represented his one potential source of income. Constrained from ordering Paul McCartney's wife to shape up, especially in her own kitchen, he thought of a neat psychological ruse to achieve the same effect.

Paul's former fiancée, Jane Asher – now married to cartoonist Gerald Scarfe – had also recently entered the cookery field with a best-selling book about cake-making. Cox would bring along a copy of *Jane Asher's Party Cakes* and casually flip it open whenever Linda's attention started wandering. The thought of Paul's old flame being a cookbook ahead never failed to concentrate her mind.

For Paul, the priority in 1988 was making an album to erase the disappointing performance of *Press to Play*. But before work even began, he scored a surprise hit in the last territory he expected.

Auditioning possible musicians at the Hog Hill studio during the previous summer, he'd started with the usual work-out of old rock 'n' roll numbers, like 'That's All Right Mama', 'No Other Baby' and 'Twenty Flight Rock', his audition-piece for John and the Quarrymen in 1957, all of which sounded so good that he decided he had an album right there. His new manager, Richard Ogden, that experienced record company boss, successfully argued it would be too much like John's *Rock 'n' Roll*, released 13 years earlier, and he should go for a polished studio album instead.

To mollify him, Ogden had the idea of issuing the rock 'n' roll tapes as a bootleg dressed up to look like an illegal import from Communist Russia. When EMI and MPL's lawyers objected, Ogden licensed the album to a real Russian label, Melodiya, which released it under the title *CHOBA B CCCP* (Back in the USSR) after Paul's Beach Boys pastiche on the Beatles' White Album.

The Soviet Union, under its final president, Mikhail Gorbachev, had relaxed many of its old restrictions, but pop music remained in short supply, especially from such a name as this. *CHOBA B CCCP* sold half a million and became the Communist record industry's most successful export of all time. When Paul did a phone-in for his Russian fans on BBC radio's World Service, he received five times more calls than the prime minister, Margaret Thatcher, in a similar programme a few weeks earlier.

At 46, he was keener than ever to find younger collaborators to keep abreast of modern trends and reinvigorate him in the recording studio. And in 34-year-old Elvis Costello, he found the most promising yet. This one and only pretender to The King's Christian name – confusingly arrayed in Buddy Holly glasses and playing a solid-body guitar – was one of Punk Rock's more worthwhile survivors. Paul had first met him in 1982, when they both had albums engineered by Geoff Emerick, and formed a high opinion of his songwriting abilities. They'd also coincided at Live Aid, where Costello performed a solo version of 'All You Need Is Love', cheekily introducing it as 'an old northern English folk song'.

In the summer of 1988, he came to Hog Hill to work with Paul on the album that would become *Flowers in the Dirt*. Linda was equally pleased to see him since he'd converted to vegetarianism largely due to her assurance that it wouldn't be 'like joining a weird society'.

There was first an intensive songwriting session, just Costello and Paul in a room above the studio, with two acoustic guitars, an electric piano and a large notebook. The two guitars, the notebook – above all, the figure in horn-rimmed specs on a facing seat and 'the great sarcastic quality in his voice' – gave Paul a sense not of déjà-vu so much as reincarnation. 'I would sing a line and [Elvis] would come up with some witty, acerbic foil to it,' he later recalled. 'I said, "My God, that was my and John's whole style." I'd write some romantic line and John would write the acid put-down.'

As a rule, Paul's collaborators were overawed by his fame and terrified of challenging him, a state of affairs he resolutely refused to acknowledge. But Costello told him things straight as only John ever had before. Indeed, told him very much what John always used to: that he should spend less time on being a PR man and more on his music. 'There's no denying that he has a way of sort of defending himself by charming and smiling and thumbs-up and all that bit,' Costello would later observe perceptively. 'I said once I thought he should step from behind that.'

Egalitarianism had its limits, however. Having co-written an album's worth of songs with Elvis Costello and given Costello his head as producer, Paul decided against releasing it. Instead, he decided to make a completely different album under his name alone, to be called *Flowers in the Dirt*.

As studio musicians, he could easily have called back the Wings line-up he'd suspended in 1980. But, deciding to start from scratch yet again, he asked Richard Ogden if he 'knew anyone'. Ogden immediately thought of lead guitarist Hamish Stuart, formerly of the Average White Band, who could also play bass and sing and was tough and worldly-wise enough to handle the politics of sharing a stage with Paul and Linda.

Stuart now lived in Los Angeles, so was not fully up to speed concerning the McCartneys' strict stance on animal rights. When Ogden met him at Heathrow airport, he was wearing a fur coat, leather trousers and snakeskin boots. Hasty re-outfitting had to take place before he could be delivered to Hog Hill Mill. Stuart recommended his friend, guitarist Robbie McIntosh, formerly of the Pretenders, who in turn recommended keyboard-player Paul 'Wix' Wickens. Drummer Chris Whitten had been hired for the rock 'n' roll sessions and kept on the payroll since,

Paul at this time was still embroiled in litigation with George, Ringo and Yoko over his extra one per cent from EMI on Beatles back royalties. Paradoxically, he was soon to be responsible for enriching each of them, as well as himself, by some \$6.5 million.

Since 1981, the world's fastest-growing computer company had been allowed to use the same name as the Beatles' Apple organisation on condition that their equipment featured no music or entertainment content. But in 1988, Apple Computers launched the Musical Digital Interface, a microchip which enabled PCs to create, record and store music. The result was a lawsuit from Apple Corps which took up 116 days in the High Court in London – and featured the playing of 'Lucy in the Sky with Diamonds' on an Apple computer (one up to John, if he'd only known) – then moved to the Court of Appeal and the European Court in Brussels before being settled out of court for around $26.5 million.

And all because in 1967 Paul had loved a Magritte painting of a pristine green apple and borrowed it to name and brand the Beatles' short-lived Garden of Eden.

On days when no chauffeur-driven car was available to collect Peter Cox from Hampstead, he went to Sussex by train to work on Linda's 'little side project' of a vegetarian cookery book. At Rye station, he'd usually be met by the Peasmarsh Land Rover which, like some American bomber in the Cold War, remained operational virtually around the clock. 'Fans of Paul's, especially Japanese ones, were continually turning up in the district, then getting hopelessly lost. The Land Rover would gather them up, take them to the station and put them on the right train back to London.'

If the Land Rover wasn't available, Cox had to take a taxi – no easy task since most of the drivers had been terrified by reports of the ferocious security at 'Paulditz' and refused to go near the place, no matter what proof of being a bona fide visitor he showed them. 'One guy who did agree to take me wanted to let me off at the beginning of the road up to the front gate, where there was this field full of the most beautiful wild flowers. When I told him I wanted to go right to the house, he said, "What about all the machine-guns?" Ironically on that particular day, there was *nobody* at the front gate.'

The lax security was all the more surprising given Paul and Linda's chequered career as drugs-bustees. But, as Cox discovered, neither of them ever smoked dope around the house, because of the children, although Paul did so liberally in the recording studio.

'Next to the phone, they had a list of contact numbers for all the local police, so it didn't seem as if they were expecting any trouble from that quarter.'

While Cox worked with Linda in the kitchen, Paul was usually at Hog Hill with his new band, making *Flowers in the Dirt*. 'I preferred it when he wasn't around,' Cox recalls. 'When he walked into a room, he had the most powerful charisma of anyone I'd ever known. At those moments, all work came to a stop and everything centred on him.'

Friendly and blokeish though he seemed, Cox always sensed 'this question mark, as if he was always thinking "I am Paul McCartney, you want something from me and I am going to find out what it is." He once said to me, "If I gave you a million pounds, would you eat a hamburger?" I said "No" and he said "You're lying". I thought, what does that say about him – that he thinks everyone has a price?

'I once saw him give Linda a Cartier watch that had cost £20,000. But she never seemed to have any money for day-to-day expenses. She'd often ask me, the impoverished hack, to lend her a fiver or a tenner.'

Where cost never mattered was in gratifying some passing whim of Paul's. 'Once he decided he fancied a kind of pizza you could only get from a particular place in New York, so he had one flown over on Concorde. The odd thing was that, although we were in a kitchen, with unusual amounts of food lying around everywhere because of the book, I never once saw Paul eat. And other people he worked with every day said the same.'

Another time, when Sussex was shrouded in thick fog, he told his staff to charter a helicopter to fly him to London. 'MPL found a pilot who'd flown helicopters in the Falklands War but even he said it would be crazy to go up in conditions as bad as that. Because it was Paul McCartney, the guy agreed to take him but for safety's sake never flew higher than about 40 feet; they went all the way just skimming over the tops of hedges.'

Among all the people Paul dealt with every day, professionally and personally, Cox can recall only two who weren't putty in his hands. One was George Martin, with whom he'd worked since 1962 and on whose musical wisdom he still relied. 'George knew just how to handle Paul, just like he had the Beatles. With both those things on his CV, he could have sorted out the Middle East, no problem.'

Somebody else who'd always known how to handle Paul was his youngest daughter, Stella, now 17 and, says Cox, 'a focused girl who always knew where she was going. She was the one of his kids who was most like him and the only one who stood up to him. Once, he was giving her a bollocking because she'd overspent her allowance. "Do you think I'm *made* of money?" he said. To which the answer was "Well, yes, actually, Paul."'

Relationships between celebrity authors and their editorial 'ghosts' can easily turn sour, but Cox grew fond of Linda – even a little concerned about her. 'She really was the most generous person you could ever want to meet. When my wife Peggy and I needed a holiday, Linda lent us the farm in Kintyre for three weeks. We lived on potatoes and a specially potent brand of local Scotch because that was all there was. The water out of the taps came from a thousand-year-old spring; it was amazing, but full of little wriggling creatures.'

His concern came from a feeling that the McCartneys' marriage was going through a difficult patch. While Linda was totally content with life at Peasmarsh with her horses and animal waifs, Paul often complained of feeling isolated and of missing the London life that used to keep his 'cultural antenna' vibrating.

Cox began to suspect that he himself might be part of the problem; that Paul resented Linda giving undivided attention to the cookbook that could have been spent on him, even felt insecure about the hours she spent closeted with her co-author. Sometimes when Cox arrived, she wouldn't be in the kitchen but out in the front drive, in tears. Once or twice when the Land Rover met him at Rye station, he was told she couldn't work on the book that day, but no explanation was given.

The tension only surfaced when Paul decided to tour again. For whereas he'd once been unable to face life on the road without Linda, he now seemed rather ambivalent about having her along.

'It was like a psychological war between them,' Cox recalls. 'Linda would ask him "Do you want me to come?" and he'd sometimes answer "Yes", sometimes "No". That went on for about two weeks before it was settled that she'd go.'

Paul would later say he'd felt no special urge to return to live shows after a lay-off of ten years. But by 1989, the financial inducements had become irresistible.

Tours had once been looked on simply as a means of promoting albums, but were now huge moneymaking operations, grossing double-figure millions from merchandising (a sphere in which the Beatles had earned practically nothing) and the sale of film, television and radio rights. There was also a growing trend for commercial sponsorship – as if plutocratic rock bands were cash-strapped charities – with leading retail brands and business corporations bidding fortunes to have their names printed on concert programmes and tickets. The Rolling Stones' upcoming Steel Wheels world tour, for example, was guaranteed around $99 million before Mick Jagger had sung a note.

It was a propitious moment, for *Flowers in the Dirt* had proved the 'comeback' album Paul had so much needed and wanted, reaching number one in the UK, charting around the world – though not yet high enough in North America – and containing a string of potential hit singles that live concerts could exploit.

To Richard Ogden now fell the ticklish task of finding a corporate sponsor as impressive as Paul demanded which did not in some way or other offend against his and – especially – Linda's ethics. The tour was itself to be a means of promoting the environmental pressure group Friends of the Earth to which they both now belonged; a magazine-format souvenir programme, given away free to audiences, contained several pages on FOE's work and at every press conference Paul extolled the work they were doing to save the planet.

Ogden seemed to have found an ideal commercial partner in American Airlines and was about to seal a thumping deal when Paul suddenly told him to break off negotiations. The reason was that Linda's mother, Louise, had died in an American Airlines passenger jet which crashed soon after take-off from New York in 1962. By that late stage, the only alternative, found by the tour's American booker Alex Kochan, was the Visa credit card company. Their upfront offer was $500,000, which Paul considered a paltry sum compared with what the Rolling Stones were getting. But he accepted when Visa promised a nationwide TV campaign to promote the tour's American leg.

It was to be in no sense a revival or reinvention of Wings: Paul went out under his own name with only Linda representing the old line-up and his *Flowers in the Dirt* band – Stuart, McIntosh, Whitten and Wickens – as anonymous sidemen. It opened in Oslo, Norway, in September 1989 and over the next ten months gave 103 shows to 2.3 million people across the UK, Europe, North America, Asia and South America, travelling 100,331 miles, taking with it 178,000 kg of freight, filling 17 trucks, a road crew of 250 and 365 security staff including seven bodyguards for Paul, Linda and their children, Stella and James.

It was also to be an 'all veggie' tour, promoting Linda's just-published vegetarian recipe-book, *Linda McCartney's Home Cooking*. Such a thing was not totally unknown in rock; the Smiths had made their 'Meat Is Murder' tour in 1985, forcing their road crew to abstain from hamburgers and even forbidding the sale of hotdogs at gigs. The McCartneys took a softer line, serving Linda's meat lookalikes to the crew and at media receptions. 'The vegetarian catering was really great, so it was no hardship,' Hamish Stuart remembers. 'But there were quite a few raids on steakhouses on our nights off.'

Above all, it celebrated the band Paul had spent so many years trying to escape. Richard Lester, the director of the Beatles' two abidingly popular cinema features, *A Hard Day's Night* and *Help!*, had been hired to create a film-montage which opened the show with clips of Beatlemania and concurrent news events. The set list included 16 Lennon–McCartney songs including their Swinging Sixties apotheosis, 'Sgt. Pepper's Lonely Hearts Club Band'. Despite 'Sgt. Pepper's' vaudeville atmosphere and direct address to its listeners – 'You're such a lovely audience' – it had never before been played to a live audience.

The Beatles segment began with a ceremonial reintroduction of Paul's Hofner violin bass, which had spent years under lock and key at Peasmarsh. It became the show's high point when he exchanged his Fender bass for that so-familiar skinny silhouette and tore into 'Please Please Me' as a 60ft-high image of his long-ago mop-topped, round-collared self lit up behind him.

But as well as recreating history, he was out to correct it; specifically, the stubborn myth that John had been the experimental, avant-garde Beatle and he merely the soft, safe, 'tuneful' one. In the free souvenir programme – of which a million were distributed – readers turned from current Friends of the Earth campaigns to an interview with Paul, pointing out that he, not John, had been the first into experimental musicians like John Cage and Luciano Berio, painters like Magritte and sculptors like Takis. 'I do think John's avant-garde period . . . was really to give himself a go at what he'd seen me having a go at.'

The itinerary included the Tokyo concerts Paul had been prevented from giving in 1980 by an over-zealous customs officer at Narita airport. Coincidentally, his first single from *Flowers in the Dirt* was an Elvis Costello co-composition called 'My Brave Face', something his fellow inmates at Kosuge Prison would well remember. The accompanying video was a veiled reference to his ordeal: a Japanese businessman showed off a collection of McCartney memorabilia, including ancient colour Beatles-footage, then was carted off to jail by police for stealing the violin bass. But this time, he took care with his packing and his Japanese fans were not denied their ration of 'Paur'.

In America, where he hadn't been seen onstage for 13 years, ticket sales were at first only middling. Then the promised TV ads from his sponsor, Visa cards, began to kick in prime time across the nation. There was none of Visa's usual cleverness, just a straightforward sequence of him onstage with the band in LA. 'A concert like this doesn't take place every day,' the voice-over said. 'And they *don't* take American Express.'

It proved a trump card: from playing to an average of 20,000 people per city, Paul went to double shows in full-to-capacity 50,000-seat arenas, outselling concurrent tours by Madonna and Janet Jackson. His two nights at Berkeley's California Memorial Stadium earned $3.5 million, the nation's top gross that year. Visa's magic carried over to Brazil, where he was appearing for the first time; at Rio de Janeiro's giant Maracanã Stadium, his audience numbered 184,368, the largest stadium crowd ever recorded.

On 28 June 1990, he returned to Liverpool, performing on a specially-constructed stage at the long-disused King's Dock. John would have turned 50 that year, and a month previously Yoko had organised a tribute concert for him at the Pier Head in aid of her Spirit Foundation charity, which had drawn much adverse comment for too-pricey tickets, irrelevant performers like Kylie Minogue – and the absence of any other ex-Beatles in person. Paul and Ringo merely provided videotape clips while George refused, as he put it, to 'dabble in the past'. Still, an ever hopeful American entrepreneur had invited the three to mark the reunification of Berlin with a reunion concert at the Brandenburg Gate.

Paul's own homecoming tribute to 'Someone we all loved – very much' included some quintessential John tracks: 'Strawberry Fields Forever', 'Help!' and 'Give Peace a Chance'. To mark John's fiftieth on 9 October, he was also to put out a live version of 'Birthday' from the White Album (one of their late collaborations which John had subsequently dismissed as 'a piece of crap').

The night after Liverpool, at Knebworth Park, Hertfordshire, the music business took a last little poke at Linda. During 'Hey Jude', a mischievous sound-recordist isolated her backup vocal, put it onto a tape entitled 'Linda McCartney Sings!' and circulated it, to general hilarity.

Admittedly, the crowd singing along were more in tune – but by then her musical abilities had ceased to be an issue. *Linda McCartney's Home Cooking* was top of the UK hardback bestseller list and would go on to become the Bloomsbury imprint's top-selling title until it found Harry Potter.

43

'I work my arse off, I do. I work my bloody arse off'

The 1980s had not been kind to Liverpool. Incessant strikes had crippled its surviving industry, raising unemployment to twice the national rate, and race riots culminating in orgies of arson and looting had brought police baton-charges and CS gas to its streets. A far left-dominated city council waged guerrilla war on Margaret Thatcher's Conservative government while essential services teetered on the edge of bankruptcy and 15 per cent of the once-proud Victorian metropolis lay derelict. There were thousands of decent, hard-working Liverpudlians who were horrified by the state of things, but the Thatcher propaganda machine portrayed them all as gobby layabouts content to sponge off the benefits system while their habitat disintegrated around them.

That stereotype was enshrined in *Bread*, Carla Lane's TV comedy series whose Dingle-dwelling Boswell family possessed all the Scouser's supposed fecklessness and bombast in excelsis. Yet out of the show came an event which can be said to have started Liverpool on the road back to self-respect.

After Paul and Linda's cameo appearance, they had become friendly with Jean Boht, who played the Boswells' matriarch. And it happened that 'Ma Boswell's' real-life husband was the American composer and conductor Carl Davis, famous in Britain for scoring prestigious television series like Thames TV's *The World at War* and silent movie classics like Abel Gance's *Napoléon*.

Soon after the McCartneys' appearance in *Bread*, Davis found himself conducting the Liverpool Philharmonic Orchestra, one of the city's last uneroded bastions of excellence. The gig resulted in an invitation to compose and conduct something to mark the orchestra's 150th anniversary in 1991. Remembering his wife's recent pleasant working experience with the world's greatest living Liverpudlian, he suggested he should write that something in collaboration with Paul.

Classical music had run through Paul's work ever since the string quartet on 'Yesterday' and the piccolo trumpet on 'Penny Lane'; he'd marshalled whole symphony orchestras for both Beatles and Wings tracks, and lost count of the number of his songs which had been scored for strings and woodwind. George Martin had always believed him capable of creating some large-scale classical work and repeatedly urged him to try. But he'd always hesitated, feeling himself disqualified by being unable to read or write music and put off by the 'posh' aura of the conductors and virtuosi with whom he'd have to work.

Carl Davis was not in the least posh with his television and movie themes and cheery boast that 'if it moves, I'll score it'. Before meeting him through his wife, Jean, Paul had seen him on a talk show and remarked to Linda, 'One of these days, I might get in touch with that guy.'

An invitation with Jean to Peasmarsh offered Davis an opportunity to pitch the Liverpool Philharmonic idea. Unfortunately, a crowd of Paul's Liverpool relatives also happened to be there, making it difficult to get him on his own. There was an awkward moment, too, when he asked Davis to name his favourite Beatles song and Davis could think only of 'A Hard Day's Night', written by John.

At first, the chance to co-compose a choral work for the Liverpool Phil's 150th anniversary did not seem to excite him. But later, around the tea-table with his relations, he started reminiscing about his days at Liverpool Institute High School; how on hot summer days he would 'sag off' class and sneak into the nearby cathedral graveyard to sunbathe on the tombstones. This triggered the idea of a musical autobiography on a scale far beyond 'Penny Lane'.

Davis expected merely to be Paul's amanuensis, translating raw ideas into musical grammar as George Martin had always done. To begin with, he adopted a somewhat pedagogic air, explaining technical terms such as 'rondo', sometimes pausing to say 'Let me give you a lesson . . .' 'He tried to sit me down one day with Benjamin Britten's Young Person's Guide to the Orchestra,' Paul would remember, '[but] I said, "No, Carl, it's too late for that, love."'

He'd also presumed they would be working separately and he'd take the musical lead, pastiching Paul's style in the same way he'd matched 1920s-ish music to Hollywood silent movies. For the first movement, 'War', set in the year of Paul's birth, 1942, he composed what he thought were sweet, tuneful McCartneyesque cadences, only to have them rejected out of hand. What Paul wanted to evoke was the Nazi bombing of Liverpool as shown on grainy old black and white cinema newsreels, 'with planes coming over and dropping their bombs and the fire brigade rushing around and bells ringing'. 'My God, you're turning me on,' Davis said, beginning to scribble new notes. After that, the two worked together almost as closely and interactively as Paul once had with John.

Some time passed before Paul knew exactly what it was they were composing. 'I'd say to Carl, "Is this a symphony?" He'd say, "No, that's slightly different." "Is it a concerto then?" He'd say, "No, it's not." "Is it a suite?" "Oh, no, God, no."' Then by chance he read an inflight magazine article which mentioned the oratorio form, a narrative work on a religious theme, like Handel's *Messiah* or Verdi's *Requiem*. After checking with Davis that that indeed was what they were about, he titled it the *Liverpool Oratorio* – the first use of the city's name for artistic purposes since 'the Liverpool Sound'.

Close collaborators that they had become, Davis was expecting a Lennon–McCartney-style 50–50 credit. But Paul made it clear that he wanted the billing to be 'Paul McCartney's *Liverpool Oratorio*'. As he later explained: 'I was getting paranoid that Carl would be up on the podium like Stravinsky on heat and I'd be coming over as the scruff from Speke who couldn't read music.' Speke was the blue-collar suburb where he'd lived as a small boy before his mother's job as a midwife allowed them to move to a better area; how revealing that 40 years on, for all the immensity of his fame, he should still have felt its caste-mark.

He worked on the oratorio for two and a half years, longer by far than he'd ever devoted to a single project, somehow finding time for sessions with Carl Davis between making the *Flowers in the Dirt* album, setting up two further ones and going on that ten-month, 100,000-mile world tour.

It told the story of his early life but not any part of his musical career, which he'd ruled out as 'too boring'. Its hero therefore had a fictitious name, Shanty, a dual reference to Liverpool seafarers' songs and the humblest type of dwelling, more so even than a Speke council house with an outside toilet.

The core of the piece was Shanty's education at Liverpool Institute, which mirrored Paul's own; its leitmotif was the Inny's Latin motto, 'Non Nobis Solum Sed Toti Mundo Nati' – 'not for ourselves alone but for the whole world were we born' – an apt prophecy for two pupils (George as well) destined to be Beatles. There was also a recreation of the Spanish teacher, Miss Inkley, whom Paul's class believed to have been a wartime secret agent, and her little song about three bunny rabbits in a tree, 'Tres conejos en un árbol'.

Other autobiographical touches were more oblique. In boyhood, Shanty did not lose his mother as Paul had but his father, commemorated in what could have been an epitaph for 'Gentleman Jim' McCartney: 'Your spirit will keep us moving in the right direction'. Later, the adult Shanty received a vision of his mother in a graveyard which morphed into his future wife, both of them named after Paul's maternal patron saint, Mary.

And despite the moratorium on Beatle history, there was no preventing John from sneaking into the libretto. Shanty's declaration that 'the most important thing I've done was sagging off' meant more than just cutting class to sunbathe on gravestones; it meant forging the Lennon–McCartney songwriting partnership in the tiny front room at 20 Forthlin Road.

At the end, Shanty's pregnant wife Mary suffered an accident and was taken to hospital where a kindly nurse (Paul's other patron saint) asked her, 'Do you know who you are?' It is the emergency services' first means of assessing trauma in an accident victim. After John's shooting by Mark David Chapman, he'd been asked the same question in the back of a New York police car as it rushed him, unavailingly, to Roosevelt Hospital.

While Liverpool Institute was being thus celebrated in words and music, it presented one of the saddest symbols of the city's decline.

The Inny had closed in 1985 after 140 years. Officially, the reason was declining pupil numbers caused by an oversupply of modern schools round about. In reality, the feeling of privilege it gave its pupils was anathema to Liverpool's hard left city council (none more so than the Trotskyist deputy leader Derek Hatton, who'd once been among them). Nor did the Inny's demise put an end to this official malevolence: for six years, its neoclassical building in Mount Street had simply been left to rot.

When Paul first embarked on the oratorio, he'd paid a return visit to his alma mater to refresh his memory for the music, and had been shocked by the desolation he found. In fact, the Inny had contributed little to his musical development beyond putting him on the other side of a wall from John in the adjacent art college. Still, he recognised the superlative education in English and languages that he'd jettisoned to go with the Beatles to Hamburg.

At this point, it must be said, he was not exactly famous as a public benefactor, least of all in his home city. During the late Seventies, when the school launched a redevelopment appeal, his old English teacher, Alan 'Dusty' Durband, had asked him to contribute and been disappointed to receive a cheque for just £1000.

His reputation as a tightwad hardly bore scrutiny; as a co-founder of the Beatles' Apple organisation, he had given away more money than any pop star before or since. But overt acts of philanthropy like, for instance, Elton John's had never seemed his thing. 'I know any number of people and organisations he's helped,' says his old Liverpool friend, Joe Flannery. 'But never a word about it has got out. I sometimes said to him, "Paul, why don't you tell some of these people who think you're tight with your money?" He always said, "It's not the point."'

Lately, that had begun to change. In 1990, when Rye's small hospital was threatened with closure, he and Linda joined in local efforts to save it, including a protest march in company with Spike Milligan. He subsequently donated £1 million to build a new 19-bed care centre, to which Linda sent flowers every day.

So now he felt it was up to him to do something about his old school, little dreaming how much it would end up costing him. His first idea was merely to replace the Inny's roof which had been stripped of its lead even more thoroughly than Apple's old head-quarters in London, allowing rain to compound the ruin below. But to safeguard the building in the long term, some new use for it would have to be found.

Historically the only way for pop artistes to learn their craft – as the Beatles learned theirs – had been by trial and error in front of live audiences. But in America during the 1980s, the idea took root that pop vocalising, songwriting and instrumentation could be taught in the same way as English or algebra. This notion of star-dom as being open to everyone inspired Alan Parker's 1980 film *Fame*, about hyper-competitive students at the New York School of Performing Arts. Irene Cara's title song had since become an anthem for millions of young people to whom fame had never before seemed an option: 'I'm gonna live for ever . . . I'm gonna light up the sky.'

Yet British versions of that 'Fame academy' had been slow to take root. The first, prophetically enough, was at Liverpool University which opened its Institute of Popular Music in 1988 with Paul's brother, Mike, on its steering committee. The idea then spread to

secondary education, notably with the BRIT School – named after
the UK's annual pop awards – in Croydon, south of London, which
offered performing arts courses, sponsored by the record industry,
alongside conventional subjects.

The BRIT School was the brainchild of a former teacher and
publisher with the very un-rock 'n' roll name of Mark Featherstone-
Witty. Inspired by Parker's film, Featherstone-Witty had set up the
Performing Arts Trust, a body dedicated to bringing it to life in the
UK, whose supporters included Parker himself, Richard Branson,
Joan Armatrading and George Martin.

Martin had received the most rigorous classical music education
at London's Guildhall School. But he'd never forgotten the torrent
of raw talent that had come out of Liverpool in the Sixties in the
Beatles, Cilla Black, Gerry Marsden and dozens more. Hearing
of the Inny's predicament from Paul, he suggested it would be a
perfect site for a fame school like the one Mark Featherstone-Witty
was putting together in Croydon.

By then, Featherstone-Witty had bowed out of the BRIT School,
which had made use of his ideas but then failed to appoint him
principal. At a loss professionally, and in 'a deep depression', he
was contacted by Richard Ogden, and invited to a meeting with
Paul. Thus from the mildewed classrooms and sodden textbooks
of Liverpool Institute High School for Boys was born the Liverpool Institute for Performing Arts, or LIPA. As its 'lead patron',
Paul pledged £1 million of start-up money in staged payments;
Featherstone-Witty was to be its founding principal and head its
fund-raising campaign.

The moment could not have been more opportune. By 1991 the
city council had recovered from its long amnesia about the Beatles
and realised the potential of their name to attract tourism and generate business. LIPA therefore received enthusiastic support from
City Hall, if no concrete promise of funding. The city's evening
paper, the *Echo*, also took up the cause, conducting a readers poll
which showed overwhelming enthusiasm for the project. In a
letter to the *Echo*, Paul stressed that the new school would be for

Merseyside's young talent above all. 'I got a great start in life at the Institute, and would love to see other local people do the same.'

Confirmation of the Inny's rescue came in the run-up to the *Liverpool Oratorio*'s premiere in June 1991. Paul had further announced that when LIPA was established, he himself would teach classes there. No one imagined such a thing could really happen, but it swelled the already huge media interest in his classical debut. For the first time in many years, the name 'Liverpool' in a story signified something other than strikes, motormouth politicos and benefits cheats.

The oratorio was not to be performed at the Philharmonic Hall, its orchestra's usual home, but in the Anglican cathedral whose stark sandstone bulk towers over the heights of Georgian Liverpool. Paul had been rejected by its choir at the age of 11, instead joining the rather less exalted one at St Barnabas' Church near Penny Lane.

To sing the four solo parts, his simple instruction to Carl Davis was 'Get the best in the world'. Grand opera had boomed in popularity since Luciano Pavarotti's heart-stopping performance of Puccini's 'Nessun Dorma' during the 1990 World Cup; however, Pavarotti and the other tenors of the so-called 'Football Three', Placido Domingo and José Carreras, all had Latin accents too strong for the work's Scouse idiom.

Paul got his wish nevertheless; the line-up was headed by Dame Kiri Te Kanawa, the world's best as well as best-loved soprano, in the role of Shanty's wife, Mary, supported by the American tenor Jerry Hadley as Shanty, the great West Indian bass-baritone Willard White and the South African mezzo-soprano Sally Burgess.

In March, Davis began rehearsing the finished 90-minute piece with its 90 musicians and 150-strong choir, augmented by the cathedral's own 40 choristers (one of whom was actually named Shanty). Paul was there throughout with Linda; rather than commute to and from Sussex by private jet, they used the house on the Cheshire Wirral that Paul had originally bought for his father, then turned over to his brother, Michael.

He himself very nearly joined the four international opera stars who were to sing the sort-of story of his early life. Dame Kiri was all for it, suggesting he took the role of the Institute headmaster. He tried a few bars, but decided the competition would be too great.

Although Davis was the one on a podium with a baton, Paul effectively ran the rehearsals. He was concerned that the orchestra shouldn't think themselves on a soft wicket, having overheard Davis tell leader violinist Malcolm Stewart, 'Don't worry . . . It's not concerto-level.' The fourth movement, 'Father', particularly exercised him as it featured trumpets, his dad's old instrument. If anyone forgot a note, he instantly supplied it in a perfect falsetto. Linda sat to one side, singing along word-perfectly.

And of course the resources at hand far exceeded any normal choir-practice. When Kiri Te Kanawa sportingly volunteered to sing 'I'm going to have a baby' in a Liverpudlian accent, Ma Boswell from *Bread*, aka Mrs Carl Davis, was brought in to coach her.

The premiere was to be filmed and also recorded for release as an album. The extra generators that were needed almost drowned out the music, so a sound-engineer suggested muffling them with bales of hay. 'Paul snapped his fingers and said "Get hay",' Davis recalls. 'In an hour or so, a lorry load arrived.'

At the outset, Paul's biggest worry had been hearing his words sung by 'fruity' voices, the kind he'd always poked fun at (never more zestfully than in John's company). But as the days passed, he discovered how that fruitiness could move him in ways the most poignant pop track he'd written never had. For instance, in the chorale where Shanty, Mary and their child looked ahead to the future, the Fifties and Sixties, he admitted, 'I had to bite my lip a bit. I didn't want to start crying there in the middle of everyone.'

In fact, none of the words came near 'Penny Lane' level. But world-class operatic voices and the cathedral's magnificent acoustics lifted the tritest of them to a higher dimension – like tenor Jerry Hadley's spine-tinglingly sweet and poignant delivery of 'I can say that looking back the most important thing I've done was sagging off.'

One of the journalists allowed to observe the rehearsals was Russell Miller of the *Sunday Times Magazine*. At first, Miller hardly recognised Paul, seated alone in the top tier of the choir stalls:

> To judge by his appearance he could belong to Liverpool's legion of unemployed, could have crept in off the street to warm up for a bit. He wears a brown tweed overcoat that has definitely seen better days . . . His hair is long and greying and he carries his possessions in a cheap green nylon rucksack.

To Miller he came across as his usual unpretentious, light-hearted self, mocking his own presumptuousness in a Scouse voice more lumpen than any of the Boswells': '*Oratorio!* Orright Paul wazza noratorio when it's at home? Wasn't he the bloke who shot Moby Dick?' Yet his anxiety was palpable: Miller noticed how he kept shifting in his seat, crossing and uncrossing his legs, running his hands through his hair, picking at his fingers and chewing his nails.

His involvement in the Rye hospital campaign had been big enough news to be still worth asking about. 'It's not a worry for me, I could build my own bloody hospital if I wanted, but it's for the people who really need that hospital . . . because I'm one of them really. I don't see any reason to become middle class or upper class because I've got some money. People say to me, "You're not really working class any more." I say, "I bloody am, you know. I work my arse off, I do. I work my bloody arse off."'

He took the opportunity once again to correct the 'huge misconception' about his character in relation to John's: the cute, middle-of-the-road Beatle versus the avant-garde artist and iconoclast. While he'd been co-founding the Indica gallery and funding the *International Times*, he said, in an untypical outburst, 'John was living on a golf course in bloody Weybridge . . . I suppose [the mistake] is to do with the way I am, the way I was brought up, sort of jolly. . . . I'm a great believer in time. There's a lot to be found out about who did what, but I think it will come out in time.'

Linda was there as always to defend him. 'A lot of the artistic and creative things that John got the credit for were done by Paul, but you can't prove that . . . I keep saying it doesn't matter what people think, he knows who he is and what he's done. But he still resents it.'

The final run-through was watched by all four McCartney children, 21-year-old Mary in her new capacity as her mother's assistant at MPL. 'They just seemed a very ordinary family, if you forgot they'd just flown in by private jet,' Russell Miller remembers. 'The boy, James, had a basketball with him and kept looking around the cathedral as if assessing its potential for a game.'

A block of VIP seats had been set aside for Paul's Liverpool relations. His favourite aunt, Gin, had died in 1987, so the clan matriarch was now Auntie Joan, wife of his dad's whispering brother Joe, who'd helped care for him and Michael in the first shock of their mother's death when it seemed doubtful that Gentleman Jim could ever recover.

Paul's real affection for these elderly and frail survivors was what most impressed Miller. 'They may not look much, there are no stunners among them,' Paul said, 'but by God they've got something – common sense in the truest sense of the word. I've met lots of people, I've met Harold Wilson and Maggie Thatcher and most of the mayors in America, but I've never met anyone as fascinating, as interesting or as wise as my Liverpool family.'

The premiere of the *Liverpool Oratorio* on 28 June was also an opportunity to publicise the Liverpool Institute for Performing Arts. Margaret Thatcher had resigned as prime minister in 1990 and under her less bellicose, more culturally-aware successor, John Major, there were prospects of government funding for LIPA.

Before the recital, Paul gave Major's Inner Cities Minister Michael Portillo a guided tour of the Inny building to show what huge renovation it needed. In one of the derelict classrooms, he mentioned the Spanish song 'Tres conejos en un árbol' which he'd learned there as a small boy and now put into the oratorio. (Portillo, whose father was born near Madrid, came back in disconcertingly fluent Spanish.) As a further gift to the media, he said he himself might take a LIPA course 'and finally get some letters after my name'.

The audience of 2500 in the cathedral that evening was believed to be the largest congregation in its history. As Carl Davis lifted his baton, the massed television lamps and recording equipment caused a power overload and every light in the place went out. But after a few moments, as if through divine intervention, perhaps by an angel named Mary, they came on again.

At the end, there was a ten-minute standing ovation. Paul joined Davis on the podium and they hoisted each other's arms aloft like boxing champs. The biggest challenge in his solo career had brought its most successful collaboration. He'd even ceded a share of the glory: the posters outside read 'Paul McCartney's *Liverpool Oratorio* by Paul McCartney and Carl Davis'.

The classical music critics who provided the bulk of the reviews were almost as sniffy about Davis's background in populist TV and film as about Paul's in pop. The *Guardian* called their work 'lacklustre and embarrassing'; *The Times* said the oratorio had some 'sweet tunes, but the churchy choral passages and laboured orchestral interludes made Brahms's *Requiem* sound like a hotbed of syncopation'.

Five months later, it received its American premiere at New York's Carnegie Hall – where the Beatles had famously appeared in 1964 – with Barbara Bonney taking Kiri Te Kanawa's role and the Liverpool Cathedral choristers replaced by the Boys Choir of Harlem. The *New York Times*'s reviewer Edward Rothstein was little more impressed than his British colleagues, calling it 'a primitive assemblage of material gussied up through some clever scoring', and noting how 'the kind of musical and emotional simplicity that make a pop hit can sound barren in the concert hall'. Complimenting and admonishing Paul in the same breath, Rothstein quoted the reply of the great classical composer Arnold Schoenberg during the 1930s when he was asked for composition lessons by George

Gershwin. 'But why do you want to be an Arnold Schoenberg? You're such a good Gershwin already.'

As so often with Paul's pop releases, bad reviews had no effect: the two-disc live recording made all 25 of America's most important classical music charts and even appeared in some pop ones. Professional and amateur orchestras around the world instantly put their own versions into rehearsal, creating EMI's first surge in sheet music sales since the early Sixties.

He may have failed to become an Arnold Schoenberg and had to settle for being a modern Gershwin – but he had given his birthplace something precious beyond price. It was there in the oratorio's second movement like an audible turning of the tide, when the cathedral choristers sang the Inny's Latin motto, 'Non Nobis Solum Sed Toti Mundo Nati', then its English translation with six extra words.

'Not for ourselves alone but for the whole world were we born,' chorused the boyish trebles with – yes – pride. *'And we were born in Liverpool.'*

44

'Everyone wanted to be the icing on the cake. No one wanted to be the cake'

On 30 July 1991, Linda's father, Lee Eastman, died of a stroke, aged 81. As his *New York Times* obituary noted, he had effectively created MPL and in 20 years as Paul's lawyer and business adviser had brought huge assets into the company through his knowledge of music publishing. To be sure, his combination of toughness and taste would have made him an excellent manager for the Beatles; one in whose hands their partnership might never have ended in the messy, anticlimactic way it did.

Cheated of that prize by Allen Klein, he still hadn't done badly from a client-list which included other major music names like David Bowie, Billy Joel and Andrew Lloyd-Webber as well as 'Bill' de Kooning and most of America's highest priced modern painters. He left an estate valued at $300 million with a $30 million art collection containing works by Picasso, de Kooning, Mark Rothko and Robert Motherwell, and a Rolls-Royce presented to him by his appreciative son-in-law.

Although a tragedy for his second wife, Monique, his four children and three stepchildren, Lee's passing had no repercussions on Paul's legal or business affairs. Long in poor health, he had turned over the family law firm to Linda's brother John, to whom Paul had been close since they'd joined forces to break up the Beatles' partnership in 1971. John Eastman remains his lawyer to this day, paying unstinted tribute to 'a great client who always listens to advice and realises when it makes sense'.

Paul and Linda flew to Long Island for Lee's funeral despite the fact that Hurricane Bob was currently devastating America's eastern seaboard. By the time it reached East Hampton, the hurricane had spent much of its force, but still gave the family's mourning a Shakespearian atmosphere with high winds, driving rain and frequent power-cuts, when even the Hamptons' super-rich were forced to live by candlelight and cook on open wood fires.

Paul, as usual, rather enjoyed roughing it and, while the electricity was out, wrote several songs on acoustic guitar. One of them, inspired by the dramatic meteorology, he named 'Calico Skies' and put away in his huge bottom drawer. It showed that at 49 he hadn't lost the madrigal simplicity and sweetness that created 'Blackbird' when he was 25.

Linda's share of her father's estate made her now an extremely wealthy woman. And an even greater fortune was about to come her way, bringing with it a thaw in any remaining public chill towards her.

The surprise runaway success of *Linda McCartney's Home Cooking* had transformed her status at MPL, turning what had been patronisingly viewed as her 'little side project' into a potentially major growth area for the company. After the book topped the UK bestsellers list, Peter Cox, Linda's co-author and nutritionist, was summoned by Paul and asked to set up and run a 'food company' to package her vegetarian recipes and put them into the shops.

Cox spent several months compiling a feasibility study based on food retail methods all over the world. 'In the end, I told Paul there were only two ways that a food-producing company could work,' he recalls. 'Either it had to be very small and niche, like cheese- or honey-makers, or some huge organisation like Nestlé. The only other alternative was to franchise the McCartney name, which he was very much against. "I've *never* done that," he told me, "and I *never* will."'

Initially, Cox had enjoyed his immersion in the rock-star world where pizzas were flown in from New York on Concorde, but now he was glad of a chance to escape from it. Besides, the tension he felt from Paul over his collaboration with Linda was bringing out the Macca side at its worst. 'One day when I had to speak to him about something, he kept me waiting for hours while he just messed around in the studio. When he came out, he was very high, and said something extremely sarcastic to me. I snapped back what right did he have to treat people like that because he was Paul Mc-Cartney? It brought him up short because as a rule, nobody *ever* talked back to him. And later, he did apologise.'

Cox's contract for *Linda McCartney's Home Cooking* had been a straight 50–50 split with Linda, but now he had to agree to a not-very-generous buy-out of his share. 'It wasn't a pleasant experience, dealing with people at MPL who'd previously seemed to be my friends but were now putting me under serious pressure.' He'd also been credited as co-author in the UK edition, but on a visit to America he chanced on a copy of the new US one and saw that his name had been removed.

After Cox's departure, various ideas for marketing Linda's food were discussed, from building it its own factory to buying the Cranks chain of vegetarian restaurant/takeaways as a ready-made outlet. In the end, the deal negotiated by Richard Ogden was a franchise such as Paul had initially ruled out: Linda's recipes would be sold as ready-to-eat frozen meals by Ross-Young's, a division of the United Biscuits corporation and the UK's third-largest producer of frozen foods. By a happy coincidence UB's newly-appointed chief executive, Eric Nicoli, also happened to be a non-executive director of Paul's record company, EMI.

Selling the idea to Linda was not easy, since any mass-market frozen food producer would be heavily reliant on the inhumane livestock and poultry farming methods she so abhorred. She insisted on paying a personal visit to Ross-Young's factory in Grimsby, Lincolnshire, and gave the green light only after assurances that production of her ready meals would be completely segregated from that of meat-based ones. Those would be processed and packaged by day and her recipes during the night, using stringently cleansed and purified machinery and surfaces.

Linda McCartney vegetarian frozen food was launched in 1991, initially consisting of six items: lasagne, Ploughman's Pasties, beef-less burgers, Italian-style toppers (sauces), Golden Nuggets and Ploughman's Pie. There was a lavish reception at London's Savoy Hotel where music journalists mingled incongruously with VIPs from the grocery trade to sample Linda's creations and hear Paul testify to having himself cooked her Golden Nuggets with mash. Boxed sets were also sent to those of his northern relatives, like Mike and Bett Robbins, who still remained stubbornly carnivorous.

The range went straight into Sainsbury's, one of Britain's largest supermarket chains, and was as instant a hit as Beatles records had once been. Within a year, it was bringing more money into MPL than did music.

Linda was infinitely more passionate about the frozen meals bearing her name than she ever had been about playing in Wings or even photography. She fronted the television ads herself, this time attracting no criticisms for her performance. Though others had to be trusted to prepare her recipes, she acted as a one-woman quality control, paying incognito visits to supermarkets to check that they were being displayed properly and hadn't passed their sell-by date. When meat-free sausages were added to the range, Carla Lane reported that one of her friends found them 'a bit greasy'. Linda got straight on the phone to Ross-Young's senior management, demanding the sausages be removed from sale immediately, which they were.

The most serious slip-up was never explained, but thought to be deliberate sabotage by a Ross-Young's employee, possibly with a lingering grudge against the Woman Who Married Paul. A large batch of shepherd's pies containing lamb were put into Linda McCartney purple boxes instead of their rightful green ones and sent out into the world without further checking. The subsequent mass recall was more suggestive of the motor trade than the freezer cabinet.

*

Paul's fiftieth birthday in July 1992 found him in uniquely good shape for a rock star of his vintage. His face still kept its boyish heart-shape, his smile its impish exuberance – ever reinforced by two upraised thumbs – his brown eyes their puppy-soulfulness, his voice its lightness and purity. His hair remained as abundant as when he was a teenager, albeit now winged with grey above the ears. For the moment, he decided to let it be.

The continuing autobiography of his songs was now to take more tangible form. A few months earlier he had agreed to authorise a biography of himself, written by Barry Miles who had given him his entrée to avant-garde art and music in the mid-1960s. From the Indica gallery and *International Times*, Miles had gone on to author a string of books, from anthologies of pop-star quotes (including by the Beatles and John Lennon) to a critically-acclaimed life of Allen Ginsberg.

Paul was not the first top-echelon rock star to take this step, normally associated with royalty, politicians or major figures in literature or the theatre. In the early 1980s, Mick Jagger had received £1 million for his life story from the illustrious house of Weidenfeld & Nicolson, but then come up with so little interesting information that the book was aborted and Jagger had to repay the whole advance. An official McCartney biography would therefore be starting a new genre.

Despite the hopes of the Bloomsbury imprint, Linda's publisher and MPL's next-door neighbour, the book was signed in the UK by Secker & Warburg, a division of the Random House group. Paul at first wanted it to deal solely with his 'London years', from the onset of Beatlemania to the end of Apple, but Miles persuaded him to include his childhood and to continue the story after the Beatles' break-up, though it was still not to be a detailed chronology of his life with Linda or of Wings.

Biographers normally rely heavily on written sources like letters and diaries. But even with someone of Paul's literacy, pop-star life had left little time for correspondence bar the odd picture postcard or letter home to his dad from Hamburg. This dictated the form of the book, which was to be based on extensive interviews with its subject and include lengthy direct quotations, making it as much autobiography as biography. Images of his childhood were in equally short supply; the fans who'd got inside Cavendish over the years had stolen most of his family photographs including almost every one of his mother.

Evelyn Waugh once wrote that the famous write their memoirs or authorise biographies of themselves only when they have lost all curiosity about the future. But despite the gargantuan achievement behind him, all that mattered to Paul was moving forward, staying current and keeping contact with live audiences by every possible means.

The previous decade had seen the rise of America's Music TV cable and satellite channel, initially playing non-stop pop videos but increasingly a medium for performance that no big name in the business could afford to ignore. In 1991, Paul had been invited to appear on an *MTV Unplugged*, or all-acoustic, show with his new band: guitarists Hamish Stuart and Robbie McIntosh, 'Wix' Wickens (his first bald sideman) dividing keyboards with Linda, and drummer Blair Cunningham (his first black sideman since Billy Preston) replacing Chris Whitten, who'd left to join Dire Straits.

Previous *Unplugged* invitees had slipped in a bit of electricity somewhere, but Paul insisted that his performance should be totally au naturel. Recorded before a youthful audience of just 200, it mixed Beatles material with old rock 'n' roll and R&B and included the public debut of 'I Lost My Little Girl', his earliest attempt at songwriting, aged 14. Grief-stricken though he'd been by his mother's death at the time, it was an upbeat little country ditty with a Buddy Holly hiccup.

The 51-minute set was then turned into an 'official bootleg' album – with the same kind of deliberately dodgy-looking cover as Paul's Russian one in 1988 – which quickly charted and would have gone higher if he hadn't made it a limited edition. Along with that came six more 'surprise' live shows, alternating dates in Spain,

Italy and Denmark with unlikely British venues such as Westcliffe-on-Sea and St Austell in Cornwall. This was not a man showing the least inclination to rest on his forests of laurels.

In the Liverpool Institute for Performing Arts fund-raising campaign, the first task of its founding principal, Mark Featherstone-Witty, was to send appeals to several hundred celebrities and public figures, including the Queen. 'The letters had to seem to come directly from Paul,' he remembers, 'so it was rather like one of those "Write an essay in the style of . . ." exercises I used to set my class when I was teaching. Paul looked through them and altered a word here and there, but mostly they went out as I'd drafted them.'

The cost of launching LIPA had now been set at £12 million. And in the months that followed, Featherstone-Witty found that having Paul McCartney's name attached to the project was no magic key to success. 'The Arts Council wouldn't get involved because they viewed it as a purely commercial venture for an industry already awash with money. A lot of prospective donors, including Liverpool City Council, assumed that Paul would be meeting most of the costs and saw themselves as the icing on the cake – which was just how Paul saw himself. Everyone wanted to be the icing on the cake. No one wanted to be the cake.'

With Paul's help, Featherstone-Witty had an impressive list of celebrity supporters, among them the Hollywood stars Jane Fonda and Eddie Murphy and the designer Ralph Lauren. George and Olivia Harrison made a donation through their charitable foundation (although George remembered the Inny only for being caned on the hand and persecuted over his clothes, and took no interest whatsoever in its renaissance). EMI pledged £100,000, a modest enough quid pro quo for the millions Paul had earned for the company over the years. The Queen responded to her fake 'Paul' letter with a cheque signed by an official known as the Keeper of the Privy Purse. 'It wasn't for much,' Featherstone-Witty recalls, 'but the PR value was enormous.'

Paul did his bit by attending four fund-raising lunches, two in

London, one in Japan and one in Brussels to solicit help from the European Commission. Yet still only the tiniest dent had been made in the £12 million LIPA needed and Featherstone-Witty was 'scrabbling around for money', with little in view but a handout from the National Lottery's projected arts fund. Then a name from Paul's distant past came forward to help.

Back when he and John used to long for a tape recorder to preserve their songs, rather than just a school exercise book, the most desirable make was a German Grundig. In 1992, the company was still in business and looking to rejuvenate that very 1950s reel-to-reel image by sponsoring sport or pop music. Grundig offered LIPA a million Deutschmarks a year for five years in exchange for 'title sponsorship', meaning that its name would appear below the school's logo. 'Paul didn't like that idea at first,' Featherstone-Witty recalls. 'He said he wasn't putting his name on LIPA, so why should anyone else? But we were suddenly being handed what amounted to about a fifth of the total building-cost, so he accepted it.'

Paul in fact was having serious misgivings about the project, not least his choice of someone with so elaborately double-barrelled a name to be his representative in Liverpool. And the ebullient Featherstone-Witty was not always as feather-footed around him as protocol required. Granted the high favour of inclusion at MPL's Christmas party, he brought along an uninvited friend who happened to be very loudly camp. That bothered Paul less than the ruckus the intruder was making, and he sent Richard Ogden over with a terse request to keep it down.

Several times he told Ogden he was unhappy with the way LIPA seemed to be shaping and feared it wouldn't benefit working-class kids, as he'd intended, but that 'Mark will fill it with gay ballet dancers'. But Ogden convinced him to have faith: it would be his legacy.

The 1989–90 world tour had been a massive earner which put Paul back on top as a concert attraction and turned *Flowers in the Dirt* into his biggest album since *Band on the Run*. An unexpected extra dividend had come from the monitoring of record stores along the way, which revealed a major accounting mistake in his foreign royalties from EMI. The resulting back-payment ran into millions.

So in 1993 he was to go out again, visiting the parts he hadn't reached before, notably Australia and New Zealand (which he now designated as 'Oceania'), and exploiting the market that had opened up in Latin America. The 77 shows on this seven-instalment New World Tour would keep him performing, with only short breaks, from February to December. The Beatles in Hamburg hadn't worked so hard – and then he'd been a teenager.

The accompanying album, *Off the Ground*, made at Hog Hill Mill through 1992, was co-produced by Paul and Julian Mendelsohn, a gifted young Australian engineer who'd worked with Jimmy Page, Bob Marley and the Pet Shop Boys. Mendelsohn's brief was that it must have a raw, spontaneous feel, with as many tracks as possible nailed in a single take (the same ambition Paul once had for the Beatles' *Get Back*). Despite an excellent new band, his list of instrumental and sound effects credits was the longest yet (guitar, bass, sitar, piano, Wurlitzer, electric piano, celeste, Mellotron, ocarina, drums, percussion, congas, mouth percussion, whistling) with Linda's not far behind (Moog, autoharp, celeste, clavinet, harmonium, percussion, keyboards, train whistle).

As usual, a proportion of the material came from Paul's irreducible bottom drawer. Two tracks were left over from the Elvis Costello sessions (one with an added horn section scored by his new classical mate, Carl Davis). For hardcore Beatles fans, there was even a memento of the Transcendental Meditation era, written during their visit to India in 1968.

But his main concern at 50, as he said, was to shake off any last suspicion of 'cutesiness' and get to grips with the issues which Linda had made important to him. So serious was he that he asked his friend the poet Adrian Mitchell to vet the album's lyrics 'as if he was an English teacher. I went through them all with [Adrian] and I can now say they're poet-proof.'

Thus 'Looking for Changes' was an attack on animal testing,

represented by 'a cat with a machine in its brain' and a cigarette-fed monkey 'learning to choke'. 'Long Leather Coat' was like a rewrite of John's 'Norwegian Wood', about a man lured to a tryst by an enigmatic young woman, only to have his leather coat – that one-time symbol of Beatle chic – drenched with red paint. 'Big Boys Bickering' employed Paul's first recorded four-letter word to denounce politicians for 'fucking it up for everyone'.

The New World Tour was to be the largest and most expensive he had ever undertaken. At the time, the band with the costliest, most grandiloquent stage-set was U2, but he ran them close with special effects including a pod that swung him out over the audience with a single musician beside him (an idea picked up from Mick Jagger).

Once again, the gospel of vegetarianism was to be spread at every show and press conference. For photo-ops, Paul and Linda often wore T-shirts with red traffic-lights saying 'STOP EATING MEAT' or green ones saying 'GO VEGGIE'. But this time, the McCartneys' animal-rights agenda had a much harder edge. Underlining the theme of 'Looking for Changes' in *Off the Ground*, the tour proclaimed their solidarity with People for the Ethical Treatment of Animals – PETA – the hard-line pressure group against animal testing. PETA's message was woven into the show's back-projections: joyous sequences from *A Hard Day's Night* or *The Beatles at Shea Stadium* segued to harrowing footage of actual cats 'with machines in their brains' or monkeys 'learning to choke'.

The tour was also to be a fund-raiser for the Liverpool Institute of Performing Arts. In America, there would be a special $1000 ticket which entitled the holder to attend the sound-check – when Paul might well come over and say 'hello', though this wasn't guaranteed – as well as watching the show proper from a block of elevated seats in front of the sound-mixing desk. That money would not be part of the tour revenues but go directly to LIPA.

In 1989–90, the tour arrangements had been largely in the hands of Barrie Marshall, a British promoter uniquely skilled both in selling rock shows to the public and handling everything on the road, including the budgeting. Despite the huge profitability of that outing, and Marshall's efficiency and total honesty, Paul decided that on the New World Tour the budgeting should be done in-house at MPL.

It was to prove a major error, for MPL's people based their figures on the huge attendances in 1989–90, unmindful of how circumstances had changed meantime. Then, Paul had been returning after an absence of a decade; now it was only two and a half years. Nor would he be touring on the back of a hit album: *Off the Ground* had not sold badly but, compared to *Flowers in the Dirt*, it had been a commercial and critical disappointment.

A large part of the tour's massive overhead was to have been absorbed by a sponsorship deal with Volkswagen cars – a seemingly perfect match as VW's most famous model was the Beetle. However, Linda objected that linking up with a car manufacturer would compromise the McCartney stance on protecting the environment (as if their own vehicular fleet and frequent flights by Concorde, the most polluting aircraft ever, didn't already do that). So at the eleventh hour, with a major advertising campaign ready to roll, the deal was called off.

With no time to find a new commercial partner, the only option was Grundig, to date the main corporate funders of LIPA. They agreed to re-allocate a year's worth of LIPA money to sponsor the tour in Europe, but there was further delay while Linda satisfied herself that tape recorders posed no threat to the planet and Paul was persuaded to do a low-key ad for the company. He didn't sign the contract until four days into the tour, backstage at the Festhalle, Frankfurt.

With LIPA thus firmly embedded in the tour, he began to have fresh doubts about the whole project, the money it was costing him and whether star quality in the performing arts really was something that could be learned. His unease had been fed by a conversation with the Christians, the new-era Liverpool band with whom he'd appeared on a charity single, 'Ferry Cross the Mersey', after the Hillsborough football stadium disaster. Despite their youth, they all held the traditionalist view that rock couldn't be taught but had to be learned on the job.

The result was another uncomfortable Macca-moment for LIPA's principal-in-waiting, Mark Featherstone-Witty, who was in Germany scouting for prospective students. 'Backstage before a show, Paul suddenly put me on the spot about my background in education and theatre,' Featherstone-Witty recalls. '"Go on," he said. "Do some Shakespeare." I tried to explain I was going to be the principal, not head of acting.'

The real malaise set in in 'Oceania' – Australia and New Zealand – where ticket sales had been unaccountably light and Paul frequently found himself playing to crowds of 30,000 in spaces built for 50,000. The next stop was America, which this time promised no free TV ads from Visa cards, only an anticlimactic $1 million from the Blockbuster video store chain. Both Richard Ogden and the US promoter, Alex Kochan, urged him to bypass the giant stadiums on MPL's itinerary and play smaller arenas where he'd been guaranteed a capacity crowd. But to the man who'd (twice) effortlessly filled the Maracanã in Rio – and who, in other circumstances, was happy to perform for the tiniest audience – that was tantamount to admitting failure in advance. Consequently in America, too, he found himself playing to blocks of empty seats.

There, too, the show's animal-testing footage created a media controversy which PETA's representatives – very different from the gentle, personable Friends of the Earth on board last time – exploited to the maximum, turning off audiences still further. Even Paul's most loyal American fans didn't care for the sermonising which interrupted the magic Beatles moments they'd paid top dollar for. The special $1000 LIPA ticket created further bad press after some holders claimed not to have had the expected meet-and-greet with Paul. One aggrieved party went so far as to wave a banner saying '$1000 LIPA SCAM' when he was in mid-performance.

Determined to change the mood, Paul extended the tour until 16 December. 'Not that I need the money,' he took care to stress, 'but I still feel that if we bother to get out there like everyday working people [sic] we'll see some kind of reward.'

He also released another album, *Paul Is Live*, with highlights from his American and Australian shows earlier in the year, packaged with a blatant Beatles come-on. Its title referenced the 'Paul is dead' rumour in 1969 and its cover pastiched the 'clues' to his alleged demise on *Abbey Road*. But here his only companion on the famous zebra crossing was an Old English sheepdog named Arrow, one of Martha's offspring. For hardcore Beatlemaniacs, there were differences from the original image to spot; for instance, that he now wore shoes instead of walking barefoot and had his left, not right, foot forward. Nonetheless, it proved the lowest-selling live album he'd ever released.

The New World Tour brought a terminal rift with Richard Ogden, his manager (and Linda's) since 1987 and the main reason for his latter spectacular revival. Despite having argued against most of the tour's unwise decisions, Ogden felt the blame was being unfairly put on him. After returning from the Oceania and US legs, he received the massive snub of being told by Paul to 'stay home' during the remaining ones. He therefore handed in his notice. The next day, Paul called him in and fired him, having apparently not seen his resignation letter. As he was clearing his office, he received a phone call from the editor of the *News of the World*, Piers Morgan, offering him £150,000 for 'the inside story of Paul and Linda's marriage'. He declined it.

The following morning brought a letter from Morgan, upping the offer to £250,000. Again Ogden declined it. The music business doesn't make 'em like that any more.

45

'This letter comes with love from your friend Paul'

Just after the Beatles' break-up, Neil Aspinall, their former roadie, now Apple's managing director, had begun compiling a definitive film record of their career. The resultant 90-minute cinema documentary, entitled *The Long and Winding Road*, could have been released in the mid-Seventies but, thanks to the conflicting demands of its stars – *Magical Mystery Tour* syndrome reborn! – it had sat on the shelf as numerous unofficial film biographies came and went.

By the time of John's death, Aspinall's plan had changed to a television documentary which, even John seemed to accept, must reunite the four of them in some way. Although that idea had perished on 8 December 1980, there clearly was still vast commercial potential in bringing the three survivors back together on-screen. The problem was the bitterness George still felt towards Paul.

George's solo performing career might have tailed off, but he'd seemingly found ample fulfilment elsewhere. HandMade Films, the company he'd started with his manager, Denis O'Brien, produced some of the most successful British movies of the 1980s, from Monty Python's *Life of Brian* and *Time Bandits* to *Mona Lisa*, *The Long Good Friday* and *A Private Function*.

His second marriage, to Olivia Arias, had proved happy and calming, and given him a son, Dhani. He remained a stalwart of the Transcendental Meditation movement (which latterly had claimed to give converts the power of flight). With his friends Bob Dylan, Roy Orbison, Jeff Lynne and Tom Petty he'd formed a spare-time supergroup called the Traveling Wilburys, playing a gentle brand of country-rock which the music press dubbed 'skiffle for the Eighties'. Yet all these years on, he still seethed about the way he'd been treated in the Beatles; how his songs had always been pushed to the margins by the Lennon–McCartney juggernaut and, most of all, how Paul used to boss him about in the recording studio.

The documentary idea resurfaced in the late Eighties, then immediately sank again when Paul got his extra one per cent on Beatles back royalties from EMI and George, Ringo and Yoko joined forces to sue him, George most determinedly of all. EMI settled the dispute simply by giving the litigants their own extra one per cent each. Yet the old grudge continued to smoulder. 'Paul McCartney ruined me as a guitarist,' he told an interviewer on BBC radio – though it evidently hadn't stopped him playing. He seldom missed an opportunity to take a poke at Paul, whether for suggesting (around the time of *Flowers in the Dirt*) that the two of them might write together or for doing so much Beatles material onstage: 'He's decided he's the Beatles. I'm not interested. It's in the past . . . There won't be any reunion as long as John Lennon remains dead.'

But by 1990, when Aspinall raised the documentary idea yet again, things were rather different. HandMade Films had suffered a run of costly flops, like *Shanghai Surprise* starring Madonna, and, having underwritten the company personally, George faced possible bankruptcy. A surge in Beatles interest, and Beatles income, thus was manna from Heaven, albeit with Macca attached. His one proviso was that the project's McCartney-saturated title *The Long and Winding Road* should be changed, which it was, to the neutral *The Beatles Anthology*.

Still, when the *Anthology* was publicly announced – by Paul – in May 1991, George denied that it signified a reunion, in terms suggesting he hadn't softened all that much: 'No, it can't be possible because the Beatles don't exist. It just comes every time Paul wants some publicity.'

The multipart documentary combined the film footage Neil Aspinall had collected – much of it never aired before – and 'talking-head' interviews with Paul, George and Ringo and TV and audio clips of John. There would be testimony from a few close associates like Aspinall himself, George Martin and their former press officer, Derek Taylor (who had come out of retirement to handle the project's publicity), but no wives, present or past.

There was a conscious effort to avoid the nostalgia of unofficial Beatle film-histories and make it all feel crisp and contemporary. The director, Geoff Wonfor, had previously worked on Channel 4's outré pop show, *The Tube*, where he'd come to Paul's notice after doing an item on one of Linda's photographic exhibitions that particularly pleased her. The interviews were to be conducted by Jools Holland, the famously irreverent musician and former *Tube* presenter who'd first found fame in the New Wave band Squeeze.

Alongside the documentary, three double CDs were to chronicle the Beatles' career on record, with out-takes and alternate versions of songs etched on the memory of millions, mixed with snatches from old radio and TV shows and studio chatter. The first, covering the years 1958–64, included their first professionally recorded tracks: Buddy Holly's 'That'll Be the Day' and Paul's surprisingly mature country song 'In Spite of All the Danger'. There were also items from the audition tape that got them turned down by Decca in 1962 for eccentric choices, usually traceable back to Jim McCartney, like 'The Sheik of Araby' and 'Besame Mucho'.

Here and there, history was somewhat rewritten. The CD's collage-style cover – created by their old Hamburg friend Klaus Voormann – had an image of the band in their black leather days, but with the head of their then drummer, Pete Best, obliterated and Ringo's superimposed.

In 1962, when the Beatles were on the brink of fame, Best had been brutally sacked in favour of Ringo, without any compensation then or ever afterwards. The rumour at the time had been that he was too good-looking for his bandmates' peace of mind and that Paul in particular had chafed at the adoring screams of 'Pete!' wherever they appeared. After fronting his own band for a while, he'd drifted out of music and spent 20 years as a local government official with the most tragic eyes in Liverpool.

However, when the Beatles made the Decca tape, Best had still been with them, so was due a share of royalties from ten tracks used on the *Anthology*. The first he knew about it was a phone call from the one who'd been so keen to get rid of him – the first time they'd spoken since it happened.

'Some wrongs need to be righted,' Paul told him. 'There's some money here that's owing to you and you can take it or leave it.' Best took it.

As Paul was beginning a double journey through his past with interviews for *The Beatles Anthology* and his own authorised biography, he received some news which gave it special poignancy. Ivan Vaughan, the boyhood friend whose birth-date he shared, had died from pneumonia.

'Ivy' had been Paul's classmate at Liverpool Institute and lived over the garden wall from John. It was he who brought those two very different friends of his together at Woolton church fete, with such momentous consequences for music and popular culture.

Studious Ivy, in fact, had followed the career path which once beckoned to Paul, reading classics at London University, then becoming a teacher. From time to time, he would find himself pulled into his old school friend's rarified world, as when his wife, Jan, provided the French words for 'Michelle'. Later, he'd been one of Paul's only two travelling companions to LA for the first, top-secret tryst with Linda. And when Apple Corps' first idealistic prospectus included a school, to be run on hippy lines utterly unlike the Inny, he was the obvious choice as its head.

After the axing of the Apple school project, he and Jan had moved to Cambridge, where he became a lecturer at Homerton College.

Then, in his late thirties, he was diagnosed with Parkinson's disease. His courage and fortitude were shown in a 1984 television documentary, *Ivan: Living With Parkinson's Disease*, narrated by Jonathan Miller and subsequently turned into a much-admired book.

Paul had always kept in touch with him, just as John had from New York; indeed, there were moments when concern for Ivy seemed about all they had left in common. 'Ivan still talked to both of them in a kind of weird private language they'd used when they were kids,' Jan Vaughan remembers. 'It was more like a code, because no one else could understand a word of it.'

He and Paul last met at the *Liverpool Oratorio*'s London premiere, a glitzy gala occasion at the Royal Festival Hall. 'By that time, Ivan found going anywhere very difficult. But he was determined not to miss Paul's classical music debut.'

He died in August 1993, while Paul was in the midst of the New World Tour. Though not a surprise, the news was devastating for one whom that shared birth-date made practically a blood brother. Yet it also stirred fond memories of skiffle-playing days a million miles from high-tech stadium rock; of tinny acoustic guitars, checked shirts, church halls and a tea chest bass whose player disguised his lack of musicality with the proud inscription 'JIVE WITH IVE THE ACE ON THE BASS'.

Paul had already been spurred by Spike Milligan to try his hand at poetry; now the passing of his friend made him do so again, this time showing more emotion than he ever had in words before. The blank verse ode he sent to Jan Vaughan was entitled simply 'Ivan':

Two doors open
On the eighteenth of June
Two babies born
On the same day
In Liverpool
One was Ivan
The other – me.
We met in adolescence

And did the deeds
They dared us do
Jive with Ive
The ace on the bass.
He introduced to me
At Woolton fete
A pal or two
And so we did
A classic scholar he
A rocking roller me
As firm as friends could be.
Cranlock Naval
Cranlock pie
A tear is rolling
Down my eye.
On the sixteenth of August
Nineteen ninety-three
One door closes.
Bye-bye Ivy.

When the verse appeared in print some years later, 'Cranlock Naval/Cranlock pie' would be puzzled over as much as any Beatles lyric of yore. 'I recognised it immediately as part of the private language Ivan and Paul used to speak to each other,' Jan Vaughan remembers. 'But I never had any idea what it meant.'

The Beatles Anthology was to absorb almost all Paul's attention during 1994 and spell the end of the post-Wings band that had worked so well since 1989. 'He told us he had to go away and be a Beatle again for a year,' lead guitarist Hamish Stuart recalls. But in case it appeared that he'd totally succumbed to nostalgia, he left behind some music showing himself still very much in the present.

By the early 1990s, ubiquitous hip-hop and 'dance' music – as if no one had ever danced to music before – was changing the record producer's role, for so long defined by figures like George Martin.

Producers of the modern school were sonic scavengers who no longer devised original vocal and instrumental configurations, but remixed existing tracks and sampled – i.e. filched – scraps of old pop classics displaying the old-school producer's art as ironic punctuation to a tuneless machine-made beat.

No one stood for the traditional studio system, and melody, as strongly as Paul but, as always, he was determined to stay current. After the New World Tour, he had approached one of Britain's foremost young performer-producers, Martin Glover, who played bass with the band Killing Joke but remoulded sound for the dance music crowd under the pseudonym Youth.

Paul's initial idea was merely for parts of *Off the Ground* and Wings' farewell album, *Back to the Egg*, to be remixed for the huge venues where dance music was played. Instead, he ended up collaborating with Youth on a whole album of 'sound-collages', reviving the love of experimental music which John Cage and Luciano Berio had implanted in him during the Sixties.

There was a strong mystical strain in Youth and he was surprised to find one in Paul also. Their recording sessions were always timed to coincide with pagan festivals like the Summer Solstice or the Equinox. 'I thought of him as a Master Bard – but at the same time, I got a strong Catholic feeling from him, too. I remember him telling me once how much he disliked the Tarot.

'One day he had to go off somewhere with Linda, so he left me alone working at the Mill. When their helicopter came back, it was very late, they'd had a few glasses of champagne and their kids were with them. Paul said to me, "Do you mind if we stick around and watch?" as if it wasn't his studio I was using. They all stayed, dancing around to the music until the sun came up.'

The finished album was titled *Strawberries Oceans Ships Forest*. As Paul had undertaken not to release anything under his own name during *The Beatles Anthology*, it was credited to The Fireman – descendant of the one in 'Penny Lane' with the hourglass and 'in his pocket . . . a portrait of the Queen'.

★

A crucial element in the *Anthology* was the good relationship he now seemed to have with Yoko Ono after years of mutual coldness and mistrust.

Their rapprochement had begun in 1988 when the American author Albert Goldman published an unauthorised biography entitled *The Lives of John Lennon*. In 800 vitriolic but ill-informed pages, John was portrayed as a schizophrenic, epileptic, autistic, hyper-neurotic, bisexual thug whose several crimes of maniacal violence included an unprovoked attack on his friend Stuart Sutcliffe, adduced to be the direct cause of Sutcliffe's death from a brain haemorrhage in 1962. Musically, he did not come out well either; according to Goldman, his songs mostly employed the structure of the same nursery rhyme, 'Three Blind Mice'.

The biography was simultaneously an attack on Yoko so savage that she considered suicide (though, strangely, not legal action). Paul rallied to her support, dismissing Goldman's more ludicrous claims and urging Beatles fans to boycott the book. Largely because of that, she had consented to the *Anthology* and allowed it to go forward without trying to influence its format or even seeking to take part. By late 1993, Paul, George and Ringo had agreed to record some new music to go with the out-takes and rarities on its CD series. But, clearly, such an exercise would be pointless unless it included John. Yoko's goodwill would thus have to be tested even further.

In his five years of so-called retirement from music between 1975 and 1980, John had continued writing songs on the treadmill of competition with Paul that nothing could ever halt. At the Dakota Building, his widow was sitting on a cache of his home-demos, some known to hardcore fans via bootlegs but all justifiably described as 'unknown' Lennon tracks. On New Year's Day 1994, Paul phoned Yoko to say that he, George and Ringo were thinking of doing 'a little instrumental' for the *Anthology* but getting 'cold feet at the thought of a three-quarters Beatles reunion'. Would she consider handing over something by John for them to work with? Neil Aspinall – of whom she thought highly – had already made the same request.

As she told me at the time, her first thought was how fiercely John had dismissed any idea of a Beatles comeback performance when the world was clamouring for one. 'He used to say they'd just be four rusty old men. But I decided it would be wrong to stand in its way. The Beatles were John's group. He was the band leader and the one who coined [their] name.' The sheer irony of the situation also helped sway her. 'I had the reputation of having broken the Beatles up. Now I was in a position where I could bring them back together . . . it was kind of a situation given to me by Fate.'

On 19 January, he and Paul found themselves together in a room for the first time in many years. John was to be posthumously inducted into the Rock and Roll Hall of Fame – a first for an individual member of a band which had already received that honour – and Paul was to give the induction address.

This took the form of an open letter to his old soul-mate and arch-competitor, recalling their first meeting at Woolton fete thanks to Ivy Vaughan; John onstage, making up lyrics to the Del-Vikings' 'Come Go With Me'; his beautiful mother Julia with her red hair and captivating prowess on the ukulele; songwriting sessions at 20 Forthlin Road, fuelled by Typhoo tea-leaves smoked in Jim McCartney's pipe; journeys to early gigs in freezing vans when the only way to keep warm was to lie on top of each other in a 'Beatle sandwich'; the 'little look' they'd exchanged before singing 'I'd love to turn you on' in 'A Day in the Life', knowing the consequences but not caring.

The woman who'd come between them received only the briefest, most tactful mention. One day in the Sixties, 'a girl named Yoko Ono' had appeared, soliciting a Lennon and McCartney manuscript. 'I told her to go and see John,' Paul said, adding with masterly understatement: 'And she did.'

At the end, he spoke directly to John about their reconciliation, as it proved just in the nick of time. 'And the joy for me, after all the business shit we'd gone through, was that we were actively getting back together and communicating again. And the joy as you told me how you were baking bread now. And how you were playing with your little baby, Sean. That was great for me, because it gave me something to hold on to. And now years on here we are assembled to thank you for everything you mean to us all. This letter comes with love from your friend Paul.'

Afterwards, he and Yoko embraced a little gingerly, but there was no doubting how moved she had been. Later that night, she gave him tapes of four songs by John and her blessing for the surviving Beatles to overdub vocals and a backing.

So the reunion that millions had awaited for almost a quarter of a century was finally to happen, albeit only on record and with what the British press termed 'the Threetles'. After the news came a flurry of speculation that they mightn't stop there. One report claimed that they'd been offered £20 million each for a single live show with Julian Lennon replacing his father; others, that they were being courted by reincarnations of both the Woodstock and Isle of Wight pop festivals.

The best song on the tapes was judged to be 'Free as a Bird', a pensive ballad which John had recorded with just his own piano accompaniment sometime in 1977. Augmented by Paul, George and Ringo, it would be the *pièce de résistance* of the first *Anthology* CD as well as coming out as a single. Although George Martin was compiling the archive music, he felt unable to produce this late addition to an *oeuvre* he had done so much to foster. Martin was now 68 and four decades of fastidious listening had taken their toll: his hearing was beginning to fail.

Instead, the job went to Jeff Lynne, George's companion in the Traveling Wilburys (whose former band, the Electric Light Orchestra, had been called 'the Beatles of the Seventies'). The sound on John's archaic cassette was of such poor quality that Lynne first had to take it to his studio in Hollywood to be cleaned up and digitised. The song being too short as it stood, Paul and George between them supplied a middle eight, for each would sing in turn. So, despite George's earlier snarkiness, they did end up writing together.

The overdubbing took place in February at Hog Hill Studio. It was the first time the two of them and Ringo had played together since George's 'I Me Mine' in January 1970.

Still the soul of tact, Paul had done his best to forestall any last-minute interference by Yoko. 'I said, "Don't impose too many conditions on us,"' he would recall. '"It's really difficult to do this spiritually. We don't know, we might hate each other after two hours."' But she imposed no conditions and didn't even attend the session. Different days indeed from when she'd whispered in John's ear through the White Album and he'd had a bed rigged up for her on the studio floor during *Abbey Road*.

Playing and singing along with John's voice was an eerie experience for all of them. 'I invented a little scenario,' Paul was to remember. 'He'd gone away on holiday and he'd rung us [and said], "Just finish this track for me, will you?" It was very nice and it was very irreverent towards John . . . not too "Aah, the fallen hero." . . . John would have been the first to debunk that. "A fucking hero? A fallen hero? Fuck off, we're making a record."'

Some of the *Let It Be* tension resurfaced nonetheless. Paul had initially thought 'Free as a Bird' should be a big orchestral number, but George wanted to give it a yearning steel guitar riff like his famous one on 'My Sweet Lord' (belying his supposed 'ruination' as a guitarist). Paul gave way after hearing the riff and, with impressive self-restraint, offered no suggestions as to how it might be improved.

Three months later, the same team reassembled at Hog Hill to overdub a second John home-demo, 'Here and There', for the second *Anthology* CD. The session was abandoned after one afternoon because of the song's weakness, although it gave Paul a chance to sing along with John in the headphones, feeling 'as if he was in the next room'.

In the end, it wasn't until February 1995 that they came back to work on 'Real Love', which John had taped in 1979 in six different voice-and-piano versions, some under the alternate title 'Real Life'. Paul played the stand-up bass used by Bill Black on Elvis Presley's 'Heartbreak Hotel' that Linda had bought him in Nashville.

Relations with Yoko continued to be excellent, so much so that at the time of the 'Real Love' sessions she paid a visit to Peasmarsh with her son Sean, now aged 19. She and Paul even recorded a track together at Hog Hill Mill, something that neither of them could ever have imagined.

That August, it would be 50 years since the dropping of the atom bomb on Yoko's homeland. 'Hiroshima Sky is Always Blue' somewhat recalled that emblematic John-and-Yoko anthem 'Give Peace a Chance', with Sean, Linda and the McCartney children joining in; there was also a touch of the seance in Yoko's introductory words, 'John, we're here now, together. Bless you, peace on earth and Strawberry Fields Forever.'

She took the lead vocal – simply a repetition of the title segueing into her characteristic sound effects – with Paul on string bass, audibly respectful. The piece would be broadcast by Japanese public radio on the anniversary of Hiroshima's incineration.

Sean Lennon had grown up feeling that the father he'd lost at the age of five belonged more to the world than to him, and that his only private time with John came through playing the piano. Among Hog Hill Mill's collection of historic musical instruments was the Baldwin spinet John had used on the *Abbey Road* track 'Because'. When Paul invited Sean to play it, he didn't stop for hours.

The Dakota Building was not alone in yielding up lost recordings for *The Beatles Anthology*. As a teenager Paul had occasionally been able to borrow one of those so desirable Grundig tape recorders, belonging to two brothers, Reginald and Charles Hodgson, who lived around the corner from him in Allerton. That August of 1995, the brothers were clearing out their mother's attic after her death and came upon the Grundig and an ancient spool tape. On it were the nameless band that had helped to bridge the gap between the Quarrymen and the Beatles: John, Paul, George and Stuart Sutcliffe.

The Hodgsons contacted Paul's old friend Joe Flannery and arrangements were made for the tape to be brought to Peasmarsh by Reg Hodgson's son, Peter. Sure enough, it contained a whole recital, apparently in the front room at 20 Forthlin Road, by the drummerless quartet who vainly used to assure local dance promoters that 'the rhythm's in the guitars'. Paul's contributions included Eddie Cochran's 'Hallelujah, I Love Her So' and Les Paul and Mary Ford's 'The World Is Waiting for the Sunrise', a memory of his and John's brief career as The Nerk Twins. To add a bit of percussion, his brother Mike could be heard bashing on anything to hand.

Paul was intensely moved by what he heard and asked to buy the tape (subsequently paying the Hodgson family a reported £260,000). To show his gratitude, he gave Peter Hodgson a guided tour of Hog Hill Mill, pointing out the Bill Black double bass, the 'Because' spinet and the Mellotron he'd played on 'Strawberry Fields Forever'. To Hodgson, the room above the studio seemed 'like a museum', for Paul's old school desk was also there (scratched with the initials 'AA', for Arthur Askey); the walls displayed what were evidently genuine Picassos and against one wall stood a chair which, he learned, had once belonged to Vincent Van Gogh.

As a special concession, the famous Hofner violin bass was taken from its secret underfloor compartment for the visitor to hold. Taped to its back there was still a piece of Senior Service cigarette-packet with Paul's scribbled setlist for the Beatles' last-ever live concert, at Candlestick Park, San Francisco, in 1966. 'Don't drop that,' he warned. 'It's insured for two million.'

He also revealed himself as a Beatle memorabilia-collector to beat the most obsessive. The cover of their 1963 debut album, *Please Please Me*, had shown four cheery, innocent lads leaning out over a metal rail at EMI's London headquarters in Manchester Square. Six years later, while making the abortive *Get Back* album, they had a cover prepared of their no longer innocent or cheery selves similarly leaning out over the same rail.

When the EMI building was demolished, Paul had bought the rail. He kept it at Hog Hill with a blow-up photograph of John, George, Ringo and himself, positioned to look as if they were leaning over it.

*

'Free as a Bird' was premiered by BBC Radio 1 on 21 November 1995. There probably has never been a record that more people wanted to love. And the general disappointment was palpable. All Jeff Lynne's technical expertise had been unable to integrate Paul's and George's overdubbed voices with John's; faint and uncharacteristically diffident, it seemed to come from a separate studio beyond the grave. The extra McCartney/Harrison words had a pang of real sadness: 'Whatever happened to/ the love that we once knew/ Can we really live without each other?' Trouble was, everyone knew they didn't mean it.

The song was lead track on the first *Anthology* CD, then, after a brief interval, released as a single to catch the Christmas market. It sold 120,000 in its first week, reaching number two in the UK – denied the top spot by Michael Jackson's 'Earth Song' – and number six on the *Billboard* chart. All well and good if one forgot the era when Beatles singles routinely sold a million *before* release.

On 19 November, the first *Anthology* documentary was aired by ITV in Britain and ABC in America. The Beatles always used to possess perfect timing, but now it had deserted them. The next evening, on BBC1's *Panorama* programme, Diana, Princess of Wales gave a sensational interview admitting that her supposed 'fairytale' marriage to Britain's future king had been a sham and that Prince Charles had been carrying on with his mistress, Camilla Parker-Bowles, throughout it.

From then on, the only story for the world's media was beautiful, brave, batty Princess Di taking on the House of Windsor and showing every sign of triumphing. Different days again, when the Fab Four could be kicked off the front pages by royalty.

The documentary's talking-head interviews left no doubt which Threetle had worn best. Recovering alcoholic Ringo now sported a cropped head and a beard which gave him a weird resemblance to the Palestinian leader Yasser Arafat. Extensive dental work had left George with a rather camp, cosy smile that went with his homespun coloured woollens – though not the gall that leaked into his reminiscences. Thirty years on, he revealed how insulted he'd been by the Beatles' MBE awards (an unprecedented honour at the time). 'For all we did for Great Britain, selling all that corduroy and making it swing, and they just gave us a bloody old leather medal with a wooden string through it.'

Paul, however, seemed unchanged, particularly since all traces of grey had vanished from his hair. While the others looked like retirees, he came across as still busy and engaged with life, sitting in his recording studio, surrounded by guitars, or piloting his converted fishing trawler *Barnaby Rudge* around Rye harbour.

As an interviewee he gave the same good value as always. But juxtaposed with archive footage of the London Palladium or *The Ed Sullivan Show* or Shea Stadium, his articulacy, candour and humour were the more striking. It seemed hardly possible for someone to have gone through all that, and infinitely more, yet ended up so very normal.

At the close of the final documentary, each of the three summed up what the Beatles meant to him. Ringo, surprisingly, showed the most emotion. 'It was magical,' he said, choking back tears. 'There were some really loving, caring moments between four people . . . a hotel-room here and there . . . a really amazing closeness . . . four guys who really loved each other . . .'

'[The fans] gave us their money and their screams,' said George, 'but the Beatles gave their nervous systems.'

The final – and, perhaps, best – judgement came from the one whose nervous system was apparently still fine.

'To me,' said Paul, 'the Beatles were always a great little band. Nothing more, nothing less, for all our success. When we sat down to play, we played good.'

46

'She radiated hope'

There was to be a second superstar named McCartney. On 1 May 1995, Paul's youngest daughter, 23-year-old Stella, graduated in fashion design from Central St Martins school of art and design in London. Her graduation fashion show made international headlines, everything in it was bought by the super-chic Tokio boutique and orders came pouring in from top British and US stores like Browns, Joseph, Bergdorf Goodman and Nieman Marcus.

Stella had known exactly where she was going since, as a small girl, she used to creep into her parents' communal walk-in wardrobe and spend hours studying Linda's don't-care-that-much clothes on one side and Paul's care-very-much ones on the other. She'd designed her first jacket aged 13 and three years later was interning with the Paris couturier Christian Lacroix, creator of the puffball skirt, as he prepared his historic debut collection in 1987.

From her Sussex comprehensive school she'd gone to Ravensbourne art college in south-east London, then on to Central St Martins, her studies punctuated by further high-end placements with *Vogue* magazine, Betty Jackson and Joseph. Unusually, too, she served an apprenticeship with a men's bespoke tailor, Edward Sexton, whose premises had formerly been in Savile Row, a few doors from Apple, and who made the suits worn by both Paul and John on the *Abbey Road* album cover.

Her designs struck a genuinely new note, mixing extreme femininity and sexiness with the formality of classic men's tailoring

– plus, now and then, the defiant bagginess or wild incompatibil-
ity of pattern she recalled from her mother's stage-wardrobe on
Wings tours. Stella herself struck an equally new note, waif-like
yet voluptuous, with eyes whose pedigree couldn't be doubted, and
a talent for networking ditto. The media coverage of her graduation show was not due solely to the presence of her proud father,
who composed a song, 'Stella May Day', for its audio soundtrack.
Her clothes were premiered on the catwalk by three supermodels,
Naomi Campbell, Kate Moss and Yasmin Le Bon, all donating their
services for nothing.

There were to be no more prodigies among Paul's children.
Stella's older sister, Mary, now 26 – and more than ever like a reincarnation of her namesake grandmother – had turned into an
accomplished photographer, yet seemed uninterested in public
recognition, preferring to work at MPL and take charge of Linda's
photographic archive.

When a son had come along with Linda's straw-coloured hair
but Paul's cherub face, his family had naturally wondered whether
musical genius might strike a second time. But James McCartney
had grown up seemingly more interested in sport – and with an
adventurous streak that caused his parents some moments of high
anxiety. In 1993, when he was 16, he went windsurfing with three
friends on Camber Sands, off the Sussex coast, and triggered a full
air-sea rescue alert after being (mistakenly) reported to have lost
control of his surfboard and be helplessly drifting out to sea. A few
months later, he overturned a Land Rover he was driving on the
estate and Rye's fire brigade had to be called to free him.

Paul did not try to steer James towards music, as his own father
had steered him. He was too much aware of the pressure on Julian
and Sean Lennon to emulate John and the feelings of inadequacy
which Julian especially – the sad inspiration for 'Hey Jude' – had
suffered in consequence. But a home that pulsed with music and
thronged with great musicians and superb musical instruments
had an inevitable effect. By his mid-teens, James had started teaching himself piano and guitar (proving to be right-handed on the

latter) and aged 17, only three years later than Dad, he wrote his first song.

Although all four children had their ups and downs with their parents, the only real source of anxiety was Heather, who by her late twenties still remained unsure what she wanted to do or who she was. She certainly had not lacked love or security. Paul never made any distinction between her as his adopted daughter and Mary or Stella while Linda always gave her the firstborn's dividend of affection and attention. Yet despite their efforts to raise their brood with as much normality as possible, the McCartney name could not but hang heavily over all of them.

It hung heaviest over Heather, who had been teased and bullied about it far worse than the others at her various schools and was least equipped to deal with it as an adult. In truth, she was very much like Linda at her age, a rather dreamy, folksy young woman with none of Stella's drive or Mary's efficiency, quite happy to spend her time around animals. Over time, she'd come to dread the initially blank look on the faces of people she met and their instantly-blossoming reverence on learning who her father was.

When she was 25, this lost and overwhelmed feeling triggered such a crisis in her that Paul asked several people, including the nutritionist Peter Cox, to recommend a psychologist who might help. In the end, it was Heather who took the initiative by checking herself in to a clinic in Sussex, but the underlying problem remained unresolved.

She'd never seemed to have been damaged by Linda's divorce from her biological father, Joseph Melville See, which had happened when she was barely two. 'Jojo', better known as Mel, still lived in Tucson, Arizona, pursuing his work as a geologist and anthropologist with none of the California wanderlust mentioned in 'Get Back'. However, Paul and Linda's purchase of their Tanque Verde property, just a few miles away, had brought him and his lost daughter little closer, for Linda still felt some residual bitterness towards him and kept their social contacts to a minimum.

Then in 1988, at the end of a family holiday in Tanque Verde,

Heather suddenly announced that she didn't want to go home but to remain in Tucson and finally get to know her father. A delighted Mel invited her to stay with him and his partner, Beverly Wilk, for as long as she wished. Beverly, a terse but kindly woman, made no objection. 'She was a very nice person – just like her mother was.'

The visit did create a bond between Heather and Mel, opening her eyes to the passion for anthropology, archaeology and indigenous art that had taken him away from her when she was a toddler. Along with his huge knowledgeability – and formidable physical toughness – he was a thoroughly nice man who, as Beverly recalls, 'never said a nasty word about anybody'. To Beverly, Heather often seemed like a fugitive: she used an alias throughout her stay and was wary of strangers. One day, she got into a panic after drawing some money from a bank and forgetfully signing her real name.

Mel See's special anthropological study were the Huichol Indians from western Mexico, whose culture dated back 15,000 years and survived largely intact. He had co-produced a much-praised film about the Huichol, entitled *People of the Peyote*, and made regular field trips to their communities in the remote Sierra Madre mountains, accompanied by Beverly. On the next one, Heather went with them.

She spent several weeks living with the Huichol, wearing their brilliantly-coloured clothes, sharing their food and being introduced by the omniscient Mel to their age-old ceremonies and exquisite religious paintings and bead-patterned masks and ceramics. No one asked or cared who her adoptive father was; everyone accepted her for herself. It was therapy that money couldn't have bought.

Afterwards, she felt confident enough to move out of Mel and Beverly's and acquire a flat in Tucson, evidently meaning to settle there. But after two years, Mel told her firmly it was time to go home. She was so much happier when she returned to Peasmarsh that Linda had to concede he'd finally come good as a father. Inspired by the Huichol's bead-embroidered bowls and jugs, she decided to become a potter – an occupation widely practised in the

Rye area. She moved into a cottage on the estate and, a runaway from her surname no longer, set up her own company, Heather McCartney Design.

Paul and Linda had celebrated their twenty-fifth wedding anniversary in March 1994 and, other than during Paul's imprisonment in Tokyo in 1980, had never spent a night apart. They and their four children were an exceptionally close and united clan who showed one another affection and said they loved each other in a way that Paul's Liverpool family, though no less loving, seldom did. When one of them was driving off somewhere, all the others would line up outside the house to wave goodbye. And, grown up and widely different as the children now were, they still needed and relied on their mother as much as they always had.

In December 1995, Linda felt unwell and consulted her local doctor in Sussex. He said she had a cold, gave her some pills and told her to come back in two weeks. When she did so, feeling no better, he referred her to a London specialist, who found a malignant tumour in her left breast. A mammogram test would have picked it up earlier, but she'd never bothered to take one.

The same illness had claimed Paul's mother at the age of 47, seven years younger than Linda was now. The devastating news could not but bring with it memories of a 1950s hospital ward . . . the ominous screens and reeking ether-smell . . . the horrible truth no adult would tell him, but that he already knew . . . his father's shockingly uncharacteristic tears.

But that had been almost forty years ago and breast cancer survival-rates had hugely increased since then. Linda was immediately admitted to the Princess Grace Hospital in London for surgery to remove the tumour. By the time the story broke, she was recuperating back at Peasmarsh. Emerging to speak to reporters massed in Starvecrow Lane, Paul said the operation had been '100 per cent successful . . . the doctors have told her now just to get some rest'.

In fact, the cancer hadn't been caught in time and had already spread to her lymph nodes. The family spent a miserable Christmas and New Year and early in 1996 she began an in-patient course of chemotherapy at the London Clinic under the supervision of an oncologist from Bart's Hospital. Paul stayed with her throughout and slept in her room.

None but her family and close friends knew what she was going through and even to the closest she gave little away. One day when Carla Lane arrived at Peasmarsh, Linda beckoned her into the house as if to plan their latest rescue of some unhappy bullock, cat or duck. 'I have cancer,' she announced, then, before Carla could reply, put a finger to her lips, went 'Ssh' and never mentioned it again.

To make matters worse, many of the drugs used in her chemotherapy had been tested on animals in the ways she so abhorred. Indeed, later that year she and Paul were to receive a lifetime achievement award from PETA, the body most militantly opposed to animal testing which they'd publicised on the New World Tour. But Paul would not hear of her refusing the treatment.

Her illness was also a blow to her crusade for vegetarianism, just after its biggest breakthrough yet. In October, she and Paul had appeared as characters in America's world-syndicated cartoon series *The Simpsons*, opening thoughtful Lisa Simpson's eyes – as their own had once been – to the connection between frisky little lambs and lamb chops. The major benefit of going veggie Linda had always stressed, latterly on the packaging of her frozen meals, was increased resistance to cancer.

Peter Cox, her collaborator on *Linda McCartney's Home Cooking*, had since become a vegan, convinced the disease could be triggered by over-consumption of dairy products. Remembering all the butter and cream he'd seen her load into omelettes, Cox couldn't help wondering if the trouble might have started there.

Throughout this time of private anguish, Paul's musical life remained as crowded as ever, his ability undiminished to juggle several totally different projects at once.

Since the *Liverpool Oratorio*, he had hankered to compose a second large-scale classical work, this time more independently than was possible with Carl Davis as a collaborator. *The Beatles Anthology* gave him time to pursue the idea as he was pledged not to release any new music under his own name during the two years when its three CDs would be appearing. Coincidentally, EMI had asked him to write something to mark the company's approaching centenary.

In 1995, the publishers Faber & Faber, who had issued the *Oratorio* score in book form, put him in touch with the British composer/arranger David Matthews as a possible new collaborator. Matthews had once worked with Benjamin Britten, whose works Paul hugely admired, and had also been involved in a celebrated arrangement of Mahler's unfinished Tenth Symphony.

His first composition under Matthews' guidance was a short piano piece entitled 'A Leaf'. 'He thought in the most extraordinary musical colours, and his ideas were often quite eccentric,' Matthews recalls. 'But he was lacking in confidence because of having had no formal musical training. I saw my job as explaining the dynamics of a piece of music – things like the way phrasing works – so that at the end he could feel he'd done everything himself.'

'A Leaf' was premiered on 25 March at an intimate one-man show given by Paul at Kensington Palace, the Prince and Princess of Wales's London home, in aid of the Royal College of Music. The Prince was in attendance and afterwards presented him with an honorary fellowship of the Academy. So never again would the classical music world be able to condescend to him.

By this time, a theme for the major work had come into his mind – autobiographical, like the *Liverpool Oratorio*, but more indirectly so. Since he'd bought his first small farm in Kintyre, he'd been fascinated by the monolithic 'standing stone' on the hillside, commemorating the religion and culture of the people who lived there in pre-Roman times. Linda's photograph of the stone had been in the cover-montage of his first solo album, *McCartney*. And it was there, or nearby, that she'd won him by saying, 'I could make a nice home here.'

The piece would be called *Standing Stone* and celebrate Paul's Scottish roots, his love of Kintyre and its long-ago Celtic inhabitants. While producing the score with David Matthews, he was simultaneously working on *The Beatles Anthology* and creating 'sound collages' for dance music raves with Youth. 'I had no idea he was doing any of that other stuff,' Matthews recalls. 'Whenever we worked together, his focus was always total.'

Even this didn't satisfy Paul's appetite for multitasking, especially now that memorialising 'Ivy' Vaughan had turned him to verse. 'I started thinking of it as a poem,' he would recall. 'Every day, I'd get a couple of lines and scribble them down until I had about 20 pages, which turned into sort of a long epic poem.'

Among the rarities on the second *Beatles Anthology* CD was take one of 'Yesterday', recorded on 14 June 1965. Of all Beatles tracks, it was easily the best-known; in the *Guinness Book of Records*, it had long since displaced Irving Berlin's 'White Christmas' as the most-covered song in history with around 2000 alternative versions and more coming out all the time.

Yet it wasn't a Beatles track at all; Paul had dreamed it complete in his attic room at Jane Asher's parents' house and recorded it on his own with a string quartet and input from no one else but George Martin. So alien to the Beatles' image did it seem in 1965 that it hadn't come out as a single in the UK, but been buried on their *Help!* soundtrack album despite not featuring in the film.

The song had huge significance for Paul, epitomising as it did the whole mystery of how music came into his head. Certainly, he never tired of singing it. A couple of years earlier at London-Heathrow Airport, word had got around that he was there to take Concorde to New York, and a crowd instantly formed outside the supersonically-exclusive Concorde Lounge. After a few minutes, Linda came out to announce that he wouldn't sign any autographs. 'But,' she added, 'he'll play for you.' The mini-concert that followed, amid the chime of departure- and security-announcements, ended with 'Yesterday'.

Nonetheless, for all this time it had carried the Lennon–McCartney credit all John and Paul's Beatles songs received, irrespective of how much, or little, each had contributed. Being thought the co-writer of 'Yesterday' actually became somewhat of a trial to John: once, he'd had to sign the violin of a restaurant musician who'd serenaded him and Yoko with it while they were at dinner.

The injustice, as Paul saw it, went on bothering him for years after the Beatles' break-up, even after his creation of a band as big as they'd ever been. On the *Wings over America* album in 1976, the five of his Beatles songs included were credited 'McCartney–Lennon'.

Now he thought it reasonable to ask for the same for the 'Yesterday' out-take on *The Beatles Anthology 2*, especially since the CD already contained a departure from the Lennon–McCartney formula: 'Real Love', the Dakota home demo which opened side one, and was to be released as a single, bore John's name only.

It was only a few months since Yoko's pleasant visit to Peasmarsh with Sean, so Linda telephoned her on Paul's behalf, asking if, 'as a special favour', she would allow the credit to be reversed for just this one track. She refused, arguing that Paul on his side had gained glory from songs by John that he'd had little or no hand in, like 'Norwegian Wood' or 'I Am the Walrus'. But her reaction was a visceral one; as inheritor of John's estate and guardian of his legacy, she would do nothing that even remotely suggested his diminution.

The release of *Anthology 2* in March 1996 brought the Beatles back to the headlines, though not in a way Paul relished. BBC radio's pop network, Radio 1, which had excitedly premiered 'Free as a Bird' the previous year, announced that 'Real Love' would be excluded from its playlist. 'It's not what our listeners want to hear,' a spokesperson explained. 'We are a contemporary music station.'

The ban could not stop 'Real Love' reaching number four in the UK, but undoubtedly affected its long-term sales. Paul mounted

a vigorous rebuttal of the suggestion that the Beatles were out-
moded and irrelevant: his press representative, Geoff Baker, issued
a statement claiming that 41 per cent of *Anthology 1*'s buyers had
been teenagers, while he himself wrote an 800-word polemic for
the *Daily Mirror*:

> If Radio 1 feels [the Beatles] should be banned now, it's not
> exactly going to ruin us overnight. You can't put an age-limit
> on good music. It's very heartening to know that, while the
> kindergarten kings of Radio 1 may feel that the Beatles are too
> old to come out and play, a lot of younger British bands don't
> seem to share that view . . . I can hear the Beatles in a lot of the
> music around today.

With the third and final *Anthology* CD and the compilation of a
group autobiography made up of quotes from all four, the reunion
had apparently run its course. The all-important peace between
Paul and Yoko had broken down and George had become bored
with the project even before 'Real Love' was finished. Other than
Paul, only Ringo seemed to want to keep the groove going.

After decades of having little but their Beatleness in common,
there was now the saddest of bonds between them. In December
1995, the same month that Linda's breast cancer was diagnosed,
Ringo's first wife, Maureen, had died from leukaemia, aged 47.
Though long since remarried to Barbara Bach – as Maureen was
to Isaac Tigrett, founder of the Hard Rock Cafe chain – he had
rushed to her hospital bedside in Seattle and been deeply upset by
her passing.

Paul had always liked 'Mo' Starkey, an unassuming woman
who'd made no waves in the Beatles' inner circle, least of all when
she was expelled from it. Her three children with Ringo, Zak,
Jason and daughter Lee, were like cousins to the McCartneys and
to comfort them as well as remember her he wrote a song called
'Little Willow', containing one of his special flashes of intuition:
'No one's out to break your heart/ It only seems that way.'

In May 1996, Ringo returned to Hog Hill to record two tracks with Paul, produced by Jeff Lynne. The first, 'Really Love You', they co-wrote on the spot; the second, 'Beautiful Night', had been in Paul's bottom drawer since the mid-Eighties. It was another adoring anthem for Linda, in direct line from 'Maybe I'm Amazed' and 'My Love': 'You and me together/ Nothing feels so good . . .'

Only by now, their nights were no longer beautiful but full of pain and dread and helplessness.

The Liverpool Institute for Performing Arts was opened by the Queen on 7 June. Its final cost had been £18 million, of which £3 million came from Paul. Yet until the last minute, he'd still had misgivings about the project and doubts as to whether its chief fund-raiser and founding principal, Mark Featherstone-Witty, could really make it happen.

'He was very cautious, obviously not wanting to be associated with a failure,' Featherstone-Witty recalls. 'Even when I got as far as putting together some pilot courses, he wouldn't let LIPA's name go on them. I had to make them look as if they came from our validating body, John Moores University.'

All such tensions were forgotten as the VIPs poured through the Inny's unchanged neoclassical portico in Hope Street. Within, the grim Victorian classrooms had been replaced by bright, airy studios and rehearsal-spaces. The former assembly hall, where generations of black-blazered boys had fidgeted through morning prayers, was now the Paul McCartney Auditorium, with sound and lighting to rival the best rock venues. Yet the old school had not been totally obliterated. Room 31 was designated 'the Alan Durband Room' in memory of the English teacher who'd piqued Paul's imagination with the bawdy bits in Chaucer's *Canterbury Tales*.

One hundred and ninety students were waiting to begin courses in dance, drama and music. And what had seemed no more than hype at LIPA's inception five years earlier was there in the prospectus, though already massively over-subscribed: a songwriting class taught by Paul himself.

He arrived alone wearing a formal black suit but no tie – still defying the rigid dress code of his old headmaster, 'the Baz' – and seemingly in euphoric mood, giving not only thumbs-ups but two-fingered peace signs and strums of air-guitar. Speaking from a lectern in the Paul McCartney Auditorium, he brushed lightly over LIPA's protracted birth-pangs. 'It's been a hard day's night, but we can work it out . . . Obviously, one of my feelings now is how proud my mum and dad would have been if they could have been here . . . but I won't go into that because I'll start crying.'

On the inside, he already was. Linda's first bout of chemotherapy had not been successful and she was facing a second one. The side-effects were so debilitating that she'd been unable to accompany him today.

It was a sign of how grave the situation looked that a month later, she made her will. As she'd always kept her American citizenship, it would be filed in New York, and thus exempt from punitive British inheritance tax. Everything was left to Paul, and to the four children equally after his demise, in a trust fund that would virtually escape US taxes. The 18-page document was signed at Hog Hill Mill – appropriately, on 4 July – with Paul's assistant, John Hammel, and his studio engineer, Eddie Klein, as witnesses.

Between treatments, she tried to live as normal a life as possible, finding the same total happiness as always with her horses and handling her chemo's most upsetting side-effect with a horsewoman's practicality. Rather than wait for her golden hair to fall out, she shaved her head and swathed it in a bandana.

'It always struck me that there was a parallel between the way Linda dealt with her cancer and the way she dealt with the overwhelmingly hostile reaction to her marriage to Paul,' her friend Danny Fields would later write. 'She looked very carefully at her situation, considered the indignities and possibilities and, although there were moments when it seemed she might go under, she came out of her corner, fully expecting to win in the end.'

The media remained totally unaware of her condition and blind to the occasional inadvertent clue. In November, a new book of her photographs, *Roadworks*, was launched with an exhibition at New York's International Center of Photography, hosted by her daughter, Mary. Linda had arrived with Paul by car but at the last moment didn't feel well enough to go in.

By now, she had turned to New York for treatment and was in the care of the city's leading oncologist, Larry Norton, at Memorial Sloan Kettering Hospital. Staff there later recalled how 'she radiated hope' that lifted her fellow patients' spirits. Some even thought she'd already recovered from cancer and was around simply to show others it was possible.

47

'Let Me Love You Always'

Nineteen ninety-seven should have been such a good year . . .

It began climactically: in Britain's New Year's Honours list, Paul was knighted for 'services to music'. Although commonplace in other spheres of entertainment, the award was still rare in pop. Bob Geldof had received an honorary knighthood for Live Aid in 1986 but, as an Irish national, was disqualified from using the medieval title of 'Sir'. The saintly Cliff Richard had become Sir Cliff in 1995 and George Martin had been similarly recognised for his own prodigious services to music in 1996.

The British honours system normally demands a spotless record, so for someone with Paul's chequered drug history to be made a KBE (Knight Bachelor of the British Empire) set a remarkable precedent. However, it was felt his creation of LIPA and philanthropy towards Rye hospital before that – not to mention his contribution to overseas exports, both in and out of the Beatles – more than redressed the balance.

Actually, initial resistance to giving him his 'K' had been on less serious grounds. One can nominate people for honours by filling out a form and submitting it to the government committee which decides the awards. This had been done on Paul's behalf (without his knowledge) by LIPA's principal, Mark Featherstone-Witty. 'But hasn't he already got the MBE?' queried a committee official, as if that should have been enough.

Through his press spokesman, Geoff Baker, he made it known

that he wouldn't be using his title in connection with his work and still wanted to be plain Paul to his fans. Many newly-created knights, especially the theatrical and literary kind, affect such simplicity while privately throwing tantrums if ever the 'Sir' is left out. In this case it was sincere – and anyway, his name already had infinitely more clout than any honorific could confer.

In March, only two years after leaving art college, Stella McCartney was appointed creative director of the Parisian fashion house Chloé. Following her headline-grabbing graduation show, she had been approached by Chloé to design a younger 'second line', but had suggested she should take on their entire output. At 25, she would be replacing 65-year-old Karl Lagerfeld, a legendary figure with his sculpted snowy hair, high clerical collars and never-removed dark glasses.

Throughout the couture world, never noted for its charity, there were mutters that Stella had been chosen more for who she was than what she could do. 'Chloé should have gone for a big name,' Lagerfeld himself commented waspishly. 'They did – but in music. Let us hope she is as gifted as her father.'

On 11 March, Paul went to Buckingham Palace to receive his knighthood from the Queen. The crowds outside were not as wild as when the Beatles had collected their MBEs from the same sovereign in 1965 (afterwards claiming to have smoked a joint in a palace washroom) but were still large and vocal. As his limo swept in through the gates, a thumbs-up replaced the palace's more usual royal wave.

When his turn came, he knelt on a scarlet footstool before his sovereign and received a symbolic touch on each shoulder with the sword of King Edward the Confessor. Watching the ceremony made even the usually super-cool Stella burst into tears. 'It was just like the end of a beautiful film,' her sister Mary later remembered. 'I will never forget that moment.'

At the photocall in the palace yard afterwards, he dedicated his award to the other Beatles and the people of Liverpool, joking that George and Ringo had taken to calling him Your Holiness (though not speculating what John might have called him). He summed up his emotions as 'Proud to be British, wonderful day . . . and it's a long way from a little terrace in Liverpool.'

May brought the release of his first album since the poorly-received *Off the Ground* in 1993. The title, *Flaming Pie*, was borrowed from a skit John had written for *Mersey Beat* in 1962 about how the Beatles had supposedly acquired their name. 'It came in a vision. A man appeared on a flaming pie and said unto them, "From this day on you are Beatles with an A."'

Having agreed to release no new songs while *The Beatles Anthology* was coming out, Paul had a backlog of titles like 'Little Willow', the tribute to Maureen Starkey, and 'Calico Skies', written on Long Island in the aftermath of Hurricane Bob in 1991. Trawling through the Beatles' oeuvre for the *Anthology* had also made him want to recreate their old spontaneity and sense of fun in the studio. To that end, *Flaming Pie*, co-produced by Jeff Lynne, included his two recent collaborations with Ringo, 'Really Love You' and 'Beautiful Night', as well as guest appearances by Lynne and Steve Miller. His son James debuted as a professional guitarist, playing lead in 'Heaven on a Sunday'.

The album was a commercial and critical success, Paul's first in the US Top 10 since *Tug of War*, 15 years earlier. In Britain, it reached number two, kept off the top spot by those newest 'new Beatles', the Spice Girls.

Yet the highest accolade his country could grant and the new bounce-back in his career seemed equally beside the point now that every waking moment was a line from 'Yesterday', written so lightly 30 years ago: 'There's a shadow hanging over me'. Linda's latest bout of chemotherapy had left her too weak to accompany him to the ceremony, by which she too was ennobled as Lady McCartney. Before he left for the palace, she gave him a watch inscribed 'To Paul, my knight in shining armour'.

Flaming Pie held its own clues to the underlying heartbreak. Linda's cover photograph was a black and white head shot in which

Paul looked atypically gaunt and haunted, more like his brother Michael. In the credits she was listed only for background vocals, as if she lacked the stamina to play keyboards any more.

The video for 'Beautiful Night' turned it into the most uplifting of love songs, acted out by a young married couple against a panorama of nocturnal Liverpool. A band performance by Paul and a gang of teenagers, plus Ringo, segued to a McCartneyesque family sing-song around the piano. But here and there were hauntingly sad glimpses of Linda, her golden hair all gone, aiming her camera from inside an old-fashioned red telephone kiosk.

Standing Stone, the classical piece on which Paul had been working for almost four years, along with everything else, was now finished at last. The final stages of rewriting and refining put an extra edge on the anguish he was suffering, for so much of the score had first been drafted when Linda was still well.

As always strictly compartmentalising professional and personal matters, he said little about the situation to his collaborator, David Matthews. But Matthews' then wife, the American musician Jean Hasse, became friendly with Linda and knew the magnitude of what she and Paul were dealing with. 'At that stage,' Matthews recalls, 'he had the greatest confidence that she'd get better.'

The 3000-year-old monolith on his Scottish farm had inspired a 75-minute symphony which, in Paul's own half-modest, half-hubristic words, was 'an attempt to describe the way Celtic Man might have wondered about the origins of life and the mystery of existence'. David Matthews had been his amanuensis for most of the composition process, but towards the end he'd sought help from four other noted classical arrangers, Steve Lodder, John Fraser, John Harle and finally the great Richard Rodney Bennett. 'He used to call us all his Politburo,' Matthews recalls.

For all this committee-input the music was entirely Paul's and, for Matthews, 'a remarkable piece of work ... It wasn't just a collection of short passages like pop songs; it had an inner cohesion and themes that repeated themselves all through.' Although a choral work like the *Liverpool Oratorio*, it told no explicit story and utilised only a small part of the epic poem Paul had written alongside it. Here, too, the best possible outside help had been mobilised; on Allen Ginsberg's advice, he asked the award-winning poet and librettist Tom Pickard to act as his sub-editor. However, the poem would appear only in printed form as a commentary on the music.

Because it was Paul, even this most mystical and cosmic of themes bore an unmistakable personal signature. The passage about human evolution, for instance, was entitled 'Cell Growth', the basis of every day's anxiety about Linda. And at the end, an andante passage called 'Celebration', supposedly about the EMI centenary, was really yet another dedication to her, involuntarily touched with sadness: 'Love is all that matters in the end/ Whatever time I have to spend will be with you.'

Standing Stone was premiered on 14 October with a gala performance at the Royal Albert Hall by the London Symphony Orchestra, conducted by Lawrence Foster. With the CD version came a new portrait of the standing stone by Linda, this time in colour, silhouetted against a threatening Kintyre sky. It topped the classical music charts – even registering on some American pop charts – but its 75-minute length was an awkward one for the concert-stage and it would not be performed live anywhere near as often as the *Liverpool Oratorio*.

October was a month of triumphs for the McCartney name, albeit underlaid by continuing sadness and anxiety. After five years' preparation, Paul's authorised biography by Barry Miles was published in a characteristically classy hardback edition. Titled *Many Years from Now* – a quotation from 'When I'm Sixty-Four' – it was an immediate bestseller, though many readers wondered why he'd chosen to end it before the Wings era, so omitting most of his years with Linda, with a brief coda about John's death.

In the same week, Stella's first collection for Chloé was shown in Paris with the help of her 'mates' Kate Moss, Naomi Campbell and Yasmin Le Bon. Paul and Linda were both seated beside the catwalk: he in the novel position of applauding someone else, she still with close-cropped hair, the result of prolonged chemotherapy, which gave her face a new gentleness and repose.

True to family principles, Stella's clothes made use of neither fur nor leather and, despite their exalted mannequins, were designed for ordinary young women who wanted style but not to be shackled by it. The rave reviews were led by the famously particular Anna Wintour, editor of American *Vogue*. 'This is one designer who shows that you can have it all,' Wintour wrote. 'She's sexy and modern and truly her own person . . . The Stella look is that of the girl who, when she gets dressed, puts on her favourite pair of Manolos, a T-shirt dress she wore in high school, then rifles through her grandmother's attic for a spare family tiara.' It might have been a description of Linda onstage with Wings in the Seventies.

As 1997 ran out, the disease that had made Paul no longer the most envied of mortals suddenly seemed to be striking all around him. George had discovered a lump in his neck which was diagnosed as throat cancer, the result of a lifetime's heavy smoking his Indian mysticism had never checked. After surgery and radiation treatment, he was pronounced in the clear. Not so fortunate was Derek Taylor, the Beatles' former press officer – recently re-enlisted to work on *The Beatles Anthology* – who died in September from the same cause.

On 19 November, *Standing Stone* received its New York premiere at Carnegie Hall (where once Beatlemaniacal stomping had shaken crooked the portraits of classical maestros on its walls). Afterwards, Paul took Linda to Arizona for the best therapy of all, her horses.

At Thanksgiving, her first husband, Mel See, came over to Tanque Verde for a barbecue, bringing his partner, Beverly Wilk. Softened by what Mel had done for their daughter, Heather – and the realisation of how short life was – Linda was friendlier to him than Beverly had ever seen her. He apologised for his failings as a husband and she did the same for having borne him ill will all those years. 'The two of them made their peace,' Beverly remembers. 'Mel was always glad they both got to say their sorrys.'

*

Christmas marked the second anniversary of Linda's diagnosis. Along with protracted bouts of chemotherapy, she had endured a bone-marrow transplant and tried numerous homeopathic remedies and alternative therapies, stopping short at swimming with dolphins, as one well-meaning friend recommended. She had even given up pot, even though it was the one thing that dulled the pain and the terror. Now there were grounds for cautious hope based on the fact that when talking about her cancer, her doctors did not use the dread word 'aggressive'.

Paul's Christmas gift to her was a pair of Shetland ponies and they held a large drinks party at which even the reclusive Spike Milligan made an appearance. Mary McCartney had just become engaged to a young television producer/director, Alistair Donald, and Linda was already starting to plan the wedding, scheduled for late 1998.

In March, she and Paul were back in Paris, with Ringo and Barbara, to see Stella unveil her spring and summer collection for Chloé. The show was another huge hit, squashing murmurs that her October debut had been beginner's luck and that Chloé were only employing 'a big name – in music'. Every journalist who asked Stella to name her greatest fashion influence got the same reply: 'My mum.'

During the visit, the McCartneys had lunch with Paul's tailor, Edward Sexton, who'd been part of Stella's training. Sexton thought Linda had lost weight, but seemed 'buoyant' and, despite all the chemotherapy she'd been through, her hair was starting to grow back again.

It was an illusion. Her latest examination showed that the cancer *had* become aggressive and metastasised in her liver. There was no more hope.

Life kept an appearance of normality for a while. At Hog Hill, Paul was just finishing a second album with the young producer known as Youth under their alias of The Fireman – as before, recorded only on pagan festivals like the Summer Solstice and Hallowe'en. This album, *Rushes*, was not merely remixes of old Wings tracks but original 'sound-collages', and Linda also took part. 'I recorded her talking about her horses, even outside, galloping past on horseback,' Youth recalls. 'The album was all about Linda, though I didn't realise until later.'

Though he knew she was gravely ill, the subject was never discussed. 'I just got this incredible vibe of melancholy. One day in the studio, Paul started singing an old song of his called "Let Me Love You Always", and it was obvious who it was about and what he was thinking.'

Linda also recorded songs she had written for what she and Paul acknowledged would be a posthumous album. One, 'Appaloosa', celebrated the breed of speckled American horse she loved most. Another, 'The Light Comes From Within', was a belated bite-back at her detractors down the years, tinged with Dylan Thomas's 'rage against the dying of the light': 'You say I'm lazy, you say I'm a hick/ You're fucking no one you stupid dick'.

Otherwise, she faced the inevitable with stoical calm. She had already made her will, nine months previously, and now looked to a future she would never see, discussing the further development of Linda McCartney Foods with its managing director, Tim Treharne, choosing work for a new exhibition of her photographs, even making arrangements for the first Christmas Paul and the children would have to spend without her. It was perhaps the most poignant of all the echoes of his mother: while dying of the same disease, Mary McCartney had made sure he and his brother Michael would have washed and ironed clothes after she'd gone.

To provide long-term security for Linda's first and most vulnerable child, the title of a cottage on the estate was transferred to Heather's name. The date of Mary's wedding was brought forward to May – though, alas, even that would prove too optimistic.

She wanted to be in the place where she was always sure of complete privacy, so at the beginning of April Paul took her back to their simple, secret hideaway in Arizona. Just before they left, she took part in a photo-session with her friend, Chrissie Hynde. When they parted, Linda held back from her usual loving embrace, which told Chrissie she was saying goodbye for ever. 'She didn't want to be sentimental about it. She didn't want to be sad.'

She kept up her anti-vivisection campaign to the last, spending £8000 to free some beagle puppies who'd been bound for the laboratory. Her final call – literally as the airport-bound helicopter powered up – was to her old animal-mad crony, Carla Lane. She told Carla only that she'd be away for five days and then would be wanting even more 'rescued' chickens to run around the garden. With Paul calling to her to hurry, she suddenly and uncharacteristically added, 'I love you, Carla.'

At Tanque Verde, it became clear that she had only days to live – clear, that is, to everyone except Linda, who continued to go out riding until 15 April when her strength finally failed and she had to take to her bed.

Paul was faced with the decision of whether to tell her how close the end was, and decided against it. 'I talked it over with her doctor and he said, "I don't think she would want to know. She is such a strong, forward-thinking lady and such a positive girl that I don't think it would do any good."'

She died in the early hours of 17 April 1998, aged 56. 'The kids and I were there when she crossed over,' Paul would remember. 'They each were able to tell her how much they loved her. Finally I said to her, "You're on your beautiful Appaloosa stallion. It's a fine spring day and the air is a clear blue . . ." I had barely got to the end of the sentence when she closed her eyes and gently slipped away.'

The international media were still totally unaware of Paul's Arizona home and he was determined to keep it that way. The statement he issued via Geoff Baker, which was unquestioningly broadcast and printed around the world, said Linda had died in Santa Barbara, California, 400 miles to the west. 'Santa Barbara' had always been the code used at MPL whenever the family were vacationing in Tanque Verde.

The ploy was only revealed when reporters and TV news crews descended on the alleged scene of the tragedy for follow-up stories.

Santa Barbara's sheriff's department possessed no record of Linda's demise and no death certificate in her name had been issued by the local coroner. Even when the *Arizona Daily Star* belatedly pinpointed the correct state, Tanque Verde was not mentioned and Pima County's coroner would not officially confirm the issuing of a death certificate, such details being protected by Arizona's privacy laws. This led to reports that police were investigating a possible case of assisted suicide, for whose 'assistant' they clearly wouldn't have to look far.

Paul then issued a second statement, admitting his subterfuge but still trying to protect the family sanctuary: 'When Linda died last Friday with her family around her, it was in a place that was private to her and her family ... In an effort to allow the family time to get back to England in peace and in private, it was stated that she had died in Santa Barbara. The family hope they can maintain this, the one private place that they have in the world.'

Geoff Baker dismissed the assisted suicide story as 'complete and absolute rubbish' while Dr Larry Norton, contacted by America's Cable News Network, said that to his knowledge death had been from natural causes.

Early in May, a small group from the Society for the Preservation of Ancient Buildings had permission to visit Hog Hill Mill and inspect the restoration work being carried out on its seventeenth-century fabric. The visit had to be cancelled, for that was the day Paul chose to scatter Linda's ashes over the hillside.

There's a photograph of them together at that same spot, taken a few years earlier in high summer. He reclines on the ground, chewing a blade of grass; she sits on her Appaloosa in a rather formal orange dress, bareback and barefoot. Never happier.

PART FIVE

Back in the World

48

Lonesome Town

In all the songs Paul wrote about Linda he showed most of his heart in 'Waterfalls' on the *McCartney II* album in 1980, long before any shadow hung over them: 'And I need love/ like a second needs an hour/ like a raindrop needs a shower'. His voice, usually so measured, climbs to an unusually high register as if sensing the desolation ahead: 'And it wouldn't be the same/ If you ever should decide to go away'.

The boy who lost his mother to breast cancer had got through it by 'learn[ing] to put a shell around me'. For the 55-year-old father of four, thankfully, there were other means. On the night after Linda's death, for instance, he didn't have to face the yawning loneliness of the bed they'd shared almost without a break for 29 years. 'I thought it would be too sad for Dad to sleep alone,' his son James would recall, 'so I kept him company.'

This time, he could admit his 'total heartbreak' and give way to the tears that kept welling up. He could talk of nothing but Linda. 'Wasn't she great?' he sobbed down the telephone to her old journalistic crony, Danny Fields. 'Wasn't she beautiful? Wasn't she smart and together and wonderful and loving?'

After returning from Arizona, he went to ground at Peasmarsh, his usual prodigious creative energy at a total standstill. 'Friends of mine and some of the doctors said, "Throw yourself into your work. Get busy. Do stuff, do stuff,"' he would recall. 'And I just couldn't. So I didn't do anything. I just let it all happen.'

The few people he saw were mainly those who'd been closest to Linda, like Carla Lane and Chrissie Hynde. His only pronouncement, via Geoff Baker, was to thank people for their sympathy and ask those wishing to pay tribute to Linda to donate to breast cancer charities or 'go veggie'.

Many went further. In Tel Aviv, Britain's new Labour prime minister, Tony Blair, took a break from talks with Israeli premier Benjamin Netanyahu to praise Linda's 'extraordinary courage' and 'tremendous contribution across a whole range of British life'. Blair's wife, Cherie, daughter of the Liverpudlian actor Tony Booth, added: 'Everyone has been inspired by the courage Linda has shown through her illness. She brought comfort to women everywhere who are suffering from this terrible affliction.'

Her obituaries could not have been further from the hostility, mockery and denigration she'd suffered from jealous Beatles fans and malevolent media for so many years. Indeed, the tearfully reverent outpourings of newspapers, television and celebrity sound bites somewhat recalled the recent death of Diana, Princess of Wales, even though the two tragedies had nothing but their victims' blonde hair in common. At the 1998 BAFTA awards ceremony in London, the film director Sir David (later Lord) Puttnam led a standing ovation in Linda's memory. Jennifer Aniston from the *Friends* television show called her 'a pioneer woman'. Candle-lit vigils for her were held all over America, including one in Santa Barbara, California, the 'decoy' location of her death.

Paul's first public appearance in more than two months was at her memorial service, which took place on the rainy evening of 10 June, a week before his fifty-sixth birthday, at the Protestant church of St Martin in the Fields in London's West End. The 700-strong congregation included George, Ringo, Sir George Martin, Pete Townshend, Sting, Elton John (now also knighted) and the two Shetland ponies, Shnoo and Tinsel, who'd been Linda's last Christmas gift. Outside in Trafalgar Square, animal-rights activists from as far afield as France, Germany and Italy held a candle-lit vigil with placards reading 'GO VEGGIE FOR LINDA'.

The order of service was as meticulously planned and arranged as a McCartney album tracklist. Eulogies were given by Carla Lane and Pete Townshend; the actress Joanna Lumley read Henry Scott Holland's poem 'Death Is Nothing at All' and the photographer David Bailey read, a verse by Spike Milligan. The church choir sang the 'Celebration' andante from *Standing Stone*; the Brodsky Quartet played 'The Lovely Linda'; a piper from Campbeltown played 'Mull of Kintyre'; and a student group from LIPA sang 'Blackbird', just as Paul had for Linda their very first night at Cavendish, while fans eavesdropped at the front gate.

His address summed up his state of mind very simply: 'She was my girlfriend and I've lost my girlfriend and that is very sad. I still can't believe it but I have to because it's true . . . After she died, I was thinking of her and I thought of her as like a diamond, a big orange diamond, and if you look at all the facets of a diamond, as with every facet you look at, she was greater.

'She said one day, "If I could save just one animal, that is all I would like to do." She was the first veggie tycoon . . . They [Linda McCartney Foods] tell me they have sold 400 million meals, so that is a couple of animals she has saved.'

George and Ringo's presence inevitably created headlines about the three former Beatles' first public reunion, as opposed to in the *Anthology* television documentary and on record. The hymns in which the congregation joined ('All Things Bright and Beautiful' and 'Let It Be') made it possible to say they'd sung together for the first time since the Apple rooftop concert in 1969.

A second memorial service took place on 22 June at New York's Riverside Church, attended by Linda's brother, John, her sisters, Laural and Louise, and Manhattan notables ranging from Ralph Lauren to Mike Nichols. The church had initially vetoed Paul's wish for her favourite Appaloosa to be present, but relented so long as it was led in by a side door rather than down the main aisle. The eulogies by Neil Young and Chrissie Hynde reduced her old friend Danny Fields to tears which earned a brisk punch on the arm from

Stella McCartney. 'Stop it!' she hissed. 'Mum wouldn't want to see you like that.'

Like everyone who loses their life-partner, Paul now discovered how difficult it is to adjust to solitude. Many times each day he would instinctively turn round to ask Linda something or reach for the phone to call her, then realise afresh that she wasn't there.

His marriage, once so disapproved of and denigrated, was hailed as a shining example, not only in the pop business but the wider world. Although for most of it he had been the world's most adored and desired man, there had never been even a suspicion of infidelity on his part. Yet the inveterate perfectionist and secret worrier now berated himself for his shortcomings as a husband. 'Whenever someone you care about dies, you wish you'd been perfect all the time,' he would reflect. 'I wasn't.'

He was also racked with guilt for not having told Linda in those last days in Arizona what a short time she had left. It affected him so badly that he received professional counselling – a huge step for someone so dedicated to the double thumbs-up.

In July, he returned to LIPA to see the first crop of graduates receive their degree scrolls. During the day, he told his old friend Joe Flannery that Linda was there with him. LIPA's principal, Mark Featherstone-Witty, had been at the London memorial service. 'Afterwards, people like Elton John and Pete Townshend came up to Paul and told him what a great thing he was doing for kids in Liverpool. I think that was the first time he fully realised what an achievement the place was.'

Coincidentally that same month, the National Trust opened 20 Forthlin Road to the public as a historical monument ranking alongside Britain's greatest stately homes. But Paul preferred not to view the meticulous recreation of the simple bachelor establishment he'd shared with his father and his brother Michael. It would have added too many sad memories of his mother's death to those of Linda's.

She was with him too, he felt, on 27 September when he drove their daughter Mary in a vintage Hispano-Suiza car to Peasmarsh's

ancient church of St Peter and St Paul for her long-postponed marriage to the TV director Alistair Donald. Mary was pregnant, just
as her mother had been with her on her wedding day: it was the
best possible reminder that life goes on.

Linda's death had given fresh impetus to the campaign to raise
awareness of breast cancer, a subject hitherto shrouded in fear and
embarrassment. In the week afterwards, the UK's national Cancer
BACKUP helpline logged double the usual volume of calls, 64 per
cent, from women spurred by the thought that if Paul McCartney's
wife could fall victim, how much more vulnerable were they? In
October, Paul gave his support to an initiative by Cherie Blair and
former Spice Girl Geri Halliwell to make women 'enlightened, not
frightened' by taking mammogram tests that can detect tumours
at the early stage when they can still be contained.

An interview for the *Sun* to publicise the campaign included his
first public reflections on Linda: 'As a wife, she was the best that
anyone could want. She was there for me all the time. She was
comfortable, she was never difficult. She was one of the kindest
people.'

After her death, he shrank from returning to the Eastman holiday
house in East Hampton, Long Island, where they and the children
had spent so many idyllic summers with Willem de Kooning just
over the way. Yet he was loath to give up 'the Hamptons' with their
Norman Rockwell towns and long, white, misty beaches, and mid-
town Manhattan just a couple of hours distant. So in December
1998 he bought a property in Amagansett, the ocean-front hamlet
adjacent to East Hampton. Like all his rural retreats, 11 Pintail
Lane was an unpretentious structure, originally two barns, in the
midst of forest even more concealing than Peasmarsh's. His neighbours had no inkling he was there until some local children set up
a roadside lemonade-stand and he stopped to buy a glass.

For now, his only work project was completing *Wild Prairie*, the
album of Linda's songs they'd begun assembling together in March,
knowing it would be released posthumously. An accompanying
six-minute cartoon she had devised with the director Oscar Grillo

was premiered at that summer's Edinburgh International Film Festival, then put on general release with Robert Redford's *The Horse Whisperer*.

The album's 16 tracks had mostly been laid down in the Seventies during Wings' globetrotting studio-sessions. Among the newer ones were 'Cow', an attack on slaughterhouses with lyrics by Carla Lane, 'Appaloosa' and 'The Light Comes From Within', that belated broadside at her critics, recorded in the very shadow of death with Paul and their son, James.

Her four-letter words on 'The Light Comes From Within' guaranteed that it wouldn't be played by the BBC, though Paul was so angered by the rejection that he fired the unfortunate plugger who'd tried to get it programmed. However, some airplay was given to 'Seaside Woman', the first song she'd ever written, originally put out in 1972 under the pseudonym Suzy and the Red Stripes.

Such was the sympathy for her – and him – that *Wild Prairie* was respectfully reviewed and made the middle reaches of both the British and American Top 100. With the best will in the world no critic could say it revealed a previously undervalued musical talent but, as *Rolling Stone*'s Stephen Thomas Erlewine wrote, it was legitimate tribute to 'a woman who, from all accounts, was kind, generous and loving'.

The previous year, Britain had elected its first prime minister who was an overt – indeed, besotted – rock music fan. That Tony Blair had once sung with a student band named Ugly Rumours and enjoyed playing air-guitar in front of his wardrobe mirror contributed significantly to his landslide victory in the polls. After John Major's stumbling, sleaze-ridden Conservative administration, Blair's rebranded 'New' Labour seemed like a breath of Curved Air.

This hip, even hippyish, young premier gave the nation's morale a lift somewhat like the one it had received (also with an incoming socialist regime) three decades earlier. Where the media then had talked about Swinging Britain, they now talked about Cool

Britannia and a similar explosion of youthful creativity in art, fashion and design. There was a resurgent 1960s look, especially among men. The national flag became a 'fun' item all over again, reproduced on coffee-mugs, kitchen aprons and plastic shopping bags.

The déjà-vu was nothing to the déjà-entendu. The UK's late-1990s music charts teemed with so-called Britpop bands, heavily guitar-based and singing songs with British themes in unapologetic British accents just like those who had reigned supreme between 1964 and 1969. Now the latest 'new Beatles' – Oasis from Manchester – made no bones about replicating the old ones with their fringed foreheads, high-buttoning suits and tough-tender harmonies. Their rivalry with Blur, from London, recalled that of the Beatles with the Rolling Stones, although this time, the northerners were the loutish ones. And although Blur had more affinity with the Kinks or Small Faces, the video for their single 'Parklife' showed them trooping over a zebra crossing in homage to *Abbey Road*.

Tony Blair quickly proved even more starstruck than his Old Labour predecessor Harold Wilson, when Wilson courted popularity by sucking up to the Beatles. Britpop stars like Oasis's Gallagher brothers, Noel and Liam, were invited to receptions at 10 Downing Street to be fawned over by as devout a groupie as they would ever meet. Several were persuaded to become proselytisers for New Labour, most notably Bono from U2 (who'd been among the first to mimic the Beatles' concert on the Apple roof). In a future keynote speech at New Labour's party conference, he was to hail Blair and Chancellor of the Exchequer Gordon Brown ludicrously as 'kind of the John and Paul of the global development stage . . . Lennon and McCartney changed my interior world. Blair and Brown can change the real world.'

Nineteen ninety-nine brought Blair the ultimate perk of his job. LIPA still needed money and Paul came to him in person with a request for government funding. 'Each of them dressed for the other,' recalls Mark Featherstone-Witty. 'So Paul turned up in a

suit to find Blair in casual clothes, trying to look rock 'n' roll.' Half
an hour or so of prime ministerial hero-worship was a small price
for the funding package LIPA later received.

This year, too, Paul's need to be constantly generating music
was all but extinguished by grieving for Linda – and concerns
about their oldest and youngest children. Mary and Stella seemed
to be coming to terms with their mother's death, one helped by
a new marriage, the other by a glittering career, but 21-year-old
James and 35-year-old Heather, in their different ways, were still
struggling.

James had virtually given up college, where he was studying art,
photography and English, to be with Linda in her last months. Despite his facial resemblance to Paul and passion for music, he was a
more sensitive, less driven character; unable to put a shell around
himself like his father in the same situation, he sought escape in
alcohol, drugs and listening to Nirvana, the American grunge
band at the furthest extreme from the Beatles and sunny Britpop.
At Mary's otherwise idyllic wedding there had been an awkward
moment when James rocked up to the church, Kurt Cobain-style,
clutching a bottle of Jack Daniel's.

It was even worse for Heather, whom Linda had always protected
so carefully – and unnecessarily – from any favouritism by Paul
towards his biological children. After her mother's death, she later
said, she 'could see no reason for living any more' and retreated
into her cottage on the Peasmarsh estate with only her animals for
company.

Heather's chief solace was her one-woman design company,
largely inspired as it was by healing memories of living among the
Huichol Indians. In January 1999, she was persuaded to launch her
range of Heather McCartney Housewares in person at a trade fair
in Atlanta, Georgia. Paul – 'my real daddy' as she always referred
to him – went along to help her handle the inevitable heavy media
interest, shamelessly plug the (very attractive) rugs, cushions and
ceramics she had designed and get her into and out of places as
efficiently as one of his own roadies.

He now had a daughter he could lean on in his turn. In March, he was inducted into the Rock and Roll Hall of Fame in his own right – something Linda had started lobbying for after his induction of John five years earlier, not slackening her campaign even after she became ill.

In contrast with that heartfelt yet beautifully diplomatic 1994 tribute to John, his acceptance speech was his first-ever public appearance visibly under the influence. 'I would like my baby to share this with me,' he slurred. 'She wanted this . . . You've got John in there. OK guys, how about George and Ringo?' Finally, he called Stella up to join him; the new darling of Parisian couture dressed down in a white T-shirt lettered 'IT'S ABOUT FUCKING TIME'. 'She doesn't give a shit,' her father remarked admiringly. As they left the podium, Stella had one arm wrapped tightly around him.

On 10 April, to mark the first anniversary of Linda's death, her friends Chrissie Hynde and Carla Lane staged A Concert for Linda: Here, There and Everywhere at the Royal Albert Hall, with proceeds going to her favourite animal charities. A week earlier, in a nice coincidence, Mary had presented Paul with his first grandchild, Arthur Alistair. The concert, later shown on BBC television, featured Elvis Costello, the Pretenders, George Michael, Marianne Faithfull, Tom Jones, Sinéad O'Connor, Des'ree, Lynden David Hall, Chris Elliott, Johnny Marr from the Smiths, Neil Finn from Crowded House, Heather Small from M People and the South African choir Ladysmith Black Mambazo. Surveying the galaxy of talent, old and new, emcee Eddie Izzard quipped, 'Some bunny rabbit's gonna go, "Hey, these guys rocked for *us*."'

There were echoes of Linda and her loss throughout the marathon setlist. Chrissie Hynde and Johnny Marr duetted on the Smiths' 'Meat Is Murder'. Before delivering a version of 'The Long and Winding Road' almost as good as the original, George Michael revealed that his mother, too, had recently died from breast cancer. Neil Finn and Sinéad O'Connor joined in Finn's doubly resonant 'She Goes On'. Tom Jones lustily revivified a half-forgotten 'Paul' Beatles track, 'She's a Woman'. Elvis Costello recalled his nervousness on arriving at Hog Hill to work with Paul, and how welcoming and kind Linda had been.

Paul himself was not scheduled to perform but, buoyed up by the homage of his fellow musicians and the waves of Linda-love from the 5000-strong audience, he decided to close the show, backed by the Pretenders and Costello. He dedicated his set to 'my beautiful baby and our beautiful children, who are here tonight' and added a proud mention of his week-old grandson.

Surprisingly, he didn't open with any of the Beatles, Wings or post-Wings songs he had written for Linda. Instead, he chose Ricky Nelson's 'Lonesome Town', a piece of saccharine American pop – the kind the Beatles would ultimately annihilate – which the two of them had listened to, thousands of miles apart, when it came out in 1958.

The lyrics were self-dramatising teenage drivel, typical of their time. But there wasn't a heart that didn't ache for him as he sang:

> Maybe down in Lonesome Town
> I can learn to forget.

A month later to the day, he was at the Dorchester Hotel in London for a further tribute to Linda. The occasion was the *Daily Mirror*'s first Pride of Britain Awards to people who had performed acts of heroism, faced up to fearful challenges or in some way 'made a difference'. Paul was to present a Linda McCartney Award for Animal Welfare to the crusading vegetarian Juliet Gellatley.

One of the awards for 'outstanding bravery' went to 24-year-old Helen Smith who had lost both legs and both hands to meningitis, yet managed to lead a fulfilling life, studying biology, even learning to play the piano. She was introduced by another symbol of triumph over disability, the model and charity campaigner Heather Mills whose left leg had been partially amputated after a traffic accident in 1993.

Paul was at a stage-front table with the *Mirror*'s editor, Piers Morgan – the same who, as editor of the *News of the World*, had offered his ex-manager, Richard Ogden, £250,000 for the inside story on his and Linda's marriage. Now he beheld a spectacular young woman of 31 wearing a tight red top and white trousers which accentuated her curvaceous figure, yet with an air of being too busy to care about her appearance. Her prosthetic lower left leg was unnoticeable as she sprinted onto the stage and, brushing aside her short golden hair, began an impassioned speech about the plight of amputees in a north-eastern accent that is as soft and lilting as Liverpudlian is harsh.

If Linda had been viewed in some ways as a temporary stand-in for Diana, Princess of Wales, Heather Mills seemed like an ongoing surrogate. In Diana's final months, her main charitable cause had been the landmines which still infested the world's war-zones, past and present, maiming thousands of innocent victims each year, a high proportion of them children.

Heather had since taken over as the embodiment of Britain's anti-landmine movement – although her involvement with the campaign actually predated Diana's and had placed her in far greater danger. Impatient with the bureaucracy and mismanagement of established charities, she had started one of her own, the Heather Mills Health Trust, to raise money for child landmine victims and lobby the National Health Service for better amputee-care in the UK.

Paul had never run across her before, and had to ask Piers Morgan who and what she was. They weren't introduced at the awards ceremony, but shortly afterwards he contacted her, saying he'd like to discuss her charity projects with a view to offering help. They had two or three business meetings, as a result of which Paul agreed to donate £150,000 to the Heather Mills Health Trust. Then he invited her out to dinner, discovering that, as a result of homeopathic treatment for her leg, she had recently become a vegan.

Heather's autobiography, *Out on a Limb*, published four years earlier, had created a sensation. It described a horrendous upbringing in the north-eastern town of Washington by a feckless mother and an unloving, cruel father, in which she witnessed habitual domestic violence, engaged in pretty crime and spent some time with her younger sister, Fiona, in a local authority children's home. When she was nine, her mother ran off with another man, leaving her and her two siblings at the mercy of her father, who was subsequently imprisoned for fraud.

She recounted how at the age of 13, by then living with her mother in London, she had run away from home, first getting a job with a funfair on Clapham Common, then living rough, stealing food from supermarkets and sleeping in a cardboard box in the hobo-city under the arches at Waterloo station, with alcoholic tramps urinating only inches from her head.

At the age of 18, while working as a waitress in a Soho club – just around the corner from MPL – she met a businessman named Alfie Karmal, ten years her senior, who encouraged her to take up modelling and to whom (at her own suggestion) she was briefly married. After she had suffered two ectopic pregnancies, Karmal sought to cheer her up by sending her on a skiing holiday to Yugoslavia. The gesture backfired when she fell in love with her instructor and refused to return home.

As a result, she was there when Yugoslavia splintered into its pre-Communist Balkan states in 1991 and numerous vicious civil wars broke out. Having come to love the region and its people, Heather set up a refugee crisis-centre in Slovenia and accompanied food and medical convoys into neighbouring Croatia where the suffering was even worse, often under fire and with the dead and dying all around her.

With her return to London came the episode that would change her life. One sunny Sunday afternoon in August 1993, she and her then boyfriend, Raffaele Mincione, were walking from De Vere Gardens in Kensington towards Hyde Park. As Heather crossed the intervening main road on a pedestrian crossing, she was struck by a police motorcyclist travelling at speed – part of a convoy rushing to answer what later proved to be a false alarm from Princess Diana at nearby Kensington Palace. The impact tore off her left leg below the knee; as she lay on the ground, she could see her severed foot a few yards away, with traffic swerving to avoid it.

In hospital, more and more of her leg kept becoming infected and having to be amputated, to the point where she feared she might lose the knee also. At this time, a female social worker paid her a visit and, in the guise of kindliness, warned that she must prepare never to be attractive to men again. 'If I lost my arms and my legs, darling,' Heather replied, 'I'd still be more attractive than you.'

In fact, the hideous misfortune proved to be the making of her. From her hospital bed she sold her life story to a Sunday tabloid, achieving national, then international fame as the '£200,000-a-year catwalk model with a golden future' that had been so cruelly terminated.

She bought her first artificial leg off the peg for $1500, mastered it with phenomenal speed and was soon back jogging, skiing, horse-riding, scuba-diving, rollerblading, playing tennis and climbing, using a differently-crafted prosthesis for each. 'MODEL OF COURAGE', the tabloids named her.

Her formerly private welfare work in the Balkans now took place under the eye of television cameras, as when she organised a convoy of 4500 second-hand artificial limbs from Britain to help landmine victims in the Croatian capital, Zagreb. With that same echo of Princess Diana, she toured hospitals, bolstering the spirits of children struggling to walk with new artificial limbs and kicking off her own false shin and foot to show she was no different.

Paul also got involved in the Balkans relief effort in 1995, rounding up a crew of younger chart stars to make an album – borrowing the name *HELP* from the Beatles' one of 20 years earlier – whose proceeds were sent to help injured and homeless children in Bosnia-Herzegovina. Recorded in a single day, in the manner of John's 'Instant Karma', it featured a version of 'Come Together' by a supergroup named the Smokin' Mojo Filters including Paul, his namesake Paul Weller and Noel Gallagher from Oasis. Amid the publicity surrounding this new *HELP* album, he might easily have met Heather Mills. But it never happened.

By 1999, Heather was Britain's best-known 'charity celebrity': she'd received a *Daily Star* Gold Star for courage from the then prime minister, John Major, taken part in a swimathon organised by the Olympic swimmer Duncan Goodhew and been tipped for the British team at the next Paralympics. Ever more impressive news stories swirled about her: that a Hollywood film about her life was in production; that she could look forward to a future government post as Secretary of State for Health; that she was in the running for a Nobel Peace Prize.

Many theories would later be advanced about how someone normally so shrewd and cautious could have fallen so quickly and heavily. One was that after his long monogamous relationship with Linda he was in a particularly vulnerable state and the combination of a powerful, seductive woman with a social conscience was irresistible. Not to be discounted either was the relief of being with someone totally unawed by his Beatle fame. Heather was too young to have known Beatlemania; indeed, she claimed to have hardly been aware of the Beatles, although she'd liked Wings.

But the real answer seems to have been the caring side of him, passed on by his mother, that selfless nurse and midwife, and so much in play during the three years of Linda's illness.

Even at this early stage, many people close to Paul – notably Neil Aspinall – warned that he might himself be walking into a minefield. But he was deaf to all such advice, as a man might well be who'd made 'Mull of Kintyre' sell a million during the Punk Revolution.

Ever supportive, Paul helps Linda launch her vegetarian range which was to become a top-seller in supermarkets. But the couple alienated many Wings fans with their 'Go Veggie' banners at concerts *(below)*.

Hard Day's Knight: Paul receives his 'K' from the Queen, 1997.

The strain of Linda's illness is etched on both their faces as they watch one of daughter Stella's wildly successful couture collections.

Linda where she was always happiest, riding one of her beloved Appaloosa horses.

Paul is caught on camera, shopping with Heather Mills. After months of insisting they're just good friends, he admits 'I love her' on a British TV show. People soon notice how Heather seems to do most of the talking.

(*Above*) Out on the town together when everything still looked rosy. (*Below*) Paul swears the international media to secrecy on the eve of his Irish wedding to Heather in 2002.

Paul with daughters Mary and Stella, 2006: 'When you're going through Hell, keep going'.

'Shake it up, baby': the American tabloids uncover his relationship with New York trucking heiress Nancy Shevell.

Paul with his musician son, James, on whom his fame will always cast 'a shadow like Mount Everest's'. His marriage to Heather caused a rift between them but with the advent of 'new mum' Nancy, they grew close again.

2011: Paul marries Nancy at London's Marylebone Town Hall – where he had married Linda in 1969.

49

'I've just got a leg missing.
I've still got my heart'

To all appearances, he remained in deepest mourning for Linda and concerned only with ensuring she would not be forgotten. One of his first acts after her death was to divide $2 million between New York's Memorial Sloan Kettering Hospital and the Arizona Cancer Center in Tucson, at both of which she had received impressive long-term care, on condition that if the money were spent on research no animals would be used. He made it known that he remained totally committed to her crusade for vegetarianism and would use his name to oppose animal cruelty wherever it was found – as proof, writing to India's prime minister Atal Bihari Vajpayee to protest against that country's illegal export and slaughter of cows for the leather industry.

Outside bodies were creating their own Linda memorials, if not funded then personally vetted by him. At the Royal Liverpool University Hospital, a Linda McCartney cancer treatment centre was nearing completion; the Rock and Roll Hall of Fame was to mount an exhibition of her photographs; her artist friend Brian Clarke had created a 62-foot-long stained glass window in her memory for permanent exhibition at the Corning Glass Museum in New York.

After the Albert Hall rock spectacular, the classical world, to which Paul now firmly belonged, paid its own tribute. In July 1999, Charterhouse school in Surrey was the setting for A Garland for

Linda, a recital of ten specially-written pieces by composers such as John Tavener, David Matthews and the newly-dubbed Sir Richard Rodney Bennett, together with a new McCartney one, entitled 'Nova'. Proceeds from the performance and the album which followed went to a cancer charity, the Garland Appeal.

Everything he did in public proclaimed that Linda had been the love of his life and that no one could ever take her place. The fact remained that he was the world's most eligible widower, his 57 years no obstacle to women of any age. There was a flurry of tabloid speculation when the (married) textile designer Sue Timney – who'd been a good friend of Linda's – was noticed paying regular visits to Peasmarsh. Paul put out a terse statement that they were merely working together on an exhibition of Linda's photographs and that suggestions of anything more were 'scurrilous' and 'mean-spirited'.

Heather Mills, meanwhile, seemed back on her own very different trajectory – and already spoken for. The day after the Pride of Britain awards, she'd travelled to Cambodia with the Duchess of Kent to make a television documentary on its landmine problem with British director and anthropologist Chris Terrill.

She was wont to say that, disability or no, every man she met wanted to marry her within a week. Actually, it was ten days into the trip, aboard a fishing boat on the Mekong River, when Terrill proposed to her. She replied with one word: 'When?'

The two showed off Heather's engagement ring on Esther Rantzen's television show, for which they'd made the Cambodia film, and set their wedding for 8 August. With just a week to go, after Terrill had had his stag night, the wedding was called off.

In a sequel to her autobiography, published after her life had changed beyond recognition, she would describe making a casual arrangement with Paul to meet up in America, going there with her sister, Fiona, and contacting him from an hotel near his summer home in Amagansett, Long Island. As the sisters lay on the beach, she recalled, he joined them by boat – not the luxury yacht they expected but a tiny Sunfish dinghy with a multicoloured sail.

By this account, he and Heather spent the next few days together, with Fiona playing gooseberry. His wooing of her began in earnest when he brought his guitar to the beach and serenaded her as they sat together on a lifeguard's high-level observation-chair. However, in future divorce papers, she would say she'd gone to America with him so that he could show her his property in Pintail Lane.

That autumn, they began a clandestine affair, conducted mainly in Rye, the small, rather literary seaside town a couple of miles from Peasmarsh. There Paul owned a cottage named The Forecastle, once occupied by Radclyffe Hall, the first openly lesbian novelist (who sometimes used the pseudonym 'John'), and her lover, Una Troubridge.

From September 1999 to January 2000, he and Heather spent several nights a week at The Forecastle, which they nicknamed Lizzie because of its Elizabethan half-timbering. There also were trysts at a London hotel where he would have the most luxurious suite specially prepared for them. On 31 October, she arrived to find he'd had it filled with Hallowe'en pumpkins and lanterns.

Heather still seemed to have no idea of his magnitude as a recording artiste. Her sister, Fiona, owned a small record label named Coda and to publicise her campaign on behalf of amputees she planned to release a single of herself talking about it, backed by some kind of music. 'I was thinking of gospel singers but I couldn't find any,' she would recall. 'So I asked Paul if he knew anyone and he said ,"I'll do it."'

The result was 'Voice', a kind of disco rap for which he provided a highly-polished dance track and backup vocal to Heather's spoken plea for amputees to be treated as real people. On the accompanying video, she did a sexy dance in her white trousers, which ended with her kicking off her prosthetic leg.

Fleet Street first scented something early in November when she and Fiona attended the Guy Fawkes Night party Paul always threw at Peasmarsh, both of them staying over for two nights in a cottage on the estate and Heather hiding her face from photographers as she left. By this time, too, there was a CD and video around in which he seemed to be 'doing a Wings' with her.

Paul promptly issued a statement denying any romantic interest in either sister: 'Because I work with these ladies does not mean I have anything more than a business relationship with them. I will continue to work with Heather Mills on the record project and even though this story of romance is not true, I hope it will bring attention to her efforts for the disabled worldwide.'

A statement on Heather's behalf repeated that they were to-gether only on 'Voice': 'She needed a backing vocalist and that is where Paul McCartney came in.' Paul attended the single's launch party on 22 November (coincidentally the thirty-first anniversary of the Beatles' White Album) but took care to be photographed only with Fiona.

Like all older men who take much younger lovers, he felt re-juvenated and energised and told himself the age difference was irrelevant. Although never a sporty type, apart from horse-riding, he resolutely joined Heather in the vigorous outdoor activities her disability hadn't curtailed. On their first skiing holiday together, he asked her, 'How fast can you go?'

'Ninety-three kilometres an hour,' she replied.

'You'd better go first then,' Paul laughed, little imagining how she would take him at his word.

The affair gave a further boost to the work ethic he'd all but lost during the year after Linda's death. During the last quarter of 1999, he put out both a new pop and a new classical album and gave his first live show since he'd shared a stage with her.

The pop album, released in October, was *Run Devil Run*, named after a 'funky' pharmacy he'd seen in Atlanta, Georgia, which sold potions to ward off the evil eye. Made back at Abbey Road, it was mostly cover versions of old rock and skiffle hits including some long-forgotten ones like Charlie Gracie's 'Fabulous' and the Vipers' 'No Other Baby', played with the euphoric spontaneity of long-ago Beatles sessions. But grief still glimmered in a new song, 'Try Not to Cry': 'All day, I try to be a man/ Help me to do it, show me the plan'.

Then in November came *Working Classical*, a collection of his past pop hits, plus three new compositions in the *Standing Stone* mould, arranged by Sir Richard Rodney Bennett and Jonathan Tunick and performed by the London Symphony Orchestra. Its title was a typical McCartney pun, but still slyly suggestive of his triumph; the working-class Liverpool lad who'd conquered classical music as completely as he had rock 'n' roll.

There recently had been a further surge of Beatlemania in Britain with the re-release of the *Yellow Submarine* animated film and soundtrack album. To promote *Run Devil Run* – and round off the twentieth century – Paul decided to give a live show in Liverpool: not at the Empire this time but in some intimate venue redolent of Beatle times past. His first choice was the flat in Gambier Terrace which John and Stu Sutcliffe had shared as art students. Then his PR, Geoff Baker, suggested the facsimile Cavern, opened in 1984 to replace the original subterranean 'home of the Beatles', filled in to make way for a car park in 1973.

Paul was initially unenthusiastic, pointing out that the new Cavern was located on the wrong side of Mathew Street as well as eight feet deeper underground with modern refinements like a front and back stage – and an alcohol licence. He relented after assurances from the present owner, Bill Heckle, that it still retained its old postal address, some of the bricks from the original structure were to be found in it and its back stage was only 12 feet away from the buried one the Beatles had trod.

After he announced the gig on BBC1's Michael Parkinson show, there were around one million applications for the 300 seats available. Some women in Liverpool were reported to be offering sexual favours in return for a ticket.

The performance on the evening of 14 December was filmed for MPL and broadcast over the Internet. For extra authenticity, Paul had asked the Cavern's first and most celebrated DJ, Bob Wooler, to emcee as he had countless times for the Beatles in the old days. The dignified, meticulous Wooler had given them valuable tips about stagecraft and turned them on to American soul singers like

Chan Romero, but had been left behind by the Epstein-led exodus to London, one of the saddest cases of wounded Liverpool eyes.

Now Paul's affectionate greeting and offer of a comeback wiped away some of that old hurt. Unfortunately, Wooler had a chronic drink problem which a latter, accident-prone business partnership with the Beatles' first manager, Allan Williams, had done little to help. Overcome with emotion and paralysed by nerves, he vanished into Mathew Street's unchanged Grapes pub and never made it onstage that night.

Behind Paul were the superior ad hoc band from *Run Devil Run*: David Gilmour and Mick Green on guitars, Pete Wingfield on keyboards, Ian Paice on drums. Virtuosi though they were, they fluffed the simple intro to Gene Vincent's 'Blue Jean Bop' and Paul held up an arm to stop them. 'With this band,' he said, 'if we don't get it right, we start again.' Backstage opinion was divided as to whether it had been a genuine slip or a very McCartney bit of theatre.

On 31 December, he threw a big party at 'Rembrandt', his father's old house on the Wirral, with the double object of bringing in the new millennium and introducing his children and Liverpool relations to Heather. Next morning, the pair were said by the *News of the World* to have looked 'relaxed and happy' as they left to attend a family New Year's Day lunch.

'Heather has been a rock for Paul since Linda's death and it looks like he is finally starting to rebuild his life,' an unnamed 'source' told the paper. 'They were every bit the happy couple at the party and it's a sign of their deep affection for each other that they wanted to celebrate the start of the millennium together.'

In the early hours of 30 December, a 33-year-old Liverpudlian named Michael Abram had broken into George's Oxfordshire mansion, Friar Park, armed with a knife and a lump of statuary purloined from the garden. George had gone downstairs to investigate and in the ensuing struggle Abram had stabbed him repeatedly in the chest, equally impervious to his would-be pacifying cries of 'Hare Krishna!' and blows from a heavy lamp wielded by his wife, Olivia.

Before police came to their rescue, the couple both believed they were about to be murdered. Abram later claimed to have been possessed by George's spirit and to be on 'a mission' to kill him.

Although George played down the attack, he'd suffered a punctured lung as well as being traumatised afresh after his recent cancer. For Paul, it was a chilling reminder of John's murder by Mark David Chapman, another crazy on a supposed mission in the selfsame month 19 years earlier. Nor was it the only sign of the strides Britain had since taken to catch up America in random violence and malevolence. George's neighbour, the writer John Mortimer, later recalled seeing carloads of people pass Friar Park's front gate, cheering and applauding what Michael Abram had done.

The world's media were still pressing Paul to admit his involvement with Heather Mills, but getting little joy from the old master of equivocation and soufflé-speak. In February 2000, he took his children to the exclusive Caribbean resort of Parrot Cay in the Turks and Caicos Islands. On the day the children left for home, Heather flew in to join him for a further ten days. His publicist, Geoff Baker, refused to confirm the tryst had taken place and insisted the two were 'just good friends'.

That pretence was becoming increasingly difficult to maintain. In March, Heather gave up her five-bedroom house in King's Somborne, Hampshire, and bought a property in Brighton – using the residue of £200,000 she'd received as compensation after her accident – in order to be nearer to Rye. Walking her dog on Brighton sea front, she sometimes passed the time of day with a fellow dog-walker whose name she never learned. It was Maggie McGivern, the most secret of Paul's 1960s girlfriends. Neither woman had any inkling of the other's connection with him.

That spring, Paul was forced to admit guardedly that he and Heather Mills were 'an item'. He described Heather as 'a very impressive woman' and appealed to the paparazzi not to hound them 'because that could wreck something'. The McCartney children were reportedly pleased with the news and Paul was said to have already introduced Heather to the Ringo Starrs over dinner.

It was an odd coincidence that he should already have a Heather in his life and as the second one claimed more and more of his attention, the first suddenly had urgent need of him.

On 19 March, Linda's ex-husband, Joseph Melville See, who may or may not have inspired 'Get Back' and 'Dear Boy', committed suicide near his home in Arizona. The once indefatigable geologist and explorer had lately fallen into a depression, taking up with another woman while continuing to live with his long-time partner, Beverly Wilk, and obsessively reading the Bible and the works of Ernest Hemingway, his lifelong role model. Even his suicide replicated Hemingway's: a shotgun blast on the eve of his sixty-second birthday.

Losing her biological father – a man she'd only lately come to know and appreciate – just two years after losing her mother was a devastating blow to the already fragile Heather McCartney. In America, there was a spate of tabloid headlines about 'Linda's ex'; even reports that, because a shotgun had been involved, the local police were launching a murder investigation.

When Paul and Linda became an item in 1968 – the year of Heather Mills's birth – the backlash from his envious fans had been highly unpleasant. But Heather was to experience nothing of the kind, at least not yet. People were glad he'd found someone else, albeit rather rapidly, and thought his surprising choice looked nice and would be good for him.

The media were another matter. Not content with the life story Heather had provided ready-made – running away from home at 13 to join a fun fair, shoplifting and sleeping in a cardboard box – Britain's tabloid press began to take a more searching and increasingly less benevolent look at their former 'Model of Courage'.

They soon discovered that the modelling career, so cruelly blighted by her accident, had not been in the glamorous haute couture sphere inhabited by Stella McCartney but the more down-market one of lingerie catalogues and topless glamour poses. For one period, omitted from her biography, she had been a regular fixture at parties organized for visiting Middle Eastern businessmen like the Saudi Arabian billionaire Adnan Khashoggi.

Fearing damaging revelations were imminent, Heather went to Paul and told him that untrue allegations were about to be published – a moment which, she later said, was 'as bad as losing my leg'. But 'he listened to everything and said it didn't make the slightest difference to our relationship'.

Among her television colleagues, she polarised opinion, some regarding her as an unbearable egotist and diva, others extolling her courage, determination and generosity. One day, she appeared on the *Richard & Judy* show alongside a mother and father making the latest of many fruitless appeals to their runaway, drug-addicted teenage daughter to return home. Heather chipped in, offering the runaway a refuge for three months and support in kicking her heroin habit. That successfully accomplished, she found her a job at a leisure-centre, turning her life around completely.

Paul's four children were far from happy about his new relationship, especially James, who still missed Linda dreadfully, and Heather, who was only five years older than her namesake. All of them felt it was way too soon after their mother's death. Mary, the eldest, and most protective of Paul, feared he was falling victim to a ruthless opportunist. Only Stella felt they should give the newcomer a chance, remembering how desolate he had been for months after Linda's death.

Throughout the summer of 2000, he and Heather continued to be seen together, mostly in pursuance of her charity work. Like her, he signed up to Adopt-A-Minefield, the organisation which both campaigned against the use of landmines and carried out the dangerous work of clearance. They were joint hosts for Adopt-A-Minefield's UK launch at the BAFTA awards, using Paul's song 'Hope of Deliverance' as a soundtrack.

In September they both appeared at a United Nations conference on landmines in Geneva. Paul delivered an opening address with all the relevant statistics at his fingertips – 26,000 adults and 8000 children killed by landmines each year, 11 governments and 30 rebel groups still using them – then called Heather to the podium.

That same month, she was with him at the wedding of his Auntie Gin's granddaughter, Susan Harris, in Wallasey, when he insisted on personally chauffeuring the bride to the church.

Early in October, Heather was the subject of ITV's *Stars in Their Lives*, a knock-off of the famous *This Is Your Life*. Paul had agreed to do a surprise walk-on to talk about her work; instead, he used his appearance to confirm at long last that their relationship was serious. Heather herself professed to have had no idea he fancied her until after one of their 'prim and proper' meetings about her charity. 'I felt these eyes on my back and I thought "He's eyeing up my bum."'

'And I was,' Paul said.

'I love him,' Heather told presenter Carol Vorderman, who then turned to Paul.

'Yeah, I love her, too,' he responded, defusing it ever so slightly with some mock sentimental air-violin.

From that moment, a minor British celebrity changed into a major international one. American television's top current affairs show, *20/20*, immediately sent its star presenter, Barbara Walters, to London to report on the romance and interview Heather. The resulting programme, titled *Heather's Journey*, began with the video she and Paul had made for her amputees campaign – the sexy dance, to his backing-track, that ended with her kicking off her false leg.

Walters introduced her as someone whose life read 'like a soap opera': 'a child of the streets' who became 'a sought-after international model until a freak accident robbed her of her leg'. Once more, she recounted that nightmare childhood and teenage flight from home; there was a visit to the scene of her accident in 1993 and film of her comforting and encouraging child landmine victims 'like Princess Diana before her'. Altogether, one of the most rigorous of American interviewers was utterly captivated.

'I've just got a leg missing,' she told Walters. 'I've still got my heart.'

The dawn of the twenty-first century found Beatlemania flourishing more than ever. In November 2000, the book version of *The Beatles Anthology*, a lavishly-produced coffee-table hardback containing the interviews from the television series plus 120 rare photos, was a bestseller around the world. That same month, Apple put out a compilation of their number one singles from 1963 to 1970 (all except 'Please Please Me') simply entitled *1*, which itself performed the same feat in 34 countries and went on to become America's top-selling album of the new decade.

The London *Sunday Times* Rich List gazetted Paul as pop music's first dollar billionaire and on course to be its first sterling one by 2001, thanks jointly to earnings of £175 million from the *1* album and his inheritance from Linda. Heather would later claim he told her he was worth well north of £800 million, though a High Court judge would ultimately set the total at less than half that.

He still had more money than he could ever conceivably spend. Others in that situation, having tired of all sensory pleasures, find satisfaction in small acts of frugality – the US press magnate William Randolph Hearst having meals served on paper plates or the oil billionaire John Paul Getty installing a payphone in the vestibule of his British mansion, Sutton Place.

Paul could be enormously generous, not only to hospitals, his family and home city but to people from deep in his past. One such was Horst Fascher, the Hamburg heavy who'd watched over the Beatles during their stints on the Reeperbahn and still ran a replica Star-Club there.

In 1994, he received an SOS from Fascher, whose 11-month-old daughter, Sophie-Louise, had been diagnosed with a serious heart defect. He flew the child and her parents to London, then brought a team of specialists from New York to operate on her at Great Ormond Street Hospital, picking up a bill of around $200,000. When his biographer, Barry Miles, was found to have a torn retina, he arranged for Miles to see Britain's top eye specialist, provided a limo to take him to the appointment and paid for all the subsequent treatment.

Yet he could also have his John Paul Getty moments. Miles

happened to be at MPL when news of the 1 album's monster success came in. 'Some of the staff opened a bottle of champagne to celebrate. But Paul got quite grumpy with them for being so extravagant.'

Heather was seeing his generous side in excelsis. After a Christmas together at Lizzie, they left for a month-long holiday to India, staying in super-luxury hotels and converted maharajahs' palaces. In Jaipur, Paul went off on his own and bought a £15,000 sapphire and diamond ring for her – then decided not to give it to her just yet.

They had only just returned to Britain when a severe earthquake struck the Indian state of Gujarat. Thousands of people were buried under collapsed buildings and had to have limbs amputated as a result. In Jaipur, as it happened, Heather had been shown a new, inexpensive type of artificial leg. She immediately rushed to the earthquake scene and arranged for a supply of 'Jaipur legs' to be provided.

From there, she joined Paul in Los Angeles where he was to record a new album with the producer David Kahne. The title, *Driving Rain*, seemed an odd choice as its theme was how Heather had rescued him from tempests of grief; the tracks included 'Back in the Sunshine Again' ('You gave me the strength to get out of bed'), 'Riding into Jaipur' ('Riding with my baby/ Oh, what a delight') and 'Heather', identifying the two of them with Edward Lear's 'Owl and the Pussycat' ('I will dance to a runcible tune with the queen of my heart').

Rather than use an hotel and be plagued by paparazzi, Paul rented the Beverly Hills home of Kurt Cobain's widow, Courtney Love, a secluded French-style mansion with the delightfully apt address of 9536 Heather Road. This they nicknamed 'the Heather House' and became so fond of it that Paul later bought it for just under $4 million, implying – so Heather would later claim – that he intended to make it over to her.

His largesse was balanced by caution; despite wanting to be with her, he didn't want them to seem to be cohabiting. In May 2001, she received a loan of £800,000 from MPL to buy a luxurious seafront property named Angel's Rest in Hove, the next-door town to Brighton, said to be so posh that its seagulls fly upside-down. There she was to live ostensibly by herself, though Paul would be there much of the time. With this in view, MPL loaned her an additional £150,000 for renovations, the total £950,000 to be repaid in easy instalments of £1000 per month. As she had nothing to hang on the walls, he shipped in 30 of his own paintings.

In the British press, impressive stories about Heather Mills continued to outweigh troubling ones. That April of 2001, in an interview to the *Sunday Times*, she claimed that the Blair government wanted to give her a peerage, and all the main British political parties were competing for her services as a Member of Parliament. She also let drop that she was rated the number one public speaker in the UK and seventh in the world.

Besotted with her though Paul was, he still wore his wedding ring and grieving for Linda remained a powerful element in his work. In May, he brought out *Wingspan*, a double CD of Wings' greatest hits, accompanied by a documentary about their musical and marital partnership, filling in the conspicuous gap in his authorised biography. The producer was his daughter, Mary – now something of a celebrity after photographing Tony and Cherie Blair's new baby son, Leo – and the director was her husband, Alistair Donald.

With Mary also acting as his interviewer, the tone was intimate, at times emotional, as he recalled the fun of having 'my best mate, my wife, to sing along with'. Under her gentle coaxing, he also talked in detail for the first time about key episodes in Wings' bumpy history, such as the defection of two key members on the eve of making *Band on the Run* and how he'd been 'an idiot' with the block of marijuana at Tokyo airport in 1980.

Linda likewise permeated *Blackbird Singing*, a collection of his song-lyrics and poems between 1965 and 1999, published by the renowned poetry imprint of Faber & Faber. She had always wanted such a book to appear and had lined up the leading British poet

Adrian Mitchell to edit it as far back as 1991 when Mitchell had a guest spot on the Unplugged Tour.

There is a world of difference between a pop lyric embedded in voices and instruments – and so allowed all kinds of imperfection – and a poem alone and naked on the page. Paul had always been exceptional, along with John, Bob Dylan and a few others, in writing lyrics that read like poetry. No less a master than Allen Ginsberg considered 'Eleanor Rigby' 'a hell of a poem'; J.K. Rowling, author of the Harry Potter books (a phenomenon often compared with the Beatles), cited the words to 'Yesterday' as a model of verbal economy and discipline; the Secretary of State for Northern Ireland, Mo Mowlam, whom he'd met at the Pride of Britain awards, opined that he'd be 'an overwhelmingly popular choice' as Poet Laureate.

Yet he'd never had any idea when he wrote a song that he was producing poetry. The qualities extolled by Ginsberg, Rowling and so many others had just happened when – to quote another fine poet, Michael Horovitz – 'the craft and hard graft of writing non-stop for gigs, broadcasts and recording left hardly a wasted syllable'.

Now, with *Blackbird Singing*, here he was being self-consciously 'poetical'. And for almost every reviewer, inevitably steeped in Beatle knowledge, there was no comparison with the unknowing bard who'd created the perfect 1950s street-scene in 'Penny Lane', the mini-drama in 'She's Leaving Home' and the cosy psychedelic carnival of 'Sgt. Pepper's Lonely Hearts Club Band'.

While the lyrics were re-praised to the skies, the poems were taken to task for slackness, triteness and laboured aphorisms like 'Sadness isn't sadness/ It's happiness in a black jacket'. Horovitz was almost the only friendly voice, welcoming 'a profoundly innocent and vastly enjoyable toybox of a book' with echoes of John Betjeman, Philip Larkin and Robert Browning, and calling the verse epic written to accompany *Standing Stone* (but never performed) 'a remarkable feat of historical imagination'.

What none could deny was the power and often naked heartbreak of the pieces inspired by Linda, most written during her illness or in the aftermath of her death. One in particular, 'To Be Said', was like 'Yesterday' revisited; no longer a young man's passing angst but a mature one's dark night of the soul:

> My love is alive, my love is dead,
> I hear her voice inside my head.
> There's a lot to remember, a lot to forget.
> There's a lot to be said, there's nothing to be said.

50

'Hey, that's pretty good. Is it one of yours?'

In these last months before the world changed for ever, Paul proclaimed his commitment to Heather by taking her anti-landmine campaign international. For those who remembered the early Seventies, and another ex-Beatle pushed into political awareness by a forceful woman, there began to be a touch of John and Yoko about them.

America at that time had the world's fourth largest stock of landmines but, under President George W. Bush, still refused to implement a ban. In April 2001, Paul's name secured them a meeting with Bush's Secretary of State, Colin Powell, the first African-American in that post and a former five-star general with direct knowledge of the foul devices. Powell could not commit his country to dispensing with them, but agreed that the State Department would make a contribution to Adopt-A-Landmine (which allowed him to boast to *Harper's Magazine* that 'Paul is a bud of mine').

This new life of diplomacy and speech-making was interrupted by grim news about George. Two and a half years after being pronounced clear of throat cancer, he'd gone to the Mayo Clinic in Minnesota for a check-up and been told he had a malignant tumour in one lung. Having received treatment for that, and supposedly made a good recovery, he had been diagnosed with a brain tumour.

His last contact with Paul had been over *The Beatles Anthology* book and had brought yet another spell of *froideur* between them. According to his friend Neil Innes, George had wanted the book to be leather-bound, offending Paul by his seeming forgetfulness of Linda's animal rights crusade.

But all such petty conflicts were forgotten now. From Milan, where he was promoting the *Wingspan* CD, Paul immediately flew with Heather to the Swiss clinic at which George was to undergo yet further treatment. Ringo also arrived, staying as long as possible before returning to Boston, where his daughter, Lee, was fighting the same form of cancer.

For any British painter, professional or amateur, the ultimate accolade is to have a picture in the Royal Academy of Arts' Summer Exhibition at Burlington House in London's Piccadilly. In 2001 the show was curated by Peter Blake, the chin-bearded doyen of Sixties pop art, whose most famous work was the cover of *Sgt. Pepper's Lonely Hearts Club Band*. A 1991 abstract by Paul, *Chocolate Sunset*, appeared alongside heavyweight names like Tracey Emin and Bridget Riley and other brush-wielding musicians like Ronnie Wood, Ian Dury and Holly Johnson from Frankie Goes to Hollywood.

While admitting Paul was a friend, Blake denied choosing *Chocolate Sunset* merely to get publicity for the show. 'He has got tremendous integrity as an artist . . . and I have hung it out of respect for him as a painter.' But the waspish art critic Brian Sewell attacked 'an infuriating tendency among clapped-out old pop stars to become artists . . . They usually produce unmitigated garbage, and should stick to what they were doing.'

On 14 June, Paul was back at Heather's side to host a gala fundraiser for Adopt-A-Minefield in Los Angeles, the highlight of which was a duet by himself and Paul Simon. To publicise the event – henceforward an annual one – he did a lengthy live interview on CNN's *Larry King Live*, with Heather joining him for the last segment.

'How's George doing with the cancer?' King asked.

'He's good, he's excellent,' Paul replied. 'I saw him just a couple of weeks ago.' A statement from George himself two days later said he was 'feeling fine . . . active and feeling very well'.

Driving Rain was not scheduled for release until autumn, which left several months free for Paul to complete his third major piece of classical music. It was another oratorio, quasi-religious in tone but steeped in memories of Linda.

Back in 1997, the President of Magdalen College, Oxford, Anthony Smith, had invited him to write something for the opening of the college's new auditorium. Linda had persuaded him to accept the commission despite his virtual abandonment of work by that stage in her illness. They'd visited Oxford together and been won over by Smith, formerly a distinguished BBC television producer who'd worked with Mike McCartney's group, the Scaffold.

Linda's death had put the musical project in abeyance, but Paul's connection to Magdalen remained. During his mourning period, Smith invited him to the college's November All Souls feast, where the usual exotically carnivorous menu was replaced by a vegetarian one in his honour. At the dons' High Table, he was amused to meet Ancient History tutor Mark Pobjoy, whose father had been John's headmaster at Quarry Bank School – and a notably more sympathetic one than his own at the Inny.

In 2001, he'd returned to the piece, disregarding Smith's request for something evoking seasons of the academic year, instead using it as therapy, as he later admitted, 'to write my sadness out'. Indeed, that came across so strongly that one woman who heard an early version burst into tears despite knowing nothing about its background.

On 18 June, his fifty-ninth birthday, he was granted the heraldic coat of arms to which every British knight is entitled. The crest he chose for himself depicted a medieval helmet surmounted by a Liver Bird, Liverpool's ancient mascot, clutching a guitar in its claws. Beneath was a Latin motto he'd seen in New York's Church of St Ignatius Loyola, above a picture of Jesus: 'Ecce Cor Meum' or 'Behold My Heart'.

This now became the title of his oratorio for Magdalen College.

'At one point, he said he wanted the whole thing to be in Latin,' Anthony Smith recalls, 'so our college Latinist translated the libretto. Then he decided to use only part of the translation.'

On visits to Oxford, he and Heather would stay at Smith's house in the college precincts, which had a comfortable guest-suite for its many visiting VIPs. 'The students were very cool, and left him alone. He could go into the bar on his own, buy a drink and sit down, and nobody bothered him for autographs.'

Smith was 'astonished' by the way Heather treated Paul. 'She behaved as if she rather than he was the celebrity. And she was very highly opinionated about everything, including his music, which she had no inhibitions about criticising in a roomful of music professors who admired it. He didn't seem to mind, or his good manners prevented him from showing it.

'One night at dinner in the Senior Common Room we had a German tutor who was rather an attractive young woman and there was some eye-contact between Paul and her. Heather kept glaring at him and there was a row about it afterwards in their suite. The next morning when Paul came down to breakfast, he said she'd gone. She was needed in London by people she looked after in her charity work – or that was the story.' Heather now claims to have been unaware of any flirting on Paul's part; she says she walked out because he lit up a joint in their room despite his promise to give up the habit.

On 20 July, they were in Liverpool for LIPA's graduation ceremony, which this year significantly introduced awards to disabled students. There were also 'Companion' awards for Joan Armatrading, Benny Gallagher and the Sex Pistols' former manager, Malcolm McLaren. As had become tradition, Paul presented each graduate with a ceremonial pin, then joined them all in a group photograph.

Afterwards, he drove Heather to the exclusive Sharrow Bay Hotel at Ullswater in the Lake District where, two evenings later, he dropped onto one knee and proposed to her with the diamond and sapphire ring he'd bought in Jaipur the previous January.

Five days later, they faced the media outside Paul's now rather left-behind London house in Cavendish Avenue. He professed to have felt nervous about proposing and Heather said she'd been 'gobsmacked'. All they knew about the wedding as yet was that it would be 'sometime next year'. Heather said she didn't plan on using the title Lady McCartney ('I'm not into all that pretence') and refused photographers' requests to kiss her betrothed. 'We don't kiss to order. It's spontaneous.'

'How are your family taking the news?' one reporter shouted to Paul.

'All right,' he replied tersely, and didn't enlarge on the subject. 'We'd better be getting off now. Thank you very much.'

On 10 September, he was with Heather in New York as she received an award from *Redbook* magazine for her landmines campaign, in a ceremony attended by Hillary Clinton and the Duchess of York. Afterwards, he made one of the little off-the-cuff speeches for which he was becoming known.

Next morning, when a pair of hijacked airliners ploughed into the World Trade Center, the couple were aboard a scheduled flight at JFK Airport on the point of leaving for London. Through their window they could actually see the two silver towers, each with its obscene frond of grey smoke.

Only after they'd been evacuated from the plane and returned to Amagansett did the full horror become clear. The hundreds of market traders, office workers and restaurant staff, trapped on upper floors without hope of rescue. The last, heartbreaking voicemail messages to wives, husbands, parents and children. The decision of many to jump from eightieth- or ninetieth-floor windows, some hand-in-hand, rather than face the inferno within. The inconceivably rapid collapse of each tower in turn; the twin summits of the city's mythic skyline reduced in minutes to plunging dust.

Paul had more reason than most to love New York. It was where *The Ed Sullivan Show* had taken the Beatles into the stratosphere in 1964. And it had given him Linda.

Along with the victims inside the twin towers, 414 emergency workers, firefighters, police officers and paramedics had been buried by their fall, many while performing acts of extraordinary bravery. According to Heather, it was she who first suggested Paul should do a benefit concert for the bereaved families. He was initially reluctant, fearing he might be accused of opportunism to publicise his *Driving Rain* album.

When JFK reopened, Heather returned to London to fulfil a charity commitment, leaving him to ponder the totalitarian terrorism that had been born on that gloriously sunny September morning. As usual, words and chords came unbidden, and within minutes he had a song in the simple, anthemic style of which John had been such a master, expressing solidarity with New York and defiance of its barbaric ill-wishers. It was called simply 'Freedom'. Once he had that, he knew he must do the concert.

His first call was to the film producer Harvey Weinstein, who had remained a good friend despite the unhappy experience of *Give My Regards to Broad Street*. Weinstein proved to be already putting together such an event with the cable TV channel VH1. It was agreed that Paul would participate as co-organiser and headliner.

Other major rock names had felt similarly moved to do something. On 21 September, the main television networks joined forces to broadcast *America – A Tribute to Heroes*, a fund-raising telethon featuring, among others, Bruce Springsteen, Neil Young and Billy Joel. Then on 2 October, Radio City Music Hall staged Come Together, originally planned to mark what would have been John's sixty-first birthday, with appearances by Cyndi Lauper, Billy Preston and Alanis Morissette and a setlist heavy with Lennon–McCartney songs. This now became a 9/11 benefit, in the words of emcee Kevin Spacey, 'to keep John's memory alive and help rebuild the city'. Wherever he was, he must have been chortling to have got in before Paul.

When the Concert for New York City finally took place at Madison Square Garden on 20 October, the trauma had still barely abated. Beforehand, Paul tried to visit the mass grave now known as Ground Zero but even he was prevented from approaching it, though he could smell the smoke, melted office-partitions and death from several streets away.

The show was an immense parade of top music acts, headed by other Brits who'd found fortune in the Big Apple: David Bowie, Mick Jagger and Keith Richards, Eric Clapton, the Who. There were also appearances by Hollywood heavyweights Robert De Niro, Leonardo DiCaprio and Jim Carrey; and from television stars, top athletes and public figures like former president Bill Clinton and Mayor Rudy Giuliani, whose inspirational conduct on the awful day had contrasted so markedly with that of incumbent President George W. Bush.

Many among the 18,000 present were relatives or colleagues of the lost rescue workers and police. Paul and Heather had person-ally handed out tickets at fire stations and precinct houses. But the atmosphere was deliberately not funereal; there were even jokes about Osama bin Laden, the head of the al-Qaeda terrorist group, who had masterminded the atrocity. Paul had been especially keen on that element, instancing Liverpool during the Blitz of the Second World War and 'how they dealt with it – with humour and with music'.

He himself took the stage wearing a New York Fire Department T-shirt to perform 'Freedom' (which Heather would claim to have 'arranged a little bit'). Though every performer tried to match a song to the occasion, 'Let It Be' was the only possible finale, giving a comfort and sense of communality that had never been needed so much. In their hour of darkness, he truly seemed a light that shone on them.

During the next weeks, just one news story displaced 9/11 and the 'war on terror' declared by President Bush and blindly followed by Prime Minister Blair that was to have such dire consequences for the new century. On 29 November, George died from cancer, aged 58.

As with John's death 21 years earlier, the headlines were a size normally awarded to great politicians or heads of state. Paul faced the massed cameras in Sussex and, unlike after John's death, was word-perfect: 'I'm very sad, devastated. He was a lovely man . . . I grew up with him and I like to remember the great times we had together in Liverpool and with the Beatles, and ever since really. I'm privileged to have known him and I love him like he's my brother.'

They had last met a couple of weeks earlier at Staten Island University Hospital, New York, after George had learned that any further treatment was useless and that he wouldn't see another Christmas. Paul and Heather went to New York for the day by Concorde, and Paul sat beside George's bed, stroking his hand – something that would have been unimaginable in their macho, buttoned-up youth.

The sad irony of George's final days was that he was effectively homeless. He would not return to Britain, afraid that fans would hold a ghoulish vigil outside Friar Park, and the journey to his house on Maui in the Hawaiian islands was too complicated, exhausting and vulnerable to media-nuisance.

Obsessively private to the last, he had hired the celebrity security consultant Gavin de Becker to transport him someplace where he could meet his end with his wife and son in absolute seclusion. This end-of-the-roadie subsequently announced his death had occurred in Los Angeles, at 1971 Coldwater Canyon.

No such address existed: George had actually passed away at Paul's new property on Heather Road, Beverly Hills. In just that same way, when they were school friends at the Inny, he'd so often suggested, 'Why don't you come round to my house?'

Stella McCartney's career in fashion continued to be stellar. After only four years of designing for Chloé, she had launched her own label in a joint venture with Italy's glamour-soaked house of Gucci, which gave her total creative freedom. She was just 30, the same age at which her father had gone solo three decades earlier.

Stella still wanted to give Paul's relationship with Heather a chance, and so invited them both to her first collection under her own name that autumn. It was a tough decision, for her mother had been at her first show for Chloé in 1997 with only months left to live.

As Paul arrived, he greeted the cameras with the peace sign that he and Linda always used to make together, and Heather followed suit. There is of course no copyright on peace signs but to Stella, under the stress of the occasion, it seemed her mother's place was being usurped in the most blatant way. One of her friends later told the *Daily Mail*: 'She was so angry, she told her dad there was no way she was having Heather to the after-show party so they both had to miss it.'

From burning towers to dreaming spires: the first performance of Paul's oratorio *Ecce Cor Meum* took place at Oxford's Sheldonian Theatre only weeks after the Concert for New York City. It was sung by the Magdalen College choir, whom he had personally rehearsed, and conducted by the college's director of music, Bill Ives. The applause from the assembled academics was rapturous and at the end Paul was presented with a bouquet of flowers which, in its way, meant more to him than the most golden of discs.

Privately, he was unhappy with the performance, though blaming no one but himself. He'd composed much of the score on a synthesiser, unmindful that half the choir consisted of small boys, and many passages proved simply too tiring for them. Five more years would pass before he thought *Ecce Cor Meum* ready for a London premiere or release as an album.

At the beginning of 2002, he took Heather back to India to celebrate her thirty-fourth birthday. This time, they didn't travel around, but stayed at a luxurious lakeside resort in Kerala. On her birthday morning, Paul filled their cabin with flowers and gave her a sapphire and diamond bracelet to match her engagement ring.

Afterwards, Heather went to Vietnam on another landmine mission while he plunged into preparations for his first world tour since 1993. The ostensible purpose was to promote the *Driving Rain* album (to which 'Freedom' had become a last-minute addition). But really it marked an end to mourning and the start of a new era, for Heather was to go on the road with him just as Linda used to.

As the title of its live album would later announce, Paul McCartney was Back in the World.

Rather than use his excellent 1993 backing band, he formed yet another new one, re-hiring only Londoner Wix Wickens to play keyboards with the new title of musical director. The rest were seasoned American session men: lead guitar Rusty Anderson and drummer Abe Laboriel, Jr, both of whom had been on *Driving Rain*, and Brian Ray, a blond, suntanned young Californian doubling on guitar and bass. Ray was so awed by Paul's own bass-playing that 'I didn't dare look up from my fingering for about the first six months'.

However, there was no suggestion of Heather joining the band as Linda had, even though she possessed some skill on the saxophone. This time around, love wasn't that blind.

The first of two 'Back in the US' segments, which opened in Oakland, California, on 1 April, struck a determined note of novelty. Each show began with a performance by Cirque du Soleil, the young French-Canadian circus troupe which eschewed traditional and often cruel animal acts. As the Cirque's gold-painted acrobats and ballerinas performed aloft, remixes of Paul's dance music with Martin (Youth) Glover provided the soundtrack.

However, that was but a vigil to be patiently borne before the giant shadow of a violin bass loomed above the stage – and there once again were the eyes, still doe-like, the delicate jawline only slightly blurred, the hair as youthfully thick and shapely as ever, though now tending to not-quite-natural auburn, the T-shirt no longer saying 'GO VEGGIE' but 'NO MORE LANDMINES'. The worshipping mega-celebs sat row on row: Sylvester Stallone, Jack Nicholson, Michael Douglas, Brian Wilson. Women shrieked louder than 1963. Strong men's eyes filled with tears at the first notes of 'All My Loving'.

He felt it his mission to raise his audiences' spirits just as the Beatles had once, unknowingly, lightened the dark days after the Kennedy assassination. And it was no mere rock-star conceit. One woman he talked to in a meet-and-greet told him that after

9/11 she'd vowed never to fly again, yet had taken a plane to come and see him. And 'Freedom' was a show-stopper everywhere. 'Let's do it for all these fine people here tonight,' he'd tell the band as they went onstage, 'and keep this uplifting spirit going.'

George's death cast a lesser but still monumental shadow. Paul's tribute was to perform 'Something', his ex-bandmate's best-known song, not with its usual high emotion and big production but alone, plink-plonking on a ukulele, an instrument they both loved.

In May, he had to fly home briefly for an exhibition of his paintings at Liverpool's illustrious Walker Art Gallery. As teenagers, he and John would often play truant from school and college respectively to look at the Walker's Rembrandts, Poussins and Pre-Raphaelites. John, the so-called 'serious' artist, had later been widely exhibited, but never like this in his home city.

The Walker's Art of Paul McCartney exhibition (given premium place next to a display of Turners) comprised 70 canvases, painted over the past 20 years, and six sculptures made from driftwood picked up on the Sussex shore. The subjects were mostly landscapes, flowers and abstracts inspired by Celtic myth, though there were some rather self-conscious shockers such as *Tits On Fire*, *Running Legs With Penis* and *Bowie Spewing* – David Bowie being sick. The only one completed since Heather's advent, titled *Big Heart 1999*, was a red heart with a nude figure scratched on it.

At the press preview, Paul recalled his long-ago wanders through these same galleries with John, subtly mixing self-deprecation and yah-boo. 'If I'd said then, "I'm going to have an exhibition here someday," I think I know what he would have said . . . I'm not trying to impress anyone but myself. I think I've shown the world enough already.'

Heather was at every one of those first 27 American dates and every night Paul dedicated 'Heather' to her with its declaration of undying love: 'I could spend eternity beside your loving flame.' Yet he also mentioned Linda and aimed 'My Love', his emblematic song for her, at 'all the lovers in the house, and you know who you are'. The very lava lamp on top of Wix Wickens's keyboard was a memorial to the ones Linda always used to position around the stage.

It still amused him that – alone in the nightly singing-along masses – Heather knew almost nothing about the Beatles and recognised almost nothing he'd written for them. 'She hears something on the radio and says, "Hey, that's pretty good. Is it one of yours?"' he laughed. 'I say, "Yes, it's 'Get Back'."'

The documentary camera that shadowed them caught some affectionate moments, arm-in-arm in backstage corridors, sharing sushi aboard the tour's private jet or making friends with a chimpanzee (to which Paul couldn't resist giving a private keyboard-recital). But there were some barbed exchanges also. One hotel-suite scene shows him doing a telephone interview while Heather, a few feet away, pores over a laptop. He's musing how once life on the road used to be all about 'picking up girls', but he wouldn't try it these days. 'It's more than my life's worth. I'd get hammered.'

'You wouldn't want to,' Heather shouts from her laptop.

'I can't talk to you and do an interview,' Paul answers with rather strained politeness, but she persists: 'Say you wouldn't want to or I'll keep interrupting!'

He resorts to joke northern male chauvinism: 'Shouting from the kitchen! Get back to the dishes, woman!'

In the early hours of 18 May, they checked into Miami's Turnberry Isle hotel after the final show in that US segment. Soon afterwards, the sound of a fierce argument in their suite reached security guards patrolling the gardens below. One later claimed to have heard Paul shout, 'I don't want to marry you! The wedding's off! We'll cancel it!' He then appeared on the balcony and threw Heather's Indian diamond and sapphire engagement ring over the rail.

Contacted by hotel reception, he initially said nothing was wrong but then admitted a ring had been 'lost' and requested help in finding it. After a lengthy search of the garden by staff on all fours – in pouring rain – and deployment of metal detectors, the ring finally came to light under a bush. Paul, by then back in Britain, bought a first-class air ticket for hotel manager Rudolph Gimmi to deliver it and sent a £1500 tip to the finder.

There had been too many witnesses for the story not to get into the papers, and 'MACCA THROWS HEATHER'S RING OUT OF HOTEL BEDROOM. EXCLUSIVE' was the front-page splash in that Sunday's *News of the World*. Little credence was given to Heather's claim that they'd merely been 'having a joke with the ring . . . playing catch with it'.

If rock had been in mourning in 2001, this year in Britain at least it had something to celebrate. On 3 June, the Queen's Golden Jubilee was marked by a concert in the spacious and usually strictly private garden behind Buckingham Palace. The 50-year sovereign herself attended with Prince Philip, the Prince of Wales, his sons, William and Harry, and Tony and Cherie Blair. Twelve thousand spectators were admitted to the garden, the sound was relayed to about a million more outside in The Mall and the surrounding parks, and the event was televised live to a further 20 million.

The bill, appropriately enough, included Queen – whose guitarist, Brian May, kicked things off by playing 'God Save the Queen' on the palace roof – Elton John, Ray Davies, Phil Collins, Rod Stewart, Eric Clapton, Tony Bennett, Brian Wilson, Ben Elton and Dame Edna Everage. Paul, naturally, was the headliner, completing yet another extraordinary cycle in his life. When the Coronation had taken place in 1953, he'd won a prize for his essay about it.

His Golden Jubilee performance included a further tribute to George, though only hardcore Beatlemaniacs would have recognised its note of contrition. With Clapton he duetted on 'While My Guitar Gently Weeps' from the fractious White Album, when George had brought in his mate Eric partly as moral support against a certain bossy bass-player. He also cheekily slipped in 'Her Majesty', his one-verse Valentine from the end of *Abbey Road*.

The 'pretty nice girl' received it all with the same equanimity she had bestowed on Commonwealth prime ministers and safety-pin factories throughout her reign. 'Will you be doing this next year?' Paul joked to her.

'Not in my garden,' the Queen replied tartly.

The contretemps with Heather in Miami had been patched up and on 11 June, a week before Paul's sixtieth birthday, they were married in Ireland. The venue was Castle Leslie, a seventeenth-century pile near the town of Monaghan, from which his maternal grandfather, Owen Mohan, had emigrated to Liverpool.

A shadow was cast over the event by yet another middle-aged woman claiming to be Paul's love child from a brief and forgotten liaison long ago. A 42-year-old Frenchwoman named Michelle Le Vallier alleged he had impregnated her mother, Monique, while he was 'a struggling musician' in London.

Le Vallier had changed her surname to McCartney, recording a song entitled 'I Wanna Be a Beatle' and, as final proof of her pedigree, playing a left-handed bass. Unluckily, the date on her birth certificate was 5 April 1960, which meant Paul would have had to father her in July 1959, when he was still a 17-year-old schoolboy in Liverpool.

The media were expecting the wedding – *Hello!* magazine had already unsuccessfully bid £1.5 million for exclusive photographic access – but believed it would be at Paul's home on Long Island. Even when he and Heather arrived at Castle Leslie amid major catering preparations, he refused to admit what was going on. In the end, he was pre-empted by the castle's 84-year-old owner, Sir Jack Leslie, an eccentric baronet who enjoyed bopping in local discos. 'It's a secret,' Sir Jack said in a television interview, 'but it's on Tuesday.'

Massed photographers laid siege to the castle walls, some possibly hoping to see a ring come sailing over its battlements. On the day, 300 guests, including Sir George Martin, Twiggy and Chrissie Hynde as well as Paul's numerous Liverpool relations, had instructions to report to London-Heathrow for a special flight to Belfast. Ringo made his own way by private jet.

Mike McCartney was best man – just as at Paul's and Linda's

wedding – and all the children attended. Their father had hoped their various talents might contribute to the occasion, Stella designing Heather's wedding dress, Mary taking photographs, James playing music and daughter Heather creating some fabrics or ceramics. But he had not pressed the point. In a family group photograph, taken by Paul's former housekeeper Rose Martin, none of the four had a celebratory air, especially not Mary and Stella.

Rather than a Stella McCartney creation, Heather wore a white lace dress she had designed herself and her bridal bouquet included 11 pink 'Paul McCartney' roses. A bridal photograph was later released to the press in return for a donation to Adopt-A-Minefield. Paul's buttonhole was a sprig of lavender from a bush his dad had planted.

A lavish vegetarian meal was served on gold plates, which the guests were allowed to keep as souvenirs. Paul's converted trawler, the *Barnaby Rudge*, had been brought over from Rye and moored on the castle lake, bedecked with flowers. After the speeches and toasts, the newly-weds went on board amid hails of confetti, and sailed, or chugged, romantically off into the sunset.

A landing-stage specially installed for the occasion was known afterwards as the McCartney Jetty. It had been meant as only a temporary structure, but would outlast the marriage.

51

'You don't say a lot, do you, Paul?'

A producer friend of Paul's, a fellow Liverpudlian and pupil at the Inny, was later to recall him confiding rather wistfully what he'd hoped from his second wife. 'He said that now he was older, all he wanted was someone to be there every night when he came off-stage and say, "You were wonderful, darling."' On that score alone, he could hardly have made a worse choice.

True to her promise on their engagement, Heather did not style herself Lady McCartney; rather, she became Heather Mills Mc-Cartney, to distinguish her from Paul's daughter and also signify that she was still a celebrity and a person in her own right (though the point might have been more forcibly made if she'd continued as Heather Mills).

The Mills McCartney name was immediately employed on a new American edition of her 1995 autobiography, *Out on a Limb*, intended to counter the unfavourable press stories about her and raise money for Adopt-A-Minefield. Now retitled *A Single Step*, it contained four brief extra chapters and an epilogue covering the remarkable turn her life had taken since. The book ended at Castle Leslie on a note of rosy optimism: 'Maybe I'm finally learning to slow down . . . Now that I am finally going to settle down with my fella of a lifetime, I want to have time to enjoy it.'

As Paul wound up the second instalment of his Driving America tour in late 2002, Heather was doing an intensive round of media interviews to promote *A Single Step* and Adopt-A-Minefield (to which she had pledged its royalties). And somehow, it was she not he who kept grabbing the headlines.

Back in Britain, the tabloids were by now in full cry after her. The *Sun* had published her wedding picture alongside one of her modelling topless during the 1980s. The *Mail On Sunday* had gotten to Charles Stapley, an actor with whom her mother had lived after leaving her father (and who'd been in the TV soap *Crossroads* when Paul wrote its theme music).

Now America's top magazines and news shows offered her a chance to bite back. And by now she had some ammunition for her complaints about tabloid 'lies'. The *Sunday Mirror* had recently run a story about her supposed investigation by Britain's Charity Commissioners over the way relief funds for the Gujarat earthquake victims in 2001 had been handled. The *Mirror* had been forced to withdraw the allegation and was about to pay damages which, she told *New York* magazine, would 'drain them of all funds'. (Hardly: they paid £50,000.)

To *New York* magazine's interviewer, Andrew Goldman, she refuted the many stories in the British press about how Paul's children disliked and mistrusted her. She spoke to her namesake Heather every day, she said, and got on so 'brilliantly' with Stella that Stella had recently put out a press release saying so. Goldman later checked with the Stella McCartney company PR and was told that Stella never discussed family matters and no such release could have been issued.

True to form, her two most important television interviews left sharply conflicting impressions. The first was with ABC's Barbara Walters, who'd been so captivated by her in London two years earlier as to make comparisons with Princess Diana. Now, Walters recalls, she was a prima donna who arrived with a PA – her sister Fiona – and a female bodyguard, was 'impossible' with the show's producers and complained even about the temperature of her glass of water. (It needed to be at room temperature as she suffered from acid reflux.)

Paul had accompanied her to the studio, and watched the

interview take place, some of it in terms less than flattering to him. 'I am married to the most famous man in the world and that is very unfortunate for me . . . This is a man who has had his own way his entire life. When you become famous at 19, it's sometimes hard to listen to other people's opinions.'

This time around, Walters reverted to her usual tough inquisitorial mode. But when she tried to broach some of the issues raised by the British press, she found 'a whole other side' to the open, charming interviewee she remembered. Afterwards, she complained to her producer how 'tough' Heather had been, not realising Paul was in earshot. 'I like tough women,' he said.

The other crucial TV booking, on 30 October, was CNN's *Larry King Live*. A year ago, she had appeared with Paul, coming in only for the final segment and keeping a respectfully low profile. Now she faced a solo hour with King whose persona was that of some old-time city editor who stood no bullshit from anyone.

Yet he was surprisingly easy on her, accepting her assertion that *A Single Step* was a wholly different book from *Out on a Limb* because of its 'many more chapters', and greeting the story of the difficult upbringing told in its early pages with none of the scepticism now being voiced elsewhere. Once again, Heather reprised its most shocking episode: how, aged seven, she and a school friend had been kidnapped by their swimming teacher and imprisoned for three days in his flat, Heather being forced to watch him masturbate while the friend suffered actual sexual abuse.

To the catalogue of family nightmares, she added one previously unheard: that her mother had lost a leg at the very same age she'd lost hers, but that it had 're-attached'; and that even while her mother was on crutches, her father still beat her up or pushed her into boiling hot baths.

'Did you ever prostitute yourself?' was King's most searching question, in reference to the time she claimed to have lived on the streets.

'No, never,' Heather replied. 'Never.'

The talk then turned to her self-designed prosthetic left leg, 'which', she suddenly said, 'I'll pop off if you don't mind.' With that, she performed the trick she so often did in amputee-wards, handing the detached limb to King, then baring her stump and inviting him to feel it. 'Wow! Does that not turn Paul off?' he asked as he did so. She repeated that, disability or no, every man she'd ever met had proposed to her inside a week.

Such a display would have appalled the squeamish British, but America loved it. 'You're a gutsy broad, Heather,' King told her, so enamoured that she became his stand-in on the show a few months later. To give her appearance maximum impact, Paul fixed for her to interview the normally reclusive screen legend Paul Newman.

Since *The Beatles Anthology*, things between Paul and Yoko had gone very quiet. Anyone who asked him how they got on nowadays (as Larry King had) received only diplomatic soufflé-speak: 'We don't not get on. But you know, it's like some people you may not be destined to become good buddies with. I don't kind of ring up . . . "Hey, Yoko, what's happening, babe?"'

But, as was all too evident, they didn't fall over themselves to be in each other's company, even when they happened to be in the same place at the same time – even if that place happened to be Liverpool. The previous July, Paul had been there to greet the Queen, as she stopped off on her Golden Jubilee tour of Britain, and show her round his exhibition at the Walker Art Gallery. Yoko had been there to open the new terminal at the just-renamed John Lennon Airport.

It was an unprecedented honour: no airport in Britain had been named after a person before, and none has been since. With it went the first municipal statue of a Beatle erected in Liverpool, a seven-and-a-half-foot figure of John surveying the check-in hall. The airport logo borrowed an apposite line from 'Imagine': 'above us only sky'.

Some questioned why the honour hadn't been shared with Paul, who'd done so much for Liverpool, or else given to the Beatles collectively. The city rather feebly responded that its purpose was 'to celebrate an entire life', but Paul gave no sign of feeling snubbed – on the contrary, was all in favour of the rebrand.

A different issue with Yoko hung in the air, one about which he felt as strongly now as when it had arisen in 1995. During the compilation of the second *Anthology* CD, he'd asked for the Lennon–McCartney credit on 'Yesterday' to be reversed since he'd written and recorded it without any input from John. George and Ringo made no objection but Yoko vetoed the idea, so he'd dropped it.

For all his oceanic fame, it still galled him that half 'Yesterday's' royalties went to John's estate and that on one statement he'd seen, Yoko earned more from it than he did. Nor could it any longer be argued that he benefited in the same way from John's compositions in which he'd had no part. A 1997 Lennon compilation had included 'Give Peace a Chance', which John had written and recorded with Yoko during their 1969 Montreal bed-in but, because Beatle rules still applied, had always borne the Lennon–McCartney label. Now the 'McCartney' had disappeared.

In November 2002, he released *Back in the U.S.*, a double live album of the previous seven months' American concerts. Nineteen of the Beatles songs on it, including 'Eleanor Rigby', 'Hey Jude' and 'Yesterday', were credited to 'Paul McCartney and John Lennon'. The result was the first public row with Yoko he'd ever had. Her spokesman, Elliott Mintz, accused him of 'an attempt to rewrite history' while her lawyer, Peter Shukat, warned of 'legal recourse' to undo his 'ridiculous, absurd and petty' act, though none was ever to materialise.

Media opinion overwhelmingly took Yoko's side: a novelty in itself. Paul was criticised for small-mindedness, overweening vanity and tampering with a sacred treasure; 'McCartney and Lennon', one columnist wrote, sounded as unnatural as Hammerstein and Rodgers or Sullivan and Gilbert. Even Ringo weighed in against him, calling his action 'underhand'. He himself affected surprise at the furore, protesting that he wasn't trying to diminish John's contribution to their partnership, just provide 'correct labelling'. 'The truth is that all this is much ado about nothing and there is no need for anyone to get their knickers in a twist.'

Ringo's comment on the affair caused no rift between the two surviving Beatles, for on 29 November they appeared together in a memorial concert for George, organised by his widow, Olivia, at the Royal Albert Hall to mark the first anniversary of his death. The impressive stage-ensemble included both a symphony and an Indian orchestra, George's sitar-teacher and mentor Ravi Shankar, his best friend Eric Clapton and his son Dhani, now the image of the shy lad Paul had brought into the Quarrymen in 1957.

Paul's performance included his ukulele version of 'Something', segueing into a big production that exactly replicated the one on *Abbey Road*. He also played 'For You Blue', a little-remembered George track from the *Let It Be/Get Back* sessions in 1969.

On that score, at least, a long-standing McCartney grievance had finally been assuaged. Thirty-four years later, he still fumed over the way the album's producer-salvager, Phil Spector, had drenched two of his finest tracks, 'The Long and Winding Road' and 'Let It Be', in sickly orchestration and celestial choirs, and how his protests had been overridden by the other Beatles and Allen Klein. Now there was to be a remixed and remastered version, *Let It Be ... Naked*, with 'The Long and Winding Road' scrubbed clean of Spector's effects ('Let It Be' in its original hymn-like version had already appeared on *Anthology 3*).

Let It Be ... Naked would go platinum in the US (and double platinum in Japan) in 2003, though many critics still preferred the overdubbed version. By that time, Phil Spector's career as 'Pop Music's Svengali' had come to a bloody end. He was about to go on trial for murder after the body of a young actress was found in his mock-medieval California mansion, shot in the mouth. In 2009, he would be convicted and sentenced to 19 years to life.

Bizarrely for someone who owned so many houses, Paul embarked on his second marriage with an accommodation problem. Heather, understandably, did not want to move into Blossom Wood Farm, the home he'd shared with Linda, where her presence still lingered in every comfortably shabby couch, well-used kitchen-utensil and invunerable chicken or duck out in the yard.

The newly-weds were living temporarily across the valley at Woodlands Farm, whose grounds contained an expansive lake. Here, at Heather's behest, Paul was building a home totally unlike any he and Linda had created – a two-bedroom Norwegian-style log cabin. So anxious was he for them to move in that the build was being rushed through without the necessary permissions from the local planning authority. But thanks to luxurious extras like a gym annexe and a 'lakeside pavilion' for watching wildlife, it still was not finished.

His estate in Kintyre was even more rife with memories of Linda and, anyway, its remoteness and solitude held little attraction for the urban-minded, hyperactive Heather. The local people had received a foretaste of the way things now stood when a memorial garden to Linda was opened in Campbeltown, whose streets she loved to wander with her camera. The centrepiece was a statue of her, cuddling one of the lambs that had converted Paul and her to vegetarianism. Paul paid for the statue but did not attend its unveiling as he was performing in Mexico City.

A group of local citizens, headed by the town veterinarian, had started a fund to build an art gallery in Linda's memory, expecting that, too, would receive his support. But none came, so the project was abandoned.

With Heather, the media glare had switched to the blizzards of money she'd supposedly walked into. She was said to have alienated Paul's children even further by refusing to sign a prenuptial agreement setting out what she would receive in the event of divorce, thereby posing a potential threat to their inheritance. In fact, just before the wedding, he'd written her a letter with a ballpark figure for such a settlement, should the marriage fail. But in an interview with *Vanity Fair*, she maintained that she'd offered to sign a prenup, 'to prove I love him for him', but he wouldn't let her. 'I believe every woman should have a reserve [of money] because you never know what will happen in life. I'll never be dependent on Paul.'

Just the same, he continued to treat her with an extraordinary largesse, starting her on an annual allowance of £360,000 in April 2003, handing her a joint credit card on his account at the exclusive Coutts bank, giving her jewellery worth £264,000 in 2004 and altering his will in her favour. On top of that, she had received a lump sum of £250,000 in December 2002 and another a year later to help her keep up her donations to charity, now that her former worldwide fundraising activities were on hold.

Paul would later maintain that he considered their marriage to be 'for ever', though its volatility caused him a nagging uncertainty from the beginning. They had stopped using contraception on their honeymoon, hoping to start a family despite Heather's previous two ectopic pregnancies. She suffered a miscarriage in 2002 but they persevered and in February the following year she fell pregnant again.

Between March and June, he was on a 33-concert European tour, once again accompanied by Heather and including two venues he'd never imagined. On 10 May, he performed inside Rome's Colosseum for 400 people who'd paid £1000 each to support Adopt-A-Landmine and hear 'The Fool on the Hill' and 'Band on the Run' echo around 2000-year-old terraces where crowds had once watched Christians being torn to pieces by lions. The next night, he played outside the Colosseum walls to 500,000 people massed in the Fori Imperiali, with whom he finally had to plead to stop demanding encores and go home.

Two weeks later, in Moscow's Red Square, he was greeted by an ecstatic young multitude for whom pop music was no longer a cultural crime. Beforehand, he and a red trouser-suited Heather were given a guided tour of the Kremlin by President Vladimir Putin, to whom Paul in return gave a private recital of 'Let It Be'. The closest John and Yoko had ever come to a Russian leader on their peace campaigns in the Sixties was sending Leonid Brezhnev an acorn.

Heather was certainly there each night when he came offstage, but not just to say 'You were wonderful, darling.' Band members who'd never dare suggest he change a semiquaver were amazed to see him paying close attention as she gave him notes on his performance. 'Yeah, don't be surprised because she does,' he told an American reporter. 'She knows music and she has a good ear and she has input.'

In Britain by now, her past was no longer just fodder for prurient tabloids but the stuff of serious investigative journalism. On 7 May, Channel 4 had aired a documentary entitled *The Real Mrs McCartney*, made up of interviews with various figures from her earlier days whose cumulative effect could hardly have been more damaging to her and embarrassing to Paul.

The programme-makers tracked down a woman named Ros Ashton who'd introduced her into the circle of wealthy Middle Eastern businessmen headed by Ashton's former lover, Adnan Khashoggi. 'Heather's ambition,' said Ashton, 'was to meet a wealthy man, either Arab, English, French, Spanish, whatever would give her wealth and status.' Paul's lawyers had vainly tried to stop the broadcast, which predictably set off a further round of stories in the newspapers. He still firmly refused to believe any of them, bolstered by the many messages of support on Heather's website.

On 30 August, Stella McCartney was married to the magazine publisher Alasdhair Willis. Stella's choice of the Isle of Bute as a venue – just a few miles east of Kintyre – seemed a tacit assurance that the McCartneys hadn't completely forsaken the Scottish Highlands. The guests included Madonna, Kate Moss and Liv Tyler and the secrecy beforehand and security on the day were even fiercer than at Paul's Irish nuptials the previous year. Afterwards, a photographer caught him with seven-months-pregnant Heather in an atypical ungainly posture, off-balance and grimacing weirdly: the first bad picture in his entire life.

It would not be his only first that summer. The evening of 19 September found him having dinner in a Soho restaurant with his publicist Geoff Baker and his PA John Hammel. London at that time was being treated to the spectacle of the American illusionist David Blaine undergoing a 44-day fast while shut inside a perspex capsule suspended beside Tower Bridge. After dinner, Paul and his two aides joined the curious, often mocking spectators whom Blaine's stunt were attracting around the clock.

An *Evening Standard* photographer, Kevin Wheal, had been tipped off about the visit by Geoff Baker. As Paul arrived, Baker called Wheal over for a 'snatched' picture like 10,000 others he'd endured without demur. But this time, he pushed Wheal away, shouting, 'Fuck off! I've come to see this stupid cunt [the fasting David Blaine] and you are not going to take a picture of me tonight.' He then rounded on Baker and told him he was fired.

The fracas did not end there. There was a scuffle between Wheal and John Hammel, after which both lodged complaints of assault (though nothing came of them). A bystander asked Paul if he could shake his hand and was also told to 'fuck off'. A police officer called to the scene found him 'rather drunk and very abusive'.

Afterwards, he tried to laugh off the episode as just a high-spirited boys' night out while Geoff Baker insisted he hadn't really been fired and that he, not Paul, had been the worse for drink. The fact remained that at 61, the shining exception to drunken, yobbish rock stars had apparently started behaving like the very worst of them. The fan he'd told to fuck off, 32-year-old Vaseem Adnan, was widely quoted: 'I feel insulted, belittled and aggrieved. He is an extremely cheap man for doing that.'

He and Heather spent the final weeks of her pregnancy at his London house, 7 Cavendish Avenue, St John's Wood, which she had by now had completely redecorated and which was handily located just around the corner from the St John and St Elizabeth private hospital. There on 28 October she was safely delivered of a seven-pound girl by Caesarian section. Paul's fourth child received the names Beatrice after Heather's deceased mother and Milly after his stalwart Liverpool aunt.

The early summer of 2004 was devoted to a European tour whose 14 outdoor venues included St Petersburg's Palace Square, in front of the Russian tsars' old winter palace. It was his three thousandth stage performance since his debut with the Quarrymen at the New Clubmoor Hall in 1957, when he'd got sticky fingers and mucked up his solo in 'Guitar Boogie'.

The tour finale was an appearance at the Glastonbury Festival – another first, but this time of a more positive kind. He'd somehow missed out on all the great Sixties pop festivals like Monterey, Woodstock and the Isle of Wight, and always felt a bit inferior to other rock giants as a result. In fact, he'd offered to play Glastonbury in 2003, but the prime Saturday-night spot on its Pyramid Stage had already been claimed by Radiohead.

His appearance, on 26 June, caused a bigger than usual bout of pre-show nerves. The festival's younger competition included Muse, Morrissey, Sister Sledge, Joss Stone and PJ Harvey, and Oasis were to headline on the Pyramid Stage the night before he did. During the run-up, someone asked how he was preparing for the event; he answered wryly that he'd been preparing for it all his life.

Glastonbury weather is traditionally atrocious and Paul came onstage after a day of torrential rain which had turned the Somerset farmland to a swamp. He still drew a capacity crowd of 120,000 which stood fast throughout the further squalls that punctuated his set, waving banners so numerous, he would recall, 'it looked like the Battle of Agincourt'.

The assembled critics had been poised to file snappy pieces about old pop legends who didn't know when to quit and the irrelevance of Sixties nostalgia to the twenty-first century. But by the end of 'Hey Jude', they were na-nah-nahing along with everyone else, some holding up mobile phones so that colleagues unlucky enough to be elsewhere could listen in.

'Even those whose Glastos number in double figures,' said the *NME*, 'have never seen, heard or felt the love like the crowd on this night.' The paper had meant to put Oasis on the cover of its next issue, but hurriedly substituted a picture of Paul. The *Guardian* found his hippy-oriented onstage patter embarrassing, but could not fault his music, concluding that 'he could perform puppetry of the penis as long as he followed it with "Eleanor Rigby"'.

He was, by any measure, the world's most beloved and sought-after entertainer. Yet when he shared a stage with his wife, the spotlight showed an increasing tendency to desert him. That autumn, the London *Sunday Times Magazine* initiated the most thorough investigation into Heather's past thus far. The author was Russell Miller, a star contributor whom it had previously assigned to interview Paul about the *Liverpool Oratorio*.

As background, Miller attended the fourth annual Adopt-A-Minefield fund-raiser hosted by the McCartneys, which took place in October at LA's Century Plaza hotel. The $1000-per-ticket gala brought out top Hollywood stars like Michael Douglas and Catherine Zeta-Jones, Jack Nicholson, Rosanna Arquette and Andy Garcia. Paul was to provide the entertainment with Neil Young. But from beginning to end, as Miller later wrote, 'it was Heather's show'.

A succession of opening speakers offered gushing tributes to her ('Calling her my friend is a great honour . . .'; 'I am totally awed by her kindness and love . . .'). Two giant screens showed film of her visiting amputee-hospitals in Cambodia. Then, stepping up to the lectern 'with all the confidence of an international diplomat about to address the United Nations', she delivered a lengthy address, variously invoking the names of Princess Diana, Vladimir Putin and Colin Powell, calling for a Democratic victory in the coming presidential election and chiding the assembled celebs ('You people', as she called them) for still not having put a woman in the White House.

She went on to hijack the charity auction that was supposed to have been conducted by the talk show host Jay Leno, first auctioning her own Valentino gown, then wresting the microphone away from Leno to invite bids for his underpants. In the goody-bags under every chair were a copy of her new autobiography, *A Single Step*, and a magazine containing a long interview with her.

Paul's eventual performance with Neil Young provided some tangible return on the $1000 tickets – but, it was felt, not nearly enough. 'I might not have put up the dough,' one disgruntled guest remarked, 'if I'd known there were going to be two hours of Mrs McCartney and only 45 minutes of her husband.'

Russell Miller's *Sunday Times Magazine* article about Heather, 'The Girl Can't Help It', was published the following month. It proved a devastatingly deadpan chronicle of 'how this former model [had] managed to position herself between Princess Di and Mother Teresa in the spectrum of angels', listing the men she'd allegedly bewitched then dumped before meeting Paul, the dubious company she'd sometimes kept, and the many times her version of events had been at odds with reality.

In particular, Miller looked at the early life of Dickensian hardship that had supposedly engendered her desire to help others, finding discrepancies no one had picked up before. For example, the school friend with whom, as a seven-year-old, she claimed to have been imprisoned by a perverted swimming teacher called her account 'wildly exaggerated' – indeed, was currently suing her for breach of privacy.

And the most dramatic, pitiable section of her CV now seemed blown apart with the efficiency of any landmine. According to both her autobiographies, she'd become a penniless teenage runaway at 13. However, Miller's researches indicated that during the time when she was supposedly working for a travelling funfair and sleeping in a cardboard box she'd been attending school normally with her sister. She would later answer this by saying her mother had kept her on the school register even though she'd been absent.

Miller ended by pointing out 'the great irony of the fantasy life that Heather Mills McCartney has constructed for herself':

With her brains, beauty, energy, ambition, courage and talent, she could surely have got where she is today without rewriting her life-story. She clawed her way out of an unhappy childhood, started out with nothing, shamelessly made use of her ability to bewitch men, turned a horrific accident to her advantage, became a minor celebrity in her own right and married Paul

McCartney. The true story is just as remarkable as the fantasy.

That Christmas of 2004, Paul partnered her on a celebrity charity edition of the TV game show *Who Wants to Be a Millionaire?*, playing on behalf of Adopt-A-Minefield. Their Christmas Eve appearance ran out of time, so had to be continued on Christmas Day, and netted £32,000, enough to provide 1066 children with artificial limbs.

It was a further sign of his commitment to a worthwhile cause and wholehearted support of his wife. Yet many viewers were disconcerted to see Paul McCartney bracketed with run-of-the-mill celebs like Sir Alex Ferguson and Eamonn Holmes, and sitting silent on his high stool as Heather chattered unstoppably to the presenter, Chris Tarrant.

'You don't say a lot, do you, Paul?' Tarrant said at one point, not entirely joking.

52

'She could not afford to sue all the newspapers she would like to'

The apogee of Heather's television career in a positive sense was her appearance on BBC1's prestigious *Question Time* in February 2005. She was the kind of left-field activist with whom the programme occasionally varied its parade of heavyweight politicians and journalists, and the idea of Paul being there even by proxy guaranteed a bumper audience. Unawed by fellow panellists who included the Tory shadow Defence Secretary Nicholas Soames, the Liberal Democrat Scottish affairs spokesman John Thurso and the controversial black MP Diane Abbott, she aired her plentiful views on current issues such as Prince Charles's engagement to Camilla Parker-Bowles, Britain's bid to host the 2012 Olympics and the recent ban on fox hunting.

In the BBC's advance publicity, she was said – yet again – to have been nominated for a Nobel Peace Prize in 1996 for her relief work in former Yugoslavia. Russell Miller had attempted to verify this claim for his *Sunday Times* article but nominees for Nobel prizes, unlike those for Oscars or Grammys, are not announced and the existing laureates who form the judging panel are sworn to absolute confidentiality. 'With the best will in the world,' Miller concluded, 'it is hard to believe these worthies had heard of Heather in 1995.'

One indisputably genuine honour, held jointly with Paul in

recognition of their work for Adopt-A-Minefield, was that of United Nations Goodwill Ambassador. Unfortunately, goodwill was not something she generated much of nowadays.

In the media, questions about her life before she met Paul had given way to outrage at her supposedly detrimental effects on him – all very much what Linda had suffered during the Seventies. She was thought to have cheapened the classiest of pop stars by pressuring him into appearing on brassy TV shows like *Who Wants to Be a Millionaire?*, persuading him to dye his hair and have plastic surgery (a plastic surgeon in California instanced the level of his earlobes as irrefutable proof that he'd 'had work done'), even making him change the order of the Lennon–McCartney credit on the *Back in the U.S.* album. And if all that wasn't enough for the female columnists who were her principal assailants, why did she have to cling so possessively to his arm whenever they appeared in public?

She had also been widely blamed for Paul's sacking of Geoff Baker after 15 years as his loyal (and highly effective) PR man. Baker was said to loathe her for the damage she'd done to his carefully-nurtured McCartney image while she felt threatened by his closeness to Paul; a bond sealed by their shared enthusiasm for pot.

Baker took his dismissal in a gentlemanly spirit, forbearing to sell his memoirs to any of the tabloids who bid for them or utter a word against Paul or Heather in public. He had been a journalist before entering PR and now returned to his old profession as editor of *Golf Course News* magazine with a brief to 'sex it up'. This allowed him to give some vent to his feelings, albeit to a niche audience; the first cover under his editorship showed a Heather lookalike with a golf ball wedged in her cleavage.

As they had been trained to do since infancy, Mary, Stella, James and Heather McCartney made no public comment about their stepmother any more than on other aspects of Paul's life. But there were constant press stories from unnamed 'insiders' and 'sources' about their common dislike of Heather, dismay at her seemingly illimitable influence over him and anger at how, no longer content with amputees and landmines, she seemed intent on usurping their mother's place in the field of animal rights.

She had become not only a patron of Linda's beloved PETA organisation, but was the face of its current advertising campaign against the clothing trade's use of dog and cat fur (slogan: 'If you wouldn't wear your dog, please don't wear any fur'). In addition, Paul had introduced her to Viva!, the vegetarian pressure group to whose founder, Juliet Gellatley, he had presented the first Linda McCartney Award at that fateful Dorchester Hotel ceremony in 1999. Recently, she and Gellatley had appeared together at Oxford University's renowned Union debating society, showing horrific film footage of dogs being skinned to make fur collars and cuffs.

Paul at this stage still seemed every inch the loyal and protective husband. In February 2005, he wrote a lengthy 'note' to the many supporters Heather still had via her website, dealing with 'the cruel suggestions that flow from these [journalists'] pens' point by point.

He admitted 'colouring' his hair, but said he'd been doing so 'with varying degrees of success' for years before Heather's advent. Nor had he undergone plastic surgery at her behest, no matter what might be said about the orientation of his earlobes. His desire to reverse the Lennon–McCartney credit likewise dated from 1995, four years before he'd met her, and, anyway, was 'something I don't have a problem with any more'.

Geoff Baker's firing likewise had been nothing to do with her, but the result of a growing 'instability' on Baker's part, which had come to a head with the David Blaine incident. Their appearances on *Who Wants to Be a Millionaire?* had been a joint decision, one Paul claimed to have thoroughly enjoyed. 'It's an insult to my intelligence to imagine me being coerced into something like that.'

Heather gripped his arm not out of possessiveness but because floor-surfaces could be slippery and someone with a prosthetic leg often needed 'a little help from a friend . . . One of the most shocking recent statements,' he continued, 'was that "the best thing that ever happened to her was losing her leg". Imagine losing a leg and dealing with it as bravely as Heather has done, and having to read that on top of it!' Finally, the reports of his children disliking and resenting her were pure calumny. 'In fact, we get on great and anyone who knows our family can see that for themselves.'

On 2 July, he headlined at Live 8, a giant international concert to mark the twentieth anniversary of Live Aid and send a message to the current G8 summit of Western leaders that famine remained a pressing world problem. The show was staged simultaneously in London's Hyde Park and at nine other venues and featured 150 bands, totalling 1250 musicians, with guest appearances by the UN Secretary-General Kofi Annan and the founder of the Microsoft corporation, Bill Gates. Paul, in Hyde Park, provided the overture with 'Sgt. Pepper's Lonely Hearts Club Band', backed by U2, and its finale with 'Hey Jude'.

There, too, in the backstage VIP area, came the first public sign that his wife and grown-up children did not get on quite as 'great' as he'd claimed. At one moment, Stella was seen to turn pointedly away from Heather as if unwilling to speak to her father in her presence or run the risk of being photographed with her.

Stella and her siblings could take comfort from the fact that, after barely three years, the marriage was looking far from idyllic. Whereas disagreements between Paul and their mother had been few and far between, and generally kept private, his rows with Heather were frequent, angry shouting matches in front of them or embarrassed employees.

Still, he continued to show her great generosity over and above the £360,000 per year annual allowance and the Coutts joint credit card. In 2002 and 2003, he had made her two cash gifts totalling £500,000 which enabled her to purchase a luxurious riverside apartment in the Thames Reach complex in west London for use as an office. His largesse extended to members of her family: he took out a mortgage to buy her sister, and now PA, Fiona, a

£421,000 house, and bought her cousin, Sonya, a £193,000 property in Southampton.

Characteristically, his first outward qualms about the relationship were expressed through music. In September 2005, he released a new album, *Chaos and Creation in the Backyard,* packaged with yet another dose of Beatley nostalgia. The cover was a black and white photo by his brother Michael of his schoolboy self in the backyard at 20 Forthlin Road (titled 'Our Kid Through Mum's Net Curtains') sitting with his guitar under lines of washing pegged out by their diligent dad.

The producer was Nigel Godrich, a young British musician/ engineer best-known for his close association with Radiohead. Unlike any other producer since George Martin, Godrich refused to be overawed by working with Paul McCartney, dismissing his stage band from the sessions, even daring to suggest some of his new songs weren't quite up to standard and should be rethought.

Paul initially bridled at this 'cheekiness', but then accepted it. His reward was a commercial and critical success which spent 21 weeks in the US album charts, peaking at number six, and later was Grammy-nominated in four categories including Album of the Year.

Much of its impact came from a very noticeable lack of usual McCartney lightness and optimism. The tone was bleak and self-deprecating; the lyrics teemed with images of insecurity and confusion – getting hooked, hanging his head, running and hiding, biting his tongue, not knowing what to say. 'Riding to Vanity Fair', in particular, was like the premature epitaph to a relationship: 'I was open to friendship/ But you didn't seem to have any to spare/ While you were riding to Vanity Fair'.

During their appearance on *Who Wants to Be a Millionaire?*, Heather had mentioned his knowledge of English literature, little thinking it might be turned against her like this. In *The Pilgrim's Progress*, John Bunyan's great Christian parable, Vanity Fair is an array of merchandise which looks alluring from a distance but at close quarters proves worthless. And in William Makepeace

Thackeray's Victorian novel of that name, the central female character, Becky Sharp, is a cynical, duplicitous social climber who ruthlessly uses her charms to fascinate and seduce older men.

In October, Faber & Faber published his first children's book, *High in the Clouds*, written in collaboration with the noted children's author Philip Ardagh and illustrated by Geoff Dunbar, the gifted animator of *Rupert and the Frog Song*. Its story touched all the pro-animal, pro-environment themes closest to Linda's heart: a young squirrel sees his woodland home destroyed (and his mother killed) by developers' bulldozers, then leads his friends on a quest for an animal Paradise bearing a strong resemblance to Peasmarsh.

Paul launched the book personally in the UK by reading its opening pages to an audience of children, then taking questions; in America, the first print-run was half a million.

The rest of 2005 was spent on an American stadium tour, promoting his new album literally to the skies. At his concert in Anaheim, California, on 12 November, one of its tracks, 'English Tea', together with a Beatles oldie, 'Good Day Sunshine', was beamed up to the Russian/American crew of the Mir space station.

Just now, anyway, there was other, more pressing trouble in the family. Two years earlier, Mike McCartney, then aged 60, had been accused of sexually assaulting a 16-year-old waitress during a party at a pub near his Cheshire home. The young woman claimed he'd groped her from behind while requesting more tempura prawns; he said he'd touched her merely in 'a fatherly gesture of thanks'.

Seventeen months passed before Mike's trial took place at Chester Crown Court, in February 2006. After three days, the judge halted the proceedings, ruling that sexual assault had not been proved, and castigating the Crown Prosecution Service for wasting public money on the case and for the long delay before the hearing. Acquitted 'without a stain on his exemplary character', Mike kept up his tradition of close-mouthedness about Paul, simply thanking 'my big brother, who has been a rock of support during this attempt to soil our family's name'.

Where campaigning at least was concerned, Paul and Heather still presented a united front. In March, accompanied by a BBC film crew, they flew to Canada to protest against the annual slaughter of harp seal pups off the coast of Newfoundland. Wearing matching orange thermal suits, they lay on an ice floe with one of the sad-eyed, mewing little creatures soon to be clubbed to death for its fluffy white fur. Afterwards, they went back onto *Larry King Live* to confront Newfoundland and Labrador's state premier, Danny Williams, about the inhumanness of the hunt, seeming more a team than usual – for this time Paul managed to get several words in edgewise.

In April, Heather needed 'revision surgery' on the stump of her left leg to reattach muscle-tissue to the bone. She disappeared from view for some weeks, provoking a spate of press stories that the marriage was in trouble. Then she reappeared, saying she'd merely been hiding from photographers seeking pictures of her on crutches and any idea of a rift with Paul was 'hilarious . . . of course we're together. Paul and I are together a hundred per cent.'

A week later, on 17 May, they issued a joint statement that they were to separate. 'Having tried exceptionally hard to make our relationship work given the daily pressures surrounding us, it is with sadness that we have both decided to go our separate ways. Our parting is an amicable one and both of us still care about each other very much, but have found it increasingly difficult to maintain a normal relationship with constant intrusions into our private lives, and we have actively tried to protect the privacy of our child . . .

'We hope for the sake of our baby daughter that we will be given some space and time to get through this difficult period.'

A separate message from Paul on his website continued to defend Heather against those who'd always said she only married him for his money. 'There is not an ounce of truth in this. She is a very generous person who spends most of her time trying to help others in greater need than herself. All the work she does is unpaid, so these stories are completely ridiculous and unfounded.'

Heather just then was in the midst of publicising her latest book, a self-help manual entitled *Life Balance: The Essential Keys to a Lifetime of Wellbeing*. Three days later, the *Guardian* magazine's Life and Style section published a promotional Q&A with her which had already gone to press when the announcement was made:

Q. What is your favourite smell?
A. The McCartney rose . . .
Q. What or who is the greatest love of your life?
A. My husband, my baby daughter and my sister . . .
Q. When did you last cry and why?
A. Watching the film *The Dreamer* with my husband asleep on my knee . . .
Q. How often do you have sex?
A. Every day. Doesn't everyone say that?

As a 14-year-old, Paul had written a song full of cosy images of his then-inconceivable old age – doing household chores and gardening, just like his dad, while a placid spouse 'knit[ted] a sweater by the fireside'; going for Sunday drives and holidays at 'a cottage in the Isle of Wight'. But now he actually was 64, very different imagery lay in store.

The milestone moment on 18 June brought an orgy of journalistic birthday greetings with metaphorical Valentines and bottles of wine. Contrary to the song's prediction, he wasn't losing his hair, even though its colour might be a little suspect. And the question 'Will you still need me?' produced a resounding unanimous 'Yes'.

The separation never looked other than permanent. By the time it was announced, Heather had already left Peasmarsh with two-year-old Beatrice and moved into a £500,000 property named Pandora's Barn, a few minutes' drive away, which she bought by selling Paul back the west London apartment his cash gifts had bought her in 2004. She also still had Angel's Rest, the £1 million beach-front property in Hove that he'd financed as a love-nest for them in 2001.

Paul, meanwhile, sought solace with his daughters Mary and Stella and the three grandchildren they'd between them put 'on his knee' – not Vera, Chuck and Dave, but seven-year-old Arthur, three-year-old Elliot and 18-month-old Miller. To add to the air of finality, Rother District Council had discovered that the lakeside wooden cabin he'd built for Heather and Beatrice was erected without proper planning permission and had ordered him to demolish it.

The semblance of an 'amicable' split was short-lived. On 29 July, Paul began divorce proceedings on the grounds of Heather's 'unreasonable behaviour', accusing her of being argumentative and rude to their staff, and refusing him sex (despite her recent claim to the *Guardian* that it was a daily occurrence). So exploded the final roseate vision of 'When I'm Sixty-Four': 'And if you say the word/I could stay with you.'

Practical measures were swiftly taken to prevent it. On 2 August, Heather took advantage of his absence from their London home, 7 Cavendish Avenue to go there, accompanied by Beatrice, and remove some of her possessions. She found the lock on the front gate had been changed and staff had been instructed not to let her in. Her bodyguard climbed over the wall to open the gate from inside, whereupon Paul's security people called the police. A photographer was on hand to snap Heather in the street, arguing with a bemused female constable.

After the media love-in for the sixty-fourth birthday boy, and her own recent disastrous nudity-attack, Heather realised her need for specialised PR help in the coming battle. She therefore followed Paul's example in hiring a press spokesman who was an ex-tabloid journalist and therefore understood the 'red top' psyche inside-out. Blind to irony, she chose Phil Hall, a former editor of the *News of the World*, the very scandal sheet she had announced she would be suing.

By Hall's account, Paul tried to warn him off taking the job. '[He] rang me up and said, "I hear you're going to be handling Heather's PR. I'm not very happy about that." I thought it was wrong for this man to try to stop Heather being advised when she clearly was going to face an absolute onslaught from the press.'

Hall's advice was to acquire a lighter touch than she'd previously been known for, responding to the charge of argumentativeness by conceding that she could be 'feisty and opinionated' (so making Paul seem a grumpy old chauvinist) but mostly keeping her head down and focusing on her charity work.

After the Cavendish Avenue lock-out, Hall told the papers she'd laughed the incident off. However, he did confirm other reports of McCartney vs. McCartney conflict on matters both major and minor: Paul had frozen their joint bank account at Coutts, and also sent Heather a stern legal letter about her removal from Peasmarsh of 'three bottles of cleaning fluid' to her new office at Pandora's Barn.

His lawyers had initially proposed a quickie divorce with no blame imputed to either party that could go through with a minimum of damaging publicity. However, the absence of a prenuptial agreement meant that – just as his children had warned – Heather could lay claim to a substantial part of his fortune, as much as 20 per cent according to some reports.

In Britain, the preparation of divorce actions normally takes place in absolute confidence. But this one was to have a literal *deus ex machina*. On 17 October 2006, fax machines began to chatter out inside information about the case in three locations where it could reach the widest possible readership in double-quick time: the UK offices of the Press Association and Bloomberg news agencies and the press room at London's Royal Courts of Justice in the Strand.

There were nine pages of a 13-page document, apparently compiled by Heather's solicitors, Mishcon de Reya, in response to that offer of a quickie 'no blame' action. It contained her response to the brief, unspecific allegations in Paul's petition, followed by a list of counter-claims which, by contrast, went into devastatingly intimate detail. These portrayed him as a controlling and selfish domestic tyrant, indifferent to his wife's special medical needs, who had treated her in a 'punitive, vindictive manner' and, on four occasions, subjected her to peculiarly unpleasant physical violence.

The general rebuttal of his petition denied she had 'withdrawn sexual intimacy' from him save on just one occasion in seven years when she had been physically exhausted. She had been, it said, a committed wife 'who sacrificed many of her own projects' for his sake. Any scenes in front of their employees had been caused by his 'controlling and possessive behaviour' and unreasonable demands that staff should work late or at weekends. Furthermore, he had continued to 'use illegal drugs' and 'consume alcohol to excess' despite a promise not to do so when she agreed to marry him.

The itemised allegations of ill-treatment dated back to late 2002, only four months after their wedding, when they were both in America, Paul on tour and Heather promoting her book, *A Single Step*. The trigger was said to have been her television interview with Barbara Walters, by now no longer an admiring fan but a searching, often hostile interrogator on the subject of her early life.

Afterwards, she had been upset but, it was claimed, Paul had reacted unsympathetically, drunkenly accusing her of 'being in a bad mood' in front of other people. The argument had continued in private, with increasing heat, until he 'grabbed her by the neck and pushed her over a coffee table . . . He then went outside and in his drunken state fell down a hill, cutting his arm (which remains scarred to this day).'

In May 2003, by now four months pregnant, Heather had been with him in Rome for his two concerts at the Colosseum. At their hotel on the morning of the second show, she had been upset by a newspaper article about her, but Paul had allegedly reacted 'coldly and indifferently' and in the ensuing argument 'became angry and pushed her into the bath'.

When she threatened to boycott that evening's performance, he made his staff badger her into going. However, she refused to attend the after-show party, preferring to have dinner at a restaurant with her sister Fiona and her female bodyguard. In reprisal, Paul allegedly withdrew her bodyguard and car, leaving her with a 30-minute walk back to the hotel 'exposed to a crowd of 500,000'.

That August, when they'd been married only just over a year, had brought a steep escalation in the level of physical violence claimed. On holiday in Long Island, Heather had asked Paul if he'd been using marijuana despite his pre-wedding promise to stop. He 'became very angry, yelled at her, grabbed her neck and began choking her'.

The birth of their child, it was claimed, only made matters worse, for Paul had had 'no regard to Heather's emotional or physical (and especially her disability) needs', often treating her with an uncaringness his first wife would not have recognised.

Despite her exhausted and fragile state after Beatrice's Caesarian delivery, he still 'insisted she should accompany him everywhere'. Once, she'd had to postpone an operation for two months so as not to interfere with his holiday plans. After the revision surgery on her stump, he'd talked her into a plane trip with assurances that special disabled facilities would be provided – but none was. Even the aircraft steps had turned out to be too narrow for a wheelchair, obliging her to board on her hands and knees.

Similarly, a man who'd already lovingly – and thoroughly – parented four children was portrayed as the most selfishly squeamish novice in the nursery. He'd allegedly told Heather he didn't want her to breastfeed Bea because 'they are my breasts' and 'I don't want a mouthful of breast milk'. She did so anyway, but after six weeks his 'constant interrupting . . . often in the presence of a midwife' became 'so intolerable to her that she gave up'.

He was also said to have turned her into a domestic slave, forcing her to prepare two different dinners each night, one for him, another for the baby, and objecting to her employing any help.

Even while suffering from a broken pelvic plate, in December 2003, she'd still had to make a meal for him on crutches and 'in agony'.

This despotism, it was claimed, even followed her into bed. Though she was an inveterate early riser and Paul addicted to rock-star lie-ins, he didn't like her to get up until he did. There were times when she needed to use the bathroom after having taken off her prosthetic leg and, rather than have to crawl there, she'd asked if she could use an 'antique' bedpan. He allegedly objected that it would be 'like an old woman's home'.

His former generosity towards her had seemingly evaporated. He'd recently bought a property in New York, a handsome town-house on West 54th Street whose lower floors were to provide offices for MPL but whose top storeys were a luxurious apartment where he could stay instead of using hotels. Heather had asked for one of its commodious spare rooms as an office, so that she could work on her own projects while staying close to Beatrice. But Paul had allegedly turned down her request, instead offering her office-space a 20-minute walk away that was too small for her pur-poses and, when she declined it, calling her 'an ungrateful bitch' in front of their chauffeur.

The protective husband who'd spoken up for her online seven months earlier was portrayed as far from consistent. On receiv-ing advance warning of Russell Miller's damning *Sunday Times Magazine* article about her in 2004, she'd hit on a seemingly quick and easy way to stop it. The *Sunday Times'* proprietor Rupert Murdoch also owned America's Fox Television network, whose broadcast of the annual Super Bowl always featured a major pop act performing at half-time. Paul was due to play at the next Super Bowl and, so she thought, could have threatened to pull out unless Murdoch killed the *Sunday Times* piece. According to her statement, he refused, though it seems he did make personal representa-tions to Murdoch and the article was pulled from the magazine. But it was then reinstated on the orders of the *Sunday Times'* editor.

By far the most extreme ill-treatment of which he was accused had taken place at the Cabin, the lakeside home he'd been so eager to build that he couldn't wait for planning permission. There in April 2006, while Heather was still recovering from her revision surgery and using a wheelchair, a drink-fuelled argument had allegedly culminated in his pouring 'the balance of a bottle of red wine' over her head and throwing the residue in his glass at her. He was said to have grabbed her glass so violently that the bowl snapped off the stem, and 'lunged' at her with the broken stem, cutting her arm just above the elbow so that it bled 'profusely', then 'mishandling' her, putting her into her wheelchair and pushing it outside, shouting at her to apologise for 'winding him up'.

On the night of 26 April, it was claimed she'd asked Paul not to go out as he'd refused to employ a nanny and she couldn't cope with Beatrice on her own. He'd gone anyway, and when she'd phoned begging him to come home he had 'mocked her pleas in the voice of a nagging spouse'. He hadn't returned until late that night, allegedly so drunk that she had to help him undress and get into a hot bath.

By her account, she'd then phoned his psychiatrist – a personage whose existence had been unsuspected hitherto – who advised her not to try to move him in case she injured herself but (shades of John's 'Norwegian Wood'!) to leave him to sleep in the bath. Because her left leg hadn't yet healed sufficiently to wear a prosthesis, she'd had to crawl up to their bedroom to fetch pillows and a duvet.

On her return, she claimed, she found that he'd vomited over himself. Fearing he might do so again during the night and choke to death, she'd somehow dragged him upstairs to bed, terrified that the strain would damage her pelvic plate or break the stitches from her recent surgery. The next day, far from showing any contrition, he'd 'made a joke of it'.

On 28 April, it was alleged, he'd gone to London, promising to be back in time to help put Beatrice to bed, but had not done so, obliging Heather to call on 'a friend' for the backup she needed. He had finally returned at 10 p.m., 'slurring his words and demanding his dinner'. She had told him it was on the stove but that she would no longer cook for him because he didn't respect her; he'd accused her of being 'a nag' and gone to bed.

It was then that she'd decided their marriage had 'broken down irretrievably' and left their log love nest for good – on her hands and knees, 'dragging her wheelchair, crutches and basic personal possessions out to her car'.

The two news agencies to which the claims had been leaked did not instantly disseminate them to dozens of publications, as the anonymous sender had evidently expected. In Britain, divorce proceedings, celebrity or otherwise, are protected by the Judicial Proceedings Act of 1926, which expressly prohibits the reporting of such intimate details prior to the hearing. There was even a possibility that the document was a hoax. Though it seemed genuine, it had not been signed nor filed with the court, and Heather's solicitors, Mishcon de Reya, refused to confirm its authenticity.

In the event, both the Press Association and Bloomberg decided the story was too legally hazardous to put out. But the *Daily Mail* – which had received the document independently – had no such inhibitions, splashing it over numerous pages the next morning. After weighing up the legal risks, the BBC and independent broadcasters took the same decision.

The initial assumption was that Heather herself was the leaker. However, her press spokesman, Phil Hall, insisted that she'd had nothing to do with it and was 'utterly flabbergasted'. Her solicitors announced she would be taking legal action against the *Mail*, its stablemate the *London Evening Standard* and the *Sun*, adding, 'She could not afford to sue all the newspapers she would like to.' They also made public a letter from the *Mail On Sunday* to her sister, Fiona, offering 'a substantial sum' for inside information about the divorce.

From Paul, there was no talk of retributive lawsuits, only a brief statement via his own solicitors, Payne Hicks Beach: 'Our client would very much like to respond in public and in detail to the allegations made against him by his wife and published in the press but he recognises, on advice, that the only correct forum for his response is the current divorce proceedings. [He] will be defending these allegations vigorously and appropriately.

'Our client is saddened by the breakdown of his marriage and requests that his family will be allowed to conduct their private affairs out of the media spotlight for the sake of everyone involved.'

If Heather had not leaked the document – which certainly wasn't in her best interests to do – then who had? The explosive fax turned out to have been sent from a public-use machine in a newsagent's shop in Drury Lane, central London, not far from Mishcon de Reya's office. The shop-owner recalled the sender vaguely as a woman 'aged between 35 and 45, tall and brunette with a "different" accent, possibly American or Canadian'. But her identity and motivation remained a mystery, and still do to this day.

Paul and Heather's daughter, Beatrice, fortunately was too young to understand fully what was happening; and, whatever their feelings about each other, they made conscientious efforts to preserve an air of harmony in front of her. On 30 October, they co-hosted her third birthday party at an adventure play-centre in Hastings, taking a full part in the activities provided and chatting and joking with each other. 'If I didn't know what had been going on in their marriage in the past few months, I never would have guessed,' commented one of the other mums present. Afterwards, Bea left to spend time with her father while Heather thriftily took away the remains of the birthday cake.

The tabloids, however, stuck to the line of a couple at each other's throats, with Paul – as *People* magazine noted – 'cast as the Queen Mother and Heather as the Wicked Witch'. In November, the *Mail On Sunday* said she had told 'a close friend' that she'd discovered

Paul had also physically abused Linda during their seemingly idyllic marriage.

The *Daily Mail* subsequently reported a clandestine meeting between him and Peter Cox, Linda's collaborator on her first vegetarian cookery book, at which Cox had handed over a large brown envelope. According to the *Mail*, this contained audio tapes she'd made with Cox on which she'd talked of her victimisation by Paul, and which he was now buying for £200,000 to prevent them being used against him in the divorce. In fact, the envelope contained only a copy of Cox's book, *Why You Don't Need Meat*, containing a foreword by Linda that Paul had never seen.

Two people who might have been expected to know if he was a wife-beater immediately came forward to dismiss any such notion. Carla Lane, Linda's close friend in the late Seventies and early Eighties, said if it had been the case, she certainly would have told her. Paul's long-time PR, Geoff Baker, concurred: '[He] doesn't hit women. He doesn't eat flesh, let alone beat it.'

Other impressive character witnesses added their own timely testimonials. Former US president Bill Clinton proprietorially claimed him as 'an American icon' and called his music 'a unifying force'; Microsoft's Bill Gates compared him with Bach; rapper Jay-Z described him as 'a genius writer [who] changed music'; even America's National Space Agency lauded him for filling the Mir space station with 'Good Day Sunshine'. The tributes were collected on a DVD of his 2005 American tour, entitled *The Space Within US*.

At the same time, his classical oratorio *Ecce Cor Meum* finally completed the journey it had begun during the last months of Linda's life. Five years after its first, low-key performance at Magdalen College Oxford, it was premiered at London's Royal Albert Hall with Magdalen's choir augmented by that of King's College, Cambridge, the orchestra of the Academy of St Martin in the Fields, the London Voices choir and soprano Kate Royal. It would go on to a second premiere at Carnegie Hall, New York, and the award for best album at the 2007 Classical Brit Awards. After the Albert

Hall recital, *Record Collector* magazine reported that Paul 'took to the stage amid a confetti burst to thank one and all, happy that his vision had been fulfilled'.

If only the same could have been said of 'When I'm Sixty-Four'.

53

'Even by British tabloid standards, the nastiness has been extraordinary'

It was inevitable that the divorce would be likened to Prince Charles's from Diana, Princess of Wales in 1996. Here were a comparably exalted husband suffering an unprecedented intrusion into his private life, and a golden-haired wife who had often seemed to cast herself in the princess's image. The opposing solicitors were the same as in the royal case, Paul being represented by Fiona Shackleton of Payne Hicks Beach, who'd acted for Charles, and Heather by Mishcon de Reya's renowned Anthony Julius, who'd secured Diana's £17 million settlement. The difference was that no infidelity on either side had been alleged – and public opinion this time overwhelmingly favoured the prince.

A preliminary hearing took place on 27 February 2007, in the family division of the High Court before Mr Justice Sir Hugh Bennett. Paul's last visit to the Royal Courts of Justice in the Strand had been in 1971 when, with Linda beside him, he'd ended the Beatles' partnership. Then he'd been a 28-year-old, awed by the elderly-seeming grey-wigged figure on the bench; now he and the judge were equals, both in their mid-sixties and knights of the realm.

Before Christmas, Mishcon de Reya had indicated that Heather would accept a settlement of £50 million. Payne Hicks Beach, for Paul, had come back with an offer of £16.5 million which, together with the properties he'd already provided for her, would take the total to around £20 million. But it had been rejected.

The hearing before Mr Justice Bennett consisted mainly of testimony from accountants. Heather's £50 million claim was predicated on her estimate of Paul's net worth, which she claimed he had always told her was in excess of £800 million. However, detailed investigation by two firms of accountants had suggested it was less than half that, below £300 million. An important factor in the case was how much his relationship with Heather might have benefited his career and thus increased his fortune. The judge ordered a report on his assets in March 2000, when the relationship had begun in earnest, adjourning the hearing meantime.

The proceedings were held in camera, with strict security to ensure nothing leaked to the reporters massed outside. Nonetheless, lurid reports attributed to 'inside sources' dominated the next day's front pages. It was said that Paul and Heather had ended up screaming at each other after he produced a detailed dossier of her 'lies' since they'd met. Their respective lawyers took the unusual step of issuing a joint statement, condemning the 'misreporting', notably in the *Sun*, and rather naively appealing for them to be given privacy 'as they work out the outstanding issues between them'.

Since their separation, Heather's £360,000 per year allowance from Paul had continued and in the current year she'd already received £180,000. On 1 March, he terminated the allowance, paying her £2.5 million on account of her final settlement and so freeing himself from responsibility for her day-to-day expenses other than their daughter Beatrice's school fees.

Against her legal team's best advice, Heather was already finding the court of public opinion hard to resist. Some weeks before the first court hearing, a message had appeared on her website, signed by her sister Fiona, saying that she and Beatrice were in actual physical danger because of the 'vicious agenda' of tabloid photographers who'd hounded them 'practically every day for the past 253 days'. One had actually been convicted of assaulting her as she cycled through Hove the previous July. Since then the persecution had become so bad that she'd resorted to filming those attempting to snatch pictures of her. She was also said to have received death threats. As she had 'no money', she was asking Paul for the same protection given to other members of his family.

Part of Phil Hall's PR strategy was to remind people of Heather's courage in overcoming her disability and the range of demanding physical activities at which she was a match for anyone. Hence in April she appeared in the American TV show *Dancing with the Stars*, partnered by professional dancer Jonathan Roberts. Despite her supposed impecuniousness, she donated £50,000 of her £110,000 appearance-fee to the Viva! animal charity.

Wearing a succession of slinky gowns that made no attempt to hide her prosthetic leg, she lasted until the fifth round of the elimination contest, coming an overall seventh out of 11 celebrity couples. Her partner praised her stamina and dedication – she was commuting between London and LA during the series – and the judges, somewhat different from Mr Justice Bennett, gave her a standing ovation when she ended a mambo routine with a backflip.

True to past form, having won admiration for her indomitability, she undermined it with a self-regarding Oscar-style farewell speech ('People keep coming up me and saying, "My God, now *I* want to dance"') and an appeal to her audience to go vegan.

The result was vicious ridicule from American comedy shows like *Jimmy Kimmel Live*, which doctored the series' footage so that her prosthesis appeared to fly off midway through a samba, clubbing a young female audience-member bloodily in the face. A similar parody online intercut the footage with a horrified-looking Paul, covering his eyes and pleading 'Stop! Stop!', a snatch of 'Money', that old Beatles Cavern favourite, and a giant dollar sign.

The British press performed a characteristic volte-face, attacking the 'cruel' Americans for mocking disability. Back home, jokes about 'Mucca', as the tabloids nicknamed Heather, didn't have to be funny to bring the house down. 'She's such a fucking liar,' quipped chat show host Jonathan Ross, 'I wouldn't be surprised if we found out she's actually got two legs.'

A month earlier, the final dividend on Paul's Magritte painting of a green Granny Smith apple had been added to the Beatles' already incalculable exchequer. Since 1978, their company Apple Corps had been fighting a copyright war with the Californian electronics corporation whose logo was also an apple, albeit with a leaf and a bite-mark. In that time, Apple Inc. had diversified from chunky desk-top computers into a range of portable entertainment, information and communication devices, tagged by a lower-case letter 'i', which seemed to grow sleeker and 'smarter' almost by the minute and which no fashion-conscious person of any nationality could bear not to possess.

Following the last court battle with Apple Corps in 1991, Apple Inc. had been allowed to retain its name and logo on condition its products had nothing to do with music. It had then promptly created the iTunes system for sending the stuff directly to its global orchard of iPods, iPads and iPhones.

Yet another court action in London in 2003 had ended with a ruling that Apple Inc. had not breached the 1991 agreement; so the 'i's had it. But hostilities between the two companies continued, much to the distress of Apple Inc.'s CEO, Steve Jobs, a passionate Beatles fan who had used Paul's 'Lovely Rita' as a soundtrack to his unveiling of the iPhone.

Finally, in March 2007, an out-of-court settlement was reached whereby Apple Inc. bought out the name and logo from Apple Corps – for an undisclosed sum, said to be $500 million – then licensed the name back to it. A delighted Jobs said, 'We love the Beatles and it has been painful to be at odds with them.' Apple Corps' managing director, Neil Aspinall, added: 'It is great to put this dispute behind us and move on. The years ahead are going to be very exciting for us.'

But not, unfortunately, for Aspinall himself. Immediately after the settlement, it was announced he had decided to 'move on' from Apple Corps and would be succeeded by Jeff Jones, formerly a vice-president at Sony/BMG with special responsibility for back-catalogue reissues.

There had been many claimants to the title of 'fifth Beatle' but none so deserving as the terse, hollow-cheeked man who, like Paul and George, had attended Liverpool Institute and whom John had mischievously nicknamed 'Nell'. He'd served the band continuously for 46 years, starting as their driver when they played pound-a-night gigs on Merseyside, circumnavigating the world as senior of the two roadies who were their only protection in the mayhem of Beatlemania, then retiring into Abbey Road studios with them to minister to their every need and, incidentally, suggest the concept for *Sgt. Pepper's Lonely Hearts Club Band*.

Through all their fights and feuds, Aspinall had retained the liking and trust of each one and, even more impressively, gotten along with all their wives. As their de facto manager during the multiple lawsuits following their break-up, he had suffered stress that brought on two heart attacks (after the second of which he awoke to see John's ghost standing beside his bed). And never once by word or gesture had he betrayed their confidence, collectively or individually.

As scheduler of their reissues and repackagings, he had been criticised for not supplying as many as their fans demanded – though the final decision in such matters didn't rest with him but the two ex-Beatles and two widows who constituted his board of directors. But what he did put out in their name was of unfailing quality and classiness, like the 1 album, the recent film of George's Concert for Bangladesh and, most notably, *The Beatles Anthology*.

The last project he'd overseen was the Love musical, a Beatle-themed Cirque du Soleil show in Las Vegas, which George had first suggested to the Cirque's French-Canadian founder, Guy Laliberté, in 2000. Sir George Martin, the natural choice as its musical director, now suffered from severe hearing problems and in his place other Apple executives had suggested the British DJ-mixer Fatboy Slim. But Aspinall had insisted on having Martin, with his son, Giles, to help him.

The result was a brilliant soundtrack that mixed and matched long-familiar Beatles songs to produce fascinating new effects, Paul's guitar intro to 'Blackbird' for instance segueing into 'Yesterday', and the Gothic melodrama of 'Eleanor Rigby' into 'Julia', John's broken-hearted hymnlet for his lost mother. In between were snatches of the four's studio chatter; those droll, offhand Scouse voices in mega-decibel sound, somehow even more affecting than the music.

The production, in a purpose-built theatre at Vegas's Mirage hotel, required a public display of friendliness between Paul and Yoko, for they both were heavily involved in its rehearsals and previews. Its first night on 30 June 2006 saw the largest ever public assembly of the Beatles' so often dysfunctional 'family': Paul, Ringo, Yoko, Olivia Harrison, Barbara [Starr], John's first wife, Cynthia, his two sons, Julian and Sean, George's son, Dhani, and Paul's brother, Mike. The show was rapturously greeted, as were the family when they took a bow afterwards. Paul requested 'a special round of applause for John and George'.

In fact, Aspinall had not decided to move on; he had been forced out of Apple because of his firm resistance to anything that he believed would cheapen the Beatles brand. The breaking-point, ironically, had been a proposal to make their catalogue available through Apple Inc.'s iTunes.

After his 46 years of service, Aspinall was treated far from generously. The single token of appreciation came from Paul, to whom he'd always been less close than to George and John. It was a solid gold wristwatch whose bulk humorously suggested the gold pocket watches traditionally presented to long-serving employees up north. Its two-word inscription combined the baby word for 'thank you' with the fondest of Liverpool endearments: 'Ta, la'.

Paul's motto during the past months had been a saying of Winston Churchill's: 'If you're going through hell, keep going'. Amazingly, therefore, the spring of 2007 found him with a new album ready for release. Its title was a message he sometimes saw flash up on his mobile phone which also suggested the epic content of his cerebral microchip: *Memory Almost Full*.

Throughout the Beatles' recording career, they stayed with EMI, the company which had signed them at a minuscule royalty rate in 1962. Since going solo, Paul had tried other record-labels but finally returned to the place where his partnership with John had reached its apotheosis and which was situated so conveniently around the corner from his London home.

However, EMI nowadays was very different from the mighty bureaucratic organisation that once had seemed almost like an alternative BBC. It had signally failed to meet the challenges of the computer age in which record-sales from stores were massively reduced by digital downloads; having recently announced record losses, it was about to be bought by a private equity group, Terra Firma.

Before the sale took place, Paul jumped ship – taking all his solo song-copyrights with him – but landing with none of the conventional record companies eager to sign him. The colossal Starbucks coffee bar chain had recently set up its own record label, initially for making compilations of tracks licensed from outside. He was to become Hear Music's first contract artiste and *Memory Almost Full* its first original release.

Some of the album had been recorded before *Chaos and Creation in the Backyard*, when he was still writing love songs to Heather rather than stern letters about misappropriated bottles of cleaning fluid. Two stayed on the tracklist: 'Gratitude' (for ending his 'cold and lonely nights' when he was 'living with a memory') and 'See Your Sunshine' ('Step out in front of me, baby/ They want you in the front line').

The newer material showed no scars from his recent travails, either in bitterness of tone or substandard performance. On the contrary, stress seemed to have sharpened his lyrics to the point where some definitely crossed over into poetry. 'That Was Me' evoked his boy-Beatle self, 'sweating cobwebs under contract in the cellar on TV'. 'The End of the End' talked about his own death, when he wanted 'jokes to be told . . . and stories of old to be rolled out like carpets/ That children have played on and laid on'.

On the day of its American release, 5 June, the album played continuously in Starbucks' 13,500 establishments around the world (including 400 in China) and thereafter to a weekly latte- or espresso-sipping audience of around 4.4 million. It went top five in Britain, America and half a dozen other countries, and prompted a bout of Sgt. Pepper-y rune-reading. Another track, 'You Tell Me', mentioned the 'bright red cardinal bird' commonly found in both Arizona and Long Island where he'd spent some of his happiest times with Linda. The word went around that *Memory Almost Full* was a deliberate anagram of For My Soulmate LLM (Linda Louise McCartney).

On 30 June, the Love musical celebrated a year of sold-out performances in Las Vegas with a lavish party at the Mirage hotel. Neil Aspinall, the man who'd done most to make it happen, was left off the guest-list.

'When Paul found out about it, he was livid,' Aspinall's widow, Suzy, recalls. 'He phoned Neil and told him, "Never mind what anyone else says. You're coming to that party with *me*."'

The divorce action proper was set down for February 2008, but legal activity continued meantime. In June 2007, the combatants went before a local district judge in Sussex on the question of Beatrice's custody. Paul feared that, in a spirit of vengefulness, Heather might be planning to take the little girl abroad, to America or her old stamping ground, Croatia. Now she gave assurances she had no such intentions.

After a three-day hearing, the judged agreed to a shared parenting arrangement whereby Beatrice would live with her mother but spend an equal amount of time with her father. Heather wanted her to be brought up in the Brighton area, but somewhere more secluded than busy and pap-plagued Hove. Paul therefore provided a further £3 million to buy them a second home in nearby Pean's Wood, close to where Beatrice had been enrolled at her first (private) school, and guaranteed continuing payment of her school fees.

On 11 October they returned to the High Court for a mediation session with a different matrimonial judge, Mr Justice Coleridge, to try to set the parameters of Heather's financial settlement. Security was even tighter than at the preliminary hearing in February. They arrived in separate cars at the rear of the building – Heather with a blanket covering her head – and used the judge's private stairs to court number 13, where the noticeboard did not show their names or the judge's and even the spyhole in the door had been blocked up.

But after legal argument variously reported to have lasted eight and ten hours, negotiations stalled yet again. The main reason was said to have been Paul's insistence that Heather sign a confidentiality agreement preventing her from ever publicly talking or writing about their marriage.

The divorce proceedings being *sub judice*, she was legally constrained from commenting on it, and had managed to remain silent throughout the continuing deluge of press rumour and counter-rumour all that summer. Then on 30 October, the *Sun* ran a 'Mucca' story too far. It said that a '£10,000' firework display she'd organised for Beatrice's fourth birthday party in Pean's Wood, two days earlier, had given her next-door-neighbour's dog, Glow, a fatal heart attack and stampeded the 15 horses kept in an adjacent field.

Heather's response was to volunteer for GMTV's daily breakfast show, which made her its main item the next morning. With her she brought an album containing some of the 4400 newspaper articles she claimed had been published about her and video films she and her team had taken of omnipresent skulking paparazzi.

Encouraged by interviewer Fiona Phillips, she dissolved into tears as she reflected on 'eighteen months of abuse . . . I've had a worse press than a paedophile or murderer . . . been called a whore and a liar . . . and I've done nothing but charity for 20 years'. She said she'd been 'living in a prison' and owed legal bills of £1.5

million, yet was still having to borrow money to hire security for herself and Beatrice that Paul ought to have been providing.

In addition to the death threats previously alleged by her sister Fiona, she claimed the police had warned of danger from an 'underground movement', presumably of resentful Paul fans. For Beatrice's sake, she'd even considered suicide, 'because if I'm dead, she's safe. She can be with her father.' As a victim of tabloid persecution, she bracketed herself not only with Princess Diana but Kate McCann, whose five-year-old daughter, Madeleine, had recently been kidnapped in Portugal and had disappeared without trace. On behalf of all such unfortunates, she added, she'd returned to campaigning mode and was organising a nation-wide petition against media excesses to present to the European Parliament.

'Heather's GMTV rant' (as it still lives on YouTube in three parts), especially her apparent identification with Kate McCann, brought a ferocious response from the organs she had denounced. In the forefront were the midweek female columnists known as 'the Wednesday Witches', whose unbridled bitchiness even turned the stomachs of some Fleet Street colleagues. The *Daily Telegraph* called it 'an ugly form of public bullying . . . even by British tabloid standards, the nastiness has been extraordinary'.

Heather's press spokesman, Phil Hall, had not been consulted before the GMTV appearance and now resigned, stressing they were still 'mates'. In Hall's place, she engaged as her 'world spokes-person' Michele Elyzabeth, a New Yorker of purportedly noble French ancestry who combined PR with marketing a range of beauty produces like 'caviar facials' and her own 'Comtesse Michele Elyzabeth' champagne.

Not that spokespeople for Heather Mills McCartney were kept very busy at present. The following week, she gave a long inter-view to *Hello!* magazine, accusing Paul of being mean. 'This is a man who hangs on to his money. He wouldn't be as rich if he didn't.' She also mentioned the confidentiality agreement she was allegedly being pressured to sign and her insistence on retaining the right to tell her story. 'He wants me gagged and they won't give me a divorce until I'm gagged.'

Then, speaking by video link to America's *Extra* TV show, she attacked Stella McCartney with whom, she said, she had 'tried and tried' to form a relationship without success. 'Every week, [Stella] tried to break up our marriage. She was so jealous. She wasn't interested in her dad's happiness. I can't protect her any longer. She's done some evil, evil things.' Now Stella was supposedly afraid the divorce would eat into her and her siblings' inheritance from Paul and that Heather would get 'all the planes and the diamonds'.

Extra received a bonus not vouchsafed to GMTV or *Hello!* Heather claimed to possess damaging material about someone she did not name, stored in a safe. 'I'm protecting that party because I still care about that party . . . but if it's going to carry on, I'm going to have to tell all the truth.'

As a finale, via her worldwide spokeswoman Michele Elyzabeth, she renewed her attack on Stella, for the first time giving chapter and verse on her stepdaughter's supposed hostility. When buying Stella McCartney clothes, she'd been allowed a discount of only 10 per cent. And when she'd wanted to put Stella McCartney perfume into the goody-bags for an Adopt-A-Minefield fund-raiser, Stella had turned down her request.

No word of response came from Paul, who had escaped to his Long Island home some time previously. But even there he was no longer safe from paparazzi. A couple of days after Heather's GMTV appearance, a zoom lens caught him in East Hampton, kissing a dark-haired woman in the front of a parked car. From then on, his wife's media meltdowns were pushed off the front pages by:

MACCA AND THE MARRIED MILLIONAIRESS

MACCA SMACKER WITH A MARRIED CRACKER

BEACH STROLLS, BREAKFAST AND TENDER KISSES

The 'married cracker' was quickly unmasked as 47-year-old

Nancy Shevell, a wealthy businesswoman whom Paul had known socially for some years past. With her lawyer husband, Bruce Blakeman, she belonged to the circle of wealthy city people with summer homes in the Hamptons that he'd met through his Eastman in-laws and often barbecued or sailed with. Now they found themselves in the same boat: Nancy had recently separated from Blakeman after 23 years of marriage.

She and Linda had been good friends with much in common though, unlike the Eastmans, Nancy did not hide her Jewishness behind WASP-y gentility. She had grown up in New Jersey where her father, Mike Shevell, a self-made man in the Lee Eastman mould, founded the trucking company New England Motor Freight or NEMF (just one letter different from the Beatles' first management, NEMS Enterprises).

After attending Arizona State University, a generation after Linda, she'd joined the family firm and risen rapidly in the male-dominated trucking world to vice-president at NEMF and member of New York's Metropolitan Transportation Authority. By a delicious irony, her second cousin was the television journalist Barbara Walters, whose 2002 interview with Heather produced one of the divorce claims against Paul which had been so mysteriously leaked to the press.

Nancy, too, had been diagnosed with breast cancer, a year after Linda but at a much younger age and with a type which, fortunately, responded to treatment. Since then, she and her husband had been prominent supporters of the Long Island Breast Cancer Action Coalition and its resources centre, Hewlett House.

Paul had reportedly turned to this familiar but still highly attractive woman for solace after the stressful courtroom scenes behind closed doors with Heather.

A week after her appearance on Britain's GMTV, she was back on the show, no longer tearful but feeling 'like a prisoner who's been let out on parole'. Signatures to her online anti-tabloid petition had been flooding in, she said, and personal messages of support had come from the McCann family and the prime minister, Gordon

Brown. When she'd taken Beatrice to Disneyland Paris on the Eurostar a couple of days earlier, her fellow passengers had given her a standing ovation.

Though she'd still heard nothing from Paul about security arrangements – or anything else – she adopted a magnanimous tone about his East Hampton trysts; far from erupting into 'tears and tantrums' as press reports had suggested, she'd wished him 'all the best' when handing Beatrice over to spend time with him.

As the *sub judice* rule was flouted time and again, the British legal profession could only watch, stupefied. 'It has spiralled out of control,' a leading divorce lawyer, Virginia Platt-Mills, told *People* magazine. 'I can't remember such a high profile case being splashed in the papers like this. It's Armageddon.'

54

'His wife, mother, lover, confidante, business partner and psychologist'

Paul maintained a typically upbeat exterior as the climactic hearing approached. 'I'm going through great struggles but I'm feeling pretty good,' he said. 'I have a lot of good support, particularly from my family . . . There is a tunnel and there is light and I will get there.'

Actually, the stresses of 2007 had contributed to his only recorded health problem since 1973 (that 'bronchial spasm' from the Nigerian heat and too many cigarettes while making *Band on the Run*). In November, feeling vaguely unwell, he'd consulted a Harley Street cardiologist, who discovered an obstruction in the blood-flow to his heart. Unknown to anyone outside his family, he'd undergone a coronary angioplasty, in which a fine tube, or stent, is threaded into the aorta via the groin, then inflated like a balloon to disperse the build-up of fat.

The procedure had been completely successful, with no lingering after-effects: he was well enough to perform at London's Great Ormond Street children's hospital in December and to appear with Kylie Minogue on Jools Holland's BBC2 New Year special. When the story finally got out, he minimised what had been a potentially grave condition, writing on his website that he hadn't had surgery – only 'tests for a minor irregularity' – and was 'feeling fine . . . and enjoying all the sympathy'.

The divorce hearing began on 11 February 2008, in court number 34 of the Royal Courts of Justice and, like its two preludes, was closed to the press and public. At its outset the judge, Mr Justice Bennett, warned sternly that any further leaks could result in prosecution for contempt of court. It still risked turning into a litigational sieve, thanks to Heather's libel actions against the *Daily Mail* and *Evening Standard* (for printing the leaked claims from her cross-petition) which were due to start in open court any time now. And if either side in the divorce appealed against Bennett's judgement, that, too, could be fully reported.

In addition to the Prince of Wales's solicitor, Fiona Shackleton, Paul's courtroom team comprised Nicholas Mostyn QC – known as 'Mr Payout' for his success on behalf of wives suing affluent husbands – and a junior counsel, Timothy Bishop. But Heather was no longer represented by Anthony Julius, Shackleton's highly effective opponent in the Charles–Diana divorce. She had dismissed Julius after the failure to reach a private settlement at the preliminary hearings – and now faced a legal bill of around £2 million.

Instead, she chose to conduct her own case, supported by what British law in such situations terms 'McKenzie Friends': her sister, Fiona, a British solicitor named Michael Rosen and an American attorney, Michael Shilub. So, as well as being cross-examined by Paul's barristers, she would be directly cross-examining him.

Her claim amounted to around £125 million, far outstripping Charles and Diana and almost tripling insurance magnate John Charman's recent £48 million payout to his wife, Beverly, to date the largest divorce settlement in British legal history. She estimated her 'reasonable needs' for herself and Beatrice as £3.25 million per year. These included £499,000 for holidays, £125,000 for clothes, £30,000 for 'equestrian activities' (although she no longer rode), £39,000 for wine (although she did not drink alcohol), £43,000 for a driver, £627,000 for charitable donations, £73,000 for a business staff and £39,000 for helicopter flights to and from hospitals. The most important component was round-the-clock security for Beatrice, on which she claimed to have already spent almost £350,000 from her own pocket and estimated at £542,000 per year in the future.

As well as her present homes in Hove and Pean's Wood, she claimed two American ones of Paul's: 11 Pintail Lane, Amagansett, and the 'Heather House' in Beverly Hills, which she said had always been promised to her. She was seeking £8–12 million to buy a home in London, £3 million to buy a property in New York and £500,000–£750,000 to buy an office in Brighton, plus title to the houses Paul had provided for her sister, Fiona, and cousin, Sonya. In all, that would give her seven fully-staffed properties with full-time housekeepers costing £645,000 annually. She further asked the court to 'place a significant monetary value on compensation for loss of earnings, contribution [to his career] and [his] conduct'.

Paul had come back with an offer worth around £15 million, giving her Angel's Rest, the Hove seafront property, Pean's Wood, the inland one, and both the Fiona and Sonya houses. He would also pay 'a balancing lump sum' on condition that 'certain art' (the paintings by him that adorned Angel's Rest) was returned to him. His provision for Beatrice, over and above her school fees, health insurance and 'reasonable extras', would be £35,000 per year plus £20,000 for a nanny, to continue until she was 17 or finished secondary education, whichever came sooner, and the security costs for her and her mother for two years at a limit of £150,000 per year.

His lawyers claimed this was not a case where marital assets should be shared because of the wife's contribution to the husband's success. He had been enormously wealthy before meeting Heather and their relationship of only short duration. Indeed, one of the bones of contention was whether they had cohabited for four years or six. According to Heather, they had begun to do so when Paul bought Angel's Rest in March 2000, whereas he said it had not been until their marriage in June 2002.

Each side accused the other of misconduct and leaking the sensational claims in Heather's cross-petition which had found their way onto news agency fax machines in October 2006. She stood by her accusations that Paul had treated her abusively and/or violently, abused drugs and alcohol, been jealous and possessive and insensitive towards her disability and failed to provide her with proper security and protection from the media. He countered that her 'leaks, lies and breaches of confidentiality' since their separation had been part of 'a concerted campaign to portray herself as a victim and him as a hypocrite and a monster' and were in themselves tantamount to an act of violence.

Crowds massed in the Strand for each of the hearing's five days. Heather arrived in a black 4x4 with blacked-out windows, preceded by a white van which was used to block photographers as she disembarked. With her, she brought an entourage of five: her three 'McKenzie Friends', plus a Hollywood beautician and her personal trainer, Ben Amigoni.

Paul by very deliberate contrast had no visible security, strolling in through the Gothic front entrance with a smile and a wave or thumbs-up.

Wearing a pinstripe trouser-suit and peach-coloured shirt, Heather opened her case by showing Mr Justice Bennett a short video film of the photographers who pursued her, often in atrociously-driven high-speed vehicles like those which had harried Princess Diana to death in a Parisian underpass. At the film's end, however, it was a paparazzo who suffered a car crash. Alas, that would be a metaphor for much of her subsequent performance in the witness box.

Her contention was that when she met Paul, her modelling, charity campaigning, TV presenting and public speaking had made her almost his equal as a celebrity (in proof of which she carried a large folder marked 'fan mail'). She'd also been independently wealthy from her autobiography and sponsorship deals with a penthouse flat in London's Piccadilly, two cars, a driver and assets worth £2–3 million. One year, she'd once earned $1 million for just 14 days' work. Paul's attitude to her during their marriage, she said, had been one of 'constriction' and her career had declined as a result. She thus merited compensation for 'loss of career opportunity' and 'commensurate with being the wife of and the mother of the child of an icon'.

Cross-examined by his silky QC, Nicholas Mostyn, she amended the tally of her pre-Paul assets, saying the £2–3 million had been money in the bank. She was asked for corroborative bank statements but could not produce any, explaining that as much as 90 per cent of her earnings had gone directly to the charities she supported. Again, there was no paperwork, such as effusive letters of gratitude, to prove it.

In a sworn affidavit before the hearing, she'd claimed she had to continue using her own money after marrying Paul but that he made her turn down '99 per cent' of the business opportunities she received, on the grounds they were just attempts to cash in on his name. 'When I was asked to design clothes, create a food line, write books, make a video, write music or do photography, Paul would almost always say something like "Oh, no, you can't do that. Stella does that or Mary does that or Heather [his adopted daughter] used to do that or Linda did that."'

In April 2001, she alleged, he'd vetoed a £1 million contract for her to model brassieres for Marks & Spencer. However, the only documentary evidence was an e-mail from an advertising man that made no mention of money, and Paul testified that he doubted whether it really had been worth as much as that. He said they'd discussed the M&S offer but agreed that, at a time when they were just starting a relationship, it would be inappropriate for her to start modelling bras, though he wouldn't have stood in her way if she'd insisted.

An even larger business opportunity he'd allegedly denied her was a series of television ads for McDonald's, promoting new vegetarian options in their restaurants. But a McDonald's executive testified the project had stalled because of 'her personal inability to be accessible as was necessary'.

In terms of her public profile, she said, Paul had 'put a stop to my dream of hosting the biggest TV show in the world and what would have been a huge and lucrative career-move for me'. In November

2005, she'd been asked to become a regular stand-in for Larry King on his hugely-watched CNN programme. Paul, she claimed, allowed her to present one show but then said she'd be 'a bad mother' if she did the two or three per week that were proposed because they would take her away from six-month-old Beatrice. He'd then 'dragged' her and Beatrice around America on his current tour.

Paul denied ever suggesting she was 'a bad mother': he'd been sceptical about the idea because of negative reviews she'd received when she stood in for Larry King in 2004, interviewing Paul Newman. Nonetheless, in return for her company on the tour, he'd agreed to spend three months in Los Angeles to see how things worked out. King's verbal offer had not turned into a contract and, anyway, they'd both decided that, for Beatrice's sake, they didn't want to relocate to LA. Heather, he said, had never mentioned the matter again – something she vigorously disputed in her cross-examination of him.

To complete the litany of selfishness, her affidavit said that Paul had 'turned down many opportunities to help my charities' and his 'refusal to commit' had made his appearances on behalf of a charity much less effective than they might have been. Further, he 'often promised to make financial contributions to charities, but later refused to follow it through'.

However, in court she admitted that he'd donated £150,000 to her personal charity, the Heather Mills Health Trust, soon after they'd first met and that two cash gifts from him totalling half a million pounds had been partly to allow her to keep contributing to charities. She accepted his QC's estimate that between 2001 and 2005 his direct or indirect contributions to Adopt-A-Minefield – from organising and performing at fund-raisers to wearing red 'No More Minefields' T-shirts throughout his Back in the World tour – had been worth around £3.5 million to the campaign.

By her own account, she'd been an 'exceptional' wife who'd rescued him from a morass of mourning for Linda, enabled him to 'communicate better' with his children (especially her namesake Heather) and given him back his confidence as a performer. She'd helped him write songs and accompanied him on all his tours at his insistence, contributing to their set-design and lighting, even suggesting he should wear an acrylic fingernail on his left (strumming) hand to prevent wear and tear on the real one. She had been, in her own words, 'his full time wife, mother, lover, confidante, business partner and psychologist'.

Paul acknowledged that she'd comforted him in the aftermath of Linda's death, just as his family and friends had done, but denied that he'd lost his confidence, that she'd encouraged him to return to touring or had any creative input into the lighting or stage-sets at his shows. A live album DVD which listed her as 'artistic co-ordinator' had, he said, merely been 'a favour to her, a romantic gesture'.

She claimed that, from being a millionairess when she met Paul, her earning capacity was now zero, thanks to the 'vilification' she had suffered in the media. She had attempted a return to public speaking, at which she claimed once to have earned £10–25,000 per hour, but found no takers. Her current assets amounted to some £7.8 million and were shrinking rapidly; in recent months, she'd spent £184,463 just on private planes and helicopters.

Her closest cross-examination of Paul thus concerned the exact size of his fortune, which independent accountants had estimated at around £400 million but which she continued to maintain was more than double that. He said his art collection of works by Picasso, Renoir, de Kooning and many other masters was worth around £25 million. She then tried to read out a report she'd commissioned from a firm of art-valuers which appraised it at £70 million. When Mostyn objected that no prior permission for the report had been given, the judge disallowed it, but she continued – as lawyers say – to 'press' him on the subject. He told the judge that the collection had been acquired before he met Heather and he wanted to keep all of it.

There was a further clash over the 30 of his own artworks he'd hung in their Hove love-nest, Angel's Rest, where Heather now lived alone. She claimed them as hers but he wanted them back – all but two that he'd given her, 'the flower photographs' and 'the Isle of Man stamp design' – in order to leave them in trust for Beatrice and his other children.

Her claim of £542,000 per year for security for Beatrice and herself contrasted with what Paul had spent on his own protection in 2005 – £125,908 in the UK and £264,000 in America. In an affidavit, he said that before their marriage, he'd generally had a 'limited, low-key' security presence. 'There were never any bodyguards at Peasmarsh. The general farm employees kept a look-out for anything suspicious. There was virtually no security at Cavendish Avenue. At the office complex in New York, there would be one guard on the door . . . There was an off-duty police officer who provided night cover when I was in Long Island and on trips to and from the airport. There was no permanent close protection during this period . . . unless I was on tour or attending high-profile events. That was how I had lived with my first wife and our four children.'

But after Beatrice's birth, Heather had begun 'demanding increasingly stridently far more security to protect her from what she regarded as press intrusion. She did not suggest she needed [it] for her or Beatrice's personal safety. Rather, her aim was to erect a barrier between her and the photographers . . .' In essence, he said she had the same attitude to the paparazzi as Princess Diana and many other celebrities less battle-hardened than himself, basking in the camera-flashes at one moment, complaining of 'intrusion' the next.

Since their separation, he continued, 'I have, to my great relief, been able to revert to the security arrangements which were in force for most of my "celebrity" life . . . There are no bodyguards. The only person with me on a permanent basis is my PA, John Hammel, who has been with me for 30 years. The court will be aware that Heather now maintains several members of staff including a driver and a personal trainer. Mr Hammel is with me only during the day or when I am working in the evenings. I am alone at night (apart from when Beatrice is with me).'

His real concern in resisting 'Heather's demands for bodyguards

24 hours a day is our daughter. Unless on tour, my older children had very little security. They all attended state schools. It is not healthy for a child to have security 24/7. It sets them apart from their peers and makes them an object of curiosity and, at times, ridicule. Such children live in gilded cages. I do not want this for Beatrice. She needs as normal an upbringing as possible.'

The hearing did not end on Friday, 15 February, as scheduled, but had to continue into a second week. When the court rose that afternoon, a middle-aged fan named Joe approached Paul, asking him to autograph a copy of the Beatles' White Album, but was refused. On persisting with his request, he was turned away by . . . security.

Later, he also approached Heather, who had no hesitation in writing 'To Joe, lots of love, Heather Mills' in the proffered auto-graph-book. The small PR victory was rounded off when she heard what had just happened with Paul. 'That's a pity,' she said, making sure her voice carried as far as possible. 'You're the sort of person who has made him what he is today.'

Mr Justice Bennett's judgement, covering 58 pages, was e-mailed to both parties in advance – more than likely by Apple computer – then read out in the High Court in their presence on Monday 18 February. It began on a highly positive note for Heather, calling her 'a strong-willed and determined [but] kindly person, devoted to her charitable causes [who had] conducted her own case with a steely yet courteous determination'. But there the compliments ended.

Paul, on the other hand, received only praise for the 'balanced' way he had given evidence. He had expressed himself 'moderately, though at times with justifiable irritation', Bennett observed. He had been 'consistent, accurate and honest'.

But the same could not be said of Heather. 'Having watched and listened to her give evidence, having studied the documents and given in her favour every allowance for the enormous strain she must have been under (and in conducting her own case), I am driven to the conclusion that much of her evidence, both written and oral, was not just inconsistent and inaccurate but also less than candid. Overall, she was a less than impressive witness.'

The judge described her claim of having been worth £2–3 million when she met Paul as 'wholly exaggerated'. Her tax returns showed that in that year, 1999, her gross turnover from modelling and acting had been £42,000 and from public speaking, £6000. Far from 'losing business opportunities' after they got together, her income as Paul McCartney's girlfriend, then fiancée, then wife had substantially increased.

The judgement quoted instances where Paul had been 'supportive of or furthered' her career and also cited 'compelling evidence that no one tells her what to do'. He had not 'dragged her on his tours'; she had gone of her own free will because she liked the excitement and attention, but had not made any artistic contribution to them. For her to suggest she had been his business partner was 'make believe'. To claim she had been his 'psychologist', giving him back his confidence and motivation to perform, was 'typical of her make believe'.

He ruled Paul's fortune to be around £400 million, that the couple had begun cohabiting in 2002, not 2000, and that the wealth Paul had built up between then and now amounted to approximately £39.6 million. On that basis, he awarded Heather a lump sum of £14 million plus £2.5 million to buy a London home to help rebuild her professional life (which he expressed confidence she could do by adopting 'a less confrontational attitude to the media').

That made £16.5 million, just above what Paul had offered prior to the hearing. Taking her two existing homes into account, she would have assets of around £23.4 million, or more than £700 for every hour she had spent with him. He would also pay £35,000 a year for Beatrice's expenses over and above her education and childcare.

The judgement ended with a warning to other litigants who might feel tempted to represent themselves as Heather had:

'This case is a paradigm example of an applicant failing to put a rational and logical case and failing to assist the court in its quasi-inquisitorial role to reach a fair result.'

Throughout the hearing, Paul had shown very obvious regard for Fiona Shackleton, the solicitor masterminding his case. Known among her male colleagues as 'the Steel Magnolia', she was a highly attractive woman with a blonde mane very like Princess Diana's which, fortunately, never had to be dulled by a barrister's grey wig.

Well before winning him such a favourable result – in cash terms, less than her former client the Prince of Wales paid Diana – Shackleton had aroused Heather's ire. Now as the proceeding broke up, she seized one of the courtroom's full water-jugs and tipped it over the solicitor's golden head. The gesture rather misfired, for Shackleton laughed it off and (like Diana) looked just as good with water-slicked hair as with a coiffure.

Having cut the most conventional of figures to this point, Mr Justice Bennett made a highly novel proposal: that rather than remain confidential in the usual way, his judgement should appear in full on the Royal Courts of Justice website. Paul agreed at once, even though it would reveal the most intimate details of his private life and finances. Of far more importance to him was the vindication it contained.

He left the court through the rear entrance, accompanied by a dampened but smiling Steel Magnolia, shouting to journalists, 'All will be revealed.' Then Heather emerged from the front door into thickets of microphones to announce she would appeal against making the judgement public; it would compromise Beatrice's safety by disclosing things like the name of her school, and was 'against everything to do with human rights'.

While hailing the result as 'incredible' for her, she claimed to have faced prejudice for conducting her own case, that the judge's mind had been made up in advance and Fiona Shackleton had handled Paul's case 'in the worst manner you could ever imagine . . . She called me many, many names before meeting me, when I was in a wheelchair . . . she is not a very nice person'. The £35,000 per year for Beatrice outside education and childcare was cited as very much less than 'incredible'. 'She is obviously meant to travel B-class while her father travels A-class.'

Both parties had been legally bound not to speak publicly about the case without permission from the other. Heather now rehashed parts of it nonetheless, still insisting that Paul was worth £850 not £400 million, that they'd cohabited for six years not four, and that, apart from one interview with GMTV, she'd already 'stayed quiet' for 18 months (*Hello!* magazine, the *Extra* TV show and a second GMTV appearance having evidently slipped her mind). She even dragged in their former log cabin love-nest at Peasmarsh, which she accused him of demolishing from spite, although it had been by order of the local planning authority.

Her loyal sister Fiona also spoke to reporters, claiming that all the negative stories about her had been orchestrated by Paul and adding, 'I can't believe a man could be so low.' For corroboration, she jogged the hacks' memory about the litigation he'd brought to this same place in 1971 to dissolve the Beatles' partnership: 'He sued his three best friends, remember.'

The next day, three judges in the Court of Appeal supported Mr Justice Bennett's decision to make his judgement public on the court website (where it remains for the edification of posterity). Four months hence, a decree nisi would be granted in the case of McCartney vs. McCartney, allowing headline-writers throughout the English-speaking world to say it had been a long and winding road through the divorce courts, but they'd finally agreed to let it be.

Paul's relief at finally reaching the end of the tunnel was tempered by sadness, both for himself and someone he had come to care about. On 3 March, Nancy Shevell's brother, Jon, a fellow executive in the family trucking firm, was found dead in his room at the Beverly Hills Hotel, apparently from a drugs overdose, aged 50.

And on 24 March, Neil Aspinall died in New York, aged 66.

Tragically soon after laying aside his Apple burden, he had been diagnosed with lung cancer that proved terminal. Paul had paid for him to have the best available medical care and, despite the pressures of the divorce, had flown over to see him and, just once more, say 'Ta, la'.

55

'There's always that moment of "Can I do it?"'

The stories of musical superstars tend to be harrowingly tragic, witness Judy Garland, Charlie Parker, Edith Piaf, Hank Williams, Buddy Holly, Maria Callas, Elvis Presley, Jimi Hendrix – and John Lennon. But Paul McCartney, whose superstardom passes all known limits, seems on course for a happy ending.

His wedding to Nancy Shevell took place on 9 October 2011 at Marylebone Town Hall in central London, where he'd married Linda 42 years earlier, the assembled crowds now cheering and clapping rather than weeping and keening in anguish. The bride wore an ivory knee-length Stella McCartney dress and the official wedding photo was taken by Mary McCartney – proof of how both approved of the match. Paul's seven-year-old daughter Beatrice was bridesmaid and, for a third time, his brother Michael was his best man.

To the vast public which still took a proprietorial interest in his affairs, Nancy seemed a perfect choice; elegant, discreet, independently wealthy and devoid of either competitive ego or over-possessiveness. In other words, the someone he'd wanted to be waiting each night when he came offstage and to say 'You were wonderful, darling.'

Few couples marrying at their age – 69 and 51 – are fortunate enough to merge lives so unproblematically. As a long-time friend of Linda, Nancy was known and liked by Paul's Eastman in-laws, to whom he remained close, particularly his brother-in-law and attorney, John. Her 20-year marriage to Bruce Blakeman, over well before she met Paul, had left no lingering acrimony and he easily forged a rapport with their 18-year-old son, Arlen.

Nancy's greatest fan among his children was his own son, James, who, since Linda's death, had struggled with alcohol and drugs and even spent some time in rehab in Arizona, symbolically close to the place where she'd died. James's dislike of Heather had created a rift with his father which only ended when Paul underwent the angioplasty in 2007. Now he said Nancy was like 'a new mother . . . we all adore her'.

James, too, was a musician, songwriter and singer, at which trades he would have to exist in a shadow as vast as Everest. He had played on a couple of Paul's albums and on Linda's posthumous one, *Wild Prairie*, but did not start solo recording and gigging until 2009, initially under the pseudonym of Light (much as his Uncle Michael had once used that of 'McGear' to avoid being unfairly helped by the McCartney name, or damned by it).

His first album under his own name finally appeared in 2013, when he was 35. Simply entitled *Me*, it had strong echoes of Paul along with more modern influences like Nirvana and Red House Painters, and was praised by *Rolling Stone* for its 'strong emotional competence'. One track, 'Strong As You', struck a poignant note of filial hero-worship mixed with deference: 'Am I strong enough to see it through/ Strong as you?' Paul bigged it up to the point of being an embarrassing dad, jumping onstage at one of James's solo gigs, accompanied by Rolling Stone Ronnie Wood, affectionately pinching his boy's cheek, then settling at the piano, taking the audience's whole attention with him.

From time to time, someone floats the idea of putting James together with John's younger son, Sean, and George's son, Dhani, to form a Beatles Mk. 2 (Ringo's two sons, Zak and Jason, being disqualified by age). But the essence of the Beatles was something their children can never know: they were hungry.

With Nancy's wholehearted approval, Linda has been regularly commemorated, both as an animal-rights campaigner and photographer. In 2009, Paul, Mary and Stella together launched a Meat-Free Monday campaign that afterwards became a cookbook to which they contributed a foreword. Whenever Paul is questioned on the subject, he uses Linda's old mantra: 'Anyone who saw inside a slaughterhouse would never eat meat again.'

In 2011, father and daughters joined up again for *Linda McCartney: Life in Photographs*, a major retrospective compiled from some 200,000 images, exhibited at London's Phillips de Pury gallery and collected into an opulent art book. Mary recalled how, whatever they might be doing as a family, Linda's camera never stopped snapping. 'It was her way of talking to you.'

The Peasmarsh estate, and Hog Hill Mill, remained the centre of Paul's life in Britain. But after Linda's death, he seemed to have fallen out of love with the Scottish Highland hideaway he credited with saving his sanity after the Beatles' break-up, and of which he'd once sung 'My desire is always to be here'.

Consequently, his interlocking farms on the Kintyre Peninsula became little more than a nature reserve which, in the harsh economic climate of 2013, his financial advisers decided was a too-expensive luxury. As part of a rationalisation plan, estate manager Bobby Cairns and the caretaker of High Park Farm, Jimmy Paterson, between them boasting 55 years of service, were fired and Paterson received three months' notice to leave his rent-free cottage. A *Daily Telegraph* reporter visited the memorial garden to Linda in Campbeltown containing the statue of her cradling a lamb. He reported the spot to be in need of some care and attention.

After the divorce, Paul refrained from any public comment about Heather: they had to continue communicating in their joint custody of Beatrice – and he never made any complaint about her qualities as a mother. In 2009, *Q Magazine* asked point-blank if the marriage had been the worst mistake of his life. He replied that it would have to be 'a prime contender . . . But I tend to look at the positive side, which is that I got a beautiful daughter out of it.'

Heather, meantime, had receded to the margins of celebrity – at least, in everyone's eyes but her own. In 2009, she opened a vegan café named VBites in Hove, announcing it to be the first link in a worldwide chain and purchasing a vegan food company to supply it and its planned successors. The similarities with another Beatle wife-turned-ready-meals-tycoon did not escape the *Daily Mail's* acerbic columnist Jan Moir. 'One can't help but suspect,' wrote Moir, 'that Heather is her own meat substitute for Linda Mc-Cartney who did all this years ago.' Yet, despite Moir's assertion that its chicken nuggets resembled 'albino goose-droppings' and its pepperoni pizza had an air of 'trodden vegan roadkill', the VBites company was to grow and prosper.

Heather returned to the news in a positive way in 2010 by lasting five weeks in another tough television dance competition, ITV's *Dancing on Ice*, then announcing her ambition to join the British Paralympic ski team at the 2014 Winter Olympics in Sochi, Russia. By way of a warm-up, she won four gold medals at the US Adaptive Alpine Skiing National Championships in Aspen, Colorado. Then, as so many times before, negativity kicked in: during training with Paralympic hopefuls in Austria, she walked out after a row over the special left ski boot she planned to use.

Echoes of the McCartney divorce were stirred by the government inquiry into tabloid newspaper misbehaviour, specifically the illegal hacking of celebrities' phones, chaired by Lord Justice Leveson in 2011 and 2012. Although Paul was not called to give evidence, he suspected his phone had been hacked by several papers while the divorce was in progress. 'When I thought someone was listening, I'd say, "If you're taking this down, get a life!"'

One strand of the Leveson Inquiry involved Piers Morgan, formerly editor of the *Daily Mirror*, who claimed – inaccurately – to have introduced Paul to Heather at the paper's Pride of Britain awards in 1999. Two years later, in less benign mood, Morgan had written an article based on listening to a private voicemail Paul had left for her after an argument on which he'd sounded 'lonely, miserable and desperate and sung "We Can Work It Out" into the answerphone'. Morgan refused to disclose who had leaked the voicemail, but hinted it had been Heather herself.

Summoned before the inquiry, she said that following their return from India in 2001 – the trip on which he'd secretly bought her an engagement ring – Paul had left her 25 phone-messages, including 'a ditty', begging her forgiveness after a row. She denied leaking the voicemail or authorising anyone else to do so.

After Leveson, a large number of celebrities whose phones had been hacked received substantial damages, the most predatory of the tabloids, Rupert Murdoch's *News of the World*, closed down, and the others were forced to radically clean up their act. (To give Heather her due, she had called for such measures almost a decade earlier, only to have it dismissed as 'a rant'.)

Contentment with Nancy was not to diminish Paul's work ethic, any more than had his heights of euphoria and depths of misery with Heather. There have been two further classical compositions: *Stately Horn*, written for the horn virtuoso Michael Thompson, was premiered at London's Royal Academy of Music in 2010, and *Ocean's Kingdom*, his first ballet score, by the New York City Ballet in 2011, with costumes designed by Stella. A new animated film is promised, based on his children's book *High in the Clouds*.

His father's enduring influence was marked by his 2012 album *Kisses on the Bottom*, a collection of jazz standards like Fats Waller's 'I'm Gonna Sit Right Down and Write Myself a Letter' whose innocent double entendre ('Kisses on the bottom/ I'll be glad I got 'em') he and John used to chortle over as teenagers. It reached number three in Britain and five in America and was streamed as a live performance on iTunes. *Rolling Stone* likened it to John's 1975 *Rock 'n' Roll* album as 'the sound of a musician joyfully tapping his roots'.

For all his taste and sophistication, he remains primarily a musician who functions best late at night and is happiest among others of his profession, though no longer a pot-smoker for fear of setting a bad example to Beatrice and his grandchildren. And beneath the melody and sentiment is the same anarchic spirit that took the Beatles closest to heavy metal with 'Helter Skelter'. In 2013, he swapped his violin bass for a cigar-box guitar – weird great-great nephew of skiffle tea chest basses – to join the three surviving members of Nirvana in a jam called 'Cut Me Some Slack', which won a Grammy for best rock song the following year.

He is still avid to work with all the newest young talents, just as they are to work with him. The four-producer team for his 2014 album, *New*, included Mark Ronson, who'd been Amy Winehouse's indispensable recording partner, and Paul Epworth, who produced Adele's *21*. In 2015, he recorded with Lady Gaga and shared a stage at the Grammys with Rihanna and Kanye West, the latest in a long line of outrageous rappers. As they sang Rihanna's 'FourFive Seconds' with the lines 'If I go to jail tonight/ Will you pay my bail?', it wasn't the outrageous rapper who'd really been there.

Afterwards, on Irish television, Heather broke a lengthy silence to accuse him of struggling to stay relevant because these days he wasn't nearly as famous as she. 'Most of the time I have people coming up to me in the street and going "Oh my God, you're a ski racer" or "You help the animals." Half of them don't even know who he is.'

The start of everything maybe wasn't rock 'n' roll, but winning that prize as an 11-year-old for his essay about the 1953 Coronation. 'All my life,' he reflected on turning 73, 'I've been trying to win a school prize or trying to do OK in an exam or trying to get a good job, something where people go "You're good."'

Quite an armful of school prizes: eighteen Grammys, eight BRITS, one Academy Award, honorary doctorates of music from Yale and Sussex universities, the US Library of Congress's Gershwin Prize for popular song (presented at the White House by President Barack Obama during a private performance there); a Kennedy Center Award; the National Academy of Recording Arts and Sciences' MusiCares Person of the Year; the *New Musical Express* award as 'Songwriters' Songwriter'; the French Légion d'Honneur; the Peruvian Grand Cross of the Order of the Sun; a street and a rose named after him; a star on the Hollywood Walk of Fame . . .

In 1963, answering a questionnaire for the *NME*, he gave his personal ambition as 'to have my picture in *The Dandy*', the British comic book he and the other Beatles read throughout their childhood. In 2012, as a 70-year-old, he appeared in a *Dandy* strip, shaking hands with its most famous creation, Desperate Dan, then leading 50 of its other characters in a singalong of 'Hey Jude'.

John evidently still looms as large as ever in his consciousness. In 2009, Neil Young performed in Hyde Park, closing his set with a version of 'A Day in the Life' that proved peculiarly suited to his soul-stirring backwoods wail. Paul came out to sing the 'woke up, fell out of bed' passage looking almost as dishevelled as Young and stayed for the rest of the song, leaping and lurching around and flailing his arms as he never had even on the drunkest teenage night in Hamburg. None of his own songs, one felt, could have generated the same emotion.

'When John got shot,' he told British *Esquire* magazine in 2015, 'aside from the pure horror of it, the lingering thing was OK, well now John's a martyr, a JFK . . . I started to get frustrated because people started to say, "He was the Beatles." Like Yoko would appear in the press: "Paul did nothing. All he did was book the studio." Like "Fuck you, darling. All I did was book the fucking studio?"'

Despite professing himself reconciled to the Lennon–McCartney blanket credit, he's still galled to see it on songs John had little or no hand in writing, the more so in an electronic age when screens are sometimes too small for the text they display. His iPad once rendered it as 'Hey Jude by John Lennon and'. But he's made no further attempts to have it reversed.

'If John was here, he would definitely say, "That's OK." Because he didn't give a damn. But I've given up on it . . . in case it seems like I'm trying to do something to John.'

During 2014, the turmoil in Iraq and Syria and the rise of the so-called Islamic State brought the strangest and sickest proof of John's posthumous power. As ISIS stunned even the blood-hardened twenty-first century with its medieval barbarities, it emerged that four young British converts, employed jointly as jailers and killers, had become known to their captives as 'the Beatles' and been given the nicknames John, Paul, George and Ringo. Even here, the traditional pecking-order was maintained. The one who achieved world notoriety for publicly beheading a series of innocent hostages, until killed by an American drone strike in 2015, was Mohammed Emwazi, aka 'Jihadi John'.

Esquire caught up with Paul in Osaka, Japan, during another world tour, named Out There, which had already lasted almost two years and played to around two million people in the US, Poland, Italy, Brazil, Chile, Uruguay, Ecuador and Costa Rica. He had no plans to come off the road any time soon, he said. 'It's what I do. It's my job. And it's nothing to what the Beatles used to have to go through. Compared to that, I have it easy.'

The nightly fix of mass love was not his sole motivation, he added. 'I kind of get to review my songs, and they go back quite a way. So if I'm singing "Eleanor Rigby", I'm me now reviewing the work of a twentysomething and I'm going "Whoa, that's good . . . wearing the face that she keeps in a jar by the door . . ."'

Since 1996, the Liverpool Institute for Performing Arts has become one of the world's most celebrated fame schools, turning out graduates who have won distinction in the technical as well as creative arms of music, theatre and film, even a few who went on to work for Paul himself. He never misses a graduation ceremony if he can help it, sometimes flying thousands of miles to present the graduates with their lapel-pins and bid each one 'Wear it with pride'.

For all the ever-multiplying multitude of popular songwriters, the ability to write an original melody remains as rare as ever, and no one since George Gershwin and Richard Rodgers has possessed it in such abundance. Indeed, Paul belongs to an ever tinier elect, like Louis Armstrong and the great jazz drummer Gene Krupa, who seem made of music more than of flesh and blood.

He continues to teach a songwriting class at LIPA, fulfilling what was once thought his true vocation. There's little conventional teaching involved, as he's never taken for granted a process one of his few peers, Brian Wilson of the Beach Boys, says can be 'as natural as swallowing a glass of milk'. 'I always tell my students, "Look, I don't really know how to write a song. There's no set way. What I do know is how to work on and finish a song." All I can say is "Let's hear what you've got."'

He admits still getting a thrill from hearing milkmen whistle his songs. Once, he swears, he even heard a bird chirp a bit of 'From Me to You'.

'Songwriting is still something I deeply love to do, but at the beginning, there's always that moment of "Can I do it?" To start with, there's nothing – just me at the piano or with a guitar and then, if you're lucky, this amazing feeling of "Hey, I've written a song!" The feeling when you do that . . . there's nothing like it.'

EPILOGUE

'See ya, Phil'

Fifty years have passed since the scene at Newcastle-on-Tyne City Hall with which this book opened. On 28 May 2015, an evening almost as chilly as that of 4 December 1965, I'm waiting outside Liverpool's Echo Arena, for my second face-to-face encounter with Paul McCartney.

Back then, he was 23, the Beatles were still a touring band and Britain had barely begun to swing. Now, three weeks before his seventy-third birthday, he's near the end of his Out There tour, a journey lasting two years on which he will have given 91 shows across four continents with an estimated total gross of $225 million. But the basic elements are the same: a concert-venue in the north of England and a capacity crowd with the added fervour of being his hometown one.

I've spent the past two and a half years as his biographer with his 'tacit approval', not authorised but not discouraged either. The job has involved no conversations nor any direct contact with its subject. At his time of life, it was hardly to be expected he'd be willing to sit down and plough through the Beatles' history in detail yet again. But that tacit approval has been a unique concession, opening the door to family members and close friends who otherwise would never dream of speaking on the record. Anyone contacting his office to check me out has been told 'It's up to you but it's OK with Paul.'

As a result, I've been able to uncover a Paul McCartney very different from the one the world thinks it knows; a workaholic and perfectionist who, despite his vast fame, has been underestimated by history and who, despite his undoubted genius, is in his own way as insecure and vulnerable as was his seeming total opposite, John Lennon. While recognising his foibles, I've come to respect – frequently admire – the man for whom I was once seen as cherishing such animosity.

However, his touring schedule has delayed this meeting until I've all but completed my manuscript. And it's come about that I have something to impart to him which strangely reprises our only other meeting, half a century ago.

When I got into the Beatles' Newcastle dressing-room as a 22-year-old *Northern Echo* reporter, he gave me an exclusive by throwing me his Hofner violin bass to try out. No other rock star has ever remained so faithful to a single instrument. He still starts every show on the violin bass, then tosses it in that same casual way to his PA, John Hammel, who's never yet missed the nerve-racking catch of an instrument as valuable as a Stradivarius. On flights the bass always has a seat to itself and Hammel sleeps with it in his hotel room – not the kind of overnight company usually associated with being on the road.

Actually, there were two violin basses. The first Paul bought in Hamburg in 1962 and played throughout the Cavern Club era; then in 1963, the Hofner company gave him an improved model as thanks for making their brand internationally famous. In 1969, when the Beatles started the *Get Back* album, he took both instruments to the sessions, hoping it might assist the hoped-for rediscovery of their roots. And the older of the two, known to Beatles historians as 'the Cavern bass', was stolen and never recovered.

One of the many new sources for my biography has been a Liverpool taxi-driver named Peter Hodgson, whose father and uncle were contemporaries of Paul's, lived round the corner from him in Allerton and would sometimes lend the Quarrymen their Grundig tape recorder. A massive McCartney fan, Hodgson has been trying to track down the Cavern bass for years, even starting a special Facebook page to appeal for information about it.

Recently, he's e-mailed me that he may have located it in Ottawa, Canada, in the possession of someone who was not the thief. This personage, with a Tolkien-esque flourish, calls himself The Keeper, suggesting the guardian of some sacred relic, rather than a possessor of stolen goods who expects someday to return it to its rightful owner.

Paul has always paid big money for mementoes of his early career – which often belonged to him in the first place – and for one as iconic as this, the sum involved would clearly be astronomical (the newer bass is insured for more than £2 million). Hodgson seeks no monetary gain for himself, just the joy of seeing the Cavern bass in action again, but is concerned that if and when its hand-back takes place, his years of detective work might get overlooked. So, rather than contact some faceless MPL person, he's asked me to tell Paul about it at our fortuitously-timed meet-and-greet.

Outside the Echo Arena, two broad queues stretch across the bleak concrete plaza of what used to be King's Dock. Near a ticket-window, there's a sudden flurry of excitement and a brief illusion that the star himself has emerged to check how business is doing. But it's just a Paul lookalike, one of several with roughly similar eyes and pixie features who derive a steady income from posing for photographs with pilgrims outside his childhood home.

My companion is Peter Trollope, formerly crime correspondent with the *Liverpool Echo*, the evening paper for which this ultra-modern, eco-friendly structure is implausibly named. Among the crowd, he spots two one-time big names from the city's gang-ridden southern quarter and another still very much active.

After several fraught mobile phone exchanges, I manage to ren-dezvous with Stuart Bell, the boyishly youthful (but impressively long-serving) McCartney publicist. 'I've just seen Paul standing on his head,' Bell tells me as we head to the stage-door. It takes a moment to realise this must refer to pre-performance yoga.

I follow him past two security checks – only two – and through a warren of corridors blocked by giant equipment-containers and thronging with young men and women in black. On the floor, strips of pink tape point the way to 'Band Room' and the special accommodation set aside, as always, for 'PM Family'.

Those whom Paul is to meet and greet assemble in a small side room containing a refrigerator full of soft drinks and a couple of rather shabby sofas on which no one feels sufficiently relaxed to sit. Two of its walls are covered in tacked-up Oriental-looking fabric, the third consists only of a plain black cloth, beyond which the 15,000-seat arena can be heard filling up with an oblivious, steady roar.

All our group has some connection or other with music. Here's Tom Meighan, the lead singer with Kasabian, a band who are all unabashed McCartney-worshippers, often seen attending him at *Q* magazine awards ceremonies. Yonder is Ben Hayes, a mixing maestro like Paul's sometime collaborator, 'Youth', whose creations include fusing 'Helter Skelter' together with Led Zeppelin's 'Whole Lotta Love'. Belying this electronic audacity, he's a stolid, rosy-cheeked boy in a tweed sports jacket who still lives at home and has brought his mum up from North Wales with him.

The tension is lightened by two of Paul's stage band, keyboard-player Paul 'Wix' Wickens and bassist Brian Ray. After all the chopping and changing with Wings in the 1970s, he's kept the same line-up of Wickens, Ray, lead guitarist Rusty Anderson and drummer Abe Laboriel, Jr for 12 years without a sign of discontent on either side. 'They're such a pleasure to play with,' he recently told *Billboard* magazine. 'We all enjoy each other's company and the musicianship.'

Wickens, the band's only British member, is amazed by his leader's stamina, undiminished at almost 73. 'He doesn't eat anything before a show, then he does three hours, 38 songs, and I've hardly ever seen him take a sip of water onstage. Though he does like his Margarita afterwards.'

Out in the corridor a female assistant, aptly named Michele, is briefing three more meet-and-greetees, a man and two women, on the protocol of the ceremony. Smartphones, set for selfies, already glow in their hands. 'You can't take any pictures of your own,' Michele says. 'Our photographer will take your picture with Paul and if he approves it, a copy will be sent to you.'

'I *am* a professional photographer,' one of the women protests.

'Sorry, but that's Paul's rule.'

Half a century ago at Newcastle City Hall he came along a back-stage corridor towards me, and so he does again tonight. Knowing all that I do about him without knowing him, it's a surreal moment, like seeing the hero of some epic novel, *David Copperfield* or *Tristram Shandy*, suddenly step out of its pages. The reality of him in the flesh prompts a sudden awful thought: what if nothing I've written in the biography – none of those exhaustively worked-over 270,000 words – got it right in any way at all?

He's wearing a grey tweed suit with a Nehru collar, a distant des-cendant of Beatle stage-wear, with a creamy open-necked shirt and Beatley black suede boots. He uses coffee-coloured stage make-up, but otherwise gives off no whiff of septuagenarianism from the side-swept, faintly auburn hair to the match-thin limbs, smooth, unspotted hands and jivey walk. Full-face, he still looks much as he always did. But in profile his once retroussé nose has grown beakier, his eye deep-set and downturned, his cheek furrowed; he's become his dad.

He starts along the receiving-line in traditional royal film prem-iere style, a handshake and a little light banter at each stop. Some of it concerns his suit, for he turns back one coat-lapel in obvious satisfaction; the first words I catch from him are 'Charcoal grey'.

'Hello, Philippe,' he greets me. 'We've spoken on the phone.' He means his call to me out of the blue in 2004 when, despite my repu-tation as 'anti-Paul', he magnanimously agreed to help me with my biography of John. Amazing that he remembers.

'I've been living your life for the past two and a half years,' I say. 'How's it going?'

'I've been astounded by the work ethic.'

He grimaces and recoils slightly; meet-and-greet exchanges clearly aren't meant to be so nitty-gritty. Tom from Kasabian, who joins us at that moment, demonstrates the proper tone: 'Hey, is everything cool, Paul my man?' That he already said it a few minutes ago makes it no less apropos.

Even so, I outline my tale of the Cavern violin bass; how, 46 years after its theft from the *Get Back/Let It Be* sessions, it has apparently turned up in Ottawa in the possession of someone who wasn't the thief and on whom it bestows an almost mystical aura. Inured though he is to hardcore Beatlemaniac weirdness, he seems amused by that concept of 'The Keeper'.

'Well,' I continue, 'he's got it and . . .'

Another wrong note: my words are echoed with a derisive laugh. 'He's *got* it!'

'. . . and he seems to want to return it.'

I'm left wondering whether my great reveal has made any impression at all. But as he moves on, his security director sidles up with a mobile phone to take further details.

When the now met and greeted line up for their pictures with him, taken by his official photographer – and, subject to his approval, sent on later – I realise I'm expected to join them. As the photographer bobs down before us and a film camera comes in from the side, he slips his arm round me. Automatic as the gesture is, it somehow conveys that all has been forgiven.

'I don't usually smile,' I say. 'But that time, I was.'

'Yeah,' he replies, astonishingly. 'I never know what to do in photographs.'

As he leaves to go onstage, there's a moment of pure McCartney; whether natural or calculated hardly matters. I call 'Goodbye', thinking myself inaudible in the general chorus – but he turns with a wave and says, 'See ya, Phil.'

I've been to many rock concerts, but never one quite like this. When he walks on, all 15,000 people in the Echo Stadium rise to their feet with a roar and stay standing for the next three hours.

However, this is Liverpool, where even patron saints are never allowed to get above themselves. The arena-floor has two

Mississippi-like aisles, both of which throng with traffic through every song as people exit and return with giant plastic beakers of beer or soft drinks and tubs of popcorn or nachos.

For the past couple of years, it's been widely reported that his voice has gone and his non-stop performances are now just mass yearning for yesterday. But the voice is here in full with hardly a blemish, so familiar that one no longer notices its peculiar quality, its lightness yet robustness, its feminine powers of empathy and compassion mixed with never-for-a-second-to-be-doubted masculinity. And Wix Wickens wasn't exaggerating; in the whole 38-song, non-intermission show, he doesn't take so much as a sip of water.

The costly stage set he's recently taken through Europe, Asia, North, South and Central America seems almost irrelevant. Likewise the excellent band, other than in its power to create perfect facsimiles of recorded classics. This evening, he's just plain Paul, singing for the 'Pool. After his third song, 'Got to Get You into My Life', the perfect charcoal grey jacket is discarded, the wondrously creamy blouse turns into workaday shirtsleeves; he could almost be back at the Cavern, kicking off one of its famous all-nighters.

'Everywhere I go around the world, I say, "Tonight, we're going to have a party,"' he tells his permanent standing ovation. 'But tonight, we *are* going to have a party.'

Twenty-three of the songs are Beatles ones, digging still deeper into the Lennon–McCartney vaults with 'Another Girl', 'All Together Now', 'Being for the Benefit of Mr Kite', from *Sgt. Pepper*, whose words John copied straight off a Victorian theatre-bill. In front of me are four hefty young men in head-to-toe Gap, clearly mates of long standing, who might be thought more at home cheering on the city's sacred football team at its Anfield pitch. While fiercely hetero, they're physically demonstrative as Scouse lads of the Beatles' generation could never be, clinging together and singing the words from the stage directly to each other. Not 'LIV-ER-POOL!' but 'blackbird singing in the dead of night . . .'

There are a few Wings tracks and the odd cult item like

'Temporary Secretary', from the 1980 *McCartney ll* album, which *Rolling Stone* rates his thirty-sixth best post-Beatles song (a high placing) and the *NME* calls 'wonky electro-pop that doesn't seem so much ahead of its time as out of it'.

He's resigned to giving up his usual stringent image-control while he's onstage; since the arrival of mobile phones, nothing can stop audience-members photographing or filming him. But most do so only during the songs that are dearest to them. 'Whenever I do a Beatles number, all the phones come out,' he observes wryly. 'But as soon as I start something more experimental, it goes dark.'

As always at his shows, he's confronted by a medieval-looking array of waving banners. He reads out a selection of their messages, ranging from the sexual come-ons that never cease to the most innocent confidences. 'We love your butt . . . My name is Claire and I am seven today . . . Happy birthday, Claire.'

His Liverpool accent grows stronger by the minute: after becoming the first rock act to perform in Moscow's Red Square, he recalls meeting 'members of the Rooshen goovernment . . . When I was a boy, growing up in Forthlin Road, if anyone had told me that one day I'd be meeting members of the Rooshen goovernment . . .' It's redeemed from bragging by its punchline: 'The Defence Minister told me the first record he ever bought was "Love Me Do". He said, "We learned to speak English from Beatles songs. Hello, Goodbye."'

Absent friends are commemorated, John in 'Mr Kite' and also 'Here Today', the tribute song almost no one noticed; George with 'Something' on the ukulele. 'I wrote this next song for Linda' introduces 'Maybe I'm Amazed', still redolent of being blown away by love for the very first time. After a decent interval comes the quieter ardour of 'My Valentine', written for Nancy, who's in the audience tonight (and, doubtless, will be waiting afterwards to say 'You were wonderful, darling').

In 'Hey Jude', he's long accustomed to audiences singing along word-perfectly and in tune. With the present 15,000, the echo is so true, he gives them a test, going 'Oh-kay . . . All right . . . Wow-wow wowowow . . . woo-oop . . . uh-uh-uh' at erratic volumes, rising and falling in odd places to see if they can match him. They do time and again until eventually he gives up and moves on to 'Day Tripper'.

After three hours on my feet, I decide I've had enough, and head for the exit. Generally at rock concerts, lots of people leave just before the end to beat the rush for restaurants and public transport. Outside on the windblown plaza, a giant coffee-and-burger wagon is open for business; police reinforcements mass in clumps of sherbet yellow; taxis with lit foreheads glide by the dozen along the old dock road. But inside the Echo Arena, no one else is going anywhere.

'You're not leaving, are you?' says the elderly security man who unbars a door for me. 'He's still got another six songs to do.'

ACKNOWLEDGEMENTS

My thanks firstly to Sir Paul McCartney for allowing me to write this biography without seeking any editorial control over it. I am grateful to his stepmother, Angie McCartney, and his stepsister, Ruth, for their memories of his father, and to his cousin, Ian Harris, for recollections of both his mother and his beloved Auntie Gin. I received generous help, too, from his brother-in-law and lawyer, John Eastman, who figures in every account of Apple Corps's disintegration and the Beatles' break-up but who, in 47 years, has never before spoken on the record.

Inevitably I have drawn on my interviews with leading characters in the Beatles' story dating back to 1969: Mike McCartney, Yoko Ono, Mimi Smith, Cynthia Lennon, Allen Klein, Sir George Martin, Neil Aspinall, Mal Evans, Andrew Oldham, Peter Brown, Clive Epstein, Queenie Epstein, Dick James, Derek Taylor, Robert Fraser, Tony Barrow, Sir Joseph Lockwood, Richard Lester. Larry Parnes, Bob Wooler, Ray McFall, Astrid Kirchherr, Tony Sheridan, Bert Kaempfert, Klaus Voormann, Jurgen Vollmer, Alan Durband, Michael Lindsay-Hogg, Pete Best and Mona Best.

But *Paul McCartney* is primarily the product of new research and conversations with people who have been close to its subject at different moments, for different reasons, many of them sharing their insights for the first time. My warmest thanks to Keith Altham, Peter Asher, Suzy Aspinall, Dot Becker (formerly Rhone), Stuart Bell, Tony Bramwell, Iris Caldwell, Sandra Caron Howie Casey, Alan Clayson, Charles Corman, Peter Cox, Mark Featherstone-Witty, Joe Flannery, Johnny Gentle, John Gibb, Martin Glover (aka Youth) Brian Griffiths, John Gustafson, Colin Hanton, Bill

Harry, Peter Hodgson, Steve Holley, Ian James, Lesley-Ann Jones, Laurence Juber, Frieda Kelly, John Lang, John Lowe, David Litchfield, Maggie McGivern, Robbie McIntosh, Reggie McManus, David Matthews, Barry Miles, Russell Miller, Humphrey Ocean, Chris O'Dell , Denis O'Dell, Natalie Percy, Brian Ray, Denny Seiwell, Don Short, Guy Simpson, Anthony Smith, Bernice Stenson, Hamish Stuart, Jan Vaughan, David Watts, Peter Webb, Bruce Welch, Paul 'Wix' Wickens, Beverley Wilk and Roy Young.

Once again I must pay tribute to my researcher, the indomitable Peter Trollope, who conducted several crucial interviews (the only person I would trust to do so) and who insisted on continuing work despite a bout of serious illness. In Tokyo, Nikki Uzumi was invaluable in helping piece together the first full account of Paul's prison ordeal there in 1980.

The world is full of Beatles experts, poised to pounce delightedly on any authorial error however inconsequential. My text has been fact-checked, wholly or in part, by eleven people, among them the indisputably expert Bill Harry, Barry Miles, Johnny Rogan, Alan Clayson and Ian Drummond. However, no book can hope to be 100 percent error-free and on that score the responsibility is mine alone.

For permission to reproduce copyrighted material on pp 39, 95, 111, 131-2, 418-20, 612, 662-3, 682 and 727, the author and publisher are grateful to MPL Music Publishing.

The excerpt from Derek Taylor's memoir, *As Time Goes By*, appears by kind permission of his widow, Joan.

Finally I wish to thank my literary agents and dear friends, Michael Sissons in London and Peter Matson in New York; my publishers Alan Samson and Lucinda McNeile of Orion and John Parsley of Little Brown; and Rachel Mills and Alexandra Cliff of the PFD rights department.

This book is dedicated to Sue and Jessica, the audience I try hardest to please.

Philip Norman, London, 2016

PICTURE CREDITS

The author and publisher are grateful to the following for permission to reproduce images:

Getty Images: p.1, p.2 (below left and right), p.3, p.4 (above), p.5 (below left), p.6 (top), p.8, p.10 (top), p.12, p.13 (top and below), p.15, p.18, p.20 (below), p.22 (top), p.24 (top), p.25 (below), p.29 (below), p. 31 and p. 32
AKG Images, p.17
Lebrecht, p.4 (below), p.6 (below)
Mark Hayward, p.5 (below right), p.14, p.16 (below)
Alamy, p.7 (below), p.23 (below)
Rex Features, p.5 (top), p.10 (below), p.11, p.19, p.22 (below), p.25 (top), p.28, p.30
PA Images, p.7, p.9, p.16 (top), p.23 (top), p.24 (below), p.26 (top), p.27
Corbis, p.13 (middle), p.29 (top)
Apple Corps, p.20 (above)
Photoshot, p.21 (top)
Camera Press, p.21 (below)
Scope Features, p.26 (below)

INDEX